# COPING WITH PSYCHIATRIC AND PSYCHOLOGICAL TESTIMONY

## FIFTH EDITION

## JAY ZISKIN, Ph.D., LL.B.

with chapters by

*David Faust*
*Michael K. Gann*
*Mitchell Earleywine & Michael K. Gann*
*John C. Yuille, Judith (Cutshall) Daylen,*
*Stephen Porter & David Marxsen*
*Ralph Underwager & Hollida Wakefield*
*Christopher D. Webster & Natalie H. Polvi*
*J. Ric Gass & Samuel H. Solomon*

## Volume III

## PRACTICAL GUIDELINES, CROSS-EXAMINATION AND CASE ILLUSTRATIONS

**LAW AND PSYCHOLOGY PRESS**
Post Office Box 24219
Los Angeles, California 90024
(310) 475-2108 — FAX (310) 474-5938

Library of Congress Catalog Card Number: 95-78594
International Standard Book Numbers:
Volumes I, II, and III: 1-879689-04-9
Volume I: 1-879689-05-7
Volume II: 1-879689-06-5
Volume III: 1-879689-07-3

PRODUCTION STAFF

| | |
|---|---|
| Editor: | Janet Cornwell |
| Coordinator: | Richard D. Burns |
| Book Design: | Mark M. Dodge |
| Typesetting: | Regina Books |

LAW AND PSYCHOLOGY PRESS
Post Office Box 24219
Los Angeles, California 90024
(310) 475-2108
FAX (310) 474-5938

Manufactured in the United States of America.

# PREFACE TO VOLUME III

Volume III of *Coping with Psychiatric and Psychological Testimony,* Fifth Edition, is intended to provide practical guidance for the lawyer in dealing with opposing psychiatric/psychological evidence. Generally, this involves exposing the vulnerabilities of these professions that are inherent in the current "state of the art" and exposing deficiencies in the procedures or conclusions of the clinician in the particular case.

Use of this volume presupposes familiarity with Volumes I and II, which include almost 2000 references from the scientific and professional literature documenting the various deficiencies or challenges that are inherent in the present state of the mental health professions. Volume III indicates how this material can be applied to depositions or cross-examination at trial.

In addition, Volume III provides suggestions for conducting investigation in cases involving, or likely to involve, psychiatric issues. It also suggests a number of items to look for, or be aware of, in reading and analyzing the clinician's reports.

Tactics and strategy for dealing with these experts are discussed as well as description of some of the more common tactics employed by the experts and ways of dealing with them.

Detailed suggestions are provided for depositions and cross-examination in general as well as in particular types of cases, such as criminal, personal injury and child custody.

Illustrative case materials, including clinical reports, transcripts of testimony from actual cases, and comments by the author, are provided in four appendices at the end of the volume. Each case, whether it be criminal, personal injury or whatever, should be worth reading regardless of the reader's particular interest, as each case contains points which are generalizable to other kinds of cases, but may appear only in that single case.

These four appendices provide examples of actual reports and/or testimony in different types of cases—custody, personal injury and criminal—along with the author's analyses and suggestions for dealing with the material. Although some are lengthy they are worthwhile for the lawyer, as they demonstrate many of the points made in this book as well as points that would have application in other cases. They are also worthwhile for mental health professionals who testify and, in addition, could be used in programs for training forensic psychiatrists and psychologists.

We wish to acknowledge and express appreciation to J. Ric Gass and Samuel H. Solomon for Chapter 14 on the effective use of visual materials.

JAY ZISKIN
Los Angeles, CA
May, 1995

# Summary of Table of Contents

## Volume III

## Appendices

# Contents: Volume III

# CHAPTER 1

# Introduction

There are two broad avenues for attacking or deflating the credibility of psychiatric/psychological evidence involved in legal matters. One of these avenues approaches the task from the standpoint of revealing the lack of validated knowledge or data base and deficiencies of evaluation methodology that at the present time are inherent in the mental health or behavioral science fields. Against this background, the other avenue approaches the task in the direction of revealing specific errors of omission or commission or misconstruction of the data or bias of the evaluator in the specific case at hand. The scientific and professional literature, consisting of well over 1500 references documenting the inherent problems, has been provided in Volumes I and II. Both of these avenues are explored in this volume; however, before getting into the specific operations for negating the psychiatric/psychological evidence in a specific case, a brief recapitulation of the inherent problems is worthwhile.

Psychiatry and psychology currently lack a comprehensive, reasonably well validated and widely agreed upon theoretical or conceptual framework for understanding or evaluating human behavior. These deficiencies might be overcome if a classification system existed which made it possible to accurately place people into classes which would then justify making statements about their behavior based on known relationships between class membership and behavior. Such a system does not exist. The *Diagnostic and Statistical Manual of Mental Disorders (DSM-I, -II, -III, III-R* and now, *-IV*) produced by the American Psychiatric Association has not succeeded in this task.

Clinical judgment, usually the principal source of conclusions, suffers from problems of such range and magnitude that little confidence can be placed in conclusions derived from this process.

The clinical method of assessment itself is highly vulnerable to attack, particularly in view of the well-documented operation of both situational and examiner effects, the influence of which cannot be determined at the present time. Psychological tests can be shown to suffer from the deficiencies of the clinical method, and are vulnerable to questions designed to show that there is a large body of negative scientific and professional literature concerning most of the tests and that their status is at best controversial.

There is substantial literature on the unreliability of psychological/psychiatric assessment. The lack of research, or general negative thrust of the literature, on validity of such assessments provides another avenue of attack.

While in most areas experience is an impregnable bastion for the authority of the expert, there is an abundance of literature in the mental health field indicating that experienced practitioners are no more reliable or accurate than novices.

Even if these problems did not exist, it is often difficult to bridge the gap between psychological findings and legal issues.

In addition to these inherent problems, many clinicians (psychiatrists and psychologists) compound the problem by failure to do a thorough and adequate job within the limitations that exist. These specific errors, omissions and misconstructions create a major and sometimes dramatic vulnerability of clinical evidence. The lawyer who is in opposition to the psychiatric evidence has available a number of operations and approaches with which to deal with these vulnerabilities at all stages of the proceedings. These measures cover the utilization of a consultant expert, the investigation, analyzing the report, taking depositions, objecting to admission of the evidence, and cross-examination. Dealing with the ploys or tactics of the opposing expert is also necessary. The remainder of this book attempts to delineate some specifics of "how to do it" in regard to each of these matters.

The lawyer who is willing to devote the time, energy and resources to adequately preparing himself in terms of both the inherent deficiencies of psychiatry and psychology and the specific suggestions which follow should have relatively little difficulty in diminishing if not destroying the credibility of opposing mental health experts. These suggestions are based on the author's experiences as expert witness and/or consultant expert in a number of cases involving clinical evidence.

The term "consultant expert" as used in this text requires explanation. This term is used here to designate a psychiatrist or psychologist who is employed by counsel to analyze the strengths and weaknesses of evidence to be proffered by other psychiatrists or psychologists. The consultant expert does not examine the litigant nor offer opinions as to litigant's psychological condition (except, possibly, to indicate equally or more tenable alternatives to the condition described by other clinicians).

He may or may not be expected to testify. For example, such an expert may testify to matters described in Volumes I and II, e.g., inefficacy of experience, test errors, etc.

We use the term "rebuttal expert" or "clinician expert" to designate a clinician who examines the litigant and renders opinions as to his mental condition, usually differing from the opinion of the other side's clinicians.

# CHAPTER 2

# Making Use of Ethical Principles, Guidelines & Standards

Since the publication of the 4th edition of this book, various professional associations have published ethical principles, specialty guidelines, and standards which we think can be extraordinarily useful in presenting the kinds of challenges suggested in this book.

## ETHICAL PRINCIPLES OF PSYCHOLOGISTS

The current Ethical Principles of Psychologists and Code of Conduct was adopted by the American Psychological Association effective December 1, 1992. We will present some relevant excerpts. The entire document was published in *The American Psychologist*, December, 1992, pp. 1598-1611.

Several principles are relevant to our suggestion to frame questions in terms of the scientific and professional literature whenever possible.

### Principle A: Competence

Psychologists strive to maintain high standards of competence in their work....They maintain knowledge of relevant scientific and professional information related to the services they render, and they recognize the need for ongoing education. Psychologists make appropriate use of scientific, professional, technical, and administrative resources.

### 1.05 Maintaining Expertise

Psychologists who engage in assessment, therapy, teaching, research, organizational consulting, or other professional activities maintain a reasonable level of awareness of current scientific and professional information in their fields of activity, and undertake ongoing efforts to maintain competence in the skills they use.

**1.06 Basis for Scientific and Professional Judgments**

Psychologists *rely* on scientific and professionally derived knowledge when making scientific or professional judgments or when engaging in scholarly or professional endeavors. (emphasis added)

**2.04 Use of Assessment in General and With Special Populations**

(a) Psychologists who perform interventions or administer, score, interpret, or use assessment techniques are familiar with the reliability, validation, and related standardization or outcome studies of, and proper applications and uses of, the techniques they use.

(b) Psychologists recognize limits to the certainty with which diagnoses, judgments, or predictions can be made about individuals.

2.05 requires that psychologists indicate any significant reservations they have about the accuracy or limitations of their interpretations. This should be read with 2.04(b).

It does not seem possible that a psychologist could deny "reasonable" familiarity with and *reliance* on the scientific and professional literature without being in violation of the above ethical principles. Obviously, the psychologist need not know every publication but is required to be familiar with the general state of the literature. Thus, if questions are framed, "Doctor, isn't there a body (or substantial body) of scientific and professional literature indicating that (whatever)," the witness would have to acknowledge that there is such a body of literature. If he says he does not know or that there is not such a body of literature, and you can establish the existence of such information (if necessary, you can call a consultant expert), you can then establish that he is not in compliance with the ethical principles. If the witness says he only pays attention to literature or information directly related to assessment or treatment, he can be asked if he bases his opinions on his experience and clinical judgment, which almost all will acknowledge; and then, literature on experience and clinical judgment are clearly areas of information and knowledge that are important to and distinctly related to his field of activity, to services he provides, and scientific or professional judgments he makes.

7.04(a) In forensic testimony and reports, psychologists testify truthfully, honestly, and candidly and, consistent with applicable legal procedures, describe fairly the bases for their testimony and conclusions.

7.04(b) Whenever necessary to avoid misleading, psychologists acknowledge the limits of their data or conclusions.

The above two sections are under a general heading "Forensic Activities." These sections are very important in relation to cross-examination which seeks to establish the bases for conclusions. They should preclude efforts to employ tactics of evasion, such as being overly general or lumping "all of the data" together as the basis (see below). In the same connection, Section 7.02 requires that forensic assessments be based on information sufficient to provide appropriate substantiation for the findings. 7.01, still under Forensic, requires that psychologists base their work on appropriate knowledge of areas underlying such work.

Occasionally when records and raw data are requested, a psychologist will state that he does not make or retain notes and that once he has interpreted tests, he does not retain them. This is a violation of the ethics principles.

### 1.23 Documentation of Professional and Scientific Work

(a) Psychologists appropriately document their professional and scientific work in order to facilitate provision of services later by them or by other professionals, to ensure accountability, and to meet other requirements of institutions or the law.

(b) When psychologists have reason to believe that records of their professional services will be used in legal proceeding involving recipients of or participants in their work, they have a responsibility to create and maintain documentation in the kind of detail and quality that would be consistent with reasonable scrutiny in an adjudicative forum.

Principle D requires awareness of differences associated with special populations (age, race, gender, etc.) which we have pointed out in Chapter 16, Volume II.

Standard 2.04(c) requires identification of situations in which particular assessment techniques or norms may not be applicable or require adjustment because of factors such as gender, age, race, ethnicity, national origin, religion, sexual orientation, disability, language, or socioeconomic status.

Standard 2.07(b) bans use of tests or measures that are obsolete and "not useful for the current purpose." This suggests that use of any but the latest version or form of a test may be unethical.

Standard 1.07(a) requires use of language that is reasonably understandable to the recipient of the services. We would view this as a proscription against the use of "jargon" in most forensic situations.

## SPECIALTY GUIDELINES FOR
## FORENSIC PSYCHOLOGISTS[1, 2]

## COMMITTEE ON ETHICAL GUIDELINES
## FOR FORENSIC PSYCHOLOGISTS[3]

The *Specialty Guidelines for Forensic Psychologists,* while informed by the *Ethical Principles of Psychologists* (APA, 1990) and meant to be consistent with them, are designed to provide more specific guidance to forensic psychologists in monitoring their professional conduct when acting in assistance to courts, parties to legal proceedings, correctional and forensic mental health facilities, and legislative agencies. The primary goal of the *Guidelines* is to improve the quality of forensic psychological services offered to individual clients and the legal system and thereby to enhance forensic psychology as a discipline and profession. The *Specialty Guidelines for Forensic Psychologists* represent a joint statement of the American Psychology-Law Society and Division 41 of the American Psychological Association and are endorsed by the American Academy of Forensic Psychology. The *Guidelines* do not represent an official statement of the American Psychological Association.

The *Guidelines* provide an aspirational model of desirable professional practice by psychologists, within any subdiscipline of psychology

---

[1] This document is reproduced from *Law and Human Behavior, 15,* No. 6, 1991 by permission of Plenum Publishing Corporation.

[2] The *Specialty Guidelines for Forensic Psychologists* were adopted by majority vote of the members of Division 41 and the American Psychology-Law Society. They have also been endorsed by majority vote by the American Academy of Forensic Psychology. The Executive Committee of Division 41 and the American Psychology Law Society formally approved these *Guidelines* on March 9, 1991. The Executive Committee also voted to continue the Committee on Ethical Guidelines in order to disseminate the *Guidelines* and to monitor their implementation and suggestions for revision. Individuals wishing to reprint these *Guidelines* or who have queries about them should contact either Stephen L. Golding, Ph.D., Department of Psychology, University of Utah, Salt Lake City, UT 84112, 801-581-8028 (voice) or 801-581-5841 (FAX) or other members of the Committee listed below. Reprint requests should be sent to Cathy Oslzly, Department of Psychology, University of Nebraska-Lincoln, Lincoln, NE 68588-0308.

[3] These Guidelines were prepared and principally authored by a Joint Committee on Ethical Guidelines of Division 41 and the American Academy of Forensic Psychology (Stephen L. Golding [Chair], Thomas Grisso, David Shapiro, and Herbert Weissman [Co-chairs]. Other members of the Committee included Robert Fein, Kirk Heilbrun, Judith McKenna, Norman Poythress, and Daniel Schuman. Their hard work and willingness to tackle difficult conceptual and pragmatic issues are gratefully acknowledged. The Committee would also like to acknowledge specifically the assistance and guidance provided by Dort Bigg, Larry Cowan, Eric Harris, Arthur Lerner, Michael Miller, Russell Newman, Melvin Rudov, and Ray Fowler. Many other individuals also contributed by their thoughtful critique and suggestions for improvement of earlier drafts which were widely circulated.

(e.g., clinical, developmental, social, experimental), when they are engaged regularly as experts and represent themselves as such, in an activity primarily intended to provide professional psychological expertise to the judicial system. This would include, for example: clinical forensic examiners; psychologists employed by correctional or forensic mental health systems; researchers who offer direct testimony about the relevance of scientific data to a psycholegal issue; trial behavior consultants; psychologists engaged in preparation of *amicus* briefs; or psychologists, appearing as forensic experts, who consult with, or testify before, judicial, legislative, or administrative agencies acting in an adjudicative capacity. Individuals who provide only occasional service to the legal system and who do so without representing themselves as *forensic experts* may find these *Guidelines* helpful, particularly in conjunction with consultation with colleagues who are forensic experts.

While the *Guidelines* are concerned with a model of desirable professional practice, to the extent that they may be construed as being applicable to the advertisement of services or the solicitation of clients, they are intended to prevent false or deceptive advertisement or solicitation, and should be construed in a manner consistent with that intent.

### SPECIALTY GUIDELINES FOR FORENSIC PSYCHOLOGISTS

## I. PURPOSE AND SCOPE

### A. Purpose

1. While the professional standards for the ethical practice of psychology, as a general discipline, are addressed in the American Psychological Association's *Ethical Principles of Psychologists,* these ethical principles do not relate, in sufficient detail, to current aspirations of desirable professional conduct for forensic psychologists. By design, none of the *Guidelines* contradicts any of the *Ethical Principles of Psychologists;* rather, they amplify those *Principles* in the context of the practice of forensic psychology, as herein defined.

2. The *Guidelines* have been designed to be national in scope and are intended to conform with state and Federal law. In situations where the forensic psychologist believes that the requirements of law are in conflict with the *Guidelines,* attempts to resolve the conflict should be made in accordance with the procedures set forth in these *Guidelines* [IV(G)] and in the *Ethical Principles of Psychologists.*

### B. Scope

1. The *Guidelines* specify the nature of desirable professional practice by forensic psychologists, within any subdiscipline of psychology (e.g., clini-

cal, developmental, social, experimental), when engaged regularly as forensic psychologists.

a. "Psychologist" means any individual whose professional activities are defined by the American Psychological Association or by regulation of title by state registration or licensure, as the practice of psychology.

b. "Forensic psychology" means all forms of professional psychological conduct when acting, with definable foreknowledge, as a psychological expert on explicitly psycholegal issues, in direct assistance to courts, parties to legal proceedings, correctional and forensic mental health facilities, and administrative, judicial, and legislative agencies acting in an adjudicative capacity.

c. "Forensic psychologist" means psychologists who regularly engage in the practice of forensic psychology as defined in I(B)(1)(b).

2. The *Guidelines* do not apply to a psychologist who is asked to provide professional psychological services when the psychologist was not informed at the time of delivery of the services that they were to be used as forensic psychological services as defined above. The *Guidelines* may be helpful, however, in preparing the psychologist for the experience of communicating psychological data in a forensic context.

3. Psychologists who are not forensic psychologists as defined in I(B)(1)(c), but occasionally provide limited forensic psychological services, may find the *Guidelines* useful in the preparation and presentation of their professional services.

## C. Related Standards

1. Forensic psychologists also conduct their professional activities in accord with the *Ethical Principles of Psychologists* and the various other statements of the American Psychological Association that may apply to particular subdisciplines or areas of practice that are relevant to their professional activities.

2. The standards of practice and ethical guidelines of other relevant "expert professional organizations" contain useful guidance and should be consulted even though the present *Guidelines* take precedence for forensic psychologists.

## II. RESPONSIBILITY

A. Forensic psychologists have an obligation to provide services in a manner consistent with the highest standards of their profession. They are responsible for their own conduct and the conduct of those individuals under their direct supervision.

B. Forensic psychologists make a reasonable effort to ensure that their services and the products of their services are used in a forthright and responsible manner.

### III. COMPETENCE

A.   Forensic psychologists provide services only in areas of psychology in which they have specialized knowledge, skill, experience, and education.

B.   Forensic psychologists have an obligation to present to the court, regarding the specific matters to which they will testify, the boundaries of their competence, the factual bases (knowledge, skill, experience, training, and education) for their qualification as an expert, and the relevance of those factual bases to their qualification as an expert on the specific matters at issue. [Author's note: This seems to echo the Ethics Code, requiring a volunteering to the court of information as to limits of competence, *seemingly* including limits of the knowledge base.]

C.   Forensic psychologists are responsible for a fundamental and reasonable level of knowledge and understanding of the legal and professional standards that govern their participation as experts in legal proceedings.

D.   Forensic psychologists have an obligation to understand the civil rights of parties in legal proceedings in which they participate, and manage their professional conduct in a manner that does not diminish or threaten those rights.

E.   Forensic psychologists recognize that their own personal values, moral beliefs, or personal and professional relationships with parties to a legal proceeding may interfere with their ability to practice competently. Under such circumstances, forensic psychologists are obligated to decline participation or to limit their assistance in a manner consistent with professional obligations. [Author's note: This section seems to clearly recognize the operation of examiner effects. It also may pertain to dual relationships such as forensic evaluator and therapist—see also IV(D)(1).]

### IV. RELATIONSHIPS

A.   During initial consultation with the legal representative of the party seeking services, forensic psychologists have an obligation to inform the party of factors that might reasonably affect the decision to contract with the forensic psychologist. These factors include, but are not limited to

1.   the fee structure for anticipated professional services;

2.   prior and current personal or professional activities, obligations, and relationships that might produce a conflict of interests;

3.   their areas of competence and the limits of their competence; and

4.   the known scientific bases and limitations of the methods and procedures that they employ and their qualifications to employ such methods and procedures.

B.   Forensic psychologists do not provide professional services to parties to a legal proceeding on the basis of "contingent fees," when those services involve the offering of expert testimony to a court or administrative body, or when they call upon the psychologist to make affirmations or representations intended to be relied upon by third parties.

C.   Forensic psychologists who derive a substantial portion of their income from fee-for-service arrangements should offer some portion of their professional services on a *pro bono* or reduced fee basis where the public interest or the welfare of clients may be inhibited by insufficient financial resources.

D.   Forensic psychologists recognize potential conflicts of interest in dual relationships with parties to a legal proceeding, and they seek to minimize their effects.

   1.   Forensic psychologists avoid providing professional services to parties in a legal proceeding with whom they have personal or professional relationships that are inconsistent with the anticipated relationship. [Author's note: This seems to virtually preclude a treating therapist from being an evaluator, and vice versa. That is, objectivity as an evaluator is impaired by the usual therapist's role as "helper," and the role as helper may be impaired if an objective evaluation is not supportive of the patients's claim. The rapport or necessary relationship may be harmed by an objective report.]

   2.   When it is necessary to provide both evaluation and treatment services to a party in a legal proceeding (as may be the case in small forensic hospital settings or small communities), the forensic psychologist takes reasonable steps to minimize the potential negative effects of these circumstances on the rights of the party, confidentiality, and the process of treatment and evaluation.

E.   Forensic psychologists have an obligation to ensure that prospective clients are informed of their legal rights with respect to the anticipated forensic service, of the purposes of any evaluation, of the nature of procedures to be employed, of the intended uses of any product of their services, and of the party who has employed the forensic psychologist.

   1.   Unless court ordered, forensic psychologists obtain the informed consent of the client or party, or their legal representative, before proceeding with such evaluations and procedures. If the client appears unwilling to proceed after receiving a thorough notification of the purposes, methods, and intended uses of the forensic evaluation, the evaluation should be postponed and the psychologist should take steps to place the client in contact with his/her attorney for the purpose of legal advice on the issue of participation.

   2.   In situations where the client or party may not have the capacity to provide informed consent to services or the evaluation is pursuant to court order, the forensic psychologist provides reasonable notice to the client's legal representative of the nature of the anticipated forensic service before proceeding. If the client's legal representative objects to the evaluation, the forensic psychologist notifies the court issuing the order and responds as directed.

   3.   After a psychologist has advised the subject of a clinical forensic evaluation of the intended uses of the evaluation and its work product, the psychologist may not use the evaluation work product for other purposes without explicit waiver to do so by the client or the client's legal representative.

F.  When forensic psychologists engage in research or scholarly activities that are compensated financially by a client or party to a legal proceeding, or when the psychologist provides those services on a pro bono basis, the psychologist clarifies any anticipated further use of such research or scholarly product, discloses the psychologist's role in the resulting research or scholarly products, and obtains whatever consent or agreement is required by law or professional standards.

G.  When conflicts arise between the forensic psychologist's professional standards and the requirements of legal standards, a particular court, or a directive by an officer of the court or legal authorities, the forensic psychologist has an obligation to make those legal authorities aware of the source of the conflict and to take reasonable steps to resolve it. Such steps may include, but are not limited to, obtaining the consultation of fellow forensic professionals, obtaining the advice of independent counsel, and conferring directly with the legal representatives involved.

## V.  CONFIDENTIALITY AND PRIVILEGE

A.  Forensic psychologists have an obligation to be aware of the legal standards that may affect or limit the confidentiality or privilege that may attach to their services or their products, and they conduct their professional activities in a manner that respects those known rights and privileges.

  1.  Forensic psychologists establish and maintain a system of record keeping and professional communication that safeguards a client's privilege.

  2.  Forensic psychologists maintain active control over records and information. They only release information pursuant to statutory requirements, court order, or the consent of the client.

B.  Forensic psychologists inform their clients of the limitations to the confidentiality of their services and their products (see also Guideline IV E) by providing them with an understandable statement of their rights, privileges, and the limitations of confidentiality.

C.  In situations where the right of the client or party to confidentiality is limited, the forensic psychologist makes every effort to maintain confidentiality with regard to any information that does not bear directly upon the legal purpose of the evaluation.

D.  Forensic psychologists provide clients or their authorized legal representatives with access to the information in their records and a meaningful explanation of that information, consistent with existing Federal and state statutes, the *Ethical Principles of Psychologists,* the *Standards for Educational and Psychological Testing,* and institutional rules and regulations.

## VI.  METHODS AND PROCEDURES

A.  Because of their special status as persons qualified as experts to the court, forensic psychologists have an obligation to maintain current knowledge of scientific, professional and legal developments within their area of claimed competence. They are obligated also to use that knowledge, consistent with accepted clinical and scientific standards, in selecting data collection methods and procedures for an evaluation, treatment, consultation or scholarly/empirical investigation. [Author's note: This section seems to require familiarity with the professional and scientific literature either by direct reading or continuing education. Further, it requires the expert to *use* that knowledge, i.e., to *rely* on that knowledge, of which the literature must be a part.]

B.   Forensic psychologists have an obligation to document and be prepared to make available, subject to court order or the rules of evidence, all data that form the basis for their evidence or services. The standard to be applied to such documentation or recording *anticipates* that the detail and quality of such documentation will be subject to reasonable judicial scrutiny; this standard is higher than the normative standard for general clinical practice. When forensic psychologists conduct an examination or engage in the treatment of a party to a legal proceeding, with foreknowledge that their professional services will be used in an adjudicative forum, they incur a special responsibility to provide the best documentation possible under the circumstances. [Author's note: This seems to require making and keeping "the best documentation possible." However, VI(B)(1) may be sending a message to "be careful" about what one puts into the documentation. This is not clear.]

   1.   Documentation of the data upon which one's evidence is based is subject to the normal rules of discovery, disclosure, confidentiality, and privilege that operate in the jurisdiction in which the data were obtained. Forensic psychologists have an obligation to be aware of those rules and to regulate their conduct in accordance with them.

   2.   The duties and obligations of forensic psychologists with respect to documentation of data that form the basis for their evidence apply from the moment they know or have a reasonable basis for knowing that their data and evidence derived from it are likely to enter into legally relevant decisions.

C.   In providing forensic psychological services, forensic psychologists take special care to avoid undue influence upon their methods, procedures, and products, such as might emanate from the party to a legal proceeding by financial compensation or other gains. As an expert conducting an evaluation, treatment, consultation, or scholarly/empirical investigation, the forensic psychologist maintains professional integrity by examining the issue at hand from all reasonable perspectives, actively seeking information that will differentially test plausible rival hypotheses. [Author's note: This seems to require the expert to consider alternative explanations, thus putting him in the position of acknowledging other possibilities, and it opens him to questions on the basis for accepting one and rejecting any others.]

D.   Forensic psychologists do not provide professional forensic services to a defendant or to any party in, or in contemplation of, a legal proceeding prior to that individual's representation by counsel, except for persons judicially determined, where appropriate, to be handling their representation *pro se*. When the forensic services are pursuant to court order and the client is not represented by counsel, the forensic psychologist makes reasonable efforts to inform the court prior to providing the services.

1.   A forensic psychologist may provide emergency mental health services to a pretrial defendant prior to court order or the appointment of counsel where there are reasonable grounds to believe that such emergency services are needed for the protection and improvement of the defendant's mental health and where failure to provide such mental health services would constitute a substantial risk of imminent harm to the defendant or to others. In providing such services the forensic psychologist nevertheless seeks to inform the defendants counsel in a manner consistent with the requirements of the emergency situation.

2.   Forensic psychologists who provide such emergency mental health services should attempt to avoid providing further professional forensic services to that defendant unless that relationship is reasonably unavoidable [see IV(D)(2)].

E.   When forensic psychologists seek data from third parties, prior records, or other sources, they do so only with the prior approval of the relevant legal party or as a consequence of an order of a court to conduct the forensic evaluation.

F.   Forensic psychologists are aware that hearsay exceptions and other rules governing expert testimony place a special ethical burden upon them. When hearsay or otherwise inadmissible evidence forms the basis of their opinion, evidence, or professional product, they seek to minimize sole reliance upon such evidence. Where circumstances reasonably permit, forensic psychologists seek to obtain independent and personal verification of data relied upon as part of their professional services to the court or to a party to a legal proceeding.

1.   While many forms of data used by forensic psychologists are hearsay, forensic psychologists attempt to corroborate critical data that form the basis for their professional product. When using hearsay data that have not been corroborated, but are nevertheless utilized, forensic psychologists have an affirmative responsibility to acknowledge the uncorroborated status of those data and the reasons for relying upon such data.

2.   With respect to evidence of any type, forensic psychologists avoid offering information from their investigations or evaluations that does not bear directly upon the legal purpose of their professional services and that is not critical as support for their product, evidence or testimony, except where such disclosure is required by law.

3.   When a forensic psychologist relies upon data or information gathered by others, the origins of those data are clarified in any professional product. In addition, the forensic psychologist bears a special responsibility to ensure that such data, if relied upon, were gathered in a manner standard for the profession.

G.   Unless otherwise stipulated by the parties, forensic psychologists are aware that no statements made by a defendant, in the course of any (forensic) examination, no testimony by the expert based upon such statements, nor any other fruits of the statements can be admitted into evidence against the defendant in any criminal proceeding, except on an issue respecting mental condition on which the defendant has introduced testimony. Forensic psychologists have an affirmative duty to ensure that their written products and oral testimony conform to this Federal Rule of Procedure (12.2[c]), or its state equivalent.

1.   Because forensic psychologists are often not in a position to know what evidence, documentation, or element of a written product may be or may lend to a "fruit of the statement," they exercise extreme caution in preparing reports or offering testimony prior to the defendant's assertion of a mental state claim or the defendant's introduction of testimony regarding a mental condition. Consistent with the reporting requirements of state or federal law, forensic psychologists avoid including statements from the defendant relating to the time period of the alleged offense.

2.   Once a defendant has proceeded to the trial stage, and all pretrial mental health issues such as competency have been resolved, forensic psychologists may include in their reports or testimony any statements made by the defendant that are directly relevant to supporting their expert evidence, providing that the defendant has "introduced" mental state evidence or testimony within the meaning of Federal Rule of Procedure 12.2(c), or its state equivalent.

H.   Forensic psychologists avoid giving written or oral evidence about the psychological characteristics of particular individuals when they have not had an opportunity to conduct an examination of the individual adequate to the scope of the statements, opinions, or conclusions to be issued. Forensic psychologists make every reasonable effort to conduct such examinations. When it is not possible or feasible to do so, they make clear the impact of such limitations on the reliability and validity of their professional products, evidence, or testimony.

## VII. PUBLIC AND PROFESSIONAL COMMUNICATIONS

A.   Forensic psychologists make reasonable efforts to ensure that the products of their services, as well as their own public statements and professional testimony, are communicated in ways that will promote understanding and avoid deception, given the particular characteristics, roles, and abilities of various recipients of the communications.

1.   Forensic psychologists take reasonable steps to correct misuse or misrepresentation of their professional products, evidence, and testimony.

2.   Forensic psychologists provide information about professional work to clients in a manner consistent with professional and legal standards for the disclosure of test results, interpretations of data, and the factual bases for conclusions. A full explanation of the results of tests and the bases for conclusions should be given in language that the client can understand.

a.   When disclosing information about a client to third parties who are not qualified to interpret test results and data, the forensic psychologist complies with Principle 16 of the *Standards for Educational and Psychological Testing*. When required to disclose results to a nonpsychologist, every attempt is made to ensure that test security is maintained and access to information is restricted to individuals with a legitimate and professional interest in the data. Other qualified mental health professionals who make a request for information pursuant to a lawful order are, by definition, "individuals with a legitimate and professional interest."

b.  In providing records and raw data, the forensic psychologist takes reasonable steps to ensure that the receiving party is informed that raw scores must be interpreted by a qualified professional in order to provide reliable and valid information.

B.  Forensic psychologists realize that their public role as "expert to the court" or as "expert representing the profession" confers upon them a special responsibility for fairness and accuracy in their public statements. When evaluating or commenting upon the professional work product or qualifications of another expert or party to a legal proceeding, forensic psychologists represent their professional disagreements with reference to a fair and accurate evaluation of the data, theories, standards, and opinions of the other expert or party.

C.  Ordinarily, forensic psychologists avoid making detailed public (out-of-court) statements about particular legal proceedings in which they have been involved. When there is a strong justification to do so, such public statements are designed to assure accurate representation of their role or their evidence, not to advocate the positions of parties in the legal proceeding. Forensic psychologists address particular legal proceedings in publications or communications only to the extent that the information relied upon is part of a public record, or consent for that use has been properly obtained from the party holding any privilege.

D.  When testifying, forensic psychologists have an obligation to all parties to a legal proceeding to present their findings, conclusions, evidence, or other professional products in a fair manner. This principle does not preclude forceful representation of the data and reasoning upon which a conclusion or professional product is based. It does, however, preclude an attempt, whether active or passive, to engage in partisan distortion or misrepresentation. Forensic psychologists do not, by either commission or omission, participate in a misrepresentation of their evidence, nor do they participate in partisan attempts to avoid, deny, or subvert the presentation of evidence contrary to their own position.

E.  Forensic psychologists, by virtue of their competence and rules of discovery, actively disclose all sources of information obtained in the course of their professional services; they actively disclose which information from which source was used in formulating a particular written product or oral testimony.

F.  Forensic psychologists are aware that their essential role as expert to the court is to assist the trier of fact to understand the evidence or to determine a fact in issue. In offering expert evidence, they are aware that their own professional observations, inferences, and conclusions must be distinguished from legal facts, opinions, and conclusions. Forensic psychologists are prepared to explain the relationship between their expert testimony and the legal issues and facts of an instant case.

## CHILD CUSTODY EVALUATIONS GUIDELINES

See Chapter 25, Volume II, for Guidelines for Child Custody Evaluations.

## ETHICAL PRINCIPLES FOR PSYCHIATRISTS

Ethical principles for psychiatrists are contained within *The Principles of Medical Ethics With Annotations Especially Applicable to Psychiatry* (1993). They appear to be much less detailed than the psychologists' ethics are and more related to treatment than assessment. They contain no provisions specifically for forensic psychiatrists and little that seems relevant for lawyers. The one relevant provision is Section 5 (p. 7).

**Section 5**

*A physician shall continue to study, apply, and advance scientific knowledge, make relevant information available to patients, colleagues, and the public, obtain consultation, and use the talents of other health professionals when indicated.*

1. Psychiatrists are responsible for their own continuing education and should be mindful of the fact that theirs must be a lifetime of learning. [Author's note: Section 5 and subsection 1 would seem to require continuing familiarity with the scientific and professional literature, e.g., "continue to study...scientific knowledge."]

One way to approach the minimal statements of ethical principles for psychiatrists is to introduce the principles for psychologists as a basis for comparison. For example, a psychiatrist could be asked if psychiatrists are less ethical than psychologists or should be held to lesser standards. If the psychiatrist denies this, he might then be asked if the principles represent good practice and then the door might be open to questions arising out of the principles.

# CHAPTER 3

# Investigation

Most lawyers are aware of the importance of thorough investigation and preparation in lawsuits. The acquisition of facts that are accurate and as complete as possible is frequently one of the keys to a successful outcome. This is particularly true where opposing psychological evidence may be anticipated. Our experience has been that for the most part clinicians do an inadequate job of ascertaining relevant background or behavioral data. Therefore, it is valuable to have as much information as possible about a litigant's background and general life functioning.

One of the uses of this information is to be able to produce facts that are inconsistent with or directly contradict some of the psychological conclusions or the facts on which the conclusions were based. For example, in one case the clinician alleged in his report that plaintiff's marriage had broken up because of her loss of sexual interest which was due to the injuries received in the accident. A search of court records showed that plaintiff had filed suit for divorce three weeks prior to the accident. Of course, this eliminated the marriage break-up as an item of damages. However, it had the additional effect of impairing the psychologist's credibility on various other matters to which he testified when he was confronted with this obvious error on the witness stand. In another case, psychiatrist reported plaintiff never had sleep problems prior to the accident. However, a review of medical records revealed a period when sleeping pills had been prescribed for her. This affected the credibility of both the plaintiff and the expert.

Another aim of the investigation is to provide background data with which to establish alternative explanations for the psychological findings. For example, in one case the psychological findings were that among other things, the litigant was suffering from depression as a result of the accident. Biographical information revealed that the woman was 50 years old, divorced, had an unhappy relationship with her only child, a 19-year-old daughter who rarely spoke to her, had recently undergone a hysterectomy, was severely conflicted in her relationships with men, both wishing for and fearing marriage, and that she disliked her work and was recently particularly unhappy over the fact that a co-worker had been promoted over her head to a supervisory position. One does not need years of specialized education and experience to recognize that this woman had plenty to be depressed about even in the absence of the accident. An expert who attempts to insist that she was not depressed prior to the accident is unlikely to be believed.

Specific areas for investigation may not become apparent until the clinician's reports have been received. For example, in a child custody case, the psychologist's report stated that the father was likely to be somewhat withdrawn and to have difficulty in social relationships. The litigant promptly presented his attorney with nearly a dozen witnesses who would attest to a full and lively social life. However, neither the litigant nor his lawyer could have anticipated the need to prepare in advance for an assertion of this kind. Generally speaking, however, there are certain areas for exploration that are likely to pay off such as relationships with family members and others, the state of a marriage if relevant, work history, and attitudes and observations of co-workers, hospital records, medical records, school records, military records, prior psychological testing, if any, and any data about typical behavior or functioning prior to or following the event in question; in other words, a behavioral description of the litigant and his life situation rather than a psychological description.

In different types of cases there are specific kinds of information one would want to look for.

## CRIMINAL CASES

In criminal cases, the arresting and/or investigating officers can be one of the most important sources of information concerning defendant's mental status, especially if the arrest is made within a short time after commission of the crime. A psychological or state of mind defense is most likely to occur in cases of a serious crime where it seems fairly clear that defendant is the perpetrator. If the arrest is made within minutes or hours of the crime, the arresting officers are in a position to perform at least a layman's mental status examination that will be proximate to the time of the crime, in contrast to the mental health expert whose examination is usually considerably removed from the time of the crime. It might be useful to have the officers carry a checklist of the items of information that may be helpful. If the officers do not record this information, as soon as the investigator is on the case, he should attempt to obtain such information.

Generally speaking, mental status examination focuses on the individual's cognitive and emotional functioning as indicated by his behavior; therefore the kinds of information one would hope to obtain from the arresting officers would be the following:

1. Is defendant oriented as to time, place and person? That is, does he know who he is, who the officers are; does he know where he is and does he know at least what day of the week it is?
2. Does he speak and communicate coherently?
3. What kind of emotions or feelings does he display? In particular, is he similar to or markedly different from most other people that the officers have had occasion to arrest?
4. Is his behavior bizarre or inappropriate under the circumstances?
5. Do his memory and thought processes appear to be within the normal range?
6. Is he able to maintain control to a reasonable extent over his behavior?
7. Is he able to act in a purposeful, goal directed manner?
8. Were there any efforts to avoid detection as the perpetrator?
9. Was there any acknowledgement of wrongfulness of act?

In addition to obtaining the above information from the arresting officers, as soon as possible the investigator should attempt to obtain information about the defendant's general functioning from those people who were in a position to observe him in everyday life, and witnesses, if any, who may have observed his behavior within a short time before the crime. Here the thrust should be to determine if defendant's behavior appeared to be within the rather broad range of normality, such as to indicate that he was capable of functioning as most other people do. Co-workers and personnel at places where defendant does business are often in an excellent position to provide information of this kind; that is, they are in a position to say that there was nothing in defendant's routine behavior to mark him as radically different from the rest of the population or if such is the case, that there is behavior which marks him as a "weirdo." That is, if he goes to the grocery store and selects several items, brings them to the checkstand, stands in line waiting his turn and produces the money to pay for them when the bill is rung up, all of this behavior would indicate that he is capable of appreciating that it would be wrong or criminal to simply walk out of the store with the goods and also that he is capable of following the ordinary rules of making purchases in a grocery store. We are aware that some clinicians will assert that being able to carry out these routine functions can exist even though the individual is seriously psychologically disturbed. Of course, the issue is not whether he is psychologically disturbed or not but whether he possesses the requisite capacities to be held responsible. Some clinicians do go as far as to say that the capacities for understanding that one is supposed to pay for merchandise in the store and to wait with average patience in the check stand line are different from the capacities to understand that shooting someone is wrong or being able to refrain from shooting someone. As far as we know there is virtually no evidence to support that notion; that is just the psychiatrist's fantasy. Some clinicians also assert that the ability to drive to the market, pick out the required goods, take them to the checkstand and so on is not evidence of the capacity to plan ahead or have "intent" with regard to a homicide. Again, we are aware of virtually no scientific evidence to support such a distinction. The mental processes in carrying out either of these two sets of operations appear similar if not in fact identical.

Friends and relatives may also be a source of the above kinds of information. However, they may be less reliable witnesses once they are aware the defendant is in trouble, out of their perfectly natural desire to help him and to avoid harming him. In any event, it is probably a good idea to get a statement from them as soon as possible in order to know how they view defendant and in some cases, to have a record of their perception of defendant prior to their being interviewed by opposing counsel or clinicians, who may wittingly or unwittingly influence their perceptions.

Where psychiatric defense can be anticipated, obviously it is desirable to have an evaluation by a psychiatrist or psychologist as soon as possible—the closer to the time of the crime, the better.

Another excellent source of information that may become relevant are jail personnel who have an opportunity to observe the defendant's behavior while he is incarcerated. It might be desirable to have them keep a running record of the kinds of information stated above for the arresting officers to obtain.

Exploration with witnesses should also be performed to determine if there is some kind of conventional motive operating in connection with the crime. For example, in connection with family killings, quite often the motives are readily obtainable, such as anger with a spouse, resentment, jealousy, and so on.

## PERSONAL INJURY CASES

In personal injury cases where psychological consequences are claimed or may be anticipated, investigation should be focused on several areas. What evidence can be found concerning plaintiff's psychological condition prior to the injury; what evidence can be found regarding plaintiff's psychological condition subsequent to the injury;

what evidence indicates alternative explanations for plaintiff's present psychological condition, if any.

Toward this end, all hospital, medical, psychiatric, and psychological records should be closely scrutinized for evidence that plaintiff may have been having psychological problems prior to the injury. Sometimes out of a large volume of medical records there may be only one line indicating such problems but it is nevertheless important not to overlook it. Complaints indicating anxiety, depression, difficulty sleeping, and so on are not uncommon in previous medical records. Similarly, occasionally one will find a prescription of tranquilizers or other psychiatric medications suggesting some psychological problem. Evidence of prior injuries or illness that plaintiff has withstood without "psychological breakdown" is also important as indicating plaintiff's capacity to withstand the stresses of such injuries or illnesses.

Co-workers can be an important source of information, particularly concerning plaintiff's attitude towards his job. For example, evidence of dissatisfaction with a job or even, in some cases, the existence of a plan to try to claim disability under Workers' Compensation laws have been uncovered. Such information may become particularly relevant in connection with any other data that suggests malingering. Also, job dissatisfaction might account for some of the symptoms of psychological distress that are reported as consequences of the accident. Co-workers may also provide information as to plaintiff's general behavior patterns and personality patterns, which may at times conflict with the description given by family members that he was wonderful before the accident but has become irritable and forgetful and so on since the accident. Supervisors' ratings, where available, may provide similar kinds of information.

Family members are another source of information in cases of this type, although it should be recognized that they may well have a stake in the outcome of the quest for damages. Investigation with family members should take place as early as possible and include within it not only material related to the injury and any physical consequences but also should, in an open-ended way, solicit information regarding psychological state. For example, after dealing with physical injuries, a rather loose question such as how does he seem to be getting along otherwise may establish that there is little by way of psychological consequence, at least at that time. A follow-up investigation a few weeks later may be worthwhile to establish that from a psychological standpoint, plaintiff's condition is unchanged. It may be possible to show in some cases that the psychological problems developed only after plaintiff's retention of counsel.

Particular attention should be paid to reports of initial examining or treating physicians, as frequently these will contain no reference to the psychological symptoms that are later "discovered" by a psychiatrist. For example, most physical examinations will include questions about the patient's sleep patterns. In several cases on which we have consulted, the examining physician reported no sleeping problem, although some months later a psychiatrist reported that plaintiff had all kinds of sleeping problems.

An important area to investigate is that of marital relationship. Sometimes where impairment of this relationship is claimed through psychiatric examination, facts will indicate that the marital relationship was already impaired. This is obviously not the easiest kind of information to obtain but sometimes neighbors, relatives or co-workers are able to provide some information based on statements of plaintiff or plaintiff's spouse. Occasionally where the investigation is early, plaintiff or spouse will candidly acknowledge that the marriage leaves much to be desired. This may also indicate alternative explanations for some forms of psychological distress. Also, problems with children (e.g., drug use, criminal behavior) may be revealed as alternative explanations.

Periodic observation of plaintiff's behavior and activities is also important as it sometimes turns out that some behavior is contra-indicative of a condition the psychiatrist diagnoses. In our experience this is most often discernible in connection with a diagnosis of depression. Typically, depression involves a slowing down of activity and movement. Such seemingly innocuous behavior as walking with a brisk step or working vigorously in the yard or smiling and laughing can become relevant in this context. Clearly, regular participation in recreational activities such as golf, tennis, etc. also tends to be contra-indicative of depression, as the person is generally described as having a loss of interest in normal or usual activities. Thus, detailed notes of an investigator who has observed plaintiff's behavior can be quite valuable. In a number of cases this will turn out to be a waste of time, but over the long run it pays off often enough to make it worthwhile.

Investigation of caffeine use may be productive as caffeine has been established as capable of producing most of the symptoms of anxiety and depression and even cognitive impairment.

## CHILD CUSTODY CASES

The major thrust of investigation in child custody cases is toward obtaining facts concerning the nature of parent-child relationships and the emotional or psychological functioning of litigants prior to the time the divorce action was instituted and, if at all possible, prior to the emergence of the marital problems which led to the divorce action. This kind of information is important because typically at the time an evaluating psychiatrist or psychologist sees any of the people involved, they are in a situation which often is extremely stressful and produces changes in otherwise normal functioning. Thus, it is important to be able to establish that the clinician's evaluation is based on an examination of the people in an abnormal and highly stressful situation. Evidence of different behavior functioning or psychological status under more normal circumstances can be useful to show that the clinician's conclusions as to the psychological status of the people or the manner in which they will function in the future cannot be relied on due to the overpowering situation effects on the data that he obtains in that examination. Friends, neighbors, coworkers, and school personnel are frequently good sources of information in cases of this type.

It is also important to know the physical aspects of the different custodial arrangements. That is, the clinician should have knowledge of the physical facilities of the home, how many bedrooms, the neighborhood and other such pragmatic matters as such things also bear on the welfare or best interest of the child.

## CIVIL COMMITMENT

The nature of investigation in civil commitment cases is defined by the bases for such commitment. Typically, statutes provide for commitment if the individual is found to be dangerous to self or others or is gravely disabled. The trend in dangerousness is for statutes to require overt acts or threats of violence along with a psychiatric opinion that the individual is dangerous.

With regard to dangerousness, investigation should be oriented towards establishing the fact that other than for the one act of violence for which there may have been at least minimally adequate provocation, the litigant has been non-violent. Where the basis is threats of violence not acted upon, the thrust of investigation should be that several such threats may have been made over a period of time without any overt act.

Regarding the "gravely disabled" basis, this is almost entirely a factual issue. That is, it almost always rests primarily on a showing that the litigant in fact has not provided for the necessities of life for himself or herself. The role of the psychiatrist is almost pro forma because if the basic facts can be established all he really testifies to is that it is due to a mental disorder. In rare cases, it may be possible to develop facts showing that while the litigant is caring for himself in a manner most of us would view as very poor, he is doing so on the basis of conscious philosophical choices.

## INVESTIGATION AND YOUR EXPERTS

An issue to be decided by the lawyer and his own experts is the extent to which the lawyer will provide the experts with data obtained as a result of his investigations. This is not an issue with that type of expert that we designate as a consultant expert; that is, one who is *not* going to testify or provide reports concerning the mental status of a litigant. His role is that of a consultant to the lawyer advising him as to flaws and vulnerabilities in the examinations and conclusions of opposing experts or possibly in testifying in court as to such flaws, and thus he should be fully informed. The issue is more likely to arise where an expert is being retained for the purpose of rendering a conclusion about a litigant which may or may not be at odds with opinions of experts retained on behalf of the litigant.

Some clinicians do not wish to have advance information about a person they are examining on the premise that it may bias their examination and conclusions. The chapters on clinical method and judgment in Volume I of this text strongly support that view. Although there is no firm division, this position is more likely to be taken by psychologists who wish to draw conclusions from test data uncontaminated by other information than it is to be adopted by psychiatrists whose examination inevitably involves the taking of a history and thus inevitably deals with factual information. It seems unwise to tamper with the clinician's usual diagnostic procedure. For one thing, deviation from his normal procedure is likely to impair the quality of his examination. For another thing, if he is honest, he may be confronted with a question as to whether the examination was performed in his usual manner and an answer in the negative will make it appear as though the lawyer was running the clinical evaluation rather than the clinician.

However, where the purpose of the examination is to determine if there is a difference of opinion among clinicians as to the litigant's state of mind or psychological status, usually on the premise that there is or that one can anticipate a clinical opinion from the other side establishing the psychiatric or psychological claim, our view is that it is best that the potential rebuttal expert have available all of the factual material possible. This will enable him to conduct a more thorough and complete examination than is ordinarily done. This subject will be dealt with at more length in Chapter 5, Strategy and Tactics.

Possession or lack of factual information is a two-edged issue. It is true that certain information may bias or influence the clinician. It is also true that factual knowledge is necessary in order to evaluate the data of the clinical examination. At the minimum, conclusions that are demonstrably wrong can be avoided. One compromise is to first perform the evaluation uninformed and then to reevaluate with the relevant factual information. This may not help much. For lack of information, the clinician may fail to explore relevant areas. Also, if the facts force him to alter some conclusions, his credibility may be affected. The likelihood of biasing effects may have to be accepted as the lesser evil.

# CHAPTER 4

# Analyzing the Clinician's Report

We have almost invariably found the clinician's report to be a gold mine of material with which to challenge his conclusions. A careful review of the report should be done with sensitivity to omissions as well as conclusions. Our practice in analyzing a report is to read it through in its entirety and then go back through it making notes of any material that may be useful in affecting the expert's credibility. Not uncommonly, material in one part of the report will be discrepant with material in another part or one report may differ from another. Obviously, any material that is discrepant to known facts should be noted.

Even the form and style of the report can provide useful information. Some reports are so brief that it is impossible to determine the foundations on which the conclusions rest. When we see a report of that kind, we usually suspect that we are dealing with a clinician who is not very thorough, who does not really expect to be challenged and who probably is not very well prepared to support his conclusions. On the other hand, some reports are minutely detailed or contain statements that seem as though they are lifted directly from textbooks.

For example, in one psychologist's report, there was the statement, "His CF on the Rorschach was greater than his FC therefore indicating that he has poor emotional control." In these cases we suspect that the clinician is insecure or lacking in genuine knowledge of his methodologies and is forced to attempt to bolster his opinion. A commonly seen phrase, "In my professional opinion," suggests to us that the individual is relying primarily on an impressionistic and authoritarian approach. Such clinicians are likely to be relying on "gut" reactions and will probably be hard pressed to justify their findings. Many clinicians find it difficult to verbalize the basis for their findings. This phrase may also indicate considerable insecurity on the clinician's part and represent an attempt to bolster his opinions by making sure everyone knows that it is rendered by a "professional."

Another element to be sensitive to is frequent use of terms indicating tentativeness or uncertainty, for example, frequent use of such words as "perhaps," "may," "seems," "some," "tends," "impression," and similar words. In some cases, we have found as many as forty or fifty instances of the use of such qualifying phrases in a 10-12 page report so that almost everything the clinician has said is tinged with uncertainty. Obviously we believe that is the only honest way a report can be written in the present state of knowledge. Nevertheless, it is a cue to recognize the degree of uncertainty that exists within the clinician in the matter and to make sure that this uncertainty is made apparent in his testimony.

Sometimes even the letterhead or an accompanying vita, if there is one, can provide useful information. For example, if the letterhead reads Dr. X, "Child Psychiatry," and the report deals with the evaluation of an adult, it would seem likely that the bulk of this clinician's experience is in evaluating and treating children and one might raise some questions about his diagnostic skills in relation to adults as contrasted to one who specializes in adult psychiatry. A marked distance between the clinician's office and the litigant's place of residence or business can also contain significant implications. For example, in one case, the litigant lived in Long Beach, California, but the clinician selected for the evaluation and initiation of treatment was located in Glendale, California. While both of these communities can be viewed as being within the greater metropolitan Los Angeles area, they are some 30 miles apart, requiring travel through cross-town traffic. There are a considerable number of well-qualified clinicians in Long Beach. Coincidentally, in this case the litigant's attorney was also located in Glendale and, as it turned out, had worked in several cases with this particular clinician. The implications of such a situation are not lost upon a trier of fact.

There are several matters to have in mind when reading the report.

## 1. The Nature of the Examination

A properly prepared report will usually give the number and duration of contacts with the subject. If this information is not contained in the report, of course, the lawyer will have to get it by way of deposition or in cross-examination. Because psychological states are complex and fluctuate, a single and relatively brief examination is almost on the face of it inadequate. (If the lawyer is going to use a rebuttal expert, it is wise to suggest that he see the litigant on at least two separate occasions, or more if the case involves conditions *expected* to shift over time, e.g., cognitive dysfunction secondary to recent head injury.) Sometimes where there is a single interview, it can be determined from the report that a considerable portion of the hour was devoted to gathering mundane biographical data, such as date of birth, schools attended, family constellation, jobs held, and other such material which frequently leaves relatively little of the interview hour to be devoted to any kind of thorough exploration of the individual's psychological condition. Of course a certain amount of history taking is necessary. It is not that point which is subject to attack, but more the idea that if 20 or 25 minutes of a 50-minute interview were taken up with this pure history taking, relatively little time will be left to a thorough investigation of the current psychological condition and, where relevant, prior psychological states.

## 2. Basis for Findings

In reading the report, one should bear in mind the questions: "What information was obtained according to the report?" "What is the basis for the conclusions?" "What are the sources of information?" "How much reliance is there on self-report?" "How thorough was the investigation?" "Was there an attempt to obtain medical records, school records, and any other kinds of relevant records or information?" "Were symptoms observed by others prior to the event?" "What was the degree of probing or verifying of information by the clinician?"

A typical report contains several different kinds of information.

There may be factual information, for example, the litigant states he dropped out of high school in the eleventh grade. This information is usually obtained from the litigant and therefore it is nearly always of questionable veracity, given obvious motives of the litigant to falsify.

Some information is factual observation, for example, "during the interview, litigant's hands shook," or, "during the interview, litigant perspired heavily." Some information is judgmental in nature, for example, defendant "lacked affect," or plaintiff "appeared depressed." Information of this kind is judgmental rather than factual because it depends upon the clinician's frame of reference. Thus, what might be viewed by one clinician as depression or lack of affect might not be so viewed by another clinician.

Some information is conclusionary, for example, "plaintiff has strong dependency needs which he tries to cover over." Statements of this kind pertain to matter that is not directly observable by any clinician. Obviously, the soundest basis for drawing conclusions about the individual is the factual material available, while conclusionary material is at the other extreme—it provides the least sound basis—with judgmental material falling somewhere in between. Thus in reading the report one should estimate the amount of factual, judgmental or conclusionary material it contains and the relationships between such information and the final opinions stated. That is, sometimes there will be considerable factual material in the report but it will be unrelated to the opinions drawn.

Of equal importance is material omitted from the report or not dealt with in it. Thus, for example, in a personal injury case where the clinician claims the plaintiff is depressed or has lost sexual interest because of the injury, does the report indicate that he made any exploration of the marriage relationship prior to the injury? If it does, did the clinician find out that there were marital problems as your investigation has indicated? If he did, does the report show how he dealt with this in relation to his contention that the depression or the loss of sexual interest was the result of the injury? Failure on any one of these three points would obviously weaken the conclusion he has drawn. In the case of failure to explore, this would raise questions as to the thoroughness or competence of the clinician, or to the credibility or truthfulness of litigant. Failure to explore possible alternative explanations or conclusions would also raise questions as to the clinician's competence. Failure to be diligent in seeking disconfirming data suggests bias on the part of the clinician.

In another area, did the clinician obtain and read and consider all available medical records? Did he utilize this information in his report? If so, how did he utilize it? Our concern in this regard is whether his opinion is based largely on prior psychiatric or psychological evaluations. Given the data provided in the chapter on reliability and validity of clinical evaluations in Volume I of this text, it would be highly risky for an examiner to put much credence in such prior evaluations. In addition, there is the possibility that a preconception as to psychopathology has been established in his mind if he read these reports prior to seeing the litigant (see discussions of hindsight bias and confirmatory bias in Chapter 5 of Volume I). In one child custody case, the examining psychiatrist incorporated and therefore clearly relied on statements made by the wife's former therapist to the effect that the husband was "cruel," although that therapist had never seen the husband.

### 3. The Diagnosis

One should note whether the report contains a formal diagnosis. Most often, psychologists' reports will contain a formal diagnosis but sometimes they will not, containing only descriptive statements. Probably, the psychologist can get away with this because his report is generally not viewed as a medical procedure; however, where the psychological report does not contain a formal diagnosis, one should make a note to question the psychologist as to what diagnosis he would make. He is especially likely to get away with no diagnosis where the testing and report were requested by or done for the benefit of a psychiatrist who will normally have a formal diagnosis included in his report. Most psychiatric reports contain a formal diagnosis. Those that do not are weakened in the sense that the psychiatrist's position is that he is a physician and normally one would expect a physician to make a diagnosis. One can usually spot a formal diagnosis by the presence of a code number, usually a three-digit number, sometimes with additional digits following a decimal point, although in some cases, psychiatrists will state what turns out to be a formal diagnosis without using the code numbers. It is sloppy work if the number is not given. Where there is a formal diagnosis, one should check to see if it is one of those listed in the *current Diagnostic and Statistical Manual*. If it is not, of course, that fact should be noted. If the diagnosis is listed in DSM-III or DSM-III-R, the lawyer or his consultant should check the manual for the elements required for making that diagnosis and then check to see if the report describes those elements. In our experience, it has not been uncommon for the diagnosis to be stated even though the material in the report does not justify the diagnosis. The reader will recall from Chapter 7, Volume I, the discussion of the Rosenhan study where the diagnosis of schizophrenia was based on only one element described in DSM-II.

Obviously, in such instances, the clinician's competence is called into question. If there is a diagnosis, but it is not from the DSM, this is a matter to be questioned as there is only one official diagnostic classification system at a time and at the time of this writing it is DSM-IV. Questions here may elicit criticism of the DSM-III-R by the expert. We should note there is another diagnostic system, The International Classification of Diseases (ICD), but this is not commonly used by American psychiatrists and psychologists.

## 4. Situation and Examiner Effects

The report should be checked for attention to or omission of possible situation or examiner effects as these are almost invariably present in any examination for litigation purposes.

Under the heading "Severity of Psycho-Social Stressors," *DSM-III* includes a category of "Legal: e.g., arrested, jailed, lawsuit or trial." [*DSM-III-R* (p. 20) and *DSM-IV* (p. 29) contain similar matter.] Of course, one does not need the official declaration by *DSM-III* to know that being involved in litigation is a stressful situation for most people, as would be the case for other kinds of psycho-social stressors defined in *DSM-III*. These include: "Conjugal (Marital and non-marital): e.g., engagement, marriage, discord, death of a spouse"; "Other interpersonal: Problems with one's friends, neighbors, associates or non-conjugal family members, e.g., illness of best friend, discordant relation with boss"; "Occupational: Includes work, school, homemaker, e.g., unemployment, retirement, school problems"; "Living circumstances: e.g., change in residence, threat to personal safety, immigration"; "Financial: e.g., inadequate finances, change in financial status." The influence of one or more of these various stressors in addition to the stress of litigation in various kinds of cases seems obvious.

Thus, for example, in criminal cases, if the defendant is incarcerated, there is a change of residence and likely a threat to personal safety. There may be possible concern with unemployment or difficulty finding work if one is convicted, as well as possible alteration of interpersonal relationships.

In child custody cases, obviously conjugal stressors are present. As one of the spouses normally has moved out of the home, one of them at least has undergone a change in residence.

In the personal injury case it is the involvement in a lawsuit that is often the most significant stressor, as the plaintiff typically is in suspense over the outcome with usually a considerable amount of money and his future lifestyle at stake.

In civil commitment cases, if the litigant has been involuntarily hospitalized pending the hearing, obviously he has had a change of residence and rightly or wrongly may perceive the mental hospital as a threat to his personal safety. There may also be separation from family.

Therefore, a report that does not deal with these situational issues when they are present is inadequate. It is thus necessary to determine the extent to which symptoms such as anxiety or depression or any impairments of functioning or mood that are ordinarily thought to result from stress are due to these situational influences and therefore do not represent the individual or characterize the individual as he is under other circumstances. Although an accurate history may shed some light in this area, the findings or observations of the mental status examination and the responses on psychological tests are particularly susceptible to situational effects and there is no known way to measure the extent of those effects. In most instances, about the best that an honest report can do is acknowledge the possibility of such situational effects and acknowledge that it is not possible to determine the extent to which such effects have influenced the observed behavior.

There are some specific situation effects that are often present in personal injury cases and less often present in criminal and other kinds of cases.

The report should note whether the litigant was on any kind of medication at the time of the examination and if so, what possible effects this might have. Similarly, the presence of pain should be noted along with its possible effects. In some cases it becomes obvious that the litigant should not have been examined under those circumstances at all. For example, in one case, the litigant informed the psychologist that he was having headaches and that his back and preferred arm and hand were also causing him pain. Nevertheless, the psychologist proceeded to administer a battery of tests, some of which called for performance of tasks requiring concentration, attention and psychomotor speed and manipulation. The results were interpreted as showing considerable impairment due to anxiety. This is obviously nonsense in the face of the conditions under which the plaintiff had taken the tests.

Consumption of caffeine is also a matter that needs inquiry in any case where anxiety or depression, or sleep problems, or some cognitive impairment, is found to be a symptom or condition. The research of Greden at al. and others reported in Chapter 6 of Volume I makes it clear that excessive caffeine consumption can produce symptoms of an anxiety state. If that were not enough, DSM-III, DSM-III-R, and DSM-IV have a category of "caffeine intoxication." DSM-IV has a category of "substance induced anxiety disorder" which lists caffeine as one of the potential inducers. Therefore, an examination which fails to inquire as to caffeine consumption is inadequate in any case where anxiety is a symptom. Tobacco use has some similar effects.

One does not need to be a trained clinician to be sensitive to possible situation effects. One need only use common sense and life experience and then with regard to each finding or observation reported ask oneself whether or not one could reasonably expect such behavior of a normal person under the conditions that prevailed. It is the clinician's prerogative to assert that the defendant's behavior, mood, affect, thought processes and so on are unaffected by the fact that he is now in jail facing homicide charges, living with the knowledge of having killed a family member, and so on. It is the judge or jury's prerogative to recognize that such an assertion is nonsense. It is the clinician's prerogative to assert that the litigant experiences no anxiety based on the fact that he has brought a lawsuit for a sum of money which he hopes will allow him to live comfortably for the rest of his life without working. It is the prerogative of judge or jury to recognize that it is extremely unlikely that one would not be experiencing anxiety over the outcome of a matter of such importance.

Examiner effects are not as easily discernible in the report as are situation effects. Bias, one kind of examiner effect that may be apparent in the report, is discussed below. Occasionally, reports will show that the way examinations were conducted did influence, or could have influenced, the data.

## 5. Base Rate Issues

Quite often, clinicians seize upon some relatively normal or predictable piece of behavior and express it in a report as an indication of psychopathology. Every description of the person's behavior should be read with the base rate question in mind. In each instance, after reading the description, the lawyer should ask himself, "What is abnormal about that," in terms of the population in general and in terms of any subpopulation to which the litigant may belong.

For example, in more than one child custody case, we have read in the report that one of the parents was "guarded" or "not open about psychological problems." Common sense suggests that most people being examined in connection with a child custody litigation are likely to try to put their best foot forward to appear as psychologically sound as possible and certainly not to go overboard in trying to reveal psychological problems. Unless the expert can cite scientific evidence in such instances that support these assertions, the lawyer can usually establish, successfully, that such behavior or reactions are commonplace and should not be attributed to abnormality. We are not aware of any research data on this issue, one way or the other, so that we cannot say with certainty that "guardedness" is normal or common, but neither will the clinician be able to cite research data to the effect that it is uncommon or abnormal. Under those conditions, common sense should prevail.

### 6. Bias

The report should always be read with the assumption that the expert may be biased, even in the case of the presumably neutral, court-appointed expert. The scientific and professional literature is overwhelming to the effect that the clinician's biases play a significant role in the way the examination is conducted, the data he obtains, the data he notes, and the way he interprets the data. Bias arises from many sources including theoretical orientation, social values and attitudes, political values and attitudes, the circumstances leading to the examination, attitudes of the examinee toward the examiner or his profession, like or dislike of the examinee, and the fact of having been employed by one side or the other. There is also a well-known "therapist bias" which arises out of the nature of the clinician's profession in which his principal role is that of "helper." That is, most clinicians have entered their profession motivated at least in part to be able to provide assistance to people they perceive as having psychological problems and in their practice this is primarily what they try to do. In the forensic evaluation, many clinicians perceive the litigant in the patient role and themselves in the helper role and thus are motivated to try to reach conclusions that will be helpful to the litigant.

Various indicators of bias may appear in the report. One indication of bias is the completely one-sided report, in which no data or material which might contra-indicate or cast doubt upon the evaluation is presented. It is a symphony of symptoms, deficiencies, psychopathology. It is rare for a clinician to encounter such clear-cut, one-sided cases; and if one does, the chances are the case is not going to go to trial because the conclusion will be evident to everyone involved. In most instances, the litigant will have at least some psychological strengths and some areas of adequate functioning, and many areas of life that encompass no greater problems than the average individual encounters in his everyday living (see discussion in Chapter 4, Volume I, of overlap between those considered abnormal versus normal). Therefore, a report in which any positive description of the litigant is absent or in which any data raising some question about the conclusions or diagnosis is absent indicates bias.

Related to the completely one-sided report is the report which mentions some data which might be contrary to the evaluation or raises some question about the conclusions but then proceeds to ignore this information or slough it off in some cavalier fashion without making clear why this data does not diminish the certitude of the conclusions. For example, in one custody case, the clinician's report, clearly favorable to the father, casually mentions that he may have a drinking problem but then does not discuss the potential significance of this or the need for further investigation, nor does the report deal with this in any way, although it is of obvious potential significance in terms of the child's welfare.

The language chosen to describe some aspect of the individual or his behavior provides another clue to bias. The clinician has great latitude in this respect. He can color the individual in any direction he wishes. Depending on how he wants to make the litigant look, he can describe behavior in terms that are either positive or negative. (See Diamond, B., Chapter 1, Volume I). This can be illustrated by an old parlor game in which the object was to describe the other person in unflattering terms but to use a complimentary term for the same characteristic in oneself, for example, "You are stubborn but I am persevering." "You are impulsive, but I am spontaneous." Therefore, in reading a report or in listening to testimony, try to play this old parlor game and substitute more favorable language for that used by the clinician. Thus if the clinician says "lacks affect," rephrase it to read "stoic or unemotional or cool." If the clinician says "guarded and suspicious," substitute "cautious or thoughtful." In one custody case, the child was described as "over-involved" in some of the mother's activities. One would have difficulty in distinguishing between "over-involved" and "enthusiastic," but the connotations of the two terms are quite different. In another case, an unwed father had been denied any visitation at all with the child, but persisted through proper legal channels of motions and appeals, to attempt to have some contact with his child. The psychiatrist described this behavior as that of a "litigious paranoid." Of course, given the magnitude of the issue involved, someone else could look at the behavior and describe it as "devotion to the parenting role" or "good old Yankee gumption and stick-to-itiveness" or other similarly positive terms.

Another clue to bias is exaggeration. For example, in one case of alleged traumatic psychosis, the plaintiff was described as a "vegetable," although the evidence clearly showed that after abandoning the world of work, the plaintiff spent his time painting, writing poetry, and learning to play the guitar, clearly well beyond the description of a vegetable.

## 7. Jargon

Many attorneys have had the experience of reading a report so filled with clinical jargon that it was impossible to understand what it was all about. One should not be discouraged by this. A report filled with jargon probably means the clinician did not understand what he was talking about either. When reports are submitted in connection with litigation, the clinician knows that those reports are going to be read by laymen and need to be couched in terminology that is understandable to laymen. If this is not done, it suggests that the clinician is not able to translate the jargon or the concepts into understandable language. Not infrequently, clinicians use excessive jargon to cover up their lack of genuine understanding of the concepts involved. The jargon is used in an effort to impress a reader or listener with how knowledgeable the clinician is when, in fact, the converse is likely to be true. For this reason, even limited amounts of clinical jargon will have to be challenged to dispel this notion of superior knowledge. In reading the report, one should note each use of jargon, being particularly sensitive to whether or not the clinician has explained what he means by the term or whether he simply rattles on with a lot of esoteric language. Note that the psychology Ethical Principles require the psychologist to use language reasonably understandable to the recipient of services (see Volume III, Chapter 2). Jargon is not likely to be understandable to a jury or judge. The challenge to jargon is dealt with below under the topic of cross-examination.

## 8. Psychological Tests

If the report is from a psychiatrist, the lawyer should note whether or not it is based in part upon psychological tests. Given the doubtful reliability and validity of psychiatric evaluations, if psychological testing was not used the psychiatrist will be vulnerable to attack for having failed to obtain this additional source of information. He will either have to assert that the conclusions were made with a degree of certainty which can be shown to be unlikely to exist or he will have to denigrate psychological tests. If he chooses to denigrate the tests, it should be possible to demonstrate that conclusions based on psychiatric interviewing are no more reliable or accurate than those based on psychological testing. In fact, if anything, the evidence shows the opposite (see discussion of Sawyer's work in Chapter 5, Volume I). Occasionally it will turn out that the psychiatrist has administered the psychological tests himself rather than utilizing a psychologist for this purpose. This is a cue to inquire as to his qualifications for administering and interpreting tests in contrast to a clinical psychologist. It is unlikely that the psychiatrist will have had training and experience with the tests comparable to that of the average psychologist; therefore, this procedure is highly questionable. One exception to this approach is where the psychiatrist has given the litigant an

MMPI, which usually only requires the examiner to read a brief set of instructions, and has then sent it off to one of the automated interpretation services. In that instance, his training or qualifications are really not relevant, and the attack can be made on the basis of questions or issues concerning the MMPI or computer interpretation.

Occasionally, we have found that when a psychiatrist, and sometimes even a psychologist, is confronted with a challenge to an opinion based in part on psychological test findings, he will state that he uses the tests only to corroborate his findings. What this seems to mean is that if the tests agree with his conclusions, he finds the test data useful. But if the tests disagree, or fail to confirm his findings, then he simply disregards the tests. This is obvious nonsense and a prime example of confirmatory bias. If the tests provide valid or useful information about the individual then that information cannot be disregarded. If they do not provide valid information, then they serve no purpose because the corroboration obtained from them is obviously meaningless. One could use an analogy to laboratory reports. It is hard to imagine a biochemist using a blood test report only to confirm his opinion of the subject's blood type and throwing out the lab report if it does not conform to his "impression" that the individual had a certain blood type. This practice also suggests the clinician felt unsure of his conclusions and needed corroboration.

If the report is from a psychologist and he has not used psychological testing, which happens occasionally, then he will probably be vulnerable to attack for failure to use the diagnostic methods in which he was trained. (Some training programs in psychology, such as behaviorally-oriented ones, may provide little training in the use of "standard" psychological tests.) Typically, however, the psychologist will have used psychological tests and most probably included among them one or another of the various projective tests. If psychological tests have been used, it is imperative to obtain the raw test data. By this we mean the actual responses of the litigant on the WAIS, the Rorschach, the TAT, drawings, and whatever other tests were administered; and in addition the scoring of any of these tests and computations of scores in connection with the tests. If the MMPI was given, the profile and the copy of the answer sheet that the litigant filled out should be obtained. This test data along with any notes made by the psychologist should be obtained as soon as possible, and one should request that the material be in legible form. If it is not legible, further requests should be made to have it typed or handwritten in a form which can be read. We have had the experience of having test data delivered a couple of days before trial only to find that it was not possible to evaluate it because the psychologist either used some personal shorthand or his writing simply could not be read.

Sometimes the clinician will assert that the raw test data has been destroyed or even that the scores and profiles and so on have been discarded once his report was written, as he will claim to have no further need for them. The same is true of psychiatrists in some instances who claimed to have made notes during their examination or even treatment but to have discarded them. There is simply no excuse whatsoever for such a practice where there is any inkling on the part of the clinician that there is or may be some kind of legal claim or litigation. The usual assertion is that there is so much paperwork it takes up a lot of space and it is not necessary. This is a feeble excuse where there is litigation involved. Any clinician of ordinary intelligence should know that his conclusions may be subject to examination by the other side and that this can only properly be done if the raw data is maintained. In all cases where the possibility of litigation was known to the clinician, destruction of tests or other examination data should be viewed as a deliberate attempt to conceal data that could be important (see Volume III, Chapter 2, re requirements to make and maintain records).

While the lawyer may be able to spot a number of deficiencies in the psychiatric report, this is a more difficult task regarding psychological test results because much of the material is technical and can only be evaluated by one who has manuals and resource books available and is knowledgeable about the tests. Therefore, it is our view that the lawyer could use the services of a psychologist, preferably one with academic interests who teaches courses in testing and/or personality assessments. This consultant expert should be asked to carefully scrutinize the test materials for errors of scoring or administration. Even where the examining psychologist has impressive credentials, these errors are astonishingly frequent and they are quite damaging to the credibility of the psychologist or to any conclusions of a psychiatrist who has relied on the test findings.

Careful examination of the MMPI, if it has been used, can be highly useful. To begin with, it has the validation scales that have been described (see Volume II, Chapters 12 and 18), and often these will cast doubt on the credibility of the litigant. In other cases, they will seem to be ignored by the psychologist or interpreted by him in the light most favorable to the litigant. We have often found that going through the answer sheet, item by item, reveals a number of responses by the litigant which either directly contradict the conclusions drawn by the psychologist, cast a certain amount of doubt upon the credibility of the litigant, or reveal problems or strengths not noted by the psychologist or psychiatrist. For example, in a case involving alleged psychological consequences of purportedly tortious conduct by plaintiff's employers, the psychologist's report contained the following statements describing plaintiff: "Plaintiff is constantly preoccupied with the incident and cannot get it out of his mind. The approval of others especially those in authority is an especially important element in holding together a rigid and fragile personality structure. Any attack by those in authority would be emotionally devastating. He sees his whole life collapsing around him as a result of the incident. He is highly sensitive to criticism. He is extremely tense, fearful and anxious. He is socially introverted and he is depressed."

Observe in this context, statements of plaintiff extracted from his MMPI answer sheet:

He is happy most of the time.

He seldom worries about his health.

His judgment is better than it ever was.

He is about as able to work as he ever was.

He is liked by most people who know him.

He is a good mixer.

Most of the time he does not feel blue.

His feelings are not easily hurt.

He is not lacking in self-confidence.

He usually feels that life is worthwhile.

He does not mind being made fun of.

He does not find it hard to make talk when he meets new people.

When in a group of people he does not have trouble thinking of the right things to talk about.

He seems to make friends about as quickly as others do.

He very seldom has spells of the blues.

The future does not seem hopeless to him.

Thus, these several statements by plaintiff flatly contradict the conclusions stated by the psychologist based on profile interpretation. The jury, for example, simply refused to believe that someone who says he is happy most of the time, and seldom feels blue, is depressed. Incidentally, in addition to these statements, plaintiff's score on the social introversion scale of the MMPI was right in the middle of the normal range, flatly contradicting the psychologist's assertion that he is "socially introverted." Checking a litigant's responses on the MMPI does not always turn up such a gold mine of information but will pay off often enough to justify the effort. This applies to any questionnaire type of test.

As a rule it is not as easy to find such concretely usable items in the projective test material. With the projective tests, one should request the consultant-expert to provide alternative ways of interpreting materials, which is almost invariably possible. In addition, the consultant-expert should be requested to provide information as to the extent to which any of the types of conclusions drawn from the tests have been validated or lack scientific validation.

## A SAMPLE CASE REPORT ANALYSIS—
## THE CASE OF THE MANIC MILLIONAIRE

The case material which follows was selected because the reports are quite brief, but illustrate a number of the points described above. This case has been effective in teaching seminars in which, after being provided with the case material, the seminar participants were invited to see how many leads they could find in the report or how many leads to areas in which to question the clinician. Then, the report would be analyzed as a group endeavor. We would suggest that for most effective learning, the reader first read through these materials and then go through them again trying to note such flaws and leads before reading the analysis which we provide. Insofar as possible the facts of the case have been altered so as to avoid identification of any of the parties.

## FACTS

This case is an action to rescind a contract on the grounds of lack of capacity to contract due to mental illness. You represent the defendant sheep dealer. Your investigation has turned up the following facts:

Plaintiff is a very wealthy, 67-year-old farmer, sheep rancher and land owner. His net worth is estimated at $15,000,000, all of which he made through his own efforts and shrewd investments. For most of his life he was a very energetic, active man and has been viewed by acquaintances in the small western town in which he resides as a somewhat eccentric wheeler and dealer. At one time he had purchased several hundred acres of purportedly worthless land for $200,000, which became known as Plaintiff's Folly, but a couple of years later, after developing the parcel, he sold it for a $2,000,000 profit. His nephew acts as foreman of the ranch, since the family persuaded plaintiff to partially retire in 1975. In late summer of 1976, he was seen by his doctor in connection with some fairly severe medical problems. The doctor was concerned that he seemed tired and sad and referred him for psychiatric evaluation as a result of which he was diagnosed with neurotic depression for which, however, he refused treatment and according to the description by his wife, apparently came out of the depression in subsequent months, shifting into an overactive state. The psychiatrist, Dr. P, saw him only during the week of August 10, 1976.

During January and February of 1977, he was traveling around the country making various business deals in which, according to the nephew, he had spent some $500,000 and obligated himself for perhaps another $5,000,000. On February 10, 1977, he entered into the transaction at issue for the purchase of sheep and equipment from defendant for $267,000. In connection with this purchase, he retained an independent sheep broker who appraised the sheep at very close to the actual sale price although very shortly afterward the price of the sheep dropped. This broker states he did not notice at any time prior to the transaction that plaintiff acted in an irrational or unusual fashion; that is, nothing beyond the way he was in the course of his everyday dealings. There are indications his family was opposed to this purchase. During the couple of months preceding his hospitalization shortly after this transaction, he had made a number of other purchases, some of which have been honored, while parties involved in the others are coat-tailing this case to see whether or not they should attempt to enforce their contracts with him.

The facts surrounding his involuntary hospitalization are as follows: Between February 10 and February 17, he continued his traveling and wheeling and dealing. Purportedly the family became concerned because he was calling at all hours of the night and they thought he was not sleeping and they became concerned about his health. They were unable to persuade him to return home so they tricked him into coming home by a ruse to the effect that his wife was quite ill and needed him. He immediately got a flight to the nearest major airport, a three-hour flight, and then rented a car and drove another couple of hours to get home, arriving in the early hours of the morning. Upon arrival, he was greeted at the door by his perfectly well wife and family and several Deputy Sheriffs. He was urged to go to the hospital and upon his refusal, was placed in restraints by the Sheriffs and delivered to the hospital. He was placed in restraints by the Sheriffs because he refused to go along with them willingly. He was also placed in restraints at the hospital as he stated that he would not stay there and would get out as soon as he could. The psychiatrist, Dr. P, was the same one that had seen him and diagnosed the neurotic depression the preceding year.

## REPORT OF DR. P, 4/25/77

Plaintiff was hospitalized at Hospital from 2/17/77 through 3/23/77, by commitment. When he arrived, he was belligerent, hostile, and had to be restrained. He refused to eat or take his medicine and it was necessary to force feed him and give his medication by injections. In addition to his hyper-motor activity, he showed flight of ideas with constant talking, changing the subject with almost every other sentence. He discussed grandiose ideas and stated that he was losing $10,000 a day in the hospital. In addition, he had an exaggerated opinion of himself and his ability.

The patient states that there is nothing wrong with him. He shows marked pressure of speech. He says that he is not going to stay in the hospital, that he is not sick, and that putting him in the hospital is keeping him from making "$10,000 a day." He further states that he will not eat, nor will he take his medicine. When told that the restraining cuff on his ankle could be removed if he would not hurt himself trying to get out of bed, he said no, he was going to get out if he could. He does not intend to stay in the hospital. He is threatening towards the hospital personnel, refuses to take any medication, continues to talk constantly with flight of ideas. Plaintiff was seen by this examiner in August, 1976 at the request of Dr. X. At this time he showed a marked depression. He remained somewhat depressed all summer and then came out of the depression in October, 1976. In November it was evident that he was beginning to get hyperactive and his mind becoming more acute but he would not return to this examiner or any other physician for medical care. He continued to gradually increase his psychomotor activity. Recently he has been traveling around the country, buying and selling in trades that involved considerable amounts of money. It became evident to his family that he was sick because he was not sleeping since he would call them at all hours of the night and since they recognized he was spending money which he could not afford. They arranged to persuade him to come home on the grounds that his wife was sick, since he wouldn't come home for any other reason.

In the hospital, plaintiff showed an overall intellectual impairment. His contact with reality was impaired and his judgment was defective in that he could not distinguish between the important and the unimportant details in his environment there in the hospital.

The above-named individual has always exhibited what is known as cyclothymic personality. That is, he has always had periods when he was somewhat depressed and withdrawn and then he has had other periods when he was very active and excited and his mind overworking,

He had a previous episode of the same illness 15 years ago and was treated by electroshock therapy.

DIAGNOSIS: Psychosis, Manic-Depressive, Manic Phase.

OPINION: It is my opinion that plaintiff had been suffering from this psychotic illness for a number of weeks before he was admitted by commitment to the hospital for therapy. This is a major and severe mental illness. No one with this illness is mentally responsible for his acts.

## PSYCHOLOGICAL EVALUATION
## BY PSYCHOLOGIST, MARCH, 1977

He was given the Wechsler Adult Intelligence Scale, Rorschach, TAT, Human Figure Drawings, and Bender Gestalt. He obtained a Full

Scale I.Q. of 109, which is in the high average range of I.Q. Verbal I.Q. is 117 or bright normal, while Performance I.Q. is 98, or average. His basic capacity is in the superior range. There does seem to be a deficit in his overall intellectual functioning, probably due to some organic brain changes as well as to his functional disturbance. His contact with reality is definitely impaired, although he can put on a very good appearance and appears quite reasonable in much of what he says. Judgment is impaired, however, he is unable to distinguish the important from unimportant details in his environment. He does appear to be rather manic at this time. His thinking becomes loose and fluid at times, although it does not really appear to be schizophrenic. Rather, instead, he does appear to be suffering from a manic illness, presumably manic-depressive variety complicated by some organic brain changes due to the aging process.

He is a person who obviously is quite ambitious, has been all of his life, who feels he has had to prove something, and now with increasing age is feeling these pressures on him even more. He is very doubting of himself as a man underneath but again has to disguise this from himself and others by his manic behavior. There is a great deal of anger and resentment underlying, and some of the manic behavior is a defense against a potential depressive condition.

He does not seem to have very much insight into himself, and he is feeling that everyone is against him because of his great success.

DIAGNOSTIC IMPRESSION: Manic-depressive illness, manic type, with some organic brain changes.

## ANALYSIS OF REPORT

The first paragraph of Dr. P's April 25 report is obviously his description of plaintiff's symptomatic behavior. The paragraph describes principally angry or grandiose behaviors. Dr. P apparently considers it psychopathological for plaintiff to be hostile and belligerent after having travelled all night to return to his presumably ill wife only to find out that he had been tricked and on top of that he has been forcibly hauled off to the hospital. We would seem to be dealing very clearly with a situation effect here and probably with base rate issues. How many people under those circumstances would not be extremely angry? Once we view plaintiff as extremely angry, rather than sick, it is easy to account for the flight of ideas and the pressure of speech. Except for people who tend to be somewhat over-controlled in their mode of expression, most of us have experienced states of extreme anger in which we engaged in more or less lengthy harangues directed toward the object of our anger in which we spoke rapidly and vehemently, hardly able to get the words out fast enough (pressure of speech) and in the course of the harangue may have thrown in all kinds of matter that is not directly relevant to the present issue, dredging up hurts from the past, making threats about the future and so on (flight of ideas). An angry tirade is rarely highly rational and well modulated. However, it is not a symptom of psychopathology. These things are symptoms of extreme anger, overwhelmingly justified in this case.

Dr. P also views plaintiff's high opinion of himself and claims that he was losing "$10,000 a day by being in the hospital" as symptoms of mental illness. There are several things to consider here. First of all, one will want to know if plaintiff really meant that he was losing precisely $10,000 a day or whether this was simply an angry man's way of saying "You are costing me a lot of money by confining me this way." Secondly, Dr. P views the declaration of $10,000 a day as grandiose, and that would probably be a correct assessment for most people, but is it correct for this plaintiff? In the days before inflation, he had made $2,000,000 in two years on a $200,000 investment. That figures out roughly to about $2700 a day. Given that he has now invested a considerably greater amount and with the kind of inflationary period that existed, it is not altogether unreasonable for him to expect that he could make thousands of dollars a day roughly stated as $10,000 a day. Is Psychiatrist P unaware of the money making capacity this man has demonstrated in the past? If he had done it before, how does Dr. P know he cannot do it again? One can safely assume that Dr. P's education, training and experience is in medicine and psychiatry and not in the fields of business and economics. What qualifies him to judge the potential profits from this plaintiff's business activities? The report does not make clear the basis for Dr. P's conclusion that plaintiff has an exaggerated opinion of himself and his ability. Possibly, it is related to the $10,000 a day assertion. One would certainly want to know just what it was that plaintiff might have said that would constitute an exaggerated opinion for a man who through his own efforts has accumulated a fortune of $15,000,000. Success of that magnitude would seem to justify the use of some superlatives in describing one's ability. Statements of this kind may also merely represent a tactic he was using in the effort to regain his freedom; that is, he may have held some hope that by letting them know that he was an important person they might yield to his demands to be released.

Moving on to Paragraph 2 of Dr. P's report, we note that Dr. P saw plaintiff in August but in this paragraph describes his condition for the rest of the summer and changes that occurred in October and November. How does he know what plaintiff's condition was at those times, particularly in view of the statement that plaintiff would not return to him or any other physician? The way the whole paragraph reads, one is impressed with the probability that the information came from family members (and in fact, later questioning showed that the primary informant was plaintiff's wife with some additional information from the nephew). This suggests a line of questioning to the effect that plaintiff's wife is not trained in psychiatry and therefore is not qualified to assess symptoms of mental illness. She could, of course, describe behavior. Anyone can determine that someone appears less depressed than they were a month or two before and could also describe the individual becoming more active, or very active, but presumably a layman would not be qualified to determine whether these behaviors fell within or without the psychopathological or normal ranges. Therefore, we are going to want to find out what were the behaviors that warrant the description "hyper-active." We will also want to find out what Dr. P means when he says his "mind is becoming more acute." Unless Dr. P attaches some unusual meaning to "more acute," one would think it sounds pretty good. In fact, looking at Dr. P's statement, "In November it was evident that he was *beginning* to get hyperactive," one wonders how it is possible to distinguish beginning hyperactivity, obviously considerably less than "hyperactivity" itself, from a high degree of involved, enthusiastic activity. This point is highlighted by the next sentence, "He continued to gradually increase his psychomotor activity." Dr. P describes plaintiff's business activities, buying and selling, involving considerable amounts of money. We have to find out if he considers that a symptom because given plaintiff's financial status and general level of business activities, this would seem to be a normal thing for him. In the next sentence, he states, "It became evident to his family that he was sick because he was not sleeping." What is the base rate for staying up late, working long hours, for people in general when they are very involved (not pathologically) in an immediate project? How many lawyers work late and get less sleep when they are in trial? They assumed that he was not sleeping because he would call them at all hours of the night and since they recognized he was spending money which he could not afford. First of all, this apparently involves a medical diagnosis by the non-medically trained family based upon an assumption that he was not sleeping, although one might recognize that if a man were heavily involved in business activities, he might be calling late at night. We certainly will need to find out what was meant by calling them at all hours of the night. Our experience in these matters is that it will turn out that it was far less extreme than it sounds. The family also diagnosed him as ill because they "recognized" that he was "spending" money which "he could not afford." We might first of all note the use of the word "spending" money which seems to be a clear misrepresentation of what was happening. He was making investments, he was wheeling and dealing as he had done virtually all of his life, and he was engaged in trying to make money. He was not dissipating his fortune on wine, women, fast cars or anything of that kind. He was, apparently, primarily putting his money into hard goods of one kind or another. Given the inflationary trend, one can at least hypothesize that this was a very wise way to invest his money. Then there is a question concerning the amount of money he could afford. We can legitimately wonder which of the medical or non-medical diagnosticians in this matter were qualified to judge how much of his net worth was appropriate for him to invest. So far as we know, none of them are graduates of Harvard Business School or Wharton Business School with advanced degrees in business; certainly the wife is not, certainly Dr. P is not; we don't know about the nephew but judging from his activities we may speculate that he is not and make a note to find out. However, on a purely common sense basis, we might well conclude that for a wealthy individual to invest a third of his assets in diversified holdings does not seem all that unreasonable. Of course the amounts of money involved here were large but they were not unreasonable in the absence of other explanation, in view of the extent of plaintiff's wealth. In any event, it would seem more reasonable to accept the judgment of the man who amassed the $15 million fortune as to how much he could invest rather than to accept the judgment of those who had not amassed a fortune such as the wife, nephew, and the psychiatrist. Recall that many years earlier, he had made millions on an investment that everybody said was crazy. Note the wording of the last sentence of this paragraph, "They arranged to persuade..." This appears to be an effort to downplay the fact that someone else viewing the fact might very well have stated it in terms that more accurately portray what really happened, such as "the family tricked him into coming home by a ruse." Obviously, such a statement would clarify probable situation effects involved in plaintiff's anger on being hauled off to the hospital. Dr. P's statement suggests some bias.

It will be important in connection with all of the information Dr. P relied on as indicated in the second paragraph to explore possible motives the family would have in attempting to portray plaintiff as sick. One obvious motive is the fact that there was a considerable amount of money which the wife and/or children and/or nephew might anticipate inheriting. It is of such a sizable amount that they might not feel there was any need to add to it and their interest would only be in protecting the amounts they could look forward to receiving. The nephew might view plaintiff's activities as somehow impinging on his own managerial role and have some resentment or need to "protect his territory." There might be other reasons which we do not know about from the information that we have. Perhaps the nephew did not want to be burdened with the management of the additional sheep.

Moving on to the third paragraph, if we have read through all of the materials and are now rereading, we sense a familiar sound to the words that are used and checking through the materials, we see that they are very similar to those contained in the psychological evaluation. Thus, both state his judgment is defective or impaired in that he could not distinguish between the important and unimportant details in his environment. This, along with the other statements in this paragraph, strongly suggest that Dr. P has read and utilized the information from the psychological evaluation report. As that report is based on a number of projective tests, along with the WAIS, it is going to be vulnerable to all of the kinds of attacks that can be made on those tests. Beyond that, a question virtually leaps from the page in the statement, "he could not distinguish between the important and unimportant details in his environment there in the hospital." One is compelled to ask, "Important or unimportant to whom?" Important to Dr. P? Important to the psychologist? Or perhaps important to plaintiff? What were the important or unimportant details demonstrating defective judgment? (As it turned out in a deposition later, Dr. P could come up with nothing more than the fact that plaintiff did not recognize that it was important for him to remain in the hospital because he was sick and less important for him to be free; whereas, apparently, plaintiff felt that it was important for him to be out of the hospital because he did not think he was sick and he had other things to do that he felt were important.)

In any event, it would seem clear that prior to his hospitalization, he was able to make responsible judgments concerning levels of importance. This would seem to be clearly illustrated by the fact that in the midst of what he undoubtedly viewed as important business activities, he was able to recognize that his wife's health was more important and to take a proper action accordingly. Thus, he not only demonstrated recognition or distinctions between more or less important matters but also the ability to control his behavior in accordance with that judgment.

In the fourth paragraph, Dr. P asserts without qualification that plaintiff has "always" exhibited a cyclothymic personality. How on earth could he know what plaintiff has always exhibited when he has known the plaintiff for less than one year and, at that, had only a very brief contact with him? We note the use of jargon although Dr. P provides some explanation for what the term means. However, without more information than is provided, the statement may be one of the Barnum effect type. In DSM-II, which was current at the time, cyclothymic personality "is manifested by necessary and alternating periods of depression and elation." The reader may recall from the Barnum effect discussion it consists of statements such as "at times you are somewhat depressed and withdrawn but at other times you are active and excited and full of energy." Is that a statement that a great many people would check as applying to themselves? Furthermore, at the time that Dr. P first saw plaintiff, he was only depressed, if that. Certainly, Dr. P has not seen him in the active and excited period prior to the present hospitalization. Furthermore, if we reread the last part of the statement, "he has had other periods when he was very active and excited and his mind overworking," which Dr. P describes as fitting with the diagnosis of cyclothymic personality, that diagnosis is given in DSM-II as a personality disorder, definitely not a psychosis. In fact, it is listed under the heading of "Personality Disorders and Certain Other Non-Psychotic Mental Disorders." What is different in this description from what plaintiff was doing prior to his return home? The evidence shows that he was "very active and excited and his mind was overworking," if we take the information given to Dr. P as true. Therefore, why is the diagnosis not cyclothymic personality rather than psychosis, manic depressive, manic phase? Manic depressive illness, manic type is described in DSM-II (the manual then operative) as follows: "This disorder consists exclusively of manic episodes. These episodes are characterized by excessive elation, irritability, talkativeness, flight of ideas and accelerated speech and motor activities. Brief periods of depression sometimes occur but they are never true depressive episodes." This is interesting. When Dr. P first saw plaintiff he diagnosed him as a case of depression. Was he wrong in that diagnosis? Secondly, looking at the symptoms, Dr. P apparently obtained no evidence of excessive elation; at least none is mentioned in the report. The irritability obviously was warranted in the situation. The talkativeness, flight of ideas and accelerated speech we have already dealt with as further situation effects.

In the fifth paragraph, Dr. P notes that plaintiff had a previous episode of the same illness 15 years earlier and was treated by electroshock therapy. Given the well-known unreliability and lack of validity of psychiatric diagnosis, we are entitled to wonder how Dr. P knows that the diagnosis was correct at that time. From what we know of psychiatric diagnosis, the probabilities are that it is as likely to have been wrong as right. In his opinion, he states that plaintiff had been suffering from this illness for a number of weeks prior to the hospital admission. This involves an attempt to assess a mental state considerably prior to the time at which the doctor saw the patient and as we know can only be of doubtful validity. He then states that "no one" with this illness is mentally responsible for his acts. We will want to question the absoluteness of that statement. There are few, if any, psychological disorders in which every individual so diagnosed is never in a condition where he could be responsible for his acts. Would there not be some fluctuation of the condition over a period of several weeks? It seems most likely that there would be so that in a more moderate phase of the cycle, one would think individuals could be somewhere within the limits of responsibility.

However, within the facts of the instant case there seems to be evidence that plaintiff was acting in a responsible manner. This is indicated by the fact that before he bought the sheep, he went to the trouble of getting an appraiser and having the sheep appraised and making the purchase only when it appeared that the price was in line. He obviously did not rush in and throw his money on the table without any regard for what the correct price for the sheep should be.

At this point, it seems likely that a pretty good case of bias could be made out. It is a completely one-sided report, all psychopathology and no indication of strengths and no efforts to consider alternative explanations for many of the symptoms such as the anger upon being forcibly incarcerated in the hospital, anger at the deception by his family, omission of any indication that the amounts of money he was doing business with might be appropriate for a man of his wealth and so on. Is there a therapist bias operating here? Keeping in mind that the sheep deal turned out to be a poor one and therefore, while the report sounds negative regarding the plaintiff, it is to his advantage to be found to be suffering from a severe mental illness at the time of the purchase.

Turning to the psychological evaluation, it is unfortunate that in this case the raw test data were not obtained so we are unable to comment concerning that. However, we note that even with this condition, his intellectual faculties were functioning at a level in the upper end of the average range with his verbal I.Q. well up in the high average range. The verbal I.Q. would probably have more significance for transacting business as it involves dealing with ideas and concepts, in contrast to the performance tests which emphasize non-verbal abilities. The statement, "his contact with reality is definitely impaired although he can put on a very good appearance and appears quite reasonable in much of what he says," gives us something to think about. The gist of it seems to be that for the most part he appears quite reasonable and looks all right. We will want to know how, in the face of this appearance of reasonableness, the psychologist was able to determine that his contact with reality was impaired. Seemingly, the basis is given in the next sentence concerning the inability to distinguish important from unimportant details which we have already covered. However, the statement is interesting from another standpoint inasmuch as the law in the jurisdiction requires for recision of the contract that the other contracting party should have had reason to suspect that the individual was not competent. If he appears reasonable and the sheep seller was not required to give him psychological tests, it would seem as though the issue would be resolved on that basis. What is interesting is that having utilized much of the psychologist's material, Dr. P, the psychiatrist, omitted any statement of this kind from his report, again possibly suggesting bias. We would also note that the psychologist gave a number of projective tests which are going to be subject to serious challenge. In addition, the psychologist comes very close to making a diagnosis of an organic brain syndrome, if he does not actually do so. However, the tests he has employed are not viewed as sufficiently diagnostic of this condition to allow for that kind of statement and he has not given any of the neuropsychological batteries which one would think would be required where brain syndrome was suspected. We might also note in this very brief report of the psychologist some statements of tentativeness: "there does 'seem' to be a deficit...probably due to some organic brain changes...he does 'appear' to be 'rather' manic at this time." (For additional sample report analyses in Personal Injury, Custody and Criminal cases, see cases at the end of this volume.)

# CHAPTER 5

# Strategy & Tactics

The basic approach of this book is oriented to accomplishing doubt, disbelief, and rejection of the testimony of psychiatrists and clinical psychologists by demonstrating serious doubts that they possess the knowledge or expertise that they profess. The scientific and professional literature provided in Volumes I and II provide ample evidence that, at the very least, the state of knowledge has not been demonstrated to be sufficiently advanced to give credence to the conclusions and opinions of members of these professions in most instances. These materials may be used in a motion to disqualify the clinician as an expert in the matters involved or in the attempt to diminish his credibility through cross-examination. In addition to the general state of the art deficiencies, any specific errors of omission or commission by the clinician should be included in the attempt to disqualify the expert either by motion or through voir dire or should be fully brought out through cross-examination.

The bases for objecting to admission of this kind of evidence are provided in Chapter 12 of this volume. For reasons that are discussed in that chapter, it is our view that this type of motion or objection can be useful in many cases. Cross-examination is discussed in detail in Chapter 8. The present chapter is concerned with more general considerations in dealing with clinical testimony.

The major concern is how to get the negative scientific and professional literature before the judge or jury. We stress the negative literature because in the face of such a quantity of negative literature, affirmative literature becomes almost irrelevant. In any of the areas described in Volumes I and II, given that there is a substantial body of negative literature, the presentation of contrary or affirmative literature can only establish that at most there is evidence both ways and therefore the issue is one of doubt and controversy within the professions themselves. In that case, as the professionals have not been able to resolve these doubts and controversies among themselves, no judge or jury should be expected to be able to resolve them during the course of a trial. In addition, for several of these issues, affirmative research evidence is either meager or nonexistent—for example, validity, detection of malingering, relationship between experience and accuracy, board certification, several of the psychological tests, DSM, and relationship between diagnosis and legal issues.

There are three ways of getting the scientific and professional literature before the trier of fact—cross-examination of an opposing expert, direct examination of your own clinician-expert, and direct examination of a consultant-expert. By clinician-expert, we mean a psychologist or psychiatrist appearing for your side of the case who will testify regarding the psychological status of the litigant, usually presenting an opinion that differs from that of the expert presented by the other side. Such an expert can testify regarding the negative literature but there are some difficulties with this approach which are described below. By consultant-expert, we mean a professional who will consult with you and/or testify not on the issue of psychological status of the litigant but only on the state of the art issues and deficiencies of procedure or interpretation in the particular case at hand. The use of this type of expert is also described below.

Extraction of the negative research and/or deficiencies of his evaluation or procedures from the opposing expert through cross-examination is the most difficult of the three approaches but potentially is the most effective. If it is possible to obtain acknowledgment of these various deficiencies from the mouth of the opposing expert, one is in the strongest position to argue to the jury that little or no credence should be given to the testimony. Unfortunately, few such experts will readily concede all or even many of these deficiencies involved. Some will not concede any. In many cases, they can easily evade questions on these various issues by denying acquaintance with the negative literature or by denying that they relied on any of it in forming their opinions in jurisdictions where that is the rule. However, since the adoption of the 1992 ethics principles for psychologists, this may be very difficult for psychologists, as the principles require them to be familiar with *and rely on* the scientific and professional literature, among other things (see Chapter 4, Volume III). The witness who denies the existence of the negative literature or is unaware of it presents no great problem. He will be shown to be ignorant in his field when your expert testifies as to the substantial amount of negative literature that does exist. The witness who denies reliance on, or use of the negative literature in forming his conclusions can be dealt with in another way. One way is simply to ask questions, for example, "Isn't there a substantial body of literature indicating that psychiatric evaluations do not have high reliability and validity?" and after a series of these questions, dropping that line of questioning and producing the information from your own experts.

However, it is possible to demonstrate through cross-examination that the expert does rely on the scientific and professional and research literature generally and that it forms part of the body of knowledge from which he draws his conclusions and therefore inevitably he has used it in drawing his conclusions. Very early in cross-examination, questions can be asked to establish that the witness' education and training involved, and was in part based upon, the scientific and professional literature—books and journals—in his field. Therefore, the scientific and professional literature forms part of one of the bases for his qualification as an expert. Questions should follow to establish what journals and books he reads as part of his keeping up with developments in his field. Few experts will assert that they do not read any of the scientific and professional literature because, obviously, no one is going to place much credence in someone who does not keep up with the developments in his field. When his reading material is established, he can be asked questions to establish the fact that this is not recreational reading but he reads the books and journals in order to apply the information provided in his practice. It may be worthwhile to ask if he reads any literature that is contrary to the position or view that he holds, and if so, whether he takes that contrary literature into account in writing his reports or giving testimony. If he says he does, clearly he should then be subject to cross-examination on such literature. If he says he does not read any of the contrary literature, he is obviously in no position to judge whether the contrary position is better supported than the one he takes. If he reads it but does not take it into account, it is obvious that he is ignoring part of the body of knowledge and consequently is taking a one-sided view or is asserting greater confidence in his conclusions or statements than would be warranted by the state of controversy that exists in the literature. However, most clinicians will concede some, if not all, of the negative literature and attempt to deal with it in a "push-pull" manner. That is, they will acknowledge there is some negative literature but then attempt to defuse its significance by one or another kind of explanation, frequently an explanation to the effect that, based on their individual experience, they disagree with the findings. This can be dealt with by going into the issue of experience, but our point here is that if they concede the negative literature you will have established what you want to establish—at least to some degree. You can then ask questions to establish that there is not a substantially better quantity of affirmative research nor is there affirmative research that is of a better scientific quality on the particular issue. (See Chapter 6, Volume III, Experts' Tactics.) This tactic presents one of the difficult aspects of attempting to extract this information by cross-examination. A cross-examiner who is well versed in the materials provided in Volumes I and II and who asks the questions in a proper form and is tenacious in holding the witness to answers that are responsive to the question in the form it was put can succeed, but it is an arduous task and very time-consuming. We believe that at least some cross-examination along these lines should take place, to establish either that the expert is not well informed in his field or that he refuses to acknowledge what the research indicates. The reader is reminded that the ethical principles require psychologists to be aware of scientific and professional literature and recognize limits both to their expertise and to the certainty with which diagnoses, judgments, or predictions can be made about individuals (see Chapter 2, Volume III).

If you are presenting a clinician of your own, he may provide an adequate avenue for introducing the negative literature. However, he is in a somewhat awkward position in this respect. He has either already rendered a diagnostic evaluation and conclusions based on the state of the art at the time questions are put to him regarding the state of the art, or he is going to testify to such issues after responding to state of the art questions. To begin with, many people who render diagnostic evaluations strongly believe in what they are doing and would not be comfortable raising the issues of the many deficiencies that exist, although it should be said that there are some who render their opinion as representing the best that they can do given the problems in the state of the art, and are willing to confess that such problems exist. It is most difficult to acknowledge that there is an inadequate knowledge base, that reliability and validity are low, that experience does not help and so on, and then assert with a high degree of confidence that one's conclusions are correct. Also, with regard to pointing out deficiencies of procedure by the opposing expert, most attorneys are aware that many professionals are reluctant to strongly criticize the work of their professional colleagues. It is also awkward for such an expert to be critical of the knowledge and techniques that he may himself be using in his practice.

The consultant-expert is the most dependable person for introducing evidence on state of the art or state of knowledge deficiencies as well as deficiencies of the examination and conclusions of the opposing expert in the particular case. This type of expert can assist the lawyer in many ways that the clinician-expert cannot or should not. This type of expert can review all of the materials of the case—historical information, investigative information, psychological tests, reports of various clinicians—and point out to the lawyer errors or flaws or deficiencies that the lawyer may not have been alert to. For example, the lawyer is not likely to recognize scoring errors on psychological tests that a psychologist consultant-expert would be able to find. Such an expert has access to restricted materials such as MMPI booklets, WAIS manuals and the like which the lawyer would have difficulty obtaining. He can assist the lawyer in preparing questions for deposition or cross-examination with regard to the specific case. This type of expert can freely testify to all of the state of the art and specific case deficiencies. Experts of this type are most likely to be found on university faculties, and we would speculate, more likely to be found on psychology faculties than psychiatry faculties. It is desirable that such an expert should have had a reasonable amount of clinical experience, either institutional or private practice, so that he is not in a position of a witness testifying about a professional activity in which he has never engaged. Some psychology faculties have professors who are disillusioned clinicians and have returned to academia after finding clinical activity unsatisfactory. Alternatively, there are faculty members who maintain small private practices or consult with clinics or other institutions or supervise trainees who, while involved in clinical work, are involved to a rather small extent, and often primarily for the purpose of staying in touch with clinical activities, so that their teaching is not entirely from the literature. This type of expert has no investment in a diagnostic evaluation he has made, nor does he have any bias due to contact with the litigant.

If the consultant-expert is to be utilized, we recommend that he be brought into the case as early as possible so that he may assist in setting up the investigation as well as reading reports and other materials and guiding the attorney at various stages of the proceedings.

Several lawyers have raised the following questions: Can you present a clinician-expert who will testify to the psychological or mental status of the litigant and also present a consultant-expert who will testify to the poor quality of such evaluations and all of the deficiencies of the clinical field? Would this appear inconsistent or would you not be destroying the credibility of your own witness? Our answer is that it can be done if the judge or jury are properly prepared for it and if the clinician-expert you are presenting is one who is not uncomfortable conceding some, if not all of the deficiencies, at least to some degree. Obviously the situation is more difficult if your own clinician-expert insists that these evaluations can be made with a high degree of accuracy, that his experience has made him accurate, that there is an abundance of validated knowledge, and so on.

One approach to this problem, of course, is not to present a clinician-expert to give conclusions contrary to those of the clinician on the other side, but to present only the consultant-expert who will testify as to the reasons why the testimony given by the opposing psychiatrist should not be given credence for lack of sufficient knowledge and inadequate methods of assessment. This approach can be effective, particularly where your investigation has developed a quantum of factual evidence that is contrary to the psychiatrist's opinion. However, even in jurisdictions where the jury is free to disregard uncontroverted expert testimony, there is still a problem of what the jury may do in the absence of an expert opinion which contradicts the description of the litigant's psychological status as given by the opposing side's expert. Still, there may be situations in which the tactic represents a good gamble. For example, if on cross-examination you have been able to elicit from the clinician many statements which are damaging to his credibility, or he has damaged his own credibility by his demeanor, or he has made statements which can be demonstrated to be outrageous by your consultant-expert, you may have a sufficient basis to take a tack with the jury to the effect, "You have heard how preposterous testimony of this kind is. I am not going to insult your intelligence by offering similar testimony on my side. I think you can see that the testimony of Dr. _____ amounts to nothing more than guesswork. I am confident that you have all had sufficient experience in life that you can take the evidence we have concerning the litigant's behavior and make your own judgment as to his mental condition. As you have been told by Professor _____, the research shows that laymen such as yourselves can do this just about as well as these fellows with all their fancy sounding titles, which as Professor _____ has shown us really does not mean that they know very much." (We have been informed by a number of lawyers that this approach has worked successfully for them.)

In a Los Angeles case a few years ago concerning the so-called Alphabet Bomber, Deputy District Attorneys obtained a jury verdict that the defendant was competent to stand trial despite the testimony of four defense psychiatrists that defendant was psychotic, paranoid (or paranoid schizophrenic), suffered from delusions, had auditory hallucinations and believed he was on trial for masturbating in a public place and, therefore, was incompetent to stand trial. The prosecution presented no experts, and the defense argued to the jury that they should accept the psychiatric opinions because they were based on their collective experience of approximately 75 years. Credit should be given to the prosecutors for their skillful marshalling of the facts of the defendant's past behavior in support of their argument that he was capable of deceiving the psychiatrists and had done so. On cross-examination, the prosecutor also elicited admissions from the psychiatrists that they had not done follow-up studies of their validity in diagnosis of this type. This enabled the prosecutors to effectively utilize the example of the golfer who gets no feedback (see Chapter 8 on Experience, Volume I), to counter defense counsel's argument for validity based on experience.

However, many lawyers feel uncomfortable if they do not produce a contradictory clinical opinion. In that case, we would suggest the following approach.

You could, first of all, try to have your examination and testimony given by a clinician whose philosophical stance is not at great disparity with the position taken in this book. There are a number of clinicians who, while they continue to practice their profession, are aware of the limitations in clinical knowledge and methods. You should forewarn this expert of your intention to attack clinical expertise. On opening or closing arguments, you should try to get the point across that it is necessary for you to offer this type of evidence because the other side has done so and the jury is entitled to know that there is conflicting clinical opinion. You could make it clear that you have little faith in such testimony and encourage the jury to disregard it on both sides if they feel so inclined, particularly based on the evidence to be provided by your cross-examination and/or the testimony of your consultant expert.[1]

---

[1]Argument to the jury could be something like the following: "Ladies and gentlemen, you have heard a good deal of psychiatric (and psychological) testimony in this case. Now you will have to decide how much weight should be given to that testimony in forming your judgment as to _____ (party's mental condition at the time in question). Let me remind you that it is your function to make the decision. The testimony of the doctors is given only for the purpose of helping you make that decision. You are not bound to accept their conclusions and, in fact, you can disregard their testimony or give it very little weight if you choose to. In fact, you have heard a good deal of evidence of lack of knowledge in psychiatry and deficiencies of psychiatric evaluation which in my opinion would clearly justify your rejection of all of the psychiatric testimony. Possibly some of you have been surprised by this testimony in view of the general image of psychiatrists that has been created through the media. However, Doctor _____ (your psychiatrist) has agreed with many of these points. In fact, the psychiatrists were able to agree more about the deficiencies of psychiatric evaluation than on the condition of _____ (the party). Doctor _____ (your expert) and/or Doctor _____, (your consultant-expert, if you have called one) has indicated that psychiatry has additional deficiencies not described by Doctor _____ (opponent's psychiatrist), such as (whatever these doctors have produced which has held up under cross-examination). It seems to me that just hearing two doctors with impressive credentials such as Doctor _____ (opponent) and Doctor _____ (your own), having examined the same party and come to different conclusions, just highlights these weaknesses of psychiatry.

"I would like to suggest in view of the infancy of the art of psychiatry and the conflicting testimony of these two psychiatrists, each with approximately the same qualifications, that the most reasonable course for you to take is to disregard their testimony. I do not see how you could decide which one is right and which one is wrong. It may even be that they are both wrong. You have all had experience in life. I think you are able to look at the behavior of _____ (the party) and determine for yourselves whether _____ (the party) was able to distinguish between right and wrong (or form an intent or has been made neurotic by this accident or is dangerous or whatever)."

# CHAPTER 6

# Dealing with Experts' Tactics

Various tactics or ploys or combinations of tactics are employed by clinicians when confronted by the kinds of challenges that are described in this work.

One approach, not too often encountered, is for the expert to candidly acknowledge the deficiencies or doubts you have raised regarding the state of the art and then simply assert that he is doing the best he can given the state. Some experts will then add that given the state of the art, they nevertheless feel quite confident in their assessments in this particular case. The lawyer can then ask questions to bring out the fact that there is research showing that there is little or no relationship between the confidence in the diagnosis and the accuracy of the evaluation, and indeed that the more confident clinicians may be among the least accurate (see Chapter 5, Volume I). However, in our opinion, this sort of acknowledgement is the best approach for the expert to take. He may in so doing diminish the weight that the jury might attach to his opinions, but he preserves his personal credibility with the jury. It is likely that he may enhance his credibility because the jury is likely to view him as, if nothing else, a very honest man and there is a reasonable chance that they are going to feel that he must know something. After all he is a professional, and despite the evidence that you have presented, he must know something. For this reason, with such witnesses, it is important to go through all of the various deficiencies and spend some time on them so that it does not pass quickly before the jury. Similarly, one should deal extensively with any misconception of skills that the jury may have based on the expert's qualifications. With such a witness, you will have to deal in closing arguments by stressing that even by his own admission, his opinions cannot be really considered other than speculative and therefore should be given little weight. This argument is bolstered where you have been able to present a quantum of objective evidence in the trial which would contradict his opinion.

Another relatively uncommon tactic at the opposite pole from the one above is for the clinician to refuse to acknowledge the existence of the negative literature. Generally this does not involve an absolute denial that the literature exists but takes the form of indicating that the clinician is not aware of any such literature or a statement to the effect that you can probably find an article taking any point of view in the field. This approach does not leave a great deal that you can do in cross-examination of such witness, at least in terms of establishing the specific deficiencies through him, except to show his ignorance of the literature. With this type of witness you will probably have to produce a consultant type of expert who will verify the existence of the research. If you are using a clinician-expert he can establish the negative literature but his position is a somewhat awkward one in view of the fact that he will be rendering opinions about the litigant's mental state; however, some clinicians taking the concession approach described above can, without appearing inconsistent, render an opinion while at the same time conceding the deficiencies that exist. One approach with the witness who does not acknowledge the literature is to ask him what journals he reads in his field and then to ask him about some of the literature that has been published in those journals. He may say that he does not read the journals from cover to cover, so that he may have missed these articles. In that event you will have at least made the point that his reading of the literature was not thorough. He may say that there are thousands of articles published and while he may have read some of these, it is impossible to remember all of the articles. There obviously is merit to that argument. However, it seems highly unlikely that one can maintain reasonable familiarity with the literature in psychiatry or psychology without some awareness of the negative literature which exists in such large quantities. It may be possible through questioning to get some admission that he relies on the general body of knowledge in psychiatry or psychology and then to try to bring out that this negative literature is part of the general body of knowledge. A variation on this type of witness is the one who acknowledges that there is some negative literature but denies the implications of this literature for the state of the art. This point might be pursued with such a witness by trying to get an acknowledgement that there is a considerable quantity of this kind of literature and dealing then in argument by pointing out to the jury that such a quantity of negative literature must create doubt about the state of the art. The two approaches described next—denigration of research and evasion—can work very well for the expert or can work against him, depending upon the skill, preparation and perseverance of the cross-examining attorney.

One of the more common tactics used by challenged experts is to denigrate the research. This may take the form of asserting that you can prove anything you want by research, or by describing the methodological problems of research in this area, or some other kind of response to generally indicate that you simply cannot place much credence in research findings or in articles by authorities. He may cite some examples where research seems to have been misleading.

Where the expert takes the denigration approach, he leaves himself vulnerable in a number of ways. Presumably you will have established earlier that, in part, his education and training were based on the scientific and professional literature and that he devotes a certain amount of his time to reading this literature, presumably with the aim of increasing or keeping up-to-date his knowledge; otherwise, it would appear to be a total waste of time if the scientific and professional literature is as meaningless as he appears to indicate. If this utilization of the literature has been established, it may be best to deal with this tactic in argument rather than through further cross-examination. Cross-examination may give him an opportunity to explain away his use of some of the literature even though he has a generally low opinion of research. For example, he may say he utilizes some of the literature because it reaches sound conclusions. You will then have to question him to show that he is employing a double standard of evidence. That is, he is no longer denigrating research per se, he is only denigrating the research which is contrary to the position he has adopted. You may then have to attempt to demonstrate that there is no better basis for accepting those findings that he accepts than there would be for accepting the findings that he rejects, which then brings him back, for all practical purposes, to the position that he is disregarding research and simply relying on his own personal opinions. This is similar to the situation where the clinician uses the test findings if they corroborate his findings, but discards them if they do not. The point that needs to be made here is that if there is literature pro and literature con, the issue must be considered to be in doubt unless the research on one side or the other is demonstrably and meaningfully superior, which is not particularly likely, and in those cases where such a difference exists, the methodological superiority usually lies with the negative literature. Also, on many of the issues we discuss in Volumes I and II, the literature is overwhelmingly negative (e.g., actuarial vs. clinical, lack of benefit from experience, etc.). However, this is a messy issue to try to deal with on cross-examination. That is why we think it may be better to attack it through a consultant-type expert or your own clinical expert. Also, where the expert denies reliance on the scientific and professional literature, this puts him in a position where all there is for him to rely on are unvalidated theories or clinical case materials which provide most of the alleged support for the various theories. If this can be established, you will be able to argue to the jury that the clinician, if he is not relying on research, can only be relying on a class of data that is demonstrably less reliable than research; that is, the accumulation of clinical cases all of which suffer from the many deficiencies of the clinical method. (In the case of psychiatrists, one may point out that DSM-III-R clearly endorses a preference for scientific data over other data.) If the clinician is not relying on case reports, all he has to rely on is his own experience which is necessarily idiosyncratic and which renders his years of education and training in the field a nullity. (An example of this approach and how it can be dealt with is given in the brief cross-examination illustration below.)

Evasion is probably the most common tactic employed by clinicians. It may appear in different forms.

A number of methods of evasion are described in a book by Dr. Stanley L. Brodsky, *Testifying in Court: Guidelines and Maxims for the Expert Witness,* published by the American Psychological Association in 1991. As we understand this book has had substantial circulation, we think it would be wise for the lawyer expecting to face a mental health expert to obtain a copy and become familiar with the tactics described. We cannot deal with the whole book here, but will attempt to cover some material that seems most salient. We should point out that for the most part, in his examples, Brodsky does not utilize questions framed in terms of the literature, as we suggest, but rather provides questions which seem to be "set-ups" making evasion easy.

One form of evasion involves conceding the correct answer the question calls for, but then going on to qualify or deny its implications. Brodsky calls this "The admit-deny." It calls for the witness to use a dependent clause for the "admit" part so that the answer can not be cut off at that point (e.g., "Thank you, doctor, you have answered the question"). The "deny" part uses an independent clause which strongly and accurately (Brodsky's term) denies the conclusion from the admit part. For example, in an earlier work, to a question regarding the negative literature on the Rorschach, Brodsky suggests the following answer, "While there are many criticisms of the Rorschach in terms of its theoretical meaning, those of us who use it regularly have found that it is an extraordinarily meaningful and important technique." If the question which elicited this answer was framed properly (e.g., "Doctor, isn't there a substantial body of scientific and professional literature that is unfavorable to the Rorschach?"), the answer is probably subject to a motion to strike. That is, the witness has not answered your question which was about the literature generally. Another approach is to repeat the question and ask if the answer is a "yes." You can ridicule a response of this type by questions designed to bring out the fact that it is obvious that those who use the Rorschach think it is useful, otherwise they would not use it. That does not prove anything about the reliability or validity of the Rorschach. Questions should be designed to bring out the fact that there are also a number of clinicians engaged in the difficult task of psychodiagnosis who do not use the Rorschach because they do not think it is useful. If they did think it was useful, they would use it, given the difficulty of the task. If necessary, questions could be asked to bring out the existence of surveys showing that substantial proportions of clinical psychologists engaged in psychodiagnosis do not use the Rorschach. Questioning should continue to bring out the fact that while some clinicians may think, believe, hope, pray or whatever, that the Rorschach is useful, it has not been possible to validate that belief over a series of some six or seven thousand research studies. You should always be prepared to ask questions, to demonstrate that clinical beliefs or clinical impressions which cannot be supported by the research do not deserve credibility. They are nothing more than speculations. In connection with the response Brodsky suggests, it might even be useful to ask a question to the effect that it may be so useful because it is so ambiguous and hypothetical that the clinician can draw any conclusions he wants to from it. One could also ask if the clinician does not find the Rorschach useful, even though there is so much negative literature, because there is nothing better. One of the better ways to deal with witness statements that a concept or method is widely accepted and widely used is to ask questions to bring out the fact that wide acceptance and wide use does not provide good evidence of the utility of the concept or method. This can be done with a series of questions to the effect that for some 200 years, physicians used the method of bleeding to cure diseases and finally discovered that it was a poor method; to bring out that it was accepted for eons of time that the earth was flat but that proved to be wrong; and similarly, that for eons of time it was widely accepted that the sun revolves around the earth until it was finally proven that was wrong. One can also bring out the history of mistaken beliefs within psychiatry (see Chapter 3, Volume I), or articles on psychological tests which indicate that popularity and validity should not be confused (see Chapter 10, Volume II). "Beliefs" have to be shown up for the superstitions that they are, and that not only do they not lead to valid conclusions, they often constitute an impediment to reaching valid conclusions. Frequently the "deny" part of an answer will not rest on well-validated scientific data and this can be brought out.

Another Brodsky suggestion is the "push-pull" which employs the martial arts principle of going with your opponent's force and making it your own. Thus, if the question is, "Doesn't the literature contain many statements indicating the clinical interview is unreliable," a "push-pull" response might be, "Good heavens, yes, those people think the interview is completely useless." Thus, rather than being defensive, the witness goes with the thrust of the question and makes it seem like his own and he does not perceive it as damaging. You might take the issue back by repeating the question, "Doctor, I take it your answer is that there is such a body of literature, is that correct?" Brodsky does warn his readers that overuse of "admit-deny" or "push-pull" may backfire. This suggests it may be useful to ask a lot of questions the witness might be tempted to answer that way.

Another form of evasion is the citation of one or two studies supporting the position the expert is trying to maintain or that are contrary to the challenge posed by the question. The simplest way to deal with this is to establish that while there may be some studies supporting the clinician's contention, there are other studies that are contrary to it, and that this leaves the issue in doubt and therefore, if it is a problem that the profession has not been able to resolve, one cannot place any confidence in the clinician's adoption of one side. Thus, for example, in one case a psychologist (see *Psychologist* No. 2, Chapter 9, Volume I), when asked if race was not a significant variable in psychological assessment, cited four studies to the effect that race does not make a difference when education is controlled for. Cross-examination in such an instance has to bring out the fact that while the four studies the psychologist cited do exist, there are also studies showing that race makes a difference even when education level is controlled for. If the witness is not aware of or fails to acknowledge the conflicting research, then he will appear either uninformed or biased when a rebuttal expert or consultant expert recites the contrary research.

A related form of evasion takes place when the clinician asserts there is research showing whatever it is that he is trying to show, but is unable to give the citations or references. If this occurs on deposition, one can ask him to supply the references prior to trial. If it occurs at the time of trial, one can ask how many such references there are, approximately when they were published and whether there is also contrary research published. If the witness is not aware of any contrary research, doubts as to his biases or credibility will become apparent when your expert testifies to the existence of contrary research.

Another form of evasion is the recitation of a single case or some kind of anecdotal material. For example, the clinician states that "In 7 out of 10 cases of learning disabilities in children, I find there is marital conflict in the home." Statements of this kind should be challenged by questions to bring out the fact that this is a very crude kind of observational research that does not begin to meet appropriate standards of scientific research and therefore does not provide an adequate basis for reaching any conclusions. The reader may recall from Chapter 2 of Volume I that one could go around the countryside and observe whether farmers using

Fertilizer A produced a greater crop yield than those using Fertilizer B. All of the deficiencies of that kind of approach are outlined in that chapter. Thus, in the example cited above, assuming that the witness can substantiate that the 7 out of 10 quantity is accurate, and not his impression of what the number is, then he is stating that he has performed research. He has done a "study" of this phenomenon and is vulnerable to all of the attacks on failure to use scientific methodology, so that his finding is of little if of any value and certainly no basis for confidence. For example, what is the base rate for marital conflict in the homes of children who do not have learning disabilities (control group)? If it is about the same or, as is more likely, if the expert does not know, he has no basis for concluding as he has done, that there is some relationship between marital conflict and the learning disability. It may simply demonstrate that, as is well known, there is marital conflict or marital discord in quite a high percentage of American families, and thus the chances are when one sees a child with a learning disability they will find marital discord, just as if they were to look into the family situations of children without learning disabilities they might well find an equal proportion of families with marital discord.

Another form of evasion consists of altering or rephrasing the question. Frequently, the expert would rather answer a question in the form he states it rather than one you have put, because he will be able to do it better or it is more likely to allow him to "prove" his point. Of course, in some instances, he may restate the question in a way that is actually better than the form you used and in such cases, one would not want to fight him on it. However, most of the time you should not allow the expert to take control of the cross-examination in that manner. You should insist that he answer the question as you have put it, or state that he is not able to answer the question as it has been asked. Many cross-examination questions are framed in a manner which allows the cross-examiner to be quite confident of what the answer must be unless the witness is uninformed or less than candid. For example, rather than putting a question such as, "Doesn't the scientific and professional literature prove that psychiatric evaluations have low validity?" we suggest framing the question in a more conservative manner, "Isn't there a substantial body of scientific and professional literature indicating that psychiatric evaluations lack high validity?" If the clinician responding to the more conservative question states, "I don't believe the literature proves that," he has changed the question; that is, he has answered a different question than the one that was asked. This can be dealt with by pointing out to the witness that he has not answered the question that you asked. You did not ask whether the literature proved low validity, you have asked whether there is a substantial body of literature indicating lack of high validity and you might then repeat the question and ask him if he would answer it the way you have asked it. An alternative approach is with a motion to strike the answer as non-responsive. If you sense that the clinician is going to try to deal with your challenging questions in this manner, the effect of several motions to strike as non-responsive conveys the information to the jury that the witness is unwilling to perform his role, which is to answer your questions if they are answerable.

Another tactic is the attempt to represent widespread general consensus or even unanimity on a particular principle or statement or imply that the principle has been scientifically established by prefacing the statement with words such as "we find" or words of similar import. For example, the statement, "We find paranoids emphasize the eyes in figure drawings," conveys the idea that this is a well-established principle and there is widespread agreement on it. Statements of this kind generally contain two misrepresentations which need to be brought out. This can be done with questions to the expert as to what is meant by the word "we." That is, do all psychologists come to this conclusion or make this finding? If it is less than all, how many less? Does the literature show substantial disagreement on the issue? The point is to not permit the expert to get by with conveying the impression that there is agreement on the point because this is most unlikely. If the clinician insists that there is agreement, questions may be asked concerning illusory correlation (see Chapter 5, Volume I).

The second misrepresentation lies in the word "find" conveying the impression of scientific precision, or the existence of some clearly and unequivocally observable relationship. This also is unlikely on most psychiatric or psychological issues. Usually questioning will demonstrate that the clinician really means that sometimes we observe or we interpret or we fantasize or we create but there is little in the way of unequivocal objective finding that is significant to diagnosis. Sometimes the phrase is, "We find such and such associated," or, "We frequently see." This inevitably raises questions about such matters as illusory correlations, base rates, and Barnum effects. It may be true that a number of people diagnosed as schizophrenic do not form close relationships. The question is, we do not know how many people who are not diagnosed as schizophrenics also do not form close relationships, so that finding has no significance. Or, in some cases, there are research findings showing a relationship of one data item to another, but those relationships may be so small that they have no practical significance.

Sometimes the statement is prefaced with "We believe," which does not connote scientific verification but still contains the impression of general agreement. The quote "we" can be dealt with as described above and the "believe" part can be dealt with by questions bringing out the issue of illusory correlation.

Another statement is the "frequently we see A in relation to B" type. This sounds fairly impressive but often masks the fact that the psychiatrist really does not know the frequency of the relationship. Therefore, it will generally be a good risk to ask him when he has used the term "frequently" just how frequently he means, and try to pin him down to a specific number or percentage. In some cases, it will turn out that by "frequently" he means three or four times out of ten, allowing you to show that it is more likely not to find the relationship than to find it. If he states a higher frequency, he should be asked how that frequency was determined, whether through scientifically controlled studies to determine the frequency or whether that is his guess, undocumented by research. If he refuses to be pinned down as to the meaning of "frequency," he can be asked if there is scientifically controlled research demonstrating any particular frequency for the alleged relationship. The term "frequently" should be recognized as a crude validity statement, and subject to all the previously shown attacks on psychiatric validity. A similar approach can be used with statements that a particular finding is "consistent" with the diagnosis. This only tells you the diagnosis is possible—not that it is correct. Most findings are consistent with several or many diagnoses and are also found in people who do not have that diagnosis (see discussion of overlap in Chapter 4, Volume I).

Sometimes when confronted with the negative research evidence, the psychiatrist will try to crawl out with a glib phrase such as, "Oh, we have learned a great deal since then…" as the research would undoubtedly have been done some period of time prior to the testimony. In such cases, it would almost always pay to pin down the psychiatrist as to any new research evidence which contradicts the previous research and which shows that the present state of research substantiates the psychiatrist's opinion. This strategy should be employed in connection with almost any type of glib disregard of the research evidence by the psychiatrist. In his practice, of course, he may choose to disregard the research and to depreciate its significance; but the fact is that in almost all cases, he will be unable to cite any better kind of evidence to support his position. He should also be asked if there is not some more recent scientific and professional literature which continues to indicate what the prior literature has indicated. A check of chapter references in this book will almost always show this to be the case. At best, the situation is left in doubt which means that no credence should be given to the psychiatric testimony on that issue.

## EVASION IN DETERMINING THE SOURCE
## OF CONCLUSIONS

One of the most difficult types of evasion to deal with develops when you try to extract from the expert the bases in the data he has obtained from which he has drawn his conclusions or descriptions of the litigant. It goes something like this. You ask questions trying to determine which data led to which conclusions. The clinician responds roughly to the effect that it was no single piece of data taken by itself but all of the data taken together. Critical analysis and considerable research show that declaration is almost surely incorrect and that there is no clinician that can come close to handling and "integrating" the thousands of pieces of information that take place or emerge in a clinical examination (see Chapter 5, Volume I). Theoretically, there is information in every word the litigant speaks, every sentence he uses, the sequence of the sentences, the way the sentences are structured, verbal or motor expressions or movements occurring at the time the statements were made, the nature of the situation, momentary changes in the way the examinee and the examiner perceive each other and the purposes of the examination, and so on and on and on, far beyond the capacity of any human brain to manage, which is one of the reasons computer interpretation systems have become popular. It is highly unlikely that the clinician has utilized every piece of information that appeared in the examination. Frequently, the report itself or, if not the report, then detailed questioning as to the bases for the conclusions, will reveal that as few as three or four items of information formed the basis for the conclusions and it is rare in our experience for more than a dozen or so bits of information to be used by the clinician. The difficulty arises when you try to extract from the clinician exactly what it was in the data that he used to form his conclusions and how he used the data to form his conclusions. Any method of dealing with this problem is likely to be cumbersome, frustrating, and exhausting for everyone concerned: lawyer, expert, judge, jury. However, unless the expert has been sufficiently discredited through some of the other approaches described in this text, it is imperative that this issue be dealt with. Note that Ethical Principle 7.04(a) requires the psychologist to candidly and fairly describe the bases for his conclusions in forensic matters.

One approach is to try to demonstrate that the clinician did not, in fact, use all of the data. That is, he did make some selection from the many bits of information that were available. One might try to penetrate that thicket by asking a question such as, "Well, doctor, the litigant walked into your office and sat down. Did you attach any significance to that, either by itself or in the context of all of the other information?" And if the clinician says he did, he should then be asked what significance he attached to it and how that significance was arrived at either for the bit of behavior itself or in conjunction with other behaviors. A series of questions of this kind will rather soon, we believe, demonstrate that the clinician has not used all of the information, that some of the information obtained was viewed as non-significant by him. Once this has been established, the field has begun to be narrowed. One can start to go through each bit of behavior that occurred and ask the clinician if it had any significance, either by itself or with the other material. And, as there begins to be an accumulation of behaviors to which the clinician did not attach any significance, it may be possible to shorten the procedure by noting this fact with the question, "Well, doctor, is it correct from what you are saying that of all the data that arose in the examination, there was some to which you did not attach any significance?" and presumably the expert will respond affirmatively to that. If he does not, there is no alternative but to proceed item by item, with behaviors in the psychiatric examination or test responses if there was psychological testing. Assuming however that he answers affirmatively, it should then be possible to ask a question, "All right, doctor, is it correct then to say that some of the information had significance and some of it did not?" Presumably that will be answered in the affirmative. One can then proceed to ask the next question, "All right, doctor, I would like you to tell us what information that you obtained did have significance for you." Then there are two alternative approaches. One is to have him elucidate all of the data that was significant to him and then question him about it, or to have him start to describe the data that was important and then at each point to ask him how that was significant in the diagnosis. The latter may be the easier procedure to deal with as it allows you to deal with the point while it is fresh in everybody's mind and does not require extensive note taking to keep track of each item the expert mentioned. Of course, at best, the examination of the witness is going to be lengthy and this is one of the reasons we suggest making the motion to bar the testimony or limit it, one of the grounds of the objection being that in order to adequately cross-examine experts in this field and to extract the bases for their findings, an inordinate amount of time will be consumed if the job is to be done properly. There is little doubt that the examiner has the right to determine from the expert the bases for his conclusions. If you have stated in a motion that this is going to require a lengthy cross-examination and the judge decides to let the testimony in anyway, he is in a somewhat awkward position intellectually to limit you in the cross-examination, particularly when it will become apparent that the difficulty lies in the expert's inability or refusal to provide the information and not with the cross-examiner.

The problem in this whole area is that the clinician wants to speak in terms of his inferences and abstractions while the cross-examining lawyer wants to determine what observable facts formed the basis for those inferences and abstractions and how they did. That is, the lawyer wants to find out if the inference or conclusion is justified by the fact or facts upon which it is based. In order to do that, he has to know upon which observable facts it was based. He also wants to know if there were other observable facts in the clinical examination which might give rise to contrary or inconsistent inferences and so he wants to know if those facts were considered and dealt with by the clinician. In order to do that, he has to be able to find out if a particular observable fact played a part in the clinician's conclusions or inferences or in some cases, if not, why not. The clinician does not want to be pinned down in this manner; he wants to say "I am a trained clinician in my field and after looking over all of the data, I have formed the following conclusions based on my professional training and experiences. You should believe me because I am a physician specializing in psychiatry or a Ph.D. clinical psychologist with an impressive set of credentials and therefore you should understand that my conclusions are correct." Yet all of the materials provided in Volumes I and II of this text cast serious doubts upon any such contention and probably negate it.

As an illustration of this problem, the reader may recall in the case of *Smith vs. Schlesinger* (see discussion Chapter 1, Volume I) that one of the clinicians utilized the fact that the litigant associated with people the clinician considered "bad company" as one of the symptoms of poor judgment supporting the diagnosis of psychotic depression. Once this basis was revealed, the court was able to determine that this was not a medical judgment but was a social judgment based on the clinician's social biases, but the court had to be made aware that this was one of the bases for the diagnosis in order to be able to make that judgment.

In personal injury or other cases where deposition can be taken, it may be preferable to deal with these cumbersome issues of bases at that time, rather than consuming a great deal of court time. For this reason, it may be well to inform the clinician and opposing counsel that the deposition is likely to take a whole day and maybe more.

The following is an example of responses of a psychiatrist which illustrates many of the tactics described above. Suggestions for dealing with such responses are given following the example.

## SAMPLE CROSS-EXAMINATION OF PSYCHIATRIST

The following examples of psychiatric cross-examination are adapted from M. Blinder, *Psychiatry in the Everyday Practice of Law,* 1973, The Lawyer's Cooperative Publishing Co., Rochester, N.Y. 14603, and were themselves adapted by Blinder from transcripts of actual testimony by psychiatrists. That book contains many examples of psychiatric testimony.

1.  Q: As a psychiatrist, your examination is limited to just talking with your patient?
    A: Yes. And observing him, too. His expressions, movements, posture and so on.
2.  Q: Do you physically examine him?
    A: Not as a rule. The psychiatric diagnosis is concerned primarily with patient's thought, feelings and behavior. These things don't show up on physical examinations.
3.  Q: So then, you depended a great deal on what Mr. Jones told you?
    A: Yes, but more on how he said it. The patterns his narrative fit or did not fit, the things he didn't say, his behavior, mood and so on. While, of course, I listened carefully to what he said, I certainly didn't take it at face value.
4.  Q: Did you check any of his statements with any other witnesses?
    A: No.
5.  Q: Don't people sometimes lie, especially when they have a great deal to gain by doing so?
    A: It happens, yes, of course.
6.  Q: So, then, a man could fool you into thinking he had a mental illness he didn't really have?
    A: Yes, but it is hard to do a credible job of simulating mental illness. A man may try to talk or act bizarrely or describe some previous occasion when he did, but speaking or acting crazy is one thing and a clinical pattern of mental illness is quite another. In any event, I do not believe Mr. Jones tried to simulate mental illness.
7.  Q: If he were successful in his efforts, you wouldn't believe he had tried to fool you either. Is that so?
    A: Yes. I suppose so. But he is not likely to be successful unless, of course, he has gotten an M.D. degree, taken an internship and a three year psychiatric residency, examined 1,000 mentally ill people and read several hundred books on the subject. I don't think Mr. Jones has done any of those things.
8.  Q: Don't different psychiatrists use quite different systems of classification of mental disorders?
    A: Yes.
9.  Q: Isn't it true that if three psychiatrists examined this man, it is likely they would come up with three different diagnoses?
    A: No. Though it is quite likely they would use different labels for the same condition.
10. Q: Then psychiatric conditions are pretty vague, aren't they?
    A: Well, no.

11. Q: Aren't they the subject of much dispute among psychiatrists?

A: No, not the conditions, the labels. This labeling problem stems from the fact that you can accurately describe the same person in different ways. If a girl 5' 5" weighs 200 lbs., you can call her overweight, fat, or an excessive eater. So it is with psychiatry. If a woman believes that she's Joan of Arc, psychiatrists might say she is confused or psychotic or delusional. But regardless of the labels, they would all mean the same thing, that most people would perceive her as crazy.

12. Q: Well, there seems to be considerably more than a semantic difference here today. Isn't it a fact that psychiatrists are frequently in substantive disagreement when they get into court?

A: Yes and no. Most cases that I've worked in, the psychiatrists have tended to agree with each other in their medical opinions. When appearing in a courtroom adversary setting, psychiatrists are often focused by opposing counsel onto different aspects of a patient's condition and into divergent legal conclusions.

13. Q: Dr., can you offer any scientific evidence that the psychiatric theories upon which you base your conclusions have some basis in fact?

A: Yes, I believe so. It depends on what you mean by scientific evidence. For example, when I did public school consultations, I found that eight times out of ten, when a previously well-behaved pupil began tearing up the class, his parents were having terrible marital problems and perhaps were on the verge of separating. Marital counseling with the parents without even involving the child usually corrected the inappropriate behavior in school. Now, I can't prove this cause/effect relationship like one can prove the slot machine odds are stacked against the player, but it is proof enough for me.

14. Q: Dr., how do you determine if your professional opinions are correct?

A: I don't know if I can answer that except to say that it would be hard to go on practicing psychiatry if I were wrong most of the time.

15. Q: Has there ever been a scientific study of the accuracy of your professional judgment?

A: I don't know what you mean by a scientific study. I examine the psychiatric data and then I reach the best conclusion that I can.

16. Q: You have never gathered evidence which indicates that the conclusions you offer in the courtroom are usually correct?

A: That's a subtle form of the "are you still beating your wife" question because there is no such evidence to gather. There is no such thing in this context as "correct." There is no answer in the back of the book against which I can check my results. No platinum bar in the Bureau of Standards in Washington. There is no ultimate authority, only the jury's verdict and that, too, merely is their best judgment.

17. Q: So you haven't, then, any idea if the diagnostic opinions you have been offering year after year are really accurate?

A: I think I have a good idea. Over the years I have treated hundreds of patients on the basis of my diagnosis and most of them get better. Many express gratitude for the help I have given them. I don't think patient response is an ideal way of assessing one's competence, but it is worth something. I have also worked closely with more experienced psychiatrists, and they have indicated that I have acquired a certain proficiency.

18. Q: So your confidence stems largely from your experience in this kind of work?

A: Yes.

19. Q: Do you consider yourself fairly experienced?

A: Yes.

20. Q: Are you aware of the great number of studies which show that more experienced psychiatrists are no more accurate in their assessments than inexperienced ones, or even lay people?

A: That is not my understanding. The studies I have read on this matter have been done largely on psychologists. Psychologists generally have a good academic background and much theoretical knowledge, but relatively little clinical training and experience compared to the psychiatrist. Most of these studies are simply not valid in my opinion.

21. Q: On what fact do you base this opinion?

A: On the fact that merely doing a study in the name of objective research does not necessarily make it valid. The tobacco companies have all sorts of elaborate, scientific studies showing that cigarettes do not cause cancer or heart disease, but smokers continue to die prematurely of these two ailments at a prodigious rate.

22. Q: I am sure we'd all agree that smoking is unhealthy, but I believe we are talking about psychiatric experience here.

A: In all due respect, we are talking about research studies which purport to show that psychiatric experience is of no particular value, perhaps a disadvantage, and I would refute that assertion by suggesting that all such laboratory studies show is how easy it is to inadvertently draft a scientific investigation so that your conclusions come out at war with common sense. For example, it would be very easy to produce a study showing that experienced brain surgeons lose a lot more patients each year than do inexperienced ones. They perform many more operations and take on more difficult cases. If you use postoperative mortality as a basis, you could easily conclude that the best one to go to for brain surgery is my barber because he has never lost a case. Nevertheless, in the unlikely event that you should develop a psychiatric problem, you would do well to come to me rather than to my barber in spite of the disadvantage of all my experience in treating emotional disorders.

## ANALYSIS OF SAMPLE CROSS-EXAMINATION

### 1. THE CLINICAL EXAMINATION

Questions 1, 2, and 3. Here the psychiatrist has told you that he utilizes behavioral observations and observations of mood and feeling and so on in arriving at his conclusions. You will want to make it clear that this material is important to arrive at the conclusion he has drawn. In regard to prior mental condition then, you will be able to point out that this important class of information could not possibly have been available regarding the mental condition at the time of the event in question or at any prior time. You may want to elicit from him a statement to the effect that one needs to be a trained psychiatrist to know what to look for in the behavior and to adequately observe the psychiatric material and thus you will preclude his reliance on the testimony of lay witnesses if there are any available. If the expert does not volunteer the information about observing behavior and so on, of course, you will have to ask questions to draw this out from him also.

You could ask why he did not take the man's statements at face value and hopefully elicit something to the effect that the statements of psychiatric patients are not particularly reliable or that he had some reason to question the statements in this case. Secondly, you can ask what statements were made that he did not believe as indicated by his statement.

Question 4. This answer indicates he did rely on what Jones told him.

Question 5. We would modify the question a little bit to include words such as "misrepresent" or "exaggerate" in addition to "lie" and the same thing applies to Question 6.

Question 6. We would change the question a little bit here to state "could fool a psychiatrist" rather than "fool you." This answer is a variation of admit-deny technique and you have to deal with it, otherwise the psychiatrist is going to sound credible on this point. First of all, you should respond immediately to the last sentence regarding no attempt to simulate as it is a gratuitous effort to promote Mr. Jones' credibility and suggests that this is not an impartial expert but, in fact, a partisan witness. To emphasize this, you could ask something like, "Why, Doctor, I didn't ask you if Mr. Jones was trying to simulate," and you might move to strike that portion of the answer as not being responsive to the question to further indicate to the jury that it was improper. Regarding the substance of his answer, you might ask if it has been demonstrated by research that it is very difficult to successfully simulate mental illness. You could ask him about the literature indicating that a high proportion of people do succeed. You might also ask if people do not have a tendency to exaggerate things where there is a motive to do so and possibly even inquire as to the problems involved with poor recall, which is aside from simulation. Also, having in mind the Rosenhan Study, and the Heaton and Albert studies, you might want to ask if there is some research showing that as a matter of fact some people have been able to very easily deceive clinicians into diagnosing mental illness or disorder.

Question 7. First of all, note his reluctance to give you a clear answer—he says "...suppose so..." to this question which calls for a clear and unequivocal affirmative. You might wish to point out the contrast between this mild equivocation and the high degree of certainty he has probably been expressing regarding his psychiatric evaluation or effect of his experience. Then again we have another example of the admit-deny technique. However, he has gone overboard on his lavish description of what it would take to effectively simulate mental illness and he has been snide to boot, which—if you wish to take advantage of it—affords you the luxury of being somewhat less polite with him than you might otherwise be. You might wish to call attention to this with a preliminary statement to a question roughly to the effect, "Well, Doctor, I think you are trying to make fun of me, but I'm sure you understand I'm merely trying to get to the truth of the matter here." If you want to play around a little on this answer, you might ask, "Well, Doctor, you really don't need an M.D. degree to simulate mental illness, do you?" And if he has not recovered his wits enough to concede that various other kinds of mental health professionals could do it just as well, you can point this fact out to him, such as clinical psychologists, psychiatric social workers, probably psychiatric ward technicians, psychiatric nurses, etc. Then you could go on down the line, that you don't suppose it really takes an internship and it doesn't really take a three-year psychiatric residency and one need not have examined a thousand mentally ill people and read several hundred books on the subject in order to successfully simulate. In other words, the way he has stated it, just about everything he has said can be challenged and you will certainly, again with Rosenhan in mind, want to ask him if, in fact, there are not a number of recorded cases where people with no training whatsoever in the mental field were able to successfully fool the psychiatrist into diagnosing mental illness. You will recall that among Rosenhan's pseudo-patients, there was a housewife, a painter, a graduate student in psychology, who might be questionable in this regard, and a pediatrician, who probably also might be questionable. But, in any event, none of these would have met the expert's criteria for being able to successfully simulate mental illness but they still fooled the psychiatrists. Further, if people without the qualifications he described had succeeded in fooling him, he would not know that such education and experience were not necessary in order to fool him.

## 2. RELIABILITY, VALIDITY AND DSM-II

Question 8 would be better phrased in terms of the literature. Further questions should be asked to establish that there is an official diagnostic classification system and to determine whether or not this expert uses it, with the attack going in either direction depending on his answer. However, we will deal with the material the way we have it.

Question 9. We do not like the form of the question here. We would not use the number 3, but simply substitute "different" psychiatrists and eliminate the second 3. We could try to establish that the label is in fact the diagnosis. Otherwise, we will not deal with the answer because it is repeated in a more lengthy fashion a couple of questions down.

Question 10. The answer here should be followed up with questions concerning the fact that psychiatric conditions are poorly defined and maybe that would have been a better way to state the question; if the expert continues his denial then you might want to ask questions concerning the Spitzer article as to how poorly defined these psychiatric conditions are. However, let's go to Question 11, where we think we can show how the expert is evading the truth. You will note that response 11 is part denial and part push-pull.

Question 11. Keep in mind here particularly the Tarter Study (Chapter 7, Volume I) because the psychiatrist is either going to have to back off of what he says or you are going to discredit him with that study. You might deal with this response with a question something like, "Well, Doctor, let me see if I understand you correctly. If one psychiatrist says the patient is psychotic and another says the patient is neurotic and another says the patient has a character disorder, they would really all be describing the same condition, just using different language for it. Is that correct?" Obviously, he is not going to agree with that and with infinite patience will probably explain to you that, in fact, those do represent different psychiatric conditions. So then, your next question should be, "I see, and it is those different conditions on which psychiatrists do not have much dispute or disagreement. Is that correct?" And we assume he is going to be consistent in his response there and say that is correct. You can then introduce the Tarter Study and others showing that, in fact, psychiatrists are unable to agree on the presence of these conditions. You do not have to deal with the last part of his response but it might not do any harm to point out that if a woman really believed she was Joan of Arc, obviously in terms of his own statement, you would not need a psychiatrist to determine she was crazy (always subject to the qualification that if she had some motive to misrepresent, everybody, including the psychiatrist, might be wrong).

Question 12 is probably unnecessary at this point, but if it's going to be asked, we would word it differently, leaving out "in court." However, if it was asked and you got the answer that was given, there is some interesting material to work with. The answer seems to state that the conclusions are determined by the lawyers rather than the psychiatrists, which is certainly an interesting state of affairs. Same for the data that the psychiatrist attends to so we seem to have a statement that so far as forensic psychiatry is concerned, the psychiatrist simply becomes a mouthpiece for the lawyer. This statement also verifies the problem of the gap between psychiatric conclusions and legal conclusions by indicating that diverse legal conclusions are possible from the same medical condition. It might be worthwhile to ask a question about a well-known case, such as the Patty Hearst or John Hinckley cases, in which it was clear from newspaper accounts that, in fact, the experts were of considerably different medical opinions after extensive examination regarding the medical condition.

Question 13. This is a badly framed question. One should not ask if there is *any* evidence—there may be some—and the open-ended nature of the question gives the expert an excellent opportunity to lecture on any available positive evidence. The question should be approached from the other direction. To establish that scientific validation of these theories is lacking, the question might be, "Taking the professional and scientific literature as a whole, isn't there a great deal of controversy about the validity of these theories so that at the very least they must be considered controversial and their status in doubt?" However, the answer proves that sometimes even a bad question can produce good results. You might first of all want to establish how he confirms the eight out of ten number, whether by an actual count or by his impression. If it is the latter, you can bring out the fact that he could be off to some degree which would reduce the significance of his conclusion. You might ask how many of these cases he conducted to see if it was a sufficient number, or large enough sample, upon which to base "scientific" conclusions. Then you might ask if he knows what percentage of children in schools display the problem he has described. Whether he knows the answer to that or not, you can then ask what percentage of parents have marital problems (roughly 50% according to statistics published). What you will want to establish here is that in fact he has done a very crude form of research study without knowledge of base rates, which are relevant, without adequate controls and generally without employing anything approaching adequate scientific methodology. If you have been able to establish that instead of eight out of ten maybe it was only seven out of ten and you take his statement that marital counseling usually corrected the situation, meaning something less than always corrected, so that of the seven out of ten maybe only six were corrected by marital counseling, then you have a rather slim basis for his conclusion. But what is particularly important here is his final statement that while this can't prove the cause-effect relationship, this crude research is proof enough for him. Also, it shows he is willing to render opinions based on evidence of poor quality. If this badly done research is proof enough for him, he is clearly not going to be in any position to effectively denigrate the research you may later wish to confront him with.

### 3. THE ACCURACY OF THE EXPERT

Question 14. We think this question should be preceded by a question to establish that the doctor is not correct 100 percent of the time. Most psychiatrists would concede that. We think you would not want to ask as open-ended a question as this one because it gives the expert the whole field to run in. However, in this case, the answer given is helpful to your cause. He has pretty much given you the answer you want which is that he does not know how to tell you how he determines that his professional opinions are correct or more accurately, he does not know how to determine if they are correct. Obviously, if he does not know how to determine if they are correct, how can the jury determine if they are correct? This is a point you will probably want to make in argument. If you wish to deal with the rest of the answer, his statement that it would be hard to practice if he was wrong most of the time begs for another mention of the practice of bleeding for 200 years, and mention of the many questionable and later abandoned treatments during the history of psychiatry. In addition, obviously, if he does not know how to determine if he is correct, then he does not know in fact that he is not wrong most of the time; but if you ask another question about it, he may give you some answer indicating that it is his impression that he is right 90 percent of the time or something like that.

Question 15. The answer here may be further explored to indicate that he does not really know how scientific studies are done, although it may simply mean that he is not sure how the examiner is using the term. If the former, the response can be used to negate any of his denigration of research on the grounds that he really does not understand it. If you want to gamble, you might ask some questions as to how scientific method could be applied to the problem of determining the accuracy of his judgments, being aware yourself that this would require experimental controls, definitions of population, definitions of criteria, some kind of quantitative measurement, and the utilization of independent researchers to avoid any bias that might be present in his own observation of his performance.

Question 16. This is a poorly stated question as it gives him an opportunity to recite single cases or anecdotal evidence if he cares to. However, once again, a poor question has produced a useful answer. When he says there is no such thing in this context as correct, you would probably want to just file that away and bring it out for use in argument. However, if you want to challenge him on it, you could make reference to the number of studies which have, in fact, assessed the degree of accuracy of psychiatric judgment, for example, Baxstrom, Plag, and others in that group which do give a precise percentage of accurate judgments.

Question 17. This is an atrocious question as it gives him the opportunity to express any basis whatever that he uses for concluding that he is correct most of the time. Of course, this is essentially what he does. A more astute response from the witness might have been something like, "I have the impression that I am correct most of the time," or, "I think I am correct 85 percent of the time," or something like that. Upon further questioning to try to challenge that, he can just keep going back on the fact that he has not made a count. You asked him if he had any idea, and his idea was that he is 85 percent correct. There is not much you can do with it except to bring out that it is an impression and not a verified fact. We have previously suggested a little better form of the question, "Well, in that case, Doctor, you really can't be certain how accurate your diagnoses are, isn't that right?" which allows the questioner to emphasize that the doctor does not know for a fact what his accuracy is and is relying purely on impression. It can then easily be brought out that the impression is likely to be biased in his favor. However, his answer here brings us down to the critical issue—his experience. We want to deal with this because we have frequently encountered similar responses when the psychiatrist is asked why he thinks he is correct. The simplest way to deal with it is with a question about bleeding and other such "cures," if you have not already beaten these to death. However, there is further material you can use to demonstrate that his experience is indeed a flimsy basis for validating his diagnoses. While we do not want to get into a discussion about the usefulness of psychotherapy, it is important for you to know, because this approach is taken so often, that there is published research (See Volume I, Berman & Norton, 1985; Smith & Glass, 1977) which casts serious doubt as to whether the improvements in therapy are, in fact, due to the experience of the therapist and presumably would apply, according to the words of this expert, to the correct diagnosis.

His statement that patient response is "worth something" may also be worth dealing with using questions to see if he considers this to be of equal value with scientific research to establish his validity, although he admits it is of questionable value. (See Chapter 8, Volume I, re: doubtful value of patient response and treatment outcome as criteria for validity.) Then he gives you a circular psychiatric argument based on the evaluation of his evaluations by more experienced psychiatrists as proof that his experience has been beneficial. Obviously, if their experience does not lead to greater validity, their support of his diagnoses does nothing to establish that his diagnoses have been improved by his experience. If you feel comfortable enough with it, you might want to ask questions here about illusory correlation which you will recall is the practice clinicians have of supporting each other's false beliefs. Question 18 should be asked before going into all this material to establish the fact that he does rely largely on his experience in making diagnoses with confidence. One may also wish to raise research which shows a lack of relationship between confidence and accuracy and which, not irrelevant to this seemingly quite confident expert, suggests that the most confident clinicians may be among the least accurate.

Question 19. This question seems to serve no purpose and we would prefer a somewhat different question, "Well, Doctor, in order to benefit from doing the diagnoses, wouldn't it be necessary to follow up those diagnoses to determine in some way if they were correct and if they were not, to determine what kinds of errors the psychiatrist was making?" It might be worthwhile to precede these questions by a question such as, "Doctor, are you saying that the diagnoses of more experienced psychiatrists are more accurate than those of less experienced psychiatrists?" and let him commit himself to an affirmative answer on that question.

Question 20. We would alter this question somewhat by eliminating the word "great" and substituting the word "indicate" for the word "show" which would make the question less subject to argument on the grounds conveyed by the words that were used. We are going to deal with the series 20, 21 and 22 together because they all contain the same elements and provide a number of bases for diminishing any credibility this expert might have had if you go after him doggedly on the answers that he gives. In the example given here, cross-examination goes off on a different tack after Question 22, so we are going to assume for discussion that the cross-examination has proceeded as given to that point. On that basis, we would then proceed to go back through the statements the expert has made one by one to demonstrate the error or misrepresentation involved.

With regard to his statement that the studies are largely concerning psychologists, you could ask if there are not several with this finding involving psychiatrists. Our book contains over ten citations with findings of no difference of diagnostic accuracy between experienced and inexperienced psychiatrists and no better rate of agreement among experienced than among inexperienced, thus making the Tarter study relevant here also. That is, if experience makes for greater diagnostic accuracy, the amount of disagreement in diagnosis among experienced psychiatrists should be much less than that among inexperienced. Otherwise the percentage of errors should necessarily be the same for both groups. There are also various studies showing low predictive accuracy that included experienced psychiatrists. Of course, you could move to strike all of that portion of his answer dealing with psychologists as not being responsive to the question and possibly add to the jury's impression that this witness is biased and is there to prove a point rather than give information. If there have been a series of such motions it may indicate that he is unwilling to play by the rules of game. However, you might find it beneficial instead to pursue him on his statement concerning psychologists. You would want to get him to commit himself openly to what he is implying here which is that psychiatrists are better diagnosticians than psychologists because of their superior clinical training and experience. As long as he has introduced the topic of academic courses, you might want to ask him if it is not true that psychologists get a great deal more formal course work in psychology than psychiatrists. Then you will want to show that his declaration that the psychologist has "relatively little clinical training and experience compared to the psychiatrist," is outright nonsense. He is likely referring to the fact that the psychiatrist does a three-year residency which the psychologist does not do. However, those three years are usually counted in the total years of experience stated by an expert. Thus, it should be brought out that obviously a clinical psychologist with 20 years of experience has the same amount of experience as a psychiatrist with 20 years of experience. We cannot think of any rational way for him to get out of that. However, if necessary, you can go further. Many of the studies evaluating the effect of experience and many of the studies on reliability and validity have employed both psychiatrists and psychologists in the same study and there are virtually none to our knowledge which demonstrate a superiority of psychiatrists over psychologists. In fact, if anything, there is a slight trend in the opposite direction (e.g., see Dershowitz, Chapters 1 and 7, Volume I), but it is not of sufficient significance to try to establish that psychologists are better than psychiatrists. You could ask if there are some studies showing psychologists a little better than psychiatrists. There are also a number of studies showing that psychiatrists evidence the same types of judgment problems or problematic habits as psychologists (see Chapter 5, Volume I). It is clear from this research that psychiatrists, despite his allegation of their superiority due to training and experience, cannot be shown to be better diagnosticians than psychologists. Also, if he has not acknowledged several studies on psychiatrists regarding experience, it might be worthwhile to ask why he has paid so much attention to those showing psychologists do not improve with experience while paying no attention, evidently, to the literature showing the same thing concerning psychiatrists.

Having stated his opinion that these studies are not valid, he could be challenged to demonstrate how they are less valid than any research he has indicated he does rely on in other respects. We do not think he will be able to do this and this will allow you, then, to raise the issue of a double standard of evidence. Or you might ask him how these studies are less valid or less well done than his study showing that eight out of ten school behavior problems are caused by marital difficulty in the home which is proof enough for him. But the main opening he has provided is by questioning the validity. In order for him to do that he would need to be familiar with the studies. So it would be appropriate to ask him to describe the methodology of each study (or as many as necessary). This would make question 21 unnecessary. If he does not know the methodology, how can he know the studies are not valid?

It is probably just as well to ignore the tobacco company research except that you might want to bring out the obvious bias and motivation of the tobacco companies in performing that research. You may later be able to contrast this bias with the fact that many of the studies showing unreliability of psychiatric diagnoses and failure to improve through experience were done by psychiatrists who likely would not be highly invested to prove that experience is of no effect in psychiatry.

With regard to Answer 22, you might want to ask if he is saying in effect that no reliance can be placed on research findings. We suspect he will not agree with that, which then brings you down to the research findings, particularly having to do with experience. We would take him up on his statement regarding scientific research that is at war with common sense. Obviously, one of the purposes of research is to test common sense notions because, as you can bring out, sometimes common sense notions are wrong (e.g., the earth is not flat, the sun does not revolve around the earth, and so on). The fact that a research conclusion may be contrary to common sense does not mean the research should be thrown out; it means that the common sense notion has to be questioned. The common sense of today is very different in respects from the common sense of yesterday, in significant part because of the corrective influence of science. There may be two other lines of questioning that you might want to pursue with regard to the common sense notion. One would be in a case where some of his conclusions are somewhat at war with common sense. For example, if this was the previously discussed case of the 50-year-old divorced woman who was depressed, you might want to pick him up on the acceptance of common sense and ask if in that kind of situation in fact all of the details of the woman's life would not tell us through common sense that she would probably be depressed even without the intervention of the accident. Or you might want to challenge some esoteric theoretical concept he has relied on, perhaps from Freudian theory.

We would also take him up on his declaration of how studies can be drafted so as to inadvertently produce a certain conclusion. You might want to bring out that much of the research on experience was done by psychiatrists who would not have any motive to design the research so as to prove that experienced psychiatrists were not very good diagnosticians. You might ask if all of the several studies were inadvertently drafted to produce this result. You might also want to point out that taking blood out of sick people is at war with common sense. You might also want to point out that it was not common sense that put astronauts on the moon, it was research that did it, and that polio vaccines were not developed and tested through common sense but through scientific research, and whatever else you care to recite to indicate that as a matter of fact, research is probably the best way to proceed rather than common sense. However, by his brain surgeon example, he has invited an elucidation of the difference between clinical observation and scientific research. As you will recall from the discussion of fertilizer in Chapter 2, Volume I, what he has described here is directly analogous to the example we gave of what would not be research performed according to scientific methodology. All he is referring to in his example is a hypothetical observation that experienced brain surgeons lose more patients than inexperienced ones. Of course, that is exactly like someone going out and observing that Farmer A using Fertilizer A produces more corn than Farmer B who utilizes Fertilizer B. Indeed, that is exactly what happens in clinical studies or case reports, which he will probably have indicated he does rely on. You will then want to point out that the example he gives suggests he does not understand scientific method because it does not represent a reasonable application of scientific research methodology in that it fails to control for obvious variables such as the number and nature of cases treated. We would want to ask questions of him to see if he understands the meaning of controls and then to ask him in what way the studies on experience have failed to reasonably represent a more appropriate scientific approach than the example he gives. If he is knowledgeable enough to give you an example or two, probably based on the amount of experience or the kinds of cases that were involved, we would then get into a discussion of the methodology in the Tarter study in which they made sure that only highly experienced psychiatrists were used, psychiatrists who were "known" to their colleagues to be highly skilled at diagnosis, and that there was no particular selection of patients; there were roughly a couple of hundred taken as they came to the hospital. They still got results similar to those of many previous studies, roughly about 50 percent disagreement on the diagnosis.

# CHAPTER 7

# Depositions

In many respects, taking the deposition of a psychiatrist or psychologist is not greatly different from taking the deposition of any other kind of expert. The object is to get as much information as you can while giving as little as possible. Therefore, many lawyers do not go very far by way of challenging the expert at this stage. There is the advantage, if the challenges are made at deposition, of finding out how the clinician will respond to the various kinds of challenges that are discussed in this book. However, if he is challenged on any particular issue, this may alert him and he may come much better prepared for cross-examination at the time of the trial. There is a further problem in that if you succeed in making him look weak on the deposition, opposing counsel may then decide to call in another expert to try to bolster his case. A possible compromise is to try out a couple of the kinds of challenges you are interested in making and see how the clinician responds to them. A major advantage of deposition is the opportunity to use more open-ended questions.

The deposition provides a good opportunity to establish any authorities or publications the clinician relies on and to establish what professional journals and publications he reads, if any. It may be worthwhile to ask the clinician, particularly if he describes himself as a forensic psychiatrist, or forensic psychologist, if he has read *Coping With Psychiatric and Psychological Testimony,* and if so which edition. If he has read the book, he will hardly be in a position to deny the existence of the literature that is cited in it. We recommend dealing extensively with the expert's qualifications on deposition. He should be questioned in detail concerning his education and training, any employment, any types of practice he has engaged in, association memberships or offices, administrative positions, and publications, particularly in areas that are relevant on the basis of his report. For example, if the diagnosis is schizophrenia, has he published in that area, or if it is his opinion that the defendant was not able to conform his behavior to the requirements of the law, has he published anything in that area? Does he have a number of publications that are on issues remote from the case at hand, thus indicating that his interests and principal knowledge lie elsewhere? What books or journals does he read? How else does he stay current?

The American Psychiatric Association publishes a directory every few years which can be found in many medical school libraries or can be obtained from the association in Washington, D.C. It is a quick source of information about a psychiatrist's education, specialties, and certification, and may indicate psychoanalytic orientation.

The American Psychological Association also publishes a directory every few years which can be found in many university libraries or obtained from the APA in Washington, D.C. It provides information regarding institution and type of degree (Ph.D., Psy.D., Ed.D.) and field of degree (Clinical, Counselling, Educational Psychology, etc.). This is important because some vitae just state, "Ph.D., Psychology," and it is important to know if the field is not clinical psychology. It lists main field and specialties and past and current employment. This is from information provided by the expert.

With both of these directories, one should use the most recent edition. However, sometimes, it is useful to look into prior directories to determine if there have been changes (e.g., a different subspecialty).

The major goal of the deposition is to establish all of the professional knowledge bases and all of the information which the expert has utilized in drawing his conclusions. This should be done exhaustively, to the point where the expert finally states that there is no other information on which his conclusions are based. It is usually worthwhile to ask questions aimed at determining whether the clinician knows of any information that would contra-indicate or be inconsistent with his conclusions, or if there are sets of recognized principles other than those he used which would contra-indicate or be inconsistent with the conclusions. Similarly, it may be worthwhile to ask if he considered any alternative explanations for the data he had available and if the answer is negative, whether any such alternative explanations exist or could be justified. Some lawyers prefer to hold questions of this type for cross-examination, particularly where their own investigation or reading of the clinician's report makes it clear that such contrary indications exist.

The sets of questions that follow are organized generally around the chapter topics of Volumes I and II. They are only suggestions and the lawyer should neither feel bound to use all of them nor feel limited to them. In addition, there is a need for questions specific to the case at hand. To the extent possible, we have tried to avoid redundancy with the chapter on cross-examination, but some redundancy is unavoidable.

Lawyers should be familiar with questions in both chapters and make judgments regarding point at which to use them.

## ESTABLISHING THE LITERATURE

It is important to establish that the scientific and professional literature is the main repository of knowledge in the field and that the expert relies on it or at least has it in mind when doing evaluations. This provides a foundation for asking questions based on the literature. As this topic is extensively covered in the next chapter, it will not be done here.

## ETHICS AND GUIDELINES

The lawyer should have the ethical principles and forensic specialty guidelines for psychologists (Chapter 2, Volume III) in mind during deposition or cross-examination. It may not be necessary to use them, but they can be very useful to counter denials or lack of candor on the part of the witness. This topic is also dealt with in the next chapter. However, because psychiatry lacks such a detailed set of principles some questions to try to apply them to psychiatrists may be useful.

Q: As a profession, is psychiatry less ethical than psychology?

Q: Shouldn't psychiatrists be held to the same ethical standards as psychologists?

Q: Are you aware that the Ethical Principles of Psychologists adopted by the American Psychological Association in 1992 require that psychologists be familiar with relevant scientific and professional information in their field? [It may be useful to cite the number of the principle(s) or have a copy of the Principles available to read from or provide a copy to the witness.]

Q: Do you believe this should not be required of psychiatrists?

Q: Isn't much of this information contained in the scientific and professional literature?

Q: Are you aware that the Principles also require the psychologist to rely on scientific and professionally derived knowledge when making professional judgments?

Q: Shouldn't psychiatrists rely on such knowledge when making professional judgments?

## GENERAL

Once qualifications and literature are out of the way, it may be useful to begin the body of the deposition with questions designed to establish the questionable status of psychiatry or psychology.

Q: Is there a substantial body of scientific and professional literature expressing concern about the lack of adequate scientifically validated knowledge in your field?

Q: Isn't there considerable controversy (or doubt) expressed in the scientific and professional literature about the usefulness of psychiatric (psychological) evidence in regard to legal matters?

Q: Is psychiatry (psychology) an art or a science?

Q: (If the above is answered "both") How much (or what proportion) is art?

Q: How much is science?

## THEORIES AND PRINCIPLES

The aim in this area is to try to establish the theoretical position that this clinician uses or primarily relies on. If he does not adhere to any particular school, then establish that he is eclectic and also establish the manner of eclecticism that he employs as described in Chapter 3, Volume I.

Q: Does the scientific and professional literature indicate that there are several different theories of human behavior?

Q: Does the scientific and professional literature indicate that all of these theories have serious flaws?

Q: What psychiatric (psychological) theory do you use in your practice (or did you use in this case)?

Q: (If the previous question is answered by stating a particular theory) Is that theory the principal orientation of the majority of people in your field (or a subject of controversy in your field)?

Q: (If the first question was answered to indicate the clinician does not adhere to any particular theory) Would you describe yourself as eclectic?

Q: (Assuming the answer is yes) What do you mean by eclectic (or how do you utilize an eclectic approach in your practice)? (The aim here is to establish whether the clinician primarily relies on one particular school of thought and brings in concepts from other theories as he sees they are helpful, or whether he limits himself to a combination of two or three theories, or whether he really has no theoretical orientation at all, using whatever he finds useful from any of the various theories he is acquainted with.)

Q: When you combine material from different theories, aren't you, in effect, creating your own idiosyncratic theory?

Q: Such a theory has not been published, has it?

Q: What theories do you use in your eclectic approach?

Q: Doesn't the scientific and professional literature indicate that those theories have not had adequate scientific validation?

## DSM-IV

Because DSM-IV was not published until May, 1994, it is likely that cases involving DSM-III-R diagnoses will continue to appear for a couple of years. Most of the questions below can be applied to DSM-III-R. In addition, it will be worthwhile to check criteria for the particular diagnosis involved to see if there are changes between DSM-III-R and DSM-IV.

Q: Is your diagnosis one of those listed in DSM-IV? (This is unlikely to be answered in the negative, but if it is, you will have to find out where the diagnosis came from, establish that it is not in the official diagnostic system, and determine why the official system was not used.)

Q: DSM-IV is quite a new diagnostic system, is it not? When was it published?

Q: Do you know how many changes were made from DSM-III published in 1980 in DSM-III-Revised published in 1987?

Q: Are you aware that there were more than 200 changes?

Q: Do you know how many changes occurred from DSM-III-R to DSM-IV?

Q: Are you aware that again there were more than 200 changes?

Q: Are you aware that in some cases, the changes involved reverting back to DSM-III?

Q: Doesn't the literature, including the manual itself, indicate that for many disorders, research support is lacking or minimal or conflicted?

Q: It will be several years before it can be determined how reliable and valid it is, is that not correct?

Q: Isn't it correct that the previous diagnostic systems were considered quite inadequate?

Q: Don't these frequent changes cast doubt on the present applicability of research done with sets of diagnostic criteria which are now changed?

Q: Wouldn't there be some question because some people in the research population with a particular diagnosis would no longer be so diagnosed, and vice versa (some, now diagnosable, would not have been in the research population because they did not meet the previous criteria for the disorder)? (See Chapter 4, Volume I.)

Q: What criteria for (the diagnosis in the case) did you find?

Q: Any others? (If there is a report, you should have checked to see if the requisite criteria for the disorder have been met. You may or may not want, on deposition, to confront the witness with any lack, but you will want to be able later to confine him to those given on the deposition.)

Q: What was the evidence for (each criterion stated)?

Q: Are there any other diagnoses that could have been considered under DSM-IV?

Q: Did you consider such other diagnoses?

Q: What was the basis for selecting (the diagnosis) instead of (alternative diagnosis)?

Q: Was it a close question?

Q: Might another psychiatrist come up with another diagnosis (or conclusion)? (If yes, what?)

Q: Did you make any finding on Axis IV (psychosocial and environmental problems that may affect the diagnosis and prognosis)?

Q: (If none) Did you consider any? (If so, what?)

## THE GAP

The "gap" refers to the fact that the diagnosis *per se* rarely establishes any relevant legal issue, other than that there is a *diagnosis* of a mental disorder. For example, a diagnosis of schizophrenia does not establish a lack of ability to distinguish right from wrong nor does a diagnosis of generalized anxiety disorder establish an incapacity to function occupationally.

Q: What does the scientific research show regarding the relationship between (the diagnosis) and (the legal issue)?

Q: What percent of people with (the diagnosis) have been scientifically demonstrated to have (or lack) (the legal issue)?

Q: What percent of people without the diagnosis have been scientifically demonstrated to have (or lack) (the legal issue)?
If the witness can answer these questions, it will be necessary to ask him for citations of the research and have them checked. The witness should also be asked if there is contradictory research. Regardless of the answer, you should have your expert or consultant expert do a literature search on this issue.
Questions can be asked at this time concerning the DSM-IV statements about its use in forensic settings, but this could be delayed until cross-examination.

Q: Doesn't the manual contain cautions regarding the use of the diagnoses in forensic matters?

Q: Doesn't the manual warn that there are significant risks that diagnostic information will be misused or misunderstood when used for forensic matters?

Q: Doesn't the manual declare that because impairments, abilities, and disabilities vary widely in each diagnostic category, the particular diagnosis does not indicate a specific level of impairment or disability?

Q: Doesn't the manual state that decision makers who are not mental health professionals should be cautioned that a diagnosis does not carry any necessary implications regarding the causes of an individual's mental disorder or associated impairments?

Q: Doesn't the manual state that if someone meets the criteria for a disorder, that does not necessarily carry any implication about the individual's degree of control over behaviors that may be associated with the disorder?

## THE CLINICAL EXAMINATION

The aim in this area is to determine what information the clinician had available, what sources of information he used, and what kind of examination he conducted.

Q: Did you perform a clinical examination of (litigant)?

Q: Would you describe how that examination was conducted? (In criminal and personal injury cases where prior mental condition is an issue, you will want to particularly extract from the psychiatrist the fact that he observed many aspects of the litigant's behavior, such as mood, affect, quality of verbalization and so on—all of the types of observable behavior that it is highly unlikely that he could have as of the prior relevant time.)

Q: Is information of that type important in making an evaluation (diagnosis, etc.)?

Q: Did you interview litigant?

Q: Are you aware of literature indicating undependability (or inaccuracies) of self-reports?

Q: Did you receive information from any source other than (litigant)?

Q: (If not) Did you attempt to obtain information from any other source?

Q: (If yes) What information did you try to get? Why would that be important?

Q: What information did you receive from (each source)?

Q: Was there any reason to disbelieve or doubt that information?

Q: Who referred (litigant) to you?

Q: Were you first contacted by (referral source) or by litigant?

Q: In making the referral did (referral source) provide any information about litigant?

Q: What information did (referral source) provide?

Q: On the basis of that information, what thoughts, if any, did you
have as to what litigant's diagnosis or problems might be?

Q: Have you performed evaluations upon referral by (lawyer) before?

Q: How many times?

Q: Have those all been evaluations of plaintiffs in personal injury
cases (or whatever type of case is involved)?

Q: Have you performed evaluations in other legal cases?

Q: What types of cases?

Q: For which side have you performed the evaluations? (If witness
says, "for both sides" he should be asked if more for one side
than the other and if so, what proportions?)

Q: Are you acquainted with the term "examiner effects"?

Q: Would you explain what that refers to? (If any effects, as described in Chapter 6, Volume I, are not mentioned, you should
ask specifically about them.)

Q: Are you acquainted with the term "situation effects"?

Q: Would you explain what that refers to? (Same as above.)

Q: What situation effects did you consider? (You can ask about any
omitted or wait for cross-examination.)

Q: How did that affect your conclusions?

Q: Did you tape record the examination?

Q: Did you take notes during the examination?

Q: Did you make notes immediately after the examination?

Q: May I have a copy of those notes (or tape recordings)? (Should
request this in advance.)

Q: Could there be some information that developed during the examination that you did not notice or record?

Q: (If notes or any data were destroyed or discarded) Were you
aware that a legal claim was being made (or was possible) in this
matter? [See Volume III, Chapter 2, Ethical principle 1.23 (b).]

Q: Did you receive information based on psychological tests?

Q: Who did the testing?

Q: What tests? (Should request raw test data in advance.)

Q: What is the status of (each test) regarding reliability and validity? (See below, psychological tests.)

Q: (If tests were not used) Isn't psychological testing used frequently as an aid to diagnosis or evaluation?

Q: Do you ever make use of psychological test data in your
practice?

Q: What was the basis for not having psychological testing done in this case?

Q: Are there any conclusions in your report that you have some doubts about?

Q: Do you feel 100% confident concerning all of the conclusions stated in your report?

Q: How much less than 100%?

Q: Isn't there a body of scientific and professional literature indicating little or no relationship between confidence and accuracy?

Q: Could another psychiatrist reasonably disagree with any of your conclusions?

Q: Is there a body of scientific and professional literature indicating that psychiatrists (psychologists) tend to over-diagnose psychopathology?

Q: Is there a body of scientific and professional literature indicating that psychiatrists (psychologists) tend to distort the data to fit the diagnosis?

Q: Describe the data from which your conclusions were derived.

Q: How were those conclusions derived from that data? (Be exhaustive.)

Q: Has a conclusion of (whatever) been scientifically validated as arising from that data?

Q: What is the known rate of error in drawing that conclusion from that data?

## RELIABILITY AND VALIDITY

The aim here is to produce an admission from the clinician that reliability and validity are low in psychodiagnostic evaluation. If he is not going to make this concession, you will want to know how he tries to avoid it, because this is an area in which you will certainly want to cross-examine at the time of trial.

Q: Are you familiar with the term reliability as it is used in reference to psychodiagnosis? (If he is not, you will have to explain it to him.)

Q: Does the scientific and professional literature indicate that there are serious problem of reliability in connection with psychodiagnosis?

Q: Are you familiar with the term validity as it applies to psychodiagnosis?

Q: Does the scientific and professional literature indicate that validity of psychodiagnostic evaluations is not very high?

Q: What is the rate of false positives shown in the scientific and professional literature for (the diagnosis or the method)?

Q: What is the rate of false negatives?

Q: (If the witness cites some supporting research) Is there also contrary research?

You may in addition wish to ask about the reliability and validity of the specific diagnoses in the particular case.

## EXPERIENCE

Nearly all testifying clinicians cite their experience as a basis for and evidence of the reliability and validity of their conclusions. Therefore, the aim in this area is to see how the clinician is going to respond to a challenge to the efficacy of experience.

Q: Isn't there a substantial body of scientific and professional literature indicating a lack of relationship between experience of mental health experts and accuracy of evaluations? (Aren't there well over 100 publications to that effect?)

Q: Isn't there a considerable body of scientific and professional literature indicating that the more experienced psychiatrists (psychologists) are not appreciably more reliable or accurate in their evaluations than are the less experienced?

Q: Have you had a scientific study of the accuracy of your evaluations done by independent evaluators?

(By scientific, you will want to have in mind that what you mean is a study in which there were objective criteria against which to validate the conclusions, suitable controls, and so on, such as in the military suitability studies cited in Chapter 7 of Volume I.)

Q: How do you know that your evaluations or conclusions are more accurate than those of most other psychiatrists (psychologists)? (This is a question most attorneys prefer not to ask on cross-examination as it gives the expert an open field to run in. However, it can be safely asked on deposition. From time to time, the answer will turn out to be poor enough that you might want to ask the question again during the trial. If the expert concedes that he really has no way of knowing that his evaluations are more accurate than those of others, then all the literature on psychiatrists and psychologists in general would apply to him as well.)

Q: Do you regularly get feedback showing whether or not your conclusions were accurate?

Q: (If yes) What kind?

Q: Do you keep a record of the times you were right and the times you were wrong?

Q: I suppose you are not correct 100% of the time, are you?

Q: Do you know for a fact how much less than 100%?

Q: (If answered "yes") If you do not have independent evaluation and keep records, how do you know your rate of accuracy?

## BOARD CERTIFICATION

You will only need to explore this area if the witness is Board Certified. The aim would be to see how much familiarity he has with the lack of research showing a high level of competence for Board Certified clinicians, or a higher level than for those who are not Board Certified. On the other hand, if the witness is not certified, you may just want to establish that he lacks this credential.

Q: It has not been demonstrated through published research findings that Board Certified psychiatrists (psychologists) are more accurate in their evaluations than those who are not Board Certified, has it?

Q: Are there several articles published in reputable journals to the effect that the Board examinations do not measure competence?

Q: Are there several articles published in reputable journals to the effect that the Boards do not know what constitutes the elements of competence that they should be measuring in the examinations?

Q: Are you aware of any publications providing evidence that Board Certified psychiatrists disagree among themselves regarding conclusions in particular cases?

Q: Are you aware of reports of cases in which the performance of a Board Certified psychiatrist (psychologist) did not indicate (or counter-indicated) a high level of competence? (If the expert has read the third, fourth or fifth edition of this book he will have to acknowledge that he has read reports of such instances.)

## THE ROSENHAN STUDY

The aim here is to find out first of all if the clinician is acquainted with the Rosenhan Study. If he is not, then it will have to be introduced in some other manner at the time of the trial. However, if he is acquainted with it, he can then be questioned as to its findings and the deposition provides an opportunity to determine how he is going to handle the Rosenhan results.

Q: Are you acquainted with the study by Professor David Rosenhan entitled "On Being Sane in Insane Places"?

Q: Could you briefly describe that study and its findings?

Q: Doesn't that study show 100% error on the part of psychiatrists? (It is likely that at some point in this questioning that clinician will volunteer his critique of the Rosenhan Study. If he does not,

further questions should be asked to elicit any arguments he is
going to advance against the study. Most of the criticisms are described and dealt with in Volume I, Chapter 7.)

Q: (If the clinician has attempted to discredit the Rosenhan Study)
Isn't the Rosenhan Study just one of several showing a very high
degree of error by psychiatrists?

Q: Are you aware of the second part of the Rosenhan Study in
which, at another hospital, a number of patients were classified
as Rosenhan pseudo-patients although Rosenhan sent no patients
to that hospital?

Q: Did Rosenhan's data indicate that the psychiatrists distorted the
information given to them by the pseudo-patients in order to
make it fit the diagnosis?

Q: What is your opinion of the Rosenhan Study? (This does not
seem dangerous on deposition.)

## SPECIAL GROUP MEMBERSHIP (WHERE APPLICABLE)

The aim here is to determine how the clinician will deal with the issue of the need for separate norms or standards for members of ethnic or
other special groups.

Q: Is the (litigant) black (or whatever minority group)?

Q: What normative base did you employ in analyzing information
about litigant?
(If the clinician has indicated considerable reliance on his experience and if the litigant is a member of an ethnic minority
group, it may be worthwhile to ask how extensive his experience
has been with ethnic minority group members or members of this
particular minority group.)

Q: Isn't there considerable controversy in scientific and professional
literature about the utilization of norms based on the white
population for members of ethnic minority groups (or the particular group involved)?

Q: Isn't there a substantial amount of research indicating that blacks
(or whatever minority group) as a group respond differently than
do whites on various elements of the examination?

You should anticipate that if the witness is familiar with the literature, either on deposition or at trial, he will assert that the findings of differences disappear when education and socio-economic status are
controlled (more or less equal). While it is true that there are studies to
that effect, there are also studies where the differences are evident even
when these variables are controlled. Thus, at minimum, there is doubt
about applying the same norms to special groups.

Q: Isn't there research indicating that even where the measures are the same for the two groups, the behavioral correlates of the measures differ as between blacks and the white normative group?

## MALINGERING OR CREDIBILITY

Falsifying or exaggerating symptoms of psychopathology are most likely to occur in criminal and personal injury cases. On the other hand, attempts to fake "psychological health" or to minimize symptoms is most likely to occur in child custody or civil commitment cases, although in the custody cases, one parent may attempt to falsify or exaggerate symptoms of the other spouse. The aim in this area of deposition is to determine what approach the clinician takes on the assessment of malingering or litigant credibility. The questions deal primarily with faking psychopathology but they can be altered for cases of faking health.

Q: Do some people involved in (type of case) try to fake or exaggerate symptoms of psychological disturbance?

Q: What would indicate (suggest) malingering?

Q: (If other than test measures) Doesn't the scientific and professional literature indicate that those indicators have not been scientifically validated?

Q: Do they sometimes succeed in fooling the psychiatrist (psychologist)? (It is likely that the answer here will involve some explanation to the effect that while it can happen, it is very rare and is extremely difficult and the clinician may volunteer that he's satisfied that it was not taking place in this case.)

Q: Is it possible (litigant) was fooling you in this case?

Q: (If appropriate) How did you make that determination?

Q: If he succeeded in fooling you, you wouldn't know you had been fooled, would you?

Q: Are there some quantitative measures of malingering?

Q: Has there been a substantial amount of research on them?

Q: (If yes) Which, and what were the results?

## PSYCHOLOGICAL TESTS

The aim in this area is to determine if psychological tests were utilized and if so, what role if any they played in the evaluation. It is also usually worthwhile at the deposition stage to see how the clinician will deal with the issues of reliability and validity with regard to the psychological tests. Although there is some overlap, the nature of questions put to a psychiatrist will differ somewhat from those put to a psychologist.

Questions described above concerning racial minority group members and faking are applicable in this area also.

Q: Was psychological testing of the litigant performed in this case?

Q: At whose request was the psychological testing done?

Q: Did you use the results of the psychological testing in forming any of your conclusions in this case?

Q: What contributions did the psychological testing make to your evaluation?

Q: (For psychiatrist) Did you receive a report from the psychologist?

Q: (For psychiatrist) Did you see the actual test results?

Q: Is this test (ask the question for each test given) the subject of considerable controversy in the field of psychology?

Q: Haven't serious questions been raised in the scientific and professional literature about the reliability and validity of this test (for each test)? (Or validity of this test for this purpose.)

Q: Isn't there a lack of published research validating this test for this purpose?

Q: (For psychiatrist where there is no psychological testing) Are psychological tests used by psychiatrists in assisting them to reach their diagnostic and psychological conclusions?

Q: (For psychiatrist) Could psychological tests have been of some help in this case? (If not, why not?)

Q: In what order were the tests administered?

Q: Does it make any difference in what order they were administered?

The following questions pertain to each of the particular psychological tests and are probably more appropriate to ask of a psychologist than a psychiatrist, although the latter can be asked. However, it is likely in asking a psychiatrist that he may say he is not an expert on tests and that he knows they are widely used and that he relied on the psychologist to select the appropriate tests. The raw test data should be obtained prior to deposition.

If the Rorschach was used:

Q: Is there more than one system for using the Rorschach?

Q: How many systems are there?

Q: What are the systems?

Q: Which system do you use?

Q: Does the scientific and professional literature indicate that the Rorschach data vary according to which system is used?

Q: According to the scientific and professional literature can the responses that are obtained on the Rorschach be different depending on which system is used?

Q: (If other than Exner's Comprehensive System was used) Aren't a large number of psychologists shifting from those older systems to Exner's Comprehensive System of the Rorschach?

Q: (If Exner's system was used) How long have you been using the Exner system?

Q: Isn't the Exner system a relatively new system?

Q: Won't it be several years before it will be possible to fully appraise how good the Exner system is?

Q: Isn't it still undergoing testing and modification?

Q: Is there any published research raising doubts about the reliability or validity of the Exner system?

Q: Are there some doubts about the validity of this system for this conclusion?

Q: Are there some components for which little or no validating research has been published?

Q: Did you utilize any of these components?

Q: Did you make use of the Comprehensive System computerized interpretation service? (If not, why not?)

Q: What was there about litigant's Rorschach performance that contributed to your conclusions?

This type of question goes to the very heart of the diagnostic process. It is not possible to deal with it in the abstract or to predict what kind of answers will be forthcoming from the psychologist. The aim of the question is to force the psychologist to make explicit, in clear and understandable language, those elements of the Rorschach performance or any other test performance or even, in the case of the psychiatrist, the examination performance of the litigant from which he formed the diagnostic conclusion. It is essential to extract every bit of information that the clinician used and how he used it to indicate whatever he feels it indicates. This can be an exhausting process for both the lawyer and the clinician but it is absolutely essential. Our experience is that when pressed far enough to make very clear the basis on which the conclusions were formed, most clinicians are unable to do so or if they do so, it will more often than not turn out that there were really only a few items of information that contributed to the diagnosis. Therefore, the next few questions are simply suggestions that the lawyer will have to decide whether to use or not depending on what kind of responses the clinician is giving.

Q: How does that (data) indicate (whatever it indicates)?

Q: Can you cite published research which supports that conclusion? (This type of question should be asked only on deposition— never on cross-examination at trial.)

Q: Is there any contrary research?

Q: Do all people who are (whatever psychologist has said) give that kind of responses?

Q: Do any people who are not (whatever) give that kind of response?

Another approach to this kind of questioning is simply to ask the psychologist what diagnostic information he got from each of the responses on the Rorschach. He is likely to say that some responses did not have any particular diagnostic significance. He may say that other responses had a certain diagnostic significance and in that case you have to find out why they had that diagnostic significance. Frequently, psychologists will evade the issue by saying no response means anything by itself, he has to take everything altogether, it is the total pattern of response. If he takes that tack, then it is necessary to find out how Response I on Card I of the Rorschach and each subsequent response is articulated with all of the other data to show the pattern. For example, if the psychologist has taken this approach, the lawyer can ask if Response I had any diagnostic significance and if the answer is "not by itself" the next question is, "Did it have any significance in relation to the other material?" And if the answer is then yes, "What significance did it have in relation to what other material and how is that significance established by viewing it with whatever other material it has to be viewed with?" Perhaps a shortcut approach to this whole problem is simply to ask a very broad and open-ended question such as: "Well, doctor, I do not understand how you derived your conclusions from the set of data that you had. I realize what I am about to ask you to do may be somewhat difficult but I'm sure you will appreciate my responsibility to determine exactly how your conclusions were derived so that they may be properly evaluated. For that reason, I am going to ask you to take us through your diagnostic process, to show us how you arrived at the descriptions and conclusions you have stated about the litigant."

It is our experience as consultants that clinicians typically cannot give an explicit, detailed account of how they thought through the data to arrive at their conclusions, and when they attempt to do this, they expose problems of bias, reliance on unvalidated theories or principles, failure to consider situation effects, failure to consider examiner effects, failure to consider base rates, failure to consider all of the material and so on.

Other questions that might be asked are as follows:

Q: Is the Rorschach a projective test?

Q: Is there some literature to the effect that the conclusions drawn from the subject's ambiguous responses to the ambiguous ink-blots are based on the psychologist's projections upon the ambiguous responses of the subject?

Q: Are there a number of studies indicating that psychopathology can be faked on the Rorschach?

The diagnostic thought process has to start somewhere. It is reasonable to ask the clinician where his diagnostic thinking started in this case, and what was the second step and the third and so on.

The next few questions deal with the TAT:

Q: How is the TAT interpreted?

Q: How did you interpret it in this case?

Q: What was it about the TAT that led to those conclusions?

Q: Is there a good deal of negative scientific and professional literature concerning the reliability and validity of the TAT?

Q: Which TAT cards did you use?

Q: Do you always use those same cards?

Q: (If "no") Why did you select those for this case? (This may reveal some pre-conceptions and possible confirmatory bias.)

Questions similar to the above can be asked in connection with any of the projective tests—figure drawings, sentence completions, whatever.

The following questions deal with the MMPI:

Q: Where did the litigant fill out the answer sheet? (This question is aimed at finding out if the test was a "take-home" test wherein the litigant was given the booklet and answer sheet and sent home with them to fill out and return to the psychologist. In that instance, no one can be sure that he filled out the answer sheet without participation of any other people.)

Q: How are conclusions drawn from the MMPI data?

Q: What conclusions did you draw from the MMPI data in this case?

Q: How were those conclusions derived?

Q: Does the scientific and professional literature indicate that all people with elevations on (a particular scale) show this characteristic or behavior?

Q: Does the scientific and professional literature indicate that all people with (this kind of profile) show this characteristic or this kind of behavior?

Q: According to the scientific and professional literature what percentage of people with (this scale) elevation show this characteristic or behavior?

Q: According to the scientific and professional literature what percentage of people with (this kind of profile) show this kind of characteristic or behavior?

Q: According to the scientific and professional literature are there people with this profile who do not show it?

Q: Did you use the MMPI or the MMPI-2?

Q: (If MMPI) When was the MMPI-2 published?

Q: Isn't there a body of scientific and professional literature indicating the MMPI is obsolete?

Q: (If MMPI-2) Did you use any research done with the MMPI in drawing your interpretations?

Q: Isn't there a body of literature indicating that a substantial percentage of people do not get the same profile (or high point scale) on the MMPI-2 as on the MMPI?

Q: Because of this, isn't there a body of scientific and professional literature questioning the application of MMPI research to the MMPI-2?

Q: Was the test interpreted by you or by one of the computerized or automated MMPI interpretation services?

Q: Which automated service?

Q: According to the scientific and professional literature, what is the current status of the automated interpretation services? (And this service if one was used.)

Q: Has their validity been established through published scientific research?

Q:  According to the scientific and professional literature, what is the status of the automated services in contrast to the interpretation by the individual clinician?

Q:  In what ways are the automated services superior to the individual clinician?

Q:  In what ways is the individual clinician superior to the automated services?

Q:  Is there any evidence in the MMPI that could be construed as suggesting malingering or an attempt to fake or exaggerate symptoms?

Q:  (If answer to above is yes) How did you determine whether or not the MMPI did involve an attempt to fake or exaggerate symptoms? (Be exhaustive here to determine whether the psychologist used any or all of the quantitative measures described in Chapter 18, Volume II, e.g., F scale, F minus K, Ds-r.)

If tests other than the WAIS, MMPI, Rorschach, TAT, DAP, or Bender-Gestalt were used, questions can be asked to show that the majority of psychologists do not use those tests regularly.

In any case where psychological testing is involved, we strongly recommend the use of a consultant. To gain maximum benefits from the use of the consultant, the raw test data in its entirety, along with any psychological reports including those of an automated interpretation service and any notes made by the psychologist, should be obtained in readable form prior to the taking of the deposition. This will enable the consultant to go over the material and advise the lawyer as to any flaws of administration or scoring as well as to point out contrary or alternative interpretations of the data or points where the data simply does not support the conclusion. Currently, most psychologists, following the Principles, will not supply raw data to others than professionals who are qualified to interpret such materials. Similarly, prior to the psychiatrist's deposition, if a consultant is being used, he should have the psychiatrist's report along with any notes or records and all of the data available about the case.

If neuropsychological tests or batteries of tests are involved, questions similar to the above can be asked. In particular, it may be useful to inquire concerning reliability and validity, extent of use among psychologists, newness of the test, and appropriateness of normative base for the particular litigant.

# CHAPTER 8

# Cross-Examination— Samples & Suggestions

Cross-examination is generally viewed as an art; therefore, it is primarily a matter of individual style and there are many different styles. The approach suggested below employs a series of systematic and methodical questions to weaken or neutralize the expert's testimony. Attorneys who are more comfortable with a different style can easily convert the material to their style.

As there is considerable overlap between deposition and cross-examination, and because in some cases deposition is not obtainable, many of the approaches and questions described in Chapter 7, Volume III on depositions are repeated in this chapter for the sake of completeness. Also, some attorneys prefer to hold some of the questions that might be asked at deposition until the cross-examination phase.

Generally speaking, cross-examination should be addressed to two broad categories of information. It should attempt to illuminate the problems or deficiencies as described in Volumes I and II that are inherent at the present time in the mental health field. Secondly, cross-examination should be addressed to any flaws of omission or commission concerning the examination or the conclusions in the case at hand. It seems obvious that the low level of credibility that is warranted by illumination of the inherent problems is reduced even further by failure of the clinician to perform his examination or draw conclusions properly.

Therefore, one of the objectives should be the demonstration that psychiatry and clinical psychology lack firmly established knowledge and that unless the individual expert can demonstrate that these deficiencies do not apply to him, he suffers from the same lack. The judge or jury should be informed that there is a lack of scientific bases for the kind of statements these experts make and that there is insufficient evidence that they possess the ability to make such statements with reasonable accuracy. Cross-examination should focus on the deficiencies of education and training and of theory and principles, and on the low reliability and validity of assessments by the professionals in these fields. It should be demonstrated that the expertise of psychiatrists is a matter of assumptions which have never been proved. Cross-examination should also aim to demonstrate that the methods of evaluation employed by psychiatrists and clinical psychologists are highly unreliable and invalid or, at the very least, are of doubtful reliability and validity. This can be accomplished with questions concerning the defects of the clinical examination and clinical judgment. Also, one should be prepared to refute the usual assumption of expertise based on experience by demonstrating that such an assumption is unwarranted in the case of psychiatry and clinical psychology. Further in the case of psychiatry, one would wish to eliminate the credence that might ordinarily be granted due to the witness' status as a physician by showing that training in the field of medicine has little relation to what psychiatrists actually do. The natural tendency to impute expertise on the basis of the expert's credentials should be counteracted by showing that little or no such relationship between the credentials and competency or accuracy has been demonstrated and that the thrust of such evidence as there is indicates that little or no relationship or even a reverse one exists.

We recommend that cross-examination on these issues utilize the scientific and professional literature as much as possible as the basic reference point. As much as possible we try to phrase questions in terms of what is contained in the scientific and professional literature and to avoid as much as possible asking for the witness's views on the above issues. There are two advantages to this. No matter what the witness replies, you can produce an expert who will be able to confirm the points you wish to make and document his testimony with citations to the scientific and professional literature. Secondly, you avoid implicitly recognizing expertise in the witness by not asking for his opinions on these subjects.

The second objective of cross-examination is to demonstrate that even within the limits of the inherent deficiencies, the clinician has not, in this particular case, performed a thorough evaluation, that he is not well qualified regarding the particular subject area, that he has failed to acquire or account for various kinds of relevant information, that he has not conducted his examination in a proper manner, that he is biased, that his data warrants conclusions other than those he has drawn, and in some cases, that he has been less than candid, and that he lacks knowledge of the literature in his field.

It may be that no single line of attack will be sufficient to impair the clinician's credibility. Therefore, one approach on cross-examination is to pile doubt upon doubt—doubt about education and training, doubt about theoretical bases, doubt about the clinical examination, doubt about reliability and validity, doubt about experience, doubt about the thoroughness and objectivity of his examination, and so on. In some cases, the expert may respond on redirect with rehabilitative efforts. These may take the form of attempting to refute damaging points by referring to contrary literature or statements by authorities or acceptance of his position by psychiatrists in general. If the cross-examiner is well acquainted with the literature provided in Volumes I and II, the expert will be able to do no more than raise some doubt concerning the various issues. That is, recitation of some contrary literature or countering the published scientific and professional literature with the witness's beliefs or impressions unsupported by research cannot erase doubt but only contribute to it. It is the existence of these doubts that works in favor of the opponent of the clinical testimony. Usually it is the aim of the opponent to eliminate or neutralize the psychiatric contention and then allow the judge or jury to decide the case on the basis of the facts demonstrated by other kinds of evidence.

In addition to attacks on general grounds, another kind of challenge can go to the capability of the expert with regard to the specific subject matter or specific psychiatric issue in the particular case. For example, a challenge can be directed to the capability of psychiatrists in general or the specific psychiatrist, to evaluate a prior state of mind. Given the literature to the effect that psychiatrists are not very accurate in evaluating a present mental state or condition, it could be made clear to a jury that they would be no better, and in all probability less accurate, in attempting to evaluate a prior mental condition or state of mind. Similar challenges can be made to efforts to predict a future course of events.

Various benefits may result from pursuing these lines of attack in cross-examination. When one succeeds in dismantling the usual bases of expertise, the judge or jury are left free to disregard the expert testimony and decide the case on the facts. In addition, under the pressure of cross-examination which increasingly reveals the deficiencies of knowledge and methods in psychiatry, the psychiatrist may become upset and take an irrational defensive stance or become quite willing to concede many points in order to demonstrate his knowledge and integrity.

It may be useful to briefly consider the psychological situation of the expert witness when he is on the stand, although obviously this can only be stated in very general terms as different witnesses respond in different ways. However, generally speaking the witness is invested in his performance. He is, after all, a professional person who certainly does not want to look foolish and for this reason, many experts are rather anxious. Most of them have some awareness of the vulnerabilities of their profession. Many attorneys have indicated their feeling that the more one can do to implement the expert's anxiety without badgering him, or behaving in a manner that will antagonize the jury, the more likely one is to precipitate blunders on the part of the expert. The more threatened he feels the more likely he is either to become very defensive or evasive, which will become apparent to the jury, or to become somewhat submissive so that he will begin to agree with the points you are trying to make in order to make it clear that he is being very honest and that he is competent and knowledgeable. Some experts take a different approach and attempt to bully and browbeat you by assuming a domineering posture, one in which they are "the experts" and they know because they are experts and that it is ridiculous for you to challenge them. Frequently, this type will buttress their conclusions with statements of "we know," "we find," "it is generally accepted" type. Many, perhaps most, clinicians prefer to be vague as to the bases for their conclusions. They dislike being pinned down to specifics. That is, they frequently prefer to say all of the data indicates the litigant is whatever they have said he is rather than respond to your efforts to get them to state that Items 1, 2, 3, etc. of the clinical data are the basis for their conclusions. Lawyers have reported to us that they have spent an entire day, sometimes more, in questioning the expert to try to extract what the specific data were that led to their conclusions and that at the end of all of that time it was impossible to get a clear statement from the expert. They have also generally reported in such cases that at the conclusion of the case the jury was clearly aware of this evasion and reported that they gave no credence to such an expert. Another thing that we think almost inevitably happens is that the experts try very hard to second guess the cross-examiner. That is, they try to anticipate where the cross-examiner is trying to go with his questions. This is not particularly a disadvantage to the cross-examiner. In fact, some cross-examiners encourage this by being a little mysterious and possibly even throwing in an occasional question that really is not going to go anywhere; however, the expert will be thinking about it. If you ask some innocuous question that really has no purpose at all, he is going to think it has a purpose and when he cannot grasp what the purpose is, it is going to be upsetting to him. Some attorneys even make a point of making a note of the answer of the expert to a question of this type so that he is impressed with the importance that you are attaching to it. It is also useful to show, by your questions, that you are familiar with the literature in the field. Sometimes this causes the expert to exercise moderation in his testimony and frequently to indicate less certainty or confidence than he might if he felt he could bowl you over with his credentials. Some attorneys have reported that they conspicuously display a copy of this book on counsel table or carry it in their hand when they are cross-examining a mental health expert and have expressed their belief that this is not without effect on such a witness. If you are using a consultant-expert and permission can be obtained or if he is not excluded from the court, a similar effect can be obtained by having him present in the courtroom when the opposing expert is testifying and if possible letting the other side know that such an expert is there. Most clinicians are aware of their vulnerabilities and become uncomfortable and considerably more cautious when they know that a fellow professional is listening to what they say. Sometimes such a consultant-expert can be brought into the courtroom if he is not going to testify himself by virtue of the fact that he is both a psychologist or psychiatrist and an attorney as well, and thus can sit at counsel table during cross-examination as co-counsel. There are now several hundred people with these dual credentials. Usually this cannot be done if the consultant-expert is going to testify. The course of cross-examination depends not only upon the individual style of the attorney but also to some extent upon the particular type of witness involved. Quacks or charlatans, as well as honest psychiatrists who are either ignorant or blind concerning research data in the field, may deny the existence of deficiencies or weaknesses which cross-examination attempts to illuminate. In such cases, it may be necessary to query the witness extensively with regard to specific research findings and statements by authorities. In dealing with this type of witness, cross-examination is useful in laying the groundwork for later calling an expert who will acknowledge the research findings and authorities and be able to support his statements with the research literature, thus demonstrating the opposing expert is simply not well informed in his field. Responsible and informed psychiatrists or psychologists are more likely to concede some, if not all, of the deficiencies and weaknesses subject to cross-examination, although in many of these cases they may attempt to grant the existence of the research but deny its implications or denigrate the research. Although charlatans are not infrequently encountered in legal proceedings, it should be stated that the vast majority of psychiatrists and clinical psychologists are not charlatans and that the number of charlatans who appear in court are probably far out of proportion to the number that exists in the population of psychiatrists and psychologists. No reflection is intended here on the ethics or moral character of clinicians, in general. Most of the examples of cross-examination which follow are based on the assumption that one is dealing with a responsible clinician.

In this section on examples of cross-examination or suggested cross-examination questions, we will be trying to provide a minimal and crude set of questions to guide the attorney in cross-examination on the various topics. These questions do not really bring out the full richness of the kind of data that is available with which to cross-examine the mental

health experts. The materials in Volumes I and II are much more voluminous and of a much richer character than can be dealt with in this section. We know that lawyers are busy people and that many of them will
not take the time to thoroughly read and digest the Volumes I and II materials. Nevertheless, we would urge them to do so and not rely on the
section of questions because in many instances, the answers to the questions will not be the ones the lawyer expects, or necessarily answers that
are correct. But without the depth of knowledge that is provided in Volumes I and II, the lawyer may find himself unable to deal with the unexpected answer. One alternative, of course, is to utilize the services of a
consultant expert and be prepared to call him as a witness to establish all
of the points that we are providing questions for in terms of cross-
examination.

In the examples that follow, we have not been concerned with technical details of evidence production (e.g., proper foundation). We assume
that practicing lawyers will be better able to recognize and deal with any
requirements.

The cross-examination approach suggested below is tedious and
time-consuming, particularly when there is a real struggle to obtain clear
answers from a clinician. It may be worthwhile on opening statement or
wherever appropriate, to inform the jury that this type of cross-
examination will take place with some brief explanation of the need for
it. It may be useful, in opening, also to indicate to the jury that if the witness will give direct answers to questions that are phrased to elicit "yes"
or "no" answers the process will be less tedious. Our experience is that
cross-examination of this type is likely to be the most effective approach.
However, we recognize there may be lawyers who prefer to cross-
examine only briefly or there may be instances in which that is more desirable. If the lawyer is planning to call an expert who will establish all
of the points to be made by the more lengthy type of cross-examination,
it may be sufficient on cross-examination to simply ask a few very general questions of the type that follows. Virtually all of the questions we
provide in this chapter call for answers in the expected direction. If these
are not forthcoming, the lawyer has available in Volumes I and II the
literature on which the questions are based.

Q: Doctor, does the scientific and professional literature of your
field constitute part of the knowledge base (or basis for expertise) in your field? (You may need to define the literature as the
journals and books in the field.)

Q: This literature provides a means for keeping up with knowledge
in the field, doesn't it?

Q: In fact, the *Ethical Principles for Psychologists* call for maintaining knowledge of relevant scientific and professional information related to services rendered? (Principle A)

Q: The principles also require psychologists to rely on scientifically and professionally derived knowledge when engaging in professsional endeavors, don't they? (Standard 1.06)

Q: When the American Psychiatric Association prepares its diagnostic manual, they state that they look to the scientific and professional literature for guidance, don't they?

Q: And the people on the various committees are considered authorities in their areas, aren't they?

Q: And they feel they need to look to the literature, right?

Q: Doctor, what journals do you read regularly?

Q: What journals do you read occasionally?

Q: Doctor, do you also sometimes read (here ask about any journals that you want to establish or from which you may wish to cite later)?

Q: Doctor, isn't there a substantial body of scientific and professional literature indicating that psychiatry (psychology) lacks an adequate scientifically validated theory of human behavior? (If there is a problem with "substantial" you can ask for the expert's definition or simply reduce the question to "a body.")

Q: There is a good deal of controversy in psychiatry regarding theories of human behavior, is there not?

Q: Doctor, isn't there a substantial body of scientific and professional literature indicating that in the clinical examination the information obtained and the information noted or recorded and the interpretation of that information is subject to considerable influence due to characteristics of the examiner? Is this referred to in the literature as examiner effects?

Q: Isn't there a substantial body of literature indicating that different examiners obtain different information and interpret it differently?

Q: Isn't there a substantial body of scientific and professional literature indicating that some of the data gathered in the psychiatric examination may result from what are called situation effects, events going on in the litigant's life situation?

Q: Doesn't that mean that the behavior which forms part of the basis for conclusions could be different if the examination were performed under different circumstances?

Q: Isn't there a substantial body of scientific information in the professional literature to the effect that many psychiatric conclusions have not been shown to be very reliable? (If reliability has not already been defined it may have to be done at this point. Also, you may want to deal with the specific conclusions in this case.)

Q: Isn't there a substantial body of scientific and professional literature to the effect that psychiatric conclusions have not been demonstrated to be very accurate?

Q: Aren't there a number of studies showing that psychiatric conclusions are not accurate?

Q: Are there several published studies in which the psychiatric conclusions were shown to be wrong more often than they were right?

Q: Doesn't the literature contain numerous publications which cast doubt on the accuracy (dependability) of clinical judgment?

Q: Isn't there a substantial body of scientific and professional literature to the effect that psychiatrists with considerable experience are not more accurate in their diagnoses or conclusions than those with little or no experience?

Q: Doctor, isn't there a substantial body of research showing that the results of the psychiatric examination are considerably influenced by biases of the examiner?

Q: (If prior mental state is an issue) Doctor, there is not, is there, a substantial body of research indicating that psychiatrists are able to determine a person's psychological state at some time prior to the examination with a high degree of accuracy?

Q: In fact, there is a body of literature indicating they lack that ability, isn't there?

The term "psychologist" can be substituted for psychiatrist wherever appropriate; however, if the expert is a psychologist and has used psychological tests, the following question can be added:

Q: Doctor, isn't it true that the accuracy and reliability of conclusions based on the tests you have used is a matter of considerable controversy within the field of psychology?

If the particular clinician has indicated that he is Board Certified, the following questions should be asked:

Q: Isn't there a substantial body of scientific and professional literature indicating that a relationship between Board Certification and competency or accuracy of conclusions has not been demonstrated?

Q: Isn't there a body of literature indicating that reliability among Board Certified psychiatrists is no greater than that found for psychiatrists in general?

Q: Is there some literature indicating a low rate of agreement among Board Certified psychiatrists?

Q: Is there some published literature describing rather poor performance by Board Certified psychiatrists?[1]

If the expert denies any of the above propositions or is unable to establish the points through a clinical or a consultant expert who will be prepared to verify these points by citing the quantity of studies or the studies themselves, if necessary.[2] Where there is a more liberal "learned treatise" rule, it may be possible to confront the witness with the relevant contents of this text or with the primary references cited herein.

The following question may be useful also:

Q: Aren't there a number of publications by legal and mental health professionals raising serious questions about the usefulness of psychiatric (psychological) evidence in legal matters?

It should be noted that most of the above are fact, not opinion, questions, and therefore, as asked, call for a "yes," "no," or "I do not know" answer. The cross-examiner should immediately try to cut off any attempt at lecturing or expressions of opinion by the expert in response to these questions, and he should insist that the doctor answer the question with a "yes," a "no," or if he does not know, to say so. We are aware that it is common practice to allow an expert to explain an answer if he feels it is necessary. It is difficult to find any such necessity in regard to questions of this type. If the witness finds the term "substantial" unclear, he can be asked for his definition or the question can be rephrased without it.

It is our personal view that a more detailed and extensive cross-examination is more effective. This type of cross-examination, described below, has the disadvantage that it can become quite tedious and time-consuming and may be more than a jury can tolerate. The lawyer may wish to reduce the cross-examination accordingly. In many cases, if you

---

[1] We are using the term "Board Certified" to describe both psychiatrists who have been certified by the appropriate psychiatric board and psychologists who have been granted the Diploma of the American Board of Professional Psychology or the Diploma of the American Board of Forensic Psychology. The latter are more commonly referred to as Diplomates in Clinical Psychology or in Forensic Psychology or where appropriate, Diplomates in Clinical Neuropsychology. That terminology would be a more precise usage in connection with psychology; however, for convenience in this text and because the meaning is the same we are using the term "Board Certified" to cover psychologists as well as psychiatrists.

[2] For the convenience of the lawyer or consultant expert attempting to establish the points made by the questions above, the number of references cited in Volumes I and II in support of these points can easily be determined by checking the number of references cited at the end of a chapter on any given topic.

are successful with two or three of the points, so that you are confident that the jury is likely to give little credence to the expert, there is not a great need to go on. However, it is our experience that most experts employ various kinds of evasion so that it is difficult to clearly establish the point. One of the benefits from the extended cross-examination is that the evasive tactics of the expert become clear to the jury. We believe that once you commit yourself to one of these points, it is necessary to stay with it until either you get the concession from the expert or it has become abundantly clear that he is uninformed, evasive or unreasonable.

The next section of this chapter deals with a general type of cross-examination that is applicable regardless of the specific type of case involved. Cross-examination in specific kinds of cases such as criminal, personal injury, or child custody cases is dealt with in later chapters.

There are no hard and fast rules as to the order of topics for cross-examination. Typically, the first material the expert presents to the jury, on direct examination, is a recitation of his education and training and other qualifications and credentials, which is designed to impress the jury with his expertise. For this reason, we feel it is important to deflate these credentials in as close proximity to the expert's testimony as possible. However, we believe the first order of business is to establish that the expert is acquainted with and uses the scientific and professional literature as one of the bases for his practice. The cross-examination presented is applicable to both psychiatrists and psychologists, with a few exceptions which will be obvious.[3] A section dealing specifically with psychologists is presented later.

## ESTABLISHING THE LITERATURE

Our approach to dealing with psychiatric and psychological evidence makes extensive use of the scientific and professional literature in these fields. Therefore, it is important to establish early on that expertise in the

---

[3] In previous editions of this book when writing sample cross-examination we used a format of questions with what we thought would be probable or required answers. However, because so many clinicians do not give the expected or required answer, we are concerned the attorneys will be lulled into a false sense of security or left unprepared to deal with the unexpected answer. Therefore in this edition, we are providing only the questions we feel are appropriate with some comments on how to deal with some answers that deviate from what should be given. However, to use this method effectively, the lawyer would be in the best position if he is fairly familiar with the contents of Volumes I and II so that when the answer is contrary to the data provided here, he can at least confront the witness with that data so that the jury will be aware that the expert's answer is not consistent with what the literature says. The other obvious approach to this problem is to produce an expert of your own who will testify to the contents of the literature, in which case the opposing expert will be shown to be either less than candid or relatively ignorant of the literature in his field.

clinician's field is based in part upon the scientific and professional literature and if possible, to establish that the particular expert utilizes such literature in conducting his practice. If a particular expert denies knowledge or use of the scientific and professional literature in his practice, particularly in the diagnostic aspects, it is not likely that a jury or judge would view this witness as possessing the appropriate amount of expertise. Some experts will attempt to play down the importance of research and of the literature with statements to the effect that they simply use what works in their practice. Of course, if everyone practiced that way, that would establish the field as primarily an art and not a science at all. In other words, if each individual is operating purely on the basis of his own experience, then there is no coherent discipline and one has to wonder what gets taught in medical school and the residency or in the clinical psychology Ph.D. program and its internship. One also has to wonder why there are so many books and journals published in these fields containing both research results and commentary articles and why textbooks and journals are used in the education and training of these professionals. Therefore, the aim in cross-examining on these topics is to establish that the scientific and professional literature contains the public collective knowledge and principles of the field and is a vitally important component of expertise. If there is doubt about obtaining the "correct" answers on this issue, it might be useful to employ *voir dire* with its implication of a possible challenge to the qualification of the witness as an expert. It is likely that in the face of such scrutiny, the witness may find it awkward to deny the importance of and reasonable familiarity with the literature. Query whether some judges would refuse expert status to someone who lacks knowledge of and does not use the scientific research in his field.

Q: The (public) knowledge base in your field is contained principally in the scientific and professional literature that is published, isn't that correct? (Some clinicians may assert that only part of the knowledge is contained in the literature and the rest is, more or less, just in the clinician's head as a result of his experience, and some may even go so far as to indicate that they really utilize only their own experience and do not pay attention to the literature in the field. In that case they should be asked the following questions. Even if there is agreement, you may want to ask some of these questions to emphasize the importance of the literature.)

Q: Were any books and journals used during your education and training in medical school? (It would be hard to imagine anyone answering "no" to that question.)

Q: And during your internship and residency, did you also make use of (or were you referred to) books and journals in the field?

Q: As a responsible professional are you expected to keep up with scientific knowledge in your field? (See Volume III, Chapter 2, Ethics.)

Q: Do you do that?

Q: Do the ethical principles require you to rely on the scientific knowledge in your field? (See Volume III, Chapter 2.)

Q: If someone in your field wanted to learn or find out about something in your field, would they be likely to look it up in the literature? (have literature search done, etc.)

Q: If someone in your field were writing a book or article in your field, wouldn't they search and make reference to the literature?

Q: When the committee of the American Psychiatric Association that produces the diagnostic manual is working to develop that manual, they refer to the literature, don't they? They state that in the manual, don't they? And the people working on those committees are considered authorities in their fields, aren't they? And they still find it important to look to the literature, don't they?

Q: Does knowledge of the scientific and professional literature constitute part your expertise in this field?

Q: Does the literature contain information about new and old methods, diagnoses, tests, and revisions?

Q: What scientific and professional journals do you read regularly?

Q: What scientific and professional journals do you read occasionally?

Q: Do you ever read (names of important journals, or journals you or your expert may want to refer to)?

Q: What other materials related to your field do you read?

Q: Do you read any research reports?

Q: How often?

Q: Do you make any use of the research reports and other scientific and professional literature in your practice?

Q: Would it be correct to state that to some extent, you have the scientific and professional literature of the field in mind when you formulate your opinions?

Q: Do you use the information (or some of it) from the scientific and professional literature in formulating your opinions?

The following question may be useful if the witness has indicated forensics as a specialty. If answered affirmatively, it may open the witness to questions about the literature in the book.

Q: Have you read a book by Jay Ziskin (or Ziskin and Faust) titled *Coping with Psychiatric and Psychological Testimony*?

Q: Doesn't that book contain more than 1500 references from the scientific and professional literature which tend to negate the expertise of mental health professionals?

## EDUCATION, TRAINING, QUALIFICATIONS & CREDENTIALS

Ordinarily, clinicians are not modest in describing their qualifications on direct examination so that one can feel fairly comfortable in assuming that they stated everything that they had. Therefore, it is important to listen carefully to the statement of qualifications not only for what is mentioned but for what is not mentioned.

With psychiatrists it is important to separate them from the more conventional fields of medicine with which the trier of fact may be familiar.

Q: Most of your patients come to you because they are having some kind of psychological problem, is that correct?

Q: These are usually problems involving some sort of personal or social or interpersonal difficulty or maladjustment, isn't that right?

Q: Are psychiatrists the only professional people who deal with problems of this type?

Q: What other professionals deal with them?

Q: And in most (this) state(s), psychologists are licensed to work with problems of this kind, is that right?

Q: A medical education and M.D. degree are not required for diagnosing or treating psychological problems, is that correct?

Q: You don't ordinarily do a physical examination of your patients, do you, doctor?

Q: You don't perform surgery, do you, doctor?

Q: What is mental illness (disorder)? (All current definitions are problematic—see DSM-IV. There are no widely accepted definitions of mental illness which stress the disease aspect. Almost all definitions usually come down to the fact that the individual is maladjusted or distressed and ordinarily the cause of the maladjustment is some failure or deficiency of learning; that is, the individual has either failed to learn how to cope with his emotions or has failed to learn how to cope with the society that he lives in, or is having difficulties in interpersonal relationships. There is no known underlying tissue pathology or dysfunction for many of the so-called mental disorders. Questioning of the witness should then continue on this point until he either admits that he cannot define mental illness or admits that he is, in fact, not talking about illness as that term is generally understood but rather about maladjustment. There is the option of asking questions concerning several of the disorders listed in DSM-III-R that are clearly adjustment problems and would not meet most people's understanding of disease.)

Q: Isn't there considerable controversy in the literature in the behavioral sciences concerning the appropriateness of a medical model for problems of adjustment or psychological problems?

Q: Are there some medical and other authorities who contend that the medical model or the concept of mental illness is not the appropriate one for understanding or dealing with individuals having psychological problems?

Q: There are also a number of publications by psychiatrists to that effect, are there not?

Q: Did you spend much of your time in courses in psychiatry studying psychoanalytic theories? (If the answer is "no," questions can be asked to determine what theory or theories his study focused on, and show that such other theory is not a commonly accepted one.)

Q: There is considerable controversy about the status of psychoanalysis even today, is that correct?

Q: (If witness has not mentioned this on qualifying) Doctor, are you Board Certified in psychiatry (or a Diplomate of the American Board of Professional Psychology)? (Some psychiatrists answer this by stating that they are "board eligible." In that case, questions should be asked to demonstrate that the term means nothing more than that the individual has five years of experience in psychiatry. It has no relation whatsoever to being Board Certified other than meeting this minimum requirement for taking the examination. Indeed, the statement of the Board specifically points out it does not recognize such a status; see Volume I, Chapter 9.)

Q: Are you Board Certified in forensic psychiatry? (Diplomate of the American Board of Professional Psychology in forensic psychology.)

The next series of questions is for Board Certified psychiatrists.

Q: Research has not demonstrated a relationship between Board certification and competence, has it?

Q: Has it been demonstrated through published scientific research that the conclusions of Board Certified psychiatrists are more accurate than those of psychiatrists who are not Board Certified?

Q: Aren't there a number of publications in reputable psychiatric journals to the effect that no relationship between Board certification and competence has been established?

Q: Isn't Board certification defined by the Board as indicating only minimal competence in the field? (Unfortunately, ABPP and the Board of Forensic Psychology have not displayed this appropriate humility, so this is not a good question for psychologists).

Q: In that case, Board certification does not indicate superior competence or accuracy of conclusions, isn't that correct?

Q: Are you Board Certified in forensic psychiatry?

Q: Are you aware that there is a Board certification in that specialty?

Q: What is that specialty?

If the psychiatrist indicates he is Board Certified in forensic psychiatry, then the following questions can be asked:

Q: That is a relatively new kind of certification, isn't it?

Q: It has not been demonstrated through research that certification indicates a higher level of competence or accuracy of conclusions than for those not so certified, has it?

Q: Isn't there some published material which suggests that the level of competence or accuracy of conclusions is not greater for forensic certified psychiatrists? (The references here are the case studies reported in Chapter 9, Volume I.)

Q: Would it be correct to state that at the present time, for lack of research demonstration to the contrary, it is not more than an undemonstrated assumption that Board Certified psychiatrists are more competent or more accurate than those who are not certified?

Similar questions can be asked of the psychologist who is a diplomate in clinical and/or forensic psychology, or neuropsychology.

Some other data presented in qualifying (or conspicuous by their absence) call for some questions to blunt the significance which they are intended to convey.

Q: Membership in APA (or whatever associations the witness has indicated) is not based on demonstration of a high level of accuracy of your conclusions, is it?

Q: The presidency of (whatever association positions the witness has stated) does not require demonstration of a high level of accuracy either, does it?

Q: Your position as chief of psychiatry at the Wonderland Hospital (or whatever other positions have been indicated) is an administrative position, is it not?

Q: What proportion is administrative and what proportion is direct service?

Q: And in the administrative aspects you deal with things like budgets, personnel selection and policies, and generally perform the functions of a manager, isn't that correct?

Q: Then, many of your credentials, such as Board certification, association memberships and offices, and administrative positions, are not an indicator of a high level of accuracy in your clinical opinions, are they? (It may be better to just save this for argument.)

Q: Have you published any research findings, or books, or articles on the subject of (any issues or disorders involved in the testimony)? (If "yes," questioning should elicit the titles and citations for these publications, so that your own expert can look them over. Our experience is that few clinicians who testify have published anything in the area and if they have, they will have stated it among their qualifying materials.)

Q: Have you published any research findings or books or articles on the relationship of (the diagnosis) and (the legal issue)?

Q: (If the witness has indicated publications in other areas) What was the subject matter of the publications you referred to earlier?

Q: (Particularly, if more than one publication is in a particular area) Would (the topic area) be your major area of interest or expertise?

Q: Judging from the fact that this is the area in which you have done the most publishing and devoted most of your interest, wouldn't my statement be correct so far as the major focus of your professional interest?

Q: Your letterhead says "children, adolescents and adults." What percentage of your practice is with each?

Q: Then you would have less experience with (whichever) than a psychiatrist who deals only with that population, is that not so?

## DISTINGUISHING SCIENTIFICALLY VALIDATED FINDINGS OR PRINCIPLES FROM HYPOTHESES, CONJECTURES, BELIEFS AND CLINICAL LORE

As much of the cross-examination will utilize scientific research or demonstration as an element of questioning, it is important to establish early in the cross-examination what is meant by scientific or research validation and how that is distinguished from what the clinician may believe or speculate or hypothesize, or how he might utilize clinical case reports or clinical beliefs as the basis for his conclusions. Cross-examination can be facilitated by eliminating any quibbling about the meaning of science or scientific method as early as possible. Therefore, questions should aim to establish that generally the scientific method involves an effort to control extraneous variables as much as possible, and some kind of quantitative measure. The essence of the scientific method is that it tests assumptions or beliefs derived from unsystematic and uncontrolled observations. A classic example that is easy to use in cross-examination is the practice of bleeding to treat disease that was employed by physicians for a couple of hundred years during the 17th and 18th centuries. Based on their observations that after bleeding a number of patients got better, physicians concluded that the bleeding was responsible for the cure and had therapeutic value. This belief was handed down from generation to generation of physicians and it was accepted that this was useful. It was only later when systematic scientific research methods were employed that it was demonstrated that except for a very few diseases bleeding did not have curative effects and often resulted in worsening or the death of some patients. This flaw of unscientific, unsystematic observation leading to erroneous conclusions can be employed in any case where the witness cannot assert that the statement he makes is clearly supported by appropriate research methods. That is, whenever he says "we believe" or "it is generally accepted" or "it has withstood the test of time" or "I have found" or any such similar statements, he can be challenged to produce the scientific research which supports and validates that statement. Anytime he produces such research he can be challenged as to whether or not there is contrary research. There will be very few instances of assertions by psychiatrists or psychologists for which there is an adequate amount of supporting research to begin with and fewer cases still where there is no conflicting research, often far in excess of supportive research. In the face of conflicting research, the issue is in doubt and will remain in doubt until the definitive research can be done which resolves the question one way or the other. Until such time, statements of the witness are nothing more than assumptions similar to the assumption made by physicians that bleeding was curing their patients.

Q: Doctor, you have some acquaintance with the field of science, do you not?

Q: In a number of questions, I am going to use the word "scientifically." Would you agree that, generally, that term denotes a systematic method of acquiring information or knowledge by using means to control extraneous variables so that one can isolate the particular issue being explored, and the use of some method of measurement or quantifying the information so that one is not guessing as to how much of the information conforms to one side of the issue and how much to the other? Would you agree with that as a crude, general statement of the scientific research approach? (In the alternative, you can ask the witness what the term "scientifically" means to him, but this may result in an extended discussion to try to establish what you are trying to establish. Probably most witnesses would be willing to agree with the definition above stated as a rather crude, general approximation of the term "scientifically.")

Q: And isn't that term generally thought to be in contrast to other bases for conclusions, such as intuition, or belief? (This is in accordance with the definition in *Webster's Unabridged Dictionary*.)

Q: And if there is scientific research evidence on one side of a proposition and scientific research evidence of roughly equal quality on the other side of the proposition, the truth or falsity of that proposition is left in doubt, is it not?

Q: So that, until the research becomes consistent or relatively unequivocal, the issue remains in doubt as to which side of the proposition is correct, is that right?

Q: Generally, the scientific research on a particular issue is contained in what I refer to as the scientific and professional literature, is that correct?

Q: In addition, the scientific and professional literature contains reviews of the literature summarizing the status of research on particular issues, is that correct?

Q: And it also contains statements by knowledgeable people, with regard to a particular issue, is that correct?

Q: In order for an article to be published in a reputable scientific or professional journal, it is reviewed by an editor or peers to see that the work is reasonably well done and that the article has sufficient merit to give it space in the journal, isn't that correct?

Q: So that, generally speaking, in order to be published, an article would have to at least pass the scrutiny of one or more journal editors or peers, is that correct?

Q: Doesn't DSM-IV state that, in its production, reviews of a number of scientific studies and field testing of various disorder criteria were employed?

## THEORY AND PRINCIPLES

Q: According to the scientific and professional literature, in psychiatry, or more generally behavioral science, there are quite a few differing theories concerning human behavior and mental condition, are there not?

Q: According to the literature does each of these schools of thought have some followers among the profession?

Q: According to the literature, taken as a whole, none of these theories have been scientifically proven to be correct, have they? (The question is put in terms of the theory as a whole because some clinicians might assert that some of the concepts have received some research validation.)

Q: Doesn't the literature indicate that clinical opinions vary to some degree according to which school of thought the clinician followed?

Q: Which theory do you follow?

Q: Has that theory been scientifically proven better than the other theories?

Q: (If no particular theory) Is that the position described as eclectic?

Q: Do you use all of the theories in your eclectic procedure?

Q: Which theories do you use?

Q: Do you mix them together, or do you sometimes use one theory and sometimes another theory in different cases; I'm trying to understand what you mean by your eclectic approach?

Q: When you do that, are you not then, in fact, creating your own theory?

Q: Well, let me ask it this way. Isn't a theory generally made up of a number of concepts which are then interrelated according to the nature of the theory?

Q: Okay, so what I am trying to get at is that when you take some concepts from Theory 1 and some concepts from Theory 2 and some concepts from Theory 3 and you combine them in a particular case or in a particular way, are you not then, in effect, creating your own theory?

Q: Well, isn't it true that if you take concepts from different theories or different sets of concepts and put them together your own way, you are essentially making up your own theory, utilizing those concepts, isn't that correct? Isn't that what we just said a theory is, taking a certain number of concepts and putting them together to provide an explanation or understanding of human behavior?

Q: Okay, then what you really are doing is using Doctor (witness' name) idiosyncratic theory of human behavior, isn't that correct, which has never been published anywhere or subject to the scrutiny of your colleagues so that one could know whether it is a correct theory or not?

Q: Isn't it a fact that there are a number of statements in the scientific and professional literature to the effect that psychiatry lacks an adequately validated theory of human behavior?

Q: Aren't there statements in reputable psychiatric journals to the effect that psychiatry as an agreed upon body of knowledge hardly exists?

## THE CLINICAL EXAMINATION

The next series of questions deals with problems and deficiencies of the clinical examination. Based on the literature cited in Chapter 6 of Volume I, the psychiatrist should be obliged to confirm the problems or defects raised by these questions. It is almost inconceivable to us that a clinician who has any awareness of the psychodiagnostic process could deny these problems, yet it does happen. If he refuses to acknowledge the influence of the various factors raised in these questions, it should be easy to discredit him with a rebuttal or consultant expert who can cite the overwhelming literature on these issues. Therefore, one could probably put these questions in the form of "Does factor X influence the clinical examination?" However, here the more conservative approach of putting the questions in the form "*Can* factor X influence the clinical examination?" is employed. It is unlikely that a clinician would answer negatively to the question put in this form.

Q: Doctor, is there a (substantial) body of scientific and professional literature indicating that the general circumstances under which the examination is conducted (time, place of examination, purpose of the examination, particular circumstances such as being in jail) affect the kind of information or data that emerges in the examination? (The only correct answer to this question is, "Yes, it can make a difference." However, many psychiatrists are unaware of or do not accept the research findings concerning situation effects. If they should answer negatively to this question, then the next few questions can be asked.)

Q: Doctor, isn't there research showing that such factors do affect the kind of information that is obtained in the interview?

Q: Doctor, are you familiar with the studies of demonstrating that these factors have an effect on the material produced in the interview? (If not, this expert will be shown to be ignorant when your expert testifies to the extensive literature establishing the correctness of this point.)

Q: Aren't these things described in the literature as situation effects?

Q: Well, doctor, wouldn't the fact that someone is in jail awaiting trial on serious criminal charges have some effect on his mental condition?

Q: Wouldn't that affect his mood and his affect?

Q: Could he be so preoccupied with his current situation that it might have some effect on the clarity of his thinking or speech?

Q: Then, wouldn't you be getting, in your clinical examination, some behaviors or emotional states that would appear under these abnormal conditions but might not be present under different circumstances? (Pendency of litigation to try to get a large sum of money for a personal injury or involvement in a child custody dispute can be substituted for the jail situation where appropriate.)

Q: In fact, doesn't the DSM describe involvement in litigation as a psychosocial stressor?

Q: Are you familiar with the term "examiner effects"? (If no, the cross-examiner will have to explain this).

Q: What does that term mean in relation to the diagnostic process?

Q: Is there a (substantial) body of scientific and professional literature indicating that examiner effects include such things as the examiner's theoretical orientation, and his personality, and his social and political values and attitudes?

Q: Is there scientific and professional literature indicating that examiner effects can occur as a result of being hired by one side or the other?

Q: According to the literature do these examiner effects have some influence on the data that is obtained?

Q: According to the literature do they also have some influence on the data that the examiner will pay attention to or record?

Q: Is there also scientific and professional literature indicating they also have an influence on the way he interprets the data of the clinical examination?

Q: According to the literature, some examiners with one theoretical orientation might get different data and record different data and interpret the data differently than an examiner of a different theoretical orientation, is that correct?

Q: And also, according to the literature examiners with different personalities might get some different kinds of information from the people they examine, isn't that correct?

Q: That's because people respond differently to different types of people, isn't that so?

Q: So, according to the literature, the material produced in the interview results, to some extent, from the conditions of the examination and the type of examiner conducting the examination, isn't that correct?

Q: If someone was being examined under different circumstances, by a psychiatrist with a different theoretical orientation and a different personality, different needs, values and biases, he might produce different data, isn't that correct?

Q: And it is the data from the examination that determines what the diagnosis is going to be, isn't that correct?

Q: There is a body of scientific and professional literature indicating that what the examiner pays attention to and remembers are all influenced by the same factors in the examiner, are they not?

Q: And according to the literature,these same factors, situation effects, and examiner effects play a role in determining the interpretation of the material of the clinical examination, isn't that so?

Q: Isn't there a body of scientific and professional literature indicating that self-reports are an undependable source of information about the person (or can be quite misleading)?

Q: Would it be fair to state that the scientific and professional literature indicates that the diagnostic process in psychiatry is subject to variation due to a number of variables that are extraneous to the litigant's psychological status?

## CLINICAL JUDGMENT AND INTERPRETATION

In Chapter 5 of Volume I, we have provided a very extensive discussion, backed by well over 100 references, of the problems and lack of validity of clinical judgment. This included such topics as clinical versus actuarial judgment, the operation of the clinicians' biases, illusory correlation, anchoring effects and many others. Where it is made clear that the witness is presenting what are in effect, his clinical judgments, it obviously is useful to bring out to the jury the nature of that process and its weaknesses and inadequacies.

With a candid and knowledgeable witness, this subject may be dealt with in a relatively brief way.

Q: Doctor, what you have provided us with on your direct examination is what could be called your clinical judgment, isn't that correct?

Q: (Or the question could be asked in this manner) Doctor, what you have given us in your direct examination, is your clinical judgment concerning (any specific issue you wish to deal with)? (In some cases, which will be rare, the witness may assert that what he is presenting is an actuarial conclusion. In that case, questions would have to be asked based on the material elucidated in Chapter 5 of Volume I to determine whether, in fact, what he has presented is truly actuarial. If that is the case, then one should be able to extract from him exactly what percentage of cases the actuarial formula correctly predicts and the basis for the actuarial formula.)

Q: Doctor, isn't there a substantial body of scientific and professional literature indicating that there are a number of serious flaws and problems with clinical judgment (or that clinical judgment lacks validity or cannot be relied upon)?

If you are fortunate enough to obtain an agreement, it is probably sufficient to let the matter drop there, however, there will not be very many cases in which a clinician will make this concession because it goes to the very heart of his profession and practice, at least so far as the diagnostic or assessment function is concerned. It may be that the chances of getting this answer would be increased by limiting the previous questions to clinical judgment in the diagnostic or assessment area and making it clear that you are not referring to clinical judgment so far as treatment procedures, although of course, many clinicians believe that treatment procedure depends on the diagnostic or valuative process. There are, however, some who do not feel that this is necessary. Many initiate therapy on the basis simply of asking an individual what the problem or problems are as he sees them.

However, with most clinicians, it is likely that much more detailed cross-examination will be necessary to illuminate this problem. Obviously it will be much easier to produce the desired material from a witness of your own, particularly someone whose orientation is from a more academic than practice viewpoint. The following questions assume that the witness has either denied the literature or has used some admit-deny type of answer which acknowledges the existence of the literature but attempts to strip away its significance or possibly has attempted to repair the damage of such literature on redirect examination.

Q: (If denial) Doctor, are you saying that such literature just does not exist or only that you are not aware of it?

Q: (If admit-deny or repair) Well, doctor, even assuming (whatever he has said) to be true, doesn't the existence of the substantial body of literature at least give rise to some serious doubts about clinical judgment?

## CONFIDENCE:

Q: Doctor, in your direct testimony you indicated that you felt pretty confident about your conclusion in this case. Are you aware of some research literature indicating that higher degrees of confidence tend to be associated with lower levels of accuracy? (or are unrelated to accuracy)

## DATA GATHERING:

Q: Doctor, in order to arrive at a clinical conclusion you need to acquire some data or information, correct?

Q: In acquiring that information, do you employ a pre-set procedure or do you determine where your investigation will go according to the data that comes up? (If the latter, it is unstandardized and does not lend itself to normative comparison.)

## INTERPRETATION:

Q: Would it be appropriate to describe the information as it comes to you as raw data?

Q: And then I presume you have to make some interpretation of what the data means, is that correct?

Q: And then I presume you have to put together your interpretations of the data, that is to integrate them in some manner, is that correct? (In the alternative one can ask, "What do you do with the data after you get it?" But that is an open-ended question which allows the witness to lecture, so we prefer the closed-end type of question.)

Q: Doctor, isn't there some research showing that different clinicians may gather somewhat different information? (If no, you have to be prepared to confront the witness with some of this literature.)

Q: Isn't there some literature showing that clinicians interpret and integrate the data differently?

Q: Doctor, isn't there a great deal of information that comes up in a clinical examination and in whatever records or other material you review?

Q: Do you use all of the data in arriving at your conclusions? (This is an important question because if the witness answers in the negative, he is then precluded later, when you ask him for his basis, from evading specific answers by saying he uses "All of the data.")

Q: Isn't it extremely difficult to integrate what amounts to thousands of items of data? (You may have to establish the fact that there are thousands of items in the examination.)

Q: Do you know how many items of data you can have in your awareness at any given time? (If the answer is yes, you will have to ask how this number has been determined so that one could rely on it.)

Q: Doctor, is there some research showing that clinicians use only a relatively small number of items of information in reaching their clinical judgments?

## ACCURACY:

Q: Doctor, aren't there several published studies showing the accuracy of clinical evaluative conclusions to be low? (less than 50%)

Q: Sometimes as low as zero percent?

## ACTUARIAL VS. CLINICAL:

Q: Doctor, did you utilize actuarial formulas in deriving your conclusions in this case? (The attorney should be alert to some claims by some clinicians that they have sent the data, particularly the MMPI, to a computer and obtained a printout which is the basis for their opinion. In that case you will have to determine whether or not the particular computer system is truly an actuarial one or whether it is a clinical model. Whether the clinician knows it or not, it is likely to be "clinical-actuarial" or clinical (see Chapter 14, Volume II). If it is an actuarial one then you have to ask what is the percent of accuracy of that actuarial formula. In most cases concerning computerized interpretations, as we know, that information will not be known. Also, in connection with the actuarial versus clinical, the attorney might want to find some way to get the quotation from Paul Meehl about how overwhelming the evidence is (see Chapter 5, Volume I) into evidence, as it is an impressive statement from an impressive source. Similarly one would want to get into evidence Sawyer's finding, also from Chapter 5, Volume I.)

Q: Doctor, are there a large number of studies showing that conclusions based on actuarial approaches are at least as accurate or more accurate than those involving the clinical judgment process? (If "actuarial" has not yet been defined, it should be before the question—see Chapter 5, Volume I.)

Q: Are there a large number of studies showing that the clinical judgment process is more accurate than the actuarial?

Q: In fact, there are virtually no studies showing that the clinical judgment approach is more accurate than the actuarial, is that correct?

## PSYCHIATRIST VS. PSYCHOLOGIST:

Some psychiatrists may claim that these studies of judgment pertain mostly to psychologists, as more studies have been done on psychologists than on psychiatrists. In that case, the following questions apply.

Q: Isn't it a fact, doctor, that there are virtually no studies that show that psychiatrists are superior to psychologists in this regard? (If denial, request citations)

Q: Well, in that case, you cannot assert that the findings with regard to psychologists are not equally applicable to psychiatrists.

Q: Well, doctor, are you aware that there have been a number of studies in which both psychiatrists and psychologists were involved and the findings are nearly universal that psychiatrists are not more accurate than psychologists? (There is not much you can do there with a negative answer. One choice is to confront him with some of that literature. The alternative is to have a rebuttal witness do it.)

Q: Aren't there some published reports indicating that psychiatrists also have these problems in clinical judgment?

## TREATMENT RESULTS AS EVIDENCE
## OF DIAGNOSTIC VALIDITY:

Many clinicians, particularly psychiatrists, will cite treatment successes as evidence of the validity of their diagnostic evaluations. Their rationale, following the medical model, is that in order to treat someone, you have to diagnose correctly what the illness or disorder is. We cannot speak with any authority on general medical matters but as a lay opinion, we would tend to agree with the proposition that in most areas of medicine, one would have to correctly diagnose the disease in order to provide the appropriate treatment. For many diseases there is a highly specific treatment or a very limited range of treatments are known to be effective. In contrast, very few mental disorders have a specific treatment, and as was shown in Chapter 5 of Volume I, recovery or improvement may occur without any treatment or may occur in conjunction with treatment for reasons that have little to do with the treatment or, even if they are the result of treatment, the treatment or the result may have had little to do with the diagnosis. The literature, in general, seems to indicate that by and large, improvement (success) in treatment is seldom related to a specific kind of treatment (see Volume II, Chapter 22). In that case, one cannot really reason back from the treatment success to the diagnosis. Patient statements are clearly not a reliable indicator.

Q: Doctor, is there scientific and professional literature which indicates that patient statements are not a sound basis for determining results of therapy?

Q: Isn't there literature indicating that in therapy patients frequently acquire a liking for and attachment to the therapist?

Q: Is it possible or probable that because of this liking and attachment the patient may tell the doctor what he thinks the doctor wants to hear?

Q: When one comes for therapy they are hoping to get better, and isn't it probable that they will then tend to believe and have faith in the therapist so that they will tend to agree with what the therapist says?

Q: Is there some research showing that while therapists tend to attribute gains to their therapeutic skills and techniques, clients mainly attribute it to "just having someone to talk to"?

Q: Doctor, isn't it true that in the mental health field treatment responses often lack specificity or fail to show clear relationships with the form of treatment that is provided?

Q: Doesn't the literature indicate that many disorders respond well (about as well) to a variety of different treatments?

Q: Doesn't the literature show that a variety of treatments have about the same level of success with many particular disorders?

Q: Isn't there a body of research showing that relatively untrained paraprofessionals have shown about as much success performing psychotherapy as psychiatrists and psychologists?

Q: With regard to various psychiatric medications, isn't it often the case that there is a good deal of trying out of this drug and that drug with a particular patient and this dose and that dose before one can arrive at something that seems to work?

Q: Wouldn't that indicate that the treatment is not specific to the diagnosis?

Q: (If appropriate) According to the literature is there a specific drug for post-traumatic stress disorder?

Q: (If appropriate) According to the literatures is there a specific drug for compulsive personality disorder?

Q: How many specific psychiatric disorders can be treated only by one drug?

Q: How many drugs are there that are specifically curative or ameliorative to only a single psychological disorder?

The purpose of some of the foregoing questions is to establish that even with medication, which is the most likely form of treatment to be confirmatory of a diagnosis or to be specific to a particular diagnosis, the evidence is weak. Regarding any specific medication, it may be necessary to consult resource materials (e.g., *Physician's Desk Reference*) as to the degree or extent or percentage of effectiveness for specific conditions. There are too many medications and too many disorders for us to attempt to deal with that topic here but there are resources that can be consulted and additionally a psychiatrist that you may be using would have access to that information. Further questioning will demonstrate that the situation is much worse with regard to psychotherapy.

Q: When patients who are not involved in litigation enter into treatment, doesn't that indicate a high degree of motivation on their part?

Q: With many conditions, doesn't that motivation itself provide considerable impetus for improvement?

Q: Doesn't the mere fact of entering into treatment with some belief in its potential for improvement, in itself, give the person some sense of relief and some sense of doing things about their problem so that this alone might result in some improvement (or feeling of improvement)?

Q: Doesn't the research indicate with regard to successful treatment outcomes in psychotherapy that the reasons for the successes are obscure and have not been established as related to a particular type of therapy?

Q: Haven't reviews of the research on psychotherapy in general expressed the theme that research in that area is very difficult and it remains uncertain what form of therapy is best for what patient?

Q: Similarly, the same articles indicate that it is uncertain what factors account for therapy responses?

Q: Doesn't the literature show successful outcomes can occur without necessarily being related to the particular diagnosis?

Q: Have you had a scientific study done by independent evaluators of the relationship between your therapy outcomes and your diagnoses?

Q: Have you had a scientific study done by independent evaluators of the outcome of your treatments?

Q: Do you keep track of the outcome of the treatment of all of your patients? (Emphasize "all.")

Q: Do you have any treatments that are not successful?

Q: How many or what percentage are not successes?

Q: How do you know if you do not keep a count?

Q: It's just your impression that most (or x percent) of your patients are treated successfully by you?

Q: Is it possible for a therapist to misjudge the success of treatments due to his own personal involvement?

Q: Is it possible for the therapist to misjudge the relationship between his treatment outcomes and his diagnosis?

Q: If you were employing someone would you rely on that individual's appraisal of their performance or success or would you try to get information from some less interested parties?

Q: Wouldn't the therapist be in a poor position to evaluate or to provide objective assessments of the outcome of his/her own therapy?

Q: Isn't there some research showing that therapists' reports on their own behavior in therapy often show poor correspondence with observations made by independent judges?

Q: Isn't there literature to the effect that therapists' accounts of their own work may be subject to various distortions and biases?

Q: Isn't there research showing that clinicians of differing theoretical orientations differ in their evaluation of treatment quality?

Q: Isn't there research showing little relationship between experience and therapy outcome?

Q: Isn't there research showing that there is little difference in outcome between professionals and non-professionals, in terms of treatment effectiveness?

Q: Wouldn't this raise some questions as to the importance of diagnosis?

Q: If treatment effectiveness is a means of validating diagnostic accuracy, wouldn't this then qualify as diagnosticians, the non-professionals who had success in treatments along with the professionals?

## ILLUSORY CORRELATION:

If the witness has cited concurrence of other practitioners in his diagnosis as evidence of validation, questions concerning illusory correlation might be appropriate.

Q: Doctor, are you aware of the term "illusory correlation"? (If he is not familiar with the term, questions can be asked concerning the phenomenon itself.)

Q: Isn't there research showing that clinicians have a tendency to confirm each other's erroneous beliefs?

Q: Isn't there research showing that clinicians continue to operate on the basis of beliefs that have not been validated through research?

Q: Isn't there research showing that clinicians continue to operate on the basis of beliefs that research has shown to be wrong (or untenable)?

Q: The facts that two "symptoms" (behaviors, items) occur together with some frequency does not necessarily mean that they are related or that the presence of one indicates the presence of the other, does it?

Q: (If answer to the previous question is unsatisfactory) In order to know that the two symptoms were related and one signified the other, wouldn't you have to know the extent to which that symptom occurred in people who did not show the other symptom?

## BASE RATES:

There is research showing that clinicians tend to disregard population base rates when evaluating case specific information. This obviously can lead to symptomization or pathologizing of behavior that is very common or normal. Therefore, after establishing a definition of base rates the following question is appropriate.

Q: Doctor, the term "Base Rates" as it is used in the mental health field or behavioral sciences, generally refers to the rate at which a particular sign or behavior occurs in a given population or in the population at large, is that correct?

Q: If you don't know what the base rate in the general population is for a particular behavior, then you have no real basis for determining that it is a symptom of disorder, isn't that correct?

Q: Do you know the base rate for (the particular behavior or symptom)?

Q: If you don't know the base rate, then you can't say for sure that the symptom is diagnostic of the disorder?

Q: If you don't know the base rates, then you don't really know if your use of the symptom or sign (or whatever evidentiary basis the clinician relied upon) results in more frequent misidentifications of a disorder than correct identifications of the disorder?

Q: Doctor, in your practice you mostly see people who are abnormal (who have some kind of mental disorder), isn't that so?

Q: How many hours a week of your professional time do you spend with people who are abnormal?

Q: Then you spend (that many) hours a day or week less with normal people than the average person does, is that right?

Q: In that case, it would be correct, would it not, to state that you have relatively little experience with so-called normal people (or relatively less experience) or less opportunity to observe normal people?

Q: In that case, doctor, isn't it correct that you would have less opportunity than most of us to observe the degree to which normal people display (whatever the behavior is that is in question) or to observe the degree to which normal people show some of the same behaviors that you view as symptoms in your patients?

Q: Is George Vaillant (see discussion in Chapter 4 of Volume I) a well-known psychiatrist?

Q: Does he have articles published in scientific and professional journals?

Q: Has he indicated in one article that certain behaviors thought to be exclusive to those with psychiatric disorders were actually common among normal individuals?

Q: Is Paul Meehl a well known psychologist?

Q: Doesn't Dr. Meehl assert that much behavior or thinking observed in disordered individuals is also common to normal individuals?

Q: Doctor, based on your clinical method of observation, if you studied chief executive officers (CEO's) of corporations and discovered that a very high percentage of them had pets as youngsters, would you have an opinion that having a pet was related to their success, or stated better that their success was related to their having had pets?

Q: You would not be able to draw that conclusion, would you, unless you also knew how many or what percentage of managers who did not become CEO's may have had pets as youngsters?

## ANCHORING EFFECTS:

Some discussion of anchoring effects can be useful, particularly if a referral was made by litigant's attorney and there was any discussion of the reasons for the referral at the time of the referral, as this would represent the first information that the witness had about the litigant and might have established an anchoring effect.

Q: Did the referral contain any information about litigant other than his name and phone number?

Q: What was that information?

Q: Doctor, does the term "anchoring effect" refer to a greater influence of information received early in the diagnostic process over information received later?

## OVER-RELIANCE ON SALIENT DATA:

Although clinicians often claim that they utilize all of the data in making their diagnosis, there is research showing that they tend to overemphasize more vivid or dramatic data and in fact in some instances one single piece of dramatic data will control the diagnosis. If there is some indication in the case that this is what has happened, the following line of questioning is suggested.

Q:  Doctor, isn't there literature showing that one particularly noteworthy item may exert considerable influence in the diagnosis?

Q:  Are you aware of studies in which clinicians were given identical information about two individuals except that they were told one was a patient and the other an applicant for employment and that in those studies, with only that difference, the difference in conclusions was considerable?

Q:  Isn't there research showing that although diagnosticians believe that they have integrated a wide range of data in reaching conclusions, that often only one or a few pieces of data primarily account for conclusions?

## HINDSIGHT BIAS:

Sometimes when confronted with an item of conflicting data the clinician may attempt to make it seem consistent with his conclusions by a declaration to the effect that, "Oh, well, that was perfectly predictable because..." whatever. Several research reports have identified this phenomenon.

Q:  Doctor, when you declare that (the particular data) is entirely predictable, is that an instance of what is known in the literature as hindsight bias?

Q:  Is there some research literature indicating that clinicians sometimes, after the fact, declare something was predictable when in fact they are not able to predict it in advance?

## CONFIRMATORY BIAS:

Confirmatory bias is a tendency of clinicians, and people in general, to maintain beliefs despite the force of counterevidence and to pay particular attention to evidence that supports their beliefs, misinterpret ambiguous or non-supportive evidence as supporting their beliefs, and disregard or dismiss counterevidence. Sometimes the beliefs are held in the face of strongly persuasive or convincing counterevidence. In such instances, it is quite likely that if a patient were to behave in such a manner, it would be described as "delusional." For example, if a psychiatrist held the belief that psychiatrists are able to assess dangerousness with a high degree of accuracy, this would be in the face of overwhelming evidence to the contrary and the officially stated position of the American Psychiatric Association, presumably representing the view of colleagues, and therefore would seem to be extremely close to the DSM glossary definition of a delusion. There are several aspects of confirmatory bias one might wish to cover in cross-examination, depending on how the direct has unfolded and what transpires in the cross. These include favoring one's initial hypotheses by emphasizing confirmatory evidence and downplaying controverting evidence, employing double standards of evidence, premature closure, gathering data in a manner to confirm the initial hypotheses and how all of these operate in the forensic area.

Before going insto confirmatory bias, it would be useful to determine what information the witness had about litigant and what if any observations he made early in the examination.

Q: What information did you have about litigant before you saw him?

Q: Did you observe anything about him in the first few minutes of your contact?

Q: Were you able to form any initial impressions from that data?

Q: Is there a body of research showing that initial beliefs are often maintained, even in the face of counterevidence?

Q: Is there a body of literature indicating that when clinicians have taken a position or adopted a conclusion, that they apply very high standards of rigor in regard to any contradictory evidence and will accept a much lower standard of rigor for any data that supports their position?

Q: Is this particularly true with regard to published research reports? (This obviously is useful when a clinician's response to contrary or negative research findings is to pick on the methodology).

Q: Are you familiar with the term "confirmatory bias"?

Q: What does it refer to?

Q: Doctor, are you familiar with the term "premature closure"?

Q: Does that term refer to a tendency to form conclusions very early in the data collection process?

Q: Does the literature show that this sometimes results in becoming resistant to data which might indicate that the initial conclusion was wrong?

Q: Is there some literature to the effect that psychiatrists frequently form diagnostic impressions of patients within the first two or three minutes of contact and sometimes even in as little as thirty seconds? (Another possibility here is to take the witness through each bit of data from the beginning of data collection and at each point ask, "Did you have any impression at that point?" You may find some who will indicate an impression early so that premature closure must be considered a possibility; or if he denies forming an impression at any point along the line until the last item of data is in, he will have made it appear that every piece of

data mentioned was important in the conclusion so that any item
that can be disproved should make the conclusion fall.)

Q: Doctor, is there literature showing that the confirmatory bias
sometimes affects the gathering of data so that information supporting one's hypotheses is more likely to be collected and noted
than information disconfirming one's hypotheses?

Q: Doctor, isn't there scientific and professional literature indicating
that in your field it is relatively easy to find data supporting most
hypotheses one might form initially, regardless of whether they
are correct or incorrect?

Q: Well, doctor, doesn't the literature indicate that most people
have engaged or do engage in behavior that could be construed
as symptoms to support a diagnosis made early in the data collection process?

Q: Is there scientific and professional literature indicating that an
early hypothesis can influence the clinician's behavior in the examination process?

Q: Is there scientific and professional literature indicating that the
clinician's behavior in the examination process can influence the
kind of data that the person being examined will produce?

Q: Doctor, isn't there research showing that clinicians distort data in
order to fit an original hypothesis or diagnosis? (We have in
mind here particularly the Rosenhan study and the Temerlin and
Trousdale studies; see Chapters 7 and 5 of Volume I, respectively.)

## INABILITY TO CONTROL BIAS:

Many clinicians will concede that bias can affect collection and interpretation of data; however, many will claim that they are not biased,
possibly on the grounds that they have been "psychoanalyzed" or that if
they have biases, they know what they are and therefore are able to control them. There is no sound evidence that psychoanalysis eliminates all
biases. The literature cited in Chapter 5, Volume I raises considerable
doubt that even if the clinician knows what his biases are, this does not
enable him to eliminate their effect.

Q: (If needed) It has not been clearly established through the scientific and professional literature that psychoanalysis eliminates all
biases, has it?

Q: Doesn't the scientific and professional literature indicate that insight into or knowledge of biases does not significantly reduce
their effect?

Q: Isn't there some literature to the effect that biases can be operating below the level of awareness?

Q: Wouldn't biases influence a clinician's judgment as to how his biases affect his judgments?

Q: An individual is not really a very good judge of his own biases, is he?

## INTEGRATING OR USING ALL OF THE DATA:

One of the major tasks of cross-examination is to pin the expert down as to precisely what data he was using in formulating his conclusions. This allows the cross-examiner then to question the adequacy or validity and in some cases, even the accuracy of those particular data as supporting the conclusion. In some cases, the cross-examiner can point out contradictory data or alternative interpretations. However, in our experience this is one of the most difficult goals to accomplish in cross-examination. The reason for this is that many, if not most, experts will attempt to evade explicating the basis for their conclusions by asserting that their conclusion is not based on any one item of data or on any one test but rather, it is based on all of the data taken together. In effect, then, they are saying that they are integrating all of the data in order to reach their conclusion. As discussed in Chapter 5, Volume I, there is little if any research supporting the notion that clinicians are able to do this and a substantial body of literature indicating that they are not capable of such integration of large amounts of data. Further, the literature indicates that while they may sincerely believe that is what they do, the research indications are to the contrary. One line of cross-examination involves asking the witness as to each datum, for example each test response or in an interview, each statement, how that data was integrated with all of the other data and to do this exhaustively. Unfortunately, it can be exhausting for all concerned, including the jury, although typically one would not have to go beyond perhaps three or four bits of data to demonstrate that in fact the clinician has not used each piece of data, i.e., has not used "all" of the data. The following line of questioning is suggested as an alternative or perhaps even an addition to the exhaustive datum-by-datum cross-examination.

Q: Doctor, earlier you indicated that you draw your conclusion by putting all of the data together, is that correct?

Q: Is it generally recommended in your profession that this kind of data integration, if that is an appropriate term, should be performed in order to arrive at accurate diagnosis?

Q: Isn't there a lack of a substantial body of published research findings demonstrating that clinicians are able to utilize large amounts of information at one time? (If the answer is that there is, you might want to ask the witness to recite a number of such studies that have been published.)

Q: Is there a body of research literature demonstrating that clinicians in fact do not use a large amount of information in forming their conclusions?

Q: Aren't there a number of studies showing that, in fact, clinicians do not use a large amount of information in forming their conclusions?

Q: Doesn't the literature show that clinicians often use only a few items of data in forming their conclusions?

Q: Aren't there a number of studies indicating that clinicians are not capable of utilizing large amounts of data or information in forming their conclusions?

Q: Aren't there a number of studies showing that given a certain minimum of information, adding more information does not improve the conclusions drawn by the clinician?

Q: Isn't there considerable research to show that a considerable amount of data is not observed or recalled by the clinician?

Q: If you take all the data into account, then this missed data would have to have been taken into account as well. So you don't know what your opinion might have been had you observed or recalled the data that was present but that you failed to observe or recall?

Note that in connection with this line of questioning, when we refer to data we are referring to "hard" data or factual data, e.g., a test score, a test response, a school record, a statement made in an interview, an observable bit of behavior and other information of that type. An observation that litigant in the interview "appeared depressed" should not be considered data as it involves an inference and might not be seen as such by all. For example, in contrast, an observation that litigant cried during the interview would constitute data.

## INCREASED INFORMATION:

Q: Isn't there some research showing that adding more information or having the clinician use more information does not increase accuracy?

Q: Aren't there studies showing that in some cases using more information decreased accuracy?

Q: Aren't there some studies showing that greater amounts of information increased the clinician's confidence in his conclusion although, in fact, such increased information did not appreciably increase the accuracy?

There may be some objection to questions of this general nature. However, in response to such objections, it should be brought out that it is essential to establish what is generally true of clinicians and then give the specific witness an opportunity to provide evidence that he is an exception to the principle as only he would be likely to be in possession of such evidence, if any exists. One certainly should be allowed to demonstrate that he is not free of these problems or inadequacies simply by virtue of being a psychiatrist or a psychologist.

Q:  Aren't there several studies showing that configural analyses do not appreciably increase accuracy?

Q:  Aren't there research findings that raise serious doubts that any configural analyses clinicians might perform contribute anything of importance to judgment accuracy beyond what could be accomplished by simply adding data together? (You may have difficulty with the terminology here with psychiatrists, as their training does not necessarily include the term configural analysis; however, most psychologists should be familiar with it.)

Q:  Are there several studies showing that individuals have severe difficulties recognizing and comprehending even relatively simple configural relationships? Even those involving only two or three variables?

Q:  Doctor, actually there are thousands of items of information in the clinical examination, are there not?

Q:  In that case, in order to consider all of them and all of the possible interactions of items of information it would involve millions or even billions of comparisons or relationships, would it not?

Q:  That really would not be within the capability of the human brain, would it?

Q:  In fact, one would not even be able to remember all of that data, would one?

Q:  You did not make a videotape of this examination so that you could record all of that data, did you?

Q:  (If there is some objectively contradictory data) Doctor, how did you integrate (the contradictory data) into supporting your conclusion?

Q:  (In response to a clinician's declaration that his awareness of his biases and erroneous judgment practices allows him to compensate for them.) Doesn't some of the research suggest that clinicians have limited awareness of the factors that actually shape their conclusions?

Q:  Isn't there research showing that objective measures of the data influencing conclusions often contrast sharply with a clinician's subjective impression of the influential data?

## COMMON COUNTER-ARGUMENTS TO
## THE JUDGMENT FINDINGS

The lawyer should be aware of some of the more common responses of expert witnesses to the judgment findings, and be prepared to challenge these arguments. We cannot cover every possibility, for we have found that experts can be extremely imaginative or creative, but the following are among the most frequent.

### It's Not Fair

Many experts claim, in essence, that the judgment research has been rigged such that psychologists and psychiatrists were handicapped in one or another way and prevented from showing their true abilities. One such argument is that experts were not used in the studies. This argument is simply incorrect. Many of the studies have used experts and judgment performance has been no better, or even worse. Quite a number of the studies discussed in Chapter 5 included clinicians with extensive experience or training. In fact, there is so much literature on this topic that we had also devoted a full chapter to experience and to training in Volume I.

Another refrain is that clinicians were placed at a disadvantage by being denied access to information critical to accurate clinician appraisal. For example, as noted previously, some of the earlier studies on the clinical-actuarial debate were criticized because clinicians did not have interview data with which to work. There may have once been some basis for this objection, but no longer. A number of the studies have allowed clinicians to gather whatever information they wished to gather and to proceed in whatever way they wished to proceed. The results have been the same, if not worse. In fact, if one considers the studies showing the limited benefits of additional information, and the work by Sawyer (see Chapter 5) showing that overall accuracy decreases when interview data are added to test data and combined clinically, then lack of interview data in some of the earlier studies does become potentially noteworthy, but for opposite reasons than most clinicians contend. Apparently, had such data been available, clinicians may have in fact shown themselves to be even more inferior to actuarial methods than results suggested.

Another complaint is that clinicians were forced to make "atypical" judgments that are not actually representative of those made in clinical practice. This assertion is somewhat baffling. The studies often involve judgments about diagnosis, or about the prediction of such matters as potential violence or various aspects of everyday functioning. If clinicians wish to maintain that these tasks are foreign to clinical practice, fine and well, but these same clinicians should not engage in such practices in the courtroom. Further, whether these types of judgments are or are not typical of clinical practice, they are precisely the types of judgments most pertinent to the forensic setting. The court obviously needs to know about such matters as diagnosis and prediction.

## I Am the Exception, or This Case Is the Exception

This counter-argument comes in various forms, but it always boils down to the same contention—the judgment research does not apply to this particular case. One may hear clinicians argue that the particular defendant has a particular type of problem and that the judgment studies did not address this particular set of circumstances. Alternatively, the clinician may try to explain why he was not susceptible to the various erroneous judgment practices, biases, or limits the studies described.

This approach leaves the expert vulnerable in various ways. For example, if he indicates that the particular judgment task involved in the case under consideration has not been scientifically examined, this obviously means that although there is no negative evidence, there is no positive evidence that the task can be accomplished either. Given such a massive body of negative evidence on related judgment tasks, what should we assume given this lack of direct evidence? Certainly, we should not assume that the odds are in favor of a positive result. At minimum, there is considerable doubt that such judgments can be performed accurately. Alternatively, if the expert argues that he is above all this judgment literature, the lawyer may wish to point out that this may well have been what other experts believed before their judgment accuracy was put to formal test. Additionally, you can raise pertinent questions about the research showing lack of insight into one's own judgment practices and the biases (e.g., hindsight bias and confirmatory bias) that make it extremely difficult for experts to form accurate appraisals of their own judgment abilities and accuracy levels. Most of all, ask the clinician to prove his assertion, or what formal evidence exists to support his claim. We have discussed at length the limits of the arguments that are likely to be offered, such as treatment effectiveness providing evidence for judgment accuracy.

## I Am an Artist

As discussed briefly above, some experts will contend that their work is as much art as science. As such, they may argue that the judgment research involves science and does not apply to the clinician's artistic abilities. Again, this places the expert in a very vulnerable position. First, clinicians in many of the judgment studies were allowed to proceed in their preferred manner—to perform their art—and yet their conclusions about the type of matters that are of greatest interest to the courts were quite commonly wrong. Second, one can ask this artist how much of what he does is science and how much is art. He may well respond by stating he does not know. One might then ask, "Thus one would not know for sure that it is wrong to assume that what you do is 90% art and 10% science."

Along similar lines, we believe the courts may wish to consider the following question: Should psychologist artists be serving as expert witnesses? Apparently, even given the same set of facts and the same individual, these artists often "paint" very different pictures. This is shown by the frequency with which the opinions of these artists clash in specific cases. Should we try to decide who is the best artist, and how are we to do this? Should the best painter or storyteller, the one whose picture *seems* most realistic, be declared the winner? When our courts are reduced to deciding matters of art, rather than fact, something is very wrong.

## I Deal with Individuals, Not Numbers or Groups

As typically uttered, this statement defies the most rudimentary principles of logic and rationality. The clinician will state something to the effect, "I know that x percent of individuals with this configuration on the MMPI have been shown, by empirical research, to grossly exaggerate their symptoms, but this has nothing to do with *this* particular individual." The clinician will go on to focus on the absolutely unique features of this individual and disregard any features he may well have in common with those on which this MMPI research was conducted.

Consider the following. Suppose you are offered a bet on a series of 100 coin tosses with an unaltered penny from the U.S. mint. If you come within 5 of the number of heads that turn up, you win $5000. Now everyone knows that every penny is unique. This particular coin may be 23 years old, contain a unique pattern of scratches and scuffs, etc. Would you decide that because of the penny's unique features, you will defy the odds (which would lead you to say 50 heads in 100 tosses) and guess, say, that only 25 heads will turn up? If you do so, you will have greatly decreased your chances of winning. Of course, it is conceivable that the result will turn up 25 heads, but the odds are greatly against it. Thus, even though this is a unique and one-of-a-kind penny, you will focus on the features it probably has in common with most pennies (i.e., it comes up heads about 50% of the time) and play the odds.

If you do not play the odds, then you are behaving exactly like the clinician who asserts that numbers or figures derived from groups never apply to individuals. As regards such practices, Meehl (1973) states:

> The vulgar error is the cliché that "We aren't dealing with groups, we are dealing with this individual case." It is doubtful that one can profitably debate this cliché in ten minutes. He who wishes to reform the thinking in case

conferences must constantly reiterate the elementary truth that if you depart in your clinical-decision making from a well-established (or even moderately well-supported) empirical frequency...your departure may save a particular case from being misclassified predictively or therapeutically; but such departures are, prima facie, counter-inductive, so that a decision *policy* of this kind is almost certain to have a cost that exceeds its benefits. The research evidence strongly suggests that a policy of making such departures, except very sparingly, will result in the misclassifying of other cases that would have been correctly classified had such non-actuarial departures have been forbidden; it also suggests that more of this second kind of misclassification will occur than will be compensated for by the improvement of the first kind. (pp. 234-235)

In other words, the clinician who departs from probabilities is more likely to be wrong than right. Of course, where clear objective facts contradict the odds (e.g., the coin is a freak with heads on both sides) one is justified in disregarding the odds. Indeed, however, in those situations no "opinion" is necessary: the conclusion is unequivocally dictated by the fact.

## Trying to Make a Real Issue a Pseudo-issue

Finally, some experts may claim that this whole matter of clinical versus actuarial judgment is an artificial creation or a "straw man," and that actually there is no conflict between the two. For example, it may be argued that most clinicians combine clinical and actuarial approaches, or integrate the two. Meehl's (1986) rejoinder to this argument makes it clear, however, that this is no pseudo-issue. He states:

Some critics asked a question...which I confess I am totally unable to understand: Why should Sarbin and Meehl be fomenting this needless controversy? Let me state as loudly and as clearly as I can manage, even it if distresses people who fear disagreement, that Sarbin and I did not artificially concoct a controversy or foment a needless fracas between two methods that complement each other and work together harmoniously. I think this is a ridiculous position when the context is the pragmatic context of decision making. You have two quite different procedures for combining a finite set of information to arrive at a predictive decision. It is obvious from the armchair, even if the data did not show it overwhelmingly, that the results of applying these two different techniques to the same data set do not always agree. On the contrary, they disagree a sizable fraction of the time. Now if a four-variable regression equation of a Glueck actuarial table tells the criminal court judge that this particular delinquent will probably commit another felony in the next 3 years and if a case conference or a social worker says that he will probably not, it is absurd to say that Sarbin and I have "fomented a controversy" about how the judge should proceed. The plain fact is that he cannot act in accordance with both of these incompatible predictions. (p. 372)

Meehl has also stated that while there undoubtedly are cases where one should depart from the actuarial rules, it is difficult to know when such a departure should be made. We would argue that such departure should only be made where there are objective facts which clearly over-rule the formula. Such departure should not be made by pitting the clinician's inferences against the actuarial inferences. Boiled down somewhat, Meehl's statement above appears to corroborate the statements we have made elsewhere and what the research has shown, which is that the clinician is more likely to be wrong than right when he departs from established empirical frequencies.

### Denigration of Research

Additionally, some clinicians will attempt to denigrate research as a means of getting around the implications of the clinical judgment research. In that case the following questions may be useful:

Q: Doctor, are you saying that scientific research in your field is worthless? (If this is answered affirmatively, obviously then, one can argue to the jury that this witness has declared his field to be a non-science because sciences are sciences precisely because they do employ scientific methodology. As we pointed out in Volume I, one might acquire knowledge by religious methods or by intuitive methods, but to be a science the knowledge must be acquired and/or verified by scientific methods.)

Q: Well, doctor, if the research isn't worth anything then isn't it the case that your field simply is not a science? (We are unable to guess how this might be answered.)

Q: Well, doctor, are you saying that some research is good and some is worthless?

Q: How does one determine what research is good and what research is useless?

Q: Are you saying, in effect, that if the research agrees with what you believe or with what you have observed in your practice then it is good, but if it does not agree with what you have observed then it is no good?

Q: Does the fact that there have been a number of studies by a number of different people of different orientations, which point to the same conclusion, have any influence on your opinion concerning the validity of the research?

Q: You have mentioned research that is contrary to that indicating deficiency of clinical judgment. If there is research going both ways, would you say that the issue is probably in doubt?

Q: If the issue of whether clinical judgment is likely to be accurate is unresolved by the researchers in your field, can the jury be expected to resolve that controversy?

Q:  If the controversy exists, then one cannot take it as a fact that clinical judgment is free of these various inadequacies that have been pointed out in the research publications, can one?

Q:  If that is the case, wouldn't it seem to be a risky venture to give credence to opinions based on clinical judgment which is a procedure of dubious value? (This is a question you probably would not want to ask; simply make the point in argument.)

## PUBLISHED RESEARCH VS. THE CLINICIAN'S OBSERVATIONS

In Chapter 2 of Volume I, we described different approaches to knowledge, among which were so-called observational methods and experimental methods. The reader may recall the agricultural example that we employed. The principal differences between the experimental and clinical-observational methods were in the utilization of control of variables and usually some kind of quantitative measurement, as well as publication of results and replication. While the term "research" has both broad and narrow meanings, we will use the term here (and you may need to define this in your questioning) in its narrower meaning, which is that of the more scientific approach which involves control of variables and some kind of quantitative measurement. We will use the term clinical or observational for those matters that clinicians claim to have established or validated or acquired knowledge of through their clinical experience or in some cases through the clinical experience of others.

Q:  Doctor, is your profession an art or a science? (The usual answer is "both.")

Q:  Can you tell us how much of it is art and how much of it is science? (Few, if any, will attempt to specify the proportions.)

Q:  (If there is a blackboard available, this question could be preceded by drawing a moderately large circle on the blackboard.) Doctor, could you step up to this circle and with the chalk, show us how much is art and how much is science? (Again, few mental health professionals will attempt this kind of specification. If one does, to this or the previous question, then the following questions can be asked.)

Q:  Doctor, are those proportions that have been established through scientific research in your field?

Q:  Doctor, are those proportions generally agreed upon in your profession?

Q:  What is the source from which you have determined those to be the proportions? (We really do not know how the clinician might answer this question other than again, to fall back upon his experience, which we find difficult to comprehend as an explanation.)

Q: Doctor, aren't there a number of published articles suggesting that psychiatry (clinical psychology) is to a considerable extent an art? ("Yes" is the only correct answer, but the clinician can probably get by by stating that he does not know.) (Once again, the lawyer is cautioned that many mental health professionals may respond to a question like this by attempting to take control of the cross-examination with a statement such as, "Well, I believe the majority feel it is more science than art." Obviously this should be subject to a motion to strike. If the motion is not granted or if the lawyer wishes to pursue this anyway, the next question could be, "What is the source of that opinion?" or "Are you aware of a substantial body of published literature which establishes that to be the case?")

Q: Doctor, directing your attention to that portion of your field which is science or scientific, would that portion be contained largely in the scientific and professional literature of the field? (It is of course possible that having established that the clinician does not know how much of his field is science and how much is art, the lawyer may not wish to pursue the topic anymore, leaving it as it is, to return in argument and point out to the judge or jury that, indeed, according to this testimony there may be very little science in the field, it may be almost entirely an art.)

At this point, assuming the answer is "yes" to the previous questions, you may not wish to ask any further questions as you have now established that the science part of the field, whatever that may be, is contained in the scientific and professional literature.

Some experts may assert that other sciences also have inadequacies. One does not want to leave an impression that therefore, psychiatry is on a level with hard science. A question such as, "Doctor, are you claiming that psychiatry is as precise and mature as chemistry and physics?" should serve its intended purpose.

Q: Doctor, would you agree with this definition of science or scientific method, that it is a way of approaching issues or questions or problems through the use of control of variables and some kind of quantitative measurement? (We recommend establishing a definition of science by your own question as it keeps better control of the situation. In the alternative, it can be done by asking the expert for his definition of science or scientific method which should come out roughly the same, but in some instances may turn out to be a definition that other experts would simply not support. Informed experts may indicate that "experimental" is the best term for work in which variables are controlled.)

Q: Doctor, are knowledge or information or conclusions acquired through the use of scientific research methods generally viewed in your field as somewhat more secure than the information of uncontrolled, unsystematic and unqualified observations based solely on the observations of a single practitioner which have never been published and thus, subjected to the scrutiny of his peers? (We feel, although we do not know, that most clinicians in the mental health field would agree with this statement. However, if the expert does not, and there clearly are some who will not, the following set of questions need to be asked. We will use the model of the fertilizer experiment for this line of questioning, although in the courtroom one might prefer to use seed A and B rather than fertilizer. Also below, we will provide another illustration of this type of questioning in connection with the topic of cross-examining the expert on his utilization of his success in treatment to substantiate his diagnostic accuracy. If you were introducing your own clinical expert or consultant expert, preferably the latter, you might have them explain to the jury the difference between scientific and clinical-observational methods, and why scientific methods lead to information that is more secure. However, if you wish to attempt this with an opposing expert, questions along the following lines might bring out the important difference. This may seem to be very much a collateral issue but hopefully you will have prepared the judge for it by making a motion to bar or limit the psychiatric testimony on the basis that if it is offered you will have to engage in this kind of detailed cross-examination in order to expose its weaknesses.)

Q: Doctor, in order to illustrate these differences for my benefit and the jury's benefit, I am going to pose a hypothetical issue and ask you some questions to determine how each method would proceed. Assume that you are a traveler who regularly goes through a few small towns in Iowa shortly after harvest time. This is an area where the principal agricultural product is corn. Actually, you are a buyer of corn for a large canning company and you notice that among the people you do business with, Farmer A consistently brings in more corn to sell than does Farmer B, although you have visited both of them and know that their farms are about the same size. You notice that after they get their money from you, Farmer A goes across the street to the feed and grain store and buys corn seed A, and that Farmer B goes over there and buys corn seed B. Now you are able to put these two things together and you think you have discovered what may be the secret of Farmer A's greater productivity. That is, pretty clearly, he is using different seeds and therefore this could explain why he is getting more corn. Actually you have noticed that several farmers whose crops are larger buy seed A in contrast to those who buy seed B. You mention this to a couple of other corn buyers and they say, "Yes, by golly, we've noticed the same thing," although one of them says, "I've also noticed that in some cases, some farmers using B seeds have larger crops," however based on these several observations and the fact that they have been shared with some colleagues in an informal way, at least two of you, with some hesitant concurrence by the third, agree that apparently seed A is superior to seed B. Would you agree that is a reasonable approximation of the observational method of acquiring information? (While "yes" is the correct answer, we cannot be sure that the expert is going to agree with it. Because it is definitional in nature, he may wish to add to it or vary it in some way. The attorney will simply have to be alert to see where the clinician goes with it and if he goes in a direction which describes what the scientific method would require and is attempting to call that observational, then it may be better to discontinue this line of questioning and rely on an expert of your own to explain this kind of thing. However, assuming the answer is affirmative, the questioning can continue.)

Q: Now, having made this discovery, you want to perform a public service and you speak to the professor of agriculture at the local university or a government agent administering agricultural assistance programs and you tell him what you've discovered and suggest that he ought to advise all the farmers in the area to use A type seeds. Now he says, to you, "Mr. Buyer, I appreciate your public spiritedness in bringing me this suggestion but I have to caution you that based on what you have observed, we really can't draw the conclusion that A seeds are better than B seeds because we don't know, for example, that the farms that are using A seeds don't have more fertile soil than those with B seeds. And we don't know whether the farmers using A seeds are more skillful or harder working farmers than those using B seeds, and we don't know whether their farms get more water, or they provide more water than those using B seeds. So you see, before we could draw that kind of conclusion (and he might go on and name some other things), we would have to do a controlled study which would allow us to eliminate all of those possibilities (variables) so that we could feel pretty secure that it really is a difference in the seeds that is making the difference, that is to be sure there is a relationship between the kind of seeds used and the amount of corn produced. And then we would have to measure the difference in output to see whether it was of a sufficient difference to make it worthwhile to change the brand of seeds. In other words, we would have to really measure the output. See, we would get a few of the farmers that are using A seeds now and have them divide their farms up into kind of a checkerboard pattern so that there would be one plot of ground where they would use A seeds and then an adjoining plot where they would use B seeds and then an adjoining A and an adjoining B and so on. So that the farm would look like a checkerboard in terms of the seeds that were used, and that way we would control for any difference in farming ability, because it would be the same farmer and we would also control for any differences in soil because we could safely assume that with this checkerboard arrangement any possible differences in soil were being canceled out and controlled in that manner. And we would arrange with the farmer to see that each plot got the same amount of water and the same amount and same kind of fertilizer and so on. We would go down the line with everything we think might affect the growth of the corn. And if we did that and then we found out by measuring the amount of corn from the A plots and B plots that the amount from the A plots was appreciably greater, then we would feel comfortable telling the farmers who use B seeds that they would get more product by using A seeds. We would say, A seeds, other things being equal, produce more corn than B seeds. There is a relationship that has been pretty well demonstrated by research methods which indicate that relationship. Of course we would limit our recommendation to farmers in this area because we don't know if the same thing would hold true in another area. For example, we wouldn't want to tell farmers in the central valley of California to use A seeds for their corn instead of B seeds because we don't know with the soil being different there, if this would hold up. In order to tell farmers in other areas, we would have to conduct this same kind of research in several areas. We wouldn't have to go to every state, but maybe go to eight or nine states where we know the climate and soil is different. If we found that A seeds produced more than B seeds in all cases, then we would feel pretty secure in making that recommendation even in states where we hadn't performed the research." Would you agree, Doctor, that is an approximate representation of what the scientific method is like? (Again, we cannot predict what kind of answers one might get but the statement, the hypothetical that was given, does represent a reasonable, brief illustration of scientific method.)

Q: Doctor, would you agree that the scientific method seems to tie down the conclusion a good deal more firmly than just the observational method? (You may not even need to ask this question because it should be obvious to the jury at this point that this is the case.)

## DSM-IV

The goal of cross-examination on DSM-IV is to disabuse the trier of fact of any belief that it is an adequate system of classification of mental disorders for any purpose, and certainly not for forensic purposes. Cross-examination can bring out its temporary and experimental nature, lack of relationship to matters of forensic relevance (see Volume I, Chapter 1, "the gap"), and the obvious concern its producers had concerning its use in forensic matters.

Q: The history of the diagnostic manuals has been pretty poor, hasn't it?

Q: They have had to revise them every few years, haven't they?

Q: It took a few years after the previous manuals were published before it was determined that they were not adequate, is that not so?

Q: All right, doctor, then given the previous history of the diagnostic manuals, isn't it going to be a few years after the publication of DSM-IV before an adequate evaluation of it will be available?

Q: Was DSM-IV published in May of 1994?

Q: Doesn't it have to be out in general use for at least a few years before it will be possible to fully evaluate the reliability (and/or validity) of diagnoses that are based on it?

Q: And until there has been enough time for an adequate amount of research to be done about it, by people other than those who produced it, we will really not know how much better than the previous inadequate manuals it is, isn't that correct?

Q: (If reference is made to the field trials) Weren't there also field trials with DSM-III?

Q: And didn't research done by others after DSM-III was published show lower reliability results for various categories than the field trials?

Q: Weren't there more than 200 changes from DSM-III, published in 1980 to DSM-III-Revised, published in 1987?

Q: And seven years later, in DSM-IV there were another more than 225 changes, right?

Q: And in some disorders, there was a return to the DSM-III positions that had been changed in DSM-III-R, right?

Some witnesses may state that the changes were minor, e.g., just matters of wording. Such witnesses should be asked if there are also a number of substantive changes, and if so, does he know how many were wording and how many were substantive.

Q: When the criteria for a particular disorder are changed, that casts doubt on the application of research done with people diagnosed under the old criteria to people diagnosed under the new criteria, isn't that so?

This may be a good place to present visuals utilizing the cases of Alice Adams, Bill Brown, Ann Atkins, and Abe Allen given in Volume I, Chapter 4.

Q: Hasn't the Chairperson of the DSM-IV production (A.J. Frances) along with others published an article titled, "An A to Z Guide to DSM-IV Conundrums" which describes a large number of unresolved issues and problems with DSM-IV?

Q: Isn't the manual produced by committee consensus?

Q: Isn't that a political rather than a scientific process?

Q: Weren't the committees for DSM-IV composed to some extent of different people from the committees for DSM-III-R?

Q: Wouldn't that give rise to the possibility that some changes were simply due to changes in the composition of the committees rather than to scientific research?

Q: Doesn't the manual state (p. xxii) that there should be no assumptions that all people described as having the same disorder are alike in all important ways even in regard to defining features of the diagnosis?

Q: In that case, you can't really draw any conclusions about a person based on the diagnosis, can you?

Q: Both DSM-III and DSM-III-R contained cautionary statements concerning the use of DSM diagnoses in legal matters, didn't they?

Q: And DSM-IV has a whole section titled Use of DSM-IV in Forensic Settings, doesn't it?

Probably the most effective procedure at this point is to simply read the first three paragraphs of this section (p. xxiii) and ask the witness to acknowledge it as the DSM-IV statement. The lawyer needs to be aware that the fourth paragraph dilutes the first three. It indicates that the diagnoses can be of assistance when used appropriately, using the example of where there is a requirement for a diagnosis as a predicate for legal action, such as in civil commitment. Finally it states that knowledge of longitudinal course of a disorder may improve decision making concerning mental functioning in the past or future. This, of course, is nonsense in view of their declaration that people with the same disorder may differ in significant ways. Note the last sentence of the first paragraph, "It is precisely because impairments, abilities, and disabilities *vary widely* within each diagnostic category that assignment of a particular diagnosis does not imply a specific level of impairment or disability." (emphasis added)

Q: When is DSM-V expected?

## RELIABILITY AND VALIDITY

The next series of questions deals with the low reliability and validity of clinical diagnosis. It is advisable to use the term "diagnosis" in these questions as the largest amount of research on reliability deals with diagnosis. It is unlikely that there will be a denial of the research on reliability of diagnosis, although some witnesses may assert that applies to diagnoses based on earlier editions of the DSM. This can be dealt with in the manner described below, basically to the effect that DSM-IV is too new to be evaluated and the best guess that could be made is that it will prove as inadequate as the previous diagnostic systems have. Other witnesses may assert that while there is disagreement on "label" there is better agreement on the dynamics or description of the individual. In that case, the cross-examiner should have in mind studies like that by Tarter et al., cited in Chapter 7, Volume I, in which highly experienced and highly reputed psychiatrists disagreed roughly 50% of the time with regard to the major diagnostic category, that is, they could not agree whether the individual was psychotic or neurotic or had a personality disorder. This is not a refinement of labelling or a simple matter of semantics but goes to important differences in diagnosing the individual. It is a basic disagreement as to the nature of the psychopathology regardless of the language used. If the expert asserts that it is only one study, you should have in mind that it is only one of the more methodologically sound of many studies which demonstrate this basic disagreement. There are a number of references to that effect in Volumes I and II. Particularly with regard to agreement and disagreement on dynamics, the studies of Goldsmith and Mandel and of Stoller and Geertsma (Chapter 7, Volume I) are highly relevant. It is important to bring out that the literature showing low reliability and validity generally pertains to present evaluations and this paves the way for establishing that the reliability and validity when assessing a prior mental state, if relevant, must necessarily be even poorer. It is well to have in mind throughout cross-examination that you do not have to prove that there is no reliability or validity. All you have to do is create considerable doubt concerning agreement among psychiatrists and the accuracy of their diagnosis.

Q: Doctor, hasn't the scientific and professional literature shown that psychiatrists frequently disagree with each other in their diagnoses?

Q: All right, doctor, I take it that your answer to the question as I stated it would be yes, is that correct?

Q: Doctor, there hasn't been a great deal of research on the validity (accuracy) of psychiatric conclusions, has there?

Q: Is there a body of scientific and professional literature indicating that psychiatry is not a very precise scientific field?

Q: Given the lack of a generally well validated theoretical system or body of knowledge and all of the problems of the clinical examinations such as situation and examiner effects, as we discussed a little bit ago, and as there is little in the way of research demonstration of a high degree of accuracy in psychiatric conclusions, it would not be very safe to assume there is a high degree of accuracy, would it?

Q: In fact, there are a number of published research studies showing a massive degree of error by psychiatrists (or psychologists), isn't that correct?

Q: Doctor, there isn't a substantial body of scientific evidence proving that psychiatrists in general are usually correct in their conclusions about individuals, is there? (Be sure the answer deals with a "substantial body.")

Q: Doctor, is there a principle in medical diagnosis that it is safer to diagnose and treat a condition which may prove not to exist, than to fail to diagnose a condition which does exist, and as a result of the failure to diagnose the patient may become worse or even die?

Q: Isn't it generally indicated in the scientific and professional literature that psychiatrists (psychologists) tend to overdiagnose psychopathology?

Q: Could that explain why it is that in several instances when it's been possible to test psychiatric conclusions against independent objective criteria, they have generally been shown to be wrong more often than they have been right?

## THE ROSENHAN STUDY

Questions concerning the Rosenhan Study flow from the previous set of questions on validity. We view this as a study that is useful in almost any case involving mental health testimony. It is likely that the witness will respond to cross-examination by presenting various critiques of the

Rosenhan Study, most likely that of Spitzer. As all of these arguments are covered in Chapter 7 of Volume I, and the rebuttal of those arguments as well, we are not going to deal with those responses in this chapter. We would suggest that the lawyer who plans to use the Rosenhan Study in cross-examination be very familiar with the contents of Chapter 7. We think the study is particularly useful because of its simplicity.

Q: Are you acquainted with the study by Professor David Rosenhan titled "On Being Sane in Insane Places"?

Q: Is that the study where 8 apparently normal people, as part of a research project, went around to 12 different mental hospitals and presented a single complaint that they thought that sometimes they heard voices saying "empty," "hollow," or "thud." And even though the rest of the information they presented was well within the normal range, they were diagnosed as schizophrenic with the exception of one hospital where the diagnosis was manic depressive psychosis, is that correct? (At some point, many experts will raise some of the specific criticisms of the Rosenhan Study, and these will then have to be dealt with using questions based on the information provided in Chapter 7 of Volume I.)

Q: Isn't it true, however, that the study was a demonstration of 100% diagnostic error by the psychiatrists? (The expert may raise the issue of people faking psychopathology under circumstances where the psychiatrist had no reason to suspect malingering.)

Q: Are you saying it's that easy to fool psychiatrists?

Q: What situations would provide a basis for suspecting malingering?

Q: Wouldn't the absence of any other symptoms of schizophrenia except possible hallucinations be a reason for suspecting the diagnosis?

Q: Well, doctor, these diagnoses were made under DSM-II, is that correct?

Q: And doesn't DSM-II describe a number of other indications of schizophrenia that ought to be present to make the diagnosis?

Q: (If the witness asserts as Spitzer pointed out in his critique of the study, after you rule out other conditions in which hallucinations might occur, the only diagnosis that is left is schizophrenia.) Well, doctor, isn't it true that in the process of eliminating explanations for the hallucinations, if the psychiatrist had seen that there was a lack of any other symptoms of schizophrenia and ruled that out before he ruled out the manic depressive psychosis, keeping in mind that at one of the hospitals that was the diagnosis, wouldn't he then be left in the position where, if he ruled out schizophrenia, the only thing left would be manic depressive psychosis?

Q: Well, doctor, isn't schizophrenia described in DSM-II as being manifested by characteristic disturbances of thinking, mood, and behavior?

Q: And the only symptom displayed by the Rosenhan people were these select hallucinations which I take it are manifestations of disturbance in thinking, is that correct?

Q: No other symptoms of schizophrenia were present, is that correct?

Q: Doesn't the diagnosis in DSM-II of manic depressive psychosis also include hallucinations and, in addition, uneasiness or apprehension?

Q: Didn't the Rosenhan people display some nervousness which would be the same as uneasiness or apprehension when they presented themselves at the hospitals?

Q: So according to the description in DSM-II, hallucinations might occur either in schizophrenia or in manic depressive psychosis but in addition, the nervousness displayed by the Rosenhan people would also fit with the manic depressive diagnosis, isn't that correct?

Q: There also are a number of other symptoms that are needed to make the diagnosis of schizophrenia, isn't that correct? Let me phrase the question this way. Of the symptoms of schizophrenia and of manic depressive psychosis, depressed type, given in DSM-II, the Rosenhan people displayed two of the symptoms of manic depressive psychosis and only one symptom of schizophrenia, isn't that correct?

Q: In fact, doesn't Spitzer, state—I am quoting: "Admittedly there is a hitch to a definitive diagnosis of schizophrenia: almost invariably there are other signs of the disorder present, such as poor pre-morbid adjustment, affective blunting, delusions or signs of thought disorder. I would hope that if I had been one of the twelve psychiatrists presented with such a patient, I would have been struck by the lack of other signs of the disorder. But I am rather sure that having no reason to doubt the authenticity of the patient's claim of auditory hallucinations, I would also have been fooled into noting schizophrenia as the most likely diagnosis." Is that a correct statement of what Spitzer had said?

Q: I am interested in his statement that other signs of the disorder were absent just as the mood disturbance was absent so far as diagnosing manic depressive, isn't that correct?

Q: In fact, at a later point in his critique, doesn't Spitzer state, "Is Rosenhan's point that the psychiatrist should have used 'diagnosis deferred,' a category that is available but is rarely used? I would have no argument with this conclusion." Doesn't Spitzer say that?

Q: That's an acknowledgement that a different diagnosis might have been more appropriate, isn't it?

Q: Immediately after being admitted to the hospital, the Rosenhan people stopped any simulation of symptoms, isn't that correct?

Q: And they were kept in the hospital on the average for almost three weeks, isn't that correct?

Q: And during that period of time, none of the psychiatrists who saw them determined that the diagnosis of schizophrenia had been erroneous, is that correct?

Q: In his report, didn't Rosenhan show how the psychiatrists distorted the information obtained from these patients to fit the diagnosis, rather than using that information to question the diagnosis?

Q: And Spitzer acknowledges that problem in his critique of the Rosenhan Study, does he not?

Q: In fact, Spitzer says that distortion of the data to fit the diagnosis goes on all the time, does he not?

Q: And while none of the psychiatrists ever found that there was anything wrong with these patients, a number of the other patients in the mental hospital were able to see that there was nothing mentally wrong with them, isn't that correct?

Q: Is it also correct that as a follow-up study, Rosenhan arranged with a different hospital where they felt they could not make such mistakes, that he would send some pseudo-patients to that hospital and, over a period of time, the staff at the hospital were instructed while admitting anyone who sought admission, to indicate if they thought the person was one of Rosenhan's pseudo-patients?

Q: And isn't it a fact that the psychiatrists, at that hospital, felt very confident that about twelve percent of the patients that were admitted were Rosenhan pseudo-patients?

Q: And is it also correct that, in fact, no Rosenhan pseudo-patients ever went to that hospital?

Q:  Actually, the Rosenhan Study is only one of several reported in the literature showing a very high degree of error by psychiatrists, isn't that correct?

Q:  And there are numerous statements in the literature to the effect that the validity of psychiatric conclusions never has been adequately established, isn't that correct?

## EXPERIENCE

The next series of questions deals with the lack of relationship between experience and diagnostic accuracy. Most people attach more weight to the experience of the expert than to any other aspect of his qualifications. They are accustomed to making the assumption that greater experience means greater expertise. When a psychiatrist or psychologist states that he has had ten years of experience or has diagnosed more than 1,000 cases, it is difficult for people to believe that such experience has not materially sharpened his diagnostic accuracy. Yet the weight of research shows that the difference between experienced and inexperienced psycho-diagnosticians is virtually nil. Therefore, it is most important to get the full impact of the research across to the trier of fact. In Volume I, Chapter 8, we cite more than 125 references to the effect that experience does not make a difference with regard to accuracy. Some of these publications are old, but about half are from the 1980s and 1990s.

One of the principal reasons that experience does not produce greater diagnostic accuracy is the lack of feedback. That is, in many if not most instances, the clinician does not get the kind of clear objective results that would enable him to determine first of all if his conclusions were correct and, secondly, if they were correct, why they were correct, and if they were in any way incorrect, what errors he may have been making or repeating that led to the inaccuracy. This is particularly true where the clinician is seeing the patient only for the purpose of evaluation as is most often the case in forensic matters. Most of the time, therefore, the clinician has little if any opportunity to make a determination as to whether his conclusions were correct. Knowledge of the verdict is of no help in this regard because the verdict could be based on many factors other than the psychiatrist's conclusions. It is also the case that even when clear and precise feedback has been provided under artificial, experimental conditions, clinicians still may show only minimal gains, likely due to biases that impede the interpretation of feedback (see Chapters 5 and 8, Volume I).

Some clinicians will assert their success in treatment of patients validates their diagnostic accuracy. There are numerous reasons why treatment success cannot be used as a validator of diagnostic conclusions.

Treatment success itself is not a well-defined entity and may well vary from one clinician to another so that what one considers a success another may not. Secondly, with very few exceptions, mostly involving the rare cases where there is a highly specific drug that is successful in treating only one highly specific disorder, treatment "success" may occur for a variety of reasons, several of which might have little or nothing to do with the diagnosis. For example, a change in the patient's life situation may relieve stresses or improve his life to the extent that he no longer finds treatment necessary and informs the therapist that he is feeling better and thinks he's okay, which the therapist may very well conclude is a result of the treatment when it in fact may be a result of the fact that the patient has inherited a million dollars from his maiden aunt or has met "the right girl" and married her or any of a number of events that can occur independently of the therapy. The patient may get better just over the passage of time, as is true of many medical conditions. The patient may actually not get any better and simply want to stop and save the rather expensive cost of treatment. However, because most therapists are likable people, the patient does not want to hurt the therapist's feelings, so instead of saying, "Doctor, I don't think you're doing me any good," he may inform the doctor that he is feeling better, doing better, whatever, so he can get out of the situation without hurting the doctor's feelings. The doctor, however, may mark this in his mind as another example of success showing what a good therapist he is and how accurate his diagnosis must have been. Finally, and most convincing of all, is the fact that there is a virtually unequivocal set of research findings to the effect that success in treatment, however it may be defined, is unrelated to the experience of the therapist. Several of these studies and reports are provided in Chapter 8 of Volume I and Chapter 22 of Volume II. Further, if it is correct, as some clinicians assert, that you have to make the correct diagnosis in order to provide the correct treatment, then numerous studies are relevant showing that relatively untrained people—the so-called "paraprofessionals"—who may have had as little as a few hours of instruction, are just about as effective in treatment as are psychiatrists. If treatment success is dependent upon correct diagnosis, then it must be the case that these untrained people are making diagnoses just as accurately as the highly trained and experienced psychiatrists and psychologists. An alternate explanation of these findings, of course, is that the diagnosis is not critical to treatment success (see Chapter 22, Volume II).

Q: You indicated that you also rely to a considerable extent upon your experience in making your evaluations. Is that correct, Doctor?

Q: Concerning psychodiagnosis, doesn't the weight of scientific research show that more experienced examiners are not appreciably more accurate in their evaluations than are the less experienced? (This appears to us to be only conclusion from the literature we have reviewed. However, the question can be asked more conservatively in terms of "a substantial body of scientific and professional literature" rather than "the weight of." The lawyer should be prepared for a negative answer from the clinician. There are not a large number of clinicians who are going to concede that experience is not helpful. Their answer is likely to be one based on their "impressions," "belief" and so on.)

Q: While I understand, Doctor, that it is your impression that experienced diagnosticians are more accurate, what I'm asking you about is the research and the scientific literature. Are you familiar with that literature (research)? (If the doctor is familiar with the literature, he really should acknowledge at the minimum that there is a substantial body of literature to this effect. If he says there is research and it does not show that experience does not improve diagnostic ability, one has the choice of either confronting him with several of the studies cited in the chapters noted above, or letting it pass and having the material presented by your own expert, at which point it should become clear that the witness is simply not being candid.)

Some witnesses may cite Brodsky to the effect that recent research has supported the benefits of experience. They can be confronted with the statement of Dr. Brodsky to the effect that when he revises his book he will change that statement (see Chapter 8, Volume I).

Q: Aren't there more than 125 publications indicating that experience is not related to accuracy?

Q: Doctor, do most psychiatrists perform quantified, scientifically controlled follow-up studies of their diagnoses?

Q: Have you done such studies concerning the validity of your diagnoses? (The answer to the last question is quite likely to be no. If the answer is yes, the investigation should then pursue the methods employed and the data obtained by such follow-ups to see if it was done in a manner giving it scientific validity. This would necessarily involve questions concerning the criteria for accuracy of evaluation—whether objective or subjective— whether independent evaluators of the accuracy of the diagnoses were used or simply the clinician's opinion of his own diagnoses and results, and all of the other methodological considerations such as are suggested in the chapter on scientific method.)

Q: (Assuming the answer was no) Well, in that case, doctor, there isn't any way for you or anyone else to know how accurate you are, is there?

Q: All we have is your guess?

Q: What you have is a belief that your experience has made you better at diagnosing, isn't that correct?

Q: Might another psychiatrist who also has many years of experience come to different conclusions than yours? (If this is denied one can refer to the literature showing disagreements among highly experienced psychiatrists.)

Q: And wouldn't he probably believe that his conclusions were correct on the basis of his experience?

Q: There are cases like that reported in the literature, aren't there? (See Board Certified Psychiatrists, Case #1, Chapter 9, Volume I.)

Q: Then we could not rely on the experience of either of you in trying to determine whose conclusions were accurate, could we?

Q: Doctor, are you familiar with the concept of illusory correlation?

Q: Illusory correlation refers to the fact that clinicians maintain certain beliefs even though research evidence is lacking or research goes against the belief, isn't that correct?

Q: And, doctor, doesn't the research show that even experienced clinicians maintain illusory correlations despite their experience?

Q: Doctor, are you aware of several studies showing that relatively inexperienced clinicians make psychological evaluations just about as well as those with more experience?

Q: Doctor, are you aware of any research evidence showing that laymen, completely untrained and inexperienced in psychiatry and psychology, make such evaluations just about as well as professionals? (Note: If the witness acknowledges such evidence, the point is made. If, as is more likely, he is not aware of the evidence, the stage has been set for your witness to present the research findings and demonstrate that the other expert is ignorant concerning an important issue in his field and that his impressions can be quite wrong in the light of objective research data.)

It seems fairly obvious that if experience were to be helpful at all, it would be principally in the area of clinical judgment. Yet there is no substantial showing that experience alleviates all of the problems associated with clinical judgment as described in Chapter 5 of Volume I, and there is even some evidence that experience tends to further entrench some of those problems in some clinicians. Therefore, the attorney may want to ask some questions relating experience to clinical judgment.

Q: Doctor, in what way does experience produce greater accuracy? (We are not recommending this open-ended question, but presenting it for the attorney who wishes to take a chance on the kind of answer he may get, which in many cases may prove to be very helpful.)

Q: Doctor, would you agree that one of the principal effects of experience is presumed to be an improvement in clinical judgment? (The purpose here is to have the witness talking the same language as you are. Once this is done, you can then introduce all of the clinical judgment material if you have not already done so. If you have, then his answer, if it is affirmative, should suffice.)

The next few questions deal with the old medical practice of "bleeding" or "blood-letting." We think that lawyers may find these questions or questions on this topic to be an effective series with which to close the set of questions on experience. However, we would caution the lawyer to make himself fairly familiar with the literature we have cited in Chapter 2 of Volume I on scientific method so he does not find himself in the position of the lawyer in Case B, cited in the appendix, where he was unable to deal with the psychiatrist's contention that seemed to imply that bleeding was a good practice or was stopped by virtue of experience.

Q: Doctor, are you aware of the practice of bleeding or blood-letting which was utilized by physicians for several hundred years as a form of treatment?

Q: (Assuming an affirmative answer) This method of treatment was used by physicians with twenty and thirty and forty years of experience. Isn't that correct?

Q: And it is now known that kind of treatment was inappropriate or not effective for most of the conditions for which it was employed. (This leaves room for the fact that in reality bleeding did have some remedial effects on a limited number of illnesses as well as having a beneficial effect as a placebo in other cases. However, it is clear from the literature that bleeding was extensively used for a wide variety of diseases without any proof that it was curative for those diseases and that physicians sometimes over their entire lifetime did not learn by experience that this was a poor treatment.)

Q: Doesn't the literature indicate that Benjamin Rush, considered by many the father of modern psychiatry, relied extensively upon bleeding in his practice?

Q: Doesn't the literature indicate that he killed George Washington by bleeding him to death?

We do not see how a clinician who is familiar with the literature could honestly refuse to acknowledge that there is a substantial body of literature to the effect that there is little, if any, relationship between experience and accuracy. Nevertheless, because experience is such a vital element of the clinician's credibility, the greatest amount of resistance can be expected on this issue. The clinician may use any one or a combination of the tactics described in the chapter on Experts' Tactics. The two approaches we have most often seen are attempts to denigrate the research or a form of admit-deny technique, roughly by acknowledging the existence of the negative literature but pointing out that this clinician treats patients, many of them successfully, and has many acknowledgements of the effectiveness of his treatment by patients, thus implying that he must after all know what he is doing. The latter tactic can be dealt with by reference to the massive survey by Glass (see Chapter 8, Volume I and also Chapter 22, Volume II) in which they found therapy outcome to be virtually unrelated to therapist experience. Questions can be directed to bring out the fact that consumer satisfaction is hardly an appropriate measure of diagnostic accuracy and also to show that similar expressions of satisfaction are given to non-mental health professionals who perform counselling functions. (See Swartz and Swartz, Chapter 8, Volume I.)

Denigration of the literature in this area may take the form of asserting that one can prove anything one sets out to prove by research, that research that flies in the face of common sense should be disregarded, and sometimes (in the case of psychiatrists) by attempting to indicate that this research applies only to psychologists. Any claim that psychiatrists are superior to psychologists should be met with questions to bring out the fact that there is no research showing such superiority in psychiatrists so far as diagnosis is concerned and that what literature there is tends to suggest that psychologists may be superior to psychiatrists, although this is by no means established. In addition, if this tack is taken by the witness, there are a number of studies cited in Chapter 5 of Volume I and over 10 additional studies cited in Chapter 8 of Volume I that involve psychiatrists and show that their experience has not made them accurate diagnosticians.

So far as the common sense argument is concerned, it should be noted that it is the purpose of research to test principles that might be derived on the basis of common sense. If common sense were an adequate guide, there would be no need to perform scientific research. Therefore, when research flies in the face of common sense, assuming that the methodology has reasonably met scientific requirements, it is safer to question the common sense notion than to throw out the research. Common sense would tell us that the sun revolves around the earth. We can see it with our own eyes; however, research has established that it is not so, it is the other way around.

Concerning the argument that one can prove anything they want to by research, it should first of all be noted that it has not been proven by research that experience does make for superior diagnostic accuracy. This is only an assumption. Secondly, it should be noted that some of the research demonstrating the failure of experience to make for superior psychiatric accuracy was performed by psychiatrists, who could hardly be thought to have set out to prove that experience was of no use. For example, in the study by Tarter et al. (see Chapters 7 and 8, Volume I) the psychiatrists who performed the research specifically state that they were trying to show that earlier research on this issue had not made use of the most experienced and most reputable psychiatrists and that their intent was to overcome that deficiency in the hope of showing that experience was effective. They point out, with some chagrin, that their results failed to accomplish their intended purpose and, in fact, showed that the rate of disagreement on gross diagnostic categories—psychotic, neurotic or personality disorder—was the same in their study as had been shown in the previous studies, roughly disagreement in about 50% of the cases. So then, in about half of the cases, one of the highly experienced psychiatrists had to be wrong.

Whether to proceed along these lines with witnesses who take this approach regarding experience or whether to simply ask the questions and rely on an expert of your own to produce and describe the research findings is a matter that would have to be determined in each individual case based on any indications that one can succeed in gaining these acknowledgements from the witness.

If the clinician, early in cross-examination, has indicated that he relies on the scientific and professional literature as part of his knowledge base, he is in a somewhat difficult position when he attacks the research. He would have to take a position that while other research is useful, the research in this area should be disregarded, and we are not aware of any basis on which this distinction can be made. If one went through study by study, one could probably find some methodological problems in any given study, However, the fact is that there are several studies pointing to the same conclusion and one cannot really justify a statement that all of that research has been badly done. The Tarter study, in particular, has been about as well done as any other research in the mental health field. Many of the judgment studies have been performed by highly respected and skilled researchers (e.g., Robyn Dawes, Lewis Goldberg, Amos Tversky). If the clinician attempts this approach, probably about all that can be done is to ask him on what basis these studies are distinguished from other research that he does rely on. One could go through each study individually and ask what are the methodological problems and what research does he rely on that is free of such problems; however, this is a difficult task to perform in the courtroom and it might be better, certainly it would be easier, to simply raise the issues and then have your own expert come on who will verify that there is a substantial body of research indicating that there is little relationship between experience and the reliability and validity of conclusions and that the methodology meets customary standards (e.g., publication in peer reviewed journals).

## ASSESSMENT OF CREDIBILITY OR MALINGERING

Most clinicians will concede that it would be possible for an individual to deceive them. However, frequently they will assert that it would not be likely for one to simulate a pattern of psychopathology without having had extensive training and experience in the field. Similarly, many will assert that they can tell whether or not an individual is being honest with them. We have found virtually no research, except some early research on psychologists trying to fake schizophrenia in the Rorschach, to support either of these contentions and have found some research to the contrary. (See Chapter 18, Volume II.) Because much of the diagnosis is based upon information obtained from the litigant who almost always has a motive to deceive, it is important to establish that there is little or no basis for the clinician's confidence that he has not been deceived. You may also be able to show the clinician was not diligent in pursuing evidence of malingering.

Q: Doctor, sometimes people involved in lawsuits are less than honest, isn't that correct?

Q: And it is possible for an individual to deceive you, isn't it?

Q: (If there is any kind of negative response) Well, if someone was successful in fooling you, you wouldn't know that he had fooled you, would you?

Q: In that case, you really couldn't know how many people involved in lawsuits have successfully fooled you, could you? (The witness may claim that in order to fool him, to simulate a pattern of psychopathology, the litigant would have to have had training in medical school and done a residency and read a lot of books on the subject and seen a lot of patients, and there are not many litigants who have had that kind of training.)

Q: Well, doctor, first of all, I imagine a Ph.D. clinical psychologist who had been out in practice a few years could do it as well as a psychiatrist, isn't that right?

Q: So one would not need to go to medical school and do a psychiatric residency, right?

Q: And I suppose a psychiatric social worker probably would know enough about the different syndromes to be able to do it also, isn't that correct?

Q: Isn't there a body of research indicating that in order to successfully simulate a mental disorder, one would not have to have training in psychiatry or psychology?

Q: Indeed, isn't there research (Hart et al.) that shows that even children can fool psychologists into believing they have brain damage?

Q: Isn't there research showing error rates as high as 100% in detecting malingering?

Q: Aren't there a number of articles in the scientific and professional literature indicating that psychiatrists (psychologists, except for some tests, see below) have not demonstrated a capacity to detect malingering?

Q: Is there literature indicating that a litigant's lawyer or a mental health professional may unintentionally provide cues as to what may be important for the litigant in trying to establish psychological disorder?

Q: Do you know whether or not plaintiff's lawyer asked him if he had difficulty sleeping (troubles with eating, with relationships, with judgment, with thinking, with memory and so on down the list of symptoms)? (This question may draw an objection on the grounds of lawyer-client privilege but note the question does not ask for the content of any conversation between lawyer and client. It only asks the expert what he knows about. He can answer this question "yes" or "no" without in any way revealing anything the client told the lawyer. As an alternative, you can ask the witness if he asked the litigant if his lawyer or anyone had discussed or asked him about the various symptoms.)

Q: If you don't know, then you would not have any way of knowing if the lawyer did in some way suggest symptoms to the litigant, would you? (Similar sets of questions can be asked regarding the expert himself and any health or mental health professional who may have examined the litigant.)

Q: Litigants (prisoners) would have access to public libraries (prison libraries), which have books describing many kinds of psychological disorders, would they not? (Most public libraries and prison libraries have at least some analog of introductory psychology texts, most of which contain descriptions of the main symptoms of the more common psychological disorders.)

Q: Aren't there a number of prisoners who are "shrink wise," that is, who know a fair amount about symptoms of various disorders?

Q: Do you know if litigant had any communication with any such?

Q: There is no single rigid set of symptoms for (the disorder in this case), is there?

## OBJECTIVE MEASURES OF MALINGERING:

Several psychological tests have built-in validity indicators, some with research support as indicators of malingering. The MMPI in particular has several quantitative measures of malingering: the F Scale, the F minus K, the Dissimulation Scale (Ds-r) and the Subtle-Obvious scales. The MMPI-2 has additional indicators but these do not yet have as extensive a research base as the older ones.

Q: Aren't there some objective or quantitative indicators of malingering or measures of malingering on the MMPI?

Q: What are those measures? (Ask specifically about any that are omitted that you plan to use.)

Q: Don't those measures have considerable (some) research support?

Q: Did you administer or have an MMPI administered?

Q: What was the score on (each) measure?

Q: What percentage of genuine or non-malingered MMPI's would be misidentified according to that result on that scale? (With all of these questions, obviously you will not want to ask them unless the scale numbers are such as to pretty strongly indicate malingering. Because there is no set score for defining malingering but a range across the studies, you may want to find out what research or whose numbers the witness is using. If they are high, you can query whether there are other studies showing lower or much lower scores as indicators.)

## CLINICAL VERSUS ACTUARIAL:

If you have not already introduced this issue, the cross-examination on measures of malingering may provide a good avenue for such an introduction.

Q: Doctor, are you familiar with the literature on actuarial versus clinical evaluations? (If the witness is not familiar with this literature then obviously there is not much more you can do in questioning him about it. This is more likely to be the case with psychiatrists than psychologists, as most psychologists would have encountered this issue in their education and training. However, if the witness is not familiar with the literature, you will need to bring it out through a witness of your own and then point out to the jury in argument that the opposing expert is ignorant in an area of considerable importance.)

Q: (Assuming the expert has answered the previous question affirmatively) Doesn't that literature show almost unequivocally that the actuarial approach is as accurate or more accurate than the clinical approach?

Q: In fact, doctor, there have been over 100 studies on this topic, have there not?

Q: There are almost no studies showing the clinical method to be more accurate than the actuarial, isn't that correct?

Q: By actuarial is meant the use of set decision or interpretive rules such that *no* professional judgment is involved, isn't that correct?

Q: The actuarial method would permit a clerk to write the conclusion dictated by the numbers, isn't that correct?

Q: Can't the F minus K Scale on the MMPI be interpreted by the actuarial method? (Same question can be asked concerning the Dissimulation scale, or any other quantitative indices of malingering that are available in the case.) (Once again, if the witness is ignorant regarding these measures, you will need to have an expert of your own available who can inform the jury about them.)

Q: The actuarial method makes it possible to state the percentage of misidentifications likely with any particular score, doesn't it?

Q: When you say that you believe the litigant was not malingering, that is just your clinical opinion (guess), is it not?

Q: Your clinical opinion is not based on an actuarial approach, is it? (If you ask this question, you have to be prepared to back it up with extensive questioning to illuminate the fact that the expert's opinion in fact is clinical and not actuarial, because some clinicians either through ignorance or other reasons will assert that their conclusion is actuarial or "clinical-actuarial." It's based on their observation that in seven out of ten cases they can detect, or have detected malingering. This is obviously nonsense because they cannot know how many cases of malingering they saw who escaped detection, unless they have had a controlled study performed, which is highly unlikely. For further discussion of the distinctions between the actuarial, clinical, and clinical-actuarial methods, see Chapter 5, Volume I.)

## UNAWARENESS OF THE LITERATURE
## & THE OBJECTIVE MEASURES OF MALINGERING:

In the situation where the witness lacks knowledge of the existence of objective measures of malingering and/or the literature concerning these measures and the literature on actuarial versus clinical methods, some additional questions may be worthwhile. This seems particularly true if the witness has represented himself as having a specialty or being a specialist in forensic psychiatry or psychology and even more so if he is Board Certified in Forensic Psychiatry or is a Diplomate in Forensic Psychology. It seems that it would be reasonable to expect someone specializing in forensics or who was Board Certified in forensics to be aware that malingering is a significant issue in that field and to be knowledgeable about all of the means of evaluating the possibility of malingering. Further, one would assume that in order to become Board Certified in this field, the examination for that certification would require a reasonable degree of knowledge in that area. The questions that follow assume the witness has indicated that he lacks knowledge of the various measures of malingering and/or the literature showing superiority of actuarial over clinical methods. The reader is also reminded of the ethical principles (Chapter 2 of Volume III) which require knowledge of and reliance on the scientific literature. It may be unethical for a psychologist, and by implication a psychiatrist, to render an opinion about malingering if he is unfamiliar with the literature on the subject.

Q: Well, doctor, isn't malingering an important issue in the area of forensic psychiatry (psychology)?

Q: In order to practice forensic psychiatry (psychology) wouldn't you need to be familiar with all of the tools that are available for assessing malingering? (If the answer is that the witness does it based on his clinical experience, skill, acumen or whatever, then lines of questioning concerning actuarial versus clinical as indicated above should be useful.)

Q: Doctor, in order to be Board Certified in Forensic Psychiatry (Psychology), didn't you have to demonstrate a knowledge of objective methods of assessing malingering?

Q: If you are not aware of these objective measures, what did you indicate in your examination that you use to assess malingering? (One of the possibilities here, of course, is that nobody asked him anything about assessing malingering when he was certified or became a Diplomate, in which case, a jury ought to be able to judge just how meaningful that particular credential is.)

Q: Doctor, aren't there some studies showing that there is little relationship between the clinician's confidence in his opinion and the accuracy of his opinion concerning malingering?

Q: Doctor, isn't there even one study showing that nine- and ten-year-old children were able to successfully fool experts into believing they had a psychological disorder although most of the experts were quite confident in their judgments? (You should be prepared for a critique of this study so you may not want to get into it although it can be defended. If you are calling a consultant expert it would be better to introduce it through him.)

The MMPI and other questionnaire type tests may also provide another kind of evidence affecting the litigant's credibility. Sometimes such tests contain answers which directly contradict the litigant's statements to the clinician. For example, he may have claimed "irritability" as a symptom following the accident but on a questionnaire item he states that he is usually calm and is not easily upset. This is not consistent with irritability. All questionnaire items should be checked for such inconsistencies.

## ASSERTION OF SUPPORTING LITERATURE

In many instances when being questioned concerning the negative literature which is recited in this text, the witness may counter with statements to the effect that there are supporting studies; that is, studies which show good reliability or reasonably good validity or that experienced clinicians do better. We have found relatively little of such research, but we have heard this assertion frequently made. It should not make any difference, because if there is research going both ways, obviously the particular scientific or professional issue is unresolved and a jury should not be expected to resolve it in the courtroom.

Q: (In response to the above assertion) Well, doctor, are you saying that there is scientific and professional literature going both ways on the issue of (reliability, experience, whatever)?

Q: Doesn't that mean that from a scientific and professional point of view, this is an unresolved question (or is a question that is in doubt)?

Q: This means that the highly trained and educated scientists and professionals in your field have not been able to resolve this issue, isn't that correct?

Q: Wouldn't it be better to resolve this question through scientific research rather than here in the courtroom?

Q: If the highly educated and trained professionals have not been able to resolve this issue, isn't it unreasonable to expect the jury, who are not trained in this field, to resolve it here in the courtroom? (This is probably an unnecessary question and better saved for argument if the previous points have been established.

The conclusion would seem to follow without any need to get it out of the witness.)

## PSYCHOLOGICAL TESTS—PSYCHIATRISTS

The previous lines of questioning should have at least established considerable doubt concerning the validity of psychiatric evaluations. The next set of questions deals with the psychiatrist's use or failure to make use of psychological testing. Either choice leaves the psychiatrist vulnerable on cross-examination. If he has used psychological testing in arriving at his conclusions, then all of the material available for attacking psychological tests can be brought out to show another instance in which the psychiatrist in drawing his conclusions is relying on methods and data of low or doubtful reliability and validity or whose reliability and validity is unknown to him. If he has not used psychological testing, it can be brought out that he did not follow a procedure that is common practice in hospitals and other agencies as an aid to evaluation. It can be stressed that in view of the low reliability and validity of psychiatric diagnosis, it would be incumbent on the psychiatrist to use every kind of additional diagnostic aid that could be obtained. His failure to do so could then suggest something less than due diligence on his part. If he says he does not use tests because of their low reliability and validity, he can then be questioned as to how their reliability and validity has been demonstrated to be any worse than that of the psychiatric interview method. He could be asked what scientific evidence there is that psychiatric evaluations are any more reliable and valid than those made from tests. One might wish to point out research, such as that cited in Chapter 5, Volume I, which suggests that tests are more accurate than interviews. It may be possible to elicit information from him showing that the grounds on which he rejects tests are equally, or more, applicable to his own methods of evaluation. The first set of questions that follows pertains to the case where the psychiatrist has not used testing.

Q: Doctor, did you obtain psychological testing to assist you in making your diagnosis in this case?

Q: Isn't psychological testing frequently employed by psychiatrists in hospitals and clinics in order to help them arrive at a diagnosis? (Note: The reference to hospitals and clinics is deliberate. Obtaining psychological testing seems to be more frequently done in institutions than is the case in private practice. Therefore, the affirmative answer is more likely to be given to the question in this form. If the answer is negative, it can be shown by a rebuttal witness that psychological testing is, in fact, frequently employed in making psychiatric diagnosis. However, it is not likely that psychiatrists would give a negative answer to the question as stated.)

Questioning concerning the lack of use of tests can probably stop at this point. These two questions are sufficient to establish that there was an additional source of information used by other psychiatrists which this psychiatrist failed to utilize in forming or supporting his diagnosis. This point can be made effectively in argument to further weaken the credibility of the psychiatrist. Where psychological testing has been employed, the line of questioning is likely to be more extensive.

Q: Doctor, did you make use of psychological testing in this case?

Q: Who did the testing?

Q: And does _____ hold a Doctoral degree in Clinical Psychology?

(Note: This question and several that follow have to do with the qualifications of the psychologist employed to do the testing and with the doctor's knowledge, or possible lack of knowledge, of his qualifications. These questions are shots in the dark as in most cases the psychologist will be a qualified person. However, on rare occasions it may turn out that the psychiatrist has used a psychologist who lacks the appropriate qualifications. The American Psychological Association Directory, published every three or four years, contains a lot of information about a psychologist. It gives his degree, where and when obtained, his main field and subspecialties, and current employment. One is not particularly hurt by a showing that the psychologist has the usual qualifications as this is only to be expected. Also, there is the possibility that even though the psychologist turns out to be well qualified, the psychiatrist is not really familiar with his qualifications and thus, it can be shown that he relied on a report from a psychologist whose qualifications were not known to him. Again, this suggests a lack of thoroughness, if not carelessness, in his approach to diagnosis.)

Q: And, is Dr. _____ licensed (or certified) as a psychologist?

Q: And does Dr. _____ possess the Diploma of the American Board of Professional Psychology in clinical psychology?

Q: Do you know what the Diploma is?

Q: It is a diploma granted upon examination by the American Board of Professional Psychology, isn't that correct?

Q: Does Dr. _____ possess the Diploma of the American Board of Forensic Psychology?

Q: Do you know what that diploma is?

Q: It is a diploma granted upon examination by the American Board of Forensic Psychology, is that correct? It is like Board Certification in psychiatry, isn't it?

Q: Does the psychological testing help you in forming your conclusions? (Note: It is difficult to imagine the psychiatrist giving a negative response to this question because there would be no reason to have the testing done unless it was felt to be of some use. However, some psychiatrists will assert that they use the test findings only to corroborate their own findings. In that case, the following questions can be asked.)

Q: Did you feel you needed confirmation of your findings in this case? (The psychiatrist may indicate his findings would have been the same without the psychological testing but it is comforting to have confirmation from another source.)

Q: By comforting, do you mean that it makes you feel more certain?

Q: So that without the testing you would be less sure of your conclusions than you are with the test results, is that right?

Q: Was the testing requested before or after your interviews with the litigant?

If the psychiatrist indicates that the tests were requested before he saw the litigant, questions can be asked to bring out whether or not this is his standard practice so that he routinely uses psychological testing in making his diagnoses, in which case it is fairly clear that he does depend on the psychological testing to at least a moderate extent. If he does not routinely use psychological testing, then questions can be asked to determine why he felt they were necessary in this case. Questioning should bring out the fact that there is additional expense involved in this procedure and there is no reason to incur that expense unless some benefits are expected from it. Typically, one would expect the answers to questions along this line to ultimately bring out the fact that there were some difficult diagnostic problems which required the additional input. This would also be the case if the testing was requested after the psychiatrist had seen the litigant as in that case the request would seem to indicate that there were difficult problems or doubtful areas in which the psychiatrist needed some additional information. It is also worthwhile to determine whether the psychiatrist formed his conclusions and/or wrote his report before or after receiving the test findings.

Q: What psychological tests were used?

Q: (If projective tests are used) Those are considered techniques rather than tests, are they not?

Q: Doctor, do you know what the reliability and validity of the Rorschach are?

Q: Actually, there are several different systems of the Rorschach, aren't there?

Q: Do you know which system the psychologist used? (Do you know if the psychologist used the most current system?)

Q: Do you know the reliability and validity of the TAT (or figure drawings or whatever)? (Note: If the witness indicates that he does know the reliability and validity data, he should be questioned to bring out the fact that they are low or undetermined for these tests.)

Q: So in that case, doctor, you have relied to some extent in forming your opinion upon psychological techniques whose reliability and validity are not known to you, is that correct? (He may assert these tests are widely used.)

Q: But the fact that they are widely used doesn't necessarily mean that they are accurate, does it?

Q: Don't psychologists disagree in their findings just the same as psychiatrists do?

Q: If there is a disagreement among psychologists, like psychiatrists, then wouldn't it also be the case that if the testing had been done by a different psychologist the finding might have been different?

Q: So then, the findings depend to some extent on who is doing the testing, is that correct?

Q: Are you aware that there is considerable controversy in psychology about the utility of these tests (particularly for these purposes)?

Q: If it could be shown that the tests are of questionable value, would your confidence in your diagnosis then be reduced somewhat? (Note: The foregoing questions serve the purpose of laying the groundwork for pointing out after the rebuttal expert has testified to the dubious value of these tests, that in the psychiatrist's words he would have less confidence in his conclusions. If the psychiatrist should answer this last question in the negative, he will simply appear ridiculous because if the tests do not contribute something to the final conclusions, there would have been no point in having them in the first place. If they do contribute something, and they are shown to be of little value, logic dictates that the conclusions should be somewhat weaker.)

## CROSS-EXAMINING THE PSYCHOLOGIST

Most of the lines of questioning addressed to the psychiatrist are equally applicable to the psychologist except those relating to education where the psychologist is probably less vulnerable. Qualifications can be checked in the APA Directory (see above). Check to see if the degree was from an APA accredited program. Any deficiency in qualifications tends to magnify errors or questionable procedures and vice versa. If direct examination has not established that the psychologist holds the

ABPP or ABFP Diploma, that may be worthwhile bringing out in cross-examination. It may even be well to do this at an early point for whatever psychological effect it may have on the psychologist when it is revealed that he does not have this qualification.

If he has the diploma, he can be asked whether it has been proven by research that diplomates are more accurate in their evaluations than other psychologists, and he can be further asked if there is not some research showing the diplomates are no more accurate than non-diplomates or even than novices.

Cross-examination should be generally directed to all of the problems of the clinical examination or judgment and reliability and validity in general and then specifically to the tests employed and the manner in which they were employed. Further questions can be directed to the standardization of the test, the appropriateness of norm groups to the individual involved and so on.

Thus, as with the psychiatrist, questions should be aimed to elicit concessions that some or all of the variables discussed in the chapters on the clinical examination and judgment were, or at least could have been, operating—time, place, circumstances, examiner effects, etc.—to influence the data obtained and the recording and interpretation of the data. Questions should also be directed to the theoretical and personal biases of the psychologist. These could generally follow the lines of questioning suggested above for the psychiatrist.

## PSYCHOLOGICAL TESTING

Use of psychological tests in forensic matters has become quite common. With a few possible exceptions in the case of computerized testing and interpretation, tests are subject to many of the difficulties that plague interviews. In particular, there is extensive research indicating that situational and examiner effects influence subjects' test performance and the examiner's interpretation of the tests. There remains considerable controversy over the use of tests for individual assessment, particularly in the case of the objective and projective personality tests. The intelligence tests seem to be somewhat less controversial when used for their intended purpose, that of attempting to predict academic capability. However, these become more controversial as they depart more from that intended purpose.

Many of the more widely used tests have recently undergone revision or are currently undergoing revision. The Exner Comprehensive System of the Rorschach is still relatively new, having appeared first in 1974, and while there is a considerable body of research being built up around it, there is still a ways to go in terms of establishing reliability and validity, and some changes appear in Exner's later editions (Second

Edition, 1986; Third Edition, 1993). The revision of the MMPI was published in 1989 as the MMPI-2. A third revision of the Millon Clinical Multi-axial Inventory (MCMI-III) was published in 1994 with extensive changes and, therefore, is still too new to be accurately and adequately assessed. In general, when revised versions of a test come out, or alterations as in the Exner System, one cannot safely apply research done with prior versions. It is as though the test is new as of the time of its revision. Of course, the same is true no matter how popular a test may rapidly become.

Further, to the extent that the conclusions from the test are based on clinical judgment, all of the problems of clinical judgment outlined in Chapter 5, Volume I are applicable.

## REFERENCE TEXTS:

There are a number of works which most psychologists would recognize as authoritative in evaluating various tests. These include the *Mental Measurements Yearbook*, the *Annual Review of Psychology*, *Psychological Testing* by Anne Anastasi, and the *Guidelines for Educational and Psychological Tests* issued by the American Psychological Association. The lawyer may wish to check the evaluations of any tests used in the case in the current edition of any of these texts before asking questions about them. Consultation with a local university professor who teaches testing may also be useful as academic people usually keep up with the literature.

Q: Is _____ a recognized reference work for evaluating tests?

Q: Are you familiar with this (these) work(s)?

Q: Did you utilize these reference works in employing the tests you used in this case?

Q: What limitations or criticisms of the test are contained in this (these) work(s)?

Q: Don't the APA *Ethical Principles* require psychologists to acknowledge limits of their data or conclusions? (Principle 704b)

Q: Did you do that in your report (direct testimony)?

Q: Have the test producers followed the APA guidelines? (The lawyer will probably want to bring out any way in which the guidelines have not been followed.)

## CONTROVERSY REGARDING TESTING:

There is, and has been for a good many years, considerable controversy within the field of psychology regarding the uses and abuses of psychological testing, particularly in the personality or psychopathology areas.

Q: Doctor, isn't there literature indicating considerable disagreement in psychology concerning the status of psychological testing? (Or over the use of psychological tests to evaluate whatever they were used for in the particular case.)

Q: Aren't there studies showing that many of the professors who teach courses in testing do not look very favorably upon testing?

Q: Aren't there published surveys showing that a number of major universities have reduced the teaching of testing in their doctoral programs?

Q: Aren't a number of questions concerning reliability and validity raised in the scientific and professional literature concerning testing?

Q: Aren't there a number of published studies and articles demonstrating the operation of situation effects on psychological testing?

Q: Were there any situation effects present in this case?

Q: What are they? (The lawyer may want to run through several situation effects which would be present in the current case and ask if such things could not have an effect on test performance.)

Q: There isn't any well validated method for measuring the effects of such situational variables (conditions) on the litigant's test performance, is there?

Q: Aren't tests subject to the operation of examiner effects?

Q: Were any such variables present in this case?

Q: To the extent that your biases might influence the testing and its products, you would not be a good person to judge your own biases, would you?

Q: So there may be an unknown amount of influence from examiner variables operating in this examination in this case? (Again, you may wish to run down a list of known examiner variables which could have been operating.)

## BATTERIES OF TESTS:

If the psychologist has asserted that his conclusions are more accurate because he has not relied on a single test but has used a battery of tests, the following questions may be appropriate:

Q: Isn't there literature indicating that batteries of tests are not more accurate than some of the individual tests? (Use of the "Isn't there" format is probably superior to the more conventional "Is there" because it suggests to the witness that the cross-examiner has knowledge of literature in accordance with the content contained.)

Q: Are there standard batteries in psychology?

Q: Is the battery you gave a standard battery?

Q: Is that a battery of tests that is used by most psychologists?

Q: Aren't there studies showing that adding more tests in some cases reduces the accuracy of conclusions?

Q: Isn't it true that the more tests the psychologist gives, the more likely he is to obtain some material which he can interpret as confirming or supporting his preconceptions or biases?

There is a lack of scientifically validated methods for combining the data from one test with the data from another test. Norms for combinations of data from different tests are lacking. This is another one of the flaws of the assertion that batteries improve validity. No one really knows how to combine the data. Most commonly it is a matter of clinical judgment. The clinician uses what he wants from each of the tests. However, many clinicians say that what they look for are consistencies across the different tests and, of course, most of the time there will be some consistencies. What they apparently do not do (or ignore if they do it) is also look for the inconsistencies across the tests. It is also somewhat problematic as to what constitutes a consistency, particularly if it is not factual data but interpretations of data that constitute the consistency.

Q: Doctor, there are no scientifically validated methods for combining the data from (the various tests), are there? (If "yes," how validated?)

Q: (If the consistency approach has been taken by the psychologist) Well, doctor, isn't the consistency you see in your interpretation, rather than in the data itself? (For example, seeing a tree without leaves on the Rorschach does not by itself become consistent with an elevated depression score on the MMPI. The consistency comes when the psychologist *interprets* the tree without leaves as a "depressive" sign and he also construes the score on the depression scale as indicating "depression." Nor is there any established actuarial relationship between these two items of data.)

Q: Well, doctor, if you looked out the window in wintertime you would not see leaves on the trees either, would you?

Q: So that response might only mean that the blot reminded litigant of the way a tree looks at the time he was tested, right?

Q: Did you look for inconsistencies?

Q: What did you find?

## EXAMINER ERRORS:

There are few things so deflating to the credibility of the witness or his conclusions as a demonstration that he has made errors in the course of the examination or has done sloppy work. For this reason, it is

ESSENTIAL TO SECURE FROM THE PSYCHOLOGIST ALL OF THE DATA OF THE TESTING. THIS INCLUDES THE RAW DATA, THAT IS, THE ACTUAL RESPONSES OF THE LITIGANT, ANY SCORING, ANY PROFILES, ANY ANSWER SHEETS, AND ANY INTERPRETATIONS OF THE DATA. This material should be submitted to a qualified psychologist, preferably an academician who teaches testing, to review for errors of administration, or scoring, or interpretation. These errors are far more frequent than one would expect. There should also be checks to determine if the test is one that is appropriate for the population to which the litigant belongs. For example, are there norms for people of litigant's classification (ethnic, cultural, educational, age, etc.)? The questions to be asked obviously will flow from whatever errors the consulting psychologist has been able to discover. In many cases, where the test has a manual which delineates proper administration and gives scoring criteria, it may be desirable to subpoena the manual along with the witness or to take steps to insure that he will bring the manual into the courtroom with him and on cross-examination have him read the section which pertains (e.g., the failure to continue a sub-test of the WAIS until a certain number of errors have been made), so that he will be revealing with his own voice that he has made an error. Alternatively, one can call a consultant psychologist who will demonstrate all of the errors and who will make less effort, of course, to defend them.

## ORDER EFFECTS:

It has been demonstrated that the order in which tests are administered can affect the performance of the individual on the tests. Therefore, it is appropriate to bring this out and make inquiry as to the order of tests.

Q: Doctor, isn't there scientific and professional literature showing that the order in which tests are given can affect the performance on the tests?

Q: In what order were the tests given to the litigant?

Q: Could the results have been different if you had given _____ test first and _____ test last (or any variations of the order of the tests)?

## TEST USE OR ACCEPTANCE:

Some psychologists, when confronted with the abundant negative literature on psychological tests and testing, may respond with declarations to the effect that some of the tests they are using are widely used and accepted by their fellow psychologists. These responses may be countered by questions to bring out the fact that either the test is not used by a majority of psychologists (there are only a few exceptions; see survey studies in Chapter 10, Volume II), or in any case that usage is no measure of the reliability or validity of the test, as there are several references to that effect (see also Chapter 10, Volume II).

Q: Doctor, haven't surveys shown that less than half of the psychologists use the _____ Test?

(or,)

Q: Doctor, aren't there surveys showing that only _____ percent of psychologists use _____ test on a regular basis?

Q: Doctor, wide usage of the test does not provide an adequate (or scientific) measure of its reliability or validity, does it?

Q: Doctor, isn't there a substantial body of literature to the effect that wide usage and acceptance does not constitute an adequate measure of reliability and validity?

Q: (Particularly if you are calling a rebuttal witness) Doctor, do you know if there is a substantial body of literature indicating that wide usage is not an adequate measure of reliability and validity of a test?

Q: Doctor, wasn't bleeding widely used by physicians for several centuries before they discovered that it was not a very good cure and in fact was harmful to many patients?

## INTELLIGENCE TESTS

This section will deal with the Wechsler Adult Intelligence Scale-Revised (WAIS-R) published in 1981 and to some extent it predecessor, the WAIS, as these are by far the most commonly used intelligence tests and the ones the lawyer is most likely to encounter. It is important to be aware that research has shown consistently that on the Verbal, Performance, and Full Scale IQs people on average will score seven, seven, and eight points lower on the WAIS-R than on the WAIS. That is an average difference which means that many people would have even greater differences, so that one cannot use a prior WAIS to compare with a later WAIS-R in order to conclude that there has been some impairment. In fact, in general, one cannot use the WAIS-R to compare with any other prior intelligence testing because we know it tends to produce lower IQs. This also raises doubts about the applicability of much research done with the WAIS to the WAIS-R. If a test other that the WAIS-R is used for assessing adult intelligence, questioning should establish that such test is not the one most commonly used for that purpose.

In general the scientific literature raises questions as to what the term "intelligence" means, or what intelligence is, and raises doubts about the use of the test for purposes other than predicting academic aptitude. The literature also raises doubts about the use of the test with special populations. The literature also has posed severe challenge to the use of the test for estimating intelligence at some prior time ("pre-morbid intelligence"). Also the literature has cast doubts on many of the hypotheses or interpretations attached to variations in the sub-test scores ("scatter"). Given the relatively recent appearance of the WAIS-R, there has not been sufficient time for accomplishment of the several thousand studies to bring it up to the level of research that has been done on the WAIS. Obviously, it should not be assumed that the WAIS-R has overcome problems or deficiencies associated with the WAIS until research has demonstrated that to be the case. It is reasonable to anticipate it may yet be several years before such extensive research will have been performed.

Q: Doctor, what is intelligence? (This is not a necessary question and one with some risk that a sophisticated and well-educated psychologist may be able to provide a reasonable sounding answer. However, it also has a potential for embarrassing many experts because there is no accepted definition of intelligence or agreement as to its nature as will be illustrated by the next question.)

Q: Doctor, doesn't the scientific and professional literature indicate considerable disagreement among psychologists as to the meaning of the term "intelligence"?

Q: Doesn't the scientific and professional literature indicate considerable disagreement over whether intelligence is a unitary thing or whether, in fact, there are several different kinds of intelligence?

Q: (If the witness attempts to argue that intelligence is a unitary process) Doctor, isn't it the case that some people are better at one kind of thing than they are at another kind of thing? (You may want to have some kind of example ready or even ask the question in terms of some sort of example such as, "Aren't there some people who are pretty good at fixing a car, but not very good at writing poetry?")

Occasionally a psychologist's report will indicate that due to the injury or psychological trauma, the individual is unable to concentrate or perform simple arithmetic calculations such as counting his change when he goes to the store. One of the subtests on WAIS, the arithmetic subtest, often provides direct refutation of this assertion. That is, one can look at the specific problems and have them read to the jury with the litigant's correct answer, sometimes even with time bonuses, which clearly indicate that he has the capability of performing the kinds of mathematical calculations that are part of daily living.

## SUBTEST VARIATIONS (DIFFERENCES):

One of the most common uses (or abuses) of the test is to base conclusions about the individual's personality or possible psychopathology on differences among the subtest scores. The reader should be aware that there are eleven subtests on the WAIS-R, which create a large number of comparisons such that there is a reasonable possibility of having one or more substantial differences entirely due to the operation of chance factors. In Chapter 11, Volume II we described the study of Matarazzo et al. (1988) which showed that in the population from whom the WAIS-R norms were derived, one-third had differences of eight and one half had differences of seven. They also found that the size of difference was related to IQ level, with people at higher IQs showing larger differences and people at lower IQs showing smaller differences on average. Introduction of this (and related studies, see Chapter 11, Volume II) is essential on this subject. It is probably worthwhile to obtain a copy of this article and have it in court if this is an issue in the case. A witness who is not aware of these findings should probably not be allowed to testify on this issue.

Q: Doctor, has it been conclusively established by scientific research methods that a difference of _____ between the score on _____ subtest and _____ subtest signifies (whatever the psychologist has said it signifies)?

Q: Haven't differences of that size been shown by research to occur, on average, in _____ % of the normal (average) population? (Refer to Matarazzo.)

Q: Doctor, with as many subtests as there are, isn't there a reasonable possibility that there might be differences this large, just by chance? (Of course, this will depend to some extent on how large the difference is and you would want to check this out with your consultant.)

Q: Isn't it a fact that the standard deviation is one measure of central tendency that is used in psychology?

Q: Isn't it a fact that the standard deviation on each subtest is three points from the mean in either direction?

Q: Wouldn't this place any score between seven and thirteen within plus or minus one standard deviation of the mean?

Q: Doctor, do you know what percentage of people show substantial differences (or a difference of the size involved in the case) between two or more subtest scores?

Q: Doctor, do you know if there is scientific and professional literature indicating what percentage of people show such differences? (There is. See Chapter 11, Volume II. The percentage of normal individuals showing scatter in the range the examiner noted is often considerably larger than the expert recognizes.)

Q: Isn't there considerable controversy reflected in the scientific and professional literature concerning the use of scatter or differences between subtest scores for the kind of conclusion you have drawn?

## ESTIMATES OF "PRE-MORBID" INTELLIGENCE:

One of the most common and pernicious uses of the subtest scores on the WAIS is to estimate "pre-morbid" intelligence. That is, the subtest scores are used to demonstrate that there has been intellectual impairment. Some of these procedures are predicated on the theory (and it is only a theory) that intelligence is unitary, that there is a general intelligence factor which in fact has been labeled "g" in the literature on intelligence. Obviously, this is only one school of thought and there are schools of thought which vigorously disagree with that conclusion and the resolution of that conflict remains for some time in the future. There are different procedures by which pre-morbid intelligence is estimated, one of the best known of which is called the "best performance" method. The estimate in this method is based on the premise that the individual's highest subtest score or scores represent his "true" level of intelligence or his "true" intellectual endowment based on the premise that, if he is able to score this high on one or more of the subtests, this represents the capability in his "g" factor and therefore, he should have been able to score at approximately that level on the other subtests, making some allowance for the fact that there can be some variation. Obviously until controversy over the general factor versus multifaceted intelligence has been resolved, this is an unwarranted assumption. Also, quite often, it does not allow for the more reasonable approach which is that the individual's mean subtest score probably represents his correct ability more than his most extreme score or his highest score (see also Matarazzo et al., 1988, above). It also flies in the face of almost everyone's life experience where they themselves and most people they know show considerable variation in their abilities. Keep in mind that the various subtests do tend to measure different abilities or factors, as shown by numerous studies demonstrating at least three dimensions or types of broad clusters into which the subtests fall. Thus, while some of the verbal subtests emphasize verbal skills (e.g., Vocabulary), others emphasize attention/concentration (e.g., Digit Span). Thus, someone who might be a whiz at writing poetry might be poor at rote memory. One of the most effective counters to this sort of estimate is to obtain the litigant's school records and determine if he has not, in fact, shown considerable scatter or variation prior to the incident in question. In our experience, we have found many cases in which an individual who, presumably, would have had relatively even estimated subtest scores prior to the incident, has run the entire gamut of grades with A's, B's, C's, D's and F's prior to the incident. Although the witness may be able to mount arguments that there may have been differences in motivation or interest or whatever, those are guesses or speculations, whereas the hard factual evidence is that the individual showed as wide a variation in his intellectual functioning prior to the incident as he has shown subsequent to the incident. Even grades of D's, C's and B's would seem to indicate that the individual showed considerable variation in his intellectual functioning, functioning sometimes at an average level, sometimes below average and sometimes above average, given the usual meaning of those grades.

Q: Doctor, in using litigant's highest subtest score to estimate his pre-morbid intellectual level, haven't you made an assumption that there is a general intelligence factor?

Q: Isn't that a controversial issue in psychology, with some people believing in the general factor and others believing that intelligence is made up of two or more independent factors?

Q: Doesn't the literature show that there is controversy on this issue?

Q: (If appropriate) Did you review litigant's grades in school? (If the answer is no, you can stop the questioning on this issue at that point and bring out later the fact that the witness has chosen to speculate or guess rather than go to a concrete source of information as to litigant's prior functioning.)

Q: Don't his grades show a considerable amount of "scatter"?

Q: Wasn't he below average in some subjects, average in others and above average in still others?

## AGE NORMS:

The WAIS-R Manual contains separate scale score norms by age group. This allows a comparison of litigant's performance on any scale with people in his age group. For people over 35, there is a good chance that their performance will look better (less impaired) in such a comparison. These scores are not used for computing IQ.

Q: Are there norms provided for the subscales for different age groups?

Q: Did you compute such scores for litigant?

Q: (If "no") Wouldn't it be important to see how litigant did in comparison to people his own age?

**SHORT FORMS:**

Fairly often you will encounter psychologists who have given only a short form or a "partial" WAIS-R. It should be recognized immediately that there is no such thing as a "partial" WAIS-R. The WAIS-R consists of eleven subtests, six verbal, five performance. If these are not all given, the psychologist has not given the WAIS-R, he has given some subtests that form part of the WAIS-R but it is not the WAIS-R, nor is it a partial WAIS-R. The WAIS manual does not allow for calculation of an IQ unless five of the six verbal subtests and at least four of the five performance subtests have been administered. Anything less than that, according to the manual, does not permit the calculation of an IQ at all. However, there are short forms (described in Chapter 11, Volume II) that are in somewhat common use. There is almost never a legitimate excuse for not giving the full WAIS-R. The usual excuse given is there was not time or the psychologist was trying to save the client's money. In any event, the literature makes clear that short forms often do not accurately reflect what would happen had a full administration been given, and of course unless one gives the full form one does not know whether the short form result reflects what the full form result would have been. Although some reasonably decent correlations are shown for short forms with the IQ, that is an average and the literature shows that large numbers of people would be misclassified using short forms.

Q: Doctor, you did not give the eleven subtests of the WAIS-R, did you?

Q: What you have done is given something called a short form, isn't that correct?

Q: Doesn't the literature say that short forms often do not accurately reflect what the person might have done on the full administration?

Q: Aren't there studies showing that many people are misclassified based on the use of short forms?

Q: Why didn't you give the whole test? (Ordinarily, this is not the kind of question you want to ask an expert witness, but unless you have reason to believe that the answer is going to be other than saving time or money, it is a safe question, in our opinion.)

It may also be worthwhile to get hold of a blank record form which has boxes with the names of all of the subtests and places for the scores or even to use the record form involved which, for example, may show three verbal subtest scores with three blank spaces for the others and two performance subtest scores with blank spaces for the other three. You can make a blow-up of that and have it standing by the witness when you conduct this sort of cross-examination so the jury gets a visual image of the incomplete way the testing was conducted, at least on this measure.

Also, the manual for the test requires the psychologist to enter the subject's responses verbatim. Many psychologists use various forms of shorthand which of course is permissible, but then you will have to get them to translate their recordings. However, some psychologists do not bother putting down the responses, they just put in a score or a check mark indicating a correct answer or a blank space meaning an incorrect answer. This violates the manual and might make any testimony based on the test inadmissible on the grounds that the information is not there which would be necessary to evaluate the correctness of the scoring and makes it impossible to cross-examine the witness on the scoring.

As noted above, the WAIS was replaced by the WAIS-R in late 1980; therefore, any administration subsequent to 1980 which used the WAIS rather than the WAIS-R would mean the psychologist was using an obsolete version of the test and this can be brought out in questioning. Also as noted above, the content and the results of the WAIS-R are quite different from the WAIS, so that questions to bring out that fact should also be asked as well as questions indicating that there has not been time for an adequate amount of research on the WAIS-R.

### OBJECTIVE PERSONALITY MEASURES (MMPI)

This section will deal briefly with the most widely used objective personality measure, the Minnesota Multiphasic Personality Inventory (MMPI), and its successor, the MMPI-2, published in 1989, and also briefly with a relatively new but increasingly popular measure, the Millon Clinical Multi-axial Inventory (MCMI), now in its third edition (1994).

As with virtually all assessment devices or techniques, the MMPI suffers from problems of inadequate reliability and validity. Despite the thousands of studies that have been performed with the MMPI, serious problems remain concerning the reliability of some of the scales. Further, the general tenor of the literature is that validities are either unknown or too low for the test to be used for individual diagnosis, although it does appear to have some value in helping to form classification groups for research purposes. Probably the most serious current problem is that the test is some forty years old. Many of the items are obsolete, the norms are based on a population that hardly anyone believes represents the modern population and, most of all, it has been declared obsolete by several of the leading authorities and proponents of the test. While these criticisms do not apply to the new MMPI-2, the fact that changes in items and norms were made raises doubts about the use of the massive MMPI research base with the new MMPI-2. This may not be a great loss because many of the ten thousand studies were not all that flattering or affirming of the MMPI. However, the point is important because often expert witnesses like to recite the fact that there have been more than ten thousand studies done on the MMPI. There are of course two answers to this. One is that with ten thousand studies, it has not been possible to establish a high degree of reliability or validity, particularly as the MMPI might be applied in forensic assessments. The second answer which should shortly be available is, more or less, "so what." Until proven otherwise, MMPI-2 is a different test. At this writing the arguments about the comparability of the two MMPIs rage on as indicated in Chapter 12, Volume 11. (See the comment by Starke Hathaway, one of the creators of the test, in Chapter 12, Volume II, regarding the impact of even small changes in items.)

It should be noted however, that there is one respect in which the MMPI is capable of providing valuable information. This is in the area of assessing malingering, which will be discussed under that heading.

Q: Doctor, does the scientific and professional literature raise serious doubts concerning the reliability of the MMPI? (We are assuming that at some point in the cross-examination or direct examination, the concepts of reliability and validity will have been explained. If not, of course, this has to be done.)

Q: Doctor, does the scientific and professional literature raise serious doubts concerning the validity of the MMPI, particularly in its use for diagnosing of individuals?

Q: Does the scientific and professional literature express these same doubts about the MMPI-2?

Q: Was the large body of research on the MMPI one of the reasons for its widespread use?

Q: Isn't there a body of scientific and professional literature to the effect that the scores or profiles that people get on the MMPI-2 are different from what they get on the older MMPI?

Q: For that reason, isn't it argued in the scientific and professional literature that you cannot safely apply research from the MMPI to the MMPI-2?

Q: Did you base any of your conclusions from the MMPI-2 on research done with the MMPI?

Q: (If "no" above) What large body of research did you base them on?

Q: Doctor, could two people obtain similar scores on the _____ scale, although they did not answer *any* items similarly on that scale?

Q: Doctor, could two people obtain similar scores or profiles and yet show different behavioral characteristics according to the scientific and professional literature?

Q: Doctor, have serious concerns been raised in the scientific and professional literature concerning the use of the MMPI with members of (whatever special population might be involved)?

## SHORT FORMS:

Some clinicians will employ short forms of the MMPI. Outside of the very rare situation in which the examinee's condition is such that giving the full test is not reasonable (in which case there is likely to be little or no research on full form performance for such individuals because they do not or cannot complete the full form), there appears to be no justification for this other than the convenience of the examiner. Even the latter is questionable because it takes virtually none of the examiner's time for the administration of the test, which the subject can take sitting in a room by himself. The literature is clear that this is a poor practice and while the witness may be able to cite reasonably high correlations of short forms with the full test, there is a general dearth of research showing that the conclusions based on short forms would be the same as on the long form or even that the profile would be the same. What research there is appears to be predominantly negative in this regard. (See Chapter 12, Volume II.)

Q: Doctor, isn't the scientific and professional literature concerning the use of short forms generally negative? (This can be stated more conservatively as, "Isn't there a substantial body of literature that is negative concerning short forms?")

Q: (Unless there is some reason to believe that there was a good reason for not giving the full test.) Doctor, why didn't you give the full form of the test? (If the answer is because of time problems, it should be brought out that it would take virtually none of the clinician's time and if the litigant didn't have or wasn't willing to give enough time to take the test, he then is not cooperating in the diagnostic procedure, unless the clinician was too lazy to set up another appointment so that he could come in and take it at the proper time.)

Q: The MMPI is a means of making some inferences about a person, isn't it?

Q: The short form is a means of inferring what the full test result would be like, isn't it?

Q: So, when you draw conclusions from a short form, you are in effect making an inference from an inference (making a guess based upon a guess)?

**THE TAKE HOME MMPI:**

In some cases, there is what we call a "take home" MMPI. That is, the clinician simply gives the booklet containing the instructions and the items and an answer sheet to the litigant and allows him to take it home to complete and bring it back or mail it in or whatever. Obviously, this is a poor practice, certainly in cases involving litigation.

Q: Doctor, did the litigant take the test in your office or elsewhere?

Q: Why was he allowed to take it out of the office and complete it (wherever he completed it)?

Q: If he did not fill in the answer sheet in your office, you have no way of knowing whether he consulted with anyone about how he should fill in the blanks, do you?

Q: As a matter of fact, I'm not suggesting this happened, but it is possible for all that you know that he could have consulted his attorney about how to fill in the answer sheet, isn't it?

**MCMI:**

Probably the best way to deal with the Millon Clinical Multiaxial Inventory (MCMI) is to bring out the fact that it is a very new test, having first appeared around 1980, with extensive revision (45 out of 175 items) in 1987 in MCMI-II and even more extensive change (95 out of 175 items) in MCMI-III published in 1994. The revised version is obviously quite new. In any event, even with the original, there has not been enough time to gather that substantial body of research data with which to thoroughly judge its reliability and validity. However, while there are some encouraging research results, there are also some studies and some commentary about the test which are quite negative.

Q: Doctor, isn't the MCMI a rather new test?

Q: Hasn't it been extensively changed every few years?

Q: There has not been time to accumulate thousands of research studies on this test as with the MMPI, has there?

Q: There are some negative research studies which have appeared, is that not correct?

Q: There already is a fair amount of negative scientific and professional literature concerning this test, is that not correct?

Q: Isn't there scientific and professional literature on the MCMI which suggests it may overdiagnose abnormality, or misclassify a large percentage of individuals as having a serious disturbance even if they do not have such a disturbance?

## THE RORSCHACH & OTHER PROJECTIVE METHODS

The status of projective methods for assessing people has been one of raging controversy within the field of psychology for several decades and continues to be so up to the present. There are ardent proponents of these methods who believe the clinician can derive large amounts of very useful material from them and there are equally ardent opponents who feel that, because of the high degree of subjectivity or "art" that is involved along with an inability so far to establish adequate reliabilities and validities in most instances, these tests may be useless and possibly worse than useless. There are some moderate voices between these extremes who feel that projective theory and method is promising, but that the work necessary to realize the promise has not yet been accomplished.

One point that should always be made is that projective methods represent techniques and not tests as the term "test" is commonly understood.

The best known of the projective techniques is the Rorschach Ink Blot Test or, as has been pointed out, because there are so many different systems of the Rorschach, the Rorschach *techniques* would be more appropriate. Until the appearance of Exner's Comprehensive System for the Rorschach in 1974, there were five well-known systems for the Rorschach which had different rules for administering, scoring and interpreting and which often produced different results. Of these, up until 1974, the Klopfer method was the most popular. A massive amount of literature was accumulated concerning the Ink Blot Technique and it is fair to say that the weight of this literature was negative toward these methods. This has been pretty widely acknowledged. In the years since its publication, the Exner System has clearly become the most widely used by psychologists, with Klopfer holding a second position but clearly being used by only a minority of psychologists at this time, according to surveys. Similarly, in the teaching of the Rorschach in academic settings the Exner text is by far the most commonly used with Klopfer a distant second, being used only by a minority of academic departments. Obviously, any other system would represent an extremely small portion of the population of psychologists. Further, as another variant of eclectic approaches, some psychologists will combine elements of different systems, thus in essence inventing their own, untested combination. (See questions regarding eclectic approaches, supra.) Other projective devices that are in fairly common use are the Thematic Apperception Test (TAT), the Draw-A-Person (DAP), and although it is misused as a projective technique, the Bender-Gestalt. These latter tests according to various surveys have anywhere from a little more than half to a little less than half of the psychologists using them.

## PROJECTIVE TECHNIQUES GENERALLY:

The theory underlying projective methods is that because, by definition, they employ ambiguous stimuli, the response of the subject must come from some characteristic within the subject and therefore provides clues to his feelings, attitudes, problems, conflicts, psychodynamics or whatever it is that one cannot otherwise see and therefore justifies the use of such a technique. As many commentators have noted, the responses of the subject to the ambiguous stimuli are themselves ambiguous, so that what you get in the interpretation of these responses are the projections of the psychologist on the ambiguous stimuli provided by the subject's responses. That is, with very few exceptions, there are no fixed and scientifically validated meanings that can be attached to the responses or configurations of responses. Lacking these, the clinician is forced to say what the responses "look like" to him, just as the subject is required to say what the ink blots "look like" to him.

Q: Doctor, hasn't the scientific and professional literature indicated that the use of projective techniques has been highly controversial within the field of psychology itself?

Q: Doesn't this controversy continue up to the present time?

Q: The scientists and professionals in psychology have not been able to resolve this controversy among themselves, have they?

Q: Is the principle on which these methods are based, the idea that because the stimuli are ambiguous, the responses of the individual reveal something about himself?

Q: Aren't there numerous statements in the scientific and professional literature to the effect that because the responses are also ambiguous, what you get out of it are the projections of the psychologist on the projections or ambiguous stimuli that the subject's responses provide? (Note this question does not ask the clinician to give his opinion on the subject. It asks him for a factual answer to a factual question as to whether or not such statements are encountered in the literature.)

Q: Doesn't the scientific and professional literature itself contain numerous statements to the effect that the weight of the research literature on projective techniques is negative? (If you wish to ask this in a more conservative way, you can change negative to "fails to support" the use of projective techniques.)

## THE RORSCHACH OTHER THAN EXNER:

Q: Isn't the Exner Comprehensive System of the Rorschach, the one used by the largest number of psychologists these days?

Q: Isn't the _____ system (whatever other system has been used) used only by a minority of psychologists these days?

Q: Haven't there been published surveys showing that only a relatively small percentage of psychologists use the _____ Rorschach Method?

Q: (If the psychologist has referred to them as tests) Doctor, these tests are more commonly referred to as techniques, rather than tests, is that not so?

Q: Isn't the Exner system the most commonly used in the teaching of psychology at the present time?

Q: (If relevant) Isn't the Klopfer system used in only twenty or twenty-five percent of the graduate training programs?

Q: Isn't (whatever other method may have been used) used by an even smaller percent, if at all, in graduate training, currently?

Q: (If the psychologist claims it does not matter what system was used, or that all systems produce the same results) Doctor, hasn't the scientific and professional literature shown that different systems produce different results?

Q: (If the witness has not conceded the previous point) Hasn't Doctor Exner, himself, in his book pointed out that different systems produce different results?

Q: There is no large body of scientific research establishing that method has a high degree of validity, is there?

## THE EXNER COMPREHENSIVE SYSTEM OF THE RORSCHACH:

If such publications are not already out by the time this book comes out, it is likely that in the very near future, surveys will show that among psychologists who use Rorschach techniques, the majority and perhaps a substantial majority are or will be using the Exner System. One possible reason for this is that because the Exner system is new, there has not been time for the accumulation of negative literature on it which burdens the other systems. Also, Exner and his associates are taking a much more scientific and rigorous approach to the Rorschach, attempting to make it more exact and less subjective. This is a vast undertaking which has not been completed in the several years since publication of this system. As Exner himself points out in the second edition of his book, a number of changes from the original edition were required as their research progressed both in terms of scores and interpretations. Reliabilities reported for various categories of the Exner System range from adequate to inadequate. The most recent version, the Third Edition, was published in 1993 and thus is quite new. Exner also notes the serious problem of preconceptions and of biasing of the data and interpretations due to characteristics of the clinician. He urges that special precautions be taken so as to minimize some of these problems, although to our knowledge the efficacy of his recommendations in reducing bias remains unproven. He also emphasizes the importance of treating the Rorschach material in a quantitative manner with extensive scoring and utilization of ratios. He also emphasizes the importance of using the test "properly" which means according to the instructions in his text.

Q: Isn't the Exner System considerably newer than other Rorschach systems, such as Klopfer's?

Q: Isn't the Exner System undergoing constant revision?

Q: Wasn't the Third Edition, the most recent, published in 1993?

Q: Shouldn't it be considered as still somewhat experimental in nature?

Q: Isn't it still in need of much more research?

Q: The thousands of studies which have been done on the Rorschach are not applicable to this new system, are they?

Q: Doesn't some of the research reported by the Exner Group show that reliabilities for a number of the scores do not meet the usual standards for adequate reliability?

Q: Aren't some of the reliabilities reported below the lower figure of .80?

Q: According to the data given by Exner himself, you could not tell from a Rorschach administered today what an individual's Rorschach might have been like a year ago (or a year from now)?

Q: (For cases involving children) Isn't test-retest reliability, especially over longer time spans, a particular problem with children?

Q: Doesn't Exner himself express cautions regarding future predictions on the basis of children's Rorschachs?

Q: In fact, aren't some of the reported test-retest reliabilities with children quite unsatisfactory?

Q: Doesn't Exner indicate that some Rorschach responses are subject to situational (state) effects? (If there are some particular situational effects you are aware of, it may be worthwhile to enumerate them and ask if each in turn could affect the responses. For example, if the litigant had a fight with his wife before coming in for testing or had a close call with death on the freeway on his way to the psychologist's office.)

Q: Doesn't Exner indicate that examiner effects can occur on the Rorschach?

Q: What information did you receive about litigant before you examined him?

Q: Did you interview litigant before you gave him the Rorschach?

Q: Did you give litigant any other test before you gave him the Rorschach?

Q:  Did (any of the above) give you some idea as to what litigant's psychological makeup was like?

Q:  Are you aware that Exner has cautioned psychologists to avoid having any information about the person that might influence their perception of his Rorschach performance? (Or alternatively, are you aware that Exner recommends doing the Rorschach "blind," meaning without any information about the subject in advance?)

The attorney or his consultant should check the psychologist's materials to determine whether or not he has scored the test in accordance with the Exner principles. The Exner System provides a sheet called a Scoring Summary which has blanks to be filled in with numbers for a large number of scoring categories and a large number of ratios. If the sheet is not filled in or if there is no such sheet in the materials, it would indicate that the test was not scored at all, which would be a flagrant violation of Exner's admonitions. If the summary is there and there are blanks that are not filled in, it means that the clinician did not carry out all of the computations that the system requires and in either case, he has failed to perform the system as Exner has designed it and therefore cannot apply any of the research attached to the test or to the Exner System. Further, because Exner argues that one *must* consider the interrelation between all test scores to achieve accurate interpretations, missing scores would make it impossible to do this.

Q:  Doctor, do you have a scoring summary sheet?

Q:  Did you score the test according to Exner's directions?

Q:  I note that there are some blanks here. Does that mean you did not compute these scores?

Q:  In that case, you have not followed Dr. Exner's instructions?

Q:  Are there any (other) ways in which you deviated from Exner's rules (instructions, procedures)?

Q:  What training have you had in the Exner System?

Also the general instructions are to take down the person's responses verbatim so that one can score them accurately afterward. Also, Exner insists on performance of the portion called the inquiry, in which the psychologist asks the subject to explain how he saw whatever it was that he saw. This is also essential in order to score the test. Many psychologists skip this part altogether or partially where they make an assumption as to how the subject saw the particular percept. Obviously, in such cases, questions should be asked to bring out that the work has not been done in a competent, thorough manner, nor as Exner has indicated it should be done. In connection with the scoring summary, if this has not been done at all, or if there are a number of blanks, it may be worthwhile to have a slide made and project this on a screen while questioning the witness about it so the jury can observe the degree to which he did not do what is supposed to be done.

Many psychologists lean heavily on the content of the responses for interpretation and particularly for illustrating some of their conclusions. Except for quite disturbed people or people with brain damage, generally, whatever it is that people see in the ink blots can reasonably be seen. If the percept can be reasonably seen by the jury, it might be worthwhile to have the psychologist show them how the subject saw whatever it was (e.g., a rocket ship taking off on Card II). Once a percept has been pointed out, nearly everybody is going to see it. It is hard to convince people that there is anything wrong with somebody based on the fact that, for example, they saw a rocket ship taking off on Card II because there is a shape in the blot that can look like a rocket ship and there is a somewhat shapeless red blotch at the bottom which could represent the flames that one sees when a rocket or space craft takes off.

If the psychologist can be led to state some interpretations of specific responses, they may appear patently ridiculous and remain so unless the psychologist can cite incontrovertible research evidence.

It seems likely that a few of the above questions along with a question about Dr. Exner's negative opinion concerning forensic psychological evaluations would be enough to establish considerable skepticism about the use of his system in such evaluations.

Q: Are you aware that Dr. Exner has stated his strong belief that psychological evaluations have no place in most litigations? (See note, Chapter 13, Volume II).

## THE TAT:

The scientific and professional literature on the TAT is generally negative, and in some cases powerfully negative, with regard to reliability and validity. There is a further problem with the TAT in that in contrast to the Rorschach Ink Blots, with all ten standard ink blots administered, the TAT consists of twenty cards containing different ambiguous pictures, but there is no standard administration of the test. That is, hardly any psychologist administers all twenty pictures. They may select five or ten from the twenty and often do not even have a standard set that they use themselves, selecting the tests in terms of some notion they have about the particular subject. In any event, one psychologist might be using cards one, three, five, seven and nine while another psychologist might use two, four, six, eight, ten so that there really is not one TAT but various TATs. It is just a set of cards that are called the Thematic Apperception Test as a clear misnomer. It has also been noted in the literature that the cards, by their nature, tend to draw "psychopathological" responses even from normal individuals. Also, as with the Rorschach, the responses of the subject are themselves ambiguous stimuli on which the clinician must project his own characteristics in order to interpret them. There is no hard core of scientifically validated principles. By and large, this technique is not scored, although there are methods of scoring for certain themes having to do with such things as achievement motivation or affiliation motivation which have been shown to be quantifiable in a moderately reliable way. However, these themes are not the ones the lawyer is likely to encounter in forensic matters.

Q: Doctor, isn't there a substantial amount of negative scientific and professional literature concerning the TAT?

Q: How many cards are there in the TAT?

Q: How many did you use?

Q: Which ones did you use?

Q: Why did you select those particular cards? (This may bring out some preconceptions.)

Q: What is the reliability data on *this* version of the TAT you used (or the exact set of cards you used)?

Q: Another psychologist giving the TAT might have used different cards, isn't that so?

Q: If he used a completely different set of the cards than you did, wouldn't he be giving a different test?

Q: This is not really a test, is it; it is a technique, is it not?

Q: Did you score the test?

Q: What does (a particular response) mean (signify, how did you interpret it, etc.)?

Q: How else could (any particular response) it be interpreted? (Usually the lawyer will be able to point out alternative interpretations.)

## THE DAP:

The literature on the Draw-A-Person Test is so overwhelmingly negative that it remains a source of astonishment to us that anyone even continues to use it. Nonetheless, we do see it fairly frequently in our consulting practice. So apparently a considerable number of psychologists either in ignorance of or in defiance of the overwhelmingly negative literature continue to use it. Probably one question will be sufficient here.

Q: Doctor, isn't there an extremely large amount of negative literature concerning the Draw-A-Person Technique?

In some instances where it is clear that the psychologist drew conclusions from the tests that are on the face of them pretty outlandish, you may want to go into some of those (See Jeffrey's example in Chapter 13,

Volume II). This might be followed with a question as to whether that particular interpretation has received substantial unequivocal scientific validation.

## THE BENDER-GESTALT:

The Bender-Gestalt was originally designed and is principally used as a somewhat gross screening device for possible neuropsychological or brain impairment. With this test particularly, most of the projective interpretations sound nonsensical on their face. For example, drawing small figures in the upper left hand corner may be construed as indicating insecurity. That is possible. However, it should be understood that while there are only nine cards in the test, these are in a pile on the table in front of the subject and he does not know how many cards there are. So it might also be an example of planning and foresight. That is, to leave enough space in case there are a large number of cards which are going to require a considerable amount of paper. In any event, there is little validation for the use of this test as a projective device and much criticism of its use in this manner in the literature.

Q: The Bender-Gestalt was not designed primarily as a projective technique, was it?

Q: Wasn't the Bender-Gestalt designed primarily as a screening device for brain damage?

Q: Isn't there a substantial body of negative literature concerning the use of the Bender-Gestalt as a device for personality measurement (or projective technique)?

## COMPUTERIZED OR AUTOMATED
## TESTING & INTERPRETATION

In recent years automated testing and interpretation has rapidly increased in both clinical and forensic areas. These procedures are capable of dealing with a great deal more information than the human clinician and carry an aura of scientific precision and backing that makes them potent evidential tools. Therefore, the lawyer needs to be aware of the shortcomings of these procedures and the ways in which they may be misused or misrepresented and the kinds of knowledge a user should have which often is lacking.

Psychiatrists (and other medical doctors for that matter) may use these procedures for assistance in evaluating a patient or litigant as no special skills or training are required to administer many of the tests, particularly the MMPI, and all the doctor has to do is send it off to one or another of the now large number of automated interpretive services. Frequently, these psychiatrists and physicians will know very little about the test itself that is being used and know very little about the interpretive service. As the literature is virtually unanimous in declaring that the user should acquire a great deal of information (see Chapter 14, Volume II), the physician user and for that matter a good many psychologists will be vulnerable to cross-examination with regard to their knowledge of the particular procedure and/or service. One justification that may be offered is the fact that computerized interpretation services are now widely used and accepted. This argument has at least two major flaws. One, probably best illustrated by the well-worn example of "bleeding," is that procedure also was widely used and accepted for two hundred years. A second flaw is that even if it were true that automated interpretations in general were established as highly accurate and reliable diagnostic tools, one would still have to have knowledge of the *particular* interpretive system that the clinician was using in order to know that it also possessed those qualities. Thus, there are three major avenues for challenging the use of these procedures. One is the lack of adequate validating research generally covering pretty much the spectrum of the various services. A second avenue is the adequacy of published validation studies on the particular service used in the case and third, the knowledge or lack of knowledge on the part of the user of those things which the literature rather uniformly indicates should be known to the user.

Another problem that may present itself in connection with computerized interpretations is the assertion by the witness that he uses the computerized interpretation only to confirm the conclusions he has already reached with his clinical interview and/or other psychological testing. Of course, this merely illustrates confirmatory bias. Also, if the clinician lacks the necessary information about the service, he cannot know whether its confirmation is worth anything. This type of response is dealt with in detail below.

Another concern is a frequently appearing statement early in the printout, to the effect that, "This profile is valid" or some other statement to that effect. This statement, which is most likely to appear in reference to MMPI interpretation, may carry with it the erroneous impression that the conclusions in the interpretive narrative have been found to be valid or are based on diagnostic principles that have been scientifically and unequivocally validated. That is not what the term "valid" means in this context. It means only that the validity indicators (or more correctly, invalidity indicators) did not reach levels required by this particular service in order to invalidate the findings. Even this can be misleading because no absolute standard has been scientifically established for this purpose and different systems do not necessarily use the same standard, although it is likely that there is some point at which all would agree that it is valid or invalid. The validity or invalidity in this sense refers to the manner in which the test-taker took the test. Invalidity refers to confusion, random responding, the so-called cry for help, malingering or excessive omissions. It must be borne in mind that the primary use to which the computer systems are oriented is as an aide in establishing a treatment program, as a very quick and efficient way of providing a treating clinician or institution with a lot of information about the individual (we are not saying the information is correct—just that there is a lot of it and that it is quick and cheap). It is unlikely that many, if any, of the automated systems would raise the question of malingering at levels where a finder of fact would be likely to consider the probability of invalidity quite high, particularly in view of the difference between the clinical situation where the individual is motivated to be honest in his attempt to get treatment and the legal situation where the individual is motivated to portray himself in whatever way will be most likely to advance his side of the case. The literature is quite clear that the purpose for which one is being examined is a significant variable that affects examination behavior and conclusions but, so far as we know, none of the computerized systems incorporate litigation motives or even the fact of litigation into their interpretations. They are almost universally based on the assumption that this is a patient seeking treatment. They are therefore more likely to interpret indicators of invalidity as representing serious disturbance rather than attempts to malinger.

In this area as well as many others, it may be useful to start many questions along the lines of, "Doctor, do you know..." or, "Doctor, are you aware of the literature..." Note that this is not an invitation for the witness to take off on a lecture on the subject. It is a "yes or no" question aimed at determining the extent of his knowledge. In some cases where the reply is in the negative, that may be all you need and questioning may be discontinued at that point.

Q: Doctor, do you know what percent of American psychologists use the Crystal Ball Automated Interpretation Service? (We are not aware of data indicating that any one service is used by a majority of psychologists.)

Q: Do you know if the majority of American psychologists use that service?

Q: Do you know if there are published studies demonstrating the validity of conclusions provided by that service?

Q: (If the above is affirmative) Do you know if most of those studies are by people other than those who are involved in the production or the marketing of that service? (Bring out financial interest of producers.)

Q: (If affirmative) How many such studies are there, that you know of?

Q: Do these studies validate all of the interpretive statements the service provides?

Q: What percentage of the statements have been determined to be correct?

Q: Is there research conflicting with those findings?

Q: What percentage of their statements have been found to be inaccurate?

Q: Are some of the statements what are known as "Barnum" type which would tend to apply to large numbers of people?

Q: Do you know what procedures are employed by this service in providing these interpretive statements?

Q: (If you have already established or asked questions concerning the superiority of actuarial over clinical interpretations of data) Do you know if these interpretations are actuarial or clinical in nature? (Obviously you will want to know the answer to this question before you ask it.)

Q: Do you know if it is partly actuarial and in fact, partly clinical in nature?

Q: Do you know what decision rules were employed to derive the particular statements in this system?

Q: Are you aware of the literature in general concerning the use of automated interpretive systems?

Q: Doesn't that literature indicate there is a good deal of controversy in psychology about the use of such systems?

Q: Aren't there a number of publications indicating that such systems should not be used in the absence of extensive published validation data?

Q: Do you know what methods were used for establishing the reliability and validity of this program?

Q: Are you aware of several publications indicating that most computerized interpretive systems rely heavily on clinical lore?

Q: (If relevant) Hasn't consumer satisfaction been criticized as a very inadequate test of validity?

Q: Do you know if all of the automated systems produce identical descriptive statements on the same individuals?

Q: Isn't it a fact that they do not?

Q: Do you know in what respects the Crystal Ball system would differ from other systems? Do you know how it would differ specifically from the Tea Leaf system?

Q: Not all automated statements are of equal accuracy, are they?

Q: Do you know the degree of accuracy associated with (each of the interpretive statements that the clinician has used)?

Q: Is Anne Anastasi a recognized authority in the field of psycho-logical testing?

Q: Has she indicated that these systems should be required to dem-onstrate the reliability and validity of their interpretations through publication of adequate supporting data? (If you're go-ing to call a witness who will cite Anastasi, you may only want to ask the previous question and not this one).

Q: Is Joseph Matarazzo a recognized authority in the field of psy-chological testing?

Q: Has he indicated that the validity of current automated interpre-tive programs has not even met, in his words, "Primitive tests of validation"? (Same consideration about this questions as with Anastasi.) (The next four questions may not apply to all sys-tems.)

Q: Does the Crystal Ball system take into account the gender of the person being evaluated?

Q: Does the Crystal Ball system take into account the age of the person being evaluated?

Q: Does the Crystal Ball system take into account the ethnic group membership of the individual being assessed?

Q: Does the Crystal Ball system take into account local norms? (These last four questions could also be put into "Doctor, do you know..." format.)

Q: Haven't the reviews in the *Mental Measurements Yearbook* indi-cated quite a number of criticisms of the automated interpreta-tion systems? (It might be necessary to establish what the *Mental Measurements Yearbook* is before asking these questions.)

## PROGRAM USE ONLY TO SUPPORT DIAGNOSIS:

In many cases the clinician will indicate that he has not used the pro-grammed interpretation in formulating his diagnosis but has used it only to support or confirm his conclusions. This may well be the case, if for no other reason than that it does take some time, at least a few days, to transmit the test responses to the automated system and get a printout returned. Quite often by then the diagnostic formulations have already taken place based on interviews and other test data. If there is examina-tion on more than one date and it seems pretty clear that the clinician has waited for the second examination until the automated interpretation has been received, which can usually be determined by the date on the report, allowing a few days for mailing, then it is a logical conclusion that the clinician was deferring his conclusions until the automated interpreta-tions were received. In that case, it seems likely that the clinician was relying on and utilizing the automated interpretation in formulating his conclusions and therefore all the lines of challenge above are applicable. However, many clinicians will reach their conclusions, or at least will assert that they had formulated their conclusions without reference to the automated printout and have used it only as a means of confirming the diagnosis or conclusions. In that case, the foregoing lines of attack are still applicable, and there are some additional issues that can be raised. One obvious one is that if the clinician thought he needed this confirmation, he must have had some uncertainty about his conclusions, and therefore, to the extent that the automated programs are inadequate, the same doubts should remain. Another possible issue is whether the printout has agreed totally with all of his conclusions or if there are some points of difference in which case he is in a position of saying, roughly, that he accepts those parts that agree with him but he rejects those parts that don't, in which case the whole project would seem nonsensical. That is, if one takes the position that the printout is accurate, one cannot disregard those portions that are not in agreement with what one has already concluded. Stated another way, if the printout is good enough to confirm, it is good enough to disconfirm.

Q: Did you rely on or utilize the Crystal Ball interpretive system printout in arriving at your conclusions? (If yes, proceed as above. If no, proceed with the following.)

Q: This service has to be paid for, doesn't it?

Q: What was the purpose of this additional expense if you were not going to use it? (Presumably at this point, if he has not already done it, the witness will say he uses it to confirm his conclusions.)

Q: I take it then that you had some doubts about your conclusions, is that not correct? (One would expect the answer to this question to be some sort of affirmative. If so, then proceed with the challenge to the automated systems as above. However, some clinicians may say that they really did not have any doubts or were not at all shaky, that they simply felt it would be a good idea to get another opinion.)

Q: Well, doctor, are you saying that you spent your client's money (or the state's money) unnecessarily, in view of the fact that you had no doubt about the diagnosis?

Q: Did you also charge for your time in reading through the printout?

Q: Was there anything in the printout that was not in agreement with your conclusions?

Q: Was there anything in the printout that sounded much less secure (more tentative) than your conclusions?

Q: (So far as any contradictory material) Did that material support your conclusions?

Q: How did that material confirm your opinion? (This can be a risky question as some clinicians are very talented at twisting the meaning of the contradictory material to make it sound as though it is confirmatory.)

Q: (If the answer has been something to the effect that the clinician only uses that portion which confirms his conclusions) Doctor, I need your help in understanding this. Are you saying that the computer printout provides accurate information?

Q: If the information that the computer prints out is accurate, isn't the information that contradicts your conclusions of equal weight with that which confirms your conclusions?

Q: Well, doctor, aren't you applying a double standard of evidence here? (It is probably not a good idea to ask this question but rather state it as a fact in argument.)

## COMPUTER ADMINISTRATION OF TESTS:

One problem with computer administrations principally is that one does not know if the norms derived from pencil and paper administrations can be appropriately applied. There is some research suggesting that people respond differently to the test when it is given via the computer, possibly due to the fact that there are still large numbers of people in the population who are not familiar with computer operations and may even feel uncomfortable with them.

Q: Are you aware of published literature to the effect that computer administration of test may result in different performance on the test, than given in its original form?

Q: Are you aware of literature indicating that one cannot then apply the same norms?

Q: Did you apply norms for computer administration or for pencil and paper administration? (At present there is little in the way of established norms for computer administrations and not likely to be much if any for all of the automated or computer administration systems.)

Q: If (litigant) had taken this test in the usual manner with paper and pencil, his responses might have been different than they were with the computer then, is that not so?

Q: Many people are not familiar with computer operations, isn't that so?

Q: Many people are uncomfortable using a computer, is that not so?

Q: Did you determine how much experience litigant has with computers?

Q: How much did he have?

## USE OF PSYCHOLOGICAL ASSISTANTS

A number of psychologists have all or part of the testing, and sometimes even some of the interviewing, performed by psychological assistants. Typically a psychological assistant is an individual who has completed formal course work for a doctoral degree but is in the process of acquiring the required hours of supervised experience in order to qualify to take the licensing examination. Obviously such an individual is not licensed and presumably therefore not qualified to practice independently. Often the supervision is minimal or almost non-existent. Further, the psychologist who has not administered the test is lacking direct observation of the manner in which the litigant performed, observations which, according to most textbooks on testing, form part of the data base from which conclusions are drawn. Also, unless the psychologist was observing the testing through a one-way mirror or other means, he has no way of knowing what improprieties or errors of administration might have been made by the trainee or what kind of examiner effect might have been operating. Occasionally it will turn out that the psychological assistant is continuing to work in that capacity because he has taken the licensing examination one or more times and not passed it. As it will ordinarily be a licensed psychologist who will be testifying, the following questions are based on that assumption.

Q: Doctor, I note that the initials (or names) after the word examiner on (the name of the test or tests) are not yours. Is that correct?

Q: Who administered these tests?

Q: What is that person's status?

Q: What does the term "psychological assistant" denote?

Q: Then these tests were administered by a person who is not qualified to practice psychology independently in this state. Is that correct?

Q: Were you present during all or part of the testing? (If this is answered affirmatively, it can be followed with questions as to what effects the presence of more than one examiner has on the test results, as most of them are standardized with just one examiner.)

The following questions assume that the psychologist was not present or observing through a mirror.

Q: Are observations of the behavior of the person taking the test of some importance in arriving at conclusions about the individual?

Q: (Assuming an affirmative answer to the above) You did not yourself observe the test behavior, did you?

Q: You did not observe the behavior of the psychological assistant in giving the tests, did you?

Q: You cannot then be sure whether or not there was behavior of the psychological assistant (examiner effects) that may have affected the performance of this litigant?

## ETHNIC MINORITY LITIGANTS
## AND OTHER SPECIAL GROUPS

There is a substantial body of literature indicating that test and interview behavior or performance of members of various specialized groups may differ from that of the normative population who provide the basis for clinical assessment. The literature indicates that differences may occur on the basis of ethnic minority group membership, age, gender, creed, national origin, socio-economic status, religion and education. That is, members of these groups may respond differently in an interview or on a test than members of the normative group, or even if they give the same responses, the responses may have a different meaning for members of such special groups. Thus, the doubts about reliability and validity in the assessment of the norm group are compounded when the person being examined falls outside of that classification.

Q: Doctor, isn't there a substantial body of scientific and professional literature to the effect that tests or interview performance may be affected by (ethnic minority group membership, gender, age or whatever may be at issue in the particular case)?

Q: Doesn't this literature raise doubts concerning the application of the usual standards (or norms) for members of this group?

Q: Isn't there a substantial body of literature indicating that special normative data needs to be gathered for use with people in (the group)?

Q: Did you employ such special normative data in this case?

Q: Do you know if such special normative data exist?

Q: What norms did you use?

Q: Don't the *Ethical Principles of Psychologists* (D) require awareness of problems with assessment of people in special populations?

Q: Don't the *Principles* (204c) require identification of situations in which particular assessment techniques or norms may not be applicable or require adjustment?

Q: (For psychiatrists—this may require some foundation) Shouldn't psychiatrists meet the same standards?

## SOME SPECIFIC COMMONLY ENCOUNTERED DIAGNOSES

Some diagnoses seem to appear more frequently in legal matters than others. These include post-traumatic stress disorder (PTSD), depression, anxiety, schizophrenia, thought disorder and borderline disorders (referring to borderline psychotic conditions). The latter three are more likely to arise in criminal or civil commitment proceedings but occasionally may occur in other matters. PTSD appears in both civil and criminal cases. Brain damage or, more technically, neuropsychological impairment is another diagnosis that is occurring with increased frequency but is dealt with separately. Depression and anxiety come up most often in personal injury matters.

### SCHIZOPHRENIA:

The literature continues to reveal a chaotic state of affairs with regard to the mental disorder of "schizophrenia." The literature shows little agreement on what it is or how to diagnose it. DSM-III-R deletes or alters several diagnostic criteria. It is highly possible that a person diagnosed with schizophrenia at one time and place would not be so diagnosed at another time and place given the instability of this diagnostic category. Further, as indicated in a comparison of schizophrenia paranoid type and schizophrenia catatonic type, two people could be diagnosed as having schizophrenia with virtually no symptoms in common. Under these conditions, it hardly seems likely that any statements could be made about a person by virtue of their "schizophrenia" that would be of any relevance in a legal matter. The classification is simply too unstable and inconsistent within itself to permit of any generalization with a reasonable degree of confidence. Stated differently, to say that someone has schizophrenia is essentially to say nothing, because the term has so many different meanings.

Q: Doctor, did you use the DSM criteria in making your diagnosis of schizophrenia?

Q: Did you use the DSM-III or DSM-III-R or DSM-IV?

Q: Haven't the criteria for diagnosing schizophrenia been changed in each of those diagnostic manuals?

Q: Doctor, a lot of people who were diagnosed with schizophrenia in the past would not be diagnosed with schizophrenia under the present diagnostic criteria, is that not correct?

Q: Doctor, isn't it hard to get research done on a disorder when the definition and criteria for diagnosing the disorder keep changing?

Q: Isn't there a substantial body of scientific and professional literature indicating that there is very little known about schizophrenia?

Q: Aren't there a number of publications suggesting that diagnosis be dropped?

Q: Isn't there a substantial body of scientific and professional literature indicating that whether or not somebody gets diagnosed with schizophrenia depends on who is doing the diagnosing, at what time, and for what purposes the diagnosis is being made?

Q: When they wrote the introduction to DSM-II, didn't they say that they didn't know what schizophrenia is, only what to call it?

Q: Doesn't the literature indicate that they still don't know what it is?

Questioning should also aim at extracting from the witness, if he has not already given them, the bases or criteria on which he made the diagnosis and these should be checked against the criteria in DSM-IV.

As some form of thought disorder is frequently an element in the diagnosis of schizophrenia, see the next section on thought disorder.

## THOUGHT DISORDER:

Thought disorder is not a formal diagnosis in and of itself but is frequently a component of some other diagnosis. We have not found a great deal of literature on thought disorder per se. What there is suggests that as with schizophrenia, the area of thought disorder is chaotic and there is little valid knowledge. One of the problems is that frequently what is or is not deemed deviant thinking or odd or disordered thinking depends on the frame of reference of the individual clinician. We are reminded of a case in which, in response to one of the cards of the TAT which is often referred to as the "operation card" because it so often elicits stories of an operation, the litigant began his story by saying, "This is a young Arrowsmith," which the psychologist immediately seized upon as a demonstration of thought disorder which played a significant role in a conclusion of paranoia. As it happened, the litigant was in a medical field and he was familiar with the novel by Sinclair Lewis and/or the movie *Arrowsmith,* which is about a physician named "Arrowsmith" and, therefore, perfectly appropriate in this case. He was however an older man. The psychologist was young and apparently unfamiliar with either the novel or the movie, and concluded that the litigant was describing the young man in the operation scene as a maker of arrows, which would appear to be a misperception of reality. Of course one could have asked the individual what he meant by an "Arrowsmith," but we are mentioning it here to indicate how controlling is the subjective frame of reference and areas of knowledge of the clinician in determining what may or may not be deviant thinking.

One should have in mind in this area the data provided by Exner (1986, see Chapter 13, Volume II) which shows a considerable percentage of normal people, that is non-patients, display one or more instances of responses that fit the category of thought disorder, many of them more than once in a Rorschach record, and there is no reason to believe the same thing might not occur in a psychiatric interview.

> Q: Doctor, do you know what percentage of the normal population displays thinking of that kind at some time?
>
> Q: (If the doctor doesn't know) Are you aware of studies which show a considerable percent of normal people display this kind of behavior at times?

**DEPRESSION:**

There are fads in psychiatric diagnoses just as there are fads in clothing, car styles, movies and other commodities. In the Freudian and early post-Freudian period, the diagnosis of "hysteria" was common. Today, one rarely hears this diagnosis. More recently we had what many described as "the age of anxiety." Currently one of the most popular diagnoses is depressive disorder. Some argue that this recent popularity of depression has coincided with the emergence of apparently effective treatment for depression in the form of the so-called anti-depressant drugs which provide relief to a considerable number of people. In almost every case of claim for psychological damages, one is likely to find the clinician asserting depression among whatever other symptoms are described. Unfortunately, there are no agreed upon research definitions of depression and no one knows the prevalence or base rate for "depression" in the general population. Surveys and studies attempting to establish the prevalence have produced widely varying figures, some ranging as high as fifty percent of the population. It is difficult to classify as a disorder something that characterizes half the population. As one famous writer once said, "Most men lead lives of quiet desperation," which would not be an inaccurate description of what is often diagnosed as depression. One of the critical problems in the field is attempting to distinguish between normal depression or feeling sad or feeling low and clinical depression, that is, depression which constitutes a disorder or abnormality.

Depression appears most often in connection with personal injury claims, and given the either unknown or apparently large prevalence of many of the symptoms of depression, one is reluctant to believe a plaintiff who says that he had no depression before the accident but all of the symptoms have emerged after the accident. Such statements are frequently supported by the plaintiff's spouse who obviously has a financial stake in the outcome. The spouse may also have a psychological stake in having an outside source to blame for the spouse's unhappiness which, in fact, over the period of the relationship, may have been partially attributable to characteristics or behaviors of the corroborating spouse.

Q: Doctor, how common is depression (feeling low, sad, etc.) in the population?

Q: Do you know how common depression is in the population?

Q: Do you know how common (run down the list of symptoms of depression) is in the population?

Q: Are you aware of studies showing prevalence rates as high as fifty percent of the population?

Q: If this condition is so common isn't there a high probability that any given individual would have had at least some of the symptoms, if not the entire syndrome, throughout various periods of his life? (The aim here is to establish that the accident was not the cause of the symptoms.)

Q: Did you determine that plaintiff had none of these symptoms ever, prior to the accident?

Q: What was the basis for that determination?

Q: Doesn't the lack of adequate base rate information make it difficult to assess the validity of various measures of depression?

Q: Doesn't the scientific and professional literature indicate that adequate definitions of depression are lacking?

Q: Doesn't the scientific and professional literature show there are many different models of depression in current use?

Q: Aren't there a number of agents that can produce symptoms of depression? (You may want to be more specific and take them one by one, such as different medical conditions or different situational or life circumstances. In particular, keep in mind the research showing that caffeine can produce symptoms of depression and that very few clinicians explore this potential causative agent. Many other medications or drugs also can produce the condition.)

Q: Doesn't the literature indicate that the more tests one gives, the more likely one is to uncover some evidence one can interpret as psychopathology?

Q: Hasn't it been shown that various popular measures of depression tend to disagree with each other to a considerable extent?

## Situation Effects

Very clearly, whenever depression is asserted, a diligent investigation should be done to determine what situational factors exist in the plaintiff's life and did exist prior to the accident or may have arisen since the accident, that would be likely to cause a normal person to feel low or depressed. Typical examples are marital problems, problems with children, dissatisfaction with employment, reaching a certain age in life with little accomplishment, health problems other than the accident, financial problems particularly, and so on as to any of the many kinds of issues people have to deal with in their lives and which take some of the joy, or even a good deal of the joy out of living. Questions along this line should try to elicit from the doctor whether or not any of these conditions which you can establish would tend to cause a normal person to feel bad or depressed.

## EFFECTS OF CHANGES AND INNOVATIONS

The decades of the 1980s and 1990s have seen a large number of changes in major diagnostic tools, procedures and classification systems. DSM-II was replaced in 1980 by DSM-III, representing a radical departure. DSM-III was replaced or at least altered by DSM-III-R in 1987, which was replaced by DSM-IV in 1994. The WAIS was replaced by the WAIS-R in 1980. In the 1980s the various formerly popular systems of the Rorschach were gradually supplanted by the Exner Comprehensive System. The MMPI-2 replaced the MMPI. The MCMI was replaced by the MCMI-II, in turn replaced by the MCMI-III in 1994. The implications of these changes are clearly relevant in the legal arena.

One aspect is the clear indication that the predecessors were inadequate. With the possible exception of the WAIS, there has been little claim that these were good tools now being more finely honed and modernized. It has been clear that they are being changed because of serious problems and inadequacies. This is one reason the years and years of research (and experience) are nullified, because of the obvious inadequacies of the methods and knowledge base employed.

A second reason the library shelves are virtually swept clean is that because of the changes one cannot have confidence that research on any class of data (patients, instruments) can be applied to similarly named classes, because the persons or instruments represented by those classes may not be the same. Thus, there is no assurance that someone diagnosed with a certain disorder under a prior DSM would receive the same diagnosis under a later DSM; therefore, one cannot apply the research findings on that disorder without redoing all of the research with patients qualifying for that diagnosis under the new DSM. Research with the WAIS cannot be applied to the WAIS-R because it is a different test and we already know it results in IQ differences of 7 or 8 points on the average.

A third aspect is that these new classification systems or diagnostic procedures or instruments cannot be considered other than experimental for many years following their publication. This gives rise to the specter that the new tools may prove to be little or no better than the old. At least, it may take as many as 10 to 15 years to adequately evaluate their status. Of course, as long as they are experimental, they should not be relied on for decision making in a court of law.

Therefore, it is useful to inform the judge or jury of these issues whenever new or revised instruments are involved.

Q: Doctor, when was (the latest edition of whatever) published?

Q: Would it then be considered a relatively new (manual, test form, procedure)?

Q: Would it not be viewed as experimental for some years after its publication? (If this is denied, questions may be necessary to bring out the fact that it takes several years to do research on any new instrument, several years for publication to appear, and several more years for cross-checking and either possible confirmation or failure to confirm.)

Q: With the new version, I suppose we will have to wait several years before we will find out whether they got it right this time?

Q: Will we have to wait a few years before we find out that while the new version may have solved some problems existing with the old version, it may have created some new problems which will require new solutions?

A similar approach can be taken with research done prior to the revised tests or manuals.

Q: Doctor, you mentioned that there have been several thousand studies with the WAIS. The WAIS-R is different from the WAIS, isn't it?

Q: If the WAIS-R is different from the WAIS, you cannot apply that research to the WAIS-R without doing the same research with the WAIS-R, can you?

Q: Isn't it true that on average people obtain lower IQ's on the WAIS-R than the WAIS?

Q: Doctor, doesn't it take several years after the appearance of a new manual or test before enough research has been done and published and replicated and published again, before one can feel that there has been a thoroughgoing demonstration of the reliability and validity of the manual or the instrument?

Q: Research (or scientific and professional literature) which was done with the earlier version has formed part of the body of knowledge in your field, has it not?

Q: That knowledge cannot properly be applied to the new procedure until it has been verified that the population to whom it is applied is the same as the population under the old version, can it?

Q: Interpretations based on research in test performance under the old test cannot be applied to test performance under the new test unless it has been determined that such test performance would be equivalent, isn't that correct?

Q: One cannot rely on data obtained under the old rules to determine what would occur under the new rules, can one?

In particular, for those diagnoses in DSM-III-R that represent changes from DSM-III, the following questions may be useful.

Q: Doctor, a person diagnosed with (whatever) under DSM-III-R might not have met the criteria for that diagnosis under DSM-III, isn't that correct?

(or conversely,)

Q: Doctor, a person who received that diagnosis under DSM-III might not receive that diagnosis under DSM-III-R, isn't that correct?

Q: And a person receiving that diagnosis under DSM-III-R might not receive the same diagnosis under DSM-IV, is that not correct?

Q: With these manuals changing every few years, isn't it difficult to know from one time period to the next, who has what disorder? Or even if somebody does or does not have a disorder? (This question is probably unnecessary and better saved for argument.)

## EYEWITNESS EXPERTS

In contrast to the clinical diagnostician, the eyewitness expert is tied to research. He cannot rely on his experience or clinical judgment. His expertise arises entirely out of principles established through research. Thus, the issues in this area include the quantity, quality, and generalizability of the research. The major issue seems to be the application of laboratory research to non-laboratory situations.

Q: Doctor, the conclusions you have stated are derived solely from laboratory based research, isn't that correct?

Q: Isn't there substantial disagreement in the scientific and professional literature regarding such application?

Q: Don't the *Ethical Principles* (7.04b) require psychologists to acknowledge limits to their data or conclusions?

Q: Isn't there some data from real life situations that contradicts some of the laboratory findings?

Q: (If applicable) Isn't there another body of laboratory research with findings that are contrary to the findings you have described? (See Chapter 21, Volume II for specifics.)

## PROGNOSIS AND TREATMENT

Issues of prognosis and treatment arise most often in personal injury cases in relation to assessing damages. These issues can appear in disposition phases of criminal cases. They can also appear in civil commitment matters where dangerousness may be relevant. This will be discussed below. In this section, we will focus on personal injury. In general, the scientific and professional literature indicates while psychological treatment is helpful, there is little relationship between type of treatment, length of treatment, frequency of treatment, qualifications of the therapist, and outcome. In this section treatment refers to some form of psychotherapy or counseling, not medication.

Q: Doesn't the scientific and professional literature indicate that for the most part the particular type of therapy is not related to the outcome?

Q: It has not been proven in the scientific and professional literature that (whatever treatment is proposed) is more effective than other therapies, has it?

Q: It has not been proven in the scientific and professional literature that long term therapy is more effective than shorter term therapies, has it?

Q: It has not been proven in the scientific and professional literature that therapy four times a week is more effective than fewer times a week, has it?

Q: Isn't there a substantial body of scientific and professional literature indicating that the training and experience of the therapist are not related to the results?

Q: Isn't there a body of scientific and professional literature indicating that the fit between characteristics of the therapist and patient is the strongest determiner of outcome?

Q: So according to the literature, less trained and experienced therapists are just as effective?

Q: Are there such therapists available in the community?

Q: Do they charge less than (the experienced psychiatrist's rate)?

Q: What do they charge on average, if you know?

## POST-TRAUMATIC STRESS DISORDER
## & BRAIN DAMAGE/ORGANIC BRAIN SYNDROME

Although issues of brain damage or post-traumatic stress disorder occasionally arise in criminal cases, they occur more often in personal injury cases. Therefore, discussion of cross-examination on these diagnoses can be found in Chapter 10 below.

# CHAPTER 9

# Cross-Examination in Criminal Cases[1]

The general deficiencies of the knowledge base and methods in psychiatry and clinical psychology as well as the more general lines of questioning indicated in the previous chapter are applicable to the presentation of a defense clinician in criminal matters. In addition, the criminal case presents two issues on which the clinician is incapable of demonstrating that he can present valid evidence. One issue is the need to establish the defendant's psychological condition at the time of the crime, which usually is prior to the time of the examination, often by a matter of weeks or months. The second issue is establishing a causative relationship between the mental disorder alleged to have existed and the legal issue, which is whether or not the defendant possessed to a sufficient degree those capacities required by the law in order for him to be found culpable. This is the issue referred to in Volume I as "the gap."

Moderately capable cross-examination along the general lines previously suggested should at the very minimum establish doubts concerning the reliability and validity of the clinical evaluations of a defendant's psychological condition *at the time of the examination*. Even where cross-examination has been unsuccessful, all of the deficiencies can be described and documented by a consultant/expert. Once the dubious validity of such evaluations in the present has been established, it should be obvious to all concerned in the absence of research demonstrating to the contrary, that an evaluation of a prior mental condition would be even less reliable and valid. At the very minimum, the clinician has available in a present examination the behavior of the defendant which he can observe for himself. The mental status examination, a significant part of a clinical examination, calls for observation of many aspects of the defendant's behavior such as his mood, his affect, the nature of his verbalization, the nature of his thought processes and so on, which could not

---

[1] See Appendix B for transcript of testimony in criminal case.

possibly be observed by the clinician at the time of the crime (with the exception of the rare case where the defendant is in treatment with the clinician at the time of the crime). The most the clinician could have would be the observations of lay witnesses concerning mood, affect and so on, and in our experience even this is rare. The clinician is in a most awkward position if he asserts that any lay witness is capable of observing and inquiring into all of these areas with the same skill that he possesses, because he will normally be asserting that it requires his years of education, training and experience to be able to do this skillfully. Few lay witnesses, for example, would be paying attention to the defendant's chain of associations and quality of verbalization, another item that is noted in the mental status examination. Thus, it would appear unreasonable for a clinician to assert that he could obtain the same information from reports of lay witnesses as he could from his own clinical and mental status examination. Some clinicians will assert that once they have been able to make the diagnosis based on their present examination, they can establish that this is a condition that is likely to have existed for some period of time and that it has certain other characteristics which they can predict or postdict from the diagnosis. This is nonsense for two reasons. One reason, as explicitly expressed in DSM-III, DSM-III-R, and DSM-IV is that people falling within the same diagnostic classification may vary considerably from one to another so that little if any prediction about the individual can be made from the diagnosis. Secondly, almost invariably, powerful situational effects are present at the time of the examination. Often, the defendant is aware of, and has to live with, the fact that he has done something really evil. Unless grossly incompetent, he is aware that he is facing serious charges which constitute a great threat to his well-being. This alone is likely to have a jarring effect on his usual pattern of living. Further, in most cases, the defendant will be incarcerated and displaced from his normal environment and living patterns. It is ridiculous for a clinician to assert that all of these things have no effect on the defendant's mood, affect, or thought processes. There is no known or demonstrated method for establishing the degree to which the behaviors forming the basis for the clinical examination result from these situational factors as distinct from behaviors in more usual life circumstances.

Even if the clinician could accurately determine the defendant's psychological disorder at the time of the crime (or in the present, for that matter), there is no validated body of knowledge which permits the leap from the diagnosis to conclusions concerning the legal issues. The legal issues are whether because of his mental disorder, the defendant lacked the capacity to distinguish right from wrong, or under the ALI rule, whether he lacked the capacity to appreciate the criminality (wrongfulness) of his conduct, or lacked the capacity to conform his conduct to the requirements of the law, or in some instances, whether he lacked the capacity to form the requisite intent. There are no known psychiatric disorders (with the possible exception of some organic conditions and some substance abuse conditions) which per se predict the lack of such capacities. The lack of such capacities is not described as an element of any of the disorders described in DSM-III-R or DSM-IV with the possible exception of Explosive Personality Disorder, which principally describes a "bad temper" (this disorder was retained in DSM-III-R despite serious doubts about it, p. 321). Further, because DSM-IV clearly states that individuals with the same disorder may vary considerably from one another, it is impossible to predict such things from the diagnostic classification. Further, there is a considerable amount of research to the effect that people suffering from psychiatric disorders (other than the antisocial conduct disorders) do not commit crimes with a meaningfully greater frequency than crimes are committed by the population in general. In the absence of adequate research demonstration that the contrary is true, therefore, assertion of a causal connection between the psychopathology and the commission of the crime or the lack of capacities requisite for criminal responsibility are sheer speculation.

In connection with crimes of violence, it seems obvious that if psychiatric diagnosis could predict violent behavior or if a relationship between psychiatric diagnosis and violent behavior existed, the prediction of violence or dangerousness by psychiatrists would not have proven to be the great failure that the literature has demonstrated it to be (see below, dangerousness).

In cases where the defendant has engaged in apparently "crazy" behavior, two approaches are possible. One approach is to establish that the defendant may have been putting on a show for the purpose of avoiding criminal responsibility and all of the literature on malingering is relevant in this regard. Secondly, it may be useful to establish that whatever "craziness" the defendant may have had is not related to the commission of the crime. This again is the "gap" problem.

It is always important to establish a conventional motive, rather than the psychopathology of the defendant, as the cause of the crime. Thus, for example, in cases of domestic violence, one can almost always establish anger and resentment as the motive and as is well known, this is a conventional motive for violent behavior. Killings in the course of the commission of robberies or burglaries also contain in most cases the conventional motive of the desire to avoid detection. Often, killings occur as the result of the defendant's anger at the world in general. Although we certainly do not accept this as a justifiable basis for homicide, it can nevertheless be shown that such individuals often have ample reasonable grounds for being angry at the world and therefore that the killing resulted not from psychopathology (unless one wants to call justifiable anger psychopathological), but from conventional motives of anger. Thrill-seeking is another well-known motive for human behavior. And while most of us do not resort to homicides to satisfy this desire, the motive is a conventional one even though the behavior is not.

Another area in which defense clinicians are frequently deficient is in their failure to obtain or adequately consider facts that may be contrary to the conclusions. This is why thorough investigation with psychological issues in mind is extremely important. Often such investigation would turn up facts that the clinician did not have, or if one has these facts, and notes that the clinician did not discuss them on direct examination, it provides a clue to cross-examination in those areas. We have not infrequently seen instances in which the clinician denied one fact after another as making any difference in his diagnosis to the point where it was easy to argue to the jury that apparently facts made no difference to that clinician.

In many cases it is possible to establish the witness' biases by demonstrating that he appears overwhelmingly for defense or for prosecution in criminal matters.

Findings that the defendant was delusional appear in criminal cases, often with a diagnosis of paranoia because of the delusion. It is sometimes possible to establish that the belief had a justifiable basis in fact. Also, there may be no connection between the "delusion" and the nature of the crime.

In connection with any diagnosis, the cross-examiner should have the current DSM, and should check the elements described by the clinician against the elements required by DSM descriptions. Of particular importance in connection with criminal matters where frequently the diagnosis is schizophrenia, DSM-IV requires that symptoms of the disorder be present for a significant portions of the time for at least one month. In many cases, the clinician will not be able to establish that duration of the symptoms.

## CLINICAL EXAMINATION

Q: Doctor, how long after the date of the crime did you examine the defendant for the first time?

Q: How many times did you see him altogether?

Q: What was the duration of these interviews?

Q: Where were the interviews conducted?

Q: Where in the jail (if there was psychological testing)?

Q: Was the physical setting comfortable?

Q: Free from distractions?

Q: Aren't these conditions important to proper administration and interpretation of tests?

Q: Did you perform a mental status examination? (Usually this will be established on direct examination with an explanation of what it consists of; if not, questions should be asked to bring out the components of the mental status examination.)

Q: As part of the examination, did you observe the behavior of the defendant?

Q: In that examination, isn't it important to observe his mood, affect, manner of verbalizing and thought processes? What else?

Q: Could the fact that he was in jail accused of this serious crime have any influence on the kind of material that would be produced in such an interview?

Q: Could that make someone depressed?

Q: Could that make someone anxious?

Q: Can anxiety (depression) have an effect on a person's concentration and attention?

Q: Could it make his thinking a little less clear than it would be if he was not anxious?

Q: Could his attention and thought processes be affected by a preoccupation with the situation that he is in?

Q: Would it be pathological for him to be preoccupied with his situation?

Q: Had you examined him under a quite different set of circumstances, could his behavior, mood and affect have been quite different?

Q: Could his mood (affect, verbalization, thought processes, etc.) have been different a couple of hours before the time of the crime?

Q: If you observed a different mood and affect and quality of verbalization and thought processes, would your diagnostic conclusions be any different? (Any answer except "yes" has to be simply ridiculous, because these observations form an important part of the diagnostic conclusion. If the observations are different, it is difficult to see how the conclusion could be the same.)

Q: You did not observe defendant prior to the crime, did you?

Q: In fact, I believe you indicated the first time you saw him was several weeks after the crime, is that correct?

Q: Then these behaviors which you observed in the clinical examination could have been quite different at the time of the crime for all you know, isn't that correct?

Q: Are you familiar with the term "examiner effects"? (Have the witness describe if he knows, or describe to him if he doesn't.)

Q: Doesn't the literature show that people react differently to differ-ent types of psychiatrists?

Q: Did you base your conclusion to some degree on the affect or emotional response that he displayed in his interviews with you?

Q: That is just the way he reacted with you under the particular set of circumstances, isn't that correct?

Q: He might have reacted differently with a different psychiatrist, isn't that correct?

Q: Who first contacted you regarding this case?

Q: What did he tell you on that occasion (or what information did you have before the examination)? (It is important to get as nearly a verbatim account of the referral as possible in order to demonstrate that a certain set has been established in the clini-cian's mind. If there is an objection to this line of questioning, the argument should be that it goes to the basis for the expert's conclusions and goes to his state of mind, which the literature has shown plays a role in the conclusions he reaches.) (What you will be looking for in the answer are any suggestions by the law-yer that the client is psychotic or insane, or any information he had given that concerned psychopathology of the defendant or that might set up a preconception.)

Q: Did that information suggest anything to you about defendant's psychological state? (If the clinician answers no to this question, further questioning should go along the lines of expressing dis-belief that one could have heard all of these facts or acquired all of this information without having some idea in one's mind con-cerning the defendant's psychological state. There is at least one study (Temerlin and Trousdale in Chapter 6 of Volume I) indi-cating that suggestion of this type does establish a set in the cli-nician. See also confirmatory and hindsight bias, Chapter 5, Volume I.)

Q: Isn't there research showing that suggestions of this kind do es-tablish a certain amount of preconception in the clinician? (Insist that the answer be to the question of whether there is research. The clinician is likely to assert that he puts all of that out of his mind. It may be particularly important to establish if the lawyer informed the clinician that other clinicians had already found the defendant psychotic, or whatever, if that is the case.)

Q: What does the term "confirmatory bias" mean in your field?

Q: Did you have in your possession any information which might suggest a conclusion contrary to the one that you reached?

Q: What information was that?

If the clinician states there was no information which would be contrary to or inconsistent with his conclusions or at the very least raise questions or doubts about it, it may be appropriate at this point to ask him if he is aware of whatever information you are going to be able to prove that by common sense would appear contrary to the conclusions, for example, at least minimally adequate functioning within a short time period prior to the time of the crime. If the witness is not aware of such information, there are the alternatives of asking if that would change his opinion or simply dropping the matter at that point and raising in argument the fact that he lacked this presumably important item of information. If the witness indicates that he was aware of the information, he could be asked how the conclusion was reached in the face of this contrary data or more conservatively he could be asked if the existence of such contrary data would tend to cast some doubts on the conclusion reached.

With regard to questions concerning the variables of the clinical examination, particularly where the questions have been phrased in the "Could it have an effect" manner, it is likely that on re-direct examination, defense counsel will ask the expert if, in his opinion, these variables actually did have an effect on his clinical examination. If the psychiatrist states with apparent confidence that none of the clinical method variables had any influence in this case, he should then be asked on re-cross-examination if it has not been stated in the literature that many of these variables have an effect and operate without the awareness of the clinician. This would demonstrate that such variables could have been operating without his awareness and therefore it is not appropriate for him to express a high degree of confidence that they were not operative in this case. For example, most of us, including clinicians, have biases that we are not aware of as biases. One can also raise research suggesting that any awareness of bias, by itself, does not alter or reduce this bias (see Chapter 5, Volume I).

## RELIABILITY AND VALIDITY OF THE SPECIFIC DIAGNOSIS

This next area of questioning is aimed to raise doubts concerning the reliability and validity of the particular diagnosis in the case. Because schizophrenia is the diagnosis most often associated with a psychiatric defense, the questions below will be framed in terms of schizophrenia but they can be used with most other diagnoses. The aim is to establish that there is anywhere from a moderate to a substantial amount of disagreement among psychiatrists in making the particular diagnosis. Most of the negative literature on reliability and validity was produced while DSM-I and DSM-II were in effect. However, even in their short lives, considerable negative literature concerning the reliability and validity of DSM-III and DSM-III-R diagnoses appeared. Of course with the advent of DSM-IV in May 1995 DSM-III-R became obsolete, although it is likely that for some years following its demise cases will continue to come to trial on the basis of diagnoses made under DSM-III-R. In that case, at the minimum, it can be brought out that the diagnosis has come out of a manual which was short lived and is now obsolete. If the diagnosis is one such as schizophrenia where a number of changes have been made, it can be noted that the criteria or the organization of criteria for the diagnosis has changed. If the defendant no longer fits the diagnosis that can be brought out. In any event, it can easily be pointed out that the diagnostic category as now defined is too new to be evaluated. Of course this will be true for any of the DSM-IV diagnoses for several years after their publication. It will take a number of years to develop a substantial body of literature on the reliability and validity of the new diagnoses. One can conclude with the bottom line, which is that there is no soundly established diagnostic system with demonstrated adequate reliability and validity.

Q: Is there a body of scientific and professional literature indicating a lack of agreement in the mental health fields as to what schizophrenia is?

Q: Haven't the criteria for the diagnosis of schizophrenia been changed every few years? (DSM-II, -III, -III-R, and -IV)

Q: In other words, no one really knows what schizophrenia is?

Q: Which set of criteria did you use in this case?

Q: Aren't there a number of reputable publications recommending that the concept of schizophrenia be discarded?

Q: Isn't there a body of scientific and professional literature indicating that because schizophrenics are so heterogenous the classification is meaningless?

Q: Doesn't DSM-IV describe completely different, and even contrary symptoms, for different types of schizophrenia (paranoid, disorganized, catatonic)?

Q: There is scientific and professional literature indicating a good deal of disagreement among psychiatrists in making the diagnosis of schizophrenia, is there not?

Q: Isn't there research showing that making that diagnosis depends to some extent on where the clinician was trained (his theoretical orientation, the particular institution or institutions at which he has worked)?

Q: Actually, aren't several years of research required in order to determine just what the degree of agreement is?

Q: Well, one study is not enough to establish it, is it?

Q: DSM-IV states that people with the same disorder can be different in many important respects, correct?

Q: In fact, there can be considerable difference between one person with schizophrenia and another person with schizophrenia. (If denied, read descriptions in manual of paranoid schizophrenia vs. disorganized vs. catatonic.)

Q: If there is difficulty in diagnosing schizophrenia in the present as indicated by the degree of disagreement, would it be correct that it would be more difficult to make the diagnosis as of some time prior to the examination? (If the witness answers negatively, he could be asked if there is literature indicating that to be the case. See, for example, Pollack in Chapter 1, Volume I.)

Q: It has not been demonstrated through scientific research methods that psychiatrists can accurately determine a condition of schizophrenia in the past, has it?

Q: (If applicable) DSM-IV states that there is no single symptom that is pathognomic (diagnostic) of schizophrenia, doesn't it?

## RELATION OF CONDITION TO CAPACITIES— THE GAP

The aim of cross-examination in this area is to demonstrate that even if the clinician could accurately diagnose the prior mental condition, the diagnosis is not determinative of possession or lack of the requisite capacities. There is literature to the effect that people with schizophrenia or other psychiatric disorders are not significantly more prone to commit crimes, particularly of the types that invoke a psychiatric defense, than people in the population without such psychiatric disorders (see Henn et al., 1975 and Phillips et al., 1988, Chapter 1, Volume I). DSM-IV states that the evidence is conflicting regarding whether frequency of violent acts is greater than among the general population (p. 280). According to Henn et al. and Phillips et al., even if the frequency is greater the difference is so small as to be meaningless. Therefore, cross-examination is directed toward establishing that people with the disorder can function within the requirements of the law, can appreciate the nature of their acts, or whatever the test may be in a particular jurisdiction. Further cross-examination should try to indicate that the particular defendant in most of his activities was able to behave within required bounds. For the sake of brevity, the questions which follow will assume a M'Naughton jurisdiction and will assume that the diagnosis is schizophrenia. For jurisdictions with other tests of responsibility, the terminology of those tests can be substituted.

Q: Commission of serious (violent) crimes by people with schizophrenia is not substantially greater or more frequent than commission of such crimes among the non-schizophrenic population, is that correct?

Q: Many people with schizophrenia can tell the difference between right and wrong, can't they? (These questions are framed to call for a yes or no answer. The cross-examiner should insist that they be answered in that manner. If the witness wishes to explain his answer, that of course is a privilege the Court can extend to him.)

Q: And many people with schizophrenia can understand the nature and quality of their acts, can they not? (In connection with the above questions, some clinicians may try to make the point that while people with schizophrenia can tell you what is right or what is wrong or that something is right or wrong they do not really "comprehend" or truly "understand" right and wrong. They may argue that while they may intellectually know what is right or wrong, on an emotional level, their emotion is separated from their cognition so they don't "feel" the wrongness of their actions. Of course this leads to the conclusion that no one with schizophrenia could ever be held criminally responsible for his acts. A question to the clinician could be put in those terms. We feel that most clinicians would be reluctant to endorse that concept because what it would mean is that an individual who in most respects and most of the time is perfectly capable of functioning out in society would either have to be put away for life or that society would have to be subjected to the risks entailed in having a person running loose who cannot in the legal sense understand the difference between right and wrong.)

Q: Many people with schizophrenia live outside of institutions, don't they?

Q: They obey traffic laws (pay for their groceries at the market, etc.), don't they?

Q: So that having schizophrenia does *not* necessarily mean that one cannot or does not know the nature and quality of his acts or cannot tell when he is doing something that is wrong, does it? (If witness elects to argue any of the points above, questions should be asked illustrating that if all of these questions do not require an answer in the expected direction, one would expect a great difference in criminal activity as between schizophrenics and the rest of the population.)

Q: People who do not have a psychiatric disorder sometimes do things that they think are wrong, don't they?

Q: And so do some mentally ill people, don't they?

Q: Is the desire for revenge (anger, financial gain, etc.) a conventional motive for a violent act?

Q: Can people with schizophrenia engage in violent behavior out of a revenge motive? (Or rob a liquor store out of a desire to get some money?)

Q: The fact that defendant may have done some things that are wrong doesn't mean that he didn't know they were wrong, does it? (The witness may add that if there were a series of crimes, this demonstrates poor judgment by the defendant. This argument can be countered with questions bringing out the fact that series of crimes are committed by many people who are not schizophrenic or not suffering from any psychiatric disorder, except possibly anti-social personality. Thus the poor judgment shown by the commission of crime is no different from the poor judgment shown by anyone who commits a crime regardless of psychiatric disorder.)

Q: Isn't there a substantial body of authoritative opinion in the literature to the effect that there is a lack of scientific knowledge or scientific method for determining the existence or non-existence of the capacities in question here? (There are several citations in Chapter 1 of Volume I and also in Chapter 4 of Volume I substantiating this point.)

If a reasonable approximation of these answers has been obtained, some attorneys choose to discontinue further cross-examination on this point as they feel that what they have is sufficient to argue to the jury with. However, there are some other lines of questioning on this issue that may produce additional useful information but create greater risk of giving the witness an open field in which to express his views. Although such risk exists, there is also the potential advantage of having the expert make statements that will be shown to further damage his credibility.

Q: Doctor, are there precise psychiatric criteria for determining the lack of (the capacity) that have been validated through published scientific research?

Q: Doctor, for what period of time prior to this crime did defendant have schizophrenia? (The terminology "have schizophrenia" is used instead of the terminology "was schizophrenic" in conformity with the policy stated in DSM-III.) (If the psychiatrist gives the likely response that he cannot say exactly, the next question follows.)

Q: I understand that, Doctor; I am looking for an approximation. Was it an hour, a day, a week, a month, a year?

Q: (Assuming the answer indicates the disorder has existed for a considerable period of time and defendant has not been involved in serious criminal activity during that period) Doctor, do you have knowledge that defendant has been convicted of a serious crime (felony) during that period of time? (Note again that this is a yes or no question, asking the clinician only about his knowledge of such criminal behavior. It does not ask for an explanation as to why this may have occurred, and nor should he be permitted to give one on cross-examination. However, one should be prepared for redirect examination in which the clinician may assert that the disorder or the effects of the disorder "wax and wane." This can be countered with a question such as "Well, Doctor, given no known criminal activity in the _____ number of years defendant suffered from schizophrenia it seems that it was all wane and no wax." Another point that can be made and does not really require a question is that if the condition waxes and wanes there is no way to determine from a present examination and diagnosis whether it was in a wax state or a wane state at the time of the crime other than for the commission of the crime itself.)

The purpose of the above question is to establish that the psychiatric disorder had been in existence for a considerable period of time prior to the crime. Once this has been established, questions can be asked to demonstrate that during that period of time, there were numerous ways in which the defendant indicated that he understood the distinction between right and wrong behavior and was able to conduct himself in accordance with those principles. For example, if defendant was employed, did he know the correct time to come into work or did he come in any old time? Did he go to the grocery store and buy groceries, or did he walk in and attempt to walk out with groceries without paying? It should be possible to establish numerous activities in the life of most people with schizophrenia showing that they were capable of understanding the difference between right and wrong or of appreciating the wrongfulness of conduct and that they were able to conform their behavior to these requirements. Otherwise, as indicated above, one would expect frequent occurrence of criminal behavior among people with schizophrenia. Where the defense is based on lack of capacity to form a required intent, similarly, behavior showing a capacity to form intent should be available. For example, if defendant buys food, could he form the intention to go to a market, select food items, wait at the checkstand, pay for the food, and return from the market to home? None of these things could be accomplished without forming an intention to do so. Some clinicians will assert that these are automatic or habitual behaviors and do not require the formation of an intent. That is highly doubtful. For example, one has to decide when one is going to go to the market.

Where the test is in terms of "substantial capacity," questions can be asked as to where the line is drawn between substantial and insubstantial capacity. Obviously, the law does not require perfect capacities in order to be culpable. Equally obvious, it does not require total absence of capacities in order to be relieved of responsibility. This is a gray area in which much subjective judgment by the clinician is involved and therefore provides much room for his biases to operate. He could be asked in this area again what the precise psychiatric criteria are for substantial capacity. We are aware of no literature which would provide such information.

It may be useful to ask the clinician to define any legal terms about which he is offering an opinion. As an example, what does "intent" mean? What does "maturely and meaningfully" mean? What are the specific psychiatric criteria for determining such things? Have these criteria been validated by scientific research? If "Yes," what is the research?

## EXPERIENCE

The aim here is to show that in addition to lack of any scientific basis for evaluating the clinician's accuracy based upon his experience, there is no evidence that would verify the accuracy of his conclusions in the particular case (see Chapter 8, Volume III for more general cross-examination on experience).

Q:  Doctor, a few minutes ago, you indicated you did not have a scientific study made of the accuracy of your conclusions; let me ask specifically with regard to your conclusions in this case, has there been a scientific study made of the accuracy of your conclusions of that type? (Note this calls for a yes or no answer.)

Q:  Isn't it true that psychiatrists frequently disagree in their opinions as to whether a person could tell right from wrong and understand the nature and quality of his acts?

Q:  That happens even when both psychiatrists are reputable, experienced doctors, doesn't it?

Q:  There have been many well publicized cases in which that has happened, haven't there?

Q:  So another experienced psychiatrist might have an opinion different from yours?

Q:  And he would probably also have the impression that he is accurate?

Q:  So, in spite of your impression that you are right and his impression that he is right, one of you would nevertheless be wrong, isn't that correct?

Q:  Impressions are no substitute for scientific objective evidence, are they?

One good source of data which often will conflict with the opinions of the clinician is the behavior of the defendant while he is in custody. Personnel involved with custody of defendants can be instructed to maintain notes concerning the behavior of the defendant, particularly with regard to whether he seems to know what the rules are and is able to conform his behavior to whatever rules exist.

## CROSS-EXAMINING PROSECUTION PSYCHIATRISTS

In some respects a prosecution psychiatrist is more difficult to cope with than a defense psychiatrist because he takes the negative side of the issue and, therefore, does not have the burden of establishing affirmative proof. Where the defense psychiatrist needs to establish by some quantum of evidence the incapacity of the defendant, the prosecution psychiatrist can get by simply by taking a position that there is not sufficient evidence on which to draw a conclusion of incapacity. Therefore, the most potent lines of attack with a prosecution psychiatrist would have the aim of establishing that he did not obtain the same information in his clinical examination as did the defense psychiatrist and that because mental condition fluctuates considerably, it is difficult for him to deny that the defendant may have been under legal incapacity at the time of the crime, although he did not show such incapacity later under psychiatric examination.

Frequently, one of the prosecution psychiatrists will be the jail psychiatrist, and quite often, in less important cases, he may be the only prosecution psychiatrist. Although generalizations are often dangerous and there is no firm proof one way or another, many people believe that the prison psychiatrist tends to be somewhat biased against the offender. Granted that he is ethical and is as objective as his profession permits, it is still a reasonable guess that his loyalties are with the prosecution side of the case, and that it will be possible to bring out this kind of bias in cross-examination.

It is also believed by some that jail psychiatrists tend to adhere more to the organic school of psychiatry than the dynamic, which would make them more prone to reject the notion of incapacity due to mental illness, where no organic pathology is observable. Probings along these lines are obviously shots in the dark, but may pay off from time to time.

Questions concerning reliability and validity of diagnosis would be similar for the prosecution psychiatrist to those illustrated above for the defense psychiatrist. The questions below pertain primarily to the problems of the clinical examination and problems related to fluctuations of mental condition.

## CLINICAL EXAMINATION

Q:  Doctor, how long after the commission of the alleged crime did you examine the defendant?

Q:  Where did the examination take place?

Q:  How many times did you see the defendant?

Q:  And what was the duration of the interview on those occasions?

Q:  Doctor, can the time and place or other circumstances of the psychiatric examination have any influence on the information that is obtained in an examination? (Note: If the answer is negative, the psychiatrist can be questioned concerning the research and scientific literature on the subject.)

Q:  And, if you had obtained different data, you might have come to different conclusions regarding his mental condition, is that not right? (Note: A negative answer to this question says in effect that the conclusion is not based on facts at all.)

Q:  A different psychiatrist might have elicited different data from the defendant, might he not?

Q:  And on that basis he might have come to a different conclusion than you have, isn't that correct?

Q:  And sometimes even with the same information psychiatrists disagree in their conclusions, isn't that right?

Q:  You did not have available to you the information obtained by Dr. _____ when you made your evaluation, did you? (Note: The prosecution psychiatrist will have revealed the basis for his conclusions in his direct examination. If it appears that the data he noted is discrepant from that obtained by the defense psychiatrist, there are two choices available at this point. One can proceed with a line of questioning to determine if the psychiatrist would come to a different conclusion if he had obtained the data that the defense psychiatrist had obtained. There is a risk in this that the psychiatrist will state that he would not change his conclusions or would change them very little on the basis of that different information. The alternative choice is to let the matter rest at this point and bring out in argument the fact that his conclusion was drawn lacking some of the information that the defense psychiatrist had in making his conclusions.)

## FLUCTUATIONS IN CONDITIONS

The purpose of the next set of questions is to bring out the fact that a psychological state is not constant and that it would be quite possible for the defendant to have been severely disturbed at the time of the crime, but not to appear as disturbed, or disturbed at all, at the time of his examination. One would also wish to bring out the fact that it is almost impossible to assess a prior mental state with any degree of accuracy.

Q: Doctor, a person's psychological state can vary from time to time, can't it?

Q: And, under severe stress, even a relatively normal person can become severely disturbed, can't he?

Q: So, the fact that a person is not showing severe disturbance when you see him doesn't necessarily mean that he could not have been seriously disturbed at some prior time, isn't that right?

Q: And sometimes the performing of an irrational act relieves an individual's psychic tension sufficiently to allow him to function somewhat better, at least for a period of time, isn't that correct?

## CAUSAL RELATIONSHIPS

The prosecution psychiatrist will probably have found some form of psychopathology in the defendant. It is not likely, where the defense can make some presentation of a psychiatric defense, that there would not be evidence of some kind of psychological disturbance. Possibly, the prosecution psychiatrist would find a different type of "mental illness" or disagree as to the severity of the illness, but it is not likely that he would find no psychological disturbance at all except where there is malingering. Many psychological disturbances are thought to involve some degree of impairment of judgment. It may be worthwhile to try to elicit this fact from the prosecution psychiatrist and then at least bring the question of ability to judge right from wrong and the quality of the act down to where it is at least a matter of opinion.

Q: Doctor, this diagnosis of _____ which you have made concerning the defendant, does that involve any impairment of judgment? That is, a person afflicted with that particular mental illness would not be able to exercise the same degree of good judgment in all respects as a normal person, isn't that right?

Q: Now, there are no numerical scales on which to measure the degree of that impairment of judgment, are there?

Q: So, it really is somewhat a matter of opinion as to just how severe the impairment of judgment is, isn't that correct?

Q: So that whether there was such impairment of judgment as to render the defendant incapable of distinguishing between right and wrong and understanding the nature and quality of his acts, would be also subject to differences of opinion?

Q: You have not done a scientific study of the accuracy of your evaluations of impairment of judgment, have you, doctor?

Q: So, you don't know for a fact how accurate your opinions in this regard are, is that right? (Note: Should the doctor deny this, questioning can then be along the lines of showing that at best he has only his impressions as to how accurate he is and that there is really no way for him or anyone else to know his accuracy. Therefore, it is unwarranted for him to be that certain about the accuracy of his diagnosis.)

## CHILD SEXUAL ABUSE

Generally in criminal prosecutions for alleged child sexual abuse, experts are called by both sides. Typically, prosecution experts examine the child with one or more methods and present an opinion that the child has been sexually abused. This opinion is usually based on the presence of some criteria which are believed to indicate or confirm the abuse, criteria for which there may or may not be adequate validating research. In almost all cases, even with some validating research, there will be a body of literature challenging the criteria. Almost all techniques or methods of evaluation are controversial at best. Because there is such a variety of criteria and methods, it would be impractical to attempt to set out questions that would meet all contingencies. We will present some generally applicable forms of questions. We urge the lawyer who has to cross examine on these issues to be thoroughly familiar with the literature in Chapter 23, Volume II. Prosecutors planning to have evaluations done should try to make sure their expert is aware of the problems indicated in Chapter 23.

Q: Isn't there a lot of controversy expressed in the scientific and professional literature in your field regarding determinations of alleged child sexual abuse?

Q: (Regarding any statements the witness has made concerning criteria or principles) Isn't there scientific and professional literature which is contradictory to (that)? (or) Isn't there a lack of scientific validation for (that)?

Q: Does the scientific and professional literature indicate that (criterion, behavior, sign) is found in children who have not been sexually abused?

Q: Does the scientific and professional literature indicate other factors that can lead to (whatever)?

Q: What are they?

Q: Can (any factors not mentioned) lead to (whatever)?

Q: The way the examination is conducted is very important, isn't it?

Q: The scientific and professional literature shows it can influence the child's responses, doesn't it?

Q: Aren't there a number of suggestions in the scientific and professional literature that such examinations should be videotaped (or at least audiotaped) so that there is no question about what went on in the examination?

Q: Without such a tape, we have no way of knowing whether you might have done something that influenced the results, do we?

Q: The use of (whatever device, e.g., anatomically detailed dolls) is highly controversial according to the scientific and professional literature, isn't it?

Q: There is a lack of normative data for (whatever device) according to the scientific and professional literature, isn't that so?

Q: According to the scientific and professional literature, there is no scientifically validated profile of a sexual abuser, is there? (Note: On the other hand a number of abusers show normal profiles on the MMPI, so a normal profile does not preclude abuse.)

## DANGEROUSNESS

Predictions of dangerousness (violent behavior) have a notoriously bad history in the mental health field, with most studies showing the predictions were wrong more often than right. Recently (early 1990s) some primarily actuarial instruments have indicated an ability to do better than that (see, e.g., Webster's adaptation of Risk Assessment Guide, Chapter 24, Volume II). We will offer only a brief set of questions as Chapter 24, Volume II contains extensive sets of questions.

Q: Haven't most of the studies on predicting dangerousness shown the mental health experts were wrong more often than right?

Q: Hasn't recent scientific and professional literature described some actuarial guides that are right more often than wrong?

Q: Did you use those?

Q: (If "yes") Which?

## POST-TRAUMATIC STRESS DISORDER AND BRAIN DAMAGE (ORGANIC BRAIN SYNDROME)

Although issues of brain damage or post-traumatic stress disorder occasionally arise in criminal cases, they occur more often in personal injury cases. Therefore, discussion of cross-examination on these diagnoses can be found in Chapter 10 below.

# CHAPTER 10

# Cross-Examination in Personal Injury Cases

Typically in injury cases,[1] clinicians will be involved in relation to allegation of disorders that are functional or organic in nature. In the first section of this chapter we will deal with brain damage claims. In the second section, we will deal with Post Traumatic Stress Disorder, the most common of the functional claims.

## BRAIN DAMAGE

Typically, the organic claims will be of the brain damage or brain syndrome type. From a defense point of view, the major line of challenge to conclusions of brain syndrome lie in determining whether or not the best diagnostic procedures were used. These procedures would utilize neuro-investigative measures such as computerized axial tomography (CT-Scan), combined with a neuropsychological test battery. A CT-Scan showing that there is brain damage is strong evidence of that fact; however, the CT-Scan alone typically cannot adequately assess the degree of impairment that is associated with the damage to the brain. That is, it is possible to have damage to the brain with little or no impairment of function.

Neuropsychological assessment may be used for one or a combination of reasons. In some cases in which neurological and neuro-investigative work-up is normal, neuropsychological testing may be used as an additional or alternative means to evaluate for brain damage. In other cases, when medical procedures have already established the presence of brain damage, neuropsychological testing may be used to try to ascertain the degree and nature of impairment. Not infrequently, an

---

[1]For analysis of vulnerabilities in reports and depositions in a personal injury case, see Appendix A.

analysis of the testing will show that the neuropsychological batteries have been abbreviated and fail to provide the full information. Administration of full or comprehensive batteries can be quite time consuming (e.g., may require ten hours). Many psychologists do not bother with the whole procedure and are subject to some challenge on that ground. Further, there is evidence that neuropsychological testing can be faked, or that brain damage can be simulated on these tests in a convincing manner (see Chapter 18, Volume II). As is the case with all psychological tests, neuropsychological tests should be checked for proper administration and scoring. Errors of these types occur with considerable frequency. Investigation should attempt to ascertain whether there have been previous head injuries, toxic exposure, illness with neurological effects, or alcohol abuse, as well as any of the common indicators of psychological consequences of such injuries such as impairments of memory or concentration, headaches, blackouts and other such symptoms, as detailed in DSM-IV. Any of these symptoms combined with a known head injury or any of the above conditions would suggest that the damage to the brain existed prior to the event giving rise to the present litigation. Obviously, if the clinician's investigation has not revealed the prior head injury or symptoms of brain damage, it can be challenged as to its competency or in the alternative, would suggest that the plaintiff has not been honest with the clinician.

Of critical importance is the issue of so-called "pre-morbid" functioning. Typically lawsuits of this kind allege impairment (loss) in both cognitive and personality functioning. Therefore the functioning of plaintiff prior to the event in question is of critical importance. Many clinicians do a grossly inadequate job of investigation on these issues, accepting the plaintiff's word, perhaps with some corroboration from a spouse, that his memory has become poor, he has become irritable, and similar kinds of symptoms. The best evidence of the plaintiff's functioning prior to the event is likely to be evidence of the way he functioned prior to the event. We refer here to hard evidence, such as performance in school, performance on the job, performance in the military service if any, and social or interpersonal characteristics as observed by disinterested persons. Any prior testing or medical records obviously can be of great importance.

In this chapter, we will provide a modest set of questions of general application. The field of neuropsychological assessment has such diversity and complexity, it is not feasible to do more within the confines of this book. We think the lawyer who wants to be well-prepared to cross examine in this area needs to become fluent with the contents of Chapter 15, Volume II. He should also review relevant portions of

Chapter 8, Volume III, which are not repeated here (e.g., establishing the literature, challenging experience, etc.).

## BRAIN DAMAGE (NEUROPSYCHOLOGICAL) ASSESSMENT[2]

Claims for brain damage arising out of a particular event are different from claims for so called "psychic" injuries because they have injury to an objective physical part of the body as a reference point. It is easier for a trier of fact to give credence to such claims when they can be connected to a head injury or exposure to toxic substances. Also in many cases it is possible for the plaintiff to present physical evidence of such damage through the use of such techniques as CT-Scan or PET. However, as noted in Chapter 15 of Volume II, there can be damage or injury to the tissues of the brain without any necessary consequences such as impairment of functioning in one or more spheres of life. Similarly, there may be damage to the brain which does not show up using these advanced techniques, but which nevertheless is revealed in terms of impairment of functioning. Neuropsychological evaluation can be important in the former case where there is, for example, a positive finding on a CT-Scan, in determining the nature and extent and rehabilitation potential with regard to the consequences of such damage. Although family and other people who knew plaintiff prior to the event can provide us with evidence of impairment in functioning that they have observed, in the case where physical evidence has failed to support the notion of brain damage, neuropsychological evaluation is virtually indispensable to establish the plaintiff's case.

The field of neuropsychology has expanded rapidly in recent years, and thus most of the research and literature we cite is of recent vintage, much of it occurring within the ten years prior to the publication of this book. The general thrust of the literature is to the effect that given the enormous complexity of the brain and its functioning, we are a long way from having the kind of understanding and methods of assessment that would warrant a reasonable degree of certainty in rendering conclusions (except, of course, in the more extreme cases).

## QUALIFICATIONS

Because there are no specific requirements for one to call himself a neuropsychologist or to do neuropsychological evaluations, these are being done in many cases by people who have little or no training or qualifications for this specialty. Therefore at present and for some time to come, probably the first point for the attorney to cover is to investigate

---

[2] See Appendix A for a sample brain syndrome case.

the qualifications of the psychologist doing the evaluation. Most attorneys prefer to do this in deposition.

Q: Doctor, would you describe your education, training and experience in neuropsychological evaluations. (The lawyer should be diligent in not accepting general statements and in attempting to pin the witness down to exactly what courses he took in his academic training, if he took any, exactly what seminars he attended and when, and the stature of the person presenting the seminars and whatever other claims he makes to have been educated or trained in this field. We have often seen attorneys allow the witness to get by with a statement such as, "I took courses in neuropsychology in my doctoral program and I have attended several lectures and seminars." Upon closer scrutiny, it turns out that the witness has only taken one course, of which only a portion dealt with neuropsychological evaluation, and may have attended one one-day seminar. Obviously, this is grossly inadequate compared to the kind of training and education that the better qualified neuropsychologist would present. It would be helpful to have the INS-APA Division 40 Standards (see Chapter 15, Volume II) in a printout to compare with what the witness describes.

Q: Are you a member of the Division 40 of Clinical Neuropsychology of the American Psychological Association (and/or INS)?

Q: (If the witness does not meet the requirements of the Standards) Are you aware that standards for education and training of neuropsychologists have been published by INS and Division 40?

Q: You did not have (anything missing according to the Standards)?

Q: Isn't that called for by the Standards?

Q: What percentage of your practice is neuropsychological? (The "real" neuropsychologist's practice is, to a large extent, in the area of neuropsychology.)

Q: (If less than 50%) Isn't there scientific and professional literature indicating that most neuropsychologists have more than half of their practice in neuropsychology?

Q: (If more than 50%) For how many years have you devoted your practice to neuropsychology to that extent? (Given the quantity of research evidence to the effect that experience does not make for greater accuracy, which we have provided in Chapter 8 of Volume I, we are not suggesting here that experience is a significant variable in relation to accuracy of conclusions. We suggest the above questions because the research evidence does not show that lack of experience increases accuracy either, and generally lack of experience will be viewed by a trier of fact as detracting from the witness's credibility.)

Q: Are you a diplomate in clinical neuropsychology? (Much time can be saved regarding qualifications of the witness if he is requested in advance of the deposition or trial to bring a copy of an up-to-date vitae or resume.)

## GENERAL STATE OF SCIENTIFIC KNOWLEDGE IN NEUROPSYCHOLOGY

The jury should be made aware that there are literally billions of cells in the brain and that the number of possible relationships among the cells becomes astronomical. Given the enormous complexity of the brain and the relatively recent expansion of research in the area of the brain and its functioning, it should become clear to the jury that so much is unknown that the accuracy of conclusions must be in doubt in most cases. In Chapter 15 of Volume II we have provided a number of references speaking generally to this point, many of them appearing within the last few years.

Q: Doctor, there are literally billions of cells in the brain, is that not so?

Q: Aren't the possibilities for interactions between the cells greater by some multiplier of these billions?

Q: Isn't the brain and its functioning an enormously complex subject matter?

Q: Aren't there a number of statements in the scientific and professional literature indicating that the state of knowledge in neuropsychology is still in a preliminary stage?

Q: Don't the Ethical Principles require psychologists to recognize and acknowledge limits of their data and the certainty with which diagnoses or conclusions can be made? (See Chapter 2, Volume III, principles 204b, 704b.)

Q: Doesn't the scientific and professional literature indicate a number of unresolved theoretical and philosophical controversies concerning brain function and its assessment?

Q: Doesn't neuropsychological assessment require some theoretical underpinning and adequate classification system?

Q: Neuropsychology is not the same as neurology, is it?

## ALTERNATIVE EXPLANATIONS

The literature is clear that it can be extremely difficult to distinguish brain syndromes from other psychological disorders and particularly difficult to distinguish between brain dysfunction and depression. Many poor performances on neuropsychological tests can be accounted for as well by depression as by brain damage.

Q: Doctor, don't a number of authorities indicate that it can be quite difficult to distinguish between brain damage and some other psychological disorders?

Q: (If there is evidence of depression) Doesn't the scientific and professional literature indicate it is particularly difficult to distinguish brain damage from symptoms of depression?

Q: (If applicable) Doesn't the diagnosis of (whatever mental disorder) fall in the field of clinical psychology? (The Directory of the American Psychological Association contains descriptions of the various fields.)

Q: Your doctoral degree is not in clinical psychology, is it?

## CAUSAL RELATIONSHIP ("THE GAP")

The fact that there are symptoms associated with brain damage and that there has been a head injury in the event (or exposure to some potential brain damaging agent) does not necessarily mean the brain damage symptoms were caused by the event. There is, for example, literature indicating that very large numbers of people, millions and millions, suffer mild head injuries every year and millions more are exposed to toxic elements. It is also a fact that once into middle or older age everyone is suffering from a certain amount of brain damage, that is, a certain number of brain cells die off, yet most people are affected little, if at all, in their everyday functioning.

Q: Doctor, isn't it a fact that many millions of people suffer mild head injuries every year?

Q: Isn't it a fact that millions of people are exposed to toxic elements every year?

Q: Did you determine that plaintiff has had no head injuries of any kind during his lifetime prior to (the event at issue)?

Q: Have you determined that plaintiff has never been exposed to any potentially brain damaging toxic elements prior to (the event)?

Q: Have you determined that plaintiff has had no such injuries or exposures subsequent to the event involved in this case?

If the witness indicates he has made the determinations above, it may then be a worthwhile gamble to ask him how he made such determinations, as it will sometimes turn out that he made the determinations simply on the basis of litigant's self report.

Q: It is possible, is it not, to have injury to the head or the brain without necessarily having any significant impairment of function?

Q: Isn't there some literature to the effect that there is a lack of research demonstrating that specific neuropsychological tests measure abilities that are required in particular aspects of patients' everyday functioning? (You may want to focus on one or two tests that on their face appear to have little relationship to everyday functioning.)

## NEUROPSYCHOLOGICAL TESTS

There appear to be two general approaches to neuropsychological testing. One involves the use of fixed batteries such as the Halstead-Reitan or the Luria-Nebraska which are fixed and set standardized tests. Other authorities argue for flexible batteries, adapting the testing to the particular individual, in which case of course there is no standardization and each set of tests may be idiosyncratic or nearly so based on the clinical judgment employed by the neuropsychologist.

Q: According to the scientific and professional literature there is no standard approach to neuropsychological assessment, is there?

Q: The literature indicates that there is considerable diversity, doesn't it?

Q: Doctor, do you use a standard fixed battery of tests or a flexible approach?

Q: (Whichever way the above question is answered) Aren't there a number of authorities who disagree with that approach?

Q: (If either the Halstead-Reitan or the Luria-Nebraska was given) Doctor, what is the rate of agreement between the Halstead-Reitan and the Luria-Nebraska?

Q: Doctor, that would indicate then that there a number of cases in which these two leading test batteries would disagree with one another, right?

Q: In that case whether or not plaintiff is found to have brain damage might depend on which of these leading test batteries was given to him, mightn't it? (This question may not be necessary as the point can be made in argument.)

Q: Published surveys have shown that only a minority of neuropsychologists use (whichever test), is that correct?

Q: (If a "flexible" battery has been used) Doctor, do the tests you use constitute a standard battery of tests?

Q: Do I understand correctly that you select the test according to your judgment about what will be most appropriate for the individual? (Assuming this is answered affirmatively, all of the material on clinical judgment can be used.)

Q: Doctor, aren't there a number of authorities in your field who feel that a standard battery is better?

Q: There are no norms for overall performance on the set of tests you have selected to use with plaintiff, are there? (It should be made clear that this refers to overall performance, not necessarily to the performance on any individual tests as there may be norms for that.)

Q: Aren't there published surveys showing that only a minority of neuropsychologists use the flexible (or process/qualitative) approach?

Q: On the Halstead-Reitan battery, poor performance on one or two of the subtests would not be sufficient to classify the individual as brain damaged. Is that correct?

Q: The fact that the individual performed poorly on one or a few of the tests you administered then also would not, according at least to Reitan standards, constitute brain damage, would it?

It is worth noting that on the Halstead-Reitan ordinarily poor performance on three or more of the subtests would be required in order to classify the individual as brain damaged. In other words, the Halstead-Reitan, which is one of the most widely used approaches, can be used to demonstrate that one or two poor performances is not sufficient to diagnose brain damage.

Q: Isn't there scientific literature to the effect that poor performance on some of these neuropsychological test batteries falls far short of an adequate description of specific, intellectual or cognitive difficulties and their impact on everyday functioning?

While this is less likely to occur now than in the past, there are still some psychologists who will do neuropsychological assessments based on IQ tests and personality measures. The research is clear that neither of these forms of testing is adequate for assessing brain damage.

## MALINGERING OF BRAIN DAMAGE

Several published studies (See Chapter 18, Volume II) have demonstrated that it is possible for untrained ordinary people to fake brain damage on neuropsychological tests such as the Halstead-Reitan battery. We would add as anecdotal evidence, for whatever that is worth, that we have also observed demonstrable faking of some of the symptoms in cases we have worked on. We cannot be certain if the individual did not have brain damage, but in at least one case we know one of the symptoms was he was unable to count his change when he went to the grocery store. Because of the presence of some indices of malingering, two independent private investigators were employed, each of whom separately observed plaintiff working behind the counter at his brother's liquor store, and each of whom bought a bottle of liquor giving plaintiff a large bill for which he made change without any difficulty whatsoever, even though he was using an old fashioned cash register which simply rang up the amount of the sale and required him to count out the change from the cash box in the cash register. This was a significant symptom to the neuropsychologist (who incidentally was a diplomate) who had given him a battery of neuropsychological tests and concluded that he was not malingering and indeed was brain damaged and significantly impaired. Ordinarily we give little weight to anecdotal evidence of this kind. However, it is of some use in countering declarations by experts that without exceptional training and knowledge, no one would be able to fake brain damage. Based on the studies and our experience, this is obviously not true.

Q: Doctor, isn't there some published research showing that untrained people are able to fake brain damage on neuropsychological tests?

Q: Doesn't this research show that experienced neuropsychologists are unable to detect that malingering with a high degree of accuracy?

Q: Isn't there some published anecdotal literature showing also that untrained people are able to fake symptoms of brain damage?

## EXAMINER AND SITUATION EFFECTS

The research is clear that examiner and situation effects operate in neuropsychological assessment just as they do in psychiatric or clinical psychological assessment of other disorders. As questions on these effects have already been illuminated in the Chapter 8, Volume III, we will not repeat them here, but simply remind the reader that questions on these issues are available in this book and can be used with regard to neuropsychological assessment.

## SPECIAL GROUPS

There is literature indicating that variables such as age, gender, cultural background, minority group status, education and intellectual level all potentially affect the meaning of neuropsychological test results and thus constitute grounds for challenging the generalization of any validity data on neuropsychological measures absent normative data for such groups.

Q: Does age (gender, cultural background, etc.) have any effect on the outcome of (any particular neuropsychological test)?

Q: In that case, isn't there some question about generalizing research which does not provide normative data for people in the particular category of this specific person being examined?

Q: Isn't data on the generalization of conclusions to such individuals generally lacking?

## ILLUSORY CORRELATION AND BASE RATES

It has been noted in the literature that a determined search for abnormalities may produce positive evidence in almost any case regardless of whether the individual is brain damaged or not. Many of the symptoms of brain damage are commonly found among the "non-brain damaged" population, particularly with regard to forgetting items and appointments. These are quite common among normal individuals and, while used by clinicians to indicate brain damage, in the absence of clear knowledge of the base rate for normal people, such use is inappropriate.

(See Chapter 8, Volume III for questions.)

## DETERMINING PREMORBID LEVELS OF FUNCTIONING

Probably the most vulnerable area in the whole field of forensic neuropsychology is the near inability of the neuropsychologist to determine the litigant's functioning prior to the event giving rise to the lawsuit. A frequent way this is attempted is by using the so-called "best performance" method in connection with the WAIS. That is, the clinician looks at the scores on the subtests of the WAIS and concludes from the best score that it represents the innate capacity of the individual at which he would have performed prior to the event, and therefore to the extent that other scores are appreciably lower they indicate impairment; this standard is also used as a basis for comparison with results on other tests in the neuropsychological battery. Thus, for example if an individual receives a score of 13 on the comprehension subtest of the WAIS the conclusion is drawn that his intellectual level is at high average. Then failure to perform at that level on other subtests or any tests other than the WAIS, is taken as evidence of impairment. The lawyer should understand that the term "impairment" means a loss or reduction from a prior level of functioning, not that one is not able to function well in a certain area. The basic premise for the best performance measure is that there is a general intelligence factor that should enable the person to perform at about the same level on most or all intellectual functions. This theory of "unitary" ability has been widely challenged and is a matter of great controversy in the field of psychology. Also the use of this test involves what is called "scatter" or "intertest variability" on the subtests of the WAIS-R, that is, there is variation among the subtest scores, some being higher, some being lower and some being in the middle of the individual's performance. Matarazzo et al. (1988) (see Chapter 11, Volume II) have demonstrated that differences or seven or eight points between high and low scores for members of the standardization population for the WAIS-R were not at all uncommon. If the best performance basis is applied to them, it would have to be concluded that they are all impaired. Other methods of estimating premorbid intelligence are based on assumed "hold/don't hold" subtests or on tests assumed to measure functions impervious (or relatively so) to brain damage or the specific damage under consideration, but these methods have not been validated.

The best evidence that can be obtained concerning premorbid functioning would of course be an identical set of tests administered prior to the event. These are rarely available, although inquiries should be made to see if some of them are, as it is quite possible that the individual has had IQ tests and may have had some personality tests. Absent some identical tests, the best kinds of evidence come from school, employment and military records, and these should be obtained in virtually every case of a claim of brain damage as they will often be the fulcrum on which the case will revolve. These are useful in showing the typical level of performance for this individual prior to the event and, in particular, may be useful in showing that he previously exhibited the same variability in his performance in different areas as he showed on the WAIS or on the neuropsychological battery. (See Appendix Case A.) Also, school records, particularly elementary school records, often contain descriptive comments by teachers which may reveal that the individual displayed many of the characteristics early in life which are alleged to have resulted from the event in question. Also they will often contain the results of one or another kind of IQ test, or at least tests that appear related to intellectual level.

Q: (Assuming the doctor has indicated use of scatter or the best performance method) Doctor, the method you have used to determine plaintiff's premorbid level is an estimate based on some of the test results, isn't that correct?

Q: That estimate is really a guess, isn't it?

Q: (If applicable per norms in Matarazzo) Actually a substantial portion of the people who were used to establish the norms for the WAIS-R showed differences (this large), didn't they?

Q: So, using the "Best Performance" method on them, you would have to conclude that the average person in this normal population was impaired, wouldn't you?

Q: Did you obtain any other kind of evidence concerning plaintiff's premorbid functioning? (Throughout this type of questioning you may wish to use a term such as "prior level of functioning" rather than "premorbid" which seems to constitute some acceptance the plaintiff is now "morbid.")

Q: Did you obtain school records?

Q: Did you obtain military records?

Q: Are there any other kinds of records that might shed some light on plaintiff's premorbid functioning?

Q: Wouldn't it be better to utilize such objective evidence rather than trying to guess from present test results? (This is probably an unnecessary question, as the point can be made in argument and there is no good reason for giving the witness an opportunity to lecture.)

Sometimes the witness will have interviewed family members or others and obtained statements from them that plaintiff is more forgetful or more irritable or that he never used to forget anything or whatever information they may have which is used to "establish" premorbid levels. Obviously in the case of family members, the statements are coming from people who have an interest in plaintiff and in the outcome of a lawsuit and to that extent may be unreliable informants. It is usually the case that before the event nobody was paying any particular attention to how good plaintiff's memory was, or was not, or how irritable plaintiff was or was not. Life was just going its normal way for those people, but subsequent to the accident, and particularly where there is some awareness that there is a claim for damages and in particular a claim for brain damage, everybody suddenly becomes extremely sensitized to any evidence which would support the claim. Therefore, while they are not necessarily lying, and may feel they are telling the truth when they describe changes, the fact is that there may not have been any change. It is just that they have become more aware of any functional problems that plaintiff has than they were before. Questions can be asked of the witness to establish that he has no way of ruling out these possibilities that the information he has obtained is not accurate. Once again, this is a poorer quality of evidence than would be the objective evidence from school, military or work records prior to the accident.

Another method of estimating premorbid level is from the educational level obtained or from the occupation of the plaintiff. The lawyer should be aware that it does not take more than average intellectual level to obtain a college degree. Many people who do not test out with above average intelligence have obtained college degrees. They may have had to work a lot harder than those with IQ's of 120 and up, but we think most people know that by hard study and by hard work one can get through college. Insofar as occupation is concerned, obviously there are very few people who have IQ's of less than 100 who become lawyers or doctors or obtain advanced degrees, but people with such degrees tend to be rare among plaintiffs claiming disability. Most often the occupation is at a lower level, perhaps involving some kinds of technical training and, quite often, while the clinician has used the occupation as the index of high or relatively high intellectual capacity, the case is as with college degrees, that people of ordinary intelligence are capable of acquiring the necessary skills to perform in those occupations. Also, quite often the clinician is unable to answer questions as to just how much intellectual ability or cognitive capacity is required for the job. They simply do not know. In that case they are making a guess based on a guess.

Because neuropsychological assessment is almost a subject unto itself, we have really only scratched the surface of the kinds of questioning that could go on in such cases. We would recommend strongly that the attorney involved in such cases thoroughly review and digest the contents of Chapter 15 in Volume II. There are more extensive and detailed resources such as Muriel Lezak's *Neuropsychological Assessment,* Third Edition (Oxford University Press, New York, 1995), and S.B. Filskov and T.J. Boll, *Handbook of Clinical Neuropsychology* (John Wiley and Sons, New York, 1981). A well-written introductory text on the Halstead-Reitan, that is not unduly long and should serve the lawyer's purposes, has been written by Paul E. Jarvis and Jeffrey T. Barth (*Halstead-Reitan Test Battery: An Interpretive Guide*, Psychological Assessment Resources, Inc., Odessa, FL, 1984). Faust et al. (1991) discuss neuropsychological assessment in a forensic context.

## POST-TRAUMATIC STRESS DISORDER (PTSD)

The most common claim of psychological injury in the past has been the so-called "traumatic neurosis" which was never officially recognized. It is important to keep in mind that post-traumatic stress disorder (PTSD) is a new diagnosis that appeared for the first time in DSM-III in 1980. While psychological consequences of traumatic events, particularly those occurring on the battlefield or in natural disasters, had been observed prior to that time and sometimes diagnosed with labels such as "traumatic neurosis," or "combat neurosis" or "shell shock," the specific diagnosis PTSD and the specific criteria for establishing the diagnosis were not formulated prior to DSM-III in 1980. It was therefore an experimental diagnostic classification; it underwent several changes in DSM-III-R, which obviously indicates that it was inadequate in its original experimental form, necessitating those several changes. However, it should be equally obvious that the "new" PTSD published in 1987 was also an experimental classification, which also underwent several changes with the publication of DSM-IV in 1994. Given this history of rapid changes, PTSD in the DSM-IV version should not be considered other than experimental. Of course, during this changeover period from

DSM-III-R to DSM-IV, many cases will come to trial in which the diagnosis of PTSD will have been made on the basis of the DSM-III-R criteria. Obviously, these should be checked to see if DSM-IV criteria are met.

DSM-IV divides criteria (symptoms) into several categories with varying numbers in each category required for the diagnosis. The diagnostic criteria for post-traumatic stress disorder are as follows:

A. Exposure to a traumatic event in which both of the following were present:

   (1) the person experienced, witnessed, or was confronted with an event or events that involved actual or threatened death or serious injury, or threat to the physical integrity of self or others.

   (2) the person's response involved intense fear, helplessness, or horror.

(Note that this is a much more specific description of the required stressor than in DSM-III-R.)

B. The traumatic event is persistently reexperienced in one (or more) of the following ways:

   (1) recurrent and intrusive distressing recollections of the event, including images, thoughts, or perceptions.

   (2) recurrent distressing dreams of the event.

   (3) acting or feeling as if the traumatic event were recurring.

   (4) intense psychological distress at exposure to internal or external cues that symbolize or resemble an aspect of the traumatic event. (Note: Internal cues is a change from DSM-III-R.)

   (5) physiological reactivity on exposure to internal or external cues that symbolize or resemble an aspect of the traumatic event.

(Note: Internal cues is a change, and also this criterion was D (6) in DSM-III-R.)

C. Persistent avoidance of stimuli associated with the trauma and numbing of general responsiveness (not present before the trauma) as indicated by three (or more) of the following:

   (1) efforts to avoid thoughts, feelings, or conversations associated with the trauma.

   (2) efforts to avoid activities, places, or people that arouse recollections of the trauma.

   (3) inability to recall an important aspect of the trauma.

(4) markedly diminished interest or participation in significant activities.

(5) feeling of detachment or estrangement of others.

(6) restricted range of affect (e.g., unable to have loving feelings).

(7) sense of a foreshortened future (e.g., does not expect to have a career, marriage, children, or a normal life span).

D. Persistent symptoms of increased arousal (not present before the trauma) as indicated by two (or more) of the following:

(1) difficulty falling or staying asleep.

(2) irritability or outbursts of anger.

(3) difficulty concentrating.

(4) hypervigilance.

(5) exaggerated startle response.

Most of the symptoms listed in (C) above are similar to those found in depressive reaction and several of those in (D) above appear in generalized anxiety reaction. The distinctive features of PTSD are the existence of the specification of the adequate stressor and the re-experiencing of the trauma as indicated under (A) and (B) above.

The reader should also be aware that there is a great deal of similarity in the symptomatology of PTSD and Adjustment Disorders. From a forensic standpoint, it makes a great deal of difference which of these diagnoses is made because adjustment disorders are defined as expected to end when a particular stressor has stopped or the individual has adjusted to it, in contrast to the frequently predicted long-term, maybe lifelong, effects of post-traumatic stress disorder. The principal distinction between PTSD and adjustment disorder, as well as between PTSD and other anxiety disorders, is the presence of intrusive thoughts or recollections or nightmares, specifically involving the traumatic event or the reliving of the traumatic event.

Faking or exaggeration of these symptoms is always a strong possibility in cases of this type due to the subjective nature of the symptoms. The potential financial gain is an obvious motive for malingering. It is important to determine whether these complaints arose before or after interviews by plaintiff's attorney. Questioning in these areas may cue the plaintiff as to what may be to his financial advantage in the case, or in some instances may provide a basis for the argument for "iatrogenic" disease, based on the suggestion by the lawyer through his questioning that these symptoms may exist. In the referral for psychiatric examination, if the lawyer stresses these symptoms to the psychiatrist, it is quite possible that the psychiatrist will also focus on them in his examination.

This may further augment the suggestion that these symptoms may be worth money, or further augment the iatrogenic disease concept by the additional emphasis on such symptoms. Because of the possibility of malingering, information from the MMPI validity measures should always be obtained. If plaintiff's examination has not utilized this instrument, the defense examination should do it. Failure of plaintiff's examination to utilize this instrument, which provides one of the best bases for detecting malingering, can be raised during trial.

Basically, there are four issues to contend with in cases of this kind. These are whether plaintiff has a psychological disorder, whether it was caused by the accident or event, how disabling or detrimental it is, and what the prognosis is.

With regard to the existence of a psychological disorder, all of the problems of reliability and validity and of the clinical examination are relevant. In particular, the clinical examination should be explored for incompleteness which we have found to occur frequently in cases of this kind. Also, one should have in mind the caution contained in the DSM-IV regarding the use of any of the classifications of mental disorders for forensic purposes. Also, with regard to reliability and validity, there are not only such questions concerning diagnosis, but, also concerning prognosis. The prognosis necessarily involves prediction, which is a notoriously weak area in psychiatry.

With regard to causation, assuming that there is some genuine psychological disturbance, one of the most important areas to explore is the existence of alternative explanations for the disturbance, or pre-existing symptoms, or symptoms that are largely situational. Just the fact of being involved in litigation is a stressor and can be the source of symptoms (see DSM-IV, p. 29). Frequently, investigation will show that there are a number of other stressors in plaintiff's life that could account for the disturbance, for example, marital problems, job problems or dissatisfaction, problems with children, aging, and others of that type, such as financial problems. Thus, for example, it would not be unusual to find that an individual had sleep problems related to marital problems or job dissatisfaction. Such problems may well cause anxiety, tension, and/or depression. Consumption of caffeine can also produce symptoms of psychological disturbance. Not infrequently, an individual was employed prior to the event, then ceases employment and has a good deal of idle time on his hands. Much of that time is spent in passive activities, such as watching television, with a concomitant consumption of caffeine from coffee, soft drinks, aspirin, and other sources. Thus, caffeine is a factor which might account for the symptoms seen by the psychiatrist or described to him, although in our experience psychiatrists rarely inquire about this area. Another possibility, where there is painkilling medication for physical injuries, is that some alteration of the plaintiff's mood may simply be a result of the use of that medication and will change when the medication is discontinued. The clinician may fail to inquire whether the plaintiff is on some kind of medication at the time of the examination, with the result that he will not know whether the behavior he has observed is the result of, or has been affected by, the medication.

Regarding degree of impairment, many people with mild to moderate anxiety or depressive disorders continue in their employment and in social and recreational activities. This is not to say that there is no discomfort involved, but it illustrates the fact that people with these complaints are often able to work and have a reasonably normal life despite problems of this type, perhaps related to motivational factors. Quite often it can be developed that plaintiff disliked his occupation, and the event that has occurred provided him with the so-called "million dollar wound" which will take him out of that job by providing adequate financial resources. Intelligence or neuropsychological tests can sometimes demonstrate that the impairment of concentration and attention is not as great as alleged or does not even exist. For example, the plaintiff may perform adequately according to his intelligence level on any of the subtests thought to require attention and concentration, such as arithmetic and digit span.

With regard to prognosis, anything the clinician says is likely to be speculative. Prediction is a notoriously weak area in the mental health professions. Prognosis may also depend to some extent on the type of treatment proposed or initiated. It has been established that in many cases of recent onset of anxiety symptoms, particularly as a result of trauma, behavior or desensitization therapies can ameliorate the difficulty in a relatively short time. It is also well known that in at least some cases, the symptoms disappear once the lawsuit is concluded. The anxieties and tensions associated with the pendency of important litigation are an important situational factor in the problems of the clinical examination in cases of this kind and may subside when the matter is concluded.

In addition, of course, as with the criminal case, there is the problem of assessing a prior mental state; that is, in order to establish causation the clinician would have to know what plaintiff's condition was prior to the event. As indicated elsewhere, this assessment is not one that can be made with a high degree of accuracy, particularly in cases of this kind where data are almost totally dependent on the description given by the plaintiff. Clinicians are particularly vulnerable if they have not obtained corroborative evidence from family, friends, co-workers, and employers, although obvious biases exist with regard to family and friends. However, as such corroborative evidence is given by lay persons who are not trained in psychiatry or psychology, it is subject to some challenge on the grounds that these people do not possess the training to have noticed the presence of such symptoms prior to the event. The type of investigation regarding "pre-morbid" functioning suggested for brain damage cases is recommended here also.

## RELIABILITY AND VALIDITY

Q: The scientific and professional literature on psychiatric diagnosis has indicated a good deal of disagreement in diagnosis, has it not?

Q: The diagnosis of post-traumatic stress disorder that you have made in this case first appeared in DSM-III in 1980, is that right? (If the witness asserts that the disorder existed prior to DSM-III, questions will have to be asked to bring out the fact that it was not diagnosed according to the criteria in DSM-III nor was that particular designation used.)

Q: Weren't there a considerable number of changes in the criteria for diagnosing PTSD in DSM-III-R in 1987 as compared to DSM-III?

Q: And it was changed again in 1994 in DSM-IV, was it not?

Q: So that because it is new, the diagnosis of post-traumatic stress disorder will require some years of research to establish what its reliability and validity are, is that correct?

Q: And they may have to change it again in a few years in DSM-V, right?

Q: Wouldn't it have to be considered an experimental diagnosis because it is so new? (If this is answered negatively, questions need to be asked to bring out the fact that it takes years to do research and years to get the research published and years more to get possible rebuttal research evidence done and published to take it beyond the experimental stage.)

Q: Some people diagnosed with post-traumatic stress disorder under DSM-III might not meet the criteria for that diagnosis under DSM-III-R. Isn't that correct?

Q: And some people diagnosed with post-traumatic stress disorder under DSM-III-R, may not meet the criteria for that diagnosis under DSM-IV. Isn't that correct? (It should be useful to have visuals of the Alice Adams, Bill Brown, and Ann Atkins examples to illustrate this point (see Chapter 20, Volume II).

Q: Because the people who may receive this diagnosis keep changing, it is not appropriate to use research done with people diagnosed under an earlier manual for people diagnosed under a later manual, isn't that correct? (There may have been no Alice Adamses or Ann Atkinses in the earlier research studies, or there may have been a lot of Bill Browns. Few, if any, prior studies would have recorded such information, so now there is no way to know.)

Q: In the absence of research done with people diagnosed under the current criteria, it is risky (inappropriate) to draw conclusions about people diagnosed under the current criteria, isn't it? (Be aware that in some cases the witness may be able to show that litigant also meets the earlier criteria. Criteria reported or known to exist should be checked before using this question.)

Q: Is there a diagnosis of adjustment disorder in the diagnostic manual?

Q: What are the criteria for diagnosing adjustment disorder? (It may be useful to have this read in full from the manual.)

Q: The criteria for adjustment disorder are considerably similar to the criteria for PTSD, aren't they?

Q: Aren't adjustment disorders generally expected to be of relatively short duration (or to remit when the stressor ceases)?

Q: The diagnosis of PTSD depends to a very large extent on the subjective reports of the litigant, does it not?

Q: Isn't there research showing that self reports are not very dependable (are often quite inaccurate)?

Q: The only information you have as to whether he re-experiences the event is by what he tells you; is that correct?

Q: Is there research showing that sleep disturbance is a fairly common problem among the normal population? (Or about a third of the normal population has some sleep disturbance.)

Q: Is some amount of depression fairly common among the normal population?

Q: Do you know anything in litigant's life prior to this event which might cause an ordinary person to have some of the symptoms you have described?

Q: Anything occurring after the event?

Q: Is being involved in litigation a stressful situation?

Q: Can the stress of being in litigation cause someone to have difficulty sleeping? (be irritable, etc.)

Q: Can the stress of being involved in litigation cause someone to experience tension or anxiety (or depression) symptoms?

Q: Do you know of research which clearly validates a particular method or formula for distinguishing between situational anxiety and anxiety resulting from a traumatic event? (Note: In this question, it is probably wise to ask the question in just this manner, where the question is not whether the clinician was able to separate these, to which many of them may answer "Yes."

Rather, the question is directed to whether or not they have knowledge of research establishing a method for making this separation, which to our knowledge does not exist.)

Q: Isn't there some research showing that people who are in traumatic events for which there is no basis for a legal claim, show far less psychiatric disturbance than people who are involved in events for which they are able to make a claim for damages?

## ALTERNATIVE EXPLANATIONS

Q: Were there any other kinds of stressors that plaintiff was undergoing prior to the accident (or prior to your examination)?

Q: Are you aware that he was having considerable marital difficulties with his wife? (job, money, children, any other stressors?)

Q: Did you ask about this?

Q: As a hypothetical question, if a man was having serious marital problems with his wife, might he suffer from sleep disturbance and feelings of tension or anxiety?

Q: Did you inquire about any other possible sources of stress?

Q: Wouldn't it be important to find out about other sources of stress? (If the doctor indicates that he did inquire and plaintiff denied any other sources of stress which you would be able to prove through other evidence, then plaintiff is established as dishonest in the interview. If the doctor indicates he did obtain some other evidence of stresses, such as marital or occupational problems, he can be asked if those problems might not account for some of the symptoms that were observed and whether he mentioned these in his report.)

Q: In part, you base your conclusion that this condition is the result of the injury on the fact that plaintiff had a previously good working history and was steady on the job prior to this accident, is that correct?

Q: Aren't there a number of people who are diagnosed as having anxiety or depression who continue to work?

Q: So, plaintiff's good work record would not necessarily indicate that he was not suffering with some of these problems prior to the accident, is that correct?

Q: Do some people with some anxiety or some depression continue their social and recreational life despite those problems?

Q: Was your diagnosis based partly on indications of mood or affects such as anxiety or depression in the plaintiff's behavior when you were examining him?

Q: You would have no way of really knowing for sure whether he displayed those same behaviors indicating anxiety before the accident, would you?

Q: (If expert indicates wife corroborated prior absence of symptoms) Well, his wife is not a qualified psychiatrist or psychologist, is she?

Q: And, you underwent a great deal of training to be able to evaluate these things, didn't you?

Q: And his wife has a financial interest in the outcome of this case, does she not?

## THE CLINICAL EXAMINATION

If general questions have not already been asked concerning the mental status examination and the operation of situation and examiner affects on the clinical examination, they should be asked at this point. The following questions assume they have already been asked as indicated in the section on general cross-examination.

Q: Is this lawsuit quite important to plaintiff?

Q: Has he been hoping to get some of money out of it?

Q: Didn't you inquire about that?

Q: Couldn't that have some bearing on any anxiety or tension he was experiencing?

Q: Let me put it as a hypothetical question, Doctor. If an individual has a lawsuit pending in which he hopes to get some financial benefits and the outcome is in doubt, might not a normal person experience a certain amount of tension or anxiety due to that situation?

Q: If he knew that the outcome of your examination might mean a great deal to him in terms of the money he would obtain, could that make him nervous?

Q: Does DSM-IV describe involvement in a lawsuit as a stressor? (problem which can be a source of symptoms)

Q: If he was trying to fake or exaggerate symptoms and had some fear of detection, could that make him nervous also?

Q: Might that cause him to have some difficulty sleeping also?

Q: Doctor, are you familiar with the term therapist bias or therapeutic bias?

Q: That refers to the general desire of people in your profession to help people who come to them, does it not?

Q: You have testified in a number of personal injury cases, have you not?

Q: Have you testified mostly for the plaintiff or mostly for the defense?

Q:   In what percentage of your cases have you testified for the defense?

Q:   So that most of your testimony has been on the plaintiff's side of the case, is that correct?

Q:   When is the last time you testified on the defense side?

Q:   Did plaintiff seek you out on his own to get psychiatric help with his problems?

Q:   Who referred him to you?

Q:   Was he referred to you for evaluation or for treatment?

Q:   Have you been treating him?

Q:   Don't the specialty guidelines for forensic psychologists indicate that one should avoid dual relationships and not treat and also provide evaluation for forensic purposes for the same person?

Q:   Isn't there concern that objectivity may be compromised in such a dual relationship?

Q:   How often have you been seeing plaintiff? (Deposition should have obtained the doctor's appointment records to ascertain whether plaintiff has been keeping his appointments, or whether there are a number of missed appointments and/or fairly long gaps such as three or four weeks between sessions. If so, the following questions can be asked:)

Q:   Doctor, plaintiff has not been diligent in keeping his appointments with you, has he?

Q:   How many appointments has he missed in the last six months?

Q:   What is the longest period of time he has allowed to lapse between sessions?

Q:   Is failure to cooperate in the treatment program one of the indicators of malingering stated in the DSM?

Q:   Is another criterion for malingering examination in the context of a lawsuit?

Q:   Does the DSM indicate that any combination of these factors strongly suggests the possibility of malingering?

Q:   It's possible for someone to fool a psychiatrist regarding symptoms, isn't it?

Q:   Do you know whether or not litigant's attorney, or anyone else, asked him if he had trouble sleeping?

Q:   Do you know whether or not litigant's attorney asked him if he felt tense or anxious?

Q:   Do you know whether or not litigant's attorney asked him if he was depressed (or any of the symptoms of depression)?

Q:   Do you know whether or not plaintiff's attorney asked him if he had nightmares about the accident? (Or had intrusive thoughts

about it, or re-experienced it, or avoided situations which reminded him of the incident.)

Q: (A series of similar questions) Do you know whether or not his
attorney asked him (concerning each of the symptoms of PTSD
that he purports to have)?

Q: Wouldn't it be important to know if the attorney or anyone else
mentioned these symptoms to litigant?

Q: Wouldn't it be important in doing your evaluations to know if
someone, even inadvertently, gave litigant some cues regarding
symptoms that might be advantageous for his claim? (See general cross-examination for questions on malingering.)

Q: (If there is no MMPI) Did you obtain an MMPI in this case?

Q: Doesn't that test provide some numerical indicators of malingering?

Q: Wouldn't it be useful to have such indicators in a case like this in
addition to your own subjective judgment? (Questions on malingering and inability of psychiatrists to detect it can be asked at
this point as indicated in the general cross-examination section in
Chapter 8, Volume III.)

Q: Does the research evidence show the MMPI indicators are less
accurate than a psychiatrist's clinical judgment?

Q: Aren't the MMPI indicators the only measures which have had
published research validation?

Q: Did you obtain information from any witnesses other than plaintiff, his wife and his lawyer?

If an MMPI has been administered, it is useful to have someone go
through it item by item to determine if there are statements that contradict the clinician's conclusions, as in the example given earlier of the
individual diagnosed with depression who continually asserted on MMPI
items that he was "happy," seldom "felt blue" and so on. Also, of course,
the quantitative indicators of malingering should be calculated.

## DISABILITY

If not already asked, the following questions can be utilized in indicating plaintiff is not as impaired as he appears to be.

Q: Doctor, do you see any patients in your practice who suffer from
anxiety? (Tension, depression, sleep problems, etc.)

Q: Do some of those people continue to carry on their occupation?

Q: And do some of them carry on some social and recreational activities? (Many patients in psychiatric practice generally are suffering from symptoms of anxiety or depression but nevertheless

are able to carry on most of the normal functions, albeit with some discomfort.)

Q: And do some, even with moderately severe problems, carry on with the help of minor medications?

Q: Wouldn't it be good for litigant to be involved with work (or other activities? (Obviously some of these questions would be best asked on deposition.)

With regard to causation, the same difficulties exist with determination of prior state as described in the section on brain damage, and the same approach can be taken in dealing with claims that litigant is now worse that before the incident.

## PROGNOSIS AND TREATMENT

Q: Sometimes the stress reactions go away just with the passage of time, do they not?

Q: And where treatment is initiated, there is no body of validated scientific research indicating how long the treatment will take, isn't that correct?

Q: According to the scientific and professional literature it is very difficult to make predictions in psychiatry, isn't that correct?

Q: What type of treatment are you employing with plaintiff?

Q: Does the research evidence show that such therapies are more effective than the behavior or desensitization therapies?

Q: Does the research evidence show that the duration of treatment you predict is necessary is more effective than shorter term treatment?

Q: Does the research evidence show that therapy of the frequency you say is necessary is more effective than less frequent therapy sessions?

Q: Do the symptoms in cases of this kind sometimes subside once the lawsuit is concluded?

# CHAPTER 11

# Cross-Examination in Child Custody Cases

In child custody disputes, clinical testimony is usually oriented to the basic issue of the best interests of the child. This issue may revolve around questions of fitness or unfitness of a parent which might be detrimental to the child; however, in most cases both parents are found to be fit and the principal issue is which parent would provide the most advantages or benefits to the child's development. Recent trends in the professional literature and the law are in the direction of maximizing contacts between the child and both parents.

When the issue is unfitness, the clinical testimony usually revolves around a finding of psychopathology in one or the other of the parents, and the effect of such psychopathology on the child. All of the problems of psychiatric diagnosis or evaluation are relevant here, as well as predictions of psychiatrists and other mental health professionals. The problems of the clinical examination are almost invariably important in the child custody situation. In terms of situation effects, the break-up of a marriage, particularly where children are involved, is often a highly stressful situation for most normal people, both parents and children. Anger, anxiety, and defensiveness are common. In addition, there is a radical upheaval of the life of the parties. Often one moves out of the house and commences living in a new place and for those who remain, the character of life is altered by the absence of one important family member. It might be noted that DSM-IV describes marital break-up as a psychosocial problem that can affect diagnosis and prognosis.

Behavior observed under these circumstances certainly may not be representative of the individual's behavior under more normal, less highly stressful circumstances. Ordinarily, the marital problems which led to the divorce action will have existed for a period of time, usually years, prior to the filing of the divorce action so as to constitute situation effects during that period of time. Historical data obtained from the parties or from friends or relatives is likely to be biased. In addition, because it is necessary to go back for some period of time to get data concerning the behaviors in the more normal circumstances, the distortions of memory that occur with the passage of time constitute another problem in the data gathering. The problems of reliability and validity of diagnoses are obviously multiplied when multiple diagnoses have to be made as in the custody situation where each parent and child needs to be evaluated, further compounded by the need to evaluate interactions between each parent and child. In our experience, many clinicians simply did not spend enough time to make an adequate evaluation of the various parties. They rarely have made sufficient observation of the parents and children together to enable them to draw conclusions about the nature of the relationship. Even should adequate time be spent in these observations, the observation of the behavior of child and parent under these strained circumstances and the additional strained circumstance of the clinical examination will provide little basis for a valid assessment. Quite often, clinicians get no information from sources other than the parties, which is obviously of doubtful reliability in cases of this kind. Failure to adequately evaluate stepparents or potential stepparents or other surrogate parent figures, and the interaction between such persons and children, is very common—although such figures may play a role nearly as important, if not as important as the natural parents.

Examiner effects are also extremely important in custody cases. Because the evaluation almost always involves prediction and because prediction in this field is overwhelmingly speculative, there is enormous room for the biases of the clinician to operate. (See, for example, Psychologist, Case 1, Chapter 9, Volume I.) Many clinicians base their conclusions on unvalidated and speculative theories of child development. Many clinicians have biases concerning the appropriate role for women in today's world.

Frequently, clinicians concern themselves very little with pragmatic considerations such as the nature of living arrangements in the home and such matters.

An additional problem in custody cases is the fact that such cases are heard by a judge rather than a jury. While many judges are open-minded concerning the capabilities of clinicians, there are many others who have a strong tendency to defer to their judgment. With such judges, it is probably wise to focus the attack on any deficiencies of the examination and to produce an expert for your own side whose conclusions will disagree with those of the expert for the other side. It is worthwhile to advise your expert of the kinds of attack you plan to make on the examination conducted by the other side's expert and hope or encourage him to make sure that he is less vulnerable regarding such deficiencies. If psychological tests have been used, all of the attacks available on tests should be employed. In particular, if the MMPI has been used, it should be gone over item by item to determine if there are any items which directly contradict the conclusions of the clinician.

No assumption should be made concerning the lack of biases in the case of court-appointed experts who frequently appear in these cases. Although the bias that arises from being employed by one side or the other is absent, there are many other kinds of biases—social, personal, political, attitudinal, theoretical—that exist even within the presumably neutral court-appointed expert. In cases in which we have been involved, we have not yet found one in which evidence of bias was not apparent in the clinician's report. Where the clinician is not court-appointed but has received the case upon referral from one of the attorneys, it is important to determine what may have been said in connection with the referral. Often the attorney will bias the clinician by his description of the individuals involved. (For research evidence that such biases and preconceptions take place, see Temerlin and Trousdale in Chapter 5, Volume I.)

Where a psychiatric diagnosis of a child is involved, the lawyer should be aware that the reliabilities for diagnoses of children and adolescents almost uniformly fail to achieve the acceptable reliability levels.

There are different and competing theories of child development, each with a number of followers and with some research support; however, the existence of the competing theories indicates that none of them has been adequately validated through scientific research and therefore to the extent that the clinician relies on a particular theory, his opinion is necessarily speculative.

One of the most important things to have in mind is that there are few, if any, perfect parents. Most parents have some of the flaws or deficiencies that the clinician will describe but nevertheless manage to accomplish reasonably normal child rearing. In the absence of gross significant disparities between the parents, the child is likely to grow up reasonably normal regardless of which one has custody so far as the personal characteristics of the parents are concerned. This is particularly true with adolescents who have arrived at a point in life where parents likely have relatively less influence on their development and peer associations considerably more impact. Often, the clinician's conclusions represent a very fine distinction between one parent and another which is probably not warranted by the state of knowledge that exists. If the point can be established that there will likely be little difference which parent has custody so far as the clinical variables are concerned, this leaves the Court free to make a decision based on other, non-psychiatric, considerations.

Where there is no substantial showing of formal psychopathology it can be brought out that the child has been living with both of these parents without any unusual detriment other than perhaps for such disturbance as may be associated with the marital discord and break-up.

## THE LITERATURE

While the general literature applies to custody evaluations, this is an area in which the literature has been particularly negative.

Q: Doctor, isn't there a substantial body of scientific and professional literature to the effect the mental health field lacks an adequate body of knowledge for rendering opinions in custody cases?

Q: Isn't there a substantial body of scientific and professional literature to the effect that clinicians exceed the limits of scientific knowledge when they do custody evaluations?

Q: Isn't there a substantial body of scientific and professional literature to the effect that there is a lack of standard (or adequate) methods for doing custody evaluations?

## APA GUIDELINES

In 1994, the American Psychological Association adopted Guidelines for Child Custody Evaluations in Divorce Proceedings (see Chapter 25, Volume II). While not mandatory, they are built upon the more general ethical principles, most of which are mandatory (see Chapter 2, Volume III). In any event, clinicians who do not abide by the guidelines should need to defend such deviation.

Q: Are you familiar with the APA Guidelines for Child Custody Evaluations?

Q: Doctor, what education, training, experience and supervision have you had in the area of child and family development? (Same question for child and family psychopathology and for the impact of divorce on children.)

If answers indicate less than the guidelines call for, questions can be asked to bring out the deficiency.

Q: Do you use current knowledge of scientific and professional developments? (This would seem to require familiarity with the literature.)

Q: (If applicable) Don't the guidelines state you should not do these evaluations with someone you have had a prior relationship (therapy or other) with?

Q: What methods of data gathering did you use?

Q: (If applicable) Don't the guidelines call for use of multiple methods?

Q: How many sources did you get (some important information) from? (Guidelines require at least two if important and reliability is questionable).

Q: Have you acknowledged any limitations in the methods or data you used?

Q: Don't the guidelines state you should do that?

Q: (If applicable) Don't the guidelines state you should not render opinions about anyone you have not personally evaluated?

Q: Are you familiar with the APA *Standards for Educational and Psychological Testing*?

Q: Did you adhere to the APA *Standards for Educational and Psychological Testing*?

## THEORY AND PRINCIPLES

Q: Doctor, Doesn't the scientific and professional literature indicate that within the disciplines dealing with child development, there are differing theories (schools of thought) regarding child development?

Q: Could you briefly describe the major theories (or differences among major theories)?

Q: Which theory or school of thought or position do you favor? (See Cross-examination in general for those who describe themselves as eclectic.)

Q: None of these theories have received full validation through scientific research methods, have they?

## RELIABILITY AND VALIDITY

Q: Your conclusions and recommendations in this case are essentially of a predictive nature, are they not?

Q: There is not a substantial body of scientific and professional literature indicating that psychiatric (psychological) predictions generally are made with a very high degree of accuracy, is that correct?

Q: In fact, doesn't the scientific and professional literature indicate that is one of the weakest areas of your field?

Q: In fact, there are some studies of psychiatric prediction which show that the prediction is more likely to be wrong than right, isn't that correct? (Affirmative answers to the above questions are the correct ones, but the lawyer should not expect the clinical witness to be simple and direct. He will probably wish to offer some qualifying statements. These will have to be dealt with according to their nature in any given case. However, after the witness has made whatever explanation he cares to, he should be drawn back by a question re-establishing the fundamental facts as indicated above.)

## THE CLINICAL EXAMINATION

Q: As part of your clinical examination, do you observe the behavior of the person being examined?

Q: Do you observe such things as the person's mood, affect, emotional responsiveness, manner of verbalization, thought processes?

Q: Does that information play a part in forming your conclusions?

Q: Is the break-up of a marriage where there are children involved a stressful situation for many people?

Q: Can the stresses and feelings associated with the break-up of the marriage have an effect on the behavior of people in that situation?

Q: That behavior, mood, affect might have been different prior to the emergence of the marital problems, is that so?

Q: And it might be different once the matter has been resolved and the people have had a chance to settle into their new life?

Q: You did not have an opportunity to observe the behaviors of the people in this case prior to the break-up of the marriage, did you?

Q: So that so far as their functioning under more normal circumstances, you would not have that important set of data, is that correct?

Q: Did you obtain information from anyone other than the parties involved? (If the witness has not, questions can proceed to bring out the fact that he is relying solely on information from people, at least so far as the parents are concerned, who may be motivated to misrepresent or whose emotional involvement in this situation may cause them to distort the facts.) (An affirmative answer calls for an exploration of possible biases of the informant, questions as to the informant's degree of opportunity to observe and problems of what lay people would attend to and remember.)

Q: There is a considerable amount of scientific and professional literature to the effect that the examiner's biases, values or attitudes influence the examination and the conclusions, is that not so? (Where there are demonstrable bases for bias, questions could follow to bring out such probable biases. See, for example, the case of Psychologist 1, in Chapter 9 of Volume I, where the examiner was a Ph.D. psychologist and father also had a Ph.D. The data obtained on the father and also obtained from the qualifications of the psychologist show both to be highly achievement-oriented people, preference for large city residence, and so on.) (In the alternative where the biasing data is quite clear, it may be just as well not to question the witness, which could allow him to try to explain it away, but to simply present it in argument to the Court.)

## PARENT CHARACTERISTICS

Q: There are not many perfect parents, are there, doctor?

Q: Most parents have some characteristics that are less than desirable, isn't that correct?

Q: And most children manage to accomplish reasonably normal development anyway, isn't that correct?

Q: (If indicated by the facts) The child in this case does not show any serious psychological problems (possibly other than upset over the marital break-up), does he?

Q: And he has been living with both of these parents all of his life, isn't that correct?

Q: In fact the child has been doing pretty well considering the marital discord in his home, hasn't he?

Q: Wouldn't that suggest that he is psychologically sound?

Q: And he would be likely to do all right with either of the parents, isn't that correct?

Many clinicians continue to view gender of the parent as an important variable. Research in this area has not substantiated such a view, and it is, at best, equivocal.

In some cases, the issue is not that of custody per se, but concerns the nature and quantity of visitation. Generally speaking, the considerations are the same in either case. There are problems of situation and examiner effects, biases of witnesses, continuing discord between parents, and so on.

# CHAPTER 12

# Motion to Bar or Limit Testimony

The contents of Volumes I and II strongly suggest that psychiatry and psychology have not yet reached the state of knowledge and methods which would allow practitioners to qualify as experts according to legal criteria. At the minimum, those materials create such massive doubt concerning knowledge and methods as to preclude the granting of the status of experts in legal matters. However, the fact is that members of these professions have been accorded such status. Efforts to alter the situation must be viewed as a long-shot, uphill battle at best. We had considered eliminating this chapter. However, the Supreme Court decision in *Daubert vs. Merrell, Dow* (see Chapter 1, Volume I) has potentially changed the nature of the game, at least in federal courts and such state jurisdictions as elect to follow it. In any event, we believe it may be valuable to make a motion to bar or limit the testimony of these professionals in almost all cases. We will try to explain the rationale for making such motions which are likely to be denied by describing several purposes or potential gains that may be achieved.

A full dress motion complete with statements of all of the deficiencies of psychiatry and clinical psychology supported by documentation will sometimes persuade the judge to grant wide latitude in the cross-examination of such experts. Denial of the motion is usually accompanied by a statement that the issues raised go to the weight rather than the admissibility of the evidence. Having made such a statement, the judge is in an awkward position concerning his intellectual integrity if he were to refuse to allow extensive questioning on these matters which he has described as going to the weight of the testimony. In fact, one of the points to be raised in such motions is that if the testimony is allowed, it will be necessary to extensively pursue these lines of inquiry so that the trier of fact will be able to appropriately judge the weight to be given to the testimony.

Even if the motion does not succeed in precluding the clinical testimony, it may be successful in persuading the judge to limit the scope of such testimony. For example, there is the overwhelming case to be made regarding any testimony concerning mental condition prior to the examination or as to the ultimate questions in criminal cases.

One question is almost invariably raised by jurists, lawyers and clinicians who acknowledge that the deficiencies exist and that they are serious. In response to the assertion that clinical testimony should be barred, they ask who, if not psychiatrists and psychologists, will provide evidence on the issues that the law has created. The implication is that there are issues of mental state or condition and there is no one better qualified than psychiatrists and psychologists. We view this as an example of illogical, inconsistent, reverse thinking. There are other issues in litigation for which the testimony of experts would seem desirable. Truthfulness of a litigant, for example, is one such issue. There is no evidence that there is any better way of determining this issue than through the use of the polygraph. Yet, the courts have consistently refused to admit such evidence, citing the flaws and deficiencies attributed to that procedure, none of which are in any way worse than those of psychiatry and psychology. Expertise cannot be established by default. If it could, there would be experts in a multitude of areas where no demonstrable expertise exists. Unfortunately, myths and superstitions are seldom destroyed by facts.

Although there may be benefits derived from making such a motion, there may also be disadvantages. Some lawyers prefer not to reveal their intentions so far as challenge to the testimony is concerned, preferring to wait and do it on cross-examination. The more thorough the motion, the more will be revealed to the witness and the more opportunity he will have to better prepare to meet these issues. We do not view this disadvantage as a serious one, particularly where the motion is accompanied by a voir dire examination. The responses of the witness will be on record and should he change them later, his credibility will be affected thereby.

We favor an approach which outlines all of the deficiencies of psychiatry and psychology in a written motion supported by the references contained in Volumes I and II. A caveat is in order. Some of the references we have cited indicate that while the authors state or refer to certain deficiencies, they are generally favorable toward clinical and even toward forensic evaluations by clinicians. As there are plenty of references cited without using ones of that type, the lawyer may feel that his brief is weakened by including such references and may choose not to include them.

We think the most effective way to make the motion, in addition to describing the general deficiencies and the authorities in support of the deficiencies, is to conduct a voir dire examination of each expert. Sometimes they will concede the deficiencies. At other times, in their attempts to argue the state of the literature, they will demonstrate such a lack of knowledge or candor that they may be disqualified on that ground alone. It is useful in connection with these motions to present testimony of consultant/experts who will be able to verify the state of the literature as well as pointing out flaws of procedure or conclusions in the instant case.

## FORM AND CONTENTS OF THE MOTION

The discussion which follows is oriented toward testimony by psychiatrists, but with some obvious modifications it can be adapted for psychologists.

The form of the motion may vary somewhat from jurisdiction to jurisdiction but in general should lead off with a statement of the intention of the motion and a recapitulation of the law as it pertains to expert evidence in the particular jurisdiction. The motion should then set forth the deficiencies in general with appropriate documentation. We prefer to place dicta from appellate court decisions after this material, but some attorneys may feel that it may have more impact at the beginning of the motion. Given a demonstration of serious doubt concerning psychiatric expertise, the motion might conclude with descriptions of demonstrable errors of omission or commission in the specific case at hand. The question arises as to how complete the documentation should be. Some attorneys prefer a few striking quotations to document a point. Others prefer to recite as many references as possible. The issue is a question of how lengthy one can be without running the risk of losing the judge's attention. A possible compromise is to cite a few striking references and then add that the point is further documented by additional references, simply citing them without quoting them.[1] The body of the motion should contain the points described below.

## 1. Psychiatry Lacks a Validated Body of Knowledge

Psychiatry is not an established science and lacks a substantial body of established or accepted facts, principles or theories. Psychiatry consists of a conglomeration of highly disputed and conjectural theories, schools of thought and principles each differing from the other and each of which has substantial numbers of followers. None of these theories

---

[1] We have had to face the same problem in connection with preparation of this chapter. In order to avoid undue length and excessive repetition of materials already provided in Volumes I and II, we have elected to omit the documenting material from the points described in this chapter. The reader who wishes to be inclusive in his motion can easily find large numbers of references under the appropriate chapter title in Volumes I and II. The one exception we have made to this is in the presentation of appellate court dicta.

has been validated through appropriate and reliable methods. If psychiatry can be considered a science at all, it must be considered a young and emerging science, too young for use in a court of law. Psychiatric data and principles must be considered still in the experimental stage. They have not crossed into the twilight zone between the experimental and the demonstrable. The psychoanalytic approach which has had wide acceptance in American psychiatry is a highly disputed theory which despite its relative popularity cannot be considered to be accepted among the scientific community, nor has it been scientifically validated. Indeed, the literature generally indicates that it is not testable (thereby failing one of the *Daubert* tests). Other theories of behavior or personality have not been adopted by a majority of mental health professionals. Thus, although it is recognized that experts in other fields may at times disagree in the application of established principles to the facts in a particular case, the deficiency in the case of psychiatry is more serious as there is not even agreement as to the correct principles ("Psychiatry as an agreed on body of knowledge hardly exists."—L.L. Havens, Twentieth Century Psychiatry: A View from the Sea, *The American Journal of Psychiatry*, Volume 138, No. 10, 1981, pp. 1279-1287.)

Psychiatry has failed to accomplish even the most basic step in the establishment of any science which is an adequate system for the classification of its data. The *Diagnostic and Statistical Manual of Mental Disorders* is the officially endorsed system, published by the American Psychiatric Association. Its history is one of frequent revisions such that each edition becomes obsolete before there is enough time for an adequate body of research to accumulate. With each revision, research done with the prior version(s) has to be discarded or redone to prove that it generalizes to the new edition. Thus, it is constantly in the state of being "experimental." The authors of the current version, DSM-IV (See Frances et al., 1991, Chapter 4, Volume I), note there is controversy over whether the manual should be "categorical," which it is now, or "dimensional" (quantitative), which it now is not. This controversy, however, suggests they do not really know what approach is best. They note that the more field trials (which they employ) strive for internal consistency and research rigor, the less likely they will achieve external validity. They express concern that so little validation was available for many of the most crucial decisions. They also describe their current classification decisions as "temporary." The manual itself warns that when DSM-IV material is used for forensic purposes, there is a significant risk that diagnostic information will be misused or misunderstood. The manual states that because impairments, abilities, and disabilities vary widely within each diagnostic category assignment to a particular diagnosis does not imply a specific level of impairment or disability. Given that impairment or disability are the forensic issues to which psychiatric evidence is most often directed, the manual declares itself unable to answer such questions. The frequent changes in the diagnostic manuals mean that litigation is often resolved on the basis of diagnoses that might be appropriate at the time but would be inappropriate within a short time later.

If psychiatry is in a constant state of flux and lacks an agreed on body of knowledge and lack an adequate classification system, how can it meet any minimally rational test for admission as expert evidence?

## 2. Psychiatry Is Not a Typical Field of Medicine

Psychiatry is unlike traditional fields of medicine. There are no scientifically established and clearly defined mental disease entities other than neurophysiological pathology. The subject matter of psychiatry is not disease in any common meaning of the term but rather involves problems of psycho-social adjustment or deficiencies of learning. In the absence of demonstrable organic pathology there is no basis for including problems of psycho-social adjustment within the province of medicine.

## 3. The Psychiatrist Lacks Appropriate Education and Training

The subject with which the psychiatrist deals is that of psychology or perhaps sociology. Medical training is largely irrelevant in problems in these areas and does not qualify anyone as an expert in psychology and/or sociology. The psychiatrist gets little formal education in psychology and sociology.

## 4. Psychiatric Opinions Are Speculative & Conjectural and Cannot Be Made with Reasonable Medical Certainty

There is no substantial body of scientific evidence demonstrating that psychiatric diagnoses and evaluations can be made with a high degree of validity (accuracy). There is a substantial body of scientific and professional literature indicating that psychiatric diagnosis and evaluations are seriously deficient in validity. There is a substantial body of scientific evidence demonstrating that the psychiatrists can neither predict nor postdict behavior or mental condition with a reasonable degree of accuracy. There is a body of evidence indicating that there is as much or more chance that the psychiatrist will be incorrect as there is that he will be correct. Stated differently, it is not infrequent that one could achieve equal accuracy by flipping coins. Therefore, it cannot be said that psychiatric evaluations can be made with reasonable certainty. For lack of reasonable certainty in psychiatric evaluation and diagnosis, it must be concluded at the present time that psychiatric diagnoses and evaluations are speculative and conjectural and therefore are inadmissible. The validity of psychiatric diagnoses and evaluations has almost never been demonstrated to be higher than the reliability and validity of evaluations based on the use of the polygraph and the latter have consistently been held to be inadmissible.

## 5.   Psychiatric Experience Is Not a Basis for Expertise

The psychiatrist is not qualified by virtue of his experience to make assessments or evaluations concerning mental condition or state. There is a substantial body of research evidence demonstrating that reliability and validity of psychiatric evaluation are not related to the experience of the evaluator and that relatively inexperienced evaluators are about as reliable and accurate as those with considerable experience.

## 6.   Unreliability of the Clinical Examination

The psychiatric examination is fraught with danger of distortion, bias and inaccuracy in the collection, perception, memory and interpretation of the data obtained in such an examination.

It has been scientifically demonstrated that the data obtained in the clinical examination are readily subject to the influence of temporary situational variables that do not accurately reflect the behavior or mental state of the individual under other conditions. These factors include the time, place and nature of the clinical situation, the purpose of the examination as perceived by the subject, the theoretical orientation of the examiner, the values and attitudes of the examiner, the personality of the examiner and the race and socio-economic status of the subject and the examiner. What the examiner perceives, remembers and records is also subject to influence, distortion and bias due to the theoretical orientation of the examiner, the values and attitudes of the examiner, and the race, sex, social class and personal characteristics of the subject. Further, the interpretation of the data is subject to influence, distortion and bias due to these same factors. Therefore, essentially no confidence can be placed in the data produced in the clinical examination, in the psychiatrist's perception and recall of the data of the clinical examination, nor in the psychiatrist's interpretation of the data of the clinical examination.

## 7.   Psychiatrists Are Not More Accurate
## in Psychological Assessments than Laymen

The scientific and professional literature does not support a belief that psychiatrists are more accurate than laymen in evaluating psychological condition.

There is some scientific evidence demonstrating that psychiatrists are not appreciably better than laymen in making psychological evaluations.

"If the subject is one of common knowledge and the facts can be intelligibly described to the jury and they can form a reasonable opinion for themselves, the opinion of an expert will be rejected." (31 Am. Jur.2d 494) In several cases courts have held that the jury could disregard psychiatric testimony and accept testimony of lay witnesses on the issue of insanity (see *People vs. Teague*, 439 N.E. 2d 1066; *People vs. Jones*, 440 N.E.2d 261; and *Taylor vs. State*, 440 N.E.2d 1109). These cases constitute judicial recognition that the issue of insanity or the ability to distinguish right from wrong can be determined as well, or better, from lay testimony as from psychiatric testimony. On that basis, therefore, psychiatric testimony does not meet that test for admissibility.

## 8. Psychiatric Testimony Confuses and Misleads

Psychiatric testimony tends to confuse and mislead rather than assist jurors and provide more valid conclusions than their own. It is well known that in a large percentage of cases jurors tend to disregard psychiatric testimony, particularly in cases where there is conflicting testimony. Further, in view of the problems and deficiencies stated above, the introduction of psychiatric testimony will necessarily lead to extensive collateral investigations on the validity of such testimony. The too hasty acceptance of psychiatric testimony, considering its stage of development, has brought complications and abuses that over-balance whatever utility it may be assumed to have. The present necessity for elaborate exposition of the deficiencies of psychiatric theory and demonstration of its lack of reliability, together with the problems of the psychiatric examination and the need for attacks on the soundness of its underlying theories, may easily result in the trial of the psychiatrist rather than the issue and the cause.

## 9. The Gap Between Diagnosis and Legal Issue

Even if psychiatrists could accurately diagnose mental disorders there is virtually no scientific evidence of a relationship between such conditions and any legal issue. (This statement would not apply in psychic injury cases.)

## 10. No Relationship Between Credentials & Competence or Accuracy

There is virtually no scientific evidence demonstrating a relationship between the psychiatrist's credentials, including Board Certification, and the competence with which he conducts his examination or the accuracy of his conclusions.

## 11. (If the Litigant Is a Member of an Ethnic Minority Group) Lack of Adequate Normative Data for Ethnic Minority Members

All of the problems described above are compounded when the litigant is a member of an ethnic minority group. There are serious doubts as to whether adequate normative data exist with which to evaluate the mental condition of such individuals. (This statement can be altered to apply to other special populations based on such variables as age, education or gender.)

## 12. Lack of General Scientific Acceptance: Conflicting Literature

Even where there is conflicting scientific and professional literature on any of the above points, the very existence of such conflicts demonstrates that the issues are in doubt and such doubts, within the scientific and professional community, render the testimony inadmissible on the grounds that it has not reached the level of general acceptance within the scientific community and has not crossed from the experimental to the demonstrable. The jury is required to decide scientific controversies concerning psychiatric issues which the scientific and professional communities have not been able to resolve.

## 13. The Dubious Status of Psychiatric Expertise

Appellate courts have rarely been asked to rule on the admissibility of psychiatric evidence. Therefore, there are virtually no appellate court opinions denying admission of psychiatric opinion (but see below, *Harper vs. State*). However, there are several appellate court opinions which at least by way of dicta describe such evidence in terms that would render it inadmissible.

In *Washington vs. the United States*, 390 F.2d 444, (1967), the court states (p. 452), "Even after McDonald, though we allowed the experts to state whether they felt the defendant had a mental disease or defect, we assumed that the expert could separate the medical judgment which he was supposed to make from the legal and moral judgments which he was not supposed to make. It has become abundantly apparent that this theory has not worked out."

In *In Re Ballay*, 482 F.2d, 648, (1973), the court states that psychiatric testimony either diagnosing mental disorder or predicting future dangerousness is "far from satisfactory" and "has never been characterized by a high degree of accuracy."

In *People vs. Burnick*, 14 Cal.3d 306 (1975), the California Supreme Court states, "It must be conceded that psychiatrists still experience considerable difficulty in confidently and accurately diagnosing mental illness. Yet those difficulties are multiplied manifold when the psychiatrists venture from diagnosis to prognosis and undertake to predict the consequences of such illness." (p. 325)

In *Smith vs. Schlesinger*, 13 F.2d 462 (D.C. Cir. 1975), the court states, "the literature concerning impact of social value judgments upon psychiatric diagnosis is immense," (p. 475) and the court states further, "Psychiatric judgments may disguise wittingly or unwittingly, political or social biases of psychiatrists."

In *Suggs vs. La Vallee*, 570 Federal Reporter 2d (1978), (pp. 1092-1120) the concurring opinion of Judge Kaufman refers to the problem presented by the case as "an emerging and highly significant problem in the law, namely, the troubled relationship between the vagaries of psychiatric evaluation and the difficulties of judicial determinations of incompetence." Judge Kaufman states further, "Of course, psychiatrists are invariably enlisted to aid in such determinations, yet psychiatry is at best an inexact science if, indeed, it is a science, lacking the coherent set of proven underlying values necessary for ultimate decisions on knowledge or incompetence."

In *Conservatorship of Roulet*, 23 Cal.3d 219 (1979) (p. 234), the Court states, "'Mental illness' is generally acknowledged to be a vague and uncertain concept. Categories of mental disease are notoriously unclear, often overlap, and frequently change. The experts themselves often disagree on what is an appropriate diagnosis."

## 14. The Position of the American Psychiatric Association Concerning Lack of Demonstrated Expertise

In *Tarasoff vs. The Regents of the University of California*, 17 C.3d 425 (1975), the American Psychiatric Association filed an amicus brief joined by several other mental health organizations. In this brief, the American Psychiatric Association chastises the court for making an assumption that mental health professionals are more qualified than the general public to predict future violent behavior. The brief cites authorities to the effect that the assumption that the psychiatrist can accurately predict dangerous behavior lacks any empirical support and they also quote authority to the effect that if the psychiatrist or any other behavioral scientist were asked to show proof of his predictive skills, objective data could not be offered. Thus, in its brief, the American Psychiatric Association seems to set for the courts a standard of demonstrable validity as the criterion of expertise. Such validity cannot be demonstrated in other than organically based conditions. The brief seems to clearly warn against assumptions by the courts concerning expertise that has not been empirically demonstrated.

### 15. Verifiable Expertise as the Appropriate Test

In *Harper vs. State,* GA., 292 S.E.2d 389, 1982, the Georgia Supreme Court rejected the longstanding criterion from the *Frye* case of "general acceptance within the scientific community." The court substituted in its place a determination as to whether the procedure or technique has reached a scientific stage of verifiable certainty. It is here submitted that with the advances in scientific techniques and methods even within the behavioral sciences that this is the proper test for admissibility. It is further submitted that no psychiatrist nor psychologist be permitted to testify as to any matter regarding which it has not been scientifically demonstrated that such an opinion can be rendered with verifiable certainty.

## PSYCHOLOGISTS

If the case involves a psychologist, obviously the points concerning medical education are not relevant. However, in the case of the psychologist, if he has employed psychological testing, some or all of the tests may be vulnerable to challenges based on lack of adequate validation, particularly for the purpose they are employed for in the particular case.

## *DAUBERT* ISSUES

One of the criteria of admissibility cited in *Daubert* is that the court should consider known or potential error rate. There is no published research establishing a known or potential error rate for most of the conclusions psychiatrists proffer.

Another criterion in *Daubert* is that the theory or technique can be (and has been) tested. There is no basis for believing that any current theory or technique for determining that a person could not distinguish right from wrong at some time prior to the examination can be or has been tested.

## DEFICIENCIES IN THE SPECIFIC CASE

Within a framework of the inherent general deficiencies of psychiatric evaluation, any deficiencies of the examination in the specific case become magnified. While such deficiencies are usually viewed as going to the weight of the evidence, given the framework of doubt as to the validity of psychiatric evaluation at best, such deficiencies of procedure ought to be relevant on the issue of admissibility also.

Revelation of such deficiencies may enable a judge who is favorably disposed to granting the motion but fears to do so on the general grounds to disqualify the particular witness as either lacking competence or having performed a poor examination; that is, while the judge may fear reversal if he were to bar the testimony on the general deficiencies of psychiatry alone, he may be less fearful in employing his discretion to determine that this particular witness does not qualify as an expert in view of the deficiencies of his examination that are revealed (e.g., errors of administration, scoring or interpretation; ignorance of psychometric properties of a test; ignorance of normative data). Along the same line, a demonstration on voir dire in connection with the motion showing that the clinician is not familiar with the relevant literature such as that provided in Volumes I and II may also enable the judge to disqualify the particular witness on the grounds that he is not adequately qualified or informed in his field.

# CHAPTER 13

# Responses to Criticisms of the Fourth Edition

This special note is being written so that readers will not be caught unaware or unprepared to deal, if necessary, with some publications that appeared after the publication of the fourth edition of *Coping with Psychiatric and Psychological Testimony*. One is the end document (until now) of a series of publications involving Dr. Joseph Matarazzo, a former president of the American Psychological Association, and ourselves. Another is the publication of a book by Dr. Stanley Brodsky, Professor of Psychology at the University of Alabama. Both of these psychologists are critical of (some of) our writings. While there is some overlap, these critics differ considerably in their approach and therefore, to the extent possible, we will try to deal with them separately. A third and somewhat different approach is taken by Rogers et al.

However, it may be anticipated that other publications will appear that also attempt to denigrate or counter this book. Probably, information in this note can be adapted to any such publication, as there seem to be some consistent themes in such works.

The most prevalent attack seems to be that the book is one-sided. This is true for the reasons stated in the preface and in this note—that in the presence of so much negative literature, and/or lack of adequate research support, generally there is too much doubt on basic issues to give much credence to mental health expert testimony. This can be brought out in regard to most critiques. The very large amount of literature cited in the book does exist and cannot legitimately be denied.

A second theme has to do with statements that question whether such testimony should be admissible under rules of evidence. This is not really the major thrust of this book and while such views may have been tenable under older rules, we do not necessarily argue that this is the case under more recent and liberal rules (but see *Daubert,* Chapter 1, Volume I).

The reader should be aware that at times critics treat as identical the 2,000 page, three-volume set of books, and a four-page article by Faust and Ziskin in *Science*, which had space and citation constraints that the book did not have. Any witness discussing our work should be asked to specify the work to which he or she is referring.

## MATARAZZO

Some chronology is necessary in order to make sense out of the Matarazzo-Ziskin and Faust exchanges. In the main text of the 4th Edition, published in April of 1988, we cite statements made by Matarazzo in a number of publications on issues of reliability and validity of psychiatric or psychological diagnosis or evaluations. Thus, on page 420,[1] we cite his chapter in a textbook on clinical diagnosis (Matarazzo, J.D., "The Interview: Its reliability and validity in psychiatric diagnosis." In B.B. Wolman [Ed.], *Clinical Diagnosis of Mental Disorders: A Handbook*. New York: Plenum Press, 1978). On page 424, we cite an article by Matarazzo (1986a), a reply to that article by Fowler and Butcher (1986), and a response to Fowler and Butcher by Matarazzo (1986b). (See Volume I, pp. 438 and 441, for these references.) In July of 1988, the journal *Science,* Volume 241, pp. 31-35) carried an article by Faust and Ziskin titled "The Expert Witness in Psychology and Psychiatry." In Matarazzo's presidential address to the American Psychological Association presented in August of 1990 and published in the *American Psychologist* in that same year ("Psychological assessment versus psychological testing: Validation from Binet to the school clinic and courtroom." *American Psychologist, 45,* 999-1017), he commends us for "accurately, candidly, and commendably" stating in the preface to our three-volume book that it consisted almost entirely of negative literature and that there is some supportive literature which we did not include because we thought it irrelevant in a legal context (p. 1013). He then chastises us for omitting from our *Science* article a similar statement and expresses great concern because of the great prestige of *Science*, suggesting that the article might get more credence than if it had been published in a journal with a less prestigious reputation in the scholarly and scientific community. In some ways, we are happy to have this expressed view of Dr. Matarazzo that *Science* is a highly prestigious journal that lends considerable credibility to a work, although we are not entirely

---

[1] Page numbers for *Coping* in this chapter refer to the Fourth Edition and the 1991 Supplement. These same references can be located in the Fifth Edition by referring to the Index of Authors.

convinced that the article is more credible for being published in *Science* than it would be if published in any other journal which employs peer review. (However, one of us—Ziskin—would like to point out that if publication in *Science* lends an author credibility, then the reader should be aware that the co-author of the 4th Edition—Faust—has had a second article which he co-authored published in *Science* [March, 1989].)

Prior to Matarazzo's 1990 article, he, as President elect, and Ray Fowler, as then President of APA, published in *Science* a response to our *Science* article. This response and our response to their response appeared together in a November, 1988 issue. Their response is focused principally on the issue of the "overly narrow conclusion that the courts should consider excluding psychologists and psychiatrists as expert witnesses." (p. 8) Since Supreme Court Justice Byron White's opinion in *Barefoot vs. Estelle* (see main text) to the effect that no one will be denied admission as an expert unless they have been proved to be "always" wrong, not just wrong most of the time, this issue seems to be academic. For that reason, and because the focus of the Fowler/Matarazzo response is on the *Science* article only and not on our major work, *Coping with Psychiatric and Psychological Testimony* (hereafter referred to as *Coping*), we feel no need to deal further with that article than we have already done in our response published in *Science*. However, as it will become relevant below, we would like to point out that in their response, Fowler and Matarazzo refer to answers to clinical questions, taking into account many complex factors and providing as complete a "picture" of behavior as possible. We would ask the reader to keep this in mind when we discuss Matarazzo's statements concerning the ten- to twenty-page *portrait* of the individual typically involved in expert evidence.

Following Matarazzo's 1990 article, we submitted a response to be published in the *American Psychologist* with the understanding that Matarazzo would have an opportunity to respond to our response. Our reply and Matarazzo's reply to our reply were published in the August 1991 issue of the *American Psychologist*.

It is advisable for readers to be able to deal with our reply (1991) to Matarazzo's 1990 article and his reply (1991) to our reply.

In his 1990 article, Matarazzo complains that in our *Science* article, we failed to "accurately, candidly, and commendably" include a statement that is in our book that the book consists almost entirely of negative literature but that there may be literature that is supportive of forensic psychiatry and psychology. We noted, however, that he omitted the immediately following paragraph, in our book, which explained why we viewed such supportive evidence as irrelevant in the legal context, as it would ultimately require a jury to decide scientific and professional issues that the scientists and professionals have not been able to resolve.

We also noted that the *Science* article was not altogether devoid of mention of supportive evidence, although indicating there was less supportive than negative evidence. For example, we noted that some studies on diagnosis demonstrated more satisfactory levels of reliability, the actuarial method is of proven utility; some studies show that professionals reach more accurate clinical judgments than laypersons (although other studies show otherwise), and indices developed for the MMPI are sensitive to the exaggeration or simulation of disorder. We also called attention to the fact that the focus of our article was on clinicians in their role as expert witnesses and not in their many other roles (e.g., as therapists).

A substantial portion of his article that is of relevance for us deals with the issue of reliability. We would note that in his article, Matarazzo states that about 50% of the studies published in the past decade show good to very good reliability. We pointed out the obvious, then, that the other half do not show good or better reliability, i.e., are not so good, and we raise the question as to what a jury is to do with this kind of unresolved basic issue. Indeed, in their own reply to our *Science* article, Spitzer (Chair of the *DSM* Committee) et al. (*Science*, November, 1988) noted that the reliability of psychiatric diagnosis continues to be a problem. Matarazzo goes on to discuss validity, which is the principal issue as far as courtroom evidence is concerned. Reliability, i.e., agreement among clinicians, does not establish that they are correct. After noting that less research is available on validity than on reliability, Matarazzo stated, "Therefore, in regard to the critical issue that the validity of *DSM-III*-type differential diagnoses has not been adequately established, Faust and Ziskin and I are in agreement." (p. 1015) However, he then accuses us of taking passages from his previous writings out of context, stating, "They correctly quote my belief that currently there is no body of research that indicates that psychological assessment across the whole domain is valid or is other than clinical art." (p. 1015) He then indicates that what we neglected to include in those same passages was his "equally relevant opinion" that in that regard, psychology is little different from other professions such as engineering or medicine. We responded that psychiatric and psychological assessments cannot be made more valid by noting that other areas may have similar problems.

In his article, Matarazzo further stated, "What I am discussing in the present section is the reliability (and thus the potential validity) of a discrete, one- or two-word differential diagnosis (e.g., manic depression, obsessive-compulsive disorder, and schizophrenia). That is, because no such body of research has yet been published, I am not discussing the clinician-to-clinician reliability and thus the validity of the personal, social, medical, and psychological portrait of the individual that is typically contained in the comprehensive 10- to 20-page psychological or neuropsychological assessment of a patient involved in the increasing number of cases also being adjudicated in our nation's courtrooms." (p. 1012) We noted that the 10- to 20-page assessment or portrait that Matarazzo says is the typical forensic contribution of clinicians lacks published reliability (and, according to him, thus potential validity) research. In describing his purpose in the article, he then goes on to say, "Rather, it was to point out that because a beginning scientific scaffolding currently exists, reliable and valid psychological assessment, especially of cognitive functioning in brain injury, *is* being carried out. In the earlier sections of this article I have been critical of my own work and that of other clinicians involved in such assessment; however, even without adequate validation that research of the type I predict will be done before long, my experience in the courtroom has persuaded me that when such assessment is well done, it is patently obvious to all involved...that what such a psychologist-expert-witness concluded was valid (true) within the reasonable degree of certainty required in such litigation." (p. 1015) We then commented that his prediction of imminent adequate validation appears to be another indicator that validation has not yet been accomplished. He stated further, "Research published much earlier showed that the types of one- or two-word differential diagnoses, characterizations, and predictions then extant were judged to be lacking in validity. Reviews of more current studies...including an excellent recent update of the use of one's head instead of formulas...reaffirm that conclusion." (p. 1016) Note that this is the third statement in this particular article in which Matarazzo states either that validity is unknown or has been shown to be poor. He goes on, "However, I know of no research...to date regarding the validity of the psychological portraits offered as expert opinion of the type involved in the two aforementioned cases: that is, assessment done by a well-trained clinician familiar with the types of literature I discussed earlier in this article and one who takes such diagnosis as seriously as is suggested by..." (others and himself). We point out that he has again stated that he knows of no research regarding such validity. We stated, "Need we state the obvious—that without such research on such validity, the validity is unknown. If the validity is unknown, testimony based on it should be given no weight in the courtroom." (p. 881) He then goes on to describe his "hope that empirical research on such state-of-the-art psychological assessment will soon be undertaken." (p. 1016) Again, he seems to be saying the research has not yet been done. We stated our opinion that belief is not a substitute for the needed research. We note that he has now in several different places and at several times and in different contexts made similar statements with regard to validity. Given these numerous statements, we feel that no credible case can be made for his challenge to our works, whether they include or do not include a disclaimer concerning the positive literature, inasmuch as Matarazzo has too often stated that such evidence on the key issue—validity—does not exist.

In his reply (1991) to our reply, Matarazzo notes that in his 1990 article, he included two serious criticisms of the writings of Ziskin and Faust. First, in reference to our *Science* article, he argues that we violated a sacred standard by not including a disclaimer of the type that appears in the preface to our book concerning the focus on negative literature. It is clear that his criticism in this regard is not related to the book but only to the *Science* article and we feel we have dealt with that above. We remind the reader that our article was reviewed on behalf of *Science* by one or more editors and peer reviewers who elected to publish it despite the absence of any such disclaimer. Apparently, the reviewer(s) did not feel such a disclaimer was necessary or that its absence violated a "sacred standard."

His second major criticism of our writings is that when we refer to his opinions regarding psychological assessment, we use selective passages that do not reflect what he has communicated in his writing. He urges readers to compare the statements we have quoted concerning reliability and validity with some passages which he asserts are only several of many examples from his article that accurately reflect his views in the context of the whole article. The first of these statements is, "Specifically, it is my position that, after years of unacceptably low levels of agreement, the test-retest reliability of clinician-to-clinician diagnosis for a number of disorders has improved considerably during the past decade. Although more improvement is necessary and current trends indicate that this improvement will continue over the next decade, research published to date indicates that the levels of reliability now achieved demonstrate moderate to good levels of confidence in many such diagnostic judgments." We note in this passage his statement that more improvement is *necessary* which, in our understanding of ordinary English usage, means that improvement is mandatory, that it must take place, that one cannot get along without it. We have difficulty reconciling Matarazzo's use of the words "necessary improvement" with regard to reliability with any notion that adequate reliability has been established. If adequate reliability had been established, improvement might be *desirable,* but not *necessary.* We also note his statement that published research demonstrates *moderate to good* levels in *many* diagnostic judgments. Obviously, if both words were used, "moderate" does not mean "good." (See also Spitzer et al. [1988], supra.)

He goes on to declare that, "Anyone with a passing acquaintance with the literature on reliability acknowledges that there exists a massive literature that demonstrates that, taken in toto, *DSM-III* Axis I diagnoses (e.g., schizophrenic disorder, major depressive disorder, and generalized anxiety disorder) show high clinician-to-clinician agreement." (p. 883) We would first note that at the time our fourth edition and the *Science* article were written, *DSM-III* was essentially history, as *DSM-III-R* had been published in 1987, so there is almost no point in even discussing *DSM-III* diagnoses because so many of them, including some of those used as examples by Matarazzo, were changed in *DSM-III-R*. As *DSM-III-R* was published only one year before our book and the *Science* article, and no reliability data were reported in the manual, too little time had passed for sufficient research to be done on the changed diagnoses for anyone to know their reliability. We would further point out, as well documented in our book (the *Science* article did not deal with schizophrenic disorders), that the diagnosis or category of schizophrenic disorder or schizophrenia has remained controversial even outside of the legal context and this was being stated in 1989 and 1990 by professionals who could be said to have more than a passing acquaintance with the literature on reliability. For example, as noted on page 162 of our Supplement to *Coping*, Sarbin [1990], a psychologist of considerable stature, has stated, "The failure of eight decades of research to produce a reliable marker leads to the conclusion that schizophrenia is an obsolescent hypothesis and should be abandoned." (p. 259)

Even were it true that high clinician-to-clinician agreement could be established for the diagnosis of schizophrenia or schizophrenic disorder, such a demonstration of reliability would still have little value within the expert witness/legal context. This is so because competent attorneys are unlikely to let the expert get away with a diagnosis as broad as schizophrenic disorder. They are going to ask the obvious next question pertaining to *which* schizophrenic disorder. That is, they are going to require the expert to be more specific, as well they should, given the substantial body of literature to the effect that schizophrenia ia a heterogeneous disorder. A diagnosis of schizophrenia could answer very few, if any, questions that would be relevant in the courtroom. We call attention to the declaration on p. 182 of *DSM-III*, "It should be noted that no single feature is invariably present or seen only in schizophrenia." *DSM-III* lists five different subtypes of schizophrenia, some of which, as we have pointed out elsewhere (see main text, Volume II), are so different from each other as to cause wonderment that they could be grouped in the same classification. We note that further in his reply, Matarazzo states, "*Specific subclassifications* of these two axes, as well as the presence or absence of discrete symptoms (e.g., jittery or jumpy) in such subtypes show poor levels of agreement." (p. 883) Note that this statement is not limited to sub-categories of schizophrenia. Further, in that paragraph, he restates his astonishment that anyone knowing the literature could deny that for the most prevalent disorders, similar to those above, the *DSM-III-R* clinician-to-clinician agreement is other than good to excellent and "thus, more than adequate as a basis for today's treatment strategies or other clinical decisions, including legal opinions as appropriate." (p. 883) We mention this only to fairly represent that Matarazzo was not limiting his praise of reliability to *DSM-III* alone but was also including *DSM-III-R*. We are unable to determine if he included within the statement about *DSM-III-R* that a "massive literature" had demonstrated *its* reliability in the short time that elapsed between publication of that document and the present book and articles. We are also somewhat concerned about his declaration that establishing good reliability provides an adequate basis for treatment strategies or legal opinions. He seems to overlook the fact that reliability is not the major issue but only a preliminary requirement to the major issue, which is validity.

Coming then to the main issue—validity—he notes that he did include in his 1990 article the following opinion, "They correctly quote my belief that currently there is no body of research that indicates that psychological assessment across the *whole domain* is valid or is other than clinical art." (p. 1015) We should make clear that in this instance, it is Matarazzo who is italicizing "whole domain." One interpretation of "whole domain" would be that, indeed, there is in the whole domain no body of research that indicates that psychological assessment is valid. However, we think that Dr. Matarazzo meant by his italics to imply that his statement only referred to the fact that not everything in psychological assessment had been established as valid by research. In that regard, we would note that on page 424 of *Coping*, we quote from a separate article of his (cited in our text as Matarazzo, 1986a), as follows: "Psychological assessment is currently almost exclusively a still-to-be-well-validated work of a legislatively sanctioned, clinician-artisan." We would take those words "almost exclusively still-to-be-well-validated" to mean that with few exceptions, psychological assessment, with no qualifying phrase, had not yet been validated and not the converse implication of his present italicized "whole domain" statement, which implies rather the opposite. We also again wish to call attention to his statement in response to Fowler and Butcher (see the citation to Matarazzo, 1986b, on page 424 of *Coping*), in which he essentially repeats this same matter, "*No* evidence has been published indicating that a credentialed clinician's signed test interpretations are any more valid than are the typically unsigned clinical psychological test interpretations being printed by today's computer software" (p. 883) which he had earlier, in the first paper, indicated had not met primitive tests of scientific validation. There is nothing about "whole domain" or any other limitation in that statement— it seems to cover the "whole domain."

In the next paragraph of his response (p. 883), he makes frequent mention of sizeable bodies of literature relating to the validity of psychological assessment. Most of the studies he describes involve relating intelligence tests and other cognitive tests to a variety of variables, many of which seem to have little to do with typical legal issues (e.g., monozygoticism versus zygoticism, birth weight, sex linked chromosomes). He does not indicate the degree of relationship. However, as *we* have not indicated that there is no supporting evidence of the relationships he describes, we see no need to respond further on this issue.

In the last portion of this paragraph, he cites numerous published studies regarding the efficacy of differential pharmacologic or psychotherapeutic treatment of serious disorders such as schizophrenia and manic depression, indicating that they are an impressive addition to the literature on validity. In *Coping*, in our chapter on experience (Chapter 8), we deal at length with the flaws in using treatment outcome to demonstrate the validity of diagnosis (also, see below, Beutler [1989], indicating little relation between diagnosis and treatment outcome).

In his next paragraph (p. 883), in response to our (1991) reply re-emphasizing that our focus on the *Science* article was on clinicians in their role as expert witnesses and not in their many other roles (e.g., as therapists), he states he thinks that most citizens would find it curious that we would assign a higher social value to professional activities in the legal arena than to the diagnosis and treatment of millions of our citizens each year. We find no basis for him to conclude that we assigned a higher social value to any one topic than the other. We simply wrote about the topic that was of interest to *us* and which we felt was within our area of expertise. We find it curious that he would find it curious that we would focus on the clinician's role as an expert witness in the courtroom in an article about the expert witness in the courtroom rather than to focus on or to assign a higher social value to the functions of the clinician in his role as a therapist in an article on the expert witness in the courtroom. This is like assuming an entomologist who writes on his area of interest necessarily assigns a higher value to fleas than humans. This non-sequitur by Matarazzo in this reply to our article suggests to us that there may have been more heat than light operating in his reply. (See below, Brodsky's mention of clinicians who are angry with Ziskin and Faust). He then raises the question that if we really do not believe in the validity of diagnosis and thus in the treatment of mental disorders, would we leave a family member at home untreated who had one or another of the disorders included in the diagnostic manual, and notes that we would be among an unusually small percentage of mental health professionals who by that action would deny that there is any validity to today's diagnosis and treatment of such disorders. Whether it be in the legal or broader societal domains, we still do not wish to involve ourselves any more than we have to in the issues of the literature on treatment, as it is not necessary to the focus of our work. We think this personal question is inappropriate in a purportedly scientific context. However, we think that if such a situation were to arise, we would act regarding treatment as we have regarding diagnosis—we would look to the scientific and professional literature in this (and, perhaps, other) fields to determine an appropriate course of action.

In his next paragraph (p. 883), he again asserts that we again misrepresent his views regarding the validity of what can be done now and states that the following passage more accurately represents his views than do the passages we quote (note the date of its publication was 1990): "However, I know of no research…to date regarding the validity of the psychological *portraits* (italics added) offered as expert opinion of the type involved in the two aforementioned cases." (p. 1016). (See below, Dawes, 1991, for a description of these two cases.) Actually, we have exactly that same quote to our reply (p. 881), and regardless of anything said at any place else, we could probably rest our case on Matarazzo's statement that he knows of no research evidence for the validity of the types of psychological portraits offered as expert opinion in the two cases he mentions. Readers should also note the statement in his 1990 article, "Therefore, in regard to the critical issue that the validity of *DSM-III*-type differential diagnoses has not been adequately established, Faust and Ziskin and I are in agreement." (p. 1015) He also indicates in the same place that considerably less research is available on validity than on reliability. The claim that his statement about psychological portraits better represents his beliefs leads us to once more refer to his statement in his 1990 article, "That is, because no such body of research has yet been published, I am not discussing the clinician-to-clinician reliability and thus the validity of the personal, social, medical, and psychological portrait of the individual that is typically contained in the comprehensive 10- to 20-page psychological or neuropsychological assessment of a patient involved in the increasing number of cases also being adjudicated in our nation's courtrooms." (p. 1012) Thus, he has now made this statement in two different places and assuming that it now "accurately" reflects his views, we still cannot escape the conclusion that Matarazzo has in several places stated in essence that evidence of validity for the kinds of opinions that are offered by mental health professionals in the courtroom is lacking. As those were the kinds of opinions (portraits and *DSM* diagnoses) that our *Science* article was about, in contrast to relating intelligence tests to monozygoticism versus zygoticism or birth weight or psychological or pharmacological treatment, we feel there is little, if any, justification for Dr. Matarazzo faulting us for not including evidence which would either be of little relevance to our article or which, according to him, does not exist.

As a final note on this issue, we are including *in toto* a comment on Matarazzo's article which also appears in the same August 1991 issue of the *American Psychologist* (p. 882) by a distinguished psychologist who is not a party to this exchange. The comment by Robyn M. Dawes follows.

> In his Presidential Address supporting psychological testimony about individuals in legal settings, Matarazzo (September 1990) pointed out that the research evidence evaluating categorical judgments of professional clinicians yields negative results (p. 1016). He dismissed such judgments in favor of what he termed "valid psychological assessment (portrait) findings" (p. 1015). As evidence of validity he cited two extreme cases: One was of a woman who scored at the 98th percentile on aptitude tests and was Phi Beta Kappa in college, prior to a serious automotive head injury, and who subsequently tested in the 3rd percentile on an intelligence test; the other was of a man whose intellectual abilities were totally unchanged after exposure to neurotoxins in the workplace. Not surprisingly, everyone involved with these two cases agreed that the first person had suffered significant neurological impairment and that the second had not. Using these two extreme anecdotes, Matarazzo concluded that
>
>> When such assessment is done well, it is patently obvious to all involved (i.e., juries, judges, and attorneys for *both* plaintiff and defense) that what such a psychologist-expert-witness concluded was valid (true) within the reasonable degree of certainty required in such litigation. (p. 1015)
>
> Actually, however, Matarazzo made the reverse argument: Because it is patently obvious in these two cases, it must be true overall. That is, the validity of what is done is illustrated by the lack of a need to do it when the conclusions are obvious. He maintained that "psychology is little different from medicine, engineering, or other professions" (p. 1015) because of the faith society places in it—as if such faith should be evidence of validity, rather than that faith should be based on evidence of validity.
>
> Worst of all, however, is Matarazzo's dismissal of findings of research that has actually been conducted in favor of *hypothetical* research yet to be done.
>
>> They [Faust & Ziskin] correctly quote my belief that currently there is no body of research that indicates that psychological assessment across the whole domain is valid or is other than clinical art (p. 1015). [But,] it is my hope that empirical research on such state-of-the-art psychological assessment will soon be undertaken. When it is, I firmly believe that research will reveal that acceptable levels of validity do now exist for these modern comprehensive assessments. (p. 1016)
>
> The validation of expert opinion is expert opinion and hope about the results of research not yet conducted!

Suppose that hope is not realized. Then what? Are Matarazzo and his colleagues to return to all the courts in which they have testified, apologize, and request new hearings for those involved?

Matarazzo and other forensic psychologists are willing to testify in ways that have a profound effect on the lives of others *prior* to the existence of any evidence that such testimony is valid. Earn now; learn—or maybe don't learn—later. If Matarazzo's defense of this practice is the best around, such testimony about people in legal proceedings constitutes a serious violation of their civil rights.

## BRODSKY

In Brodsky's book (*Testifying in Court: Guidelines and Maxims for the Expert Witness.* [1991]. Washington D.C.: American Psychological Association), he criticizes our work, which may create problems if a witness cites his book as a reference in derogation or contradiction of our text and other works. Brodsky also provides strategies and tactics for expert witnesses that may create difficulties for the unprepared attorney as well as creating a possibly false sense of security in experts who attempt to use these tactics. We will attempt to deal with each of these matters in turn.

In his book, Brodsky conveys the impression that our work does not represent the view of even a "respected" minority of psychologists. However, based on subsequent discussions one of the authors had with Dr. Brodsky, it became clear that this assertion was *not* intended to apply to our work in general but rather to our opinion regarding the admissibility of mental health testimony, and then only to a position he *infers* from our article in *Science*. To clarify the limits of his statement in this regard, Dr. Brodsky, in a letter dated September 3, 1991, graciously wrote, "Please consider this letter a formal statement that on p. 202 of my *Testifying in Court* book, the 'respected minority' comment referred to the *Science* article conclusion about admissibility of psychologists and psychiatrists as expert witnesses." Therefore, any attempt to discredit our book as contrasted to the article in *Science* on any issue other than admissibility on the basis of this statement in Dr. Brodsky's book is inappropriate and should be confronted with this later declaration by Dr. Brodsky. We should note that any statements we may have made anywhere concerning admissibility were based on long-standing criteria for admissibility which, however, have been changing in recent years to the point of markedly liberalizing admission of testimony, probably to the point where issues of admissibility in the mental health field have (at least for now) largely become academic. In any event, in view of Dr. Brodsky's clarifying statement, there seems to be no need to pursue this topic any further.

In his book, Brodsky expresses certain views or guides that might be considered idiosyncratic or that a judge or jury might find surprising. Some lawyers have indicated in discussions with us about the book that introduction of these statements might, by themselves, be sufficient to diminish any effect of this book as a reference work. For example, on page 37, when discussing the issue of malingering, Brodsky states, "Unfortunately, the term *fake* hints of illicit or manipulative motivations. My position is that the desire to achieve a goal that is reasonable by all social criteria, such as avoiding a long prison sentence, getting a large financial reward, or getting out of a psychiatric hospital, is altogether legitimate." He notes that these efforts at impression management should not necessarily elicit any automatic assignment of a psychopathological label. On page 199, he notes that when he is on the witness stand and the lawyers are making arguments before the bench and there is little to do as an expert witness, he has his own way of dealing with this situation. His description of this follows:

> I allow myself to leave my body, to slowly rise straight up toward the ceiling of the courtroom, and to fly above the proceedings. I extend my legs straight out behind me and my arms out to the side and effortlessly glide in rectangular patterns above my body and above all of the people sitting there so seriously. I like to think that a Mona Lisa smile comes over my countenance, a slight, en-igmatic smile hinting at profoundness of thought and serenity of mind. Al-though I am interested in the proceedings, my interest is in the geometrical patterns of people sitting, in the theatrical qualities of the gesturing. (p. 199)

Lawyers have suggested that any witness who cites Brodsky as a reference should be confronted with or asked to read this particular statement and then be asked questions such as, "Doesn't Dr. Brodsky seem to be up in the air?" or, "Do you think maybe Dr. Brodsky needs to come down to earth?"

Brodsky advises witnesses to portray the Faust and Ziskin (1988) review as one-sided and unrepresentative. The term "Faust and Ziskin (1988)" would appear to refer to the *Science* article, as the citation for our 1988 book would be "Ziskin and Faust (1988)." We feel we have dealt with the "one-sided" argument in addressing Matarazzo (supra) and need say no more about that. So far as our views being unrepresentative, several issues seem to arise. One, it is not clear whether Brodsky is de-claring that all of our views or reviews are unrepresentative or only some of them. Second, how does he know that our views are unrepresentative absent a formal, properly conducted survey on that issue? To our knowl-edge, no such survey exists. One response to this is to quote Richard Rogers whose works are among the limited number cited by Brodsky in his volume (but see Rogers et al., 1993, below). Dr. Rogers has been the author of a number of respected publications in the field of forensic psychology. In his introduction to a special issue of the journal *Behavioral Sciences & the Law* (1989, Volume 7, No. 2) devoted to expert testimony, Rogers states, "A cursory review of forensic literature would suggest that the preponderance of articles question the scope and value of expert testimony." That seems to mean that articles questioning the scope and value of expert testimony are, at minimum, representative. Rogers goes on to note that practitioners have grown used to such papers and concocted the term "expert bashing" to describe them. He then mentions our *Science* article and that it raised protests and rebuttals. He then states, "What I find startling about this is that the Faust and Ziskin article is *not* controversial; none of their arguments are new and many are more than a decade old. I am left to speculate whether the anger is directed more at the medium (a widely read and highly respected journal) than the message (a good, but not extraordinary, exercise in expert bashing)." It might be worth noting at this point that in contrast to the 1,400 references cited in our book plus an additional 250 in the 1990 Supplement, Brodsky cites a total of 59 references, many of which are not from scientific journals. Further, among these 59 references, eight of them are works of his own or with co-authors, three are Ziskin and Faust works, presumably cited only for identification, and some of them have such scientifically interesting titles as "101 Bridge Maxims;" "Zen and the art of contract formation;" "The transparent self;" "Time and the art of living;" "Telling lies: Clues to deceit in the marketplace, politics, and marriage;" and "This, that, or some other place" (p. 205-208). In fairness, it should be said we do not think that Brodsky's book purports to be generally based on the scientific and professional literature but is more of a compilation of strategies he has found or believes to be useful for expert witnesses in dealing with cross-examination. However, in some instances he does make assertions with reference to the scientific literature (e.g., see discussion below on experience).

He then asserts our work comes from an "advocacy perspective in the guise of scientific objectivity." (p. 202) We assume again that this is a reference only to the *Science* article and not to the book. Certainly, in view of the very clear statement of what we are going to do in the preface to our book, no one should accuse it of being in any way disguised. We state exactly what the book is intended to accomplish and state very clearly what is included and what is excluded as well as the reasons for inclusion and exclusion. He notes that expert testimony should come from an impartial perspective and states on page 203 as part of the maxim in the chapter discussing our work that our reviews have an adversarial component. With regard to issues of advocacy and adversarial components, we take note that on page 135 of his book, Brodsky lists under the entry, "Purpose of Testimony," "Persuasion; teaching; mild advocacy of his or her findings." We do not know exactly what is meant by "mild" advocacy, but as Brodsky has argued elsewhere (Brodsky, S.L. & Poythress, N.G. [1985]. Expertise on the witness stand: A practitioner's guide. In C.P. Erving (Ed.), *Psychology, Psychiatry and the Law: A Clinical and Forensic Handbook* [pp. 389-401]. Sarasota, Florida: Professional Resource Exchange) for impartiality and against even "subtle" advocacy, this seems to represent a contradiction. With regard to adversarial components, we note that in the preface to his book, Brodsky states the intention is "to discuss common problems followed by useful resolutions and a maxim, all of which would lead to *winning testimony in court.*" (p. ix, italics added) We doubt that complete impartiality and the goal of "winning" are compatible. On page 110, he refers to a situation in which he was "less persuasive" and again on page 113, he makes reference to "the persuasive witness." We think that terms such as winning and persuasion convey a note of advocacy and adversariality.

In several places, Brodsky makes reference to the expert "taking control" of the cross-examination and recommends that the expert do this. We think this is, first of all, virtually by definition, adversarial; that is, control seems to indicate, where people are involved, someone controlling and someone being controlled which seems, by its nature, to be adversarial. We think this is contrary to the intent of our system of jurisprudence which is based on faith in the adversary process, the corollary of which is that it is up to the lawyers on each side to present to the court such matters as they feel will advance their cause. For this reason, the system is designed to give control of the testimony to the lawyers, not so that they can determine what the witnesses will say, but so that they can direct their questions to that matter which they feel is relevant to their case. The law of evidence provides for this control in a number of ways, one of which is through the motion to strike an answer that is not responsive to the question. Thus, to use an extreme example, a witness may be asked, "Did you see the defendant shoot the victim?" and the witness may answer, "Although I saw the defendant shoot the victim, nevertheless I know that the defendant is a person of good character." Obviously, the first part of the answer responds to the lawyer's question and the second part does not; the lawyer did not ask about the defendant's character. This might be something that would be addressed at another point in the testimony, but it is the lawyer's right to ask only for the information that he has requested and to determine the order in which evidentiary material appears. If there is matter that is not fully brought out, or is not brought out at all, by directly answering the question that is asked, it is the function and responsibility of the opposing attorney, not the witness, to decide whether to try to bring out such matter. We are not saying here that expert witnesses should be muzzled or that they should not be allowed to explain answers, as we know they are permitted to do that. What we are saying is that the lawyer is entitled to get a direct answer to his question if one is possible or a statement that it is not possible, if that is the case, without having his question used as a vehicle for the expert to expound on issues or tangents that the lawyer has not inquired about. Therefore, we would view Brodsky's frequent references to taking control as further evidence of his lack of impartiality and objectivity and of his motivation to "win."

We will turn our attention now to some of the specifics in Brodsky's book. Before doing so, however, we would call attention to the presence in Brodsky's book of numerous sample questions that are poor, unlikely to be asked by an experienced or competent attorney, and which not infrequently set up a situation which calls for an extended answer.

## ADMIT AND DENY

Brodsky advocates use of a tactic he calls "the admit-deny." He points out it has two steps, the first consisting of an answer which accurately admits what has been asked, but uses a dependent clause so that one cannot be cut off at the point at which the question ordinarily would be considered answered. That is, he suggests beginning a response with the words "although" or "while." In the second, or "deny" step, he recommends denying the part of the answer that is untrue by using a closing independent clause and he emphasizes the need for the denial to be accurate and notes that there should be no denial unless part of the answer calls for it. He uses as an example a question asked by an attorney in an aggressive manner in the middle of cross-examination, "Isn't it true you psychologists have an awfully long way to go before you really can account for human behavior?" (p. 2) He notes that the admit step would be to acknowledge in the dependent clause, "Although it is true we psychologists have a long way to go to account for human behavior..." (p. 2) but that this is an incomplete answer, which permits the witness to continue. Then, he adds the deny segment so that the whole answer would be, "Although it is true we psychologists have a long way to go to understand human behavior, we are proud and pleased that we have been able to work toward objective, verifiable, and standardized procedures for understanding and helping people in emotional trouble." (p. 2)

A motion to strike the second part of the answer might be granted. It does seem as though it is not an answer to the question which was asked, which is a factual question as to whether psychologists have a long way to go. Psychologists' pride and pleasure in working toward methods to improve the situation seems non-responsive to the question that was asked. Even if the motion to strike is not granted, it probably should be made anyway because through the course of cross-examination, there will likely be a number of situations in which the motion will be appropriate, whether granted or not, and will convey the message to the jury or judge that the witness is indeed an advocate and is being evasive in terms of the object of the questions that are being asked. Further, once the expert has added his little speech, the lawyer can return to the main part of the question because he has now received a double answer and he should come back with something to the effect of wishing to clarify for himself and the jury that the answer to his question is contained in the first part of the response. For example, "Do I correctly understand your answer to my question to be yes, psychologists do have a long way to go...?" In response to the same question, Brodsky provides as another possible alternative, "Although it is true that the field of psychology has a long way to go to fully understand human behavior it is my definite professional opinion, based on a careful and detailed assessment, that Elizabeth flourishes in the care of her mother and she does not with her father." (p. 3) We think that here, the independent clause should clearly be subject to a motion to strike as it is completely off the subject of the question. Brodsky indeed notes that the admit and deny technique is very powerful but will flop if the witness is seen as evasive and that it becomes ineffective if overused. Thus, one way to deal with a witness who is using this kind of method is to go through the many challenges concerning the knowledge base and methods and other problems and issues that we have raised in our book so that the witness will be in the position of either having to admit these things or to constantly use an admit and deny technique to the point that it begins to wear thin.

We would also point out that the question set up by Brodsky is a poor question and that throughout our book, we continually stress the importance of prefacing many of these questions in terms of, "Is there a body of scientific and professional literature which indicates that psychology has a long way to go in understanding human behavior?" or whatever the issue may be. We think this considerably reduces the expert's opportunity to range all over the place because the question is not what is the state of psychological knowledge, or what the expert thinks is the state of knowledge, but whether there exists a body of scientific and professional literature indicating whatever. This is clearly a "yes" or "no" kind of question and a series of such questions that are not answered in the simple manner that is called for will reveal the witness as evasive and probably biased, and his credibility can be judged accordingly.

## EXPERIENCE

Brodsky notes (p. 24) that Ziskin and Faust have developed questions to raise doubts about the relationship between experience and accuracy in psychodiagnosis and suggest that the lawyer may confront the expert with selected research findings in this area. He again provides some sample questions, some of which we think a competent lawyer would not ask. He does not use any of our questions which, as we recommend, would start with, "Is there a substantial body of scientific and professional literature, etc." The one question of his we might try to deal with is, "In fact, isn't it true that a series of scientific investigations have concluded that people with years of experience like yours are no better than untrained, unlicensed students and laypeople in assessing and treating clients?" (p. 24) One answer that Brodsky provides is, "While a series of pro and con articles about experience have appeared, my reading of the literature is that the commonsense notion that experience is important has been supported." (p. 25) One might be content with that answer and then later point out to the jury that it has been conceded that the literature goes both ways and therefore that the issue is in doubt, regardless of how Brodsky reads the literature. This also looks like an admit and deny kind of response and can be dealt with as indicated above.

Another response Brodsky suggests is, "I cannot speak for anyone else's experience, but my own professional experiences have exposed me to many different kinds of clients and situations, and these experiences have been invaluable in understanding human behavior." (p. 25) This again refers to his opinion, rather than the series of scientific studies, and should be subject to a motion to strike on the grounds that the question was not about his personal experience but about scientific investigations in the field. The same point also seemingly applies to the next possible answer, "Nobody has studied my experience. Indeed, it is not the nature of scientific study to look at individuals' experience." (p. 25) (Additionally, this response is dubious, as some studies do look at the potential impact of individuals' experience. For example, in D. Wedding's 1983 study [Clinical and statistical prediction in neuropsychology. *Clinical Neuropsychology, 5,* 49-55], the experience and accuracy of clinicians is reviewed one by one. Even when results are pooled or combined across practitioners, it would seem obvious that if a group of experienced practitioners does not surpass a group of inexperienced practitioners, then on average, experience does not increase accuracy at the particular task studied). Again, this is not what the question involved. Another answer Brodsky provides is:

> We are happy that those of us involved in training and in the field have been able to contribute enough to help today's students to a high level of competence. However, I doubt that any of our students or experienced professionals

would agree with your statement about students being as good as experienced staff. The people who conduct such studies tend to work with artificial situations, with clients who are hypothetical, and do not understand what the state of current professional work actually is. (p. 25)

The first two sentences of the answer are not responsive to the question, which simply asked if there were a series of scientific investigations which have reached that conclusion which, of course, there are. The latter part, about people working with artificial situations and so on, might apply to some of the studies but not to all of them, as some of them were done in actual operating or everyday situations (e.g., see Tarter et al., Chapter 7, Volume I).

Of course, it would be far better not to ask such questions the way Brodsky puts them, but rather to ask if there is a substantial body of scientific and professional literature showing little, if any, relationship between experience and accuracy of evaluation and get that one answered before asking about the existence of some studies showing little difference between students or lay people and professionals, if one wants to go further with the issue.

When discussing our review of the literature on experience and *diagnostic and predictive accuracy*, Brodsky contends that the material contained in our book is "selectively one-sided." (p. 25) He states further that "the witness needs to understand that a series of more recent studies have contradicted these earlier reports. Knowing the literature is the best defense." (p. 25)

In our book, we do present various studies, as well as professional commentary, indicating a lack of relation between professional experience and diagnostic and predictive accuracy. Neither author has been aware of a "recent series of studies" showing otherwise. Thus, upon reading Brodsky's statement, we conducted a detailed computer search. This did not yield "a series of more recent studies" contradicting the negative literature. In fact, the closest thing we were able to find was a single study suggesting that graduate students are better able to match the diagnostic judgments of professionals than are undergraduates, a study we have discussed in the supplement to the 4th Edition. As Dr. Brodsky provided no citations to back up his claim in his book, we then contacted him to determine his sources. He stated he was unable at that time to make a thorough search of his files. He did indicate he had read a statement to this effect in a chapter by Beutler et al. (Beutler, L.E., Crago, M., & Arizmendi, T.G. [1986]. Therapist variables in psychotherapy process and outcome. In S.L. Garfield & A.E. Bergin (Eds.), *Handbook of Psychotherapy and Behavior Change*. [3rd Ed.] [pp. 257-310]. New York: Wiley). This edited text by Garfield and Bergin contains numerous articles on psychotherapy. It does not address diagnostic or predictive accuracy, much less diagnostic or predictive accuracy for the courts and, therefore, is not germane. Indeed, in a later article, Beutler (Beutler, L.E. [1989]. Differential treatment selection: The role of diagnosis in psychotherapy. *Psychotherapy, 26,* 271-281) states:

> Psychiatric diagnoses have proved to be of little value either to the development of individual psychotherapy plans or to the differential prediction of psychotherapy outcome. The dimensions that underlie diagnoses appear to be quite different from those that govern the conduct of psychotherapy. The development of differential treatment indicators and plans entail complex relationships among nondiagnostic and situational variables. (p. 271)

In the particular chapter by Beutler et al. to which Brodsky referred, the authors state:

> The current findings suggest that while therapist experience *may* facilitate treatment processes, these effects do not readily translate to assessments of outcomes. The effects of therapist experience on outcome *may* be most observable when treating seriously disturbed individuals with very complex or intensive treatments..., although more research on this interaction is needed. The most reliable conclusion at present is that experience exerts a complex effect that is most observable either on psychotherapy process, early treatment gains, or dropout rates. (p. 287, italics added)

One might note how carefully qualified this statement is ("suggest", "may", "more research is needed"). Further, the majority of the studies these authors review do not support the contention that more experienced therapists achieve better outcomes. (See also, for example, the review by Berman and Norton, 1985, as described on page 477 of *Coping*). We think it will be clear to someone who reviews this literature which, we repeat, focuses on psychotherapy as opposed to diagnostic and predictive accuracy, that even the literature on the relation of experience to treatment outcome is at best mixed, and that it does not constitute a *recent series of studies* which overthrows or contradicts the numerous studies showing low or negative relations between experience and accuracy. Thus, although Brodsky indicates that knowing the literature is the best defense, we would suggest that for the lawyer, knowing the literature is often the best offense.

## OVERGENERALIZATIONS

Brodsky also makes some overly general statements in the text, which we believe would be difficult to defend. For example, on pages 120-121, he notes that "*no* knowledgeable clinician believes the Rosenhan findings apply to detailed, full diagnostic evaluations for forensic clients." (italics added) He presents this statement as part of a reply for dealing with the Rosenhan study. We cannot imagine how Brodsky would know what *all* knowledgeable clinicians believe (and here he is again purporting knowledge only about what other profession-als *believe*), and we doubt there is universal agreement with Brodsky's statement. On page 25, when illustrating a possible response to a chal-lenge on experience, Brodsky states, "I doubt that *any* of our students or experienced professionals would agree with your statement about stu-dents being as good as experienced staff." (italics added) This again seems to be an overly inclusive statement. It would certainly not conform to the experiences and observation of fellow graduate students of one of the present authors.

## EXAMINER EFFECTS

Brodsky (p. 79) appears to acknowledge that it is difficult for mental health professionals to gauge their own examiner effects and that client behavior may vary from examiner to examiner. He suggests responding to questions about examiner effects on the basis of the expert's training, supervision and objective procedures and standardized clinical inter-views. He suggests that in supervision, trainees listen to and watch tapes with their supervisors, are observed through closed-circuit television or one-way mirrors, and receive feedback, which processes serve to educate the student and thereby reduce examiner effects. We would note that he does not state that all of these procedures effectively eliminate examiner effects, so that he is not suggesting that witnesses deny that there are some examiner effects operating nor does he cite literature supporting the efficacy of these procedures. (For contrary literature, see Chapters 6 and 9 of *Coping*, especially Blakey, p. 498; and Sechrest, p. 501; and pp. 78-82 of the Supplement). On pages 80 to 82, he utilizes a sample of questions from the previous (3rd) edition of *Coping*, which are similar to questions appearing on pages 95 and 96 of Volume III of the 4th Edition. In the 3rd Edition, answers to the questions were provided, based on what one might expect from an honest and informed expert. Attempts to predict the direction of such answers was discontinued in the 4th Edition because of the great deal of variation that seemed to occur among ex-perts. It might be useful for a lawyer preparing for cross-examination to review the questions and answers given by Brodsky as stated in the 3rd Edition and as Brodsky perceives they could have been answered. The purpose would be to emphasize to the lawyer the need to come back to the exact thrust of the question and obtain an answer to that thrust. Thus, for the question in the 3rd Edition (Q2), "What does the term examiner effects mean in relation to the diagnostic process?" the answer given in *Coping* is, "It has to do with the fact that characteristics of the examiner may have an influence on the diagnostic process." Brodsky suggests that instead, the witness could have said, "It has to do with the possibility, particularly for examiners using idiosyncratic clinical procedures, that the characteristics of the examiner may influence the diagnostic process." (p. 82) Obviously, what this answer implies is that this effect does not occur with most examiners; only for those using idiosyncratic clinical procedures. Therefore, the lawyer has to come back with a question to the effect that there is literature indicating that examiner effects do occur with the use of standardized procedures, even procedures as standardized as the Stanford Binet or the Wechsler Intelligence Scales. (For material on examiner effects, see Volume I, pp. 330-335, and Volume II, pp. 532-533, of *Coping*; and pp. 56-58 of the 1990 Supplement).

For questions 7 and 8, having to do with the possibility that examiners with varying theoretical orientations might obtain and record different data and interpret it differently, and that examiners with different personalities might get different kinds of information from the examinee, Brodsky suggests an answer, "No, quite to the contrary. The nature of the clinical method and the mental status examination in mental health interviewing is to use standard questions asked in a neutral manner and tone of voice, the answers to which are compared with a substantial base of normative client replies." (p. 82) One approach to dealing with this is to come back with a "body of literature" type of question such as, "Even with all those precautions, isn't there a body of scientific and professional literature which indicates that examiner effects continue to operate despite the intent of the clinical method and mental status examination?" One could go on and challenge the statement about standard questions, as this is in reference to interviewing and again in the immediately above references, there are a number of citations to the effect that examiner effects continue to operate in interviews. If Brodsky is referring to what are called structured (pre-set) interviews, then the lawyer should be aware that there are several such structured interviews and they are not identical to each other and they do not produce identical results, so that despite an allegation of standardized questions, until the world arrives at a point where there is *a* standard interview in use, one cannot say that interviews are standardized. So far as neutral manner and tone of voice, Chapter 5 of *Coping*, which addresses clinical judgment, contains material that challenges the notion that examiners are able to be neutral.

Finally, to question 10, "So the material produced in the interview results, to some extent, from the conditions of the examination and the type of examiner conducting the examination, isn't that correct?" Brodsky suggests that the witness's explanation should focus "on how this process is influential to a tiny extent," (p. 82) noting that the question involved the phrase "to some extent." Again, the lawyer needs to be familiar with the literature we have cited. In many of the citations reference is made to important differences, so the lawyer can then ask, "Doesn't some of this literature indicate that the effects are not tiny but rather are substantial (e.g., Terrell et al. [1981] found that obtained Full Scale IQs differed substantially depending on the race of the examiner [in relation to the examinee's trust in the examiner]. Some of the obtained differences in this study averaged about 10 IQ points, a magnitude sufficient to frequently change overall classification, for example, from the average to low average range or from the borderline to retarded range).

## REPHRASING QUESTIONS

Brodsky (p. 106) suggests that at times the expert should carefully restate questions. Most attorneys are aware that they need not allow the witness to do that so that as soon as it becomes evident that the witness is changing the question, the lawyer can interrupt with a statement like, "No, that is not the question I am asking you; please answer the question I've asked; let me repeat the question" or simply interrupt with, "Please do not change the question" and thus prevent the witness from restating the question.

## MISCELLANEOUS

We think the above material should counter any citation of Brodsky's book as a reference. However, the lawyer should also be aware that Brodsky's book can in some ways aid in cross-examination. For example, on pages 30 and 40, he makes reference to base rates. He also makes numerous statements that could help in establishing the literature. For example, on page 13, he notes that, "Every expert should be a current expert," referring to the need to stay current with professional literature. In the aforementioned article by Brodsky and Poythress, they also describe the need to become familiar with relevant literature. Therefore, this should open witnesses who cite Brodsky to cross-examination with regard to the state of the literature. On page 76 of his book, Brodsky refers to the *APA's Standards for Educational and Psychological Testing*. He notes in this context, "So few of these rigorous guidelines are ever fully implemented in practice." (p. 76)

In conclusion, we would like to quote Michael J. Saks. Dr. Saks is a past president of the American Psychology-Law Society, a Division of the American Psychological Association, and a former editor of the journal *Law and Human Behavior*. He has published a number of articles on forensic psychology and on scientific or expert evidence. There is little doubt that he would be considered "respected." In a 1990 article titled, "Expert witnesses, non- expert witnesses, and non-witness experts" (*Law and Human Behavior, 14*, 291-331), based on his presidential address to the American Psychology-Law Society in August of 1989, Saks delineates the conflict between what the law says it requires of expert witnesses and what in reality and in practice it accepts (which Saks seems to indicate might represent a hidden agenda). In any event, he describes the severely negative opinions concerning expert evidence that go back as far as 1887. We should point out that his article does not deal specifically with mental health experts but really deals with experts of all kinds, although we think it could be described as somewhat oriented toward the mental health professional. He notes that this mistrust and suspicion and negative view of expert evidence continues to this day and is likely to continue for some time into the future. He concludes his article with the statement, "On the subject of expert witnesses, one cannot be too pessimistic." (p. 312)

## ROGERS, BAGBY, AND PERERA

Rogers et al. (1993, "Can Ziskin withstand his own criticisms? Problems with his model of cross-examination." *Behavioral Sciences and the Law, 11,* 223-233) do not have criticism of the book as their principal focus. They do assert that Ziskin has assumed the "controversial" role as critic of psychiatric and psychological testimony. This is the same Rogers who was cited above to the effect that the Faust-Ziskin *Science* article was "not controversial." Their first paragraph deals with the one-sidedness of the book and article, but their concern is principally with the article.

The major thrust of their article is that Ziskin has stated general principles of cross-examination but has failed to provide any validating research which they state is his responsibility. The second part of the article presents what purports to be a "preliminary" study testing the effectiveness of the Ziskin approach.

In his response, Ziskin (1993, "Ziskin can withstand his own criticisms: A response to Rogers, Bagby and Perera," *American Journal of Forensic Psychology, 11,* 17-34) states that as he has never claimed that the book presents scientific principles of cross-examination, and, indeed, indicates the opposite, he disclaims any obligation to do validating research. Lawyers who use the book will either find its contents useful or they will not. A review of books on cross examination, whether written by lawyers or mental health professionals, does not find that they contain validating research. Further, the article contains several errors concerning the book's contents. For example, the article asserts that "Ziskin-style lawyers typically expect experts to concede their incompetence in assessment, diagnosis, and clinical judgment." On the contrary, the book states:

> Extraction of the negative research and/or deficiencies of his evaluation or procedures from the opposing experts through cross-examination is the *most difficult* of the three approaches but *potentially* is the most effective *If* it is possible

to obtain an acknowledgment of these deficiencies from the mouth of the opposing expert, one is in the strongest position to argue to the jury that little or
no credence should be given to the testimony. *Unfortunately, few such experts
will readily concede all or even many of these deficiencies involved. Some will
not concede any.* (Vol. III, p. 330) (emphasis added)

The book clearly discourages the kind of expectation that Rogers et al.
describe.

With regard to their study, Rogers et al. acknowledge the study is
open to criticism on several grounds that relate to the conceptual model,
the methodology, and the conclusions. They discuss only two problems.
First, in connection with the model, they claim they do not have a full
understanding of the theory underlying the Ziskin approach. One might
understand that it is very difficult to do research on a theory you do not
understand, especially when it has not been presented as a theory. Secondly, they concede methodological problems, including lack of opportunity for the experimental jurors to deliberate together. The also note
that more extensive cross-examination might get different results. They
acknowledge the study does not disprove the Ziskin approach. However,
there are a number of other methodological problems which should viti-
ate any conclusions drawn from it.

It seems unlikely that the subjects, visitors to the Ontario Science
Center, with an average education of approximately a bachelor's degree,
were representative of typical jurors.

The cross-examination employed was of a type which gave the advantage to the witness. It was clearly not a Ziskin-type cross-examination
in that only 2 out 12 substantive questions invoked the scientific and professional literature. It was also less complete than the book recommends.

There apparently was no opportunity for an opening statement which
might have allowed the lawyer to prime the "jury" for the kind of evidence that would be presented. Nor was there opportunity for closing
argument which would allow the lawyer (assuming he had asked better
questions) to bring attention to the deficiencies.

Therefore, this article does not really challenge this book and provides no usable evidence regarding the so-called "Ziskin" approach to
dealing with mental health expert witnesses.

# CHAPTER 14

# Trying Cases Visually™
## Understanding the Effective Use of Visual
## Communications in Your Legal Practice

by

**J. Ric Gass[1] and Samuel H. Solomon[2]**

## I. INTRODUCTION

Effective and persuasive courtroom communications require that attorneys be creative in the development of visual aids to *facilitate the jury in understanding by seeing and feeling* the merits of the case. Hopefully, this overview will give practitioners some basic and powerful ideas as to how they can fill the courtroom with stimulating and compelling demonstrative aids while staying within a budget that is reasonable and cost-effective.

---

[1] J. Ric Gass of Kravit, Gass & Weber is a trial lawyer practicing in Milwaukee, Wisconsin. He has been Adjunct Associate Professor of Law at Marquette University Law School in Milwaukee, where he also received his J.D. degree. Mr. Gass is a Fellow of both the American College of Trial Lawyers and of the International Society of Barristers; is a Master of the Bench in the American Inns of Court; holds a Diplomate from and is Board Certified Trial Advocate with the American Board of Trial Advocacy; and is listed in *Who's Who in American Law* and *The Best Lawyers in America* (6th ed.). Mr. Gass is a nationally known speaker on the subject of trial practice and persuasion, notably for the *Trying Cases Visually*™ seminar.

[2] Samuel H. Solomon is President, as well as product designer and developer, for DOAR Communications of Valley Stream, NY, a firm providing trial communications, technology, and consulting to attorneys and prosecutors nationwide. Mr. Solomon has degrees in Mathematics and Philosophy from Yeshiva University and an MBA in Finance from New York University. Mr. Solomon has spoken on visual communication at over 100 conferences and seminars for educational, business and legal associations, and has written for numerous publications including *Harvard Business Review, National Trial Lawyer Magazine, Lawyers Weekly, Computer World,* and others.

This chapter is composed of three parts: "Why" and "How" to try cases visually are the first two parts. While any trial lawyers worth their salt know they need to use demonstrative evidence, there is a wealth of research that can aid us beyond our mere gut instincts concerning the power and nuances of visual communication. That is the "Why" section. The "How" section (amplified by a later section describing specific equipment) addresses the spectrum of technology that is available for the trial lawyer to communicate visually—from the simple and inexpensive to the sophisticated and larger investment.

The third section, "What" to communicate visually, is perhaps the most important. It provides guidance on how to make the difficult choices of the right kind and amount of visual evidence so that a powerful piece of visual evidence, such as the videotape of the beating of Rodney King, is not so diluted that it loses its persuasive impact.

Your audience is "media hungry." People are bombarded with thousands of visual images every day. It is how we process and evaluate the information-rich world we live in. The use of visual aids is your critical edge.

Research on effective visual presentations demonstrates that 75% of what we learn is acquired though our eyes. Only a small portion comes through our other senses [David A. Peoples, *Presentations Plus: David Peoples' Proven Technique* (New York: John Wiley & Sons, 1988)][3]. Some of these same studies show that visuals significantly improve the "action" level of participants.

One study, using color overheads as a proxy for visual presentations in general, demonstrates that action by participants to commit time and money increases significantly with visuals.[4] There is even a difference in action level as you introduce color to your visual presentation. Finally, financial commitment by the audience improves with professionalism, i.e., transforming handwritten charts to high quality visuals. In fact, sometimes handwritten material works against the presenter. *Positive action in your client's favor is the objective of every attorney—and visuals help lead you to this goal.*

Besides jury communications and action implementation, attorneys must be concerned with retention. Research studies show that retention is

---

[3] Parker (1960) puts the percents at: sight: 85%; hearing: 10%; touch: 2%; taste: 1-1/2%; smell: 1-1/2% (Thomas F. Parker, "Applied Psychology in Trial Practice," *Defense Law Journal, 7,* pp. 33-45).

[4] Douglas R. Vogel, Gary W. Dickson & John A. Lehman, *Persuasion and the Role of Visual Presentation Support: The UM/3M Study,* Minneapolis, MN: Management Information Systems Center, School of Management, University of Minnesota, 1986.

significantly improved with "show and tell." The jump in retention after three days between telling versus telling *and* showing is 55%.[5]

The end result of good visual material is to give the attorney *the edge,* especially in complex cases—the ones that end up in trial (if the case were straightforward, it would probably settle). You need that edge, especially when you sense the issues are borderline.

A very important and early part of your goal is to get beyond the information clutter that all jurors face. Your jury has to contend with *your* message among all these:

1.  They will have been exposed to 300 ads before 9 a.m. when they start to hear evidence;

2.  They will have been exposed to two million sophisticated TV ads produced at a cost of $400 billion by the time they are thirty years old;

3.  They will see an average of 24,000 supermarket items each month—all packaged to be not only the most visually appealing product, but one that will make that juror buy it;

4.  They have learned 83 percent of what they know visually and only 11 percent by hearing;

5.  They have an alert attention span of one to ten minutes;

6.  They have a comprehension rate of 600 words per minute while the normal speaking rate for attorneys is 150 to 200 words per minute.

Add to those facts that research has demonstrated that, in terms of impact on an audience, 7 percent of presentation is content, 38 percent is voice and 55 percent is non-verbal,[6] and you wonder how you can ever try a case with just words. In fact, you should not feel just wonderment, but fear. In the words of the Wizard of Id, *"Unforgettable words are seldom remembered."*

Jurors live in a visual world. They expect visual communication in the courtroom just as in the rest of their lives. The bulk of the American population has been raised on TV. If one party in the courtroom is using visual communication and the other is not, the likely winner is going to be the visual, not the verbal, communicator. The research establishes that with equal content, the average presenter using visuals will

---

[5] Presier, Stanley E. (1980), "Demonstrative Evidence in Criminal Cases," *Trial Diplomacy Journal, 4,* pp. 30-32; Wiess-McGrath Report by McGraw-Hill, cited in Dombroff, Mark A., *Dombroff on Demonstrative Evidence* (New York: John Wiley & Sons, 1983).

[6] Albert Mehrabian, *Nonverbal Communication* (Chicago, IL: Aldine-Atherton, 1972).

secure audience change in their favor of 16.4 percent while a better presenter without visuals will only secure an audience change of 11.4 percent (Peoples, 1988). What this all totes up to is that to win with today's juries, you have to *Try Cases Visually.*

There are three facets to *Trying Cases Visually.*

The first is the easiest and it is part of what we have referred to above: the machines and technology that trial lawyers can use in their own offices to produce low cost and yet highly effective visual aids for the courtroom. The science and technology has advanced to the point where no trial lawyer should be without a ProImage or exhibit system (see below) to do enlargements in-house, and your paralegals should have available the complete array of colored foam board to mount them on and know all the tricks of producing enlargements of the appropriate portions of documents to achieve the greatest impact. In court you should be using DOAR's Presenter (see below), which is essentially a live video camera connected to a TV screen so that you can show the jury whatever exhibit or document (and even X-ray) is important, and have the capability of zooming in on the one or two words that may be crucial to your case. Other technology that should be in your arsenal of visual communication includes the latest opaque projectors, lettering machines, VCR's, and other presentation technologies. All of these are discussed in Section V below.

The second facet of *Trying Cases Visually* is the ability to visualize what the courtroom presentation is going to look like. It is similar to the athlete's ability to "see" what his or her form is going to be as they compete. Whether it is the visualization of the perfect golf or tennis swing or the slam dunk, the best athletes can see what they are going to do. The 100-yard dash runner "sees" the entire race as he or she sets up in the starting blocks. The trial lawyer must have the same visual ability and must see the witness testifying and determine what visual communication will be used with the witness. The trial lawyer must be able to objectively visualize what he or she will be doing in that examination or argument and how that will impact on the communication with the jury. The entire communication package of lawyer-witness-visual aids should be *"visualized"* by the lawyer as part of the preparation.

The third facet of *Trying Cases Visually* is the ability to use words to paint mental pictures in the minds of the jurors. The great trial lawyers have all had the storyteller's ability to tell the story of the case they are trying. Before television, families would gather around the radio and "watch" *The Shadow* and *Sky King* and the other classic radio programs. Americans were thrown into a panic by their vivid imaginations during Orson Welles' *War of the Worlds.* There is a current radio advertising program called *You Saw It on the Radio,* which has a fake advertisement with such graphic description that you can "see" a gorilla climbing up the downspout of your house. All of those are examples of the power of verbal painting of mental pictures.

We, as trial lawyers, must be able to use our words to paint those pictures in the minds of jurors. Those are powerful persuaders; the jurors will hold those mental images strongly because they are a product of their minds and not just something that your opponent or another juror is trying to sell to them. But, as powerful as mental images are, the problem with mental pictures in the jurors' minds is that there is no guarantee that all of those pictures will be the same. Different words, albeit similarly evocative of mental images, mean different things to different people. We may both see "a" gorilla climbing up the downspout, but not "the" gorilla. Now, maybe the important thing is that it is a gorilla and not that yours is brown and mine is black, but frequently in trial, the color of the gorilla is as important as the fact that the picture is a gorilla.

The verbal painting of mental pictures is the art of trial work. The technology of visual communication is the *science* that helps ensure that the mental picture in all the jurors' minds is the same and that they all see the picture in the same colors. It is thus the marriage of the *art* of the trial lawyer/storyteller with the *science* of visual communication technology that today gives trial lawyers the greatest persuasive impact.

## II. WHY TRIAL LAWYERS NEED TO COMMUNICATE VISUALLY

### GENERAL PRINCIPLES

The purpose of this section is to set out some essentials of successful communication with juries. This is not an attempt to set out the definitive work on this subject. This section sketches the outline of some of the science of communication with juries but leaves to the art of trial work the filling in of the details.

What is being communicated to the jury can be referred to *in toto* as information. Remember, though, that the information being communicated is not just words, but an amalgam of facts, evidence, proofs, ideas, attitudes, inferences, conclusions, arguments, et cetera. All of these elements are subject to what follows.

The *first dimension* of good communications requires first that the information be *organized*. The receiver of the information must not be distracted from the information by having to develop a format of organization. Organizational format, whether it is chronological, geographical, personal, or whatever, depends on the case, the evidence and the trial lawyer.

Secondly, the information must be *explicit*. It is the exception rather than the rule where counsel can or must be oblique or subtle in communicating factual information to the jury. The old speaking rule of *"Tell 'em what you are going to tell 'em. Tell 'em. Tell 'em what you told 'em"* sums it up quite well.

Thirdly, information must *build* upon the information presented earlier. There should not be gaps or leaps of faith to be filled in later on by the jury. The conditional relevance doctrine in evidence law may allow admission of evidence with later connecting up or supplying of the foundation, but that runs a substantial persuasive risk of losing the jury's understanding of the evidence and its significance.

Fourth, the information has to form a *chain of logic*. It must fit together in a logical fashion. In fact, the more you have followed the first three principles of organization, explicitness, and building, the more crucial logic becomes because its absence becomes more conspicuous.

The process of a trial must start the juror with an early and clear understanding of the basic information of the case and move to the complex information only after the basic elements are clear. Trial counsel's job is to explain and/or integrate any contributing information so that agreement among the jurors is possible. For the advocate, good communication has but one end: agreement with the advocate's position.[7]

The *second dimension* in communication is visual aids, which are the attention getters and motivators which translate the passivity of words into active decision making by the jury, and the use of which is the subject of this section. Words and sentences communicate with the jury in a sequential fashion where each one must be remembered and then connected to what came before and what comes after. Visual aids communicate entirely differently: the entire concept is presented at once and the jury does not have to think sequentially as with verbal communication.

The *third dimension* of communication with the jury is *"the medium"* that is used by counsel. *"The medium is the message"* is more than just a buzz phrase. Whether the medium is the tone of voice, the body language, the visual aids, or TV/video, there is a message (of competence or incompetence, of confidence or lack of confidence, et cetera) being communicated to the jury. As you will see in this section, the use of visual aids presents counsel to the jury as a more interesting, credible, professional and persuasive advocate. Trial counsel and witnesses (whether expert or lay) are also the medium through which the message is delivered. Thus, you, and your witnesses as well, become the message.[8]

---

[7] Perhaps all these factors can be summed up in the "Persuasion Process Model" in Vogel, Dickson, and Lehman, *Persuasion & the Role of Visual Presentation Support: The UM/3M Study* (1986).

[8] An excellent commentary on this aspect is *You Are the Message: Secrets of the Master Communicators* (Homewood, IL: Dow Jones-Irwin, 1988) by Roger Ailes, who

Remember, though, that visual aids are no substitute for good cross-examination, direct examination, creation of a case theme, preparation, conviction and belief in your case, and credibility of your client, witnesses and yourself. But visual aids can overcome weaknesses in cases and create strengths, and are essential to ensure that your points are made, understood and remembered by the jury.

## JURY INFORMATION ACQUISITION

The statistics are deceptively simple: 75% of what we learn comes to us visually, while 13% of what we learn comes to us verbally (Peoples, 1988).

## JURY MEMORY

Ten percent of information delivered only verbally is remembered after three days. Twenty percent of information delivered only visually is remembered after three days. However, sixty-five percent of information delivered both visually and verbally is remembered after three days. Thus, verbally and visually delivered information is six times as effective as verbally delivered information alone (Presier, 1980).

## JURY DECISION MAKING

The first effect of visuals on group consensus is that their use increases the percentage rate of consensus from 58 percent without visuals to 79 percent when visuals are used.[9] The figures alone may not be that significant since virtually all juries do reach what would appear to be a consensus, i.e., the hung jury is a rarity. However, most jury verdicts are great compromises and not a consensus totally favoring one side or the other. Our goal, of course, is usually not a compromise but vindication of our client and we seek a jury consensus in our favor. Thus, this finding as to consensus formation is an important one to keep in mind.

An even more telling finding is that when visuals were used, decisions were reached at the time of the presentation 64 percent of the time, whereas decisions were reached only 48 percent of the time when presentations were made without visuals (Oppenheim et al., 1981). Thus, making your case without visuals not only reduces the likelihood of a favorable consensus, but delays the decisional process. For the defense this can be disastrous.

---

was one of the principal advisors for the presidential campaigns of Presidents Reagan and Bush.

[9] Lynn Oppenheim et al., *A Study of the Effects of the Use of Overhead Transparencies on Business Meetings* (Philadelphia, PA: The Wharton Applied Research Center, October 1981).

When visual aids are not used, a group consensus is delayed 52 percent of the time and only reached at the time of the presentation 48 percent of the time (Oppenheim et al., 1981). This does not mean that a presentation to a jury without visual aids will not result in a consensus, i.e., will result in a hung jury.

Rather, what it means is that the likelihood of compromise by the jury without a consensus in complete agreement with the presenter is greatly increased, as is the likelihood that the consensus will occur later rather than at the time of the presentation when visual aids are not used. That means that the jury is likely to make up its mind in your favor at the time you use the visual aids. Thus, the earlier the use (e.g., in the opening statement) the better.

In addition to making presentations more effective, the use of both evidentiary and non-evidentiary visual aids can cause a substantial reduction in the time necessary to try a case. The use of visual aids can reduce the length of a meeting by 28 percent (Oppenheim et al., 1981). While that figure may not be directly transferable to a trial, in our opinion it is probably close, especially since a trial normally has no constraints on length such as are built into a business meeting. In all probability, the savings in a four-day trial should be at least a day, if visuals are aggressively used by both sides. Use by one side probably decreases the time savings by 50 percent.

## JURY PERCEPTION OF COUNSEL & WITNESSES

The Wharton Study also found that presenters who used visual aids were perceived as more persuasive and interesting than those who did not. That fact applies not just to you as trial counsel, but also to your witnesses. To have your experts perceived as more persuasive and interesting, build visuals into their presentation. Other evidentiary charts, graphs, and models can be built in as appropriate.

Of more significance, however, is that when you are perceived as a better presenter, the audience expects more from you in the use of visuals. An average presenter using visuals is perceived as more persuasive than a better presenter without visuals. And, a better presenter using handwritten visuals is actually viewed as less persuasive than if no visuals were used. Thus, the better you become in presenting, the more you must use high quality visuals.

Visual evidence and the media we employ go well beyond their use in front of juries. Attorneys emphatically tell us that the creation of visual and demonstrative evidence helps them fine tune the theory and the development of their cases. More importantly, it improves the success at pre-trial/settlement conferences, bench hearings, arbitration and mediation. For example, the creation of video depositions and settlement brochures, evidence preservation and, finally, witness and trial preparation has been proven very effective.

Unfortunately, video depositions usually employ the "talking head" of the witness droning for hours of testimony. Aside from offering the most boring experience for jurors, this form of deposition disregards one of the most important elements of live trial—*integrating the demonstration of the evidence with the witness's testimony.* Further on in this chapter, we will explore solutions to this emerging trend in discovery.

## III. HOW TO COMMUNICATE VISUALLY

### INTRODUCTION

Once a trial lawyer has decided to increase visual communication at trial, there are many options in technologies available to the attorney. Some are old but with new twists, while others are new and as yet not widely used. The *first* emphasis in this section is on technology that, first and foremost, a lawyer can operate. Most of us are procrastinators. We end up doing the final trial preparation the week and weekend before trial. We end up not having the time to send exhibits out to be done up professionally. We need in-house capabilities to create last-minute trial visuals. Our emphasis is on *empowerment* of the attorney to produce and develop effective demonstrative aids *in-house.* Empowerment means that the attorney has direct influence on the persuasive and visual aspect of the trial—without feeling overly burdened by logistics. This is a very important goal of this chapter. The *second* emphasis is on cost. Most trial visuals produced at, for example, photo labs are very expensive. The equipment described in this chapter is not only relatively inexpensive, but it also has the ancillary benefit of saving clients money by producing the visuals at a lesser cost than can be done outside. *Third,* all of these technologies are portable and flexible, so that most can be taken to the site of the trial (hotel room or even the courtroom) and can produce visuals in a virtually instantaneous fashion, even during the examination of a witness.

### FORMS OF VISUAL AIDS

The most usual form of visual aid in the courtroom is photographic blowups, whether of photographs, documents or diagrams. The advantages of immediate availability and portability are offset by the disadvantage of cost.

Another traditional visual aid is an overhead projection transparency. Low cost, ease of creation on a photocopier, and availability usually outweigh the additional equipment needs (projector and screen) in the courtroom. Even full color photos can be copied on transparencies at low cost. The overhead's use must be balanced against the need to prepare transparencies beforehand, the lack of zooming-in for attention-getting and the issue of courtroom lighting.

Slides are considered less legible than overhead transparencies. While both are considered equal in achieving audience attention, comprehension, yielding/agreement and retention, presenters using slides are perceived as more professional, but less interesting than those using overhead transparencies.

Of course, the old standbys of models, blackboard and easel pad are still useful tools, as well.

TV represents the cutting edge of visual presentations. Its potential for use with documents and in all parts of the trial from opening to closing is growing daily. People are being exposed to this technology in the courtroom, on nightly news, CNN and Court TV. Use of TV represents the quintessence of the *"medium is the message"* principle. Color, available with TV equipment, is an essential part of visual presentation. Visuals in color are over twice as persuasive as those in black and white.

Each form of visual aid will be considered in detail in the following sections. Practical techologies to create and present visual aids, from firms such as DOAR, are extensively covered in the last section of this chapter.

## TYPES OF VISUAL AIDS

Most visual aids used in the courtroom are evidentiary in nature. That is, they are substantive evidence. They are received for their truth and must have a proper foundation, be accurate and satisfy the rules of evidence. A subcategory of evidentiary visual aids is the illustrative visual aid. It is not a photo of the accident, but a fair and accurate chart, graph, et cetera, which summarizes or otherwise accurately conveys underlying data.

The visual aids which are more important, in our opinion, are the non-evidentiary aids which visually convey, supplement, or summarize the witness's oral testimony or the argument of counsel. These aids assist in explaining an important issue to the jury, as opposed to being evidence themselves, and do not go into the jury room. They are a means and not an end as are evidentiary visual aids, but are very important as tools used to communicate with the jury.

To draw analogies: the evidentiary visual aid is the implanted medical device, while the non-evidentiary visual aids are the scalpel and saw used to do the operation; the non-evidentiary visual aids are the mechanic's tools while the evidentiary visual aids are the new spark plugs, points and condenser.

While non-evidentiary visual aids are not exhibits, they should still be marked to complete the record as to what was being used in the witness examination, statement or argument. In addition, the marking process validates the visual aid in the jury's mind as an official part of the process.

Visual aids can be used at any time since they require no evidentiary foundation. Use them in opening or closing and while examining witnesses.

The techniques that follow all involve non-evidentiary visual aids. Remember, these are not pieces of evidence. Rather, they are utilized only to enhance counsel's communication with the jury.

Since demonstrative evidence is intended to assist the expert or witness in his or her testimony and is not direct evidence in the case, establishing the foundation is usually straightforward. It is important to consider whether the specific visual aid can be construed as prejudicial by highlighting some issue out of context. With this considered, typically you will need to establish the following.

Have the witness state that:

1.  The visual aid will help him/her explain the testimony,

2.  The visual aid will assist the jury in understanding the testimony and the issues involved,

3.  The visual aid depicts a scene, object or image with which the witness is familiar,

4.  The witness testifies that, in his/her opinion, the visual aid is a fair and accurate representation of the scene, object or image involved.

Of course, if your visual aids are admitted as evidence, their effectiveness is further enhanced. If you are unclear as to the evidentiary nature of the exhibit, it may be a better strategy to consider the exhibit for demonstrative purposes only.

## PREPARATION

A more detailed presentation on the "what" to communicate is described in Section IV; however, a few words on preparation are in order here. Preparation is the *sine qua non* of trial practice, and our tendency to "leave things for the last minute" should be resisted. With jurors eager for visual material, the trial attorney must be aware of and have an accurate understanding of the visual technologies and methods available. Visual aids must enhance and endorse the critical themes of your case. Finally, one must *integrate visual aids early in case preparation* so they are organic and fit well with oral arguments, witness preparation and cross-examination.

For instance, when deposing a witness, consider questions that generate responses which will evoke good visual exhibits to support or impeach the individual. While reviewing photographs, documents or learned treatises, keep a keen eye on what would appeal visually to a jury. In a document, for example, uncover the word or sentence which best illustrates and supports the theme of your case.

Consider these five basic steps to effectively prepare and present your visual material:

1. Audience analysis

2. Determining the theme of the case

3. Gathering visual facts

4. Determining the foundation elements and witness sponsorship for each exhibit

5. Rehearsal and courtroom inspection

Trial lawyers should do all that is possible to improve their chances for a successful verdict even before presenting their opening remarks. The first step is to carefully analyze the jurors. Education level, work experience, creativity and other factors help in understanding how one should simplify and present the facts of the case. Once an attorney knows the nature of the audience, one may adapt both style and content of what will be demonstrated in order to keep the jury intrigued and alert throughout the trial process. Design visuals to entice and emphasize both the logical and emotional sides of peoples' perceptions.

Jurors want to be informed and take readily to information which helps them understand. Juror interviews reveal that they are intrigued by technologies in the courtroom (unless it is seen as deceptive or disruptive). For example, if one adds pizzazz to an overhead transparency by introducing color or uses an opaque projector to present the actual photographs, jurors become intrigued with what you are doing and are more attuned to what you are presenting. Our interviews have shown that they will also perceive you as caring and supportive.

In gathering the visual facts, consider the following issues:

- Focusing yourself, the judge and jury on only *major themes* of the case.

- *Simplifying* complexity and details, such as expert presentations, witness testimony and documentation.

- Increasing *retention* of your key points.

- Keeping the jury *attentive and awake*—color is an important enhancement.

- Creating an appropriate *psychological "response"* on the part of the jurors.

- Facilitating *favorable interaction amongst jurors* as they view the evidence as a group.

- Projecting a *professional image* regarding preparation and the seriousness of the case.

- Determining appropriate witnesses to *sponsor your visual evidence* and outlining foundation steps for each item.

*Inspecting the courtroom prior to trial* is very important. When evaluating the physical layout, you must determine the appropriateness of each presentation medium and the visual aids you will be using. Is courtroom lighting an issue? Will the judge allow flexibility in dimming the lights? Can you block out sunlight? How can you best position charts, TVs, screens and models so they can be seen by all? Do you need multiple visuals for proper viewing? How wide is the jury box for view? Will you, your associate or witness access the equipment, and how will this affect placement? How will your experts point to items on a chart or screen? Can you place a small TV by the judge for personal viewing (this is a great tactic)? It is worth a pretrial conference with the judge to ensure his/her compliance with your visual agenda.

In arranging the charts, TVs and screens, consider these issues: How do you position the media to bring you and your expert as close as possible to the jury? For example, can you position the projector in order to "enter the jurors' space" while projecting an image on the screen? Is it possible to place the TV by the jury and have your witness stand alongside it and point out the salient features of the evidence? How do you ensure that all parties can view the material adequately? This is especially important with projection screens where the projector must be a certain distance from the screen for optimal use. Try to design your layout to facilitate the most involvement by the jurors. For example, by positioning the screen to one side of the jury box and the witness on the other, with your podium as center stage, the jurors' head movement follows from you to the witness and then the screen. This "active" involvement helps the jury remain attentive and interested as they follow you in unison.

## IV. WHAT TO COMMUNICATE VISUALLY

### INTRODUCTION

With all the research on the power of visual communications and the technologies available to present evidence, there is always a danger to overreach and think you should present everything in your "briefcase" visually. From any number of viewpoints, nothing could be further from the truth. Doing that would not only dilute the visual message, but more importantly, it is based on the erroneous belief that merely displaying something to the jury is going to cause them ultimately to agree with your side of the case.

This section could have been titled *"How to Try Cases Verbally"* and it could have gone through a series of explanations about how to achieve greater range with your voice, more dramatic pausings, how to vary the tone and pitch of your voice, et cetera. We could have given you a series of exercises to make you sound like Jimmy Stewart or Ronald Reagan or John F. Kennedy. But, if there was not an emphasis on *what* to say, all that you would end up being is somebody with a good voice, but no substance. The same is probably more true with visual communication because of the added impact and communicative power of visuals. It is for that reason that this segment of the chapter, in many ways, is more important than everything else that you will read here.

## WHERE TO BEGIN:
## WHEN DO YOU WORK ON VISUAL AIDS?

Once you appreciate the necessity of visual communication in the courtroom, there is somewhat of a daunting pause as to where someone begins to decide what is needed for the visual communication aspect of the case. Many times, as you go through your normal preparation of each segment of the trial, openings, the direct and cross-examinations, et cetera, the visuals just come naturally. It might be just an outline of a witness's testimony, or there might be a schematic of the concepts that witness is going to communicate, or there may be a particular MMPI profile or part of a profile, sections of DSM, or excerpts from reports that go with that witness. At the same time, though, as you go through your preparation for each part of the case, this thought should be at the end of the verbal/substance/semantics preparation for that part of the case: *"What do I need visually in this part of the case to really communicate with the jury?"* The end result should be a series of visuals for each part of the case that, if you set them all up, would tell the story of your case and that virtually could be the closing argument for the case.

Visuals can be worked up right along with the file review and preparing of questions. However, it is best done at the end with reflection, after all other preparation is done. That is when the whole case is prepared and you can go back and *"see the forest for the trees."* That is when you can go back and: outline the opening on overhead transparencies or large sheets; outline the witness examinations; outline the closing; and select and insert copies of pertinent instructions. You could essentially, at that point, set up the entire case outline as if on story boards on easels. Remember, this is not so much what you are going to say (the substance), but how you are going to say it, and the "black letter" summaries to which you are reducing the case.

Another way of approaching this aspect of where to begin is to put yourself back to two places in the development of the case. The first is the very first time that you became acquainted with the case and the other is the first time that you had to tell somebody else about the case, whether it was one of your partners, an associate, your paralegal, spouse, or an expert.

Think back to when you first got the case and what it was that you wanted to see and what it was that you saw that made you understand the case. Maybe that understanding did not come at the very initial look at the case, maybe it came at some other time; but whatever it was that made you understand what the case was about, that is the type of visual that should have the same effect on the jury.

And then, when you think about the first time that you explained the case to someone else, think about what you showed them. Think about the criteria for a particular disorder and how they were not all present, or a conflict between different tests showing important inconsistencies—these points that you made to get across what the case was all about. That again will tell you what you need, not just to understand the case for yourself, but then to explain it to someone else. These are two excellent points to look at for understanding what it is that you need to communicate visually during the trial.

To conclude this section, whatever approach you take to organizing your case presentation, it is very important that you create a *storyline* for your case. It is your timeline of events or issues that occurred in the case in the specific order. When did the person first see the doctor, and what happened? Consider the particular scores on the WAIS that were important, the differing psychologists and their tests, and where this all stands today. To this storyline, you anchor your key evidence and decide upon your theme. It is this storyline that focuses your attention on the important visual facts you want to present and keeps your jury focused, as well, on what you will prove and where you are going.

## OUTLINES FOR CLOSING ARGUMENTS & OPENING STATEMENTS

The first technique used by Mr. Gass for non-evidentiary visual aids was outlines of opening statements and closing arguments on large (3' x 4') pads of paper, or overhead transparencies for display to the jury during openings and closings.

Depending on the trial schedule, the outline for closing can be done the night before (or during a noon recess). If using paper, counsel should start the closing with a blank sheet over the outline, do the introduction and tell the jury that the closing has been outlined, that they will be able to follow along with a written outline, and then reveal the first page. Originally, it was important that the outline be in counsel's own printing so the presentation did not appear too slick, but still keeping it legible. Since the most current research has found that better presenters must have higher quality visual aids, Mr. Gass has switched to computer-generated charts.

The outline lets the jury see where counsel is going and keeps their attention focused either on counsel or the outline. They can see how each section fits with what has come before and how it will tie into the coming sections. If counsel wants to keep them guessing, section headings are used which have catchy-sounding titles but which do not reveal what that argument will be.

Besides focusing their attention solely on counsel and the outline, the technique has the ancillary benefit of freeing counsel entirely from notes and allowing counsel to maintain absolute eye contact with the jury. It allows counsel to feel secure in that they can always look to the outline for what counsel wants to talk about next and as they look to the outline, the jury is involved in looking with counsel to the next topic.

Lastly, this technique has the advantage of demonstrating to the jury that counsel is organized and in control of the case.

Once in a while opposing counsel will use the outline to argue from. As a result, the opponent will be fighting the battle on your turf and merely repeating and reinforcing your topics and organization for the jury.

In addition, counsel can reuse the outlines that were used with witnesses. That jogs the jury's memory and reinforces what counsel did with that witness.

The same technique should be used with opening statements since jury studies show opening statements can be as, if not more, important than closing arguments in most cases. Use anatomical drawings and overlays to teach the jury about the injury and then color in the pertinent parts, or use the colored overlays from the books. Also use diagrams and photos that have been prepared and stipulated into evidence before openings.

Obviously, this technique, like all trial techniques, has to be evaluated on a case-by-case basis to see which part (or whether all) of the case is appropriate for use of the visuals.

## OUTLINES FOR EXAMINATION OF WITNESSES

The outline technique can also be used successfully with witnesses, principally in the cross-examination of opposing experts or difficult witnesses, but also for the direct of an important witness whose testimony will be lengthy.

Counsel announces to the witness the area that they are going to question on as they move from area to area. The areas can be listed out on a chart and uncovered one at a time. The other approach is to allow the witness to see all the points ahead of time and then have counsel go back and start with the first and then uncover the areas again one at a time.

The technique has a number of advantages. First, it focuses the jury as to the totality of the cross, i.e., it gives them a road map. If the areas have been uncovered one at a time, the focus is individual at first and then the whole picture is seen at the end. If all of the areas are listed out at the beginning and then revealed area by area with the whole picture apparent again at the end, repetition is achieved as well as focus. Whichever format is used, this technique signals to the jury that counsel is prepared and organized and in control. It also focuses the jury's attention on counsel, the witness, and the outline. Since the witness is only answering counsel's questions all of those are really focused on counsel. To make this technique work without legitimate objection, the area descriptions have to be fair, neutral and non-argumentative.

The one potential disadvantage of this technique voiced by attorneys who have not used it is that counsel is telegraphing the cross to the witness. That is not a problem if the area descriptions are (as noted above) neutrally stated and just cryptic enough to give only the area of questioning and not telegraph the actual questions to the witness. (Counsel also can always orally add a surprise area and insert it in the outline, as they go along.) The witness may know the area counsel is going to be examining in, but does not know how they are going to go about it. [In addition, if the yes/no technique (described below) is working, the witness is going to go where counsel leads him.]

As a side benefit, counsel will find some opposing counsel make the mistake of going through the list of areas again on redirect. As noted above, there is nothing better for the case than opposing counsel fighting the battle on your chosen turf as all it does is repeat for the jury the areas counsel has chosen as the important ones.

The one true disadvantage (if it can be called that) of this technique is that counsel has to be so well prepared that they can be free of notes for questioning and be able to work from area to area with eye contact from the chart to the witness and to the jury. That means preparation so good that they know what they want to ask and how to ask it without having to go back to notes for the questions. The outline will prompt counsel enough so that in the long run this is not a disadvantage, because it has freed counsel from keeping their nose in a legal pad and puts them in direct contact with the witness and the jury.

Lastly, counsel can redisplay the outlines and transparencies in closing to trigger the jury's recollection of an important part of the examinations.

The uses of outlines with witnesses thus include:

1. Outlines of the topics you are going to question about.

2. Charts created during their testimony of the admissions they make.

3. A chart to compare their qualifications against those of your expert.

4. The written assumptions for your hypothetical question (it gives you an opportunity to argue your case during the trial and to reinforce the verbal argument with the same information in writing).

A trial brief establishing the authority to proceed with outlines is described in the next section. For additional reading on non-evidentiary visual aids, see: Albert H. Parnell (1986), "Use of Visual Aids at Trial," DRI Defense Practice Seminar, January 15-17, 1986, Las Vegas, Nevada; Edward D. Crocker, "Demonstrative Evidence Techniques," *The Practical Lawyer,* January, 1959, pp. 45-68; James W. McElhaney, *McElhaney's Trial Notebook,* 2nd Ed. (Chicago, IL: American Bar Association, 1987), Ch. 40; Richard O. Lempert and Stephen A. Saltzburg, *A Modern Approach to Evidence: Text, Problems, Transcripts, and Cases* (St. Paul, MN: West Publishing Co., 1982), p. 1024; and Kellogg Corporation, *K-News,* Vol. V, No. 1, March 1988.

## AUTHORITY

A trial brief for the use of outlines and other non-evidentiary visual aids to allow the jury to follow counsel's opening statement, examination of witnesses, and closing argument can be based on the following principles and authorities:

1. The Court has authority, pursuant to Federal Rules of Evidence §611(a) to allow examination in a mode most effective.

2. "Persons exposed to oral stimulators alone will retain ten percent of the information given them over a period of three days. Persons exposed to visual stimulation alone will retain twenty percent of the information given them over three days. Persons exposed to both oral and visual stimulation will retain sixty-five percent of the information over a period of three days." [J.W. Jeans, Sr., *Litigation.* (New York: Kluwer Law Book Publishers, Inc., 1986) p. 514.]

3. "The use of blackboards, charts and other visual aids at a trial is common practice. Counsel for both sides should be encouraged to

present their case in a way that will be most clearly understood by the jury." [*Campbell vs. Menze Construction Co.*, 166 N.W2d 624. 626 (Mich. 1968)]

4.  "What the ear may hear, the eye may see." [*Affet vs. Milwaukee & Suburban Transport Corp.*, 11 Wis. 2d 604, 614, 106 N.W.2d 274. See also J.W. McElhaney (1987), *McElhaney's Trial Notebook,* pp. 437-446; referencing also The Honorable Patrick E. Higginbotham, United States Court of Appeals, Fifth Circuit, at the Section of Litigation Meeting, Dallas, Texas, October 1985.]

## THE COMMANDMENTS OF VISUAL COMMUNICATION

What follows is an attempt to set out some basic rules of visual communication. The following list is not meant to be definitive or immutable. Rather, it is an attempt to set out some basic rules that hopefully will help spark your imagination and point you in the right direction.

### 1. There Is No Innate Helpful Communicative Power for Every Visual

We frequently see advertisements come across the desk for various demonstrative evidence specialists or for example, books of anatomical drawings using the phrase, *"seeing is believing."*

At the same time, there is another demonstrative evidence house that advertises that "seeing is not believing, but understanding is." At the same time we frequently hear that a picture is worth a thousand words. Our problem is that we are not necessarily concerned about the thousand words, or whether seeing is believing, or whether understanding is, but rather what we are interested in is whether or not the visual aid is going to bring us a favorable verdict. And, we have to understand the mere fact that we have blown something up or we have created a visual aid is not necessarily, in and of itself, going to bring us a favorable verdict. That visual must be thought out, the message must be clear, and it must create the right persuasive response in the jury.

Seeing is not always reality. We have all seen the picture of Richard Nixon on the last trip on Air Force I heading back to California. The pause at the top of the steps, the turning to the group that had gathered there to send him off, the familiar Nixon swing of the arms over the head with the fingers spread in the "V" symbol. What we saw was a picture of an apparently triumphant politician, but the reality was that of a disgraced president forced from office.

More recently during a Nelson Mandela tour of the United States before his election, the evening news carried pictures of this dignified, apparently successful, politician and statesman. Yet, in fact, the reality was that of a person virtually imprisoned in South Africa, who could not even vote in his own country. That is important for us to remember as we both present visual aids and defend against visual aids during a trial. The mere seeing of an image does not necessarily guarantee to us that the jurors will see it the same way we do and see the same reality that we do. Thus, the teaching of this first commandment is that you must be very certain of the message that the visual carries and not make undue assumptions about its communicative power.

## 2. Visual Aids Are Not a Substitute for Good Lawyering

Visual communication can never be viewed as a substitute for a good and thorough preparation, development of case theme, credibility of witnesses and counsel, well thought out and well carried out direct and cross-examinations, and all of the rest that goes into good trial lawyering. Visual aids can help cover weaknesses and enhance strengths, but they can never be a substitute for everything that we have learned about trying cases verbally. They are an adjunct to, but not a substitute for good verbal courtroom skills.

Visuals also cannot become playtime in the courtroom. Do not become so involved with the niceties and attraction of a model or a diagram that you constantly have it in front of the jury because you enjoy it so. It should only be in front of the jury and be constantly used because it is helpful to your side of the case. Some exhibits are so enticing that you cannot seem to stay away from them. Be able to stand back and take an objective look at every exhibit and see whether it ultimately is helpful and is going to result in a favorable verdict or whether you are using it only because you like it.

## 3. While as a General Rule, Visual Communication Should Be Added to Every Case, Not Every Case Requires Visuals

For those who have seen the seminar presentation on which this chapter is based, you would think that the author tries cases only with a director in a TV trailer outside the courthouse in the parking lot, and that every trial displays a full array of every piece of the visual communication tools described in this paper. That is not the case. Every case must be looked at to determine the role that visual communication will play in that particular case. For example, a recently tried dental malpractice case involved the allegation that during the removal of a wisdom tooth, damage had been done to the plaintiff's TMJ joint, causing severe damage with resultant unremitting headaches that had now totally disabled this twenty-eight-year-old male plaintiff. The demand was the policy limits of $2 million. You would think that this would be a perfect case to use charts, models, et cetera. The anatomy is hidden and unknown to the average jury. The case was won without a single piece of visual evidence. From our side, we really did not want an informed, well-educated jury.

## 4. Technological Flexibility Is Required at Trial

It almost is a black letter rule of law that if you try to anticipate the ten visuals that you will need for trial, the first one that you will need ultimately at trial is number eleven. It may be something as simple as a page of a witness's deposition to impeach them with or to help straighten out one of your witnesses on direct examination. Certainly, we can do it verbally, but if it is that important, many times the visual aid is what we need.

What you have to do is to build flexibility into your trial presentation. It means selecting visual technology, such as DOAR's Presenter, as one of the visual tools that you will have in the courtroom. It does not mean that you will necessarily do the whole visual presentation for the entire case on DOAR's Presenter (see below), but it means that you will be able to react as needed in trial. It may be that you have the ProImage (see below) in the courtroom so that at any time, in 60 seconds, you can have a chart ready to go. Whatever medium it is that you choose, you must have exercised reasonable judgment to have the flexibility in trial to communicate visually when needed.

Technological flexibility means also that you do not lock yourself in to just one medium. By using just one medium you lose the advantages of rekindling jury interest and attention each time there is a change of media. You actually can end up diluting your message by using just one medium. You have to think also to the various points in trial where you might wish to have more than one visual displayed at the same time. Using DOAR's Presenter solely, for example, you cannot have two visuals side by side in front of the jury. Simple foam boards with enlargements would allow that. Technological flexibility allows you to be presenting to the jury with an interesting, thought-out array and package of visual media.

## 5. Visuals as Enhancement

Remember that visuals have an effect on the jury's perception of the various presenters in the courtroom. They also have an effect on each portion of the case.

That enhancement effect of visuals should be used relative to each segment of the case, each witness, and for the attorney. What we have to do is to look at each segment of the case and see how it relates to what is going to come before it and what is going to come after it and determine whether, and in what form, visuals should be used at that point in time.

We have to look to see what visuals were used in opening statements, and then look to the next witness and see if we need to vary the medium at that time or whether we can use the same medium for two or three segments of the case before we need to change it. You might also consider using the same medium relative to liability aspects, but then a different medium relative to damages. Or you might use one medium for opening statements and another medium for examination of witnesses and then a third medium for closing arguments. Or it might be that there is one medium used with direct and a different one used with cross.

You must look also at each witness's style and keep in mind the statistical research that was set forth in the first part of this paper that, for example, shows that overhead transparencies will make a witness appear more interesting, whereas slides will make a witness appear more professional. The somewhat eccentric college professor with the tweedy jacket, the uncombed hair, the pipe hanging out of his pocket is certainly an "interesting" witness already, and perhaps needs slides for "professional" balance. The cool accountant or actuary probably needs overheads to spice up his or her presentation.

Similarly, we have to look at ourselves objectively as the presenters in the courtroom and see what type of visual aid it might be that best enhances our image as the trial lawyer. We also have to look at what media we are most comfortable with and most likely to be able to handle smoothly without any fumbling.

The bottom line is that we look at the effect and power of visual communication, not necessarily just for the substance that it can convey, but also for the ancillary enhancement benefit that it carries with it for the persons who are handling it in the courtroom.

## 6. Recognize the Two Types of Visual Aids in Trial

As we have noted, there are really two types of visual aids in trial. The first category is that of evidentiary visual aids. These are actual pieces of evidence. They are the actual medical records, the part of the failed product, a chunk of the concrete, an X-ray, a photograph, the plaintiff's cast, et cetera. They will be marked with an exhibit sticker. They will be formally moved in evidence. Within the judge's discretion, they will be sent back to the jury room during deliberations. There must be a foundation for them and while they communicate visually, they are evidence in the case.

The second and perhaps more important category of visual aids at trial are what are referred to as testimonial aids. These are not exhibits or evidence. They need no foundation and do not go to the jury room. Rather, they are devices that will assist a witness in communicating clearly to the jury. Consider charts and graphs and concept boards and outlines that witnesses can use to organize their testimony and to present it clearly to the jury. These are the more powerful because this is the integrated, verbal and visual presentation. The typical standard exhibit or piece of evidence is used and then set aside. It does not have the ongoing power of the verbal-visual combination.

### 7. Avoid Both Ends of the Visual Spectrum

At one end of the visual spectrum we have "GIGO." Just as with a computer, "garbage in/garbage out" is exactly what you get if you approach visual communication in the courtroom from this end of the spectrum. This is the "blowup of everything in the briefcase" approach. As discussed earlier, that just will not secure a favorable verdict for you.

The other end of the spectrum is the tactic advocated by most demonstrative evidence specialists; it is what is called "Issue Focus." What most demonstrative evidence specialists recommend is that you isolate the issues in the case and then focus your visual aids just on pertinent issues. While that is a good general rule, it ignores the enhancement capability of visual aids on the impression that the jury has of the presenters (witnesses and attorneys) in the courtroom. Sometimes visuals are going to be used for the ancillary benefits of perhaps making a witness more interesting, rather than just for the pure substance of the visual aid.

The bottom line is that there really is no absolute rule other than to avoid the absolutes of either end of the spectrum and to tailor the visuals to the particular case, witnesses and attorneys involved. When we say "the attorneys involved," what we mean is not just to fit your visual system to yourself as the presenter, but also tailor it taking into account the personality of the opposing counsel as well. You must consider whether the opposing attorney is going to use a great amount of visual communication or not, and if you know ahead of time what type of visual media that attorney will use, you should be able to take a different tack and so gain an advantage. Remember also that each time you use visual communication, you will be establishing a track record for your next opponent. The more you become locked into a particular medium or approach, the more likely it is that your opponent is the one that will gain an advantage by tailoring his or her visual communication to your established track record.

## CREATING VIDEO DEPOSITIONS
## A JURY WILL WANT TO WATCH

### Introduction

We have all sat through them. You have watched juries and the judge snore through them. When they have been done by your opponents, you have loved it. But, when they have been your video depositions of key witnesses, you have about died—especially if your client is in the court-room watching the debacle and the video deposition was done on your recommendation.

Trial lawyers swear by live testimony, but we all know that despite its greater persuasiveness it carries risks. Sometimes witnesses bomb de-spite the best preparation. Sometimes the seemingly invincible witness is cut up by opposing counsel because they finally got to work on their case and learned how to get that witness. And, in some states, lawyers are forced by physicians to accept video depositions in place of live testimony.

Attorneys admit to a fascination with the use of the TV medium in court. There almost seems to be some deeply hidden guilt that we are not able to find a creative way to use this modern medium in an age where every other activity, except the courtroom, seems to be using improved visual teaching methods. Any such guilt or fascination is usually quickly dispelled by the next botched video we see in court. This should not be the case.

Some of the reasons for putting a witness's testimony *"in the can"* are set out above: getting their testimony before the other side develops their case, placing the witness in a less intimidating environment and de-creasing the chance he/she will bomb, and adding some "high tech" to your case. An even more important reason, from the defense side, is the fact that plaintiffs' attorneys are learning how to use the TV medium faster and better than defense counsel. Some of their cases using the lat-est TV techniques have been quite compelling: highlighting the defective coupler in the rotor assembly used in a tragic helicopter design case; detailing complex architectural diagrams in the largest asbestos abate-ment case; focusing the jury on photographs of a road scene by "zooming" down the street, giving the illusion of driving; showing hard to read X-rays of an acute fracture located at C-7 and C-8. Thus, if for no other reason than to meet the enemy and fight fire with fire, defense at-torneys have to learn how to not only use the video/TV medium, but to master it. The contemporaneous use of TV at trial is more complex and will be treated in other articles. This article looks just at how an attorney can create a video deposition that will compel jurors to watch and which will persuade them. When the witness or expert is presented via video-tape, you do not have to lose the visual impact of live testimony.

## The Video Medium

We all know instinctively what makes the usual video deposition boring. It is the singular focus on one individual: the witness. We all also know instinctively that what makes "TV" interesting is: *variety* of visual image. When trial lawyers are absolutely forced to do a video deposition (the doctor refuses to come to court, the engineer is going to be transferred to Australia, et cetera), most at least try to use some of the usual courtroom visuals. With the doctor, they bring in a view box and have the videographer try to focus on the X-ray, hoping that, even if nothing really can be seen, this will keep the jury awake. An anatomical diagram, blueprints, photos, et cetera, are all tried the same way. It is better than using nothing, but it still is not the most effective use of the video medium.

TV is a medium that has changed American life. It has a virtual stranglehold on a significant segment of American society. Commentators constantly decry the amount of time Americans spend in front of "the tube." We can do better and really grab the jury's attention by virtue of this powerful medium in the presentation of deposition testimony. We should consider TV as a medium which extends beyond entertainment to being a *teaching* environment. Within this framework, the attorney fulfills his/her role as teacher to the jury with the TV as a learning vehicle for jurors to better understand and be persuaded by the facts and foundations of the case.

The way to do this involves three facets: the place where the deposition is taken; the technology of doing the deposition; and the ability of the trial attorney to create a series of storyboards to lay out the visualization of the deposition. We start with the place to take the deposition.

## The Location of the Deposition

Most video depositions are done where we do normal non-video depositions: our conference room, the doctor's office or opposing counsel's conference room. The walls are not the kind of backgrounds that any TV producer would select. The lighting was selected not for TV, but for office activities. If this witness is so important we need to put them on video, then we need an appropriate place. We need to provide a good background for the witness, preferably a deep rich curtain of the type seen behind presidential news conferences (rich royal blue, deep maroon, et cetera). We need lighting that will bring out our witness's eyes so the jury can see the "windows to the soul." We need a chair of the appropriate height, uncomfortable enough so the witness does not get too comfortable, but comfortable enough so they are not squirming. The table has to be sized so that, short or tall, the witness looks appropriate on the TV screen.

We might go so far as to use a mock courtroom at the local law school or an empty courtroom at the courthouse so that the jury sees this witness in the same setting as all other witnesses. The best setting, though, is a video deposition room of a local court reporter who has thought of all these things in advance for you and has all the appropriate technology. The court reporter also ought to be able to show you examples of good and bad video depositions and be able to help you put variety into the visual images of your video deposition.

## Visualizing

What we want to present to the jury is a deposition that replicates the *60 Minutes* television program. This is the best example of creating video depositions that have impact. Think about Ed Bradley or Morley Safer doing a story. The typical segment is an amalgam of a little bit of Ed or Morley talking right to the camera, documents flashed on the screen with appropriate highlighting, shadowing, circling, underlining, et cetera, with photos, video clips, and interviews mixed in. A substantial portion of America sit each Sunday night, glued to the tube, to see who they are going to skewer tonight. Time the visual portions of a segment some night. See how long they allow a single image to stay on the screen. Count how many different images they use in a twenty-minute segment. Then compare that to a typical "talking head" video deposition. *60 Minutes* is the standard that our jurors are used to watching on TV. In the courtroom, when video does not measure up, the jurors switch to a different channel just as they do at home.

We can measure up, if we do what the producers of *60 Minutes* do. We need to lay out in advance the storyboards of what this video is going to look like. Obviously, we have to lay out the questions and answers. But that is just the verbal portion of the examination. That is only half of the video. The other is the visual portion. What you need to do is to divide a piece of paper vertically in half and label the left side *verbal* and the right side *visual*. Now lay out the exam topics and your questions and answers on the left side, keeping the examination as tight and to the point as possible, keeping in mind that jurors are used to the twenty-minute segments of *60 Minutes* and half-hour TV programs that have frequent commercial breaks. Now go back to the beginning and shift to the right side, and visualize and describe what visual image will be on the camera for the jury to "*see*" while they "*hear*" what is on the left side of your story. What you are now creating is the director's script of this TV show.

The idea is to make the images "come alive" to the jury in a format that is real and memorable. Using the news-investigative *60 Minutes* style to present information is both accepted and expected. It is within this context that DOAR's Presenter, projecting photos, documents, objects, X-rays, or transparencies works dramatically.

Another important aspect of video is the ability to "zoom" or focus a person's attention on a specific detail. No other courtroom visual medium can zoom like video. Zoom focuses attention in two ways. First, it shows the area of interest in a prominent manner. Second, it excludes surrounding visual information (we call it noise) which distracts the viewer. Taken together, you have an exhibit which is more compelling than any photographic enlargement or overhead projection. The image is just there. It can be told and seen—and there is no way for the opposition to avoid the facts.

The visuals do not have to be overly complex. For example, when the doctor refers to the history he took, you might just flash the history portion of the record on the screen. Or, when the doctor reaches his conclusions[10], have them in outline form to put on the screen as the doctor runs through them, and then as he or she goes back to explain each sub-part, have only that part of the outline on the screen. That could all be done through the court reporter's character generation equipment and DOAR's Presenter. As you become better at visualizing, you will find yourself going beyond the left side/right side script and dividing your exam into storyboards of the verbal and visual images of each section of your examination.

### "They Never Taught Us This At Law School"

Right now you are probably saying to yourself, *"This sounds pretty far afield from law school, and what is the judge going to say when my opponent starts objecting to all of this?"* It is far afield from law school because law school taught us law, not how to persuade. This is the stuff of trial lawyers, not law professors. This is persuasion, not admissibility.

What the judges are going to say is, *"Good for you!"* They have sat through more boring videos than any of us have, and they are increasingly recognizing their obligation under Fed. R. Evid. 611 to allow counsel to present their evidence in the most effective manner possible. You are doing nothing in this type of video deposition that you could not do in court. You are putting up exhibits and directing the jury's attention to them and to the significant parts of them. If there is an exhibit you cannot use in court, do not use it in the deposition and you will have no problem. If this pacing and variety of presentation does not sound like the way your trials *"look,"* then it is time to re-examine your trial presentation. It probably lacks the variety and impact that persuades juries—especially in the tough cases. In states with tough video deposition rules, the picture-in-picture format, which includes the constant talking head of the witness, with the time/date stamp created by the Visual Mixer's character generator, is certified by your court reporter or videographer. This should meet the most stringent video rules.

---

[10] Note: use the word "conclusion" rather than the word "opinion." Conclusion is a more forceful word with a more objective tone to it. Opinions are like noses; everybody has one.

## Conclusions

Your video depositions do not have to be boring; they can have impact and can persuade. All it takes is your office (or the court reporter's) equipped with the proper video deposition room, the proper technology of at least DOAR's Presenter (see below), and your ability to visualize and direct what the deposition will *"look"* like for the jury. (For more specific information on video deposition technology, see Section V, below.)

So,

> *"Lights, camera, action!"*

## V. TECHNOLOGIES AND EQUIPMENT: DESCRIPTION, USE, AND COST CONSIDERATIONS

The most frequently asked questions about adding visual impact to trial presentations are: what does it cost; how are we going to pay for it in these tight budgetary times; and, if you only could afford to buy one piece of this technological spectrum, which one would it be? We now will attend to answering these important questions.

All of the technology that will be discussed here is in the $1,000 to $6,000 range. The approximate prices will be set out along with the description of each piece of equipment. That range, of course, is still a substantial capital investment, especially for multiple pieces of equipment and for the smaller office. However, each of these pieces of equipment will pay for itself in a very short period of time in any office with a reasonable trial schedule. In addition, if one considers the use of these technologies out of court, such as ADR (Alternate Dispute Resolution), settlement and deposition, the investment return will be much quicker. The machines pay for themselves by means of the office charging a reasonable rental charge to the client for the use of the equipment and for the production of the visuals. For the use of any of the equipment in the courtroom, a reasonable daily rental charge is one-half of the usual and customary rates in the community. For the production of visuals, a reasonable charge would be double the supply and labor cost necessary to produce a single visual. Thus, the cost for most exhibit blow-ups or enlargements is $15 to $30, depending on the type of mounting and color and size of the foam board. This disbursement method not only provides a substantial cost savings to the client (typical enlargement prices, for example, start at $50 and go up astronomically), but adds substantial value to the case presentation and will enhance the probabilities of a favorable verdict.

What about the last question: *"If I could only afford one piece, which piece of equipment would it be?"* You really cannot consider just one piece of equipment. While each technology and technique has its own special effect, they can present substantially similar results. However, the vice of relying on one technology only can dilute your message in the courtroom. The jury can tire of one medium and individual jurors will react differently to different media.[11] In addition, each medium has its own independent message that may add or detract from a particular witness and the attorney. For example, as noted earlier, the research establishes that the use of slides makes the audience perceive the presenter as being more professional, while the use of overhead transparencies makes the audience perceive the presenter as being more interesting. Thus, no one technology alone can achieve the maximum impact. In addition, each time there is a change of medium, there is not only the attention-getting effect of a new visual, but the added attention accorded a new medium— you get two for one, or double your bang for the buck. Trying to find just one technology will be partially self-defeating. At a minimum, two technologies are needed. You do not necessarily need the entire spectrum, but the ability to produce, for example, different font styles and not just typewritten visuals is an essential ancillary support. However, that ability may already exist with an office's word processing equipment and laser printer.

One last thought about cost. While it is essential that the trial lawyer be intimately aware of how to make visuals using each of these technologies, this is an excellent area in which to develop paralegal expertise. Not only is the production work more economically performed by a paralegal, but most paralegals desire to learn a creative new talent and are very good at it. In addition, letting/having the paralegal produce your visuals makes you and the paralegal more of a team with the ancillary benefits that flow from that relationship.

## ENLARGEMENTS/FOAM BOARD

Anyone who has tried more than their first case has probably used an enlargement of some sort, whether it is a photograph, a diagram of the accident scene, a page from the hospital records, impeaching deposition testimony or statements, et cetera. The usual presentation is to have a photo lab enlarge the entire document and plaster it on a piece of white foam board. We can improve that process in two ways when dealing with exhibits that are not photos. (For photos there are other methods that carry more impact and are more cost-effective; those we will take up shortly.)

---

[11] Kevin M. Reynolds and Lou Quinn, "A Post-Mortem Examination of the Jury," *For The Defense,* October 1990, pp. 8-17.

We can reduce the cost substantially and make the enlargements in-house with the ProImage [12] exhibit making system. This machine makes 22" by 33" (or larger) enlargements from any document or black-and-white photo, and has a memory that will allow one-half of a document to be enlarged to that size, and then when the document is scanned through the machine, it will remember where it left off and blow up the second half to the same size. Seaming the two halves together gives an enlargement of 44" by 33" or 40" by 60". Each enlargement takes only two minutes. There are over twelve different paper and color combinations (available as both regular and fax-like paper) and since the paper is on rolls, the length of enlargements is limited only by the length of the paper roll. This is a nice advantage when creating a time line, for example. The ProImage has a computer interface option for an IBM PC or Mackintosh. With this, any graphics software can generate your charts and exhibits. The ProImage is quiet enough that it could be operated in the courtroom without undue disturbance.

The ProImage has a cost of about $3,495 and enlargements can be billed at between $10 and $30 for the small size and double for the 44" x 33" size. The setup and learning curve for this equipment is less than a half hour. The ProPartner Lynx sports a computer interface for illustrations or text from a Mackintosh or PC. This is $3,995. Both the ProImage and the Lynx will enlarge photographs to gray scale in fine quality.

The enlargement sheets can be displayed with an easel without mounting on foam boards and then used in a flip chart presentation. When choosing between handwritten flip charts versus machine prepared enlargements, the clear choice generally is for machine prepared material. [13]

The other method of handling enlargements is to mount them on foam board. Better yet, there is a *reusable* Velcro frame kit (available from DOAR for $40 for the 2' x 3' size and $70 for the 3' x 4' size). The

---

[12] DOAR Communications, 743 West Merrick Road, Valley Stream, NY 11580-4826; (800) 875-8705, (516) 285-1100, or Fax: (516) 285-1145.

[13] There are tradeoffs between handwritten flip chart presentations and use of pre-prepared enlargements of typed/font styled script. There is an emphatic power gained in writing everything up in front of a jury, where the lawyer and the jury are experiencing the creating of the visual together. The advantage, however, is offset by the fact that to do that takes time, is usually not all that legible, and requires the lawyer to at least partially turn away from the jury. In addition, as set out in the "Why" portion of this paper, the use of handwritten visuals by a better presenter actually reduces audience reaction as opposed to the use of no visuals. For a typical presenter, the use of handwritten visuals produces little change in the willingness to commit money, although they do produce a greater impact relative to the willingness to commit time.

Velcro frames allow you to instantly mount any exhibit and add comments without affecting the underlying exhibit.

Three basic techniques should be incorporated into the development of your charts: summarization, extraction and process. Summarizing cases that are long and complex, with numerous events leading up to the climactic results, can be difficult to convey. Being able to condense important and intricate data, and communicate it effectively to your audience, can be difficult. Condense facts and figures; compile your own synopsis of medical history; and create a colorful enlarged exhibit. This enlargement can be mounted on foam boards or placed in DOAR's reusable frames. Consider summary charts of hospitalization, procedures, costs, attending doctors, injury process, day-in-the-life events, etc.

The best way of displaying multiple enlargements at the same time is with DOAR's Wall of Evidence. It is a fabric free-standing display wall, easily set up, to which the foam boards attach quickly and simply with Velcro. It comes with its own carrying case and costs $1,500.

While there are times that an entire document needs to be enlarged, usually there is just a key word, sentence or paragraph that is essential for the jury to see. That is what you want the jury focused on, not having them have to search the entire enlargement to find the crucial portion. At the same time, the court and jury needs the comfort of knowing where this passage came from and seeing the entire document to see that the passage has not been altered. The way to achieve this with impact is to first enlarge the important passage on the office photocopier to as large as you can get it on 8-1/2" x 11" paper (turn it lengthwise to make it even bigger or retype it in a more columnar fashion to use more of the page). Then utilize colored foam board for the background. (There are some twenty different colors to choose from, including black which gives a very professional, slide-like appearance.) Now, off to one side or the top or bottom, mount an 8-1/2" x 11" copy of the entire document with the important passage highlighted. Then mount the enlargement and perhaps even add some lines coming off the passage out to the enlargement. Make the board look as if it is framed by using any of the various colored tapes available at artist supply stores, and you have a professional looking visual at a reasonable cost to your client.

Frequently with diagrams there is a need to label certain parts. One machine that will produce professional labels for you is a ProPartner lettering machine. It can make self-adhesive labels in a variety of colors, types and backgrounds. Lettering can even be created to make up an entire visual just from the lettering machine. The ProPartner costs $1,995.

## PHOTOGRAPHS

Frequently, inexperienced trial lawyers present photographs to the jury by circulating small prints or holding them up so that two or three jurors at a time can view them. While there might be some small benefit from such individual viewing, it is substantially outweighed by the time involved and the disruption of the rhythm of your presentation.

The most usual presentation of photos is via expensive photo lab enlargements. With a color print, the charges for even a minimal enlargement start at $50 or $60. In addition, to get decent reproduction at the lowest cost possible requires that you have the negative. And while foam board mounting has the advantage of being able to place several photos on separate easels before the jury at one time, these enlargements allow for no further enlarging of a pertinent photo beyond the previously selected portions.

An alternative and superior method of presenting photos to the jury is to have them reproduced on overhead transparencies. This can be accomplished simply and inexpensively at a local copying shop, as long as they have a color laser copier. Either black-and-white or color photos can be reproduced on transparencies. The usual cost is around $5.00. The quality is very high and portions of the photos can be enlarged in the process. Negatives are not needed as the transparencies are made directly from the prints.

A more flexible presentation format for photos is available with DOAR's Presenter. This is actually a live video camera, and whatever is placed under the camera will be displayed on the TV screen, which you place before the jury. What makes this system so powerful is not just the fact that there is no pre-planning of which photos to use, but that it has a zoom feature which allows the attorney to come in on the smallest detail in the photo and enlarge it to the size of the screen. In addition, there is a backlit portion on the base platform which will illuminate a slide or a negative and when the zoom feature is activated, the screen can be filled with the image on the slide or negative. The negative can be displayed in either a negative or positive mode via a switch on the unit.

In the next sections, we suggest a number of different methods of presenting photos in the courtroom, in which DOAR's Presenter will prove low-cost and very effective.

## DOAR'S PRESENTER

You have been introduced somewhat to DOAR's Presenter in the section above on photographs, but it has greater potential beyond photos. It can display anything placed under it, so any document can be displayed and zoomed in on. The display of the entire sheet, while not displaying a type size that the jury can read, is important because it gives the jury the comfort that you are quoting accurately when they see the context from which you are taking the material. Since DOAR's Presenter can switch between negative and positive settings, written material can be presented in either black-on-white or with a white image on a black background. Even more effective, while in the negative mode the color balance can be changed, and a full array of colored backgrounds with white lettering can be displayed.

DOAR's Presenter vividly displays any type of document: blueprints, diagrams, charts, tables, graphs, hospital records, monitor strips, reports, articles, and so on. With proper planning, full page documents are effectively displayed by highlighting the most important area of the document by zooming. Another solution is simply to retype the pertinent portion on a sticky-note and place it right above or below the important lines. The note is just the width of a column of type, which is a perfect width for the zoom of DOAR's Presenter. Depositions are effectively displayed if you obtain the condensed column version from your court reporter.

X-rays are a problem in the courtroom. Usually the built-in view box is so far from the jury that they cannot see the important parts of the X-ray. While a portable view box brings the image closer to the jury, it is clumsy, and all twelve jurors cannot see the image at once. In addition, neither method allows any enlargement of any portion of the image. The back-lit portion of DOAR's Presenter's base platform allows display of any joint X-ray with very good resolution and zooming.

Displays of models (anatomical, vehicles, et cetera) present the difficulty of usually being too small to display to more than two or three jurors at one time. In addition, they allow for no enlargement of any feature in and of themselves. The camera of DOAR's Presenter can be rotated backwards and the model set up to the rear of the unit. A portable X-ray view box provides a good height. The model can now be turned and via the zoom feature any small detail of the model is enlarged on the screen. Since the model is constantly in the jury's view, they can look to it whenever they need to reorient themselves three-dimensionally to the model.

The image generated by DOAR's "wireless" Presenter is a TV image in which you need a television display device in court with DOAR's Presenter. Usually a 35-inch screen is more than sufficient. TVs may be connected to DOAR's Presenter using the wireless "satellite" facility. Also, a 3-inch monitor is attached for viewing by the attorney. If the display is done on a monitor, then the cable from DOAR's Presenter can be connected directly to the monitor. If a television is being used, then a VCR must be used as a bridge for the display. Having the VCR in court presents an advantage in that frequently you will also have videotapes that need to be played in trial. Additionally, with the VCR you have the ability to record the visual display used with any witness and if the microphone function of DOAR's Presenter is used, the oral testimony of the witness describing the exhibits will be captured as well—perhaps for later use in closing argument.

DOAR's Presenter can be on counsel's table or placed on a small table at the middle of the jury box. The display device can then be set up at the end of the jury box and slightly out into the courtroom. It can then be seen by the judge and witness directly and all the jury needs to do is to swivel their heads. Additional monitors can be positioned on a shelf below the large unit facing different directions so that co-counsel or opposing counsel or the audience can see the display. An additional monitor for the judge can be provided at the bench.

DOAR's wireless Presenter is a versatile tool to be used in court, depositions, et cetera. The cost can be recouped within a year in an office with a reasonable trial calendar, by again charging a rental rate of half the commercial rate in your area. DOAR's Presenter uniquely allows you to connect a computer presentation for output to the same TV monitors. The cost of DOAR's Presenter with the built-in monitor and wireless transmission, plus ancillary equipment, is $5,895. This package includes everything you need, other than a TV for the judge and jury.

In larger metropolitan areas, and particularly in large courtrooms, the large screen projection televisions or actual projection TV units can be used with large 10' by 10' fast fold screens. There is a very portable and yet high-quality projection unit available from the DOAR Visual Spectator to us for this projection. All that the trial attorney needs to do is to hook up one cable to the VCR and plug in the power cord and you are all ready in court. The only item you need to provide is a 24-foot cable to connect to the VCR to be able to work with the courtroom layout in terms of placement of DOAR's Presenter and the display device. The Visual Spectator costs $4,495, including the screen.

A particularly effective use for the television technology capabilities is with depositions.

## VIDEO DEPOSITION TECHNOLOGY

The technology necessary to create an effective video deposition is simple. First, an on-screen lettering process, "character generation," is used so that the title of the action and the usual introduction of who is testifying, date, et cetera, should all scroll onto the screen in rich gold letters against a blue background, rather than having the usual monotone introduction provided by a court reporter stumbling through the reading of the caption and the other jargon that gets read before the deposition starts. In addition, character generation can also be used to title exhibits that will be shown on screen and to subtitle the introduction of the various attorneys who examine.

Second, the crucial piece of technology to creating a visually appealing video deposition is DOAR's Presenter. This system, which contains an image switching device, has become a dynamic tool for both live courtroom and videotape deposition display of visual evidence. The live TV camera is mounted on an arm above a base that has back lighting capability. The camera has zoom capability and, while moveable, is usually used pointed downward toward the base. Any exhibit or X-ray now placed on the base below the camera can be captured on the videotape of the deposition by merely switching between DOAR's Presenter and the camera, capturing the witness's image through the switcher, and thus giving you the choice of image at any point in the deposition. While the witness or counsel is talking, the audio is captured no matter what visual image the camera is capturing. When you or the witness refer to an exhibit (or the crucial part of it), *that* is what will be on the screen and what the jury's attention will be focused on, just as on *60 Minutes.*

There are two technical approaches to organizing the visual evidence and integrating it into the videotape deposition. The first relies upon the "Input Selection Switch" (referred to briefly above) located on DOAR's Presenter. By connecting a video camera to capture the image of the witness (as is done today to produce the "talking head") to the input connections in the back of the DOAR Presenter, you then connect the output of DOAR's Presenter to a VCR and TV for recording and viewing. By switching the *Selector Button* between DOAR's Presenter and the camera, one records each image respectively on the final videotape. The images switch between the two sources creating the integration of the visual evidence with the witness. It is no different from trial except that the jury is really able to see the image and zoom in on the important portion, and by switching back and forth from exhibits to the witness you are creating the interest that you need to keep their attention.

The second and more attractive alternative is to connect DOAR's Presenter and the other camera to DOAR's StudioVision™ mixer as now described.

## No More "Talking Heads"

DOAR's StudioVision mixer allows you to easily combine two video sources, such as the Presenter and a video camera or camcorder, in order to produce a single result for video taping or presentation. This is very helpful, for example, for video depositions where you may want the expert speaking as a "talking head" and pointing to a critical piece of evidence at the same time being displayed on the TV screen. This effect may be produced as a "picture within a picture" anywhere on the screen, or as a split screen. The StudioVision mixer will also combine the audio sources, and allow pointing and drawing on a screen to highlight key areas or superimpose text for added emphasis.

You can easily view the evidence on the entire screen with your expert in the corner or have your expert in full view. Splitting your TV/monitor to compare two documents, X-rays, or photos side by side is yet another feature of the Mixer. One may record or present live in the courtroom comparisons of signatures, photos, documents and X-rays with just a single Presenter.

DOAR's new Mixer also includes the Illustrator so you can highlight or mark an area for emphasis, drawing on the TV screen just as in Monday-night football. You may also use the StudioVision mixer to add titles. As part of your everyday office practice the Mixer is valuable for video depositions, witness and trial preparation, and settlement/pre-trial conferences.

DOAR's other visual products, which include the StudioVision mixer, Disk Partner and Image Printer, add to the effectiveness of your presentation.

## COST-EFFECTIVE IMAGE STORAGE AND RETRIEVAL

Much has been written on the use of laser disk technology for instant retrieval of large segments of images or video. However, most cases require only a few hundred images for trial and the video segments are not extensive. In these cases (which our research shows are the majority) DOAR's Visual Disk Partner is an outstanding choice. Each disk instantly records up to 50 images from the Presenter or VCR for instant access and playback in any order, or to display a sequence of images as a simple animation. Disks are inexpensive and reusable and the Disk Partner has a fully featured remote control.

Applications for the Disk Partner are many. They include recording images for organized display during summation; an excellent tool for mediation, arbitration or bench trials; simple storage of images for your case file; or, pre-storing images to be printed by the Visual Image Printer. The Disk Partner has become one of the most important tools, with power, flexibility and cost effectiveness, now available to the trial lawyer.

## COLOR REPRODUCTION OF VIDEO IMAGES

Imagine, in court, the witness identifies a critical piece of evidence on your videotape. What do you hand the jurors? Your expert zooms in to the critical areas of the photo, X-ray or 3-D object. What can you preserve for appeal?

Video depositions have become an integral part of the trial process in today's courtrooms. To persuade the jury to remember the most important segments of the video to support your claim, you can use the Visual Image Printer (VIP) to create color prints from any frame on your VCR, Disk Partner, Presenter or camcorder or live video.

To demonstrate a sequence of events (for example, if you are introducing an accident reconstruction videotape), capturing the still, millisecond frames from the onset to impact will create a strobe-like effect. The strobe effect may be generated every 1/5 or 1/15th of a second. Titles and annotation may be added to the photo, or images may be taken directly from the Presenter or Visual Microscope. These full color 3-1/2" by 5" prints are created in 1, 4 or 16 images and cost $.05 and up per image.

## OPAQUE PROJECTOR

Your memories of an opaque projector are probably that of a big, bulky piece of equipment used by one of your elementary or high school teachers to show a page from a book. The room had to be darkened and it took forever to get the book in and then the teacher had to fight to get it straight and focused. In contrast, DOAR's SuperView projector is light, portable, and easy to use in the courtroom. It is relatively low priced at $1,695, and with a DOAR custom "high gain" screen, it can usually be used without darkening the courtroom. Its chief advantage is the ability to project anything: photographs, documents, transparencies, and perhaps best of all, objects. The lid to the unit is hinged to allow an object to be placed on the lens. When the object is then draped so that the light does not cause undue glare, the image of the object with some three-dimensional quality is projected on the screen. Smaller objects obviously work better than larger ones. The unit is relatively light and has a built-in handle and two focus controls. While the opaque cannot enlarge like the Polaroid overhead or zoom like DOAR's Presenter, it is a courtroom workhorse giving plenty of flexibility for a low capital investment.

## COMPUTER PRESENTATION & IMAGING

One of the most interesting computer software products for medical evidence to reach attorneys is DOAR's A.D.A.M.™ product. A.D.A.M. is the authoritative teaching tool for gross anatomy, and attorneys are using this system for research, depositions, courtroom presentations and client education. Using DOAR's Visual Computer Link, it is simple to create videotape material from A.D.A.M. for courtroom playback or videotape depositions. Images may be recorded on the Disk Partner for playback or printed on the Visual Image Printer. Finally, pre-built animations for ob-gyn, orthopedics, and lumbar surgeries are available. The

A.D.A.M. system ranges between $2,995 and $3,995 depending upon the options.

The other product to investigate is ZapFolio, which is an Image Organization and Presentation system. It provides the attorney a simple "trial notebook" format to keep track of all the visual evidence in a trial and provide for a simple display and presentation capability. It also has ZapTalk, which is a visual conferencing feature to share images between attorneys and experts using a modem and phone line. ZapFolio comes as a "pair" set for $1,495.

## TECHNOLOGIES: CONCLUSION

All of the equipment discussed above is in an affordable range for any office having a reasonable trial calendar and the capital investment for any piece of the equipment should be recaptured within a year or two. All of the equipment is relatively simple and easy to use. Pre-practice is necessary, but no more than an hour is necessary on any piece to achieve the utmost familiarity and comfort in using it. You do have to develop a "patter" to go along with the equipment, however, because you will periodically place an exhibit upside down, or backwards, or sideways. Do not worry about it. In fact, tell the jury in advance in opening statement what technology you will be using and that you may make a mistake with it. It makes you appear humble and human—two qualities that juries appreciate in lawyers. And, do not panic when the light does not come on. Remember that, hopefully, you checked to make sure it was working before you went to court. Also carry along a help kit of power cords, extra bulbs, marking pens, et cetera, to anticipate your emergency needs. As part of that, be sure and carry a three-prong converter and a big roll of duct tape to tape down your cords in court so no one trips. Furthermore, DOAR is available 24 hours a day to support you.

## VI. CONCLUSION

We have spent a great amount of time on the science and technology of visual communication and it is appropriate at the end here to question how that science and technology fit with the power of verbal storytelling. There are many famous trial lawyers who advocate the art of storytelling as one of the most powerful tools that the trial lawyer has. There is a audio tape available done by a master storyteller, who tries to teach trial lawyers how to become storytellers. There is no question about the power of verbal storytelling.

Think back for a moment to how powerful Orson Welles' *War of the Worlds* was, broadcast on the radio. The mental images that people conjured up led to mass panic across the United States. We have mentioned *The Shadow*, *Sky King* and other famous radio programs. People sat entranced around the radios and could "see" the story going on as it was being "told" on the radio. In the current radio ad campaign titled *You Saw It on the Radio*, the announcer describes a vivid scene, and, of course, with the power of well-chosen words and phrases, you can actually see it (and of course the tag line is that that shows the power of radio, and therefore people ought to advertise on the radio).

Think also about when you went to camp. Whether it was Boy Scouts or Girl Scouts or YMCA or YWCA, at some point you sat around a campfire and counselors told ghost stories. The stories were so vivid and created such images in your mind that you were scared out of your wits and you ran all the way back to your cabin or your tent afraid that whatever it was in the story was going to jump out of the woods at you.

Think also of the prices that the portraits of the masters command today. No photograph of irises commands the millions of dollars that the painting of those same irises do. And yet the photograph is of reality and the painting is of a mental image in the mind of the painter. That tells us much about the value and worth and power of the mental image as opposed to the real image. To give another example, wildlife art, while appearing very real, is most usually the result of a series of composite mental images that the painter has seen at various places in time and which come together in the wildlife artist's painting. The ducks may have been seen over one lake at one time of the year and they become melded together with another lake scene and another weather condition from yet another time.

What does this all mean for the trial lawyer? Does it mean that we have to abandon the power of storytelling and substitute in its place the science and technology of visual communication, or is visual communication the modern day replacement for the storyteller's art? The answer really lies in the word: "*art*." That is what a trial lawyer does. The trial lawyer has learned the art and craft of persuasion and the art and craft of painting mental images for the jury. The problem with storytelling and the verbal painting of mental images alone is that while you can create very vivid images in the minds of jurors, it is difficult to be assured that you have painted the same image in all twelve minds. What we need for a favorable verdict is a shared mental image that is the same among all of the jurors. That is what the science and technology of visual communication can do. It provides a greater guarantee or assurance that the mental image that we paint as storytellers is a shared image among all the members of the jury. Thus, it is not an either-or proposition, but rather a marriage of the power of storytelling with the science and technology of visual communication through the art and craft of the trial lawyer.

# List of Appendices

# Introductory Note to Appendices

The material presented in these appendices is adapted from cases in our files. As the identities of the participants—litigants, experts, lawyers or others—are of no relevance to the purposes of this exposition, names, dates, places and other identifying materials have been altered. Some material has been added, deleted, or altered for purposes of illustration. Therefore, the materials do not and are not intended to accurately describe the behaviors of the clinicians involved. Because the report writers or testifiers may not agree with our opinion as to what is or is not important, it should be understood that our comments are based on the materials as we have presented it and not verbatim as it was given.

Where depositions are discussed, they are in the original form., uncorrected by the deponent and therefore may have been changed after submission to the deponent for corrections. Similarly with transcripts of testimony, we know that court reporters do make mistakes and some will be apparent in these records, although we have made some changes that seemed obvious and/or necessary. However, readers should be aware that statements in depositions or transcripts may not accurately portray what was said. The material is presented and discussed "as though" it has been correctly reported. The usefulness is not in whether it was said, but what its significance would be *if* it was said.

The purpose of this material is to educate lawyers and mental health professionals regarding vulnerabilities of mental health evidence, and techniques of presenting it and dealing with it. Because this book is written as an educational tool, and is not intended to be a commentary or critique of the performance or competence of any particular person or the outcome of any individual case, the comments we make or opinions we express in the book are based upon the materials as we have presented them which do not necessarily reflect the actual performance of any particular individuals.

Our comments represent what we have provided or would provide to an attorney who consulted us concerning these cases. They consist of our view of ways in which the reports or testimony are vulnerable to challenge. Given the uncertainties and ambiguities, as well as the variety of practices and perspectives employed in the mental health fields, there may be practitioners who would not agree with us.

# APPENDIX A

# Two Brain Damage Cases

*The material in Appendix A includes several neuropsychological reports and test findings. It also includes an analysis of these reports and the testimony of a highly qualified expert with author's comments on this testimony.*

The cases portrayed in this appendix involved claims for neuropsychological impairment (brain damage) arising out of exposure to various allegedly toxic substances contained in paints and/or solvents used by two industrial painters in the course of their occupation. These two companion cases are being used here for their educational value in demonstrating the nature of testimony given by a well-credentialed, highly regarded neuropsychologist and a tight, well controlled cross examination by defense counsel. The direct and cross examination were videotaped for use at the trial due to the probable unavailability of the witness at that date.

The author served as a consultant on the case, which came to be referred to as the "Painters Syndrome Case." There were numerous medical, neurological, psychological and neuropsychological examinations and test results along with voluminous records, depositions and other materials which filled three boxes. Obviously the material is too extensive for reproduction here. Therefore, we have condensed or abstracted materials likely to be relevant to the present purpose, but the lawyer reading this should be aware that much of what emerges here resulted from a lengthy and laborious perusal of these voluminous records. No one should get the idea that this data will simply spring up at once from the boxes of records and reports. The relevant reports are provided, if available, for the most part without comment because there is extensive comment in the very lengthy reports prepared by the author-consultant. Plaintiffs will be designated as "P1" and "P2." While there were other plaintiffs in the case, only these two were examined by and the subjects of testimony by this heavyweight expert who will be designated as "EW." EW is the author of a number of publications in the field of brain damage evaluations, some of which are referred to and in fact, play a key role in the consultation report and the testimony.

We will not deal with the liability aspects of these cases as indeed there will be no liability to deal with unless the jury believes that in fact, the two plaintiffs have suffered neuropsychological impairment subsequent to exposure to the products of the various defendants.

We will deal first with the case of P1. Background information concerning P1 will become apparent in the reports that are presented. Briefly stated, at the time of the examinations, he was thirty-five years old and in a second marriage of several years duration with two children. He was extremely obese and suffered from hypertension, for which he was taking medication. He had worked for the current employer for the previous sixteen years but had been unemployed presumably due to the claimed disability. For the previous several years he had been the union shop steward and around the time of the first neuropsychological examinations, had received some literature describing the symptoms of painters syndrome. He had psychological examinations in October of 1981, March of 1983, July of 1983 (by EW), October of 1983, and September of 1984. It should be noted that while EW performed his evaluation in July of 1983, his report was not written until May of 1984. However, in connection with a workers compensation claim, there was a telephone interview with EW in 1983. The reports resulting from these examinations fall in chronological order.

## GROUP HEALTH PLAN

### PSYCHIATRIC EVALUATION
Date 10/20/81

### Identifying Information:
This is the first (group health plan) psychiatric evaluation for this 34-year-old man who is referred by Dr. BA.

### Chief Complaint:
"I've talked with Dr. BA and I believe that I need to speak with a psychiatrist on how to best deal with my stress."

### Present Illness:
The patient describes a history dating back at least to February of this past year, during which time he attributes the inhalation of fumes around a chemical as being a point in time which began his episodes. The episodes consist of periods of time in which he blacks out and generally has either amnesia or automatic behavior occurring during these episodes. They have occurred approximately three to five times a week and run from a few minutes up to 15 minutes. He describes the behavior as being automatic in the sense that on one occasion he kept lifting and dropping a pen onto a pad, on another occasion he kept staring at an object and turning it around and around. He in addition feels there is a second component, namely in the past of going to a place, such as a store for food, and forgetting what his purpose was entirely, not just forgetting the specific items he was supposed to be purchasing, but forgetting why he was going there in the first place. He states this has caused a lot of difficulty between him and his wife, much more so since he has been out of work and has had to depend on her since he has been unable to drive or feel functional in his usual capacity. The patient has had two EEG reports, one which was reported to be abnormal at

_____ Hospital where he was taken during a period of unconsciousness, from which he recovered prior to being in the hospital, and that occurred on 5/12/81, and yet on a repeat EEG done on 7/1/81 done by Dr. S, no abnormalities were found on the EEG. The patient was felt by Dr. S to have more functionally caused symptoms than organic, but was placed on a trial of Dilantin and phenobarb which appeared to not alter the course of his "seizures." He was switched to Tegretol approximately three weeks ago and has seen a dramatic improvement in his episodic behavior disorder, which has cleared except for one episode within the first three days of the medication use. He feels that he is interested in returning to work if it won't be harmful to him and moreover, is quite distraught when he describes the damage this has done to him and his wife by his being so dependent and unable to do anything. He is interested in returning to work at the soonest possible time, providing his work does not place him at further jeopardy.

The patient's past work history is significant in that he has worked at the same job for the last 12 years and has reached the position of journeyman. He has worked around chemicals and sprays during most of this time and feels this may have been the final thing that capped his difficulty. He has two co-workers who were also exposed to this chemical who have had similar episodes of behavioral dysfunction. Noted in the chart are outbursts of aggression, but when asked about this the patient states that to his knowledge, this has not occurred and he believes his wife was frightened of the possibility of it occurring, since approximately three to four years ago they had gotten into disagreements and on occasion had gotten physical, although at no point in time did he hit her with a closed fist or inflict any damage. He said the two of them would push each other around, but that has not occurred for the last three to four years.

**Past History:**
Is significant—the patient was raised in _____, primarily by his grandparents, spent his summers in _____ with his great-grandparents. His father divorced his mother when the patient was approximately 3 and only visited the patient up until he was 8. His mother left for _____ when he was approximately 5 and remarried to his stepfather, who adopted him and gave him the name of 1, although his original name was _____. He has not seen his natural father since he last visited when the patient was 8. He has only brief contact with his mother, although they live in the same state. His mother had subsequently divorced his stepfather when he was in the military, and has since remarried and been married now for approximately 15-16 years. The patient himself joined the military service in his junior year of high school, got his GED there, became a drill instructor and saw action in Vietnam where he was wounded twice.

He met his wife while he was a drill instructor at _____ in 1966 and they married in 1969. They have two children, a boy age 9 and a girl age 5. The patient states he feels closest to farming as an avocation and that, given the right opportunities, that would seem more appropriate to do since he feels a fond attachment for the times he spent farming during summers when with his grandparents in _____.

**Past Medical History:**
Significant in that the patient is both obese and hypertensive. He in addition to his current history has a past history of pulmonary embolus in 1980, secondary to casting for an ankle sprain. Still further, he had an ulnar release done in 1977. He currently is on Tegretol, Oretic and Elavcin 75 mg. at bedtime.

**Mental Status Exam:**
P1 was a cooperative, neatly dressed, somewhat obese 34-year-old man who was intermittently quite tearful, particularly when speaking about how his current stress has affected his relationship with his wife. He was not loose, had no delusions, hallucinations, ideas of reference or loose associations. His memory and judgment appear to be good on crude testing. He was neither suicidal nor homicidal. His intelligence appears to be at least average, probably above average. His mood and affect were appropriate to the situation.

**Diagnostic Impression:**
Possible temporal lobe dysfunction with secondary seizure disorder.
2. Depressive reaction, secondary to physical illness.

**Discussion and Disposition:**
I plan to see P1 on one further occasion to complete the evaluation. Additionally, I have requested that he get psychological testing beginning this Friday with Mr. JW. I believe that his medication may need to be increased for his depression and/or changed, since it causes some somnolence that he would find disagreeable at work. I also believe he may need marital counselling in order to help deal with the difficulty that has arisen between him and his wife secondary to his current dysfunction. The patient is interested in any and all help he might get and feels comfortable with the plans we have begun to set up. The psychological testing would be for the purpose of establishing a baseline, since other than with any marked discrepancies on his inventory, it may not give us anything other than documentation for future use. I have discussed his case with Dr. A, who is currently in agreement that he could return to work on Monday, if he so felt, that is a modified work environment away from toxic sprays that he has been in contact with. The patient felt agreeable with this and will be calling Dr. A to corroborate our decision tomorrow. Additionally, Dr. A and I have talked about trying to see if there are any further ways to establish his contact with a potential toxin and discussed the possibility of perhaps a sperm count to determine if it has affected any of the germ cells.

S.O., M.D.
Dept of Mental Health
SO:mmf

d10/20/81
t10/22/81

## GROUP HEALTH PLAN

January 17, 1983

P1

Our File No. _____

DOB: 5/21/74 [sic] *(Author's Note: Reversals are viewed as signs of brain dysfunction by some psychologists.)*

This is in response to your letter dated January 7, 1983 regarding the evaluation of P1 and his symptoms related to his exposure to paint.

The patient has been seen through the group health plan of _____ over the last 2-1/2 years. I am his primary physician and I noted the presence of symptoms consistent with either a seizure disorder, hyperventilation or personality change of a psychological nature occurring in the last two years. His initial symptoms were that of shortness of breath. He suggested this began when he was exposed to particular types of paints and specifically, _____. This was complicated, however, by the fact the patient had a documented pulmonary embolus requiring Coumadin prior to this symptomatology. It is likely that his shortness of breath was related to his pulmonary embolus and possibly aggravated by his exposure to paint, inasmuch as he certainly would have had some pulmonary insufficiency as a result of the former. The patient also was seen for a localized rash which began at work, again relating this to the _____, this was documented in February, 1981.

The patient's shortness of breath seemed to improve over time and the rash did not recur. However, the patient began having changes in personality with argumentative behavior, irritability, headaches, "spaced-out feelings," and episodes where he would lose touch with his surroundings, consistent with either petit mal or a fugue-like state. For this he was evaluated by our neurologist. At that time he felt the symptoms were functional, and that this was probably more psychological than epileptogenic in origin. The patient did have a normal electroencephalogram at that time, which was repeated by our department, having been done initially on the outside. This showed nonspecific slowing without definite seizure-like activity. Despite the functional diagnosis, Dr. S (neurologist) did begin him on phenobarbital and Dilantin and eventually, because of adverse reactions, he was placed on Tegretol.

Subsequently the patient was followed fairly closely by myself and Dr. S and his symptoms of amnesia and feeling out of touch, losing his train of thought, etc., were improved. In fact, he stopped taking his medication (Tegretol at the time) and within four days had a major seizure. P1 certainly would not have known the pharmacology of Tegretol to feign a seizure at the appropriate interval when his medication would have been at the lowest amount in his bloodstream. It is this type of evidence that leads me to believe he did have a true seizure process that was controlled with Tegretol.

In terms of his laboratory evaluation, the patient has never experienced any bone marrow depression, change in renal function or abnormalities of liver function. He has not demonstrated any eosinophilia during his subsequent course. He has had only one complete blood count amongst many where he had 4% eosinophils; this was not quantified. Chest x-ray has never demonstrated any infiltrates. Electrocardiograms have been done on several occasions and been within normal limits. A CT scan of his brain was performed and was normal. His electroencephalogram, although initially thought to show some slowing, was not reproducible.

The patient currently is doing fairly well. He has been seen by a psychologist and psychiatrist. The entire symptom complex including his pulmonary embolus has worn on him psychologically. He had some difficulty in his marriage, but currently is still married. They did separate temporarily.

Sincerely yours,

A, M.D.
Department of Internal Medicine

## UNIVERSITY HOSPITAL

## PSYCHOLOGICAL EVALUATION
3/3/83

P1 is a 35 year old white male who was referred to Medical Psychology by (Occupational Health Clinic) for a psychological evaluation. P1 has previously presented with numerous somatic and psychological complaints and has had a history of working with industrial solvents. Medical Psychology was asked to provide information on neuropsychological functioning. Assessment included administration of the Halstead-Reitan Neuropsychological Battery [Wechsler Adult Intelligence Scale-Revised (WAIS-R), Lateral Dominance Scale, Sensory Perceptual Examination, Strength of Grip Test, Finger Tapping Test, Tactual Performance Test, Speech Sounds Perception Test, Seashore Rhythm Test, Aphasia Screening Test, Trail-Making Test, Categories Recognition Test, and Minnesota Multiphasic Personality Test (MMPI)], the Rey Auditory Verbal Learning Test (Rey AVLT), Rey-Osterrieth Complex Figure Test, and the Cornell Medical Index.

### Interview with P1

P1 presented with numerous somatic and psychological complaints which included, fatigue, anxiety, forgetfulness, dizziness, and seizures. He described seizures as periods of "spacing out" during which he seems to lose consciousness temporarily and is observed by others to stare and drool. After these seizures he is left with a dull headache. Other problems include a constant metallic taste in his mouth and noticeable deterioration in reading comprehension. Mood has also changed recently; P1 reports going from highs to lows much quicker than he has before.

He left school after 11th grade to join the Army. He stayed in the service for five and one-half years where he earned a GED and earned an E5 rank. He sustained wounds in Vietnam. He subsequently worked for 11 years for Company until he was laid off in September 1982. Although he had been exposed to numerous toxic aerosols while employed as a painter, he believes that a "paint preservative," may have contributed significantly to his current problems. He was rushed to the hospital after exposure to this substance and experienced subsequent loss of consciousness. P1 also described having been exposed to Agent Orange during the war.

P1 noted difficulty in adjusting to being unemployed, and especially to having his wife help him through his forgetfulness and momentary confusion in social situations. In addition, he has been identified as having delayed stress from his Vietnam experiences. He is currently involved in group therapy at the VA to learn to cope with this problem and apparently is making progress and is very invested in following through with this course of treatment.

To cope with his reported cognitive difficulties he has taken to keeping notes on a pad he keeps in his shirt pocket. This is a practice first began in his military days, but one he has come to rely on more and more lately.

## Behavioral Observances

P1 presented as a heavy set man of stated age. He was well-groomed and casually dressed. He wore a hunting vest on both visits with a hunter's safety instructor's patch on it. He cooperated with all evaluation procedures, and seemed open and sincere in his response style. He demonstrated a normal range of affect. He tended to become frustrated with tasks requiring immediate memory or visual spatial organization abilities, though he stuck with them and appeared to try his best as requested.

## Test Results

*Intellectual Functioning:* On the WAIS-R, P1 obtained a Verbal IQ Score of 91 (27th percentile), a Performance IQ score of 92 (30th percentile), and a Full Scale IQ score of 91 (27th percentile) which places him in the low end of the average range of intellectual functioning. P1's area of greatest strength is verbal abstract reasoning. Areas of greatest weakness include: general knowledge, immediate auditory memory, and visual-motor attention and immediate memory. Attention and concentration ability is spotty as demonstrated by the average Arithmetic score while Digit Span (auditory immediate memory) and Digit Symbol (visual-motor speed) were impaired. P1's subtest scores (mean 10; SD3) were:

|  | Scaled Score |
|---|---|
| Information | 6 |
| Digit Span | 6 |
| Vocabulary | 10 |
| Arithmetic | 11 |
| Comprehension | 7 |
| Similarities | 14 |
| Picture Completion | 10 |
| Picture Arrangement | 8 |
| Block Design | 10 |
| Object Assembly | 10 |
| Digit Symbol | 6 |

*Memory Functioning:* The results of Rey AVLT (Learning Trials I: 4; II: 5; III: 8; IV: 9; V: 8; Distractors: 4; Recall: 6; Recognition: 6) suggests that immediate recall is within normal limits but ability to learn across trials is erratic and subsequent recall and recognition of words is impaired. The results of the Rey-Osterrieth (Copy: 25th percentile; recall (3 minutes): 25th percentile) indicate impaired visual-motor integration with subsequent poor memory for visual reconstruction. Memory testing seems to confirm the WAIS-R subtests suggesting that memory and attention is impaired and that learning new information is difficult.

*Neuropsychological Functioning:* P1 is right hand dominant. On the Sensory-Perception Examination tactile suppressions were found in the finger tips of both hands. This impairment was relatively worse for the 4th and 5th finger of the right hand, though it should be noted that he has had carpal tunnel surgery which may have affected sensory perception in those fingertips. Even so, the level of errors in both hands suggests some general peripheral neuropathy. While no lateralization of deficits were noted by the strength of grip (R: 43 kg; L:37) or Finger Tapping Test (R: 45; L: 44), the performance on the latter test suggests some motor slowing. On the Tactual Performance Test, a timed complex psychomotor task using tactile and kinesthetic cues from the right (preferred) hand (10 min., 40 sec), left hand (7 min., 0 sec.), and both hands (1 min., 30 sec.), he performed significantly slow with both hands separately, though he performed within Average limits when using both hands together. Impairment in this area therefore is probably bilateral. Ability to discriminate speech sounds (7 errors), as well as rapidly presented rhythmic patterns (5 errors) was mildly impaired. Performance on the Category Recognition Test, which assesses the ability to perceive stimulus interrelationships (66 errors) and Trail-Making Test B (90 sec), assessing overall cortical functional integrity, were significantly impaired. However, Trail Making Part A (24 sec) was within average limits, which suggests that under simple conditions he can still organize and perform a visual scanning task. The Aphasia Screening Test results suggest mild dysarthria (mispronunciation of repeated words: "Massachusetts," "Methodist Episcopal") and mild spelling dyspraxia (misspelling of "Triangle").

*Personality:* The results of the MMPI are valid (2137"8'95-64/0: F'KL:) and indicate that P1 is emotionally distressed. The pattern suggests that he is depressed and anxious. A high level of somatic concerns were endorsed, and dizziness, insomnia and general fatigue are commonly noted with such a profile. It is likely that he worries and ruminates over concerns. Feelings of inadequacy and low self-esteem are also indicated. The high level of somatic concerns, however, probably tend to defend against suicidal ideation which may be expected to follow from depression and feelings of hopelessness. An individual with this MMPI pattern is likely to become passively dependent, and a constrictive defensive style only serves to make gaining social nurturance under the given circumstances that much harder. Subsequent marital and sexual adequacy problems are likely to follow from such dynamics.

## Summary

P1 is a 35 year old, white male of average overall intelligence. Psychoneurological impaired functioning tends to be diffuse and bilateral. Deficits exist in both auditory and visual attention and concentration. Some peripheral sensory suppression was also noted. It is likely that ability to learn to perform complex tasks which require ability to shift from one conceptual frame of reference to another is significantly impaired.

His method of adaptation to his cognitive deterioration was to attempt to become more organized (e.g. keeping a notebook) and more rigid. However, subsequently, level of emotional constriction and anxiety has also increased, which in the long run has increased his level of fatigue; depression, and somatic concerns. It is likely that marital/family problems also exist as a result of this, and psychotherapeutic support should be offered. His cooperative style and past success in his VA group therapy, which he should continue, should make him a good candidate for individual and/or marital counselling. Additionally, vocational assessment and counselling will be required, concurrent with psychotherapy, to aid in his rehabilitation.

3
Intern in Medical Psychology

Dr. 4
Professor of Medical Psychology

### G HOSPITAL & MEDICAL CENTER

## MEDICAL RECORD REPORT
## NEUROPSYCHOLOGICAL SCREENING

Name: P1

Number: _____

Attending Physician: Dr. 5, Ph.D.

Date: 10/18/83

### Background Information

P1 is a 35 year-old, right-hand dominant, obese, white married male who has been married twice, the first marriage lasted only a short time while he was in the service and the second marriage now in its 15th year. He decided to join the Army after completing the 11th grade and stayed in the service for 5+ years, ultimately earning an E5 rank and his GED in the process. His tour of duty included time in Vietnam; he was located in an area that was exposed to Agent Orange. P1 reported having subsequently experienced difficulty dealing with Vietnam-related stresses and still participates in group therapy sessions weekly; however, he stated that, because of the group flexibility, he was now using the therapy sessions primarily to assist him in dealing with the changes which have occurred secondary to solvent exposure.

P1 reports having worked for company as a painter and sandblaster steadily for approximately 11 years prior to his lay-off 9/82, job termination associated with production cut-backs. He has subsequently tried working part-time with his wife in janitorial capacity, but indicated that he was asked to leave after 5 weeks because of difficulty following instructions (e.g., he would frequently forget to clean offices or become confused as to what he had actually done). He has not attempted any other jobs.

## Presenting Problems

Although unable to outline the exact sequence of symptom development, P1 reports that his current problems date back to 3/81 when he was over-exposed to a specific paint preservative while working at company. According to P1, initial symptoms include seizures and lung irritation. He characterized his seizures as "spacing-out" episodes during which he stares into space and drools; these were reported to be of brief duration (approximately 5 minutes). Following their occurrence, he is generally fatigued and disoriented; he finally begins to recover strength approximately 1 hour after the onset. He is never able to describe anything that occurs during the seizure. Available medical records also report one episode of a major motor seizure in 10/82 following which he was placed on seizure prophylaxis. Trials with Dilantin and Phenobarbital were unsuccessful. Tegritol did however eliminate their occurrence.

He is most distressed by changes which he has noticed in his working. Although once quite skilled with mechanical tasks, he now is unable to make standard repairs because he confuses parts spatially or totally forgets the sequence for putting pieces back together. He has attempted to compensate for this problem by writing down notes on the process; however, because there are some aspects which cannot be described in words but instead require visualization, his strategy is frequently unsuccessful. He also reports that he easily loses track of what he is doing, that he is unable to remember instructions or plans, and that it takes him a considerably long period of time to make decisions (regardless of how simple they are).

## Referral Question

This client was referred for a brief neuropsychological screening to determine possible neurotoxic effects secondary to exposure to organic solvents. This assessment was not intended to be a comprehensive evaluation of all areas of cognitive functioning; nor was it intended to explore the possible role of psychogenic factors in symptom development. It was exclusively designed to assess the extent of impairment of areas reported in the literature to be affected by organic toxicity. Refer to et al., "Exposure to organic solvents", *Scand j work environmental* 1980 (6); Juntunen et al., "Clinical prognosis of patients with diagnosed chronic solvent intoxication", *Acta neurol. scandinav.* 1982 (65); Bruhn, et al., "Prognosis in chronic toxic encephalopathy", *Acta neurol. scandinav.* 1981 (64) for documentation of deficits. Additional deficits may or may not exist, and a full neuropsychological evaluation would be needed to determine their presence and severity of impairment.

## Evaluation Measures

Clinical Interview, Rey Osterrieth Complex Figure (with immediate recall), Wechsler Adult Intelligence Scale-Revised (Digit Span, Arithmetic, and

Similarities subtests), Hooper Visual Organization Test, Mack Sequencing Movements and Digits, Wechsler Memory Scale Form I (Logical memory subtest & delayed recall with interference), Rey Auditory Verbal Learning Test, Gorham Proverbs Written Form I, & Tapping Test. The purpose of the assessment was explained to the client and their verbal consent obtained prior to initiating the procedure.

**Behavioral Observations**

P1 arrived promptly for his scheduled appointment. He was friendly, cooperative, and able to describe his personal history (except for events chronically [sic] related to seizure incidents) in a rather thorough and reliable manner. He was extremely embarrassed by his symptoms and broke down into tears repeatedly while discussing their effect on his life. He verbalized how difficult it is for him accept being dependent on others to make decisions for him. Although he believes that he is not currently able to make competent, reliable decisions, he nevertheless admits that the required role reversal in his marriage runs contrary to his internalized social values and is thus personally humiliating. P1 proudly characterized himself premorbidly as an assertive individual who readily assumed and performed well in leadership positions. From his perspective, he is no longer that same person. Awareness of inadequacies has reduced self-esteem, thereby increasing depressive affect, hurt, and sense of isolation. Gradual social withdrawal and lowered activity level, on the other hand, have indirectly eliminated opportunities for confidence-building. He knows that, by no longer placing himself in situations where he can obtain success, he is setting himself up to continue feeling depressed. However, he is afraid to attempt to prove himself in any way because of the risk that he will succeed only in demonstrating his incompetence once more. The distress created by existing role definitions, marital disintegration due to his inability to fulfill responsibilities, and prognostic feedback made it impossible for him to regain his composure independently during our session. It was necessary to externally re-direct him to a neutral topic before emotional control was re-established.

He made derogatory remarks regarding his performance and constantly apologized for its quality. He blushed whenever he had to admit that he did not know responses to questions asked. Yet, despite the anxiety associated with the performing and demonstrating deficits in front of an audience, he nevertheless worked diligently on all test items until completion or termination by the examiner. Although verbal expression was typically fluent, he did on occasion (particularly when stressed) show evidence of mild word-finding difficulties. There were no spontaneous attempts at circumlocution.

**Evaluation Results**

His current test performance reveals significant deterioration of self-regulatory mechanisms (attention and concentration) and abstraction from the status documented 3/83 during his assessment at the University Health Sciences Center. He is unable to adequately store new material regardless of sensory modality used for stimulus presentation (verbal vs. visual), this dramatically limiting the amount of information which can be retrieved later. Introduction of any interference or distractors between the initial presentation of information to be learned and the recall trial results in further deterioration of output accuracy. Anxiety may be at least in part contributing to the additional storage mechanism dysfunction, but it does not account for the marked (statistically significant) drop in scores.

Although his performance on tasks requiring abstraction is still above age group norms, his scores are nevertheless significantly lower than those reported 3/83 and suggest clear deterioration of client's ability to identify and manipulate concepts. He can perceive stimulus interrelationships, but his responses are less successful and seem to require considerable processing time.

Visual-spatial analysis and integration functions are impaired relative to his expected age group norms, although his performance in this area has in fact remained stable from the earlier administration. P1 specifically appears to have difficulty determining how object parts are assembled to form the appropriate gestalts and organizing his approach to visual stimuli. While he does make an effort to monitor response accuracy, he is unable to self-correct effectively. Disorganization in the initial processing of visual information may indeed also interfere with his ability to retrieve visually-coded material accurately. Motor speed has improved substantially and now is consistent with the age-appropriate performance pattern (dominant vs. non-dominant discrepancy observed).

**Summary and Recommendation**

Evaluation results document significant deterioration in the self-regulatory mechanisms and client's abstraction ability compared to the findings reported 3/83. The rate of decline is dramatic; and, while it is consistent with diffuse involvement as suggested earlier, it would be necessary to conduct a comprehensive neuropsychological assessment covering all areas of functioning to determine whether there is a specific pattern to the deterioration.

5, Ph.D.

Clinical Psychologist, (Psychology)

*(Author's Note: It appears that EW had information of P1's military service [for example, from prior reports he said he reviewed] many months before writing his report, yet chose to write the report and form conclusions without seeing military records which obviously might provide information concerning "pre-morbid" functioning.)*

## EW, PH.D.
## CLINICAL PSYCHOLOGIST

**NEUROPSYCHOLOGICAL REPORT**

Re: P1

dob: 5-21-47

5-27-84

This then 36-year-old unemployed workman was given a neuropsychological screening examination on July 7, 1983 to aid in evaluating his complaints of mental changes associated with an 11 year history of exposure to industrial solvents in the course of his employment as a painter and sandblaster. He was examined for approximately 1. hours by means of interview and the following tests: Reversed operations (alphabet, serial subtraction of 3's and 7's); Stroop test (Dodrill format); Controlled Oral Verbal Fluency Test (Benton); paragraph recall, Babcock format (Babcock and Portland paragraphs); writing sentences; Wisconsin Card Sorting Test; Picture Description and Picture Absurdities subtests (Mental Examiner's Handbook); Hooper Visual Organization Test; and Bicycle drawing. Mrs. P1 was interviewed with her husband for approximately one-half hour. The lengthy and comprehensive March 3, 1983 examination conducted at the Health Sciences University by psychology intern 3 under the supervision of 4, Ph.D. also provides data for this examination. In addition, reports from the October 1983 examinations of P1 by OM, M.D. and 5, Ph.D. have been reviewed.

## Background Information

This married veteran of the Viet Nam war is a high school graduate. He had been shop steward for his union in the course of his employment as painter and sandblaster. He had been laid off work close to one year prior to this examination. He reported that he tried doing janitorial work but made too many mistakes. He had been a hunting instructor in 1974 and 1975, but now no longer hunts because he had had two seizures while hunting a year ago. He has tried to fix things at home but can not use tools effectively anymore, giving as an example rewiring a switch backwards. He presently does little except watch television and participate in a therapy group at the Veterans (outpatient) Center. He typically only takes a drink during the holiday season.

## Present Complaints

P1 said that he loses "track of what is going on;" that he can remember only bits of what he reads, not the gist; and to illustrate problems in self-monitoring, he related how he recently gave a salesperson two $20 bills thinking he had given her $42. He has been aware of these problems since early 1981 at the time he developed a seizure disorder. At that time it "just seemed like I was losing my common sense." He also described himself as having no goals. As a result of the many changes in his physical status and life style, he reported that, "I get depressed real easy. I'm not the same person I was—I have always been active, in charge of people." He said he sleeps restlessly, often waking during the night: "Staying asleep is the biggest problem. I can be in bed 8-9 hours, get up and still be exhausted. He said his "appetite runs in spells where I won't eat for many days and then I'll binge." Of all these problems, he said that the worst of it was "feeling like I am not in charge of myself...like I lost my common sense."

## Medical History

He reported that in 1975 or 1976 he sustained a mild concussion in a car accident. He said he had blood clots in his lungs in 1979 or 1980. He has been treated for high blood pressure since March or April of 1983. He is also taking medication for seizure control.

### Interview with Mrs. P1

She described her husband as having changed markedly from a "very inde-pendent, take-charge type of person" who was well-organized, perfectionistic, "the doer and goer" in the family, to "completely opposite now." She said that now she has to tell her husband what to do "like a child." For example, she re-lated that when he fixed dinner recently she had to direct him step by step. He is also no longer able to participate in financial planning for the family. She ex-plained that he is easily distracted, can not deal with a lot of stimulation, and has difficulty concentrating. Both husband and wife agreed that there had been a role reversal in that she is now the leader in the family. On the plus side, he is no longer subject to the violent tempers for which he sought help at the Veterans' Center and is thus easier to live with. However, he now becomes depressed. She pointed out, for instance, that he takes it hard when he makes errors; because he now tends to make errors (such as the backwards rewiring noted above), he has withdrawn from undertaking activities.

### Observation

This very overweight man was casually but neatly groomed, wearing a hunting instructor's vest which he kept on. He was alert, oriented, intelligently cooperative in the examination. He spoke with a very slight speech impediment that suggested sluggish mouth movements. Language skills were unremarkable. Thinking tended to be concrete. Although he appeared to recall the elements of his personal history accurately, he was vague about the dates of even such im-portant events as a car accident or blood clots in his lungs; and of such recent events as having had high blood pressure diagnoses. He presented himself as an emotionally unexpressive man although he talked about being depressed quite frankly.

### Test Performance

His original intellectual endowment can be estimated as at least high aver-age (in the upper 25% of the population) on the basis of high average perform-ances on verbal and arithmetic reasoning tests. This estimate is supported by his history of keeping the position of shop steward for some years and having quali-fied as a hunting instructor.

*Verbal functions.* His scores on academic skills and verbal reasoning tests were in the average to high average ability range (a low average score obtained in the 3/83 examination on a test of general information was based on insuffi-cient testing and cannot be considered valid). His spelling and sentence con-structions were mostly in keeping with his education level. However, on his verbal fluency performance, in the borderline range, he blocked on two occa-sions, repeated himself once, and once forgot the letter called for in the one-minute trial.

*Perceptual/conceptual integration.* On the relatively well-structured visual reasoning subtests of the intelligence test given 3/83, he performed well within the *average* ability range. However, his performance on all other perceptual or-ganization tasks was *below normal limits*: these other tasks involve less familiar material or require more structuring and integration on the part of the subject.

Thus in his description of a picture story he identified the major figures but did not tie them together although their relationship is typically obvious to cognitively intact persons of even *low average* ability; and he failed to relate the components of another picture story that is readily comprehended by the majority of seven-year-olds. His ability to integrate fragmented pictures of common objects was *defective*. His abnormally slow responses on a test of tactile recognition and spatial organization earned him a score in the *brain damaged* range. Moreover, his piecemeal approach to copying a complex design reflect lack of conceptual organization of the material.

*Construction.* He made *average* scores on the well-structured constructional subtests of the intelligence test taken 3/83. These contrasted with a *defective* copy of the complex design and a crude, inaccurate, and rather fragmented bicycle drawing on which the pedal portion hung in space and the drive chain was omitted altogether.

*Abstracting/generalizing.* On well-structured tasks, he demonstrated a *high average* level of verbal concept formation. However, on both tests of nonverbal concept formation and conceptual flexibility his performance fell *below normal limits*. Although he seemed capable of making simple abstractions, he proved to be very slow in shifting to new concepts, could not keep track of all the elements involved in one task or maintain distinctions between differing conceptual principles on another task.

*Mental control.* He was slow to get the set of reversed operations and was unaware of errors, both of omission (leaving G & F out of Alphabet Backwards) and inattention (following 41 with 48 in Subtracting Serial Threes). Many errors compounded a very slow reading of color names; his performance was even more abnormally slowed and again punctuated with errors on the color naming form of this test: both trials in the *impaired* range reflects a high degree of distractibility as well as poor self-monitoring.

*Attentional functions.* The 3/83 examination found that his immediate span of attention was a little *below normal limits* for a man of his age; and that his performance on tests sensitive to concentration deficits were just *marginal to normal limits*. That distractibility showed up on the easier serial subtraction task but not the more difficult one suggests that concentration is erratic; that he lost track of a given letter of the alphabet within 35 to 40 seconds of hearing it and was also unable to repeat more than three digits reversed indicates how impaired is his capacity to concentrate. His very poor performance on the word and color naming test (noted above) gives further evidence of *impaired* ability to concentrate and withstand distraction. On simple visual tracking tasks P1 performed *within normal limits*. When the task is complicated, either by adding a mental tracking or an immediate memory requirement, his performance fell to the *impaired* range.

*Memory.* On all tests of memory functions excepting two of four trials on tests of immediate recall of meaningful material, he performed at *borderline defective* to *defective* levels. Particularly impaired were his immediate span of recall under stimulus overload conditions (i.e., when more information is given than can normally be immediately processed); rate of both verbal and tactile learning, retention of verbal learning; immediate recall of both visual and spatial information. Tactile recall was just *borderline to normal limits*.

### Diagnostic Impression

This man of originally *high average* intellectual endowment continues to give some evidence of his premorbid ability on well-structured tests of familiar verbal material; and his *average* scores on well-structured constructional tasks are not significantly lower. However, he shows pronounced impairments in many areas of cognitive functioning. These impairments show up most prominently as defects in perceptual/conceptual integration despite demonstrated perceptual accuracy; in mental control activities including both mental flexibility and abilities for self-monitoring and self-correction; in attentional functions in the form of blocking, distractibility, slowed and confused mental tracking, and slowed visual tracking when mental tracking or memory and learning in all (i.e., verbal, visual, and tactile) modalities. This is a pattern of cognitive strengths and deficits that can be best understood as the behavioral manifestations of organic brain dysfunction. The Scandinavian literature indicates that those deficits that remain long after removal from exposure to the toxic solvents are permanent.

In addition, on the basis of his and Mrs. P1's reports and of the nature of many of his performance errors (e.g., perceptual fragmentation, defective self-monitoring, impaired conceptual organization), this man who once took leadership roles (e.g., shop steward, hunting instructor) appears to have undergone a radical and very unwelcome personality change such that he tends to be passive, dependent on his wife for direction, lacks initiative, and has become somewhat withdrawn. Some of these new characteristics appear to reflect this once proud man's reactions to his cognitive impairments (e.g., social withdrawal; not attempting new activities); others such as inability to plan and organize his activities or to carry out a complex sequence of actions without prompting, however, probably represent the personality components of his altered mental functioning. It is not surprising, given this man's previous accomplishments and high activity level, that he is reactively depressed. Depression, in turn, may be contributing to attentional and immediate memory problems, but it is highly unlikely to affect other aspects of mental functioning to a significant degree.

A review of his deficits in the light of both his history of long exposure to toxic solvents and the recent diagnosis of hypertension suggests that while the greater part of his deficits are probably associated with solvent exposure (see a review of the Scandinavian literature on solvent exposure in publication), some of his attentional and memory problems may have been exacerbated by hypertension. However, his markedly defective ability for perceptual/conceptual integration, his impaired abilities for learning and retention, his reduced capacity for self-monitoring and self-correction, and slowing on visual tracking tasks are all deficits that have been associated with solvent exposure but not with hypertension.

The implications of this pattern of deficits for P1's future are grave. His *defective* capacity for perceptual and conceptual integration and organization will make it impossible for him to undertake any skilled craft. His greatly reduced learning capacity will make it impractical if not impossible for him to acquire new skills, whether they be verbal or nonverbal and visually guided. His impaired capacity for self-monitoring and self-correcting necessitate that he work only under close supervision or at such crude tasks that a low accuracy level is acceptable. Moreover, difficulties in making decisions, formulating plans, and functioning independently rule out future supervisory or leadership positions. Thus, by virtue of his pronounced cognitive deficits, this once bright man's vocational opportunities must be restricted to only the crudest sort of manual labor. Of course, the fact that he is seizure prone only adds further limitations to those already imposed by his mental impairments.

By _____
EW, Ph.D.

## UNIVERSITY NEUROPSYCHOLOGY LABORATORY

### NEUROPSYCHOLOGICAL REPORT

September 11, 1984

Patient's Name: P1

Date of birth: May 21, 1947

Age at time of testing: 37

Educational level: GED

Occupation: Spray painter

Referred by: Mr. G, Insurance Corp.

Dates tested: September 6 and 7, 1984

Tests administered: WAIS-R, Halstead-Indiana Battery of Neuropsychological Tests, Memory Tests, MMPI, Wide Range Achievement Test (Reading and Spelling), Kuder Occupational Interest Survey.

### Observations During Testing

P1 was cooperative and friendly throughout testing. He was adequately motivated throughout and a valid test record is felt to have been obtained.

He has been tested on several previous occasions and the neuropsychological reports from 3 and Dr. 4 (based on testing performed in March, 1983) and by Dr. EW (based on testing performed in July, 1983) were made available to us along with other medical records.

Patient is right-handed and he shows good grip strength in both hands.

### Results of Neuropsychological Examination

Performance on the WAIS places patient's current level of intellectual functioning at the lower end of the average range (Verbal IQ = 94; Performance IQ = 89; Full Scale IQ = 91).

These IQ scores are very similar to those reported by 3 and Dr. 4. Similarly the subtest scores obtained by P1 on the two testing occasions are reasonably similar. Thus he attained almost identical scores on 7 of the WAIS subtests (Similarities, Vocabulary, Digit Span, Picture Completion, Picture Arrangement, Object Assembly, and Digit Symbol); he performed somewhat better this time on two of the subtests (Information, Comprehension) and somewhat worse on two others (Arithmetic, Block Design). The correlation between the two sets of test scores is .54. Also, his scores on many of the other tests that we gave and which had also been previously administered by 3 and Dr. 4 are quite similar. The fact that his scores on these two separate occasions on many different tests are as similar as they are, adds credence to the reliability of the test data which was obtained for him. It argues against the possibility that his poor performance on either test occasion might be attributed to malingering. It also suggests that his level of functioning has been stabilized and that relatively little improvement may be expected in the future.

There was considerable variability in his level of functioning across the WAIS subtests. He performed at his best (i.e., at the above average level) on tasks demanding abstract-verbal skills (Similarities). He performed within the average range on tasks demanding general information, and simple verbal skills including vocabulary. He also performed at the average level on tasks demanding constructional ability (Object Assembly), visual accuracy, and being able to distinguish between essential and nonessential details (Picture Completion). He performed at his worst (at the dull normal level) on tasks demanding immediate attention span and on more complex perceptual-motor tasks emphasizing speed (Digit Symbol).

He experienced mild to moderate difficulties on most of the Halstead Tests attaining an Impairment Index of .9 which indicates the presence of diffuse impairments due to central nervous system dysfunction. He performed least well on tasks requiring coping with novel and unfamiliar problem-solving situations (Categories Test) and on more complex tasks requiring the subject to keep two different things in mind at the same time (Trails B). P1 experienced initial difficulties on the Tactile Performance Test (done with patient blindfolded) requiring an excessive amount of time to complete this test on the first and second trials. However, on the third trial he showed marked improvement and was able to complete this test with an amount of time that is close to being within normal limits. His performance was mildly reduced on tasks requiring simple motor speed (Finger Tapping Test) and on those requiring sustained concentration and fine auditory discriminations (Speech Perception, Seashore Rhythms). He is at his best on simple tasks which can be performed under visual control (Trails A).

The results of the Aphasia Screening examination were essentially negative. Patient experienced mild problems with the pronunciation of difficult words but then so do many normal individuals. He is able to comprehend verbal messages and he is able to express himself adequately. There was no evidence of left-right confusion. He is able to name common objects and can demonstrate their use. His ability to engage in abstract reasoning is intact. He is able to read and write letters, numbers, words, and simple sentences. The Wide Range Achievement Test places his reading at the 8th and his spelling at the 5th grade levels, respectively. His ability to engage in tasks requiring arithmetical computations is intact. Language functions may thus be said to be intact.

Patient's reproductions (by drawing) of simple geometric designs and objects are reasonably well executed and show no evidence of serious perceptual distortion. In general, one would expect him to be able to deal with everyday kinds of tasks emphasizing spatial relationships and spatial organization at a level that is consistent with his level of intellectual functioning.

On the Sensory Perception examination patient made a small number of errors (bilaterally) on the Finger Agnosia and Finger Tip Number Writing tests. There was no evidence of suppression of sensation under conditions of simultaneous stimulation. Tactile form recognition is intact.

Patient experienced serious difficulties on all of the Memory tests. His immediate attention span for both visual and auditory information is markedly reduced. He found it very difficult to master a 24-element story within ten trials. At the end of the tenth trial he only had ten of the elements correct. Retested on the story a day later he was only able to recall three of the elements. With ten additional trials he was still only able to get up to 14 correct. Questioned about memory difficulties in everyday situations patient indicated that he is experiencing problems with being able to remember what he is supposed to do (e.g., doing things at the right time like keeping appointments), with what he has heard, and with what he has seen. The laboratory findings are consistent with patient's self-report. Patient has noted a gradual increase in his memory problems since 1980-81.

Patient's scores on the validity scales of the MMPI indicate that he took this test in a valid and sincere manner and that a valid record was obtained. (It is important to note that the current MMPI profile is very similar to that which was obtained by 3 and Dr. 4 in their testing, again emphasizing the reliability of his test responses.) His current MMPI shows significant elevations on the Hysteria (T = 89), Hypochondriasis (T = 88), Depression (T = 78), Psychasthenia-Anxiety (T = 83), and Schizophrenia (T = 71) scales.

Personality characteristics associated with this MMPI profile type:

1.  Exhibits depression.
2.  Complains of difficulty in going to sleep.
3.  Reports difficulty in thinking; can't concentrate.
4.  Reacts to frustration intropunitively.
5.  Keeps people at a distance; avoids close interpersonal relationships.
6.  Is vulnerable to real or fancied threats; generally fearful; is a worrier.
7.  Psychological conflicts are represented in somatic symptoms.
8.  Complains of weakness or easy fatigability.
9.  Has feelings of hopelessness.
10. Has difficulties expressing emotions in a modulated adaptive way.
11. Obsessive thinking is present.

Critical MMPI items answered in "pathological" direction indicating:

1.  He has had very peculiar and strange experiences.
2.  He often feels as if there were a tight band around his head.
3.  He has had periods in which he carried on activities without knowing later what he had been doing.

4.  He has had blank spells in which his activities were interrupted and he did not know what was going on around him.

## Summary and Recommendations

In summary, neuropsychological testing reveals a man whose premorbid intelligence is estimated to have been within the average range and who now shows a pattern of impairments which is consistent with the presence of central nervous system impairment. Impairments were manifested most markedly on tasks requiring immediate attention span and memory processes (the amount of simultaneously presented information that he can correctly register is limited and he has marked difficulties in being able to learn and to retain longer sequences over longer periods of time), and on more complex tasks requiring mental shifts and mental flexibility. Mild impairments were noted on tasks emphasizing motor speed and sustained concentration. Language functions were found to be essentially intact. Patient was found to be able to function at his best on simple, relatively routinized tasks performed under visual control.

The MMPI indicates the presence of significant psychopathology with depression, somatic symptoms and complaints, and feelings of anxiety predominating. Neither the MMPI nor the rest of the test protocol suggests the presence of a psychotic disorganization.

Because of the severity and the extent of this man's neuropsychological impairments (especially his marked memory defect and the limitations in his ability to cope with more complex and unfamiliar tasks on which he has a tendency to become confused) it is my opinion that this man at this point in time is not capable of performing in occupational situations with normal requirements and demands. However, I would also see him as a good candidate for vocational rehabilitation with the goal of helping him to commit himself and to acquire the skills to perform in occupational situations that are consistent with his abilities and interests. Occupational planning might try to take advantage of his good verbal skills and his ability to function well in well-structured, routinized types of tasks which can be performed under visual guidance and which do not have large memory demands.

The Kuder Occupational Interest Survey has been administered and has been sent out for scoring. When the results are obtained a short supplementary report will be furnished.

Regarding the specific questions raised by _____, DDS Supervisor, Workers' Compensation Department, in her letter of August 30, 1984, I would like to respond as follows:

1.  Do you feel the conditions are medically stationary in the sense that the conditions will not improve with further treatment or the passage of time?

I feel that P1's neuropsychological condition is fairly stationary and that relatively little improvement may be expected.

2.  Are these conditions to any extent reversible?

Within reasonable psychological probabilities, I do not think that his neuropsychological impairments are reversible.

3.  Except for the obvious continued exposure to the solvents, are these patients mentally capable of resuming their former occupations of painter/sandblaster?

It is my opinion that both in terms of the neuropsychological deficits which already exist and the emotional trauma that is likely to be experienced, he is not capable of resuming his former occupation of painter/sandblaster.

4.  Are they mentally capable of learning new technical skills to enable them to begin new occupations?

This is a difficult question to answer. His neuropsychological impairments clearly limit his ability to learn new technical skills and this will seriously limit the range of occupations which are open to him. At the same time, I feel that it is important for his emotional well-being that he be assisted in gradually reentering the world of work at some level.

5.  If number 4 is no, are they then mentally capable of functioning in laboring jobs relying on past skills or are they truly incapable of engaging in gainful employment?

At this point in time, and in the foreseeable future, I do not feel that he is capable of engaging in gainful employment under conditions of normal demands and requirements.

6.  Is there any possibility of separating the effects of the damage done by the solvent and paint exposure from any preexisting damage that may have been present? It is noted that he has served in VietNam and was exposed to "agent orange."

I do not think so.

7.  The classification of impairment related to the various disorders resulting from the brain damage.

It is my opinion that he has suffered a Level II type of impairment, i.e., there is a degree of impairment of complex integrated cerebral functions such that daily activities need some supervision and/or direction. Percent impairment = 30%.

8.  Is there a cognitive retraining program that would be beneficial to either of the patients to help them adjust to their deficiencies?

His present condition is compounded by the fact that he has objective impairments and that he has not been working for an extended period of time. Reentry will thus be difficult. I feel that he would benefit from personal and vocational counseling aimed at helping him to compensate for some of his cognitive deficiencies and helping him to commit himself to a long term plan increasing his activities in a meaningful and personally rewarding way.

**Diagnostic Impression**
294.80 Mixed Organic Brain Syndrome

Dr. 6, Ph.D.
Professor of Psychology

**TABLE 1**

The following is a comparison of the results of the WAIS administered to P1 in 1981 and the three WAIS-R of March 1983, October 1983, and September 1984.

| | WAIS 10/23/81 | | WAIS-R 3/3/83 | | WAIS-R 10/13/83 | | WAIS-R 9/6/84 | | Compari-son of 3/83 and 9/84 |
|---|---|---|---|---|---|---|---|---|---|
| | RAW | SCALE | RAW | SCALE | RAW | SCALE | RAW | SCALE | |
| Information | 15 | 10 | 11 | 6 | | | 19 | 10 | +4 |
| Digit Span | 10 | 9 | 9 | 6 | 5 | 2 | 7 | 4 | -2 |
| | (6 Forward) | | (5 F) | | (3 F) | | (4F) | | |
| | (4 Backward) | | (3 B) | | (3 B) | | (3B) | | |
| Vocabulary | 52 | 11 | 47 | 10 | | | 46 | 9 | -1 |
| Arithmetic | 10 | 9 | 14 | 11 | 5 | 5 | 6 | 6 | -5 |
| Comprehension | 21 | 13 | 25 | 7 | | | 21 | 10 | +3 |
| | | | | (should be 12) | | | | | (should be -2) |
| Similarities | 18 | 12 | 24 | 14 | 22 | 11 | 25 | 14 | 0 |
| Verbal Score | | 64 | | 54 | | | | 53 | |
| | | | | (should be 59) | | | | | |
| Picture Completion | 15 | 11 | 16 | 10 | | | 16 | 10 | 0 |
| Picture Arrangement | 16 | 7 | 12 | 8 | | | 12 | 8 | 0 |
| Block Design | 34 | 10 | 32 | 10 | | | 16 | 6 | -4 |
| Object Assembly | 30 | 9 | 33 | 10 | | | 31 | 9 | -1 |
| Digit Symbol | 48 | 9 | 43 | 6 | | | 33 | 5 | -1 |
| Performance Score | | 46 | | 44 | | | | 38 | |
| Verbal IQ | | 103 | | 91 (95)* (99) | | | | 94 | |
| Performance IQ | | 95 | | 92 (97)* (97) | | | | 89 | |
| Full Scale IQ | | 100 | | 91 (95)* (98) | | | | 91 | |

Note 1.　Research and WAIS-R manual are clear that WAIS-R V, P, & FS IQ's are 7, 7, and 8 points lower than WAIS, so WAIS-R FS 91 = WAIS 99.

Note 2.　IQ 9/59 CTMM (_____ Union H.S.) Lang. 99, Non-lang. 96, total 97.

Note 3.　Iowa Test of Educational Development (_____ H.S. 1964) Composite 57th percentile—very average. Range 9th percentile to 82nd percentile—highly variable performance or scatter.

Note 4.*　These are age corrected IQ's per incorrect scale score totals. An explanation of these discrepancies, due to two different errors by the examiner, is provided on page 371.

## NOTES FOR DC ON P1

Table 1 is a comparison of the results of the WAIS administered in 1981 and the three WAIS-R of March 1983, October 1983 and September 1984.

It should also be noted that for the most part EEG and CT scan did not show abnormalities.

Prior to the preparation of a report by the author-consultant, defense counsel (DC) made the decision not to utilize the consultant as a witness, thereby preserving the report as work product and not amenable to discovery proceedings. The report follows:

In these notes I will not be dealing, except perhaps incidentally, with the issue of whether or not there is such a thing as "painter's syndrome." Nor will I be dealing specifically with the administration and interpretation of the neuropsychological tests. You should, however, clearly understand that all psychological tests are merely tools for making inferences which in reality are "informed" guesses or speculations with particular emphasis on the words guesses or speculations. If they are useful at all, it is primarily as a basis for forming hypotheses where there is an absence of objectively determinable facts or in conjunction with obtainable objective facts.

There is some evidence of malingering, understood as faking or exaggerating psychological deficits or problems which I will deal with specifically in a later portion of this report, but in general, I am sure you as well as almost anyone else, understand that there is a clear motive for malingering in personal injury claims and therefore the probability of malingering must be seriously considered and evaluated in nearly every case.

My primary focus will be on the abundant evidence that whatever P1's psychological status is at the present time and whatever difficulties he may be having, these have been present at least since his middle adolescence through his young adulthood and therefore are not the result of this so called "painter's syndrome," if there is such a thing.

It should be noted that in the neuropsychological assessments that were done and the reports of such examinations that were written, the psychologists were utilizing the better or best performances by P1 as the standard for judging what his so called "premorbid" functioning was like. That is, in the most typical example, they have utilized his best score on the WAIS-R as indicating his true intellectual endowment and therefore the level at which he probably functioned prior to suffering the brain damage which they have concluded has occurred in connection with his job as a painter. I believe the evidence will show that either these conclusions are incorrect or they are of no value in determining whether and to what extent P1's functioning has been reduced or impaired. I might note parenthetically that you will probably need to get some definition from each examiner as to how they are using the term "impaired" or "impairment" because it has two meanings. In one meaning, it indicates that the individual performs less well than the normal or average person. In the other sense, it means that the individual performs less well than he is capable of or less well than he did at some prior time. It is only in the second sense that the term impairment has any relevance for this matter, although one can argue that comparison with others provides some clues as to loss of function.

There are also two broad areas in which impairment can occur as a result of brain damage. One area is in the area of cognitive function broadly defined to include perception, memory, ability to abstract, the functions we generally think of as functions of the intellect. The other area is in the area of emotional or personality functioning broadly understood to include such areas as interpersonal functioning, social functioning, occupational functioning, motivation, coping ability, mood, self-control or self-discipline and so on. I will attempt to deal with these separately as much as possible although obviously, factors in the cognitive area can effect emotional functioning and vice versa.

Before getting into the evidence regarding P1's cognitive functioning, I think it is important to have in mind statements made by Dr. EW in an interview a few months after his examination.

"One final question, and we don't know do we whether the patterns which either one of these or both of these gentlemen exhibit are not peculiar to them as individuals and have always been with them?"

Dr. EW: "Well, we don't know it for sure but the fact that they both perform well on those kinds of activities that tend to be most resilient, suggests that at one time, they were probably performing that well, in all areas. The reasons for this is and this has been borne out over and over again since about 1905."

Doctor EW? (tape had ended)

Dr. EW: "By and large, people who do well in one thing tend to do well in other things. People who do poorly in one thing tend to do poorly in other things and it is more exceptional for someone who has not had any particular illnessess or injuries or an impoverished childhood or something like that, not exposed to the common culture, it is very rare for somebody like that to show such a difference particularly in learning ability. Here these gentlemen demonstrate that at one time they had normal learning ability and today, they don't. For instance, they had scores on vocabulary tests and tests of old learning or arithmetic, in P1's case, that represent a good ability to learn at one time." The reference to P1's arithmetic score refers to his score on the WAIS-R, I am sure, and it is rather interesting to note that in October, 1981, his scale score on arithmetic was nine. On March 3, 1983 on the WAIS-R it was eleven, which while not a significant difference, is an increase and subsequent I believe to the time that he had ceased exposure to the paint. On October 13, 1983, the WAIS-R, his scale score was five and on September 6, 1984 on the Dr. 6 test his scale score on arithmetic was six. Which of these represents P1's true ability? Very likely Dr. EW and the others would argue that his highest score represents his true ability. Which of the scores represents his most likely performance? No one can answer that question except to say that his performance apparently is highly variable and keep in mind that it is the actual performance that provides the basis from which conclusions are drawn. Raw ability, the actual performance capability of the brain cells, cannot be observed, only inferred from performance.

Turning now to the objective factual evidence concerning P1's cognitive functions, I look first at the records from _____ High School District in 1959. He apparently attended this school for two semesters obtaining, excluding physical education, three B's, seven C's and a D, indicating some above average performances, some average performances and some below average performances or at least three levels of performance. I note that two of the B's were in a course called social living which might be worth investigation as it has the sound of something that is not really an academic course at all. It does not appear to be social studies because that is a different category as indicated in the next set of rows and columns for semesters that P1 did not attend that school.

We might also note in all fairness that the D is in a shop course which ordinarily is not viewed as an academic type of course. However, it may very well have involved some of the same kinds of visual-constructive or spatial perception or manual dexterity types of functions that it is now claimed are impaired in P1. In any event, this record does show some "scatter" which is a term generally applied to the disparity among subtest scores on the WAIS. Also attached to the High School records on the second page, are the records of his performance in September of 1959 on a test described as CTMM which I would assume refers to the California Test of Mental Maturity, a widely used IQ test in the school system. On this test, P1 achieves a total IQ of 97 with a language IQ of 99 and non-language IQ 96, once again confirming a very average intellectual ability, at least as demonstrated on this test.

(For your convenience I am providing on Attachment I, all of P1's scores on the WAIS and the three WAIS-R's that he was given from 1981 through 1984 with some notes covering his scores on the CTMM just mentioned and the Iowa Test of Educational Development which will be discussed below.) Next I note the records from another High School, apparently covering approximately the years 1961 to mid-1964, which would seem to encompass P1's middle teen years, perhaps fifteen, sixteen, seventeen and up to eighteen at which time he became eligible to join the armed services. According to the deposition of November 29, 1984, of the principal and custodian of the records of _____ High School, the grading system during P1's first two semesters at _____ was a numerical one with grades from 1 through 5 representing the letter grades A through F, one being A and five being F. Counting the numerical grades and the letter grades on the transcript, I count for P1, one B (in typing), three C's, eighteen D's and six F's. Thus we have another example of a high degree of variability in P1's cognitive functioning. The grades stated above represent at least three levels of functioning, average, below average and severely below average and represent four levels if one counts the B in typing, which does represent a skill acquired through a learning process. Two conclusions seem clear from this data. One is that P1 functioned in the early sixties considerably below that of a person of average intelligence, although it is arguable that his poor grades were not a function of his intelligence but of his motivation or effort. This argument of course then provides a basis for a conclusion that P1 does not always exert a good effort particularly in cognitive or test type tasks. The second conclusion and this does not seem arguable on any basis that I can think of, is that P1 performs with a high degree of variability or "scatter" in real life. This appears to provide clear evidence that people who perform well in one thing do not necessarily perform well in other things, nor do people who perform badly in one thing perform badly in other things. And it makes it very, very clear that at least in the case of P1 any effort to predict or post-dict his cognitive functioning at a prior time based on the best of his current performances is sheer folly. On the Iowa Test of Educational Development given during his junior year at _____, apparently the 1963-64 school year, he shows a composite score which places him at the 57th percentile summing over a variety of tested areas. Once again, the 57th percentile indicates a very, very average performance. Looking at the subtests of the Iowa, we note that he ranges from a low of the ninth percentile in exposition or writing to the eighty-second percentile in social studies, with other scores at the fifty-ninth percentile, seventy-eighth percentile, fifty-third percentile, fifty-sixth percentile, fifty-first percentile, and sixty-ninth percentile, so that once again we see, above average performance, considerable average performance and way below average performance. So that once again we are seeing that, on tests, he displays a great deal of variability or "scatter."

Next I look at P1's military records, starting with a document titled, MOS evaluation, for the evaluation period August 1967, concerning subject matter dated January '67 [sic]. On the MOS evaluation, five grades are possible, very low, low, typical, high and very high. P1 obtains the following:

1.  Armored vehicle characteristics and maintenance     —very low
2.  Armored vehicle operation     —very high
3.  Small arms and amunition     —typical
4.  Vehicular mounted main weapons     —very low
5.  Communication     —typical
6.  Armor tactics     —low
7.  Common subjects     —very low

It can be seen that he performs at four different levels on these tests (the document bears the title Individual's MOS Evaluation Test Profile, so I assume these are grades on tests). It may be worthwhile, if you are able to determine what the term "common subjects" refers to. This data provides another example of his premorbid functioning at average or below average levels and of the high degree of variability or scatter in his premorbid functioning.

The military records contain further evidence of P1's functioning. I am referring to a document which is titled at the top, Project Pace 22-Jan-69 and containing scores of apptitude tests with a testing date apparently the 27th of May, 1964 with some additional tests on June 10th, 1964. There are a large number of tests. I will not run through them all but simply point out that the scores range from sixty-eight to one hundred eighteen with scores at almost all levels in between. There appears to be further testing on several of these tests at a later date which is given on the document as 75-10-06 which I would assume to mean either the sixth of October, 1975 or the tenth of June, 1975 although this is just a guess on my part. In any event, in that set of scores, he ranges from eighty nine to one hundred sixty. I do not know what these tests are and nor am I able to decipher the abbreviations. You should be aware that the scores given here may be raw test scores, it looks like they are, and for each given test might represent average performance. Just looking at the raw scores given here suggests that there is considerable variation. It would probably be worthwhile, if you are able to determine what these tests are and what the numbers mean, as I suspect they will provide still more evidence of a high degree of variability or scatter in his test performance.

To sum up this section, P1's grades in school, tests of intellectual capacity administered long before he became a painter, and military records are in complete agreement that prior to his becoming a painter, he showed a high degree of variability on these various measures of intellectual or cognitive abilities. While he occasionally showed somewhat above average performances the over-whelming bulk of measured performances show him either at average or below average levels. He shows virtually no change in measured IQ, bearing in mind that IQ as measured by the WAIS-R tends to be lower than that measured by the WAIS by about eight points. Thus he has consistently shown IQ somewhere between 90 and 100 on all tests given and relatively little variation within that range which would be of no significance anyway because it is all average and represents no kind of difference that is meaningful in terms of the way an individual could perform. That is, from the standpoint of IQ, an individual with an IQ of 91 can do just about anything that an individual with an IQ of 97 can do. They are both just average people. Furthermore, the scatter or variability of his performance on the WAIS-R does not appear to be any greater than that evidenced in prior testings, that is, prior to becoming a painter. Therefore, Dr. EW's estimate of his "premorbid" intellectual ability appears flatly to be in error. There is simply no basis for concluding that P1 is any different cognitively now than he was prior to the time that he became a painter. His cognitive performance is highly variable as it always has been. Unfortunately with regard to some of the specific measures of reproduction of geometric designs or verbal memory or some of the other specialized tests, there is no pre-morbid evidence. Therefore inasmuch as P1 does not show changes in the cognitive areas of functioning for which we do have pre-morbid measures, the most probable conclusion one can come to is that he would not show such changes in those measures where we do not have prior measures. If it is argued that his prior problems were motivational in nature that is just speculation and, it is difficult to understand why he would be motivated to perform better when he is being evaluated for the purpose of getting money in a lawsuit.

One point on the WAIS should be particularly noticed because in his interview with Dr. EW, EW reports his description of a transaction in a store recently (recall that his interview was on July 7, 1983) in which he was unable to perform some simple computations involving a couple of twenty dollar bills and a couple of one dollar bills in a store. It should be noted that on the March 3, 1983 administration of the WAIS-R, he successfully performed calculations on the arithmetic subtest items 8, 9, 10, 12 and 13, which are more difficult than the one he described. Incidentally, he was improperly given a time bonus of one additional point on item 12 for answering within 10 seconds although the record form shows he took 11 seconds. This changes his total score on Arithmetic from 14 to 13 but does not change his scale score.

It is hard to imagine that his ability to calculate would have deteriorated to that extent somewhere between the time that he was examined in March of '83 and the interview by Dr. EW. It might also be noted that a considerable amount of concentration and attention is required to perform these arithmetic problems, as they are administered verbally, so one has to pay close attention and concentrate on what is being said as well as being able to perform the calculations.

P1's military records provide some additional information which may be relevant to assessing his prior cognitive functioning as well as his prior psychological or emotional status (the latter is something I will deal with below). For the present purpose, it is noted that, in an examination in the military dated

May 26, 1964 there is a notation that he stuttered or stammered with an additional comment that he showed mild stuttering when "apprehensive." It showed that he suffered from depression or excessive worry. It showed that he had broken his arm three times. I mention this because some of the tasks on which he was currently being tested involved the use of the arms. I should mention that stuttering or stammering is often a symptom of some underlying anxiety which is interfering with the individual's functioning and which if present before may have been present during the current testing. A note from the military of November 1, 1966 shows that he was injured by a tank motor and had suffered tendinitis as a result. My limited medical knowledge, coupled with some personal knowledge of tendinitis, is that once you have it, it doesn't go away and it can interfere with your physical functioning, such that there might be some interference on some of the tests. Note, March 15, 1965, P1 suffered dizzy spells and was short of breath, again suggesting a possibility of some sort of anxiety state. Also it is obviously of importance to know that he was suffering dizzy spells before he became a painter. September 7, 1965 there was an auto accident in which he sustained a shoulder injury which may have left him with some residual loss of functioning that may have shown up on the tests. August 26, 1966 records indicate there is a weakness of the left arm, although the doctor notes there is no objective evidence of this. Apparently it was something he complained of, once again suggesting the possibility of some physical limitation which affects some of his test performances. July 31st, 1967 there is a notation of eye trouble and I believe I have commented on this, but if I haven't, there apparently is an indication that P1 needs some correction from glasses and we do not have any indication in any of the reports that he was wearing glasses when he took the tests. February 3rd, 1969 a report of chest pain that was not associated with exertion but occurs when he becomes upset or anxious. There is a notation "no shortness of breath but he becomes lightheaded," which I would assume means the same thing as becoming dizzy and apparently the dizziness is associated with anxiety. There is a further notation, December 28th 1968, dizziness, nausea and stomach cramps. While this could indicate nothing more than a bout of the flu, in line with some of the earlier reports of dizziness there begins to build up a picture of a man who suffered relatively frequently from dizziness prior to becoming a painter. However, for the immediate purpose, it would appear that at the minimum it shows a strong probability of suffering from either rather constant or at least relatively frequently occurring bouts of anxiety. It is well-known and well documented that anxiety can affect attention, concentration and memory, that is, at least recent memory, probably by virtue of its interference with attention and concentration. Also it can affect fine eye-hand coordination. Therefore, there is much in the military records that could provide some alternative explanations for his performances on some of the intelligence or neuropsychological tests. It is not clear whether any of the examining clinicians were aware of any of these prior events or conditions of P1. It seems quite likely that he would have had some degree of anxiety associated with taking these tests in view of the fact that he must have been aware that the purpose of the test was connected with his effort to obtain a substantial sum of money by his law suit. Perhaps this is as good a place as any to mention that he and some of the other plaintiffs in similar law suits were acquainted with each other and did have conversations with each other and that likely by virtue of his position as shop steward he was receiving information regarding toxic brain syndromes and would have had some awareness, whether held consciously or unconsciously, of some of the kinds of symptoms which indicated the presence of such damage. Thus, if it was his intention to present such a picture falsely, he could have done so without even being aware that he was using information he had obtained, much as we have indications that unconscious plagiarism does occur.

Of considerable additional importance is the fact that in all probability the testing performed by 3 under the direction of Dr. 4 at the University Hospital Department of Medical Psychology on March 3, 1983 should be thrown out of court on the grounds that it was performed by a trainee whose questionable competence seems evident in some of the test material. Unfortunately, a great deal of the test material is either illegible or unintelligible to me. Nevertheless, the following is clear and indicates several errors on the part of 3. It will probably help you to deal with what I am about to say, if you will have the WAIS-R record form of March 3, 1983 in front of you while reading this. First of all, as I believe I have already mentioned, on item twelve of the arithmetic subtest, P1 got the correct answer in eleven seconds which is worth one point of credit but is not worth the two points for time bonus that 3 gave him, as the time bonus is given only if the answer is obtained in ten seconds or less. Obviously it's only a matter of one second but the rule is the rule and it is wrong to give two points if it takes eleven seconds, therefore his raw score is thirteen rather than fourteen. This does not make any difference in the overall picture because, as you will note on the front sheet of the record form, a score of either thirteen or fourteen raw, equals a scale score of eleven on the arithmetic subtest.

The report of 3/Dr. 4 states, "Attention and concentration ability is spotty as demonstrated by the average arithmetic score…" This assertion makes no sense to me. How can "average" show a deficiency, particularly when it is one scale score above the mean and is his second highest score of the eleven subtests? Far more serious, if you continue to look on the front sheet of the record form, you will note under the heading "Summary," P1 has on the comprehension subtest a raw score of twenty-five which 3 translates into a scale score of seven. However, if you will look over to the left side of the page under the table of scale score equivalents, you will see that a raw score of twenty-five on the comprehension subtest equates to a scale score of twelve rather than seven. I suspect that what 3 did was glance carelessly at the scores and look at the fourteen raw for arithmetic and circle the fourteen under comprehension, thus leading to this considerable error. It makes a good deal of difference because it then makes the total verbal score for P1, fifty-nine rather than fifty-four. Even without this error, 3 had miscalculated his IQ because at the time of testing, he was thirty-five years and some months old, which means that if you turn to page one hundred in the manual to look for IQ equivalents of sums of scaled scores for the age group 35-44 you would find that for a verbal sum of scale scores of fifty-four, the IQ is 95, not 91 as 3 has presented it. And further, if you look at the performance sum of scale scores of 44, that is equivalent to a performance IQ of 97, not 92 as 3 has scored it, and a full scale score of 98 for a thirty-five year old man translates to a full scale score of 95, not 91 as 3 has presented it. I am fairly certain that what happened is that 3 carelessly glanced at the age written on the record form and, if one looks carefully, they can see that the number is 35 the upper flag of the five is almost overlapping with the heavy black line for date of birth. So that in haste, one might read that age as 33 and indeed if one looks for the IQ equivalents for ages 25-34, then, according to the verbal performance and full scale scores he has, 3 has correctly stated the IQ's. It's just that they would be wrong because of P1's correct age of thirty-five, even if 3 had not made the other scoring errors indicated. However, recalculating the IQ correctly, we come out with a verbal score as indicated above of fifty-nine which for men age 35-44 translates to an IQ of ninety-nine, the performance sum of scale scores of forty-four translates to a performance IQ of ninety-seven and the sum of scores for the full scale becomes 103, instead of 98 and this translates for a man of P1's age to a full scale IQ of ninety-eight, not ninety-one. Therefore, both in late 1981 and in March of 1983 presumably after some twelve to thirteen years of exposure to the various alleged toxic substances, P1 is performing at the same IQ level that has ever been recorded for him before and perhaps higher than had been recorded in some instances. However, inasmuch as the outcome of testing depends to some extent on the competence of the examiner, one can legitimately question whether it is safe or reasonable to use any of the testing performed by 3 as there is at least this objective evidence of incompetent performance on his part and we cannot tell all of the things that may have gone on in the testing session that may have been equal or more serious errors that do not appear in the record forms. I might add that the same might be said for any conclusions by Dr. 4 as Dr. 4 has endorsed the findings and the data obtained by 3 when he signed the report. This despite the fact that he either did not look at the evidence himself, or if he looked at it was guilty of the same error at least in not recognizing the mis-scoring of the comprehension subtest which is obvious to anyone who looked at it. What is the significance of "under the supervision of Dr. 4" if the above noted errors slip through? The report also states that 90 seconds on Trail-Making Test (B) shows significant impairment. This is wrong per the manual, which shows the impaired range begins at 91 seconds and up.

Further note on alternative explanations for P1's difficulties can be found by careful reading of the notes of his therapy for post-traumatic stress disorder at the Veterans Administration. I am going to deal with this more extensively below, but I would just point out here that there are notes of the therapist indicating that P1 was very helpful in helping the group members stay on the subject which does not seem to jibe very well with his complaints that he cannot remember what people say and that he has difficulty with short term memory. The notes indicate that he was helpful in keeping the group focused on the point and other notes indicate that he was attentive (i.e., was able to pay attention) to what was going on in the group. If you will look at page 236 through 238 in the *Diagnostic and Statistical Manual of Mental Disorders, III*, you will note that memory impairment or trouble concentrating are among the symptoms of post-traumatic stress disorder, the diagnosis that was given as "most probable" by the therapist at the Veterans Administration.

You may also be interested in knowing that while less spectacular, there were also some scoring errors on the WAIS-R administered on September 6, 1984 at the University neuropsychology lab. These are the test results that Dr. 6 used in drawing his conclusions about P1. There are two scoring errors on the vocabulary subtest which would reduce the raw score to forty-four which however does not change the scale score as any raw score from forty-three to forty-six equates to a scale score of nine. However, it is worth noting that at the top of the record form it states "tested by 7" so it seems clear that Dr. 6 did not do the testing. We do not know who 7 is, but may surmise that he or she may have been another trainee and then the question becomes which of the other tests were given by the trainee. There is another possible error, on the comprehension subtest, item number eight. One other point which I will deal with later in regard to this particular WAIS performance, is that we note that P1 on the arithmetic subtests misses items 5, 7, 8, 10, 11, 12 & 13, virtually all of which he was able to perform satisfactorily and with time bonuses, only a year and a half before, and so far as we know he has had little or no paint exposure in the interim. There is one additional scoring error on the similarities subtest and that is on item twelve. This is an additional scoring error which would reduce the raw score from twenty-five to twenty-four and make the scale score thirteen instead of fourteen, making the total verbal score fifty-two instead of fifty-three and a verbal IQ 93 instead of 94, and a raw full scale 90 instead of 91, which would then be an IQ of 90 instead of 91. Obviously these differences do not make any real difference and I am including this only to suggest some lack of competent performance on the part of the examiner as was the case with the testing by 3. I note on the MMPI profile sheet where it says, scorer's initials, would appear to be the initials 7 presumably again, Mr. or Miss 7, same person who administered the WAIS. And in fact, the information sheet from the University psychology clinic, neuropsychological laboratory indicates that the examiner was 7 on September 6th and September 7th and that 7 administered all of the tests listed on that page which would appear to be the tests of the Halstead-Reitan battery plus some of the other neuropsychological tests. In other words, it appears that Dr. 6 who is the Ph.D. and presumably the experienced person is not the one who administered the tests. You will recall from Dr. EW's talk that was attended by your associate, that he indicated it is a poor practice to have the test administered by anyone below the Ph.D. level. Of course we do not know for a fact that 7 is below that level but I suspect that to be the case. I might just add at this point so it will be clear to you that administering of these tests with the possible exception of the MMPI, is not something that can really be done adequately by a lab technician. It is not like drawing blood for blood tests where the blood is going to be sent away to be analyzed by a skilled person, it is a process which involves a good deal of interpersonal interaction. It is generally thought by many clinicians to require, if it is of any value at all, that it be performed by someone with sufficient skill and experience.

It should be noted that Wasyliw and Golden, in an article titled: "Neuropsychological Evaluation in the Assessment of Personal Injury," in *Behavioral Sciences and the Law*, Volume 3, Number 2, Spring 1985, pages 149-164, at page 152 state, "No tests or formulae claimed to be able to assess intelligence or other cognitive levels at any time prior to testing, let alone brain injury, have been sufficiently validated or replicated for general use." "Any such estimation specifically requires access to historical data such as prior academic and occupational achievements."

I am also enclosing as Attachment II, an article printed in the *Los Angeles Times,* May 7th, 1984 which describes a paper presented at the meeting of the American Psychiatric Association indicating that decrease in memory performance begins to occur around age thirty and is at its greatest between the ages of thirty and fifty. I have not seen a publication in print of this paper and it may be that you would wish to write to Dr. Albert to obtain a copy. It may be in press, as it is not unusual for it to take a couple of years for a paper to find its way into print.

With regard to the possibility of faking brain damage type deficits on the WAIS, I am enclosing as Attachment III, a portion from the 1978 article by Heaton, et al. on malingering of neuropsychological deficits which is extensively discussed in the chapter on malingering in my book. You will note from Heaton's data that the untutored group of known malingerers scored their lowest score of the verbal tests on the digit span subtest and paradoxically were significantly lower than the actual head injured patients in the Heaton study. This would tend to indicate that without any prior knowledge as to how brain damaged people might perform on the WAIS, these subjects who had been hired to fake brain damage managed to produce the low score on the test where it is expected that brain damaged patients would score low. Also while not markedly deviant, their scores on the arithmetic subtest tended to be somewhat lower than their better scores.

## PSYCHOLOGICAL—EMOTIONAL— PERSONALITY FUNCTIONING

The other aspect of P1's functioning which, it is claimed, has been impaired or in which problems have been created, is variously described as his psychological functioning or emotional functioning or personality functioning. For purposes of this discussion I will use the term psychological functioning.

There are two principal issues in this area of functioning. One of them is the question as to whether there really is any unusual amount of impairment or psychological problems in his case, and if there is, whether it can not be accounted for on bases other than brain damage. The other issue is the extent to which P1 had psychological problems or difficulties prior to his exposure to the alleged toxic substances. It seems fairly clear that the psychologists in this case drew conclusions about his "premorbid" psychological status, once again, without any reference to a fairly abundant documentation of prior complaints contained particularly in his military records.

I will deal with the evidence of prior psychological problems first.

One line of evidence suggesting earlier psychological problems lies in the relationship between his performance in school and his level of intelligence, if in fact his level of intelligence was average or high average as asserted by Dr. EW. That is, for an individual of average or high average intelligence to get almost exclusively D's and F's in his high school courses, suggests the possible presence of psychological problems of one kind or another although it can be argued that it may just represent a lack of interest in school. Some however, would consider this a psychological problem that one is willing to accept poor grades and failures in high school. However, it is noted in some of the records that P1 had a fairly disturbed childhood in terms of shifting around of parental figures and shifting from one home to another and I believe even being adopted finally. So that while this does not necessarily mean that one is going to have psychological problems, it certainly is believed to provide fertile ground for psychological problems and, indeed, further evidence that there are such problems appears in the military records.

Plaintiff's long-standing severe obesity is in itself generally viewed as a symptom of some kind of psychological difficulty. Although this condition can be a result of genetic or glandular factors, there is nothing in the records to indicate that to be the case. Therefore, the conclusion one is left with is that it is connected to psychological problems which obviously predate an alleged toxic exposure.

The military records indicate on an examination that is undated but appears to have been performed according to the next page on October 13, 1975, that plaintiff's vision in the right eye is 20 and it looks like 25, while the left eye is 20/40. The second page which is dated, 13-OCT-75, indicates that plaintiff does wear glasses, so apparently the deficiency is severe enough to require glasses and one would want to know if he was wearing glasses at the time he was examined by any and/or all of the various examiners. This examination also indicates that plaintiff has had broken bones and recent gain or loss of weight. An earlier examination on May 26, 1964, shows that the plaintiff has stuttered or stammered and suffered from car, train, sea or air sickness which almost always involves dizziness and suffered from depression or excessive worry. The second page of this examination shows that he had had a broken arm three times and that the worry and depression resulted from family problems and that the mild stuttering occurred when he was apprehensive. Thus, again indicating the presence of some psychological disorder. Stuttering usually is viewed as a psychological disorder. There is a note of November 1, 1966 for an examination indicating that in December of 1965 a tank motor fell on his chest and upper arm and he complained of constant pain in the arm aggravated by cold and lifting. Certainly it is legitimate to wonder if these numerous injuries to his arm could have had some effect on his ability to perform some of the visual-motor reproduction tests and some other of the tests which require physical manipulation of objects. Were the examining psychologists aware of these numerous injuries? There is a notation of March 18, 1965, with complaints of dizziness. There is a notation of March 17, 1966, "problem persists, patient definitely has a persistent partial radial nerve palsy which can be demonstrated by decreased strength in extension of wrist." Again, this raises questions about his ability to perform some of the physical tests, due to factors unrelated to brain damage. Note 15-March-1965, complaint of dull aching pains in chest and dizzy spells for ten days. On the next page which is undated, the notation that he states that he is having difficulty getting his breath and he breathes rapidly suggesting the possibility of some sort of hyperventilation such as could be associated with an anxiety state. Were the examiners aware of these problems and did they take them into account? A note July 31, 1967 indicates eye trouble. A note of February 3, 1969 indicates two episodes of chest pain, nonradiating, lasting one-two minutes. These are not associated with exertion, but when he becomes upset or anxious. There is no shortness of breath but he becomes light headed. The impression is that it is doubtful that there is any coronary disease and the note states, "possible anxiety reaction." There is another notation, 28-December-1968, of dizziness, nausea, vomiting and stomach cramps. Again this could represent a flu type of illness, but at least it is one of many in a substantial series of episodes of dizziness that appear to occur prior to the alleged toxic substance exposure.

On September 11, 1982, plaintiff apparently entered group therapy with the Veterans Administration with a diagnosis of probable post-traumatic stress disorder symptoms. He apparently, at that time, was complaining of marital problems and was currently separated, had nightmares about faces of people who didn't return and extreme difficulty with rage over insignificant events. Apparently during the course of the group therapy, he described recurring nightmares of battlefield events so that he does seem to have symptoms of post-traumatic stress disorder as described in DSM-III. Many of his symptoms having to do with difficulties in interpersonal relationships, memory impairment, difficulty concentrating, reduction of recreational activities, diminished interest in one or more significant activities, constricted affect, all are listed in DSM-III as characteristics of post-traumatic stress disorder. It also notes that symptoms of depression and anxiety are common with this disorder as well as increased irritability associated with sporadic and unpredictable explosions of aggressive behavior even upon minimal or no provocation. In fact, on page 237, the DSM-III states "Survivors of death camps sometimes have symptoms of an organic mental disorder such as failing memory, difficulty concentrating, emotional lability, autonomic lability, headache and vertigo." Thus, the two cardinal features described by most of the clinicians as characteristic of painters syndrome, that is memory problems and change of personality, can be attributed to post-traumatic stress disorder which seems to be established here in contrast to attributing these difficulties to painters syndrome which appears to be an, as yet, insufficiently confirmed disorder. Similarily, the depression which is alleged by some of the examiners and seen as part of the total picture here can also be attributed to post-traumatic stress disorder. In connection with post-traumatic stress disorder you may be interested in a recent publication called *Charter Quarterly Review,* Number 3, Anxiety, Panic, and Phobic Disorders. *Charter Quarterly Review* is a professional service by Charter Medical Corporation, P.O. Box 209, Macon, Georgia, 31298, and you may be able to get a copy of the pamphlet that they put out as well as the tape of a symposium which included in its members Dr. Robert L. Spitzer, who is the chairperson of the American Psychiatric Association's committee on the *Diagnostic and Statistical Manual* and is the chair of the committee working on the revision of DSM-III. He states, on the tape, that they anticipate that DSM-III-R is expected to be published sometime in 1987, to be followed hopefully by the publication of DSM-IV probably in 1993 or 94. I mention these to make you aware of the temporary and transitory nature of the diagnostic manuals and the contents thereof. Also, on the tape Dr. Spitzer mentions that there is one school of thought to the effect that post-traumatic stress disorder should not be classified as an anxiety disorder, but should be classified as a dissociative disorder. So it would appear that the committee is at least considering this sort of revision. DSM-III states, regarding dissociative disorders at page 253, "The essential feature is a sudden, temporary alteration in the normally integrative functions of consciousness, identity, or motor behavior. If the alteration occurs in consciousness, important personal events cannot be recalled. If it occurs in identity, either the individual's customary identity is temporarily forgotten or a new identity is assumed, or the customary feeling of one's own reality is lost and replaced by a feeling of unreality. If the alteration occurs in motor behavior, there is also a concurrent disturbance in consciousness or identity, as in the wandering that occurs during a Psychogenic Fugue." You can see from the foregoing that if in fact post-traumatic stress disorder is to be classified as a dissociative disorder, then some of the complaints of being lost, not knowing where one is and so on, could also be attributable to the post-traumatic stress disorder. *(Author's Note: When DSM-III-R was published in 1987, PTSD was retained among the anxiety disorders.)*

Given the number of physical problems P1 has had including several attempts to get his weight under control, it seems unlikely that there was a perfectly wonderful and peaceful relationship between himself and his wife. As anyone who has tried to lose weight knows, it is not at all uncommon for people attempting to lose weight, which usually is accomplished by some dietary restriction, to become irritable. In addition, he has periodically suffered from various other physical problems, the injuries and subsequent effects of injury to his arms. Tendinitis is mentioned in one of the military records plus the fact that he is undergoing a post-traumatic stress disorder, all of which would seem to provide a powerful combination for marital difficulties. It may well be that his wife as well as himself find it more comfortable to attribute these things to the alleged painters syndrome than to problems within him and within the relationship. Also, we seem to have been provided with virtually no information about the wife. What is she like, what was she like before, how easy is she to get along with and so on. Also, I suppose it goes without saying that she has a financial stake in the outcome of this lawsuit. As you are no doubt aware, both for her and for P1, the simple fact of being involved in litigation is a well known stressor and can cause many of the symptoms of anxiety and depression including irritability and difficulty concentrating.

I believe there is some value in looking at P1's responses to several of the items on the MMPI. I am going to provide you with responses from the 1984 MMPI, then I am going to give you inconsistent responses on either the March '83 MMPI or the 1981 MMPI. The reason for this is that while some changed responses could indicate a change in P1's psychological status, some of them refer simply to objective factual items and it seems difficult to account for changes in the answers to those items on any basis except that he was perhaps not really making a serious effort to accurately respond to the items on the MMPI and this will raise a question as to how sincere an effort he may have made on some of the other tests.

**P1's Responses to the MMPI, September 6th, 1984, Indicate:**

1. His appetite is good. I mention this item because a good appetite is not characteristic of people who are depressed although sometimes the opposite is true and depressed people have an excessive appetite. However if that argument is advanced, that is something that apparently existed prior to plaintiff's becoming a painter and then would indicate that he suffered from depression prior.

2. His daily life lacks things that keep him interested. This is characteristic of depression but note his opposite response 3/83 so that in 1983 when he was claiming depression he did not answer this in the depressed direction.

3. His sex life is OK. This raises questions about the extent of disruption of the marital relationship assuming that his sex life is with his wife. Often where there is a severe marital problem, the sex life suffers.

4. He's had very peculiar experiences. This certainly requires investigation by the examiners.

5. He does not always tell the truth, but in 3/83 he says he does. The 1983 response of course is very hard to believe as there is hardly anyone who always tells the truth.

6. Most people who know him like him but not in 3/83.

7. He has heart or chest pains. This would suggest some kind of physical problem that hardly seems to be related in any way to brain damage and it is also something that we have noted in his prior history.

8. He denies being suspended from school one or more times for cutting up, but in 3/83 he says he was. This is a purely factual historical statement, not subject to any variation in plaintiff's condition or any kind of interpretation. It is an instance where unequivocally one of the responses misrepresents the truth. I cannot think of any reasonable way for this item to be false in 1981, then true in '83 and then false again in '84.

9. He is a good mixer, but in 3/83 says he isn't. If it is really correct that he was not a good mixer in '83 but is in '84, this would indicate improvement in his condition rather than deterioration as alleged by some of the examiners.

10. He is troubled by discomfort in his stomach every few days or so. This of course could indicate some digestive problems, which in turn might have some effect on plaintiff's psychological mood or functioning or it may be an indicator of anxiety.

11. He feels he is an important person, but the opposite in 3/83. Here again if he felt important in '81 but not important in '83 but feels like he is an important person again in '84, this either shows considerable inconsistency in his responses or indicates once again that he seems to be improving rather than deteriorating. That is, certainly his self image is better in '84 than it was in '83.

12. He does not feel blue usually. It should be noted that this response was consistent on all three of the MMPI'S and one does not have to be a highly trained psychologist to understand that someone who does not feel blue most of the time can hardly be viewed as depressed.

13. He likes reading love stories, although he denies this in 3/83. It may be important to note that this statement is made in the present tense and indicates that plaintiff is as of 1984 and 1981 enjoying reading. This is contrary to

statements in some of the reports where he has stated to the examiners that he is unable to retain the theme in things that he reads or in watching television.

14. Currently he does not find it hard to keep up hope of amounting to something but did in 3/83. This is another example of either inconsistent responding or another indication that his condition is improving between '83 and '84. It is also generally not the way one tends to view someone who is depressed.

15. He is not lacking in self-confidence, but opposite in 3/83. This is another example either of inconsistency or of improvement in his general condition and self image from '83 to '84.

16. Life usually seems worthwhile to him. This is consistent across the three MMPI'S and is not what one expects to hear from someone who is depressed.

17. It is his opinion that most people would lie to get ahead, although he did not think so in '81. This seems to reflect what he feels is normal and therefore is likely to do.

18. He does not care for parties where there is lots of loud fun, but did in 3/83. It seems odd that between '81 and '83 when he was presumably getting worse and reporting depression that he would improve in this area and then suddenly get worse again in '84. Also it contradicts any claim of social withdrawal in 1983.

19. He cares about what happens to him. This is consistent on all three tests and is contrary to what one expects with people who are depressed.

20. He says he is usually happy, but says he was not in 3/83. This almost seems to speak for itself. It is difficult to reconcile irritability and depression with someone who is happy most of the time.

21. He denies ever doing anything dangerous for the thrill of it, but answers the opposite in '81 and 3/83. This seems to be another historical factual item which could not logically be true in 1984 if it was false in '83 and '81. That is, if he had done something dangerous for the thrill of it, as indicated by his earlier responses, how can he say he never did in '84? Also this tends to be old information which should not be affected by brain damage according to the experts in this case.

22. In school he was sometimes sent to the principal for cutting up but denies this in 3/83. This is another purely historical factual matter not subject to changes or variations in plaintiff's mood and one of the answers clearly has to be a misrepresentation.

23. He has a lot of stomach trouble. This is consistent across the three tests and is much more suggestive of some genuine digestive system disorder, or it is a commonly known symptom of anxiety.

24. In '81 and 3/83 he often could not understand why he was so cross and grouchy but could in 1984. I wonder if this might to be related to progress he has made in his therapy at the Veterans Administration, so that he now has some insight into the sources of his irritability if any, in the post-traumatic stress disorder.

25. He denies ever vomiting or coughing up blood, but says the opposite in '81 and 3/83. This is another instance in which on logical grounds the answer cannot be true in '84 if it was false in '83 and '81.

26. He denies ever indulging in any unusual sex practices, but in 3/83 he says he has. This is another item that cannot be true in '84 if it was false in '83.

27. At times his thoughts have raced on faster than he could verbalize them. This seems to be somewhat inconsistent with the slowing of thought processes that is alleged in some of the reports.

28. He believes that his home life is not as pleasant as that of most people, but was in 3/83. It seems strange that he would answer this way in '83 at a time when he was asserting marital problems in the therapy with the Veterans Administration.

29. He is bothered a lot by criticism and scolding, but was not in 3/83. It seems difficult to account for the fluctuation on this item from '81 to '83 to '84.

30. There are times when he feels useless but did not in '81 or 3/83. This is just inconsistency although it may be related to the fact that it is now been a longer time since he has been gainfully employed, which might suggest an importance for treatment purposes of getting him into some kind of work as soon as possible and it appears likely that there are some kinds of work he could probably do.

31. As a boy, he belonged to a crowd that tried to stick together through thick and thin but denies this in 1981 and 3/83. This is another factual, historical item which cannot be true in '84 if it was false in '83 and '81.

32. Inability to make up his mind in time has caused him to lose out on things but this was not true in 3/83. In other words, in '83 when slowing of thought processes and indications of brain damage were being noted, he was not having this problem.

33. Most nights when he goes to sleep thoughts or ideas bother him. This seems more clearly related to post-traumatic stress disorder than to brain damage.

34. He gets scared when he looks down from a high place. This was consistent through all three MMPI'S and is suggestive of the presence of phobic symptoms which are usually associated with anxiety rather than brain damage.

35. He does not have anything wrong with his mind but opposite in 3/83. Once again aside from the inconsistency this would appear to indicate that plaintiff is better in '84 than in '83 and in fact, he does not think there is anything wrong with his mind, which presumably would include memory functions, finding his way and so on.

36. He has no fear of handling money. This is consistent all the way through and is inconsistent with his assertions of difficulty dealing with change in stores.

37. When he gets bored, he enjoys stirring things up. This is generally not the way one views a person who is depressed.

38. He has no fear of losing his mind but did in 3/83. See #35 above.

39. His hearing is OK but was not in 1981 or 3/83. This seems quite strange as he has not, so far as I know, had treatment for a hearing problem. But if it is true that he had a hearing problem in '81 and '83 this might have had some effect on his performance on the tests where the instructions may have been administered orally, or where he was required to respond to verbal oral material such as on the digit span subtest of the WAIS.

40. He often has hand tremors when he tries to do something. This of course, is a common symptom of anxiety and if present, certainly could have affected his performance on some of the intelligence and neuropsychological tests although it is possible for this symptom to have a neurological basis. (See military report of palsy.)

41. He has a lot of headaches but had very few 3/83. This certainly is inconsistent on that and the '83 response of course is inconsistent with the symptomatology described for painters syndrome.

42. He has had attacks in which there is loss of control of movements or speech, but in which he was aware of what was going on around him, but opposite in 3/83. To begin with, logically this could not be false in '83 if it was true in '81. Secondly, it would seem difficult to figure out why this would stop occurring between '81 and '83 and then start again in '84.

43. He gets pleasure from several kinds of recreation and play. This hardly sounds like someone who is depressed.

44. He enjoys flirting. This also does not sound like someone who is depressed.

45. His family does not treat him more like a child than a grown-up. I mention this because it seems to directly contradict the statement of the wife made to Dr. EW in his presence to the effect that she has to treat him just like a child.

46. His parents rarely objected to the kinds of people he went around with but in 3/83 he says they did often object. Again difficult to account for this fluctuation. Also it would seem to be an objective historical fact for which the answer could not really change.

47. He is annoyed and bothered by habits some of his family have. This was consistent across the three tests and one wonders if some of these family habits could be responsible for whatever irritability plaintiff may show. Certainly it seems like something the examiners ought to have explored to see if there was some legitimate basis for the irritability. For example, does his wife nag him thus making him irritable? For lack of exploration, we do not know the answer on this issue.

48. He sometimes notices his heart pounding or shortness of breath. These are typically symptoms of anxiety.

49. He enjoys discussing sex. This does not seem to be what one would expect from someone who is depressed and it seems difficult to account for the change from '81.

50. He broods very little although he did a lot in 1981. This again is not what one would expect from someone who is depressed and if he is being accurate, it would appear he is better off in '84 than he was in '81.

51. He has had disappointments in love. For lack of information, we do not know whether this refers to his relationship with his wife or not. If it does, it might suggest another basis for some of the problems that he may have been having.

52. He is not bothered by pains although opposite in 1981 or 1983. Obviously he is better off in '84 than he was in the preceding four years. Further it seems doubtful that he would have headaches, which is one of the symptoms of painters syndrome.

53. He typically expects success in things he does. This seems inconsistent with his claimed deficits.

54. He does not acknowledge being a slow learner in school but admits this in 1981. Clearly the answer in '81 is correct according to what we know of his school records and the answer given in '84 and in '83 misrepresents the facts. Again as this is old information, it is presumably not affected by brain damage.

55. He perspires readily even on cool days. This is another well known symptom of anxiety.

56. He does not have trouble thinking of the right things to talk about when with a group. This does not seem consistent with someone who has difficulty remembering what people say, because it would seem hard to maintain a conversation under those circumstances.

57. He rarely notices ears ringing or buzzing but he did in 1981 and 1983. Another instance where he seems to be better in '84 than in the preceding years. Also in '84 it appears the tinnitis is gone.

58. He enjoyed "Alice In Wonderland" but said he did not in 1983. This appears to be another objective historical fact and therefore one of the two responses has to be a misrepresentation.

59. Life is difficult for him much of the time but was not in 1983. It seems strange that he did not find life a strain in '83 when he was representing to the various examiners that he was having all kinds of problems.

60. He thinks most people would lie to keep out of trouble. This may be an indicator of some of his attitudes.

61. Money and business are sources of worry. This again indicates the presence of anxiety which is not a direct result in any event of brain damage, although I suppose it could be argued that this worry is due to the fact that he is not employed. However the point is that he is suffering from anxiety which could be impairing some of his functions rather than brain damage. It could also indicate that he is anxious over whether or not he will get money out of this lawsuit and if so how much.

62. He is not a victim of fits of laughing and crying that he can't seem to control but was in 3/83. If this is a product of brain damage it's difficult to understand why it would be different in '83 than it was in '81 and '84.

63. He does not retain what people say to him for even a short time. This hardly seems likely if he is able to maintain a conversation as indicated above. However, if it is true, it might render some of the test results in doubt, because he might have forgotten what the instructions were. Was it frequently necessary to repeat questions or instructions?

64. Short trips away from home cause anxiety but did not in 3/83. So apparently during the periods of time when he was alleging that he got lost, he was not concerned about it.

65. He tries to retain good stories so he can tell them to other people. This seems to be a truly strange behavior for someone who earlier had stated that he forgets right away what people say to him. That was on number 63 above.

66. He has difficulty setting aside a task that he has undertaken, even for a short time. This seems hard to reconcile with difficulty concentrating and is contrary to his earlier statement that he can't keep his mind on one thing.

67. He enjoys parties but did not in 3/83. This does not sound like someone who is depressed or withdrawn.

68. He faces crises or difficulties but shrank from them in 3/83. This does not sound like someone whose deficits are preventing him from coping.

To sum up, overall there were eighty-four out of three hundred ninety-nine items changed from the March '83 to the September '84 administration of this test. (The above list does not include all 84 changes.)

Because they seem to have some relevance, I am going to provide some additional material from the 1981 administration of the MMPI. Presumably this would have been administered at the same time as the WAIS at _____ which was October 23, 1981. This may be of particular importance in view of the fact that in his report, Dr. Z indicates that P1 had "insidiously developed over several months a spectrum of emotional intellectual and behavioral symptoms approximately two years previously," noting that P1 was seen by the occupational health clinic on January 11, 1983 which would place the onset of his symptoms in January of 1981 some ten months prior to the 1981 MMPI. Indications from the 1981 MMPI follow:

1. His hands and feet are usually cold. This suggests the possibility of some sort of circulatory problem.

2. He had relatively frequent diarrhea. This can suggest digestive system problems or anxiety.

3. There have been times when he has very much wanted to leave home. This suggests a probability of some kind of domestic problems.

4. He has frequent problems with acid stomach. Again suggesting some digestive system disorder. Dr. Z does note in his report that P1 suffers from hiatal hernia, which could account for this, however, it also could be a symptom of anxiety.

5. He has frequent nightmares. This is one of the symptoms of post-traumatic stress disorder or of anxiety or depression.

6. He has no difficulty keeping his mind on a task or job. Indicating that in October of 1981, he was not having any difficulty with concentration or attention.

7. He sleeps fitfully. Again this fits the pattern of anxiety state or post-traumatic stress disorder.

8. He gets hot flashes about once a week without apparent cause. This can be a symptom of anxiety.

9. He rarely feels blue. Again counterindicating the presence of depression.

10. He has plenty of self-confidence. Indicating an adequate self-image and generally contrary to depression.

11. There are frequent quarrels with members of his family. Again suggesting the presence of domestic problems.

12. He has some worries about catching diseases. This suggests some anxiety. I might mention at this point that by far his highest score on the 1981 MMPI was on scale one, hypochondriasis, which was at a T score of approximately 95. The next highest score was on scale three, hysteria, T score of about 85, and the third highest was depression, about 81. No other scores were in the "pathological" range. Clinicians frequently refer to this as the "neurotic triad."

13. He percieves his home life as not as pleasant as that of most people he knows. Again suggesting domestic problems.

14. His eyesight is poorer than it used to be. Again confirming some visual difficulties which may raise questions about his test performance unless each of the examiners can be certain that he was wearing glasses.

15. He has no difficulty keeping his mind on a task or a job. Once again indicating that he is not having, at the end of 1981, difficulty in concentration or attention.

16. He is able to keep his mind on one thing. Same as above.

17. He experiences anxiety about something or someone almost all the time. Once again suggesting the probability of an anxiety syndrome.

18. He retains what people say to him for a reasonable time.

19. At times he has become overtired by undertaking too much. This then might account for one of the described symptoms, that of fatigue.

20. He dislikes being rushed when working. This may be relevant to his performance on some of the test tasks that were timed as there clearly is a sense of being rushed when someone is holding a stop watch on you.

21. Possible misfortunes cause him a lot of worry. Again, indicating possible anxiety state or anxious personality.

22. Waiting makes him nervous. It might be important to find out if he had to wait in any of the examiners' offices prior to being seen as is very common these days and further, whether the examiners know whether he was kept waiting prior to or at any point during the examinations, and if they are aware of this characteristic of his so that they could take it into account in evaluating his performance.

23. Sometimes worry has caused him to lose sleep. More suggestion of the anxiety syndrome in P1.

24. Frequently he memorizes numbers that are not important (such as automobile licenses). This seems like a very strange hobby for somebody who is having difficulty with memory.

25. He sympathizes with people who tend to hang on to their griefs and troubles. Again suggesting what his attitude is in this regard.

26. At times he has been excessively worried over something that really did not matter. Again suggesting the anxiety syndrome.

27. He is a tense person. Again the anxiety syndrome.

28. He gets upset when people hurry him. Again, this should be noted in connection with the fact that many of the subtests he was administered are overtly timed and do constitute for the examinee a sense of being rushed.

## MALINGERING

While the evidence in the case of P1 is not as clear cut as I have seen in some other cases, nevertheless there is a sufficient amount of evidence that I believe I should mention. There may be some difficulties of proof, but at least you should have this information.

There are quantitative measures on the MMPI which serve as indicators of malingering. One of these is the absolute height of the F scale. Another is a formula called the F - K scale which is attained by subtracting the raw score on scale K from the raw score on scale F. There is also a dissimulation index (Ds-r) and there is a comparison of differences in response to the obvious items and the subtle items on various scales. These are known as the Obvious-Subtle scales and can be calculated for five of the clinical scales, depression, hysteria, psychopathic deviate, paranoia and hypomania (D, Hy, Pd, Pa, Ma). Generally on the Obvious-Subtle scales, one looks for T scores that are higher on the obvious items than on the subtle items and for all five of the scales. The rationale for this should be clear: someone trying to fake is more likely to mark in a scorable direction those items which pretty obviously indicate psychopathology while not marking to the same extent the items on the scale which, while scorable along that dimension, are not such that an untrained person would recognize them. On the 1981 and 1984 administrations of the MMPI none of these formulas reach a level which would justify a conclusion of malingering, although it is noted on the September 1984 MMPI, the T score on obvious items on the depression scale is 82 and on the subtle items is 49 for a difference of 33, which is quite a large difference. And similarly for the items on hysteria, the obvious T score is 84, subtle is 59 for a difference of 25, also a large difference in the ratio of obviously pathological items to not-obvious items.

On the 1983 administration of the MMPI, on the F - K scale, F is thirteen and K is ten, so F - K equals three. I believe I have already provided you with a table from Gough (1950), which shows that less than ten percent of people who are taking the test in a legitimate manner would obtain an F - K of three. In other words, there is less than one chance in ten of being incorrect in calling a test with an F - K of three malingered. You will also notice in the data from Gough that only five percent of adult normals get a score of three on this measure. Also the table shows that only 17% of diagnosed neurotics score this high on F - K. So that even if we conclude that his score may be somewhat elevated due to the neurotic aspects that have been noted above, it is still less than one chance in five that he would have shown a score this high unless he was malingering, which is defined as either falsifying or exaggerating symptoms. On the dissimulation scale he obtains a score of twelve. The mean for males is 6.22 with a standard deviation of 4.33. So he is approximately 1.3 standard deviations above the mean, a score which would be too small to indicate mallingering although it leans in that direction. On the Subtle-Obvious scales for depression, he obtains an Obvious score of 86, Subtle 45 for a difference of 41. Hysteria, Obvious 79, Subtle 57 for a difference of 22. Pd Obvious 56, Subtle 50 for a difference of six. Paranoia Obvious 58, Subtle 50 for a difference of eight and Hypomania Obvious 64, Subtle 60 for a difference of four. So we note in this instance that in five out of five cases, the Obvious responses are higher than the Subtle responses and, particularly in the case of depression and hysteria, the differences are quite substantial. Thus, on this administration of the MMPI all four measures suggest that P1 is malingering. Note the 1983 MMPI was the only one Dr. EW had when he rendered his opinion.

In conjunction with the foregoing, probably the most convincing evidence are his complaints about difficulties in calculating change, which is contradicted by his statements on the MMPI that he does not worry about handling money and, more graphically, is overwhelmingly contradicted by his performance on the arithmetic subtest of the WAIS where he clearly indicates sufficient ability to perform calculations of that type.

There are also numerous contradictory and inconsistent statements noted above among the items of the MMPI.

To sum up, while no bit of evidence is strongly convincing, there are several bits of evidence which suggest that P1 may be malingering. It may be worth noting that Dr. EW, in a publication, describes malingering as a special problem in neuropsychological assessment complicated by compensation policies which can make poor health worth some effort. He declares that inconsistency in performance levels or between performance levels and claimed disabilities is the hallmark of malingering unless related to a physiological condition. He also notes that there are special techniques for testing performance inconsistencies characteristic of malingerers. It does not appear to me that he employed any of those techniques in the case of P1.

## DR. EW

There are several points on which Dr. EW's procedures and conclusions, in this case, can be questioned.

To a large extent, his conclusions that P1 has suffered impairment (here in the sense of loss of function) due to damage to the brain resulting from inhalation of toxic substances, rests to a very large extent on his "estimates" of P1's "premorbid" abilities. EW appears to have used what several writers refer to as the "best performance" method for estimating premorbid functioning. Some of these writers, including EW, indicate that estimates of original intellectual potential may be based on interviews, reports of people who know the person, from family and test scores, prior academic or employment level, military rating, school grades or an intellectual product and that "except in obvious cases the estimate should be based on as a wide range of information from as many sources as possible." You should note in the previously cited article by Wasyliw and Golden, at page 152, "No tests or formulae claimed to be able to assess intelligence or other cognitive levels at any time prior to testing, let alone brain injury, have been sufficiently validated or replicated for general use." Thus these and other authorities appear to be in conflict with Dr. EW's statement made elsewhere that such methods of estimating have been "borne out" since about 1905. For your information, Golden is a widely published neuropsychologist. In light of the foregoing, despite EW's credentials in the field of neuropsychology, his credibility in this case is seriously deflated by his failure to follow his own recommendations as well as the dictates of common sense by obtaining the existing concrete evidence of plaintiff's premorbid functioning contained in the school and military records. He has elected instead to "speculate" or make assumptions about his premorbid functioning based on the fact, principally, that he functioned as a shop union steward for several years and on some test results. I personally do not know what kinds of skills or aptitudes are required for that job and I seriously doubt that Dr. EW knows. There may be a job description somewhere that might indicate this but I suspect that it is a position one obtains through a certain amount of popularity with one's fellow union members and it may require a certain amount of street type political acumen (which I do not believe was tested by any of the tests involved here) or the kind of practical operational knowledge indicated in the article by McClelland that I mentioned earlier. I am completely convinced that being shop steward does not in any way require the ability to remember and be able to reproduce certain configurations of line drawings. In any event, none of these speculative endeavors serves to substitute for obtaining the factual evidence that could have been obtained, regarding premorbid functioning.

Turning to EW's report of May 27th, 1984 of his examination of July 7, 1983, one can at least raise a question as to why almost a year elapsed between the date of the examination and the date of the report. It seems almost obvious that it is better to prepare a report while one's recollection of the examination and interviews and so on is fresh in one's mind.

Next I note in his report, the statement that plaintiff was examined for "approximately 1. hours by means of interview" and so on. I am confused by the 1 with the decimal point following it and I wonder if there is some other figure that should have been put in there such as 1.5 or whether it was ten hours instead of 1. hours. In any event, given that he did an interview and performed several tests, it seems unlikely that it could have been done in one hour, and if it was done in one hour what was the purpose of stating it as "1."? Inasmuch as Dr. EW signed the letter, I will assume he read it. This would appear to be a visual perception mistake, which I trust is not an indication of brain damage in Dr. EW. Next I notice that he describes all of the tests he gave. None of this description includes any of the tests he describes on pages _____ through _____ of (a publication of his) to be used essentially for the purpose of detecting dissimulation or malingering. These are apparently omitted despite his statement on page _____ that the financial benefits of illness and injuries related to job and so forth make malingering and functional disabilities an attractive solution to all kinds of social and economic and personal problems for some people. If the measures he describes for detecting malingering or simulation of brain damage are indeed effective, it seems strange not to have employed them in this case where a claim for compensation is obviously involved.

I then note in the first paragraph of his report that the examination conducted 3/83 by psychology intern 3 under the supervision of Dr. 4, also provides data for this examination, indicating that he did use the data from that examination even though it was performed by an intern evidently in disregard of his statement in the lecture attended by an attorney from your office in which he reportedly stated these examinations should not be conducted by people at that level. And further, he himself notes on page three in a parenthetical statement under verbal functions that the one of the scores obtained in the 3/83 examination was based on insufficient testing and cannot be considered valid, which would seem to support his contention as well as the common sense idea that testing for this purpose should not be conducted by a novice or a trainee.

In his second paragraph, titled Background Information, he says that P1 is a high school graduate. This statement of course is clearly not correct. While he obtained an equivalency through the GED examination, that's all it is, an equivalency. It does not make one a high school graduate. Either he did not tell EW the truth or EW erroneously revised what he had said. This paragraph also shows us the example of not being able to use tools effectively giving as an example, rewiring of a switch backwards and later, as an example of his inability to function, the wife gives this same example. This of course, is the sort of thing that could happen to anybody and if it is the only example, it does not warrant drawing any general conclusions. It seems to me that a conscientious, thorough examination would have asked for some other examples in addition to this one to make sure that this was not an isolated incident. EW's history does not include many of the complaints noted in the June 29, 1984 report of Dr. Z, including, for example, such things as tinnitis, metallic taste, low level of hearing loss, burning sensation in the lungs, episodic dizziness, and so on. So, once again, it appears that Dr. EW did not do a very thorough job or P1 was not candid with him. While EW is aware that P1 was participating in a therapy group at the Veterans Center, apparently he did little to investigate what that was about and find out that the diagnosis for which he was being treated there was post-traumatic stress disorder. If he had obtained that information, I should think that a thorough report would require him to have ruled post-traumatic stress disorder out as a cause of his symptoms rather than having to do so under interogation later. In fact, he acknowledges in an interview that he really did not go into the details concerning post-traumatic stress disorder and that he did not discuss his sleep patterns and whether he was troubled with nightmares and so on, although it seems obvious that he had information on that because he states on page two of his report that he said P1 sleeps restlessly, often waking during the night. Certainly that is a cue to inquire about the nature of the sleep problems. EW did not do so.

I note under present complaints, P1 states that he has been aware of the various problems of self-monitoring and so forth since early 1981, which would be prior to the testing of 10/81 so that these symptoms should have shown up on that testing. As you will recall from the MMPI done at that time his statements contradict the existence of many of the symptoms. He says, in that paragraph, that his appetite runs in spells where he won't eat for many days and then he'll binge. However, on the MMPI, he says he has a good appetite. I think his description would call for a rather strange definition of what a good appetite is, generally meaning a healthy appetite in which one feels like eating but is not fluctuating between fasting for several days and then bingeing. I doubt that anyone would define that as a good appetite. He was able to inform EW that he has been treated for high blood presure since March or April of 1983, just a month or two before he saw EW and also that he is taking medication for seizure control. Apparently his memory for recent events was good enough for him to remember those things.

Next section deals with the interview with Mrs. P1 in which she describes a number of changes in P1. She notes that he is not able to participate in financial planning for the family. Certainly this is not due to any lack of capacity to deal with numbers as demonstrated by his arithmetic score on the WAIS. Similarily she says he has difficulty concentrating but as previously pointed out, in order to perform as he did on the arithmetic subtest of the WAIS, one would have to concentrate on the question being asked in order to arrive at the solutions as he did.

Under observations EW notes that he is very overweight but does not at any point in his report suggest any possible emotional or personality implications of that condition. He makes a note that P1 spoke with a slight speech impediment that suggested sluggish mouth movements. It is not clear how much importance he attached to that, but apparently enough to mention it and this of course, is another example where, if he had bothered to obtain the prior records, he would have known that P1 had a speech problem when he was in the service prior to any contact with paint.

Incidentally, in a section above under medical history, EW notes P1's report that in 1975 or 1976, he had sustained a mild concussion in a car accident. It would seem to me if I were assessing somebody for impairment due to brain damage, and I knew that there had been a concussion, I would not take the individual's word for it that it was mild, I would attempt to obtain medical records which might indicate the severity of such a concussion, which might give me a little pause before I blamed the brain damage on toxic substances.

On page three under test performance EW gives his estimate that P1's intellectual endowment was at least high average, in the upper 25% of the population, on the basis of high average performances on verbal and arithmetic reasoning tests. While he doesn't state it that way, I am pretty sure these are from the WAIS and it would be necessary to tie that down, but in that instance all the material I have previously discussed about such estimates would apply. Actually, none of the scores on the WAIS arithmetic subtest are above the average range—10/81 = 9; 3/83 = 11 (Note the mean is 10 with a standard deviation of 3); 10/83 = 5; 9/84 = 6 (EW did not have this when report was written). I am really somewhat surprised that he thinks that in order to qualify as a hunting instructor, one would need to have above average intelligence. This again, as in the case of the shop steward, surprises me. I would assume that someone with ordinary intelligence and experience in hunting, would be able to be a hunting instructor. It is also not clear to me the extent to which he was doing this in a professional way. I don't recall any particular documentation which verifies this other than his statement. I doubt that he was teaching hunting at the college level and I certainly doubt that it takes a high level of intelligence to teach someone how to care for and use a gun. I think many of us have had some military experience in which our instructors in the use and maintenance of rifles did not strike us as being of above average intelligence.

On page four under attentional functions, EW states that his immediate span of attention was a little below normal limits for a man of his age and that his performance on tests sensitive to concentration deficits were just marginal to normal limits, suggesting quite clearly that there is little if any impairment in these functions although EW then describes other tests which he says do indicate impaired ability to concentrate. But then as we have previously noted, variability in performance has been characteristic of P1 since at least middle adolescence.

At the bottom of page four under diagnostic impression, EW makes the statement, "This man of originally high average intellectual endowment," no longer describing this as an estimate but as an established fact. Then under the same section, the middle paragraph on page five, he uses adjectives which to me, at least, suggests that he has a bias as such adjectives really have no place in an objective report of impairment due to brain damage. These examples are in the sixth line of the paragraph. He refers to "a very unwelcome personality change" which is a value judgment, and three or four lines beyond that, he makes reference to "this once proud man's reactions." I do not believe such statements have any place in an objective report and furthermore, I do not know what evidence he has to base the conclusion on that P1 was a once proud man. At the most optimistic, what one could glean from his history was that he lived a more or less decent, fairly commonplace, life. It's difficult to see what there was that would warrant particular pride, other than simply meeting one's ordinary obligations. EW then states, "It is not surprising given this man's previous accomplishments and high activity level that he is reactively depressed." I am not clear what the evidence is for a high activity level. Seems to me he held a job, he had some recreation outlets and I have not seen evidence that he was some sort of dynamo. EW does not at any point in the report indicate any awareness that in his capacity as shop steward, P1 had acquired familiarity with symptoms of brain damage from toxic substances. In the earlier statements he indicates that so far as a connection between hypertension and symptoms of brain damage, that there is a lot of conflicting data or that the data just does not match. But in any event, there does seem to be some disagreement in the data, so that any conclusions drawn in that regard must necessarily be of a somewhat weak variety. He makes what I feel is a very careful statement, "The conclusions by several authors I can sum up, is that on the basis of the data so far documented in controlled studies, there is not sufficient evidence to attribute brain damage with persons with hypertension." Keeping in mind his later admonition that conditions can exist even though the evidence is not there, I should think this statement, so far as ruling out hypertension would not be that effective. (Author's Note: See Chapter 12, Volume 2 for studies suggesting that hypertensive medications can cause depression-like symptoms.) On page five of the report he indicated that there certainly was no obvious evidence of the kind of problem that he associates with post-traumatic stress disorder. It would appear he's likely to be wrong on this in view of the fact that that's the diagnosis at the Veteran's Center where they have more knowledge of P1's problems and did diagnose post-traumatic stress disorder. Dr. EW seems to have been pretty careless on this score. Also on page five, he describes the problems of post-traumatic stress disorder and fails to mention that DSM-III notes memory and concentration problems as among the symptoms. Similarly at the bottom of the page, he says there is no literature which suggests there are chronic cognitive changes associated with post-traumatic stress syndrome, when in fact, such difficulties of memory and concentration are mentioned as noted above in DSM-III, which I would assume is part of the literature. So that again, he seems to be wrong in this instance. For your information, this is described on page 236 of DSM-III, "Some complain of impaired memory or difficulty in concentrating or completing tasks," and on page 238 under diagnostic criteria, D (4) "memory impairment or trouble concentrating." Also note that DSM-III indicates symptoms of depression and anxiety are common in post-traumatic stress disorder and it is well-known that depression and anxiety can have effects on cognitive functioning.

As EW's testimony at times deals with both of these plaintiffs, we are at this point presenting a brief description of P2 and the reports of examinations of him and a report provided to defense counsel on P2 by the author consultant.

Briefly stated, P2 at the time of the first examination was a thirty-seven year old, single, never married, Caucasian male, who had been employed by the company for sixteen years as an industrial painter. He graduated from high school and was briefly in the military service but did not complete basic training as he was found "unfit" for the military service. He was examined in August of 1982, September of 1983 (by EW), October of 1983 and September of 1984. However, EW's report was not prepared until May of 1984. The reports of these examinations follow:

## NEUROPSYCHOLOGICAL EVALUATION
Date: 8-17-82

P2 is a 37 year old single, Caucasian male who was referred to Medical Psychology, by Dr. Z (Environmental Medicine) to establish a baseline assessment of his neuropsychological functioning as well as to assess possible neurotoxicity resulting from chronic exposure to industrial paint and solvents. P2 was initially seen in Environmental Medicine in August, 1982, presenting with reported dizziness, visual loss, distractibility, memory problems and hypertension. Assessment procedures included the Halstead-Reitan Neuropsychological Battery (Lateral Dominance Examination, Sensory-Perceptual Examination, Finger-Tapping Test, Strength of Grip Test, Aphasia Screening Test, Speech, Perception Test, Seashore Rhythm Test, Tactual Performance Test, Trail-Making Tests, Category Test), the Wechsler Adult Intelligence Scale-Revised (WAIS-R), and the Minnesota Multiphasic Personality Inventory (MMPI), the Rey Auditory Verbal Learning Test (ReyAVLT), and the Rey-Osterreith Complex Figure Test, and a clinical interview.

### Interview Data

He presented as a casually-dressed, somewhat overweight man of stated age with noticeable asymmetry of his eyes and mouth. Although he was cooperative and polite to the examiner, he did not interact spontaneously with her. His affect was noticeably blunted and he gave little indication of overt distress about his reported symptoms or performance during the seven hour testing period. However, after two hours of testing, he reportedly experienced severe dizziness which lasted approximately twenty minutes, and during which testing was suspended.

P2 reported that he was the middle sibling of a working class family. He stated that his childhood and adolescence were non-eventful, and that he graduated from _____ High School with a C-average. During high school, he stated that he worked as a janitor and had held temporary jobs with the railroad, Forestry and Highway Departments. Since 1964, he has been employed as an industrial painter at company, with seniority status since 1965, and is presently awaiting a foreman position in the company. He stated that his health was generally satisfactory until March, 1981 when he began experiencing dizzy spells which lasted ten to twenty minutes while driving home or walking after work, and parathesia initiating in the fingertips of his left hand, extending to his left shoulder. He did mention casually that prior to the onset of these symptoms, he had been hospitalized for observation on two occasions after experiencing partial anoxia, secondary to inhaling paint thinner fumes. In May, 1981, he stated that he was hospitalized for a week at _____ Hospital after "passing out while talking on the phone." Diagnostic studies (CT, EKG, EEG) were reported to be normal; however, hypertension was diagnosed. A family history (maternal, paternal) for high blood pressure was noted by him. He reported that since May, 1981, he has experienced daily episodes of dizziness and nausea with accompanying temporary loss of vision, distractibility and short term memory loss on the job, and heightened irritability. He reported two vaguely dissociative experiences (October, 1981, July, 1982) unassociated with alcohol and/or drug use. However, he denied auditory and/or visual hallucinations and no overt attention to extraneous stimuli was noted. P2 stated that he has tried marijuana two or three times and drinks an average of four beers a day and a six pack of beer on the weekend. He denied other non-prescription drug use. P2 stated that he has owned his own home for ten years and has maintained a relatively active social life and has been involved in a romantic relationship for the previous six years. In May, 1981, he moved back to his parents' home, reportedly at the advice of his physician at hospital. While his family is reportedly concerned about the etiological role his job plays in his current health problems, P2 verbalized his desire to continue working for company, possibly in an area which would reduce his contact with chemical irritants.

## Intellectual Functioning

On the WAIS-R, P2 obtained a Verbal Scale IQ Score of 93, a Performance Scale IQ Score of 86 and a Full Scale Score of 89. This places him in the low average range of intellectual functioning. His deficits in performance on the subtests most sensitive to organic impairment (i.e., Digit Span, Arithmetic, Block Design, Digit Symbol) and his satisfactory performance on the subtests more resilient to such impairment (i.e., Information, Vocabulary, Similarities) suggest that his premorbid intellectual potential may have been higher (i.e., average range). *(Author's Note: See Chapter 11, Volume II for negative literature regarding "hold" [resilient] versus "don't hold" [not resilient] subtests.)* Subtest scores were as follows (scaled scores have a mean of 10 and a standard deviation of approximately 3):

| | |
|---|---|
| Information | 9 |
| Digit Span | 7 |
| Vocabulary | 10 |
| Arithmetic | 5 |
| Comprehension | 11 |
| Similarities | 10 |
| Picture Completion | 8 |
| Picture Arrangement | 11 |
| Block Design | 5 |

|                  |   |
|------------------|---|
| Digit Symbol     | 5 |
| Object Assembly  | 6 |

Verbal IQ: 93
Performance IQ: 86
Full Scale IQ: 89

## Memory Functioning

His performance on the ReyAVLT suggests significant impairment in the ability to attend to and learn verbal information and to recognize and recall verbal stimuli following a distraction-filled interval. On the Rey-Osterreith Complex Figure Test, his copy (22.5) and Recall (8.5) scores are both below the 25th percentile, indicating severe deficits in his visual-spatial and organizational skills.

## Neuropsychological Functioning

P2 demonstrated additional deficits on several tests in the Halstead-Reitan Battery which lends further evidence of organic brain dysfunction. The result of the Lateral Dominance Examination suggest that P2 has mixed dominance; however, for the purpose of this evaluation his right hand (used for writing) was designated as the preferred hand in tasks requiring use of both hands. On the Sensory-Perceptual Examination, no tactile, auditory or visual suppressions were noted on unilateral or bilateral stimulation and no finger agnosia was detected; however impaired perception of numbers on the fingertips of both hands, as well as asterogesis to coins in both hands was observed and is suggestive of peripheral neuropathy. Mild nystagmus was observed on the right and left during peripheral horizontal gaze. Scores for the right ("preferred") hand on measures of grip strength and finger-tapping speed failed to exceed the left by the expected 10% on both tasks (Grip: R-47.5 kg, L-41.5 kg; Tapping Test: R-46.5, L-45.5). *(Author's Note: On Grip, 47.5 does exceed 41.5 by more than 10%.)* Impaired performance was exhibited on the Tactual Performance Test, a measure of complex psychomotor ability based on motor tactile, and kinesthetic information from the right (preferred) hand (994 sec), the left hand (562 sec), and both hands (461 sec) without the benefit of visual cues. Significant impairment was also observed in his processing of auditory stimuli at a rapid speed (Seashore Rhythm Test: 20 correct) and in his speech perception (Speech Sounds Perception Test: 18 errors). The Aphasia Screening Test revealed mild construction apraxia with perseveration and figure rotation (90%), acalculia, and mild central dysarthria. His performance on the Category Recognition Test which assesses the general integrity of the brain, the ability to perceive interrelationships, and to utilize abstract principles was in the impaired range (testing suspended after Trial III, 80% errors). His performance on the Trail-Making Test which assesses the interactive integrity of both hemispheres was also in the impaired range (A: 45 sec; B: 155 sec).

## Personality Data

The results of the MMPI (382-1759/40 LK/F) are valid and suggest that P2 may be in more distress than his outward behavior would indicate. He has a tendency to deny psychological problems and is invested in maintaining an overtly well-adjusted demeanor. It is likely that he is experiencing a moderate level of anxiety and/or depression and is likely to harbor fears concerning his deteriorating cognitive functions. His profile suggests some disturbance of his thought processes and difficulties in thinking clearly; however, his vague and evasive manner may mask these problems in interpersonal situations. He is likely to display a stereotyped approach to problem-solving and he is likely to have an intrapunitive response to stress and frustration. His exaggerated dependency and affectional needs may be in conflict with his traditional masculine role identification.

### Summary and Recommendations

P2 is a 37 year old, single, Caucasian male with an 18 year history of exposure to industrial paints and solvents and a one and one-half year history of hypertension. The results of this assessment suggest that he has significant generalized bilateral cortical impairment and that functional factors are not a complete etiological basis for his neuropsychological deficits. While he does exhibit numerous signs and symptoms suggestive of neurotoxicity, the possibility of a progressive cerebral vascular disorder should be considered. Longitudinal neuropsychological testing is recommended to assess any improvement or deterioration of his neuropsychological functioning and to quantify the course of his impairment over time.

### Diagnosis:

294.80 Atypical or Mixed Organic Brain Syndrome (provisional).

8
Intern in Medical Psychology
4, Ph.D.
Professor of Medical Psychology

## G HOSPITAL & MEDICAL CENTER
## MEDICAL RECORD REPORT

### NEUROPSYCHOLOGICAL SCREENING

P2
Attending Physician: Dr. 5, Ph.D.
Date: 10/12/83

### Background Information

P2 is a 38 year-old, right-hand dominant, white single male with a high school education who had been employed as an industrial painter and sandblaster by company since approximately 1966. Work history preceding employment with company consisted primarily of temporary janitorial or physical labor positions with the railroad, Highway, and Forestry departments. He reports having remained with company until recently despite his previous exposure to organic solvents. He did, however, switch to working exclusively in sandblasting where he felt there was no risk of toxicity. He was laid off from his position at company two weeks prior to this evaluation when, according to his report, the company moved back to its central location in _____. He is currently looking for another job in either sand-blasting or steam cleaning.

According to his report, education was limited but not really needed for the vocational pursuits. Academic performance was average generally Cs and uneventful. He denied any failures in school.

He currently resides with his parents. Although medical records indicate that he moved back to his parents home 5/81 at the specific recommendation of his physician. He indicated during our interview that he had basically lived on and off with them since he was 25.

Premorbid history is significant for ETOH use. He apparently usually drank a minimum of 4 beers daily (and more on the weekend) while employed. While he denied that ETOH use interfered with work performance or caused absenteeism, he did state that he had been quite aggressive at work, this occasionally getting him into trouble with supervisors. The actual timing of problems was unclear from his description; and it was impossible to r/o ETOH use, or exposure to toxic chemicals for that matter, as contributing factors. He was extremely vague regarding current use.

### Presenting Problems

P2 reports that the problems he is currently experiencing date back to 1968 when he was exposed to various chemicals and paint mixtures while employed with company. He indicated that the initial symptoms included decreased appetite, nausea, and vomiting. No other physical or neurological symptoms were described; and he was unable to provide details regarding subsequent medical problems, interventions, or hospitalizations.

In fact, according to available medical records, his problems were initially reported in 3/80. Complaints then included severe HA'S, dizziness, sense of pressure, and depression. He was taken to _____ Hospital where HTN was diagnosed (he had no prior history of HTN although there is a strong documented family history).

Subsequently, he developed intermittent tunnel vision (occurring 2-3 x mo.), L UE numbness and tingling, shortness of breath, chest pains, loss of depth perception, and syncope. He was re-admitted to _____ Hospital 5/80 following a syncopal episode and remained off work for approximately 3-4 mos. while undergoing a comprehensive medical evaluation.

Primary complaints at the time of this assessment include memory impairment, difficulty attending to tasks at hand or conversations, decreased impulse control, low frustration tolerance, and personality change. Although he characterized himself premorbidly as relatively passive, he now claims to have problems controlling his outbursts. He is verbally aggressive and excitable, resenting any comments or behaviors from others which imply personal lack of competence. He also sees considerable change in his spontaneity, reporting that those around him now have to pull information out of him. No physical symptomatology was reported.

## Referral Question

This client was referred for a brief neuropsychological screening to determine possible neurotoxic effects secondary to exposure to organic solvents. This assessment was not intended to be a comprehensive evaluation of all areas of cognitive functioning; nor was it intended to explore the possible role of psychogenic factors in symptom development. It was exclusively designed to assess the extent of impairment of areas reported in the literature to be affected by organic toxicity. Refer to Elofsson et al., "Exposure to organic solvents", *Scand j work environ health* 1980 (6); Juntunen et al., "Clinical prognosis of patients with diagnosed chronic solvent intoxication," *Acta neurol. scandinav.* 1982 (65); Bruhn, et al., "Prognosis in chronic toxic encephalopathy," *Acta neurol. scandinav.* 1981 (64) for documentation of deficits. Additional deficits may or may not exist, and a full neuropsychological evaluation would be needed to determine their presence and severity of impairment.

## Evaluation Measures

Clinical Interview, Rey Osterrieth Complex Figure (with immediate recall), Wechsler Adult Intelligence Scale-Revised (Digit Span, Arithmetic, and Similarities subtests), Hooper Visual Organization Test, Mack Sequencing Movements and Digits, Wechsler Memory Scale Form I (Logical memory subtest & delayed recall with interference), Rey Auditory Verbal Learning Test, Gorham Proverbs Written Form I, & Tapping Test. The purpose of the assessment was explained to the client and their verbal consent obtained prior to initiating the procedure.

## Behavioral Observations

P2 arrived for the assessment dressed casually. Although cooperative, he did not initiate any conversation. He sat quietly responding with brief answers and offering no additional data. Speech was fluent, of normal phrase length, and easily articulated. His report of personal history was vague and incomplete and frequently inconsistent with information reported during previous examinations. The vague quality to his report seemed to increase when potentially threatening topics were introduced into the discussion (e.g., he appeared quite defensive when questioned about work-related problems secondary to aggressive outbursts and when asked regarding his home situation). He was unable to describe events which presumably occurred during his employment with company (e.g., hospitalizations, evaluations) with any degree of reliability and could not place events into the correct temporal sequence.

Affect was flat, P2 giving no indication whatsoever of any emotional distress. He did not report any complaints throughout the entire assessment. In addition, he did not show any signs of dissatisfaction or concern over his performance quality or accuracy.

He apparently believes that he will be able to find and maintain employment despite his perceived deficits. He seemed convinced that the over-learned nature of tasks in desired occupations and his extensive work experience will allow for successful re-integration into the work force.

## Evaluation Results

This client is currently demonstrating significant impairment of perceptual, self-regulatory (attention and concentration), and cognitive functions suggestive of deterioration from premorbid level of functioning (as estimated by both educational and work history) and consistent with organic involvement. His performance during this abbreviated assessment showed no substantial change from the findings documented during a previous evaluation conducted 8/17/82, this arguing against a progressive condition of disorder (the 8/82 assessment had raised this as a possible explanation for the observed deficits).

Despite his long history of participation in manually-oriented activities which required at least adequate visuo-motor processing, he is undoubtedly at this time unable to effectively analyze visual stimuli and spatially integrate components into the corresponding gestalts. His approach is disorganized with little if any self-initiated scanning for errors; even when cued to examine for response accuracy, monitoring is deficient.

He had difficulty maintaining an active focus on task demands for any extended period of time. The fact that he tends to lose track of relevant information dramatically interferes with sequencing of behaviors. This attentional and concentration disturbance in addition limits learning of new information. His ability to retrieve material presented either verbally or visually is significantly below levels expected for his age group and premorbid history. He is unable to use contextual cues to facilitate performance, a finding which may be related to the difficulty he experiences distinguishing critical from nonessential environmental details in novel situations, or to disorganization. It should be noted that his recall is markedly impaired even if the information was presented immediately beforehand with prior warning as to the recall nature of the task. His performance does not improve in any way when provided with options and asked to simply identify previously-presented information; thus it does not appear to be strictly failure in accessing the information. When asked to recall or recognize information after a distraction-filled interval, performance deteriorates further (although not as sharply).

Motor speed is slightly improved in his dominant hand compared to the 8/82 assessment, scores now showing the expected dominant vs. non-dominant differential. However, speed most probably is depressed relative to his baseline. There was no evidence of incoordination.

## Summary

Current findings document the existence of perceptual, self-regulatory, and cognitive dysfunctions which are suggestive of significant bilateral cortical involvement. While the results, behavioral observations, and complaints are consistent with toxicity secondary to chemical or solvent exposure, one must also consider the possibility that his history of ETOH use may be contributing to the deficits found during the examination.

Dr. 5, Ph.D
Clinical Psychologist

## EW, PH.D.
## CLINICAL PSYCHOLOGIST

### NEUROPSYCHOLOGICAL REPORT

5/27/84

Re: P2

dob: 7-30-45

This then 38-year-old workman was given a neuropsychological screening examination on September 9, 1983, to aid in evaluating his complaints of mental changes associated with long-term (16-year) exposure to industrial solvents in the course of his employment as a painter and sand-blaster. He was examined for approximately one and three-quarters hours by means of interview and the following tests: Reversed operations (alphabet, serial subtraction of 3's and 7's); Stroop test (Dodrill format); Controlled Oral Verbal Fluency Test (Benton); selected subtests of the Wechsler Adult Intelligence Scale-Revised (Arithmetic, Digit Span, and Block Design); Sentence Repetition subtest of the Multilingual Aphasia Examination; writing sentences; paragraph recall, Babcock format (Babcock and Portland paragraphs); Wisconsin Card Sorting Test; Symbol Digit Modalities Test; Complex Figure Test (Taylor figure); Bender-Gestalt (Wepman memory format); and House and Bicycle drawings. The lengthy and comprehensive August 17, 1982 neuropsychological examination conducted by psychology intern 8 under the supervision of 4, Ph.D. also provides data for this evaluation. In addition, reports from the October 1983 examinations of P2 by OM, M.D., and 5, Ph.D. have been reviewed.

### Background Information

This unmarried graduate of _____ High School reported that his science grades had been best; the rest were mostly C's with a few B's. He has been employed by the same company for the last 16 years, working primarily with paints and solvents. In November 1982 his job was changed to sandblasting. At the time of this examination he was working "on call", typically less than the 40 or more hour week to which he was accustomed. He said he was spending his spare time working on his house, hunting, and fishing. Alcohol consumption has typically been four beers a day and a six-pack on the weekend.

### Present Complaints

He reported that his earlier problems that he associates now with solvent exposure occurred in the late 1960's when he experienced a stuffy feeling and just didn't eat. His main complaint now is that he has a memory problem but he could not tell how long he has had it except to state that high blood pressure was discovered some time after he was aware that he had difficulties remembering. He also said he experiences his "mind drifting;" explaining this as "things are hard to keep track of." He stated that there have been "times when I felt I was going to pass out." He also complained that he has "found myself doing weird things" such as putting things in the wrong place. He pointed out that "anything I have been doing a long time I don't have any trouble (with)" but described himself as slow to learn anything new. He said that his blood pressure has been controlled for the last two years by "cutting back on salts" and medication. He said he has also been trying to lose weight and thought he was 15-20 pounds below his maximum.

## Observations

This neatly groomed man who looked his stated age was alert, oriented, and intelligently cooperative. His demeanor was very stolid in that his face and tone of voice were unexpressive, he volunteered little information, and responded to questions with few words. Speech was unremarkable; thinking tended to be concrete; ideas were vague and poorly elaborated. He tracked conversation adequately. Although he reported that he didn't like his present situation, noting that there was not a "heck of a lot I can do about it," mood was unremarkable, affect was bland.

## Test Performance

On the basis of his self-reports and his best test performances, P2 appears to be a man of *average* intellectual endowment. However, along with many good performances, he displays a pattern of deficits from an *average* and expected performance level in a number of areas of cognitive functioning.

*Verbal functions.* Although all of his scores on the verbal subtests of the intelligence test he took in 1982 were within the *average* ability range, he displayed problems with verbal production. The three spelling errors he made on the 12 words with which he composed sentences ("pesident", "busness", "triagle") are more like errors of carelessness than due to spelling ignorance. His just *low average* rate of word production was lower than expected for a man with an *average* vocabulary.

*Perceptual functions.* He consistently displayed good perceptual accuracy for visual material, solving structured visuoperceptual problems at an *average* level. However his response rate on the test of tactile perception was excessively slow, falling into the *impaired* range.

*Construction.* P2's ability to assemble material under visual guidance or to draw either freehand or copy was consistently at *borderline defective* to frankly *defective* levels. Much of this difficulty arose from an inability to analyze and integrate the many different kinds of complex visual stimuli making up the various constructional tasks. Poor planning and unsystematic approach also contributed to his failures.

*Abstracting/generalizing.* On familiar verbal material that tends to reflect old learning, such as proverbs or identifying similarities between verbal concepts, his performance was consistently *average*. However, when the task involved unfamiliar stimuli and called for active solution of conceptual problems, he performed mostly at *borderline defective* and *defective* levels with the exception of one concept formation task which he was unable to grasp until given a demonstration.

*Mental control.* Self-monitoring and self-correcting were erratic. He tended to repeat himself when reciting word lists (both from memory and self-generated). On other memory tests he confused the elements without any awareness that what he said was inappropriate. On one arithmetic problem, this high school graduate subtracted 14 from 50 and came up with 44 as the answer, using pencil and paper. His spelling lapses are noted above.

*Attentional functions.* Except for span of simple attention *within normal limits* (digits forward = 6), P2 performed *below normal limits* on all measures of more complex attentional functions including the two Halstead battery subtests (in the 1982 examination) that are sensitive to attentional disorders. He made an abnormal number of errors on reversed operations even though he took an abnormally long time to do these tasks. He was unable to solve any but the simplest arithmetic story problems because he could not keep the story elements in mind while doing the problems in his head even when the problems were repeated for him. Only on the simple visual tracking tasks were his scores at the *low average* level; when a mental tracking component was added, his performance level plummeted to *defective.*

*Memory.* On all aspects of verbal and visual memory he displayed significant deficits. Thus immediate span under stimulus overload conditions was in the *impaired* range; immediate recall of stories was not only *impaired* but subject to confusion and perseveration of elements. His capacity for new learning of both verbal material and complex visual material was frankly *defective*; although the quantity of simple visual material recalled was *within normal limits*, more than half of his recalled designs contained errors. Moreover, interference reduced verbal recall even further. In part, his inability to recall newly learned material at any better than *defective* levels was due to an abnormally slow rate of learning; in part, it reflected an *impaired* capacity to retrieve learned information at will. Only on the tactile learning test were his recall scores *within normal limits*. However, since he was given an abnormally long exposure time, this performance can not be taken at its face value.

### Diagnostic Impression

P2 is a man of originally *average* intellectual endowment who continues to demonstrate his premorbid abilities on tests of well-learned verbal information or skills or that involve familiar, well-structured material that remains visually present. In contrast are significant deficits in constructional tasks requiring conceptual analysis and integration of unfamiliar material, in all but the simplest attentional functions, and in all aspects of both visual and verbal memory. Compounding these problems are deficits in self-monitoring and self-correcting that show up in both visual and verbal modalities and across a wide range of functions suggesting that they are pervasive.

Given his long history of exposure to industrial solvents and a pattern of cognitive deficits that is consonant with the deficit patterns documented in the Scandinavian literature (see publication), it is most probable that a pattern of deficits of this considerable magnitude reflects organic brain dysfunction due to his years of exposure to the industrial solvents. Dr. OM also pointed out that his history of symptoms of mental distress and dysfunction follow a course that is typical for toxic and metabolic disorders. The question of whether his hypertension may also have contributed to his cognitive disorder is best answered by noting that the neuropsychological literature on hypertensives indicates that response speed, immediate verbal memory (but not verbal learning or retrieval, not visual memory whether immediate or delayed), and some aspects of attention are vulnerable to prolonged untreated hypertension, particularly in older populations. In none of the studies involving patients in his age group were deficits found on visuoconstructive or perceptual integration functions. Moreover, the deficits documented for hypertensives are much less pronounced than those seen here. The question of whether his drinking habits may have contributed to his cognitive disorder can be answered again by the literature: his alcohol consumption rate comes under the category of social drinking. Again the literature suggests the pattern and severity of deficits exhibited by him can not be accounted for by alcohol consumption since memory and learning are not impaired in social drinkers, although some relationship to abstract concept formation is indicated among heavier drinkers. A careful review of the literature thus leads to the conclusion that the nature and magnitude of his cognitive deficits can best be understood as a syndrome of organic brain dysfunction primarily due to exposure to toxic solvents. The Scandinavian literature also indicates that deficits remaining long after exposure has ceased are chronic and irreversible.

As a result of these deficits, P2 is, in all likelihood, limited to doing menial kinds of work that require very little training, no constructional skills, no mental operations (e.g., mental calculations), and in which accuracy, precision, or speed are not important. He is incapable of working in "high tech" fields. Moreover, his severe learning deficits put vocational retraining out of the question, again except for menial laboring jobs that do not involve much verbal or conceptual learning. It is highly improbable that he will ever be able to perform satisfactorily at a skilled workman level.

By _____
EW, Ph.D

## DR. 6, PH.D.

### NEUROPSYCHOLOGICAL REPORT

September 20, 1984

Patient's name: P2

Date of birth: July 30, 1945

Age at time of testing: 39

Educational level: High school graduate

Occupation: Spray painter

Referred by: Insurance Company

Dates tested: September 10 and 11, 1984

Tests administered: WAIS-R, Halstead-Indiana Battery of Neuropsychological Tests, Memory Tests, MMPI, Kuder Occupational Interest Survey, Wide Range Achievement Test (Reading and Spelling), Personal interview.

**Observations During Testing**

This patient has had a neuropsychological examination by Dr. 4 and 8 in August 1982, by Dr. EW in September 1983, and a neuropsychological screening on October 12, 1983 by Dr. 5. Their reports and other medical records were available to us. P2 related to the testing situation in a positive and cooperative way. He was adequately motivated throughout and a valid test record is felt to have been obtained.

He was rather quiet and slightly defensive volunteering little information about himself. He experienced occasional difficulties with test instructions and they had to be repeated at times. There were some tasks (Halstead Categories Test, Block Design Test) on which he did not seem to fully comprehend what it is that he was supposed to do. The Kuder Occupational Interest Survey is being repeated by him because he filled it out incorrectly even though he had been given rather detailed directions. The Kuder Occupational Interest Survey has been sent out for scoring and when the results are obtained a short supplementary report will be furnished.

He is ambidextrous. He uses his right hand for writing but most other tasks are performed with the left hand.

He shows adequate grip strength in both hands.

Results of Neuropsychological Examination

Performance on the WAIS places patient's current level of intellectual functioning at the dull normal range (Verbal IQ = 86; Performance IQ = 88; Full Scale IQ = 86). There was considerable variability in his level of functioning across the WAIS subtests. There was one test (Picture Arrangement) on which he performed especially well (weighted score = 12). His variability on the other WAIS subtests was considerably smaller. Her [sic] performed very poorly (70) [sic] on more abstract perceptual-motor types of tasks (Block Design) and on those requiring arithmetical computations. He also performed poorly on tasks requiring immediate attention span (Digit Span) and on those requiring being able to distinguish between essential and nonessential details (Picture Completion). On the Vocabulary Test he attained a weighted score of 9 which corresponds to an IQ of approximately 95 and which is probably indicative of his premorbid intelligence level.

Patient experienced mild to serious difficulties on almost all of the Halstead Tests attaining an Impairment Index of .9 which indicates the presence of diffuse impairments due to central nervous system dysfunction. He performed especially poorly on the Halstead Categories Test (a nonverbal concept formation test) indicating that his ability to cope with novel and unfamiliar situations is substantially reduced. He also experienced marked difficulties on the Tactual Performance Test (done with patient blindfolded) suggesting that his ability to process kinesthetic-proprioceptive information is impaired. One would expect him to experience difficulties on tasks requiring fine motor coordination. The speed with which he can work on more complex types of tasks (Trails B, Digit Symbol) is significantly reduced. Patient's performance on tasks demanding fine auditory discriminations and sustained concentration (Speech Perception, Seashore Rhythms) is mildly reduced. On the positive side patient performed well on tasks requiring simple motor speed (Finger Tapping) and on those which can be performed under visual control (Trails A).

The results of the Aphasia Screening examination were essentially negative. Patient is able to name common objects and she [sic] is able to demonstrate their use. He is able to comprehend verbal messages and he is able to express himself adequately. However, he experienced mild difficulties with being able to understand the subtle meaning of statements (e.g., asked to explain the meaning of the statement—He shouted the warning—"He let someone know what was going on"; asked to explain the meaning of the proverb—Strike while the iron is hot— "Go ahead and move on while you have the upper hand"). Patient is able to read and write letters, numbers, words and simple sentences. The Wide Range Achievement Test places his reading at the 8th and his spelling at the 3rd grade levels, respectively. His ability to engage in tasks requiring arithmetical computations is quite limited (examples: $17 \times 3 = 32$; $14 - 8 = 7$). Patient's level of proficiency in regard to the three R's while functional is quite limited.

The results of the Sensory Perception examination were entirely negative. There was no evidence of suppression of sensation under conditions of simultaneous stimulation. Tactile form recognition is intact.

Patient's reproductions (by drawing) of simple geometric designs and objects show no evidence of perceptual distortion.

Patient's attention span and short term memory for visually presented information is at the lower end of the normal range. However, he shows evidence of a significant attentional deficit in the auditory modality. He also experienced mild difficulties on the Long Term Memory Test. After ten trials he only had 21 elements of a 24-element story correct. Retested on the story a day later he was able to recall only three of the elements. With ten additional trials he was not able to learn the story to perfect criterion (had only 18 out of 24 correct). Questioned about memory difficulties in everyday situations patient indicated that he is experiencing significant difficulties remembering what he has done, with where he puts things, with what he has heard; and to a lesser extent with what he is supposed to do in the future and with what he has seen. More specifically, patient indicates that he tends to lose track of conversations and that in the middle of working on a task he may not remember what he was doing especially when he is being distracted. The laboratory findings are consistent with his self-report. Patient needs to be encouraged to make an active effort to actively rehearse, practice, paraphrase, etc. information that is important for him to remember.

Patient's scores on the validity scales of the MMPI indicate that he took this test in a valid and sincere manner. He attained clinically significant elevations on the Psychasthenia-Anxiety ($T = 85$), Schizophrenia ($T = 76$), and Depression ($T = 74$) scales. The MMPI thus indicates an individual who is feeling anxious and depressed at a significantly elevated level.

Patient describes himself as feeling irritable and being somewhat concerned about his ability to control himself when he is frustrated. He is quite concerned about his future and about his ability to put his life back on some kind of constructive track.

**Summary and Recommendations**

In summary, neuropsychological testing reveals a man whose premorbid intelligence is estimated to have been within the average range who now shows a pattern of impairments consistent with a diffuse lesion of the central nervous system. Impairments were noted on tasks requiring mental flexibility, problem-solving ability, being able to deal with novel and unfamiliar situations, and in being able to work under less than optimal (i.e., nondistracting) conditions. He also has difficulty in working on tasks requiring sustained concentration. While language functions are intact he shows evidence of difficulties in being able to understand any but the most simple kinds of instructions and in being able to work on any but the most simple kinds of tasks. Language functions are intact but his ability to work in situations requiring academic skills is quite limited. Patient also shows evidence of a significant attentional deficit in the auditory modality and is experiencing difficulties with being able to master and retain longer sequences over longer periods of time. On the positive side patient performs best in the visual modality. He is able to work well on simple routinized tasks under visual control with little demand for memory.

Our test findings are most directly comparable to those obtained by Dr. 4 and 8 since they administered many of the same tests we have. It is important to note that the test scores P2 obtained on two separate test occasions are very similar attesting to the reliability of the test findings and to the likelihood that his condition is quite stable.

The test results indicate that he is experiencing serious emotional difficulties which are probably secondary to the fact that he has not been able to work and that he is facing a rather complicated and difficult situation.

Regarding the specific questions raised by Supervisor, Worker's Compensation Department, in her letter of August 30, 1984, I would like to respond as follows:

1. Do you feel the conditions are medically stationary in the sense that the conditions will not improve with further treatment or the passage of time?

I feel that his neuropsychological condition is stationary and that relatively little improvement may be expected.

2. Are these conditions to any extent reversible?

Within reasonable psychological probabilities, I do not think that his neuropsychological impairments are reversible.

3. Except for the obvious continued exposure to the solvents, are these patients mentally capable of resuming their former occupations of painter/sandblaster?

It is my opinion that both in terms of the neuropsychological deficits which already exist and the emotional trauma that is likely to be experienced, he is not capable of resuming his former occupation of painter/sandblaster.

4. Are they mentally capable of learning new technical skills to enable them to begin new occupations?

This is a difficult question to answer. His neuropsychological impairments clearly limit his ability to learn new technical skills and this will seriously limit the range of occupations which are open to him. At the same time, I feel that it is important for his emotional well-being that he be assisted in gradually reentering the world of work at some level.

5. If number 4 is no, are they then mentally capable of functioning in laboring jobs relying on past skills or are they truly incapable of engaging in gainful employment?

At this point in time, and in the foreseeable future, I do not feel that he is capable of engaging in gainful employment under condition of normal demands and requirements.

6. Is there any possibility of separating the effects of the damage done the solvent and paint exposure from any preexisting damage that may have been present?

I do not think so. Assuming that he was functioning well before his exposure to solvents, it is my opinion based on reasonable psychological probabilities, that his current impairments were caused by his exposure to solvents.

7. The classification of impairment related to the various disorders resulting from the brain damage.

It is my opinion that he has suffered a Level II type of impairment, i.e., there is a degree of impairment of complex integrated cerebral functions such that daily activities need some supervision and/or direction. Percent impairment = 30%.

8. Is there a cognitive retraining program that would be beneficial to either of the patients to help them adjust to their deficiencies?

His present condition is compounded by the fact that he has objective impairments and that he has not been working for an extended period of time. Reentry will thus be difficult. I feel that he would benefit from personal therapy and vocational counseling aimed at helping him to compensate for some of his cognitive deficiencies and helping him to commit himself to a long term plan increasing his activities in a meaningful and personally rewarding way.

## Diagnostic Impression
294.80 Mixed Organic Brain Syndrome
Dr. 6, Ph.D.
Professor of Psychology

### NOTES FOR DC ON P2

Table 2 shows the results obtained on the WAIS-R administered at various times to P2.

The following is the report prepared for defense counsel on P2 by the author-consultant.

I will attempt in this report to deal with the basic issue of the credibility of the several conclusions that P2 has suffered impairment due to damage to his brain as a result of exposure to toxic substances in the course of his work as a painter. I will break this down into different issues. First of all, I will attempt to deal with the issue of whether or not P2, at the time of the recent examinations, was functioning at a lower level than he was prior to the time he became a painter. I will also deal to some extent with his credibility. I will also deal with the competence with which several of the examinations were performed and the probability of accuracy of conclusions based on those examinations. I will not deal specifically with the neuropsychological testing, except as the materials I have rather clearly indicate or raise some questions about the manner in which the testing was done. I will also not be dealing with the validity of the so-called "painters syndrome."

### TABLE 2

The following are the results obtained on the WAIS-R administered at various times to P2.

| | WAIS-R 8/17/82 | | WAIS-R 10/06/83 | | WAIS-R 9/10/84 | | Comparison of 8/82 and 9/84 |
|---|---|---|---|---|---|---|---|
| | RAW | SCALE | RAW | SCALE | RAW | SCALE | |
| Information | 18 | 9 | | | 13 | 7 | -2 |
| Digit Span | 11 | 7 | 7 | 4 | 9 | 6 | -1 |
| | | (6 F) | | (4 F) | | (4 F) | |
| | | (3 B) | | (3 B) | | (5 B) | |
| Vocabulary | 49 | 10 | | | 45 | 9 | |
| Arithmetic | 5 | 5 | 4 | 4 | 5 | 5 | |
| Comprehension | 24 | 11 | | | 20 | 9 | -2 |
| Similarities | 20 | 10 | 20 | 10 | 17 | 8 | -2 |
| Verbal Score | | 52 | | | | 44 | |
| Picture Completion | 14 | 8 | | | 13 | 7 | -1 |
| Picture Arrangement | 16 | 11 | | | 17 | 12 | +1 |
| Block Design | 8 | 5 | | | 6 | 4 | -1 |
| Object Assembly | 18 | 5 | | | 18 | 8 | +3 |
| Digit Symbol | 42 | 6 | | | 42 | 6 | |
| Performance Score | | 35 | | | | 37 | |
| Verbal IQ | | 93 | | | | 86 | |
| Performance IQ | | 86 | | | | 88 | |
| Full Scale IQ | | 89 | | | | 86 | |

It should be borne in mind that the best evidence of his "pre-morbid" functioning lies in the objective evidence of that functioning such as is contained in the school and military records. It should be kept in mind that any attempt to estimate his "pre-morbid" functioning from presently administered tests or from his occupational level are nothing more than that, "estimates." That is, simply guesses for which there is little validating research support. I am not familiar with the level of skill and/or intellect required for the kind of work he was doing, that apparently of an industrial painter. I am going to make the assumption that this is not a complex technical kind of occupation and one which is essentially of a routine nature.

In order to establish the base line from which he is allegedly impaired or has had his functioning reduced, I will look first at the information provided by the records of _____ High School. These records show that he graduated number 409 in a class of 447, placing him in the bottom ten percent or stated another way, he was below the tenth percentile. It is noted that he showed some variability in his performance, obtaining two B's (one of which was in Physical Education), six C's, twelve D's and five F's, thus performing at four different levels or showing a fair amount of what psychologists refer to as "scatter." Obviously if one were to apply the "best performance" measure to determine his ability, one would have to predict that he would be a B student in high school, so that we have here a fairly dramatic demonstration of the fallacy of that method of assessing ability. What is clearly demonstrated is that the vast proportion of his high school performance was below average and a substantial portion of it was failing. Stated another way, his most probable level of performance is below average as indicated by the fact that his overwhelmingly predominant grade was D. It should also be noted that of the courses he took that involved the use of numbers, specifically general math, in which he got an F, bookkeeping in which he got an F and a course that I cannot quite make out—it's in handwriting rather than in print, but it's in the 1961-62 school year and it says math, something that looks like RES or maybe REV for math review, I do not know, but under weeks, it indicates, I think, summer session—he got a D. Thus, very clearly based on this objective data, he has always had a great deal of difficulty dealing with subject matter that involved numbers. In all probability his grade of F in bookkeeping should be included along with his grades in math as this was undoubtedly a course that also dealt extensively with numbers. Thus, he failed two out of three courses dealing with numerical operations and barely squeaked by in the third, which I note is a review course which may have been a remedial math course and one that was taken in a summer session, which as many people know, is often a little less rigorous than the course administered in regular semester. I note that this is the only time he took a summer session course. Therefore, his level of functioning with numerical operations was below his average level of functioning in high school courses, which was a little bit above a D average, and way below his best performance in a high school course, which was the B in applied science in 1963. For this reason, his low score on the arithmetic subtests of the WAIS-R and any other subtests involving numbers cannot be used as a diagnostic indicator of impairment, inasmuch as his performance on the WAIS is the same as his performance prior to his becoming a painter. Nor can his best performances on the WAIS be taken as an indicator of his "pre-morbid" intellectual functioning, as it is obvious from the high school grades that he rarely performed anywhere near the level of his best performance.

There is a further item of information in the high school record that may be relevant to some of his more recent test performances. I am referring here specifically to his grades of F in industrial art, which looks like woodshop and industrial art (looks like metalshop) in 1960-61, along with his F in typing I-II in 1961-62, although he got a grade of C in a repeat of the typing course the following year. The significance I would attach to these grades is in relation to some of the conclusions that he has difficulty with visual constructive tasks on the current neuropsychological testing, which again, is taken as an indicator of impairment. But I would make an assumption which you may be able to check out if you wish to run down these courses as they were given at the time he took them. They also involved visual constructive processes or eye-hand coordination processes as one would expect in woodshop and metalshop courses. Typing I would view also as an eye-hand motor coordination task. It is evident that he had considerable difficulty in learning in these areas and in fact, there is nothing to show that he ever did learn so far as the wood and metalshops are concerned and it took him two semesters to learn what most students can learn in one semester in typing. He was not especially good in art, obtaining one D and one C in general art courses.

The school record contains two more items of relevance so far as impairment is concerned. I note that in February of 1958, he was administered a test described as CMM which I assume to have been the California Test of Mental Maturity. In any event, whatever test it was, he obtained an IQ of 87, which is right about where his IQ tests out in the current testing. Thus, it is extremely difficult to see how one can argue that he has been impaired, if he tests out with the same IQ that he had before. It is likely that some of the clinicians will argue that this test did not tap some of the functions they tapped with the neuropsychological tests. But then we do not have any prior neuropsychological testing to compare with so the best conclusion one can come to is that given the objective evidence of non-impairment that exists, the conclusion should be non-impairment in the absence of clear evidence of present test functioning that is poorer than prior functioning. Also the school records show on the Iowa Composite, he obtained a placement at the thirty-seventh percentile which would put him in the average range but roughly in the bottom quarter of the average range. I am not familiar with any test called the Iowa Composite and am fairly confident that the reference there is to a composite score on the Iowa Test of Educational Development. If you want to use this score, it may be necessary to tie this down either by getting information from the school or testimony from one of the witnesses. You should be aware that this is not an IQ measure but a measure of educational achievement.

Turning now to the military records, I note that P2 enlisted in the Navy on October 3rd, 1963 and was discharged six weeks later on November 26th, 1963, never passing beyond the training period. He was given an Honorable Discharge by reason of "unsuitability." As an ironic sidenote, further demonstrating the inability of mental health professionals to accurately assess people, there is the document headed by the title "MEASUREMENTS AND OTHER FINDINGS" which contains the notation, "Psych. consult finds registrant fit for military service," signed _____, CAPT., MC. The report of the aptitude board, dated November 21, 1963 seems to provide dramatic evidence of the very low level of P2's functioning prior to his becoming a painter. This report indicates that according to his own statement, he had completed the twelfth grade in school with an average scholastic record, obviously a false statement. Further, according to information given by P2, his social adjustments were inadequate and his work history sketchy. He has never participated in organized social activities, he has been excessively nervous for several years. That has to be based on his own report. He was noted to be personally unclean and found to be unreliable and depressed. His grasp of instructions was poor. He frequently visited sick bay with complaints of nervousness. His overall aptitude for training was rated as poor. Psychiatric evaluation reveals an emotionally labile inadequate recruit with low self-esteem, minimal stress tolerance and marked anxiety. The report is topped off with the statement from the Company Commander, "He is unable to perform the simplest of maneuvers." Thus, we find, prior to becoming a painter, Mr. P2 was of very low competence, had little ability to learn and suffered from apparently severe emotional problems including anxiety and depression. One has to wonder how much he could have been impaired from that level without having become a basket case requiring institutionalization. The consistency between these reports and his high school records seems obvious and provides the same sort of evidence coming from two different sources.

## THE PRESENT EXAMINATIONS

There is considerable doubt as to the level of competence demonstrated by the people who performed the neuropsychological examinations in August of 1982 and September of 1984. It is noted that the 1982 testing was done by 8 who, at that time, was an intern and did not have a Ph.D. in psychology, nor a license to practice psychology, although the representation is made that she performed under the supervision of Dr. 4. It will be worthwhile to attempt to find out what the term "under the supervision" means, because there are numerous errors and either Dr. 4 did not carefully supervise what was done or his competence in this case is equally questionable. That is, what is the value of supervision if the errors to be described below are not detected? I will be focusing these comments primarily on the WAIS-R as the nature of this test and its record form make it more possible to observe errors. I will comment on some of the neuropsychological tests I believe contain clear-cut errors and will suggest some criticisms relative to the MMPI. It should be noted that none of the people conducting the neuropsychological examinations went to the minimal trouble of obtaining the high school and military records described above, which would have provided them with a sound basis for evaluating plaintiff's pre-morbid condition. They chose rather to speculate from test data which has not been scientifically validated for that purpose. The literature on estimating "pre-morbid" IQ from the WAIS is equivocal.

On WAIS-R subtest number four, picture arrangement item two, plaintiff responded by arranging the cards in the order AJNET. 8 originally scored this as a one point response but then crossed that out and scored it as a two point response. However, the correct arrangement for a two point response is JANET and the response AJNET is called an acceptable variation and is scored one point. Therefore, this constitutes a scoring error which would then make the total score fifteen instead of sixteen. This does not change the scale score, as either fifteen or sixteen provides for a scale score of eleven. However, this is the type of error that should not happen at the professional level.

Next, on the vocabulary subtest, I note first of all that 8 violated the instructions for administering the test which calls for the test to be discontinued after five consecutive failures, but looking at the scoring for this test I note that plaintiff obtained one point of credit for item twenty-nine, "fortitude" and then had three zero answers and then, apparently, was not given the additional two items to which he was entitled, but the test was stopped after three consecutive failures rather than five. There is another error in the administration of the test at item twenty-eight where the manual for the test states very clearly at page 121, that examinees giving this response should be asked for another answer. It does not appear that this was done, as the ordinary notation that is made when a question is asked is to put the letter Q in parentheses as you will note was done on item twenty-three. Therefore, the fact that no Q appears in connection with this response indicates that 8 failed to administer this item as instructed by the manual. There is also one clear-cut scoring error on item 24.

On test number six, block design, there is another violation of the instructions for administering the test which state that tests should be discontinued after three consecutive failures, but the answer sheet here indicates only two consecutive failures and then the test is discontinued prematurely. For your information, the rules for continuing or discontinuing are given in order to allow for the fact that someone might miss a couple of items, but then go on to obtain additional credits on subsequent items, so that that is the way the test was standardized. That is, all the people who took this test in order to establish the norms were given a block design problem until they had three consecutive failures and I have no doubt, nor would anyone else who has ever administered the test, that there would be some people who would miss two and then pick up on the next item and get one or two additional items correct, which would change the score. However, discontinuing prematurely deprives the individual of the opportunity to demonstrate his full ability.

The situation on subtest seven, arithmetic, is somewhat ambiguous. This also calls for discontinuing after four consecutive failures. There are only three zeros noted in the score column and then no further scores. So one might conclude that the test was discontinued at that point, the last zero being for item number eight. However, I notice that for item number nine, there is an answer written in, which is a wrong answer. So it is not clear whether the item was administered as it should have been and simply no score written in (which in itself would be an error, of course), or whether there is some other explanation.

On subtest eight, object assembly, a somewhat similar ambiguity exists in that all four items are to be given to all subjects and I note that under the column for time, there are entries for all four of the items. However, scores are entered only for items one, two and three with no score entered for item number four. You will note in looking at the sheet that, even if P2 failed to obtain any credit whatsoever on this item, there is provision for marking a score of zero. No score of any kind is marked. I should tell you this test consists of a sort of jigsaw puzzle type of test and in this instance, the object to be assembled is is found by some subjects to be somewhat difficult. But one can get partial credit (there are several pieces), and any two pieces put together would earn one point of credit and it would be a rare occurrence for someone not to be able to put at least two pieces together or a couple of pairs of pieces together so as to get some credit. Actually on the later test in 1984, Mr. P2 got credit for actually assembling almost all of the puzzle, obtaining a score of seven on that particular item. So either 8 failed to record the score that plaintiff actually obtained or she simply failed to record any score at all. In either case, this would constitute an error.

On subtest nine, comprehension, there are two scoring errors and one administration error (failure to question).

Thus on the WAIS alone, this intern, 8, appears to have committed several errors in the administration of the test and in the scoring.

With regard to the MMPI, it does not appear that either 8 or Doctor 4 did anything to follow up on a number of items on the MMPI that would seem to require further investigation (see MMPI items below).

The September 10th and 11th, 1984 examination forming the basis for Dr. 6's report of September 20th, 1984 appears to have been performed entirely by someone named 7, although nowhere in Dr. 6's report is there any mention of 7 or the fact that 7 performed all of the testing. And as far as one can determine from the report, it is not clear whether Dr. 6, in fact, ever even saw P2. The report however, is signed only by Dr. 6. There is reference in the report to some multiple examiners by use of the term "our" and "us" and "we." However, it does not seem to be entirely forthcoming of Dr. 6 not to anywhere indicate that he had not personally done the testing and that it had been done by someone else whose status obviously is not clear to us. I will make the assumption that 7 was probably an intern or a trainee as was the case with 8. In this connection, both with 7 and 8, you should keep in mind Dr. EW's reported admonition in the lecture he presented, that neuropsychological testing should not be done by people below the doctoral level and who do not have extensive experience and training in this area.

Looking first at the WAIS-R, there are seven scoring errors and one error of administration on the Vocabulary subtest. On subtest six, "Block Design" the examiner failed to circle a zero for the score on item number five, although the pass/fail column does indicate that he failed. This is certainly a very minor point. It's just sloppy work and may add to the general picture of something less than a highly competent performance by this examiner.

On subtest nine, "Comprehension," three scoring errors change the scale score from nine to eight. I have particularly mentioned the change of scores on the comprehension subtest because they were his highest on the verbal tests and some points were made in the various reports of the discrepancy between his vocabulary and comprehension scores and his arithmetic score. While a difference of four points might be viewed as having some meaning (although this is questionable in the research) a difference of three points is simply meaningless as being within a normal and expectable amount of variation.

Unfortunately in the materials that were sent to me, apparently the object assembly and comprehension subtests were copied twice and the similarities and digit symbol subtests were not copied so that I cannot comment on those tests. If you should locate these and can send them to me I will review them to see if there is anything further to add, although I would think that the above material is enough to raise doubts as to the competence of 7's administration and scoring of psychological tests in this case.

On the Halstead category test, 7 discontinued after P2's very poor performance on Set III, noting that patient had done very badly and was unable to get the idea at all and had become quite frustrated, thus justifying discontinuing at that point according to the manual as noted above. However, he then proceded to score 30 errors for Set IV, V and VI, and 15 errors for VII. I cannot figure out any basis for this. If he was prorating as the manual states, according to the performance on the first 20 items, then we note that there were 16 errors in the first 20 items and inasmuch as the number of items is the same for tests IV, V and VI, and half as many for VII, the prorating should have been 32 errors for subtests IV, V and VI and 16 for subtest VII. If he was prorating on the basis of the entire performance on subtest three then the number of errors should have been 33 each for tests IV, V and VI and 16 or 17 for subtest VII. Whichever way he was doing it, he comes out with a wrong answer, though I would assume that possibly in this case, the question could be raised as to whether if a patient did this he would be said to suffer from "Acalculia."

In connection with the MMPI it does not appear that either 7 or Dr. 6 followed up on some highly significant items on the MMPI despite having in their possession a list of critical items with at least three items circled. Normal procedure on list of critical items is to suggest that the clinician follow up on these to determine just what they mean and what their significance is. There are also other items that I think would have required some thought (see discussion of MMPI below).

## TEST DATA

Some of the material from the test data is relevant to evaluating plaintiff's claims and the opinions that have been rendered.

I note that on the 1982 MMPI all of his scores are within the more or less normal range and certainly below the pathological range, generally viewed as starting above a T score of 70. This is important because of various assertions that many of his symptoms existed prior to the time of this examination and because he is found to be suffering from organic brain syndrome on the basis of this examination. It is also noted that the examiners did not take advantage of the opportunity to obtain a computerized interpretation of the MMPI data, nor of computerized scoring. Some of the specific items are of interest and I will give the items. Just as an additional fact, you should be aware that out of the 399 items utilized on the 1984 MMPI (which was a short form), 79 responses were different from the MMPI given in '82. However, my impression is that generally the changes were in the direction of indicating more psychological disorder. The responses on the 1982 MMPI indicated:

1. His appetite is good. This is generally contrary to what one finds in people who are depressed, although sometimes they have excessive appetites.

2. He usually wakes up rested. This also is not what one expects with someone who is either depressed or anxious.

3. On a regular basis life is full of things that keep him interested. This also is not particularly consistent with depression and doesn't sound like someone who is suffering very much or is very impaired.

4. His ability to work is unchanged. It is interesting to note that in August of 1982, a time at which he is found by the experts to be suffering from impairment due to organic brain syndrome, that his own statement is that he is as able to work as he ever was. It is also interesting to note that he changes this response in 1984, possibly because of more involvement at that point with his lawsuit.

5. He is satisfied with his sex life. This generally is not consistent with depression or anxiety or with difficulty in interpersonal relationships.

6. He has no difficulty keeping his mind on a task or a job, but does in 1984. This is another instance in which at the time he is being diagnosed as having brain damage which interferes with his attention and concentration and memory, he states that he is not having difficulty of that nature, but then he changes his response in 1984.

7. He always tells the truth. This of course is generally not believable, there is hardly anyone who always tells the truth and in fact we have clear cut evidence that he does not always tell the truth because he told several of the examiners that in high school he earned average grades. We know for a fact that is false.

8. Most of the time he does not feel blue. This rather clearly indicates that he is not depressed and is not particularly suffering.

9. He is self-confident. This also would suggest that he does not see himself as particularly impaired.

10. He generally perceives life as worthwhile. This is contrary to what one expects with depression and is further evidence that he does not seem to be suffering very much.

11. He has very few quarrels with members of his family. This at least in '82 would tend to suggest that he is getting along well with his family and would be somewhat contrary to allegations of irritability and loss of temper which one would think would lead to difficulties with the family rather than getting along with them well. However, we note that this is changed in '84. But presumably the symptoms of irritability and so on were alleged in '82 despite this statement to the contrary.

12. He likes going to social events but not in 1984. This again indicates that in '82 he was not having any problems socializing and was enjoying himself.

13. Most of the time he is happy. I think this speaks for itself as far as his psychological condition.

14. He feels about as capable as most others but not in 1984. This is further indication that he does not experience himself as particularly impaired in 1982 at the time that the experts are finding him to be impaired.

15. There is not anything wrong with his mind, but this is changed in 1984. Thus in 1982 when he is being found by the experts to be impaired from brain damage, he does not think there is anything wrong with his mind, and presumably they are basing their conclusions at least in part on symptoms that he is presumably presenting to them. So either they're exaggerating the symptoms or he

is falsifying symptoms when he speaks to the examiners. In 1984, there may be an iatrogenic effect.

16. He usually does not feel weak. I think this is contrary to one of the "painters syndrome" symptoms of fatigue.

17. He rarely has headaches. Same as above.

18. He enjoys many kinds of recreational activities. That does not sound like somebody who is very much impaired or suffering very much.

19. He expects succeed in his endeavors. Again suggesting a person who does not feel particularly impaired.

20. He does not often experience life as a strain but does in 1984. Again in '82 at the time he is being diagnosed with a brain syndrome, he indicates that life is not much of a strain, which certainly would not be consistent with the idea that he has been impaired.

21. He has no trouble keeping his mind on a task but does in 1984. This again is not consistent with the impairment that is described by the experts in 1982 and I do not know how to account for the change in '84.

22. He is able to remember what people say to him, but not in 1984. This again is not consistent with the assertions that he has problems with immediate memory in 1982.

23. He rarely gets blue. This again is contrary to the idea of depression or distress.

24. It takes a lot to make him angry. This seems to be contrary to the contention that he is suffering from irritability.

25. He usually resolves things for himself without seeking help. This does not sound like someone who is very much impaired or feels impaired.

26. Usually he does not feel tired. This is not consistent with one of the symptoms of so-called painters syndrome.

27. He likes fixing things. This does not seem consistent with any contentions that he is unable to perform somewhat complex mechanical tasks.

On the September, 1984 MMPI his responses indicated:

1. He is less able to work than he was. This is a change, which makes it sound as though his condition is worse. However, it is important to note in connection with this response and any of the responses which make him sound worse that Dr. 5 examining in late 1983 concludes that his condition is not changed from the 1982 examination and that it is not a progressive condition, and also that Dr. 6 notes the high degree of similarity in the test data that he obtained in late 1984, to that obtained in 1982. So the opinion of several of the experts is that his condition was not progressing or deteriorating and therefore, it becomes difficult to view his representation of worsening condition on the MMPI other than falsifying or exaggerating his difficulties. This would be consistent with other demonstrably false information that he has given as will be discussed below.

2. He has trouble keeping his mind on a task. This is another change for the worse from his 1982 response.

3. He rarely feels blue. This again is not consistent with any notion that he is suffering very much.

4. He has no lack of self-confidence. This is not consistent with claims of impairment.

5. Most of the time he thinks life is worthwhile. This is not consistent with much suffering.

6. He usually feels happy. This obviously is not a statement of someone who is suffering very much.

7. He likes to study and read about projects he is undertaking. This would suggest that he does have capability of learning, otherwise why would he like to do such a thing?

8. Dizzy spells almost never occur. This again is a counterindication of one of the symptoms of "painters syndrome" and certainly argues against a deterioration of his condition as he earlier indicated some problems with dizziness.

9. He is capable of reading a long time. This would seem to indicate that he can read and maintain a train of thought over a long period of time, otherwise he wouldn't read for a long time and wouldn't know that it doesn't tire his eyes.

10. Headaches are rare. This again is contrary to the description of "painters syndrome."

11. He likes a variety of recreational activities. This does not sound like someone who is suffering very much or who is very much impaired.

12. He has a lot of self-confidence. This does not sound like someone who is impaired or feels impaired.

13. His eyesight is somewhat diminished. This suggests some worsening of condition and my recollection is that there was no claim of impairment of eyesight made to the various examiners. However, if he has a visual problem, that might account for some of his poor test results and one would need to know if the examiners were aware of a vision problem and took it into account in interpreting the test results.

14. His life is routinely filled with things that keep him interested. This is also a repeat of an earlier item and indicates it was not answered by mistake.

15. He often has feelings of unreality. This is another item suggesting serious disorder which requires exploration by the examiner which does not appear to have been done.

16. He enjoys going to dances. Again suggesting someone who is pretty much enjoying his life.

You should be aware that while it is argued that his test results are quite similar from 1982 to 1984, in fact his MMPI profile is really quite different. While there were no scores in the so-called pathological range, that is, above a T score of 70 in the 1982 test, he has three scores substantially above a T score of 70 on the '84 MMPI and in particular, he shows a T score above 80 on scale seven Pt, which generally is thought to be an indicator of anxiety, and he is above a T score of 75 on scale eight which is Sc, standing for schizophrenia. Along with some of the responses that were not further explored, it at least raises the possibility of something of a "schizophrenic" or "borderline psychotic" condition, and the depression scale is also elevated into the so-called pathological range and is markedly higher than it was in 1982. Also on scale ten, social introversion, he has shown a change from a T score of 47 to a T score of

61 which is a substantial movement, although all of it remains within the normal range.

It may be worthwhile to note some changes in his responses on the WAIS-R. On the information subtest in 1982 he correctly answers item 21 but fails this item in 1984. However, on the other hand he fails item 24 1982 but successfully does it 1984. In 1982 he is able to repeat six digits forward and three digits backward but in 1984 he is only able to repeat four digits forward but is now able to successfully repeat four digits backward. Most everyone recognizes that repeating the numbers backward is more difficult than forward. So it is difficult to understand how he got worse on repeating digits forward and got better on repeating digits backward.

On the vocabulary subtest he gives poorer answers on items 17, 22, 23, 26 and 27, but on the other hand he gives better answers on items four, 11 and 31. On the arithmetic subtest, he is able in 1982 to correctly perform item number five, which is a simple multiplication of a two-digit number by a one-digit number. But he is unable to do this correctly in 1984. However, in contrast, he is unable to do item seven, involving the division of a two digit number by a one-digit number, in 1982, but is able to do this more difficult problem in 1984. This does not make any particular sense if he has presumably lost arithmetic capacities that he had before. On the comprehension subtest, he performs worse in 1984 on items three, five, seven, 11, but performs better on items 12 and 13 which normally would be viewed as harder items. That is, the items are assumed to be in order of difficulty as you go up the numerical scale. Therefore this does not make any sense either. Also on test eight, the object assembly subtests where he was unable to get any credit so far as we know on item four, the on the 1982 administration, he gets almost a full credit score, that is he has made seven correct connections out of a maximum of eight that are possible, on the 1984 administration.

## CREDIBILITY

There are some items which cast serious doubt on P2's credibility. First of all, there are very clear misrepresentations to Dr. 5 and some of the other examiners regarding his level of performance in high school. He clearly represented to all of them that he was an average student obtaining mostly C's and some B's, which is a flagrant falsehood. In addition, he informed Doctor 5 that he had received no F's, which is obviously not true in the face of the five F's on his high school record. This is not something that can be accounted for by the alleged brain damage as this is old information generally thought not to be affected by brain damage. For example, the scores on the information and vocabulary subtests are believed to hold up because they are "old" information. In view of this flagrant falsehood, his representation on the MMPI that he always tells the truth becomes another demonstrable falsehood. Also note in the report of Dr. S that despite P2's claims of some visual difficulties, neurophthalmologic examination is entirely, in fact to use Dr. S's word, "resoundingly" negative. Some of the clinicians may raise the fact that P2 does not show up as a malingerer on any of the tests for malingering on the MMPI. I do not know what tests they conducted but I checked his F scale, his F - K score and his dissimulation scale score, and none of these showed him to fall into the malingerer range. However, you should be aware that on these tests, while they are quite good at ruling in malingering, they are not very good at ruling out malingering. That is, many malingerers escape detection by these measures. So the fact that these formulae for determining or indicating malingering are not positive does not mean that P2 is not falsifying symptoms or exaggerating some of his difficulties.

## THE EXPERTS' REPORTS

It is notable that there is considerable disagreement among various physicians. Dr. E in May of '81 finds malignant hypertension and a possible reaction to drugs, that is medications. June of '81 Dr. LAR finds some hypertensive retinal artery changes and suggests some type of cerebral vascular disease would be the most likely diagnosis. On August 4th of '82 Dr. Z notes a 19 year history of smoking plus moderately heavy alcohol consumption and high blood pressure. July of '83 Dr. WAT finds evidence of hypertensive vascular disease with cerebral manifestations. August of '83 Dr. CO finds a significant decrease in immediate memory function and evidence for mild peripheral polyneuropathy. Dr. LX finds evoked brain stem auditory response suggestive of sensory neurodeficit. October '83, Dr. 5 finds evidence for perceptual, self-regulatory and cognitive dysfunctions suggestive of bilateral cortical involvement. She notes while the results are consistent with toxicity secondary to chemical solvent disorder, one must consider the possibility that his history of alcohol use may be contributing to the deficits found. October '83 Dr. MA finds elements that are compatible with a slow and rather dull performance but not necessarily indicative of an organic compromise of brain structures. This of course would be compatible with the prior high school and military records. However, later in January of '84, Dr. MA seems to shift to favoring an organic brain involvement. November '83, Dr. BL does not find the vestibular findings described in the Swedish literature, but qualifies his statement by saying we would see these effects only during or shortly after acute exposure. November '83, Dr. DI finds the psychoneurologic test protocol unconvincing of any solvent brain damage and asserts the blood pressure condition is a sufficient explanation for his symptoms. Dr. EW states unqualifiedly that there are sufficient pattern deficits to reflect organic brain dysfunction due to his years of exposure to industrial solvents and states further that the symptoms are not consistent with deficits known to occur in hypertensive patients. September '84, Dr. 6 notes impairments involving mental flexibility, problem solving ability, dealing with novel and unfamiliar situations and performing work in distracting conditions, and he also diagnoses mixed organic brain syndrome. Thus summing up there seems to be a substantial amount of disagreement among various experts as to his condition and its source.

## THE EXAMINER'S REPORTS

8/4, 8-17-82

This report notes that P2 reportedly experienced severe dizziness lasting about twenty minutes, after about two hours of testing. However, the report also indicates that they went on and then tested him for an additional five hours without any further episode of dizziness. They offer no interpretation and raise no questions concerning this event, which strikes me as unusual. Inasmuch as he had a given history of prior passing out, it seems questionable that they would risk having him pass out due to the testing if they took the dizziness seriously. In any event, it seems to me the incident requires some comment beyond that of merely stating that it occurred.

The report quotes P2 that he graduated from J with a "C-Average." I do not know whether that represents a C minus or whether the dash is simply a dash, which would then indicate he was representing a C average. In either event, both are false representations as he had a D average, not a C minus average, if that is what is being stated, and certainly did not have a C average. I suspect that what is meant here is a C average as that would be consistent with what he reported to other examiners.

The report also quotes P2 as having had daily episodes of dizziness and nausea with accompanying temporary loss of vision. The MMPI items counter-indicating dizziness have been cited above. Insofar as nausea is concerned on an early item and a repeat of it later, he indicates that he is not troubled by attacks of nausea and vomiting.

This report notes that he averages four beers a day plus a six-pack on the weekend. It does note that he has maintained a romantic relationship for the six previous years which may explain why he has not married. Again, this report simply notes the fact of his alcohol consumption and makes no comment about it one way or another insofar as possible brain effects or effects on cognitive functioning.

On page 2, the report notes that his deficits are in subtests most sensitive to organic impairment, i.e., digit span, arithmetic, block design, digit symbol. His performance in digit span is simply not impaired as he obtains a score of seven, which is in the range one might expect from his IQ level. Further it is inappropriate to conclude that his block design was deficient, inasmuch as, as has been previously noted, this test was not properly administered. It was prematurely discontinued and he was not given an opportunity to perform at a higher level, if he was capable of doing so. This report appears to indicate that he is ambidextrous but uses his right hand for writing. However, the report then states that scores for the right ("preferred") hand and measures of grip strength and finger tapping speed failed to exceed the left by the expected ten percent. That is, what they have done is said that for the purpose of testing they would treat the right hand as the preferred hand, although they have, themselves, indicated that dominance is mixed. Therefore, there is no reason to expect a ten percent superiority of the right hand over the left. (Note that later in 1984, Dr. 6 points out that in fact the left hand is really probably the dominant hand except for writing, although he also describes P2 as ambidextrous.) In any event, there seems to be no sound basis for the conclusion that there is any significance to the lack of disparity in the two hands.

On page 3, the report asserts that he has a tendency to deny psychological problems and I can find no justification for that statement. Ordinarily, the basis for such a statement with regard to the MMPI would involve an elevated score on the K scale, sometimes called a defensiveness scale. But he scores simply at a T score of 55 which places him well in the middle of the average range and does not in any way suggest that he is being defensive or denying psychological problems any more than the average person.

The diagnosis of atypical organic brain disorder suggests that the symptom picture does not fit with any of the recognized organic brain syndromes.

## DR. 5, OCTOBER 12, 1983

Dr. 5 describes him as right hand dominant. She also states that according to his report, his academic performance was average, generally C's and uneventful, and further that he denied any failures in school. This of course is an outright falsehood. However, you should note that Dr. 5, as well as all of the other neuropsychologists in this case, apparently took his word for the fact that he was an average student and this in part determined the conclusions that his pre-morbid intelligence was average. The report also indicates some inconsistency in the facts concerning whether or not and for how long and when he resided with his parents. Dr. 5 also notes that the pre-morbid history is significant for ETOH use with confirmation of the minimum of four beers daily with more on the weekend. She states it is impossible to distinguish ETOH use or exposure to toxic chemicals as contributing factors. She states that he was extremely vague regarding current use. I would point out that inconsistency and vagueness are generally thought by clinicians to be characteristic of people who are malingering. According to Dr. 5, he reports that the problems he is currently experiencing date back to 1968 although he has told other examiners that they began in 1980 or '81. He also indicates to 5 that the initial symptoms included decreased appetite, nausea and vomiting. See MMPI items above to the contrary. On page 2, under primary complaints, he includes difficulty attending to tasks at hand or to conversations. (See items 32 and 57 of the MMPI above which are contrary to these assertions.) The report notes that there is considerable change in his spontaneity and that people now have to pull information out of him. This is contradicted by the item in which he indicates that he is a good mixer and by the item in which he responds that it is not hard for him to make talk when he meets new people. On page 3, Dr. 5 notes that his report of personal history was vague and incomplete and frequently inconsistent with information reported during previous examinations. She further notes that his performance on this abbreviated assessment showed no substantial change from the August '82 arguing against a progressive condition or disorder. She notes that motor speed is slightly improved in his dominant hand (according to her the right) compared to the August '82 assessment with the scores now showing the expected dominant versus non-dominant differential. She concludes that while the results are consistent with toxicity secondary to chemical or solvent exposure, one must also consider the possibility that the alcohol use may be contributing to the deficits found during the examination.

## DR. EW, SEPTEMBER, 1983
### (REPORT MAY 27, 1984)

Some question is raised by the lapse of more than seven months between the time of the examination and the preparation of the report. Obviously it would seem better to prepare the report immediately after the examination while all the data is fresh in one's mind and one may still recall some behaviors or observations that were there but may not have been recorded in one's notes. Obviously after a lapse of time and many intervening examinations, all one can go by are the notes one has made. It is also noted that among the tests described there are none of the tests that Dr. EW describes in (publication) for evaluating malingering.

EW notes on page 1, that P2 reports science grades had been his best, which is correct, and that the rest were mostly C's with a few B's, which is clearly false. Outside of science, the rest included only one B, and that in a physical education course, while the remainder of the grades were predominantly D's and F's with as many F's as there were C's. Did EW accept his version and use it in evaluating "pre-morbid" level?

The report notes that he spends his spare time working on his house, hunting and fishing. So apparently these are things he can do. The report does not contain any elaboration as to what kind of work he does on his house. If Dr. EW knows, he has neglected to inform anyone of the nature of the work which might have some bearing on P2's employability. Apparently his brain syndrome does not interfere with his hunting and fishing, as contrasted to some others. EW, as have the others, reports alcohol consumption of four beers a day and a six-pack on the weekend. He does not, however, indicate for what period of time this has been going on. He also notes that P2 has been on medication for his blood pressure but does not indicate what the medication was, what the quantities are and how these might affect his test performance. Of course, if he does not know the answers on these items, he would not be able to evaluate their effects on his test performance. EW also notes that he is somewhat overweight, as Dr. 5 did, and that he has been trying to lose weight so that if he has been dieting, as I have noted elsewhere, this might contribute to some irritability. On page 2, EW notes that on the basis of his self reports and his best test performances, he appears to be a man of average intellectual endowment. Thus, EW seems to indicate that he is relying to some extent on P2's self reports which as we know, are false and misleading. EW also relies on his best test performances and we have shown above that P2 has always displayed a fair amount of variability in his performance, so that one cannot assess his prior state from his present best performance.

On page 2, under verbal functions, EW states, "Although all of his scores on the verbal subtests in the intelligence tests he took in 1982 were within the average ability range, he displayed problems with verbal production." This is an erroneous statement as his scale score of five on the arithmetic subtest in 1982 is not within the average ability range. On page 3, under test of mental control, EW notes that on one arithmetic problem, "this high school graduate subtracted fourteen from fifty and came up with forty-four as the answer, using pencil and paper. His spelling lapses are noted above." Of course, the response to this would be that he did get problems four, five and six on the WAIS-R arithmetic subtest correct and they involve roughly an equivalent level of difficulty or even more difficulty. Interestingly, in connection with the spelling lapses, there are several spelling errors in the report of 8 and in Dr. EW's report on this page referring to P2's spelling lapses, and the date given for the report is 5-17-84 although all the other pages show the date to be 5-27-84.

Under attentional functions, EW notes that on his testing, P2 was able to get six digits forward on the digit span test. So he is indeed showing a considerable degree of variability in his performance because he got only four forward a couple of weeks later with Dr. 5 and again in 1984 with Dr. 6, although he had gotten six forward in the 1982 testing. Which is the real P2? On page 4, under diagnostic impression, EW states categorically that he is a man of originally average intellectual endowment. This of course is contradicted by the actual measure of his intellectual endowment when he was in high school which came out to be low average. EW disposes of the possible effects of drinking by asserting that his alcohol consumption rate comes under the category of social drinking. I do not know what his resource is for that conclusion, but obviously it is not one that is shared by Dr. 5 or by Dr. 4, who acknowledges the drinking may have had some effect. I would also wonder even if he was correct on the issue of alcohol alone, whether there might be some interactional affect of drinking, along with the hypertension, along with the medication that P2 has been taking. Dr. EW does not deal with the possibility of interaction effects. Also, so far as the hypertension is concerned, he acknowledges in his interview that while he sticks to the position he has taken, the research literature is not yet sufficiently complete to allow for conclusive statements.

Interestingly, on page five EW says P2 is incapable of working in "high tech" fields. I would imagine, given what we know of his intellectual functioning prior to becoming a painter, that he never was capable of working in such fields and I wonder why EW would have mentioned it here. Also so far as his having severe learning deficits, his school record indicates that he always had severe learning deficits and nevertheless managed to learn how to become an industrial painter. One would have to think that if he was sufficiently motivated, he could learn another occupation of equivalent difficulty. Once again, it would probably be important for Dr. EW to know what kind of work he was doing on his house, because presumably he could do the same kind of work on somebody else's house. Recall that one of his MMPI items was that he enjoys working on door latches, so that one must wonder if he is not capable of learning to be a locksmith. Also, it should be kept in mind that neither at the time of EW's examination nor his report did Dr. EW have the results of the September 1984 testing (or school or military records).

## 7/6, SEPTEMBER 10 & 11, 1984

It should be noted that 7 and 6 had the test reports of 4/8 of EW and of 5 available to them. It should also be noted that there is a fair probability that they would have been influenced by such reports. This report describes P2 as ambidextrous, using his right hand for writing but performing most other tasks with his left hand, which would suggest that perhaps the left hand is the dominant hand. The report states that he performed poorly on tasks requiring being able to distinguish between essential and nonessential details (picture completion) and I note that his scale score on picture completion is seven, which is in the low average range and does not warrant being called a poor performance. The report asserts that he obtained a weighted score of nine on the vocabulary subtest which corresponds to an IQ of approximately 95 and probably indicates his pre-morbid intelligence level. However it does not really matter because we have a prior IQ test in school records which shows his IQ to be 87. A prior test is better evidence than an estimate. In the first sentence of the third paragraph on page two (that is the second sentence of that paragraph) it is stated, "Patient is able to name common objects and she is able to demonstrate their use." I do not really think this error of gender is a very important thing; it is just providing you with some of the errors that were made by these very bright, highly educated people to show that everybody makes mistakes and it does not necessarily mean they have brain damage. This paragraph also states that he experienced difficulties with being able to understand the subtle meaning of statements, giving his explanation of some proverbs as examples, but these are the kinds of things that are on the comprehension subtest of the WAIS and on which he got an average score. They gave examples of his limited ability in arithmetic, showing that he can't multiply 17 x 3 or subtract 8 from 14. However, both of these are similar to tasks that he has successfully performed on the WAIS arithmetic subtest. Particularly item six, which requires the subject to discern and perform a more difficult calculation. P2 successfully solves that problem which is more difficult than multiplying seventeen by three or subtracting eight from fourteen.

## TESTIMONY OF EW

The videotaped testimony of the expert witness EW as modified for purposes of this presentation and the comments of the author follow:

MR. CA (plaintiffs' attorney): We would call Dr. EW to the stand on behalf of Plaintiffs P1 and P2.

DR. EW

Called as a witness in behalf of the Plaintiffs, being duly sworn, is examined and testifies as follows:

DIRECT EXAMINATION

BY MR. CA:

Q. Dr. EW could you tell the jury your full name and current status and place of employment.

A. My name is EW. And I am a (faculty position) _____ University.

*(Author's Note: A recitation of impressive credentials follows, including ABPP diplomas in both clinical psychology and clinical neuropsychology and numerous publications in neuropsychology and other positions and honors.)*

Q. What is the nature of that license?

A. I am a licensed psychologist in the State of _____.

Q. Now, you have before you, I believe, what has been marked as Deposition Exhibit 1—

A. Yes.

Q. —which is a copy of your Curriculum Vitae; is that correct?

A. That's right.

Q. Dr. EW, let me interrupt you because I would like you to tell the jury what—I think many of us are familiar with psychology, but I would like you to tell the jury, what is the definition or what is the concept of neuro-psychology?

A.  As a neuropsychologist I'm interested in the relationship between brain and behavior. Just like the heart is the organ for pumping blood and the stomach is the organ for digestion, the brain is the organ of behavior, the job of the brain is behavior.

One of the most sensitive ways that we have of knowing whether the brain is malfunctioning is by looking at its product, that is looking at be-havior, and this is what the neuropsychologist is trained to do, to evaluate, to examine, to understand the behavioral repercussions or behavioral mani-festations of brain damage and to distinguish them from other kinds of be-havioral disorders and from the normal range of human variability.

Q.  Dr. EW, what are, I guess, the tools of the trade that you use for this pur-pose of neuropsychology?

A.  We use everything we can get our hands on: the interview with the patient, past records and history, interview with family members; if the patient is hospitalized, we will talk to ward nurses, we talk to their physicians, and then the specialized techniques that we as psychologists have that no other professional group has are the mental tests, which allow us to make rela-tively fine-grained measurements with certain degrees of probability so that we can identify deficits on the basis of test performance.

*(Author's Note: Defense counsel might want to make note of two things in the two preceding answers. It will become important in this case and in most cases involving neuropsychologists to be aware and to focus on the fact that it is "behavior" from which the functioning of the brain is inferred. The second point to note is the declaration that neuropsychologists use everything they can get their hands on which would include past records and history, as it will become apparent as the case unfolds that this highly credentialed expert did not do so in this case.)*

Q.  Thank you Dr. EW, I would like to ask you to explain just briefly to the jury what your role is as an editor and a reviewer for these professional publica-tions, in other words how your role fits into the publication process for new papers that are being submitted.

A.  When a paper is submitted to a recognized journal, the editors of the jour-nal, the editors in chief of the journal, then send copies of that paper to three, usually three people in the field who are recognized as having some particular expertise on those topics. And the reviewer, the editorial re-viewer's responsibility, then, is, of course, to read the article and evaluate whether it's appropriate for the journal, whether it is scientifically sound, evaluate its scientific merit, its usefulness, the extent to which it makes a useful contribution and so on, and then make recommendations for publica-tion or perhaps for some changes for the author to make, to make the paper publishable, or to turn it down altogether, always with some comment so that the author can understand why, if there is rejection, why it is being re-jected. Usually you don't have to write very much if you accept it; just if you reject it, you have to explain what problems were in the paper.

Q. Thank you, Dr. EW. I would like to ask you now about your relationship with and involvement in the two cases that bring you here today, the cases involving P1 and P2.

I would like you initially to summarize for the jury how you became involved in the case, or in these two cases, what it was you did, what was your process of investigation, just in general—We will go over them independently later—what types of things you reviewed, how you spaced your examinations and things of that nature?

A. To the best of my memory, I was called by you, Mr. CA, some time in 1983, and you asked me whether I would be interested in examining these gentlemen who were complaining of behavioral changes secondary to their exposure to paints and solvents at work, and I agreed to see them. I don't remember whether it was before or—No. I'm sure, I do remember, I do know. It was before I saw them, you made available to me the complete record of Dr. 8—I know she was on one of them—and Dr. 4, 1982 neuropsychological workups on these men, and so that before I even saw them I had reviewed that material, which in part guided my decision as to what kind of examinations to do.

In Mr. P1's case, I examined him for several hours, and that examination included an interview and then testing. And I also talked to Mrs. P1 at that time—actually it was with both of them, if I recall correctly—for about half an hour, in terms of how changes that they were perceiving might be affecting their family situation.

I have had, in a sense, continuing contact with P1, as his wife has participated in the group for family members of brain damaged patients that I have been conducting for some 17 years or so. And Mrs. P1 came to the group, my guess is about a year and a half ago. She has been with the group, so that she has kept me apprised as to how he is doing, through her eyes. And then I saw Mr. P1 again last month, I think it was—Was it less? No. I guess it was less than that. It was a couple of weeks ago—last week. I'll get it straight—so that I could see how he was doing, as I had not examined him for some time, how he was doing as of now, for purposes of this hearing.

Before I saw P1 this time, I had an opportunity to review additional test data from 5, who examined him also in 1983 when I did my first examination, and from Dr. 6's laboratory. Dr. 6 supervised an examination that was conducted in 1984. So I had all of that data, as well, and reviewed all of that.

Q. Now, did you have a similar involvement with P2's case?

A. Not as much because Mr. P2 is single and I have not talked to any family members about him. But I did see P2 in 1983, about the same time that I saw P1, and I did have the material from Dr. 4's examination at the medical school and reviewed that at that time. When preparing for my examination of Mr. P2 this time, I also had data from Dr. 5's examination and from the examination that Dr. 6 supervised.

*(Author's Note: This information is contained in EW's report and establishes the fertile conditions for the operation of confirmatory bias and*

*preconception and hindsight bias [see Volume I, Chapter 5 on Clinical Judgment and Volume I, Chapter 6 on Clinical Examination]. These conditions would warrant cross examination of the witness on the scientific and professional literature concerning the operation of these variables. In addition to noting what EW had available, prior to seeing the plaintiffs and drawing conclusions about them, it is valuable to note what he did not have available, specifically school and military records. Even without EW's previous statement about "Using everything we can get our hands on," it should be obvious to anyone that in determining the functioning of these plaintiffs prior to paint exposure that such materials would be extremely valuable if not absolutely essential.)*

Q. And you also recently re-examined—

A. And I also saw Mr.—and it was a week ago Saturday.

Q. Now, Dr. EW, I would like you to take one at a time your findings, your examinations and your findings for P1 and P2 and explain to the jury, first, the specific process that you undertook as a part of your, really the two examinations, the findings from those processes, the relationship of those findings to your review of the materials that were supplied from other examinations and, of course, the conclusions that you drew from your findings.

A. Okay.

I'll start with P1, and I will present the findings in terms of areas of behavioral functioning, or cognitive functioning, mental functioning because that is the way that I find it easiest to conceptualize what goes on, and I think it has neuropsychological meaning.

The first area of examination has to do with verbal functions, and in terms of old learning and verbal skills, the examination consists of tests of vocabulary of background information, tests involving verbal habits, such as being able to name things, verbal skills, such as reading and writing. All of these are abilities that we assume are over-learned and over-practiced and by and large are not vulnerable to the effects of brain damage—or I shouldn't say that

*(Author's Note: We would simply note here that EW has made a misstatement, dealing with material which he has, we certainly could assume, over-learned and over-practiced. It is not of great importance by itself, but we would suggest to lawyers that this is frequently a happening which allows one to demonstrate that the "behavior" of the expert is not all that different from the behavior of the litigant, sometimes even to the point where the clinician looks ridiculous. We will attempt to simply point out every error made by EW in this case as we go along as there are a considerable number of them. It will be seen that defense counsel does take advantage of these to some extent in his cross examination.)*

They are minimally vulnerable, excepting where there is brain damage directly to the speech centers.

On learning and verbal skills, P1 demonstrated adequate spelling, adequate grammar, in handling a writing problem his vocabulary was, both vocabulary and background information from, were assessed as being within the average ability range. I did not do either of those tests, by the way, since

I did not want to repeat things that had already been done, and those were scores that were obtained by Dr. 6 and by—essentially by Dr. 6 and by Dr. 4.

Interestingly, in 1982 on the first examination his ability for, or recall of background information, was below average, it was in the low average range, at about the, somewhere between the 16th and 25th percentile. And when retested two years later that had come up to the average range.

*(Author's Note: Use of words such as "interestingly" should alert the lawyer to the possibility that there may be something unusual or unexpected. For example: in this instance, the witness has just testified that recall of background information is one of those areas which are not affected or only minimally vulnerable to brain damage. One would want to perhaps find out what was meant by the word "interestingly" to see if this indeed is what was meant. That is, what we have here is the fact that in 1982, P1 was low average on memory of background information but in 1984 he had come up to the average range. This is not altogether consistent with what the expert has told us.)*

His ability to generate words in 1982 was at a low average level and his, the problem areas that have shown up both in my 1983 examination and my most recent examination, had to do with a confusion in reciting the alphabet, such that in 1982—1983, I'm sorry,

*(Author's Note: Here is another error made by the expert which he does immediately correct but nevertheless he said it wrong the first time.)*

he recited it—I have people always recite the alphabet—L, M, N, O, P, Q, U, R, S, T, U, V. Most recently he misplaced the "U" again after the "Q" but left the "U" out later in his recitation. And this is something that is virtually never seen in people who are intact because you learn the alphabet and it becomes such automatic habit that you simply don't expect any breakdown in it at all.

On tests of reasoning and judgment, P1 demonstrated superior ability for verbal reasoning for Dr. 6 and high average, consistently high average ability for reasoning about verbal problems for Dr. 4. His ability to organize verbal material into meaningful sentences was within normal limits.

*(Author's Note: Note again, that on an ability presumably not vulnerable to brain damage P1 performs at a higher level in 1984 than he did in 1982, although presumably the lower performance in 1982 would not be expected on the basis of brain damage. Then note also, immediately following that EW makes another error concerning dates which defense counsel corrects for him, which is one good way to call attention to the errors as they are being made.)*

Interestingly enough, though, for Dr. 5 in 1973 in—

MR. DC: Do you mean 1973?

THE WITNESS: Thank you. 1983.

In having to respond to a fairly complex verbal reasoning task, that is interpreting proverbs, he was surprisingly concrete. He had demonstrated that on practical reasoning he is high average to superior. On fairly simple abstract reasoning he was high average to superior, and yet on proverbs, which is a more complex format, he was actually in the defective range.

*(Author's Note: While Doctor 5 gave a different proverbs test and did not utilize the portions of the WAIS-R that contain proverb problems, in fact, both the 1982 and 1984 examinations did utilize those portions of the WAIS-R and because this issue of performance on proverbs comes up in many cases, it is worth devoting some space to the following information. On the Comprehension subtest of the WAIS, there are three common proverbs for which the subject is asked to tell the meaning. Responses to these items can be scored two, one or zero. Generally speaking, a two point response is one which clearly abstracts the meaning of the saying, whereas one point is given for an answer which shows some understanding of the proverb but is not of particularly good quality, while zero is given for a response which fails to give a reasonable interpretation or fails even to recognize that the proverb is a proverb. In his fourth edition of the Measurement and Appraisal of Adult Intelligence, Professor Wechsler provides, in Appendix Three, a set of difficulty values of individual items of WAIS subtests based on 1700 cases of national standardization. We are not familiar with the Gorham Proverbs Test administered by Doctor 5, but we rather doubt that its standardization equals that of the WAIS. In any event, Doctor Wechsler's data shows that, counting as "passing" answers for which only partial credits (one point) were given, only 75% of the population get any credit, two or one, for the first proverb, only 38% get credit of any kind for the second proverb, and only 22% get even partial credit for the third proverb. Given this data, it seems clear that for most people, while there are six points of credit possible in total on the proverbs items, only two points would be obtained. Thus, less than half of the population would get any credit on the second item and only one in five would get credit on the third item. That is, most people would get one or two points on the first proverb but less than half would get any additional credit on the remaining items, therefore establishing two as the base or average for these three proverbs. On the 1982 testing, P1 received one point on the first and one point on the second, thus equating him with the average at least insofar as Wechsler's data on the WAIS is concerned. On the 1984 administration, he got two points for the first and zero for the second but he got one point for the third, which only one person in five gets any credit for. Therefore, he has gotten fifty percent more credit on the proverbs on the WAIS than the average person would get on the 1984 administration and as much as the average person would get on the 1982 administration. So it seems quite unfair to call his performance defective. Of course it might become necessary to compare the standardization and norming of the Gorham proverbs test with the standardization and norming of the WAIS.)*

Arithmetic was looked at by all of the examiners, and he demonstrated that he has a high average arithmetic ability with a high average score for Dr. 4 and for me this last time, on arithmetic problems, he was fast and he solved a number of problems that placed him in the high average range.

In contrast, on two different occasions, once for Dr. 6's technician and once for Dr. 5, his arithmetic performance on a similar kind of problems were in low average to borderline defective ranges.

*(Author's Note: We should note at this point, first of all, that up to this point, for the most part, the witness has been referring to how P1 performed for*

*Doctor 4 and Doctor 6. In this paragraph, he does specify it was Doctor 6's technician but for the most part the representation has been made as though Doctor 4 and Doctor 6 had given these tests when the fact of the matter from the test reports we have makes it quite clear that the tests were, in their entirety, administered by interns or technicians and that neither Doctor 4 nor Doctor 6 administered any of the tests. So P1 could not have performed for the "Doctors." He was performing for people of considerably less training and experience in giving the tests and certainly of considerably less status than is implied by EW's continual reference to the doctors. Defense counsel probably will not want to allow this impression to remain. More important is EW's declaration that P1 had a high average arithmetic ability with a high average score for Doctor 4. (We do not have data from EW's examination "this last time.") We do know that on the March 1983 testing (3/Doctor 4), his scale score was eleven which clearly is not in the high average range. So this high-powered expert is simply wrong on that. It should be noted at this point that later in his testimony he will state that he was using age norms rather than the scale score for the overall population, which would give P1 a scale score of 12, which EW uses as a criterion of high average. However, it is noted in the consultant's report that the raw score of 14 is in fact based on a scoring error and the true score is 13. So that even on age norms, the scale score would still be 11 and would still be in the average and not in the high average range, and inasmuch as this is one of the key criteria that EW uses for estimating pre-morbid abilities, it is a little like a house of cards. This card comes out and there is a good chance the whole house is going to come down. Further, we note EW's testimony of remarkable contrast in P1's performance which raises questions of whether this is an indication of malingering, as so many people use inconsistency as a criterion of malingering; or is this a problem of reliability; or are we seeing here an example of examiner effects, where different examiners get different results as the literature attests so well.)*

Generally on tests involving comprehending what he sees and being able to reason about what he sees, P1 performs in the average range, and this is supported by average performances on construction problems where he has to put things together with his hands, by and large.

But there are some interesting exceptions to this, and these exceptions seem to be related to the amount of structure given in the task. For instance, when having to put together pieces of a puzzle in which he can manipulate the pieces and try them out, as I said before, he performed at an average level, as well as the next guy his age.

When he has to organize these pieces, similar kinds of cut-up puzzles that are presented in a picture form, where he can't manipulate them but rather has to organize them in his head, organize them conceptually, then his performance drops to borderline defective levels, suggesting some difficulty in that kind of higher level conceptualization, visual conceptualization.

These problems in high level visual conceptualization, when not provided with a lot of structure, in other words when he is, in a sense, turned loose on his own and has to solve the problem all on his own, showed up consistently on all drawing tasks that he did. And this was consistent for all examiners, and all of us, I believe without exception—No.

*(Author's Note: This is another error by EW; it is self-corrected, but nevertheless, it was an error. It is our experience that with this number of errors, four to this point, there are some clinicians who would assert that a person who was defined as a "patient" and performed in this manner was suffering from confusion.)*

The exception is Dr. 6. But the rest of us all gave him a drawing test in which his performance was consistently at a defective level, below, in the lower 10th percentile of the population, and actually probably quite low, in the lower 10th percentile. And the same problems showed up on his drawings as, for instance, in his drawing of a bicycle, where he omitted a chain and it was crude. He simply did not think it through and did a poor job in producing it.

Another kind of perception was examined by Dr. 4 and by Dr. 6, and that is tactile perception, what he could perceive and learn by using his hands. And on these tests, where he did not, which involved putting different shapes of blocks into a form board and having to distinguish them with the eyes blindfolded so it is purely a tactile test, on these he demonstrated himself to be slow quite consistently. He did a little bit faster for Dr. 6 than for Dr. 4 and we all wonder whether there are practice effects in something like that, that is whether he now had familiarity with the task that he had done before. His performance for 4 was very slow and what he demonstrated for Dr. 4 was a moderate difficulty in recalling where he had put these pieces and an even greater difficulty in remembering just where, just what the relationship of the pieces was, so he had moderate difficulty in recalling them, a great deal of difficulty both for Dr. 4 and for Dr. 6, in the spatial organization of the pieces that he had handled.

He was given many different tests that involved attentional functions. And I'm going to break attentional functions down into three components that are meaningful for me in understanding behavior.

The first is simple span, which is a fairly passive and fairly steady ability, I mean it does not vary greatly with age or with many kinds of brain disease. Yet P1's digit span for just simple digit span—and to measure it we give people digits, a string of digits, like numbers that you would call on the telephone, only we start with three numbers and then build up. If they get three correct, we go to four and five and so on. And he recited five digits forward for Dr. 4. The next year, for Dr. 5, he recited only three forward; and the year after that for Dr. 6, only four forward which is somewhat surprising.

*(Author's Note: One would probably want to ask what was surprising about the digit span performances, however, we have another piece of data here which again shows inconsistency which may indicate malingering, may suggest some problems of reliability or may be a function of examiner effects.)*

On the other hand, he was somewhat more consistent in his span when given more information than he could grasp at one time. The way we do that is we read a list of 15 words. Practically no one can remember all 15 words at once. It usually takes three to four or five trials for the average person under the age of 70 to be able to learn all 15 words or 14 of the 15.

When we look at first trial, what we are evaluating, then, is when a person's span is not under simple span conditions but when there is the added stimulation, added burden of coping with more material than you can handle at once. And most folks will have a span, most folks of his age will have a span of seven to eight digits forward—I'm sorry, seven to eight words on the word list.

*(Author's Note: Here is another error by EW, which again he self-corrects, but nevertheless, he made the error initially.)*

His best performances on the word list were for me two weeks ago, or a week and a half ago, and for Dr. 5 in 1983, when he was able to recall five, putting his performance generously, you could call it borderline. For Dr. 4 and for me this last time, on a second word list he performed at frankly defective levels. This will happen sometimes because the second word list comes after having learned the first word list, that is after having had five exposures to the first word list. And if a person has difficulty keeping material sorted in their heads, then they will often do more poorly on the second list than the first. So that is immediate span.

Other areas of attention, a second area of attention has to do with being able to withstand distractions, to be able to focus your attention, to concentrate, and this is a much more active ability than simple span and it is more vulnerable to neurological disease. On the test most commonly used for examining distraction, the ability to withstand distractibility is called the Stroop test, and the patient is required first to read a list of words that are printed, of colored words, printed in four different colors, and all four color words are represented. So the print words are "red," "green," "orange" and "blue," and they appear in different colors but the only requirement is to read the word.

After having completed that, completed a long page of word reading, the next task is to name the color of each word that is printed. And here we have a phenomenon such that the shape of the printed word predominates greatly over the color of the word, so that while reading, while calling off a name of the color, there is a constant tug by the shape of the word that serves as a distractor and, as a result, for even the best of us, it takes about twice as long or a little more to read the color, to name the color words— I'm sorry, to name the colors of the words than to read the printed word.

And, as I said, this is a very good test of distraction. And on this test, which I gave, both in 1973 *(Author's Note: First of all we note another error which EW self-corrects, but he really does seem to have a problem in performing on giving dates. Secondly, so far as the Stroop being a good test of distraction, we would simply note for anyone who wants the information that in the Buros Mental Measurements Yearbook, Eighth Edition, this test receives mixed reviews. Apparently there is some difference of opinion on how good a test it is.)* and in—1983 and in 1986, he performed at defective levels. In other words, he had a great deal of difficulty withstanding the distraction.

The next kind of category of attentional functions has to do with mental tracking, and this is the ability to do two or more things in your head at a time and this is very vulnerable, a very sensitive ability, very vulnerable to brain damage. And mental tracking tests—and he received a variety from all of the examiners, so I'll just give you the overall picture. On these mental tracking tests he had a, on those which he had to do completely in his head without visual supports, he tended by and large to perform borderline to defective levels, and this showed up very prominently, for example, in difficulty in reciting the alphabet backward, where you have to keep track of where you are going and where you last were. It also showed up on one examination—Well, it showed up on difficulty with reverse digits.

On the other hand, he did perform within the normal limits on some of the mental tracking tasks and on visual tracking tests, that is where there was visual support. His performance varied from within normal limits to, frankly, defective on others, so that there was not a consistent picture of performance.

*(Author's Note: Here we are again being given a picture of inconsistent performance with the same issues of malingering, reliability and examiner effects as in the other instances.)*

I'm going to move over to memory tasks. I have talked about immediate span. I'm going to talk about short-term verbal memory. Memory is not a single component but it consists of a number of functions. One is the ability to hold memory in your head for short periods of time as, for instance, somebody gives you a telephone number and then you walk across the room to the telephone and you want to remember those seven digits, and that is called; short-term memory. Another aspect of memory is learning, that is incorporating that material that you learned in the short haul into some kind of permanent storage so that it's available for retrieval. And that is what happens, of course, with telephone numbers that you use very often. Pretty soon you don't have to refer to the book any more, you just know the number comes out of your head. But there are complicating factors because you not only have the ability to be efficient with the material you learned, depends not only on the amount of information you learned but on your ability to retrieve it readily, to retrieve it with facility. And so we have to look at all of these aspects of memory when examining memory.

Now, in my first examination of P1, on short-term recall of paragraphs, he performed within normal limits on both paragraphs. I gave him two paragraphs and then have him repeat as much of it as he can remember. Interestingly, on these same paragraphs, this last time his performance was in the borderline range. And for Dr. 5 on a similar task he had performed at a defective level.

*(Author's Note: Apparently we have yet another example of inconsistency on the same task, where he went from average to defective to borderline. Again, we apparently have another case of inconsistency of performance on the same task with performance at three different levels at three different times, raising all of the questions of possible malingering, questions of reliability and questions of examiner effects, although it should be noted that the first and third*

*performances were with the same examiner. On the other hand, another possible explanation for these variations could be in terms of situation effects, although no one has seemed to provide any data concerning possible events outside the testing situation which might have affected P1's performance.)*

This time he was also given a brief message to remember shortly thereafter, and he remembered to give the message and he remembered generally the message but he had twisted it so that it came back incorrect. So that is the short-term memory.

Learning, in contrast to short-term memory, his ability to learn new information, appears to be consistently in the defective range.

*(Author's Note: His learning as evidenced by school records and military records has, so far as any recorded data is concerned, always been below average. So this information simply confirms that he is presently operating on learning tasks the way he had in the past.)*

So this is an area that appears to be of great difficulty for him. He did his best on a rote learning task in which he had to learn a nine-digit number, and there he performed at a level that was close to borderline or just at borderline normal limits. And I don't remember the exact number of repetitions, but if somebody wants me to recall it later, I can. But it was repeated, the number was repeated at least six or seven times.

On the other tasks, on paragraph recall, even after hearing the paragraph twice, his recall is defective. On the rote learning task of remembering, of learning a list of 15 words, not only is his recall of those, not only does he show very little learning curve, but his recall is defective both immediately, or shortly after having learned it, and some 30 to 40 minutes later. And, in addition, he demonstrates that he has not really learned the list because his recognition is also defective, so that when he sees words, a whole bunch of words, he still only identifies a relatively small number of words, as those that he remembered from the five training trials he had had. So this is an area of consistent problems.

I'm almost done now.

He was given some tests of concept information and abstraction, by Dr. 4, by myself and by Dr. 6.

*(Author's Note: Again, EW conveys the impression that the tests were given by Doctors 4 and 6 which we know is not the case. Either Doctor EW is attempting to misrepresent the status of the people giving the test or EW is making a mistake. The latter seems more likely because immediately afterward, EW points out the poorer performance for Doctor 6's technician, than for Doctor 4's resident, indicating less of an intent to mislead and more likely the probability of making a continual error here, which of course provides an opportunity to raise questions about the cognitive functioning of EW. There may be one indication of some potential bias here in referring to Doctor 6's "technician" but to Doctor 4's "resident," as resident is usually understood as being the status assigned to a physician who has completed all of his training and obtained his medical degree and is now in the process of getting specialized training in a particular field. This was not the case of either of the two people who did the testing for Doctor 4. Neither of them had obtained their degree, which is typical*

*for people doing internships in psychology. In this case, a check of the directory indicates that 8 did not receive her degree until after this testing was done. We might also note there is another "interestingly" which may be worth a question.)*

And his performance on a test in which he has to generate hypotheses, figure out the meaningfulness of some patterned material, he performed at defective levels, interestingly performing more poorly for Dr. 6's technician than for Dr. 4's resident. But on a similar kind of task for me his performance, in which he had to figure out again, figure out the pattern of a set of responses that he was given, he was in the defective range. And his interpretation of some foolish pictures was what we call very concrete. He didn't get the overall gist, he dealt with just little bits and pieces.

I skipped talking about visual memory, and I need to go back to that because that was consistently at a defective level for everybody.

I guess I did not talk about visual memory before, but he was consistently at a defective level in both immediate and delayed recalls of the material that he had seen.

The only other thing that is covered was finger tapping, that is simple motor response speed, and Dr. 5 found that to be within normal limits in 1983. And in 1984 for Dr. 6's technician it was a little bit below normal limitation limits.

On this recent examination I reviewed—

BY MR. CA: (continuing)

Q. Dr. EW, before you go on to the recent examination, I wanted to ask you a couple questions specifically. At the time of your initial examination I think you mentioned that you spoke to P1 at length, interviewed him and interviewed his wife, took a history from him as to what he was complaining about, reviewed a variety of his medical, past medical history and literature and, of course, made observations of him in addition to the test results that you have given us.

Did you at my request prepare a written report of this examination and the history and medical documents that you had reviewed?

A. Yes, I did.

Q. And do you have—I'll hand you what has been marked as Exhibit 2 and ask you whether you can identify this as the written report that you prepared from your initial examination.

A. Yes, it is.

Q. And does this contain your findings as to the history that was given and your interview and observations of P1?

A. Yes, it does.

MR. CA: We would offer that exhibit in evidence at this time.

MR. DC: On behalf of defendant, I would object on the ground that it is hearsay and cumulative.

MR. (another defense counsel): Same objection.

MR. (another defense counsel): Same objection for.

BY MR. CA: (continuing)

Q. Dr. EW, I was hoping to avoid doing this—

MR. DC: Excuse me. I move to strike the question as improper in form.

*(Author's Note: The reader should be reminded that this is videotaped testimony to be used later at trial. No judge is present to rule on objections.)*

BY MR. CA (continuing)

Q. Dr. EW, would you go through, and before we go on to the subject matter of your repeat, or your second examination, tell us a little bit about your initial examination as far as the history that you took, your interview with P1 and apparently with Mrs. P1, *(Author's Note: It should be noted that the interview with Mrs. P1 was conducted with P1 present. This of course is an inadequate examination by itself as it would take a naive examiner not to be aware that quite often a spouse will be inhibited in the presence of the other spouse and might very well relate some perceptions of the spouse in his absence that otherwise would never be revealed.)* also, the complaints that he gave you, the particular medical, documents that you reviewed, a list of the tests, particular tests that you administered and the other information, other than the review of the test results that you have already given us.

MR. DC: Excuse me, Counsel. I would object to this witness purporting to give a medical history, as opposed to a history of background information and present complaints, on the grounds that he is not either a medical doctor nor a treating physician.

MR. CA: Can we go off the record.

BY MR. CA: (continuing)

Q. Dr. EW, let me ask you a question. Do you review as a part of your professional practice, documents that have been generated from, by medical authorities, physicians and nurses, as a matter of course?

A. As a matter of course and matter of necessity.

Q. And do you formulate any medical diagnoses or make medical opinions yourself?

A. No, I do not.

Q. Do you rely upon the medical opinions and diagnoses that are made by others in formulating your professional judgments?

A. Yes, I do.

Q. And are these medical opinions that are given by others, by medical authorities, commonly relied upon in your practice by neuropsychologists in making assessments such as the ones that you have done for us?

A. Yes. We use the criteria and the conclusions established and given by medical practitioners in evaluating our data.

Q. Dr. EW, I would ask you, then, to summarize the information that I had requested of you regarding your examination of P1.

MR. DC: Excuse me. Which examination?

MR. CA: The initial examination that is covered by the report which is Exhibit No. 2.

THE WITNESS: Okay. I saw him on July 7, 1983, and at that time I had learned—and I don't, I really don't recall where I got each piece of information in the background information. Some of it certainly was from him, some of it came from some of the records I had reviewed. But I knew he was married, he had been in the, for the Viet Nam war, and was a high school graduate.

*(Author's Note: EW states that he "knew" that P1 was a high school graduate. This is another error of fact and either EW got it wrong or P1 misrepresented his status. The former seems more likely as some of the other clinicians knew that he was not a high school graduate.)*

I knew that he had been a shop steward; and in his employment was a painter and a sandblaster, in that he had done both painting and sandblasting on his job.

He had been laid off work about one year before I saw him and he had tried doing, during that year he had tried doing janitorial work but couldn't keep up with it because he made too many mistakes.

In 1974 and in '75 he had been a hunting instructor but he could no longer hunt because previously, about a year previously, he had had two seizures while hunting and took that as a warning sign to stay out of the field. He was unable to fix things at home because when he would try he discovered he could not use tools effectively and, for example, he explained that he had just rewired a switch backward.

*(Author's Note: This is the only example that has been given of P1's difficulty using tools and it seems to be overworked. Is EW aware of other examples of his inability to use tools? Because if this is the only example or instance that is known, it tends to stand out as a sore thumb, possibly a once-in-a-great-while kind of event and not something that is actually characteristic of P1. I think almost everybody who has done work around their house at one time or another has made mistakes or done it wrong and had to redo it. This would be a base rate issue.)*

Now he does, that is at the time I saw him, he said he did very little except watch television.

*(Author's Note: This does not seem altogether true as he has indicated on the MMPI that he enjoys reading a variety of kinds of materials. The lawyer should be aware that this MMPI material is available or could be made available to any examiner.)*

And he was going to a therapy group at the Veterans' Outreach Center. And as for his drinking habits, he said that he typically only takes a drink during the holiday season.

His complaints, well, he had a number of complaints. One was that he said that he loses track of what is going on, he can only remember bits of what he reads, not the gist. And he said that he had been aware of these problems since he had developed a seizure disorder, he said, in 1981, and felt that there were times that he seemed to be just losing his common sense.

*(Author's Note: On the MMPI, P1 indicated that there was nothing wrong with his mind in 1981 and 1984, although he said there was something wrong in March of 1983. In any event on two out of the three tests, he seems to be indicating that there is nothing wrong with his mind, therefore it would not seem true that he is losing his common sense or thinks he is. If nothing else, it points*

*out the deficiency in EW's examination procedure in failing to ascertain that P1 had previous testing and in not obtaining the results of that testing, in which case he would have had available to him this response. And of course at the time of EW's testimony the 1984 examination was also available and EW could have checked on the veracity of this claim by looking at item 168. Also on the item about being afraid of losing his mind, P1 responded in the same manner on the three tests: false, true and false.)*

He described himself now as having no goals at all and pointed out that he gets depressed very easily. He feels that he was not the same person that he had been, that at the time that he became shop steward and was active in his work he had always been active and was in charge of people, saw himself as having been that kind of person, and the person that he was now was very different.

He said that he sleeps restlessly, often wakes a lot during the night, and when he wakes up he is still exhausted. He at that time he said that his appetite varied a lot and sometimes he won't eat for days and sometimes he would binge, but what he said was the worst for him was a feeling of not being in charge of himself and—a direct quote—"like I lost my common sense."

*(Author's Note: On the 1981 and 1984 MMPIs he describes himself as having self-confidence although he reverses this in 1983. However, once again on two out of the three tests, he makes a statement that seems to be contrary to the complaint that he is making to Doctor EW, and EW could have obtained this information. Item 168 noted above is also relevant. In addition, on item 257 he indicates on all three tests that he usually expects success in things he does. This seems inconsistent with this claimed deficit. On Item 301 he indicates that life is often a strain for him on the 1981 and 1984 tests but oddly not on the 1983 the time he is generally portraying himself in the worst light.)*

In reviewing the charts that were made available to me—and I had the charts from the examinations made in the Industrial Clinic at, Industrial Medicine Clinic at the _____ University, and I reviewed those charts and also we discussed some of this information. For instance, he reported to me that in 1975 or '76 he had sustained a mild concussion in a car accident. He said that he had blood clots in his lungs in 1979 or '80 and he has been treated for high blood pressure since March or April of 1983. And at the time that I saw him he was on, in 1983 he was on both high blood pressure medication and taking medications for seizure control.

He was a very overweight, neatly-groomed man. He wore a hunting instructor's vest. He was alert, he was oriented, he was intelligently cooperative, in the sense that he seemed to understand what was going on and he participated, I felt, quite fully. At that time I observed a slight speech impediment, that just seemed as though his mouth was moving sluggishly.

*(Author's Note: If this is given any significance and apparently it is by EW, he could be asked if he is aware that P1 had had a stuttering problem, as this is clearly indicated in his military records. Also, in a previous paragraph, EW indicates that P1 was on various medications when his examination took place*

*and could be questioned as to any effects of those medications on test perform-ance or behavior.)*

His language skills were unremarkable. Thinking tended to be concrete. Again, he seemed to think in terms of specifics and particulars, rather than being able to put things together in overall generalities, meaningful generalities.

His recall of his history seemed to be accurate, although he was very vague about dates of such important events as a car accident or blood clots in his lungs and even of such a recent event as having had high blood pressure diagnosed. For example, that I saw him in July and he couldn't remember whether it was March or April that he had had diagnosed this.

*(Author's Note: EW seems to be making a point of this which may provide an opportunity to poke a little gentle fun for EW's difficulty remembering when he had examined P1 the second time although only a week had elapsed in contrast to the two or three month lapse of time across which P1 was unable to remember.)*

He seemed to be emotionally, came across as being emotionally unexpressive in 1983, although he was able to talk about being depressed quite frankly.

Q. Dr. EW I think you also mentioned that you had a talk with Mrs. P1 in an attempt to get additional information about him and his background. What was the result of that?

A. She felt that she had observed a, quite a radical change, and that he had been this take-charge, get-up-and-go-getter kind of guy that he had described himself as having been somewhat earlier. And she also described him as having been very well organized and perfectionistic and now she said he is quite the opposite, he just sort of let things go. And, in fact, at that time some aspects of it seemed to be almost a welcome change for her because he was a less, seemed to be less driven and he was demanding less from the family, so he was putting less pressure on the family. But he was letting, he would just simply let things go by, as he had described. He also was having difficulty in doing some things that he should have been able to do. For example, she said when he fixed dinner recently she had to give him step-by-step directions. And he had ceased to participate in financial planning for the family.

She pointed out that he seemed to be very easily distracted, that if there were a lot of stimulation that he would get upset, couldn't handle it, and that he had difficulty concentrating.

They both agreed that there had been a real role reversal in the family, in that he had been the boss of the family before and now she had been increasingly taking over those kinds of duties. And, on the other hand, she felt that his temperament seemed to be more easy-going—This was in 1983—than at the time when he first went to the Vet Center.

*(Author's Note: The wife seems to be indicating here that in fact P1 is less irritable than he was before, thus contradicting some of these reports and certainly contraindicating the presence of one of the symptoms of the so-called painter's syndrome.)*

But she did report depression and particularly that he took it very hard when he made errors and that he was increasingly withdrawing from activities that he previously had been involved in, she felt, as much on the basis of not wanting to make errors and look foolish as anything else.

Q.  Now, Dr. EW, you were about to tell us about your findings as to this more recent examination. Why don't you go ahead and tell us about that.

A.  Going over the test performance in itself and giving an overall comparison between how he performed in 1986 and how he had previously, there is, over all there is no essential change excepting that attentional functions that I talked about before seemed to have improved a little bit so that the memory problems that he had before, that I discussed, the short-term memory, long-term memory, recognition, retrieval, are still much as they were three years ago, four years ago, when Dr. 4 conducted the examination.

His visual perceptual, visual constructional functions, his ability to do well in well-structured material and to do very poorly when structure is taken away, remains the same as it was; and he still has attentional problems. They are not as severe as they were.

Q.  Would you just say generally that the findings made in 1986 were consistent with the findings that you had made and others had made in the prior period, 1982 through 1984?

A.  Yes.

MR DC: I object to the form of the question as leading.

BY MR. CA: (continuing)

Q.  Do you have an opinion as to whether there was or was not consistency?

MR. DC: Excuse me. I object to the form of the question because it doesn't give us any understanding of what tests are being compared.

MR. CA: I guess I'll have to put everything in the question.

MR. DC: I move to strike that comment.

BY MR. CA: (continuing)

Q.  Do you have an opinion as to whether there was consistency between the examinations that you conducted and you reviewed during the period of 1982 through '84 and the most recent examination that you conducted in 1986?

A.  There is a great deal of consistency between my two examinations and Dr. 4's examination. On the other hand, P1 did poorly on a number of tests that he had done well on or later did well on for me, for Dr. 4 when examined by Dr. 6's technician also on two of the tests that he took with Dr. 5.

*(Author's Note: While this answer seems to attempt to portray the test results as consistent, the summary of it would seem to be that the test results and examination results were not consistent. This is aside from all of the inconsistencies we had noted in the consultation report to DC in the MMPI responses. However, there is some importance to attach to this because plaintiff's counsel is obviously making an issue out of consistency which should then lend more weight to all the evidence of inconsistency that can be produced. And of course the ubiquitous problems of malingering, reliability and examiner effects again arise.)*

Would you like me to comment further on that?

Q. Well, no. I'm trying to ask you just in a general sense.

A. But in general, in general there was consistency over the, what I consider to be the main tests, the first test and the two that I gave.

Q. Dr. EW, what does it mean when we talk about premorbid capacity, or premorbid functioning?

A. That has to do with an estimate, if there is not direct knowledge— Sometimes it is an estimate, sometimes it is direct knowledge—of how a person, how good a person's mental ability was at its best, whenever that may have been. When we say "premorbid" then we assume, suppose or know, that there has been some event or series of events that have compromised mental functioning so that we may see a person today who looks like a dullard or seems to have some real problems in thinking and memory and so on, and yet we, when we compare how they do now with how they did at their best, then we discover that what they are doing now represents a deficit, in other words, represents a loss from a higher level. So we attempt, whenever possible, to either get direct information concerning premorbid abilities or to estimate that from the residual areas of good functioning that we see in the present examination.

Q. Now, did you have either or both of these indicators available to you for P1?

A. I had both available to me.

Q. Could you explain to the jury what, how you use these indicators and what your estimation was of his premorbid functioning?

A. Yes. I have estimated his premorbid ability level at best was high average, that is somewhere between the 75th and 84th percentile, somewhere around there, so that he for instance—15 to 20 or so percent of the population would be brighter than he is and, you know, correspondingly, 85 to 75 percent of the population would be not as bright as he is. And this estimate is based on a number of things. It is based on a set of scores from a standardized ability examination in high school in which he obtained scores mostly in the average range and, I think, one or two in the high average range. It is based on my examination of him and the examinations of others in which he performed in the high average to actually superior levels on arithmetic and on the well-structured reasoning, verbal reasoning tasks.

So that we have both premorbid test data and we have current data that shows a man who is able to do that well. In addition, we know that as a relatively young man he was—what?—in his early 30's when he became shop steward. So that we know that he rose above his fellow workers; and that, too, would be another kind of practical support for the impression that this is a man who was just a cut above the average guy.

*(Author's Note: The above testimony is at the heart of this case and it should be possible to considerably impair the expert's credibility in this connection. First of all, EW claims to be basing the conclusion about pre-morbid functioning on the high school records as well as subsequent testing. Yet EW did not have any of these records until the morning on which this testimony began, although the opinions and conclusions were arrived at and reported as much as*

*two years earlier. Secondly, EW is being less than accurate with reference to the standardized ability examination [the Iowa test of Educational Development] in that he completely omits the fact that in addition to scores mostly in the average range and one or two in the high average range, P1 also had one at the ninth percentile, way down at the bottom, closer to the bottom than any of his above average scores were close to the top, the highest there being at the 82nd percentile. Thus, if one were using the best performance method of estimating functioning one would have had to predict that his scores on all of the Iowa tests would have been in the high average range or close to it, which is clearly not the case. This is a factual example of how prediction using the best performance method goes wrong. In addition, EW completely ignores in this portion of his testimony the well below average level at which P1 functioned in high school (i.e. on learning tasks) and also the high degree of variability that he showed in his school performance. So that again, if one were using the best performance method, they would predict a B average or close to it for P1, although this obviously would be grossly wrong. Finally, EW omits any mention in the data now available to him of the IQ obtained which showed P1 to be functioning in the average range, certainly nowhere near the high average. Certainly it can be used to create some skepticism in the jury about the quality of examination by EW in view of the failure to obtain any of these records prior to the day of the testimony. Further, there is the frequent reference to P1's attaining the position of union shop steward, which in this statement, EW asserts, shows him to be "Just a cut above the average guy." One would of course be entitled to ask, "A cut above with regard to what?" For example, is one of the criteria for becoming a shop steward an ability to interpret proverbs with greater ability than the average person? Or in fact, is becoming a shop steward based at all on above average cognitive abilities? While we have no expertise on this, this author in his younger days worked in a unionized industry and recalls quite distinctly that a position analogous to steward (in those days it was called Union Chairman) was an elective position, which means that such things as popularity or street sense or strong union loyalty or strong anti-management sentiments or whatever can be the basis on which one's co-workers elect him to be the shop steward. Clearly it is unlikely that his ability to interpret proverbs or to reproduce a set of drawings from memory or the vast majority of the test tasks that were presented would have anything at all to do with his becoming the shop steward. Therefore, it is nonsense to utilize that position as a basis for estimating his intellectual functioning. It is clearly not comparable to conclusions one might draw as to minimal level of functioning for someone who has completed medical school or graduate school with grades of B's or better when one can safely say, this person is well above average.)*

Q. Now, were you able to formulate, also, an opinion as to his current status, current mental acuity or impairment level?

A. I can't give you a single estimate because we are talking about a wide range of functions in a man who displays a pattern of deficits along with some strengths. So what I can talk about, again, is that old verbal skills are intact. When given a structured, verbal reasoning task he does fine. When you take away structure, he does very poorly. On a number of attentional tasks he does poorly—actually he is very varied—and he has consistently poor verbal delayed recall. And on visual short-term and delayed recall, verbal learning, visual learning are bad.

Q. Now, can you compare your findings as to his present status that you have just explained to us, with what you have estimated to be his premorbid status, to give us an indication of the change in those two time periods?

A. Yes. We can make an assumption, and the assumption is based on decades of research in this area, that point generally to the fact that people who are bright in one thing tend to be bright in others. People who are functioning efficiently in one thing, given no adverse situation, if you have somebody who is well-nourished, who has not had significant head injury or significant meningitis or something like that who has been exposed to what is generally available educationally in their society and so on that for the most part—and there would be sole exceptions—but for the most part if they are good in one thing they will be good in another. And I think all of us remember when we were in first and second and third grade and the teacher would divide us into Robins and Bluebirds and Sparrows and the Robins were the kids who were good in arithmetic, were the ones likely to show up in the high spelling list and were good readers. And there were some exceptions but by and large you knew that the kids who were poor in arithmetic and didn't do history very well were likely to be the poor readers and poor spellers.

So a lot of this is common sense but it has also been supported in the literature. So that is why we can take an assumption, we can go to specific test evidence, and particularly when it happens to be on functions that tend to hold up anyhow, that are not terribly vulnerable to brain damage, and look at the best thing that a person has done and generalize from that, and say this guy is probably of high average ability. And, of course, I'm always more comfortable when there are the other concrete supports such as a couple of high scores from his high school tests and the fact that he was shop steward.

*(Author's Note: Note first of all here that despite the assertion of decades of research, it is still an "assumption" that people who are bright at one thing tend to be bright in others. One would want to ascertain the source and the references on these decades of research and at least ask a question if there is not in fact, contrary research and contrary opinion provided in the scientific and professional literature. [Some of this was provided in the consultant's report.] However, in this particular instance because the expert has chosen to utilize school performance as his example, the whole issue of Robins, Bluebirds and Sparrows should be easily blown out of the water by a presentation of P1's high school records, showing his B's, C's, D's and F's, so that it would be awfully hard for anyone to say that P1 was a Robin or a Bluebird or a Sparrow or a Mudhen. The latter portion of the statement should be usable in establishing that EW would be less comfortable or less confident without the concrete supports of a couple of high scores from high school tests and the fact of being shop steward which we have already dealt with. Note the following question and answer deal with EW's confidence concerning his estimate of pre-morbid functioning; before*

*dealing with this, we would refer the reader to the chapter on clinical judgment [Chapter 5, Volume I] and the considerable research showing that level of confidence is unrelated to level of accuracy. Indeed, in a number of studies, the most confident clinicians had the lowest accuracy. Whether to confront EW with this research or produce it from another expert is a matter of the lawyer's judgment. But certainly here we have a witness who has been liberal in making reference to the literature. So perhaps a question is in order of the type, "Doctor, are you aware of literature showing that level of confidence is not related [or is inversely related] to level of accuracy?")*

Q.  So, then, I take it that you do feel confident as to your estimation of the premorbid intellectual functioning?

A.  Yes, I'm very comfortable with that.

Q.  Can you then compare that in a—I know it is difficult, I guess, to put it in a quantitative method—but can you compare that with the range of your findings as to his current level of mental functioning?

MR. DC: Object to the form of the question. It is unintelligible.

BY MR. CA: (continuing)

Q.  Go ahead.

A.  Okay. What you are asking: had he—I'm going to paraphrase.

MR. DC: You have to.

THE WITNESS: I know what I'm supposed to do.

What you are asking me is: are there any significant discrepancies between what one would expect and what one sees?

MR. CA: That's correct. Thank you.

THE WITNESS: Yes, there are a number of specific discrepancies.

I will review them. I assume that is what you want me to do.

BY MR. CA: (continuing)

Q.  If you would, please.

A.  Okay.

There is the slight breakdown in old learning that we see in alphabet, not being able to be recited with perfect accuracy as we would expect. And his reading speed on the Stroop, for example, was slow; and you would not expect that reading speed per se would have been slow.

He showed specific problems in complex verbal reasoning, that is the reasoning from proverbs, as against the simple generalization called upon by the other, by one of the other tests he took, and was defective in that. And you would not expect somebody who can do verbal generalizations at high average level or even superior level, to not be able to get the gist of proverbs and interpret them at a reasonably abstract meaningful level. But he really could not do that.

*(Author's Note: We have already provided the data from Wechsler concerning the difficulty most people have with interpretation of proverbs. We would call attention to the last sentence indicating that he really could not do that. EW has no firm evidence that he "could not" do it, only evidence that he "did not" do it. Some analogy might be drawn between EW's allegation that he had above average ability all the time he was going to school, to point out that if*

*indeed he had above average ability, nonetheless, he did not perform in a matter congruent with above average ability and perhaps that is what is happening here. Maybe he just wasn't interested in interpreting proverbs.)*

As I mentioned, immediate span, immediate memory span runs from borderline defective. Now, memory functions and attentional functions differ from the other cognitive abilities in that it's not so much a matter of being very, very bright or very, very dull, but rather that almost all adults who are not neurologically impaired and have not had, been brought up in perfectly terrible social or cultural conditions, almost everybody who is adequately socialized and has an intact brain can perform memory and learning and attentional tasks at about the same level.

*(Author's Note: Possibly the best way to deal with a statement of this sort is by asking the witness for what is already obvious, that he utilizes the Wechsler tests, and then to quote from Wechsler,* The Measurement and Appraisal of Adult Intelligence, *Fourth Edition at page 131, regarding the digit span test, normally thought to be a test of immediate memory and of attention and concentration. "Operationally defined facility in repeating numbers would seem to be almost a specific or unique ability. It is certainly true that a good auditory memory does not go with a good visual memory. Persons who can repeat a poem after one hearing often have difficulty in reproducing a picture or a design and great chess players who are known to have extraordinary powers of visualization have not shown unusual memory span for digits." And Wechsler cites a reference for that statement. So one would here have the author of the test designed to measure the abilities EW has been talking about, saying just the opposite of what EW is saying. Also, EW's statement seems to knock out the notion of a "G" factor and Robins and Sparrows if the "smart" and the "dull" are about the same in memory and learning tasks. Further, one can point out to jurors that they probably know people whose memory is better than theirs and others whose memory is worse.)*

So that when somebody drops down below the expected for their age, then we anticipate, then we can say that there is some kind of problem and we have to try to figure out what would account for it.

And so in his case his immediate span is, depending upon the task and when he took the tests, varied from borderline defective to defective. And his short-term memory varied predominantly between, within normal limits, to borderline. And his ability for verbal learning was frankly defective in all aspects of verbal learning that I examined or anybody else examined. It was consistently there, with that one exception of learning the, rote learning of numbers, and the same was true of visual recall.

His arithmetic, I find that I have to discount the lower scores because he did so well for me and so well for Dr. 4, and so I think that his arithmetic ability is just where one would expect it to be. His ability to do computations, to solve verbal problems, is high average, just at the high average level, about the 75th percentile. So no drop there.

*(Author's Note: Wait a minute! This expert cannot just throw out scores because they don't agree with what he found. This provides an excellent opportunity to ask this expert how to account for these differences in scores in the hope*

*that among other things, the expert may attribute it to examiner differences [i.e., examiner effects] or to situation effects or to malingering or to lack of effort on P1's part, or simply say that the expert is not able to account for the differences. Note that one of the poor arithmetic scores was obtained by Doctor 5, who is a Ph.D., not an intern or a technician. We did not find a test of arithmetic ability in EW's 1983 materials, so presumably that was tested just the week before the date of this testimony. However, the expert here has created a situation that many defense attorneys would dearly love, in his assertion that P1 did so well for Doctor 4, that it shows his arithmetic ability to be just where one would expect it to be, which is high average. However, because the scale score for arithmetic on the testing performed by Doctor 4's intern was eleven, it cannot on that basis be considered other than average. It is not at the seventy-fifth percentile and it is not in the high average range. We will note later that EW switches to age norms for the scale score rather than the overall norms and in that case, the raw score obtained by 3, the intern, would change the scale score to twelve, based on comparison with P1's age group. However, as we noted, there was a scoring error which reduced the raw score from fourteen to thirteen and therefore, even on the age graded norms it would still be a scale score of eleven. It would not be high average, it would only be average, so one of the props that EW has been steadily using falls, and one would think the credibility of his conclusions would fall with it. The lawyer should be aware that the arithmetic subtest is known to require both attention and concentration and if the witness were to deny this a reading of some of the problems that P1 solved would certainly make it very clear to anyone that it requires attention just to catch the problem and concentration to hold it in mind while one is solving it. So that even an average, let alone a high average, performance would indicate that P1 is not suffering from a deficit of attention or concentration. Further, if he is able to perform at an average or high average level as asserted by EW, how much weight can one give to his story about having difficulty giving the clerk the correct amount of money in a store, as related to EW and others to demonstrate his functional loss due to the paint exposure?)*

On the other hand, we have attentional functions in a sense all over the map and, as I said before, with some mild improvement noted from the time I first examined him to now, but still a number of areas—more, I think it probably could be summed up more as an inefficiency or lack of consistency of performance than just a poor performance, that what he runs into is an inability to maintain an adequate performance so that sometimes it will show up okay but he cannot maintain it.

As I said, his visual reasoning, visual and construction, so long as he was dealing with structured material, was at the average level and not so much below what we would expect. I would have to consider that those functions are not impaired and/or—I'll put it another way. These are preserved functions.

On the other hand, take away the supports, the structure, take away the, his ability to manipulate the materials, for example, to get it in the right place and force him to do the manipulation in his head, using his mind's eye, and he has difficulty. There you again see impairment and a contrast with his adequate performance on the structured tasks.

I think that is essentially it. There are a couple of other details.

Q. Dr. EW, the impairments that you have just explained to us, compared with your estimation of his premorbid level of function, in comparing those do you have an opinion as to whether this represents a brain damage situation?

A. Yes, I do.

Q. And what is your opinion?

A. My opinion is that the pattern of deficits that P1 shows is of a kind that is compatible with mental dysfunction of an organic basis.

Q. Now, by "mental dysfunction of an organic basis"—

A. Brain damage.

Q. Thank you.

A. Okay. That he has sustained brain damage.

Q. Now, I recall you giving us the history that he worked around, at least the history that was given to you, that he worked around paints and solvents for many years; is that correct?

A. Yes.

Q. Do you have an opinion as to the relationship, if any, between his work with the paints and the solvents and the pattern of deficits which you have just explained to us?

MR. DC: Excuse me. I object to that question on the grounds that Dr. EW is not a medical doctor, and attempts to elicit from him answers relating to medical causation are beyond his competence.

MR. (another attorney) I join in that objection and also add that I think that the question calls for opinions beyond the scope of what Dr. EW has been shown to be qualified to testify to, notwithstanding whether it is psychological or medical.

MR. (another attorney) We join in the objections.

BY MR. CA: (continuing)

Q. DR. EW, I think you mentioned before you are not prepared or qualified to render a medical opinion; is that correct?

A. No, I'm not.

Q. My question was whether you have formed an opinion—and I'll ask you the basis for this in a minute—whether you have formed an opinion as to whether there is or is not a relationship between the exposure to paints and solvents and the pattern of deficits which you observed for P1.

MR. DC: Same objection. And I would add to that an objection as to the form of the question, as well.

BY MR. CA: (continuing)

Q. The question was whether you have formulated such an opinion.

A. Yes, I have.

Q. And what is your opinion?

MR. DC: Same objection.

THE WITNESS: Based on my knowledge of the literature and my experience with people with neuropsychological deficits, it is my opinion that the pattern of deficits that P1 shows is of a kind, pattern of neuropsychological deficits—and that is all I can talk about—is of a kind that is similar to that which other neuropsychologists have found with other people exposed to paints and solvents which I have also observed in persons who have been exposed to paints and solvents.

MR. DC: Now I move to strike the answer as being non-responsive and irrelevant.

BY MR. CA: (continuing)

Q.   Dr. EW, I'm going to ask you a couple of questions about the basis for that, the opinion that you just gave. Have you done any studying of the particular area that we are talking about today, in other words the neuropsychological deficits that have been reported as being associated with solvent exposure?

A.   I have in two ways. One is that I have done a very thorough literature search, both in preparing the material in (publication) and for the material that I presented at the Conference. I have also reviewed a variety, a number and variety of cases of patients that I have seen and that other people have seen, as well, who have been exposed to a variety of industrial toxins, and have done this both for preparation of clinical material and for, in examining patients and evaluating their neuropsychological status, and also to prepare for a paper that I presented, I think it was years ago, in, at the Society.

Q.   Now, Dr. EW is there in fact a treatment of some sort in the current edition of (publication) on subject of neuropsychological deficits associated with solvent exposure?

A.   Yes, there is.

Q.   And is that treatment or a portion of it contained in what we have labeled as Exhibit 2, to your deposition, which is on the chart to your right?

MR. DC: That, I believe, should be 3.

MR. CA: Excuse me, that's correct.

BY MR. CA: (continuing)

Q.   Just for consistency: that would be Exhibit No. 3?

A.   That is a photograph of the paragraph out of my publication.

BY MR. CA: (continuing)

Q.   For the record, because it is probably not legible, could you review that portion for us of your study. *(Author's Note: Attorney may want to clarify this was not a scientific study.)*

A.   What I understand is that you would like me to read this?

Q.   If you would, please.

A.   (EW reads a portion of one of his publications dealing with effects of exposure to substances including paint and solvents. Several references are cited indicating most frequent effects include memory problems, fatigue, poor concentration, irritability and headaches. Also impaired ability to perform abstractions, slowing of reaction time and reduced manual dexterity have been noted.)

Q.   Thank you, Dr. EW.
     Now, in the—You have given us your opinion as to the extent of the impairment for P1. Let me ask you whether you can translate for us what that

impairment means in your experience as to the disability that he is likely to suffer in his work or in his personal life.

A.  I'll tackle work first.

Probably the most prominent deficit is the learning deficit, and since it involves both visual and verbal systems, what that means is that he is not going to learn from charts and diagrams any quicker than he is going to learn from instructions; and for him to absorb new information requires many more repetitions, would require many more repetitions than it would for some other person. And even then, as we see, he barely learned anything new, beyond what he learned the first couple of times on the word list learning task, and then he did not retain very much. That means that his ability to get into a new trade where he would have to learn new things is gravely compromised. And added to that, this is a man who had earned his living with his hands and had developed manual skills, and yet here is a man who now has difficulty—and he demonstrates it repeatedly on the testing, he demonstrates what he tells you he has problems with—he has difficulty when he has to solve a visual, spatial problem without a lot of diagrams and assists. He can't solve visual spatial problems well in his head, which means that he cannot do the kinds of activities that a skilled manual worker would be expected to do. Along with this, he has problems of fatigue and irritability.

*(Author's Note: Simply recall here that the wife in her interview with EW stated that P1 was calmer, i.e. less irritable, now than he had been prior to the paint exposure. This seems to be another instance where the expert is choosing to ignore data that is contrary to his conclusions.)*

Now, he has not had, he has not worked in many years so we don't know how they would show up in the workplace, but we know that he has difficulties with both fatigue and irritability at home at this time and so it's not hard to wonder whether these might also show up in the workplace.

I think those are the most prominent areas. But he is, he would be reduced to doing simple manual labor under close supervision, he could not learn something new. He is just not capable of doing skilled work, and issues of stamina come in because of fatigue and other problems that he has.

Q.  Now, Dr. EW, from your evaluation and review of the particular impairments that you have determined that he suffered, do you have an opinion as to whether there is any danger involved, to others, in connection with him working around machinery or something of that nature?

A.  My understanding is that he is seizure-prone. Medical, records document that he is seizure-prone, and as a psychologist who has been involved at times in working with occupational placement, I know that it's very important to not put a seizure-prone person near machinery. And he himself demonstrated good judgment about that in giving up his favorite pastime of hunting.

MR. DC: I move to strike the answer as being not responsive to the question nor directed to this witness's testimony concerning P1's neuropsychological condition.

BY MR. CA: (continuing)

Q. Dr. EW, I'm going to ask you another question regarding specifically the memory, short-term memory, and learning deficits that you have explained to us to and to whether you feel that these would involve or imply some danger to P1 as far as working around machinery of this nature.

MR. DC: I object to the question. I don't understand what "machinery of this nature" is to be or what this witness is to understand "machinery of this nature" to be.

BY MR. CA: (continuing)

Q. Let me clarify that for you, Dr. EW. I'm talking about machinery that, if not handled properly, could pose a danger either to P1 or to co-workers.

MR. DC: Same objection. That is completely abstract. The witness has no idea what that is specifically.

MR. CA: Go ahead.

MR. DC: Talking about a paint brush, Counsel?

BY MR. CA: (continuing)

Q. You may answer the question.

A. I understand you to be talking about machinery such as on a conveyor belt, or saws that cut or presses that hammer and so on. And most machinery, as I understand it, that have moving parts like that, are somewhat complicated to operate and require a person to operate, who operates them now, to be able to learn and figure out and appreciate the distances, relationships and the cautions involved in operating such machinery.

I can only answer that—this will be a general answer—that when it comes to learning new information, whether it be visual information or verbal information, and when it comes to figuring out on his own visual spatial relationships, P1 has a great deal of difficulty and he does not perform at an average level; he performs at a defective level in these areas.

MR. DC: I move to strike his answer as not responsive.

BY MR. CA: (continuing)

Q. Dr. EW, the other area of disability that I mentioned in the beginning was in the area of his personal life or his family life away from work. Do you have an opinion as to whether the pattern of deficits that you have explained to us previously have an effect on his ability to function normally in his personal and family life?

A. Yes, I do.

Q. And could you tell us what your opinion is.

A. Yes.

I see him as a man who, as a result of his deficits, has personal problems in a number of areas. As a direct, what seems to be a direct result of the brain damage—and in this his behavior follows the pattern that is indicated throughout the literature—he is irritable, has more difficulty with temper control, and this seems to be a direct kind of problem.

A lot of problems have evolved, as in his emotional reactions to the changes he has experienced the loss of status that he feels, as a still relatively young man who is no longer working, and as a result of his feeling acutely, painfully embarrassed by his, what he experiences as an inability to function efficiently.

*(Author's Note: Again, the lawyer should be aware of his response, particularly on the 1984 MMPI which would be fairly current for the time EW is now talking about in which P1 indicates that he is entirely self-confident. Certainly the opposite of experiencing an inability to function efficiently.)*

If he has difficulty recalling something, his reaction is to treat that as a sign that he is stupid, and he becomes very embarrassed because he feels that other people look at him as stupid and regard him as stupid. So that over the years since I first saw him in '83 there has been an increasing withdrawal on his part from social and community activities to the point that it's virtually impossible to get him, for instance, to even go to a PTA meeting or an assembly at school for his kids. He does not go to Little League games, although this would be very important to his son. And in just every respect, he has socially withdrawn. He does not keep up with the men that he used to be with, and he will say that he frankly feels embarrassed about it.

The embarrassment is painful; you can see it when it happens. He interprets himself as looking like a fool. And this is a man who I gather had been quite proud and, for his level of education, he had been accomplished in the early 30's, already being a hunting instructor, being a shop steward. And this is a terrific comedown for him. He is also very ashamed of not working, he feels very badly about that. It shows up in family relationships because it shows up in his resentment, in resentment of the fact that his wife has had to take over things, that he cannot do.

So that adding to a tendency to irritability is a lot of anger. It shows up in depression. He reports depression. His wife reports depression. And apparently there has been a good bit.

And it shows up in another way, too, and this is very common. I have seen this very commonly when a relatively young man with growing children in the home has brain damage. They frequently—I'll talk generally and then I'll talk about P1—they will frequently feel very threatened by the youngster who is rapidly gaining on them, getting better than they are, in so many things, while they just sit there and see themselves perhaps even getting worse, which he is not.

And another aspect of this is that young children make a lot of noise, they demand a lot of attention, there is a lot of stimulation going on, and with many kinds of brain damage—and brain damage due to exposure to solvents and paints is among these—people lose the ability to screen out extraneous stimuli so that the presence of an active, noisy child becomes a terrific irritant.

Those two things taken together frequently result in the father—and after 19 and a half years at the V.A. I still think mostly in terms of the father being the damaged person—but the father becoming very impatient with the children, no longer able to give the children support, becoming resentful and showing it in many different kinds of ways.

This seems to be, from what Mrs. P1 reports, seems to be exactly what is occurring. (The next two sentences involve another person and a possibly sensitive personal matter. As it is not very important to the case, it is deleted.)

Q. Dr. EW, is there anything related to these impairments, these mental deficits, that you have reviewed for us, that is reflected in his initial appearance to people, his first impression that he gives people?

A. No. These, like many forms of brain damage, these are subtle deficits. They don't show up, for instance, as somebody who has a stroke and has a paralysis or drooping face. And on first sight or on any kind of superficial, usual kind of examination, you go to the bakery and you buy bread, the deficit would not be apparent unless he starts fumbling with his money. And he had given at one time a story about how he had given the wrong change and had gotten confused. So it might show up there. But just on the most immediate kind of contact or just seeing a person with this kind of problem, hearing them talk for a brief amount of time and with well-structured questions so that they are prepared to give the answer well, this would not show up. It would, typically would show up in the kind of careful examinations that have been done and have been reported on. Or it shows up with longer contact with the person, where you hear them repeat themselves, where you begin to sense distractability, where they will lose a train of thought and not pick up on it again, where they will not be quick to catch on to new jokes, for instance, and be able to follow rapid mental jumps, as in fast-moving conversation.

*(Author's Note: We doubt there is much scientific research to support many of the speculations of the above type.)*

Q. Now, Dr. EW, I think that you mentioned that you had personal experience in treating or trying to help rehabilitate people who are suffering from brain damage; is that correct?

A. Yes. In terms of, what I referred to was doing some vocational counseling and some direct counseling, as well.

Q. Now, regarding this particular situation with P1, do you have an opinion as to whether there is some type of treatment or rehabilitation which would help to improve his situation?

A. There is nothing that I know of that would improve his brain functioning per se. I think that his situation would be greatly improved if he would be able to somehow learn to be more accepting of his disabilities so that there would not, there would not be the social withdrawal and the withdrawal from other activities compounding everything else. I think that would be a very realistic treatment goal that he might be able to, for instance, do some part-time volunteer work, Meals on Wheels or something like that.

Q. What about the future—No one is asking you to have a crystal ball—but as far as your estimation, or your opinion, as to what the future holds for him in terms of any improvement in his mental functioning? Do you have an opinion as to what his prognosis is?

A. I can only base an opinion on the literature because, again, we cannot see in the individual case. Certainly since we have new examinations over a four to five-year span and he is essentially not much different than he was in 1982, we can say that pretty much things have stabilized. As I said there seems to be some small improvement in attentional functions. Whether he will show even more improvement in another year or two, I don't know.

But by and large, with no change in the memory problems, no change in the visual, spatial problems, so on, I would not expect any change there.

What the literature suggests—and there have been a couple of studies now where people have been re-examined anywhere from three to nine or ten years down the road—is that most people, the bulk of people, will stay about the same, at least over that period of time. A few may show some deterioration, a few will show some improvement. But the improvement is mostly in the shorter range, that is in the one to three years or four years, and over the longer span it seemed to be less likely.

So my guess is that—It is now—what?—five, six years since he was working with the paints and solvents? My guess is that he is probably pretty much where he is going to be unless he should be one of the relatively rare, unfortunate ones that have been documented in the literature, where they have been able to follow long enough, who show, begins to show general mental deterioration.

(Discussion held off the record.)

(A lunch recess is taken.)

BY MR. CA: (continuing)

Q.  Dr. EW, just for the record here I would like to refer you to Exhibit, what I believe has been labeled Exhibit 2, which is a copy of your report for P1. You may have a copy of that in your records there, anyway.

A.  Surely.

Q.  I would like for you to review for us specifically the tests and subtests that you administered at the time of your initial examination.

A.  Surely.

I saw him for approximately one and half hours, interviewing him, and gave him the following tests:

*(Author's Note: Recall in the early portion of testimony EW indicated that he saw P1 for "several hours." Was that another error, or is the one and a half hour specified now an error? And if so, what if anything does it signify about EW's cognitive functioning?)*

a series of Reversed Operations that included alphabet, serial subtraction of 3's and 7's; the Stroop test using Carl Dodrill's format; Controlled Oral Verbal Fluency Test, which is Arthur Benton's test; Paragraph Recall, Babcock format; and I used Babcock and Portland paragraphs; writing sentences; Wisconsin Card Sorting Test, Picture Description and Picture Absurdities Subtests from the "Mental Examiner's Handbook"; Hooper Visual Organization Test and Bicycle Drawing.

Q.  Thank you, Dr. EW. Now, I believe that you have testified that the deficits that you reviewed for us earlier were associated in your mind with the solvent exposure. I would like to ask you now whether there are any other factors that in your opinion may have contributed or been involved in creating these deficits, for him again.

A.  There is always a possibility of some contributions from high blood pressure or from medications used in seizure control.

Q. Now, in this particular case have you formed an opinion as to whether either of these factors in fact played a role in creating or contributing to these deficits?

A. I have.

Q. And what is your opinion?

A. It's that there is a possibility that they may have contributed to some small degree, the high blood pressure most particularly.

Q. And when you say "some small degree," if I were to ask you to compare the contribution in terms of probability from the solvent exposure and from any possible contribution from the hypertension, which would be the predominant factor?

A. It isn't so much a matter of probability but a matter of extent of contribution, and the predominant deficits appear to be related to solvent exposure.

Q. Now, I would like to turn at this time to the case of P2. You also examined him is that correct?

A. I did.

Q. And I would like you to relate to the jury the process of your examination, the timing of it, the history or review of the history that you took, and the other information upon which you relied and then, of course, go on and indicate the findings in that examination.

A. I first saw P2 on September 9, 1983, and examined him by means of interview, interviewed him and gave him a neuropsychological, some neuropsychological tests, and then that examination took approximately one and three-quarters hours. This followed my review of a comprehensive neuropsychological examination that had been administered by 8 who was then a psychology intern at the _____ University, under the supervision of Dr. 4. And I also reviewed the examinations, report by Dr. OM, a neurologist at G Hospital, and Dr. 5, a rehabilitation psychologist, who was then associated with G hospital.

There was, he was not married, so I did not interview a wife. He had graduated from High School with something less than a glorious record. He reported mostly C's and D's, with an occasional B.

*(Author's Note: Being aware of P2's extremely poor high school record we would pay attention to EW's choice of descriptive terms here. He describes the record as, "something less than glorious." This is a very mild and certainly not a revealing way of describing a record that is mostly D's and F's. This suggests some possible degree of bias on EW's part, possibly glossing over some of this extremely poor high school performance. In addition, EW states that P2 reported mostly C's and D's, although in EW's May, 1984 report the statement is that he reported his grades were mostly C's with a few B's. Either P2 or EW is not a credible informant. It is also quite important to be aware, given EW's earlier description of utilizing prior behavior in the evaluation, that in this instance, EW started out according to his report with significantly false and misleading information as to P2's cognitive functioning. That is, in EW's mind at the initial stages of the evaluation, he was dealing with someone who had an average high school record or possibly even slightly better than average, thus working from a grossly inaccurate baseline. Of course as with P1, EW did not obtain school or*

*military records of P2 until the day of this testimony. In this instance, however, the representation of the grades in contrast to the actual grades, highlights the significance of EW's failing to obtain the school records before drawing any conclusions about P2.)*

And he had been working for the company he was working for when he stopped his employment for the last, the past 16 years. And for much of the last year that he was working for them his job had been switched from painting to sandblasting; and when I saw him he was working on what he said was on-call, in other words he did not have, he was not working his accustomed 40 hours a week but would come in when they called him. And he spent his spare time working on his house, hunting, fishing, he said.

And I did ask him about alcohol consumption and he reported he had been drinking about four beers a day and a six-pack on the weekends and that was typical for him.

His present complaints, he said, dated back to the late 1960's, when he had experienced a stuffy feeling working with paints, what he described as a stuffy feeling and there were times he didn't eat. Now his main complaint is a memory problem, and he could not tell how long he has had it except to state that high blood pressure had been discovered some time after he was aware that he had difficulties with his memory.

He also said that he had trouble with his mind drifting and stated that he has difficulty keeping track of things. There were times that he felt that he was going to pass out. And he described himself as having, having done weird things, such as putting something in the wrong place.

*(Author's Note: EW seems to treat this as a symptom. We think it is a good example of the base rate problem as we doubt that there are many, if any, people who have not from time to time put something in the wrong place and it hardly seems to classify as "weird" behavior. Nearly everybody misplaces something from time to time. Does EW know the frequency?)*

And he also pointed out that anything that he hadn't done in a long time— I'm sorry, that anything he has done for a long time he can do quite readily, but it's when he tries his hand at something new that he finds that he is slow to learn and has difficulty with it.

He said that he has been on blood pressure medication for the last two years and he has cut back on salt during that time to help control it, and he also said that he was trying to lose weight and thought that he was at the time I saw him 15 to 20 pounds below his maximum.

He was neatly groomed. He was alert, oriented and, again, intelligently cooperative in the sense of understanding what the procedures were about and working hard at what he was doing.

He came across as a man without a lot of emotional expression and his, in his face and his tone of voice he communicated in, I guess what might be best explained as a flat kind of manner. He volunteered very little. He was very responsive, very polite and cooperative. If I asked a question he would always try to respond, but he volunteered very little, he didn't elaborate very much on his responses.

His speech in itself was unremarkable; his thinking tended to be concrete, that is he would give details and be particularistic, without going into the overall pictures or make generalizations.

What ideas he did generate tended to be pretty vague and poorly elaborated. He tracked conversations adequately, in other words he did not lose himself in our immediate back-and-forth. And he said he didn't like his present situation but he didn't feel that there was a lot that he could do about it. And that was essentially as I saw him.

Do you want me to discuss this?

Q.  Yes. Did you administer the neuropsychological examination for P2?

A.  Yes, I did.

Q.  And could you review for us just very quickly for the record the tests that you administered.

A.  In 1983 I gave him the Reversed Operations, that is the alphabet and serial subtraction of 3's and 7's and the Stroop test again and the Controlled Oral Verbal Fluency Test. I also gave him several subtests of Wechsler Adult Intelligence Test Scale, the arithmetic, digit span and block design subtest and the sentence repetition subtest of the Multilingual Aphasia Examination.

I had him write some sentences. I gave him Paragraph Recall again, following the Babcock format and using the Babcock and Portland paragraphs; the Wisconsin Card Sorting Test; the Symbol Digit Modalities Test, the Complex Figure Test using the Taylor figure; and the Bender-Gestalt, using Wepman's memory format; and I had him draw a house and a bicycle.

*(Author's Note: We note that the tests given to P2 are not in all cases the same as those given to P1. It may be worthwhile to inquire of EW why different tests were administered, in view of the fact that both were assumed to be suffering from the same disorder, "Painters Syndrome.")*

Q.  Can you review for us, then, the findings that you came up with after administering these tests?

A.  After that first administration—And this is just my findings and now I'm not going to be talking about the review that I did of other people's work. Okay?

On the verbal skill and reasoning tests, which as I'm sure you remember I said before, by and large will have to do with well-learned, in fact, over-learned material, very familiar material, which will generally be the highest, represent the highest performances when there has been brain damage that doesn't involve the speech centers and, therefore, are generally good indicators of premorbid intelligence, P2 performed straight across the board within the average ability range. On the other hand, verbal fluency, the ability to generate words, was down a little bit, low average level; and his spelling left quite a bit to be desired.

His arithmetic for solving arithmetic problems mentally was at a borderline defective level, frankly depressed score.

*(Author's Note: It is noted that P2 really always had great difficulty with arithmetic as indicated by his school performance.)*

On the visual perception and reasoning tests, he performed—these are the structured tests—he performed in the average ability range. On the constructional tests, where he has to put things together, his scores dropped to the low average range. And on free drawing they dropped a little bit further, one to borderline and another to below the borderline levels.

His free drawings of the house and bicycle were both in the defective range, and his drawings of the nine fairly simple Bender designs was also in the defective level, defective copies of these drawings.

On the attentional tasks there was a very consistent separation between how he performed on the tracking tasks in which there were visual supports, in other words where he could see what he was doing and could keep track of what he was doing visually, and what he did in his head. His performance of the visual tracking tests was in the borderline, generally in the borderline defective range, not frankly defective but below normal limits, below the average range.

On the other hand, all of the concentration and tracking tests that he did were in the defective ability range. This, comparing that with immediate span, that is immediate passive attention span, his digits forward was within normal limits. But under the stimulus overload conditions of immediate span when given the long word list, his performance was at borderline to defective ranges; and he had, he was frankly defective on the sentence repetition test, which involves recalling sentences of varying lengths as accurately as possible and he was unable to do that at a normal level or even a borderline level.

As far as the memory and learning tests are concerned, his paragraph recall was defective both in the immediate, that is in the short-term, and after approximately ten-minute delay, even though the second paragraph was recalled following a second hearing of the story, he still was unable to pick up enough information to make it out of the defective range. And his performance, his performance on the word list learning test was consistently in the defective range. That has to do with the number of words he learned in the first instance, the words he recalled on a short, after a short delay, and the number of words he recalled with long delay, and also with his ability to recognize the words that he had heard five different times.

Visual recall was consistently in the defective range.

I guess I have pretty much covered the tests that I gave. There may be one that I missed.

Q. Dr. EW, as with P1, were you able to gauge or estimate a premorbid level of mental functioning for P2.

A. Yes, I was.

Q. And what was the basis of that estimation and what was your estimation of that level of functioning?

A. My estimate is that P2 has, is a man of original premorbid average endowment, average ability. And my estimate for that is based on both some documented evidence that would support that or really contribute to it, and that is a score on an achievement test that he had taken when he was in the ninth grade, I believe, on which he performed overall at the 37th percentile,

which is well within the average range, because the average range is between the 25th and the 75th percentile, by definition; and also by the fact
that he performed those tests of learning and reasoning and judgment, verbal reasoning and judgment at the average level.

Q. Now, with your estimation of the premorbid mental functioning for P2, do
you have an opinion as to whether his current status, or I should say the
mental status that you determined for him at the time of your examination,
represented an impairment or a deficit in his mental functioning?

A. Well, with reference to the 1983 examination—

Q. Correct.

A. Yes.
Yes, I did feel that he had experienced some frank cognitive deficits.

Q. Now, can you tell us, or tell the jury, the categories of those deficits, the
major deficits, and also give us an indication of the extent of those deficits,
whether they were merely mild or subtle or they were more severe?

A. The most pronounced deficits that he was experiencing showed up in both
short-term and, the short-term verbal memory and the ability to learn, to
store new verbal information. And also with visual information, the same,
he had the same problem: difficulty in storing visual information and difficulty with immediate span visual information.

He also displayed some attentional deficits, particularly, the most pronounced deficits were in mental tracking; and he had some, he showed
some lesser deficits where he had visual support for tracking. But he still by
and large performed below normal limits, not, the performance was not as
severe. When you took away the visual support, then his performance really
plummeted, but with visual supports he was at a borderline level.

I can't make much out of the arithmetic, the lowered arithmetic performance, in light of his school experience. And from his school record it
looks as though he was not a very eager student, and in light of the testing
that we have it would appear that he simply wasn't using the ability that he
had.

*(Author's Note: To say that P2 was not an eager student is pure speculation
on EW's part, he has no information concerning the effort that P2 may have
made or not made in school. We do have the information from the MMPI in both
1982 and 1984 that on item 173 P2 in both instances responded that he liked
school.)*

And I think that is all that that lower arithmetic score means.

He also showed the problems, definite problems with construction in
visual organization and construction when he doesn't have supports, when
the ground is taken out from under him, so to speak, when he has to do it on
his own.

So I believe those are the major areas of deficits that he shows.

Q. Now, Dr. EW, these areas of deficit that you have just outlined to us, when
we compare them to the premorbid mental functioning that you have also
estimated for us, are these deficits associated in your opinion with some organic brain damage?

A. This is a pattern that is associated with, that makes most sense, is understood as reflecting organic brain damage.

Q. I also want to call your attention to some other material which I believe that you have been provided You mentioned that you reviewed a neuropsychological testing by Dr. 4 or under Dr. 4's direction at the medical school and also by a psychologist by the name of 5.

A. Yes.

Q. Did you also have occasion to review the neuropsychological testing by Dr. 6?

A. The testing was not done by Dr. 6, it was done by his technician.

Q. Under his direction?

*(Author's Note: After several times having referred to the testing by Dr. 4 or by Dr. 6 or to the way he performed for Dr. 4 or for Dr. 6, the witness has now become very accurate, insisting on pointing out that the tests were not performed by Doctor 6 but by his technician. One question that could be raised is as to whether this double diplomate was confused during all of his previous testimony. More seriously, at some point or other, questions should be asked to determine whether EW knew how much direction there was by either Dr. 4 or Dr. 6, or what he means, that is, what EW means by the words "under his direction." If the answer is no, that he does not know, one has an option of asking another question to the effect, "Then, as far as you know, there could have been very little direction or supervision?" If the answer shows an adequate amount, the quality can be challenged in view of the numerous errors that came through.)*

A. Under his direction.

Q. Could you comment, then, on the consistency among the various examinations that you reviewed, including your own 1983 examination?

A. There tends to be a lot of commonalities, some differences, but a lot of commonalities in the various testings. And perhaps to keep me from getting confused because there is so much data, it would be easiest to go through again function by function, as I have been.

And on the verbal skills and the verbal reasoning—and that verbal reasoning involves one test of generalizing about words, actually a similarities test: in what way, for instance, are a dog and a lion alike? On those kinds of tests he performed consistently for everybody within normal limits, with just one single exception, again for Dr. 6, Dr. 6's technician, his score dropped a little. And I'm not giving a lot of credence for the drops that occurred with Dr. 6's technician because there is just too many of them, too much of a pattern.

*(Author's Note: There are two issues in this testimony. The statement that P2 performed consistently for everybody within normal limits except for Doctor 6's technician is simply not correct. Reference to the table of scores on the WAIS-R for P2 that show that for Doctor 4's intern, he got a scale score of ten, for Doctor 5, he got a scale score of 10 and for Doctor 6's technician he got a scale score of eight on similarities. While this is a drop, it is still a score of eight which is considered to be within the normal range and is so described by Doctor EW later in his testimony. Scale scores of eight through 12 are generally*

*recognized in the literature as being within the normal or average range. How-
ever, there is also a logic to this conclusion. This logic is based on a statistic
called the standard error of measurement, which is a statistic designed to measure the degree of chance variation that can be expected. It is understood that no
test or sub-test is perfectly (1.00) reliable, that if you tested a person on the
same test a hundred times, they would not get exactly the same score each time
but would get a cluster of scores ranging to some degree upward or downward
from an average. The standard error of measurement, which takes into account
the reliability of a test, allows one to make a statement regarding the probability
than an individual's true score falls within a certain range. The reader may recognize this type of measurement if they think about the way polls are often reported, in which range of error is described, e.g., "accurate within plus or
minus 5 points." The manual for the WAIS-R, at page 33, provides the standard
errors of measurement for the scale scores by age group and for the age group
35 to 44, which would include P2, the standard error of measurement is 1.27.
However, one cannot obtain a scale score ending in a fraction. Thus for example, one cannot say that P2's true score based on his scale score of ten in the
1982 testing would be, two chances out of three, somewhere between 8.73 and
11.27. Scale scores are only whole numbers so that the statement has to be,
"Chances are two out of three that P2's true scale score on the similarity subtests would fall somewhere between 8 and 12." Therefore, eight is considered
very definitely within the average range. Furthermore, it is not true as EW asserts concerning Dr. 6's technician that there were too many errors, too much of
a pattern, at least if this is in reference to the WAIS-R as it appears to us to be.
That is, we note that looking at the table of WAIS-R scores, P2 is two points
lower on the 1984 testing than on the 1982 testing on three of the subtests, information, comprehension and similarities. Because the standard errors of
measurement for comprehension and similarities are both greater than one, we
have to conclude that this variation of two points is not greater than would be
expected by the standard error of measurement of the test, that these are chance
variations and have no significance. While it is true that all three of the differences on the verbal subtest are in terms of the lower scale scores, this does not
hold up when the entire test is looked at as we can observe that P2 obtained
higher scale scores on two of the subtests, picture arrangement and object assembly. So it does not appear that Dr. 6's technician was performing the examination in some way so as to produce a systematic reduction in P2's
performances or scores. Further, if one were to apply the same test of acceptance to the scores obtained by Doctor 5, it should be noted that while Doctor 5
administered only three of the subtests, two out of the three had scores lower
than the 1982 examination, one was the same and none were higher. Furthermore, one of the drops on digit span was a drop of three points, a larger drop
than any obtained by Doctor 6's technician. On this basis, if EW is going to, in
effect, throw out the results of the 1984 tests (Doctor 6's technician), then on the
same reasoning, Doctor 5's results in 1983 should also be thrown out. However,
the next paragraph and the bulk of the testimony makes it clear that Doctor EW
is not throwing out Dr. 5's testing.)*

But the other thing he did do for—This was for Dr. 5—on the more difficult proverbs test, where he has to come up, where the answer is not so quickly associable as, you knew, "How are a dog and a lion alike?" "They are animals." But having to interpret the more complex proverbs, here again, he dropped down to the defective range. He just had a terrible time with handling these proverbs in anything but the most concrete and in some cases quite irrelevant manners, showing that he simply did not appreciate the bulk of the proverbs or that they were meant to be metaphoric statements.

His arithmetic was consistenly at the borderline defective level. For me in this last examination I was actually quite surprised. He had trouble doing a simple division problem, dividing one number, or one-place number into a two-place number, and he seemed puzzled at that himself, as though he knew what he was supposed to do and he set the problem out correctly but at that point he stopped. It was as though he had forgotten that operation that he once knew, had known.

His performance on the visual perceptual test was consistently, as I said, average, except he actually got one high average response, one high average score for Dr. 6's technician.

*(Author's Note: This might be another illustration of examiner effects as he is now doing better for Doctor 6's technician.)*

And his constructions were consistently, that is his structured constructions, where the answer was given and he could manipulate the material, were consistently at a low average level. And the drawings that he did, any drawings that he did for anybody, and including the two sets of drawings that he did for me, were all in the defective range and, frankly, very frankly defective, with major distortions.

On attentional tasks his immediate span was consistently for me within normal limitation. His immediate span—and for Dr. 4, as well. His immediate span under conditions of stimulus overload, that is with the 15-word list, his immediate span dropped down to average, to below average, that is borderline and defective levels. So, again, putting a load on the system, his functioning was reduced. When there was no load on the system, then it popped up to normal limits.

*(Author's Note: EW is now back to saying that P2 performed for Doctor 4, not Doctor 4's intern or as he has been saying for Doctor 6's technician. Also, there is another error in the statement, "His immediate span dropped down to 'average,' immediately corrected to 'below-average,' but nevertheless an error was made in the presentation.)*

His sentence repetition was very unreliable. And one of the things that he did this last time I saw him, which was a week and a half ago, he misheard a number of things, so that showed up, of course, quite obviously in the demand to repeat a sentence as accurately as possible. But it also showed up on other kinds of mishearings. For instance, he misheard an arithmetic problem. He had difficulty keeping the arithmetic problems in his head, even though he did ultimately do some of them. And at one point when I read a little paragraph to him that started "December 6," asking for recall, his recall of that was "September 6." So, again, either he is not focusing on what he is hearing or there is some slip, some inefficiency there in his take-in of verbal information. It is not huge, it is not gross to the point that he would miss out on everything in a conversation, but it's there and there is enough slippage as to create misunderstandings and leave him confused, I imagine, a lot of the time.

Short-term verbal recall, everybody found him to perform at defective levels.

On the learning tests his most recent performance of the list-learning was his best, and he performed that within normal limits. In other words, his learning in recall a week and a half ago of the word list was within normal limits, although his paragraph recall was still at defective to borderline levels. Now, the difference between them: with the list learning, it is rote learning, they get it five times, it is only 15 words. With the paragraph it is meaningful material and a lot of different kinds of material in a little story. There some 22 different ideas, 21, 22 different ideas in each of the stories, and he only gets to hear them twice. So it is these distinctions that probably account for the difference. In other words, simplify the situation, give him a lot of time, a lot of repetition, and he demonstrates the ability for verbal learning. And he manages to retain that information over 40 minutes or so of delayed time. But give him a more complicated message, and if he only hears it once or twice, then he is out of sight again and, of course, most communications are—you don't hear any paragraph, like list-learning, unless we have long lists when we go to the grocery store.

I skipped over attention, but I'll talk about visual memory as long as I'm on memory here. Dr. 6's visual recall test—and I'm not acquainted with that test. He has a set of verbal and visual learning tests that are unique to him and he never published widely on them, so they have never had broad distribution. I don't know what his norms are, but he reports them as being within normal limits.

On the other hand, on the tests that are in wide distribution in this country and on the continent, where there is a lot of information about the tests,

*(Author's Note: There may be a question of EW using a double standard of evidence here as the adequacy of the norms of some of the tests he uses is also questionable.)*

his immediate visual span, his immediate recall, five seconds, looking at a little design and then drawing it, there were major distortions. And his short-term recall of a more complex design was consistently defective on all three times, three examinations he had, using this design or using similar designs. And his delayed recall was also defective.

His performance of the tactile performance test—He did not do that for me. I don't know whether you want me to review it or not. But that was done by both 4 and 6, and on that he was defective in his, he was extremely, he was defective in that he was extremely slow and could not get all of the designs in place. The people his age typically will have all the designs in place within 15 minutes on the basis of three trials, and for him on the one three-trial session he required 33 and a half minutes and another session he did not complete it in 45 minutes. So he was extremely slow on that. And his recall of those designs varied really according to who gave them.

When 6's technician gave the test, he did poorly; and when 8 gave the test, he did well. So I think that is a difference in administrations.

*(Author's Note: Here EW is coming right out with the issue of examiner effects; what he is saying, as we have described in our section on examiner effects, is that the results you get depend upon who is giving the test. We also note that EW is now calling Doctor 4's intern 8, "Doctor" 8. Although at the time of this testimony, the title "Doctor" was appropriate, it was not appropriate as of the time of the testing.)*

I gave him a special behavioral memory test, as well, and he remembered objects quite well, but he had, remembering faces—and this is a very simple test—he identified one picture as one that he had seen which he had not seen.

*(Author's Note: It would probably be worthwhile to question the expert on this matter concerning the studies we have provided in the chapters on clinical judgment and clinical method, which studies have shown that when tape recordings of diagnostic interviews are played back and compared to clinician's reports or identifications of symptoms, that they report symptoms that were never present in the interview. Therefore, if this is a symptom of some cognitive malfunctioning, it is apparently something that is very common among mental health professionals. Occasionally material of this kind becomes the source of some humorous amusement in the courtroom.)*

So that pretty much covers the visual learning.

And then—I have done so much I don't remember. I guess I didn't cover the attentional functions. For me on this examination on September 6 of this month, all of the attentional tests, that I gave him were performed at borderline to defective levels and, again, the split seemed to be predominantly between things for which he had visual support and tasks that he had to do completely in his memory.

In addition, there was another piece of what I consider to be very telling evidence of an attentional deficit, that shows up not on an attention test per se but on the word list learning testing, in that he, in giving his answers, he gave many, many repetitions of words he had already said, which seems to be a hallmark of difficulty in being able to do a task and keep on track of what you are doing at the same time. So he was, I believe, able to do it. He was able to call the words out but he was not keeping track of what he said, so some words he repeated two and three times in giving those.

I think—Have we covered it all? I think we have covered my examination of him.

Q. Dr. EW, in general from your review of the earlier examinations, yours and the other psychologists who examined P2, and comparing that with your most recent examination, is there a general consistency? Is his condition stable?

MR. DC: I thought that he just spent 15 minutes dealing with that. I object as repetitious.

BY MR. CA: (continuing)

Q.  Go ahead.
A.  I'll start with the good news for P2—Okay?—and which I told him. His list-learning ability has gone up. As I mentioned, his ability to learn by rote is at least, as I understand it, verbal learning by rote, as I saw it, is within normal limits, although incidental verbal recall seems to have gone down. But by and large on other kinds of functions there is not significant change. So there is that one piece of good news.

Well, and the one piece of bad news is that I did not remember him having with—I'll use the technical term—with auditory processing, with grasping verbal information accurately, I did not recall him having that before, and he shows that problem.

Q.  Generally, then, is it your opinion that this most recent test shows a stabilization of his condition? Or are there dramatic changes?
MR. DC: I object to the form of the question.
BY MR. CA: (continuing)
Q.  Do you have an opinion as to whether there are changes that are evident in this last test?
A.  Yes, I do.
Q.  What is your opinion?
A.  My opinion is that verbal rote learning has returned to normal limits.
Q.  And as to other—
A.  And that's all. Otherwise, the deficits remain the same.
Q.  I would like to ask you whether you can, from your own experience and your findings that you have related to us, relate these deficits that have stabilized as deficits to their effect, any effect that they may have on his employability and, also, when you have completed that, to his personal and family life.
A.  As far as employability is concerned, although his rote learning has improved and his verbal rote learning has improved, we could say that he is capable of, for instance, learning instructions if he could read them over and over and over again, he is now going to have difficulty being accurate in understanding oral directions. There is some slippage there. It is slight but you don't need much more than slight slippage for problems to arise. In fact, that is usually when they occur, when slippage is slight. If somebody has difficulty, everybody talks slowly and he catches on, so on, but when there is just a little bit of error, then that is when misunderstandings are most likely to arise. So that creates a problem. He is going to have a problem dealing with oral instructions as they are usually given because he is not going to grasp them and he is not going to retain them very well.

His visual, his ability to learn visually and to deal with visual spatial, complex, unfamiliar visual spatial material, appears to be compromised, excepting that which is most simplistic. And his judgment is not going to be good in handling that kind of material. And he does have these consistent attention problems if he has to do things in his head, remembering things in his head, keeping track of ongoing events, keeping track of what he has been doing even.

He has difficulty, and it shows up, so that I think that it would make him a very difficult employee. These are not the qualities that somebody wants if they are running an efficient business. They don't want to have to repeat things all the time. They do not want somebody who will do the wrong thing because he is going to forget it or somebody that be [sic] can't carry several instructions in their head and know which ones to use and which to disregard, using judgment about the visual spatial things they are dealing with. So I think it would greatly limit whatever employment opportunities there might be, and in a competitive market where you can hire somebody who doesn't have these deficits, I would think he would be pushed to the end of the line consistently.

As far as his personal life, what seems to have happened is he has become a social isolate pretty much. For example, he said that prior to experiencing significant problems, these significant mental problems that I'm talking about, he had had some long-term relationships with women. And now whatever relationships with women he has are extremely casual, there is no consistency in them. I did not go into detail on that issue except to discover that there is, for instance, not a particular woman that he is seeing regularly, he is not developing relationships.

*(Author's Note: This testimony seems to indicate that P2 had long term relationships with women prior to experiencing the "painters syndrome" problems but that since those problems developed he has not had such relationships. However, the 1982 report at which time presumably, he was suffering all these mental problems, states on page two, "Has maintained a relatively active social life and has been involved in a romantic relationship for the previous six years." This language seems to clearly indicate present tense, so that the relationship was still ongoing at that time and apparently had not terminated because of the supposed mental problems. This may illustrate one of the problems that arise in dealing with testimony of mental health professionals. In their direct examination, often they tend to ramble on stating all kinds of things about the litigant, which they may or may not know or which may or may not be correct. Also as in this instance, it is not entirely clear what they are saying so it is hard to make a determination as to whether it is correct or not. Therefore, much cross-examination has to be devoted to establishing with precision what it is the expert is saying.)*

As far as friendships are concerned, his friendships now are limited to one guy that he feels sufficiently comfortable with, who knows what his deficits are, and that's it. And other than that he carries around a load of embarrassment with him and so is withdrawing on that account.

So he pretty much was describing himself as being socially isolate and not doing much and not going much.

Q.  Dr. EW, if a person did not know P2 and know of these deficits that you have outlined, would there be anything about the mental impairments that you have reviewed for us that would distinguish him or give a first impression that he had something mentally wrong with him?

A.  None, nothing at all. He would seem like a very alert, pleasant gentleman, and it would not be probably until you had considerable conversation and began to pick up where, that he was slipping on some of the things that you were trying to get across, or if he had to tackle some problems that you presented, that you begin to pick up.

Q. Dr. EW, you have outlined for us some mental deficits that have been the result of your findings on the neuropsychological tests and also some disabilities resulting from those impairments. Have you formed an opinion as to the relationship between these mental impairments and the solvent exposure that P2 experienced?

A. Yes, I have.

MR. DC: I object on the same grounds as I have previously objected to the same question asked of P1.

BY MR. CA: (continuing)

Q. The question was: have you developed an opinion as to the association, if any, between the impairments and the solvent exposure?

A. Yes, I have.

Q. What is your opinion?

A. That the pattern of deficits he shows fits in with the pattern of deficits described in the neuropsychological literature, the pattern of neuropsychological deficits described in the literature, on solvent exposure.

Q. Dr. EW, I would like to ask you a question at this point in time as to the role of a neuropsychologist or neuropsychology in making the type of diagnosis that has been made in these cases, in other words, associating an impairment with a cause.

A. For the solvent problems, for many of the, many people who have been exposed to solvents, the predominant symptoms that they experience are of a psychological nature, or are based just on report, feelings of fatigue, logginess, confusion—These are all verbal reports—feeling of depression; and then the cognitive problems that have been found to be associated with solvent exposure. So that the neuropsychological evaluation of these things becomes a very important, makes a very important contribution to the determination of whether or not somebody is actually suffering toxic encephalopathy due to solvent exposure.

The presentation of the problems varies greatly among patients. Some patients will have fewer of the cognitive deficits and may have more of other kinds of symptoms that will show up on neurological or radiologic or neuroencephalographic examination, for example; and with other patients the predominant symptoms may well be affecting the cognitive systems, with little or no evidence of disturbance in other aspects, in other words subsystems in the nervous system.

*(Author's Note: This appears to be a declaration that the term "toxic encephalopathy due to solvent exposure" is a meaningless term and there is no such thing as solvent or painters syndrome. That is, if the problems vary greatly among patients, there would seem then not to be a specific set of symptoms that identify this disorder, if such a disorder exists. Without going into detail, it can be shown by reference to DSM-III or DSM-III-R that virtually all of the symptoms that have been described are also associated with other disorders. Thus, it would be difficult, if not impossible, to reason backwards from symptoms to*

*cause, in particular if a range of causes are viable. If the symptoms are nonspecific and can be seen with various conditions, how can one say, by seeing the symptoms, which cause is the operative one? See also the literature in Chapter 15, Volume I, showing neuropsychologists' difficulty identifying specific etiologies.)*

Q. Dr. EW, do you have an opinion as to whether there is available any treatment or rehabilitation activities that would address or help correct mental deficits that you have reviewed for us with P2?

A. I know of none. These are deficits that people are essentially stuck with if they have them and there is not, and haven't reversed spontaneously, as, for example, his learning ability, rote learning ability, has, seems to be reversed spontaneously. But what he is stuck with, he is stuck with pretty much, and there aren't—The memory isn't a muscle and the attention isn't a muscle, and you don't improve attention, don't improve memory by exercising, any more than you can improve the acuity of your ears by listening to more music or more words.

Q. What then, would be the prognosis as far as the future for P2 and the mental deficits you have outlined for us?

A. I have to base any prognostic guess or opinion that I make on the literature because that is the only thing we have to go on, and we don't have crystal balls.

And based on the literature, where there have been studies of patients some three to six or nine or so years after the, they have left the exposure situation, most people who have been exposed stay about the same. Some tend to deteriorate, a few of those begin, a few would show a general mental deterioration, which P2 has not shown; and a few will show improvement, which he has done. So it would seem that this many years—We are now—what?—five years down the line since the exposure, that he has been out for five years away from painting, my guess is that he probably, the chances of experiencing more improvement are probably not great. He has probably gotten what gain he is going to get.

And he runs a risk of some deterioration but, you know, when you are talking about a risk, he may get it and he may escape it. I can't predict that.

Q. Thank you, Dr. EW. Let me ask you about something you referred to before, and I think you referred to a practice effect, in effect, when you were talking about neurological testing. Can you tell the jury: what is a practice effect?

A. That is the fancy name, the name you have to know for your examinations, for what your common sense tells you will happen if you do the same thing over and over again: you will get better at it, more familiar with it and remember some of the answers. And in the case of some of the tests that we give, if you can solve the problem one time, then the chances of solving it in the future not only are improved but you are likely to be faster at it because you recognize what it is, when the first time around you have to puzzle over it.

So as far as one of the things, when we are dealing with this kind of repeated examination, one of the things that we have to be aware of is the fact of practice, realize that there are some tests that are more susceptible to practice effects and some tests are not, and whenever possible to try to shift exams and use parallel kinds of examinations.

Q.  If two similar tests are given within a brief time span and the result of a second test shows better results, is this then attributable to practice effect?

A.  It depends, really depends upon the kind of test, and it depends on the amount of improvement. It's really a matter of both, because for most tests the amount of gain will be slight, noticeable but slight, and if you are using parallel forms of the same test, as for instance the design copying test, they are talking about, where I used a form that was different than the one that that 4 used or that 5 used. In the case like that, what improvement there is is probably just a matter of it may take them a few seconds less to do it because they know what is expected of them, it is not quite as strange. But, strangely, there won't be a real practice effect because they have to solve a somewhat different kind of problem.

Q.  Dr. EW, most of the tests, or many of the tests that you have explained to us seem to require the person who is taking the test to make some effort to do well or accomplish the test; is that correct?

A.  Yes, it is.

Q.  Is there any way of determining or at least focusing in on the issue of whether or not they are making their best effort on that?

A.  One method I use is to see, one way is to see whether the pattern of low scores makes neuropsychological sense or whether it is just random or whether everything is low and contradicts the impression that the person gives when you are talking to them. So it's this kind of internal evidence I think that is most useful.

There are some specific tests you can use when you suspect people of not doing their all. In the case of these gentlemen, P1 and P2, the impression they gave, very strongly, was that each of them had an awful lot riding on doing well because each of them felt very badly about their deficits, I mean they felt like they were less men than they were or wanted to be, and that is an awfully powerful motivation to do your best. And, as a matter of fact, each one of them in some areas did their best, and these were areas where doing your best makes neuropsychological sense in terms of everything else and fits in with the background of information that we know about these men. So I had no reason, absolutely no reason to question the validity of their effort with me.

Q.  Dr. EW, I skipped a part that I wanted to cover regarding P2, and that was whether in your opinion there may be other factors other than the solvent exposure that may be contributing to the deficits that you explained to us.

A.  Yes. In his case he does have high blood pressure and he is on medication, he is taking medication for his—I believe—no. In his case it is the high blood pressure and medication for high blood pressure.

Q.  Do you feel that there may have been, then, some contribution by these factors?

A. When a person has had high blood pressure over a period of time, there is always that possibility, that some, that the high blood pressure itself will make some small contribution to the overall, an overall impairment pattern.

Q. When you say "some small contribution," then can you give us a comparison as to the relative contributions from the high blood pressure or the medication being prescribed for it and the solvent exposure?

A. Based on a review of the literature, yes, I can.

Q. And what would that relative contribution be?

A. Depending upon—Well, for one thing, high blood pressure will have fewer overall effects and the effects of it are more localized, but the contribution is not very great. It shows up, when you have people who have been screened and have no other neurological problem, then it will show up on certain particular tests as some detriment in functioning.

Q. Now, Dr. EW, the trial of this case is scheduled to begin on October, 1986. Can you tell the jury where you plan to be on that date.

A. Yes. I will be in _____. I'll be at the _____ University of Medical Sciences in the Department of Neurology.

Q. And when will you at this point in time be leaving the country for that purpose?

A. I'll be leaving the country on September _____.

Q. And when is your plan to return?

A. December _____.

Q. Of this year?

A. Yes. I have committed ten weeks to the Neurology Department.

Q. Dr. EW, I need to also refer you back to something that you said about P2's examination, or at least about the history; and you mentioned in part of your history that he had consumed, I think you said, typically four beers a day and a six-pack on the weekend. What, if any, contribution is there to the neuropsychological deficits by this type of consumption of alcohol?

A. In a man of P2's height and girth, and with the relatively, the not very large quantity of alcohol intake, my guess is that it would contribute very little, if anything. And I think the fact that alcohol is not contributing shows up in the major improvement that he has enjoyed, which is in the verbal learning test, which is the one area, one of the areas that would be most sensitive to alcohol, to some kind of alcoholism problem, alcoholic encephalopathy.

*(Author's Note: The witness could be asked regarding this, if there is a substantial number of published research studies demonstrating that there are no interactional effects between high blood pressure, the particular medications that P2 was taking and the amount of alcohol he was consuming. The witness has dealt with these items only in terms of their separate impact on brain function and simply has ignored the possibility of interactional effects. We cannot say that there are any, but we doubt that there is a substantial body of literature which would demonstrate that there are not any such effects.)*

MR. CA: Thank you very much, Dr. EW.

MR. DC: Perhaps the court reporter would want to take short break before we start on cross-examination.

(A short recess is taken.)

CROSS EXAMINATION
BY MR. DC:

Q. Dr. EW, my name is DC and I'm an attorney representing the Defendant, in these cases which are being tried now before Judge _____.

Let's begin directly with a discussion of P1. I understand you have examined him twice; is that correct?

A. That's right.

Q. The first time, which was in July of 1983, you have told us that the total length of your examination of him was one and a half hours.

A. That's right.

Q. In that regard, looking at your Report of Examination, it's stated there, as I read it, that P1 was examined for approximately one hour.

A. I know. Did you see the dot after that? That is one I didn't pick up. That was on my computer, and my computer doesn't type the "1/2". I have the inexpensive Epson printer. And I didn't pick it up on proofreading; and it is "one and a half."

*(Author's Note: Two items here, one is that EW has made another error in failing to notice that the report as written was wrong about the time of the examination. What is more important is that initially in his testimony about the first examination, EW stated that it took "several" hours, which certainly conveys an impression of more than one and a half hours and so was a misleading statement or another error.)*

Q. Now, with regard to the second examination, which I understand occurred last Saturday—

A. A week ago Saturday, yes.

Q. In September of 1986?

A. Right.

Q. How long was that examination—I'm sorry.

A. That examination lasted approximately two and a half hours.

Q. What tests were given during that examination?

A. I gave him the Sentence Building subtest of the Stanford-Binet Intelligence Scale and had him write the answers. I gave him the Reversed Operations, that is alphabet and serial 7, subtracting serial 7's, subtracting serial 3's; the Sentence Repetition subtest of the Multilingual Aphasia Examination; the California Verbal Learning test; the Paragraph Recall Test, using the Babcock format and the Babcock and Portland paragraphs; the River-Meade Behavioral Memory Test the Sequence Digit Learning Test—one of Arthur Benton's tests—the Arithmetic Problem subtest from the Wells and Rusch little "Examiner's Handbook"; the Symbol Digit Modalities test, the Stroop test, using the Dodrill format; bicycle drawing test; the Complex Figure test; and I believe I used—I had better take a look and see which—I used the Ray Oscar [sic] figure.

I think that that is what the examination consisted of; and, of course, I interviewed him.

Q. Does the file which you have before you contain all of the raw data and test results from both of your examinations?

A.  Yes, this file here contains all the raw data and all the test results, everything.

Q.  Now, I have had an opportunity during one of our recesses here today to look through that folder briefly, and I see that you have recorded some of the responses of P1 and P2 in shorthand; is that correct?

A.  That's right, I do.

Q.  Well, one of the things which we are going to ask you to do at the conclusion of your testimony today is to have Xeroxed for us your entire files. And in that connection I would ask you to dictate, if you would, into English, so that we may understand it, the shorthand.

A.  I have a time problem right now and I don't know how I can. I really have a time problem. I have to leave town this Saturday morning and, I have done this before, I have done transcriptions before, and it just takes too long.

Q.  Well, I would simply ask you in the interests of being able to have your complete file before the jury when the jury makes a decision in this case, to use your best efforts in that regard, and I'll have to leave that decision as to whether you have to time to do it up to you.

A.  I'll have to see what I can do, and I don't know—Well, possibly something can be worked out.

Q.  Now, between the one and a half hours that you saw P1 in July of 1983 and September of 1986 did you see him at all?

A.  No, I did not.

Q.  I understand that you have had made available to you and you have reviewed the testing results performed by others, and I want to make sure I have a complete list of the information that you have reviewed. As I understand it, you have reviewed the work performed by two interns on behalf of Dr. 4 that would be respectively the work of Intern 3 on P1 and the work of Intern 8 on P2.

A.  That's right.

Q.  As well, you have reviewed the test results performed by some technician on behalf of Dr. 6.

A.  That's correct.

*(Author's Note: We think there was an opportunity for some high impact cross-examination here. We would like to see a set of questions along the following lines: "Doctor, in your direct examination, you frequently referred to the testing by Doctor 4 or Doctor 6 or the way P1 or P2 performed for Doctor 4 or Doctor 6. Do you know if any of the tests were actually administered by Doctor 4 or Doctor 6?" [If the answer to that is affirmative, which seems very unlikely, the next question obviously should be, which tests were administered by these doctors.] "So that when you refer to testing by Doctors 4 or 6 or performance for Doctors 4 or 6, that was not correct, was it?" [Here we would insist on a yes or no answer with an opportunity to explain, if requested. It is clearly a question that can be answered yes or no and it is very clear that the answer is that it was not correct.] "You did not intend to mislead the jury into believing that the test had actually been performed by these doctors, did you?" [This will almost certainly be answered no.] "Were you then misinterpreting the data that was right in front of you?" "Could that be construed as a distortion of the verbal material*

*that had been presented to you?" The purpose of a line of questioning such as this is to highlight for the jury that either Doctor EW was trying to mislead or was, himself, exhibiting behaviors that in a patient would be construed as symptoms of brain damage. Another alternative is that EW was being quite casual about the accuracy of the material he was presenting. Any one of the above alternatives should assist the jury in having some skepticism concerning EW in this case. Also each instance in which credibility is diminished a little can be thought of as one brick which with other bricks such as misstating the duration of the initial examination and some material which will follow can be used to construct a wall of doubt concerning the credibility to be afforded this witness.)*

Q.  Now, with regard to both of those practices, that is having interns perform the neuropsychological examinations or technicians perform the examinations, is that a practice that you approve of and condone?

A.  It depends upon the situation, the reasons for the examination, the degree of skill and sensitivity required and the maturity and skill of the technician or intern, so that I cannot make a blanket statement.

*(Author's Note: As a general rule, we do not recommend on cross-examination asking questions that call for the personal opinion of the expert witness as this one does. The object here appears to be to establish that it is not a good practice to have neuropsychological examinations performed by interns or technicians. Certainly not where there is litigation involved. It is noted in several places in the literature that neuropsychological testing in particular calls for a considerable amount of skill and experience due to the nature of the possible disorders that one may be dealing with. However, as the question was asked here, it provided EW with the opportunity to evade the question and in attempting to get at it more directly, DC went on to a specific example, the result of which was that in fact it never was established that it is poor practice, in general, to have neuropsychological examinations where litigation is involved or potentially involved done by interns. We might note additionally that when one gets this kind of answer from an expert, "it depends," it may be worthwhile to trace this down and require them to specify precisely what it depends upon so that one can obtain an answer to the objective of the original question.)*

Q.  Let's be specific, then. Perhaps I was wrong, but I gathered from the tenor of some of your comments on direct examination that you did not see fit to rely upon the examination performed under the direction of Dr. 6; is that correct?

A.  That is correct.

Q.  So you did not find that particular examiner to be sensitive enough or skilled enough or competent enough to meet your standards?

A.  I know only two things about that examiner directly, and I'll leave the hearsay out. One is that in rescoring the tests this examiner scored I found some errors in the scoring and, therefore, that would affect the whole issue. And the other was the surprising, that there were so many, particularly in the case of P1, who embarrasses so easily, there were big drops in his performance for that technician, which made me, it simply raised the question in my own mind: was there something going on between the technician and P1 that made him uncomfortable, which in turn affected his performance?

*(Author's Note: We recommend, in all cases where there is psychological testing, charts of the various test performances, especially where there is more than one examination involving testing. If the reader will refer back to the chart, given near the beginning of this case, giving the results of the WAIS and three WAIS-R's given to P1, the following can be readily noted. Compared to the performance of P1 on the testing by 3, the testing by Doctor 6's technician 7 shows that he dropped five scale scores on arithmetic, four scale scores on block design, two scale scores on digit span and one scale score each on vocabulary, object assembly and digit symbol. While the scores shown on 3's comprehension subtest is seven, we know in actuality, it should be twelve, so that would also be a drop of two from the real score although it would be an increase of three from the score shown on the record form. In addition, we note that on the information subtest, P1 increased his scale score on the testing by 7 from six to ten, or from seven to ten as the score on 3's administration is corrected by Doctor EW a few lines down. There are two points to be made here that should severely impair EW's credibility. One is that so far as something going on that was making P1 uncomfortable, this would make it difficult to account then for the increase on the information subtest, which as previously noted is a measure of old learning which presumably is not affected by brain damage. In fact, one could argue the other way, that because he did this well for Doctor 6's technician, there must have been something wrong with what was going on between 3 and P1 for him to have scored so low. We think that argument is probably as specious as several of those that EW is making, but we are presenting it in case it was missed by any reader. What we think probably is much more damaging to EW's credibility is that if he is frankly stating the reasons for discounting or disregarding the Doctor 6 technician's reports and examination, we would call your attention to the results obtained by Doctor 5, in October of 1983, much closer in time to the examination by 3. While Doctor 5 did not administer the whole test, we note that on the digit span subtest, where P1 suffered a drop of only two points from the 3 to the 7 administration, on the Doctor 5 administration, he suffers a drop of four scale score points. On the arithmetic subtest, where he dropped five points on the 6 technician administration, he dropped six points on the Doctor 5 administration. It should be obvious that these two subtests are more susceptible to practice effects than the information subtest and therefore more likely to rise than to drop. And on the similarity subtest where there was no drop at all between the 3 and the 6 technician administrations, there is a drop of three scale scores on the Doctor 5 administration. Throughout the direct testimony, EW has made several references to Doctor 5's findings, but based on the reason given for discounting the Doctor 6 technician's reports, there seems to be no basis on which Doctor 5's work could be considered acceptable.)*

Q. Did you make any attempt to assure—

A. By the way, that technician does not work for Dr. 6 any more. I have that certificate.

Q. Did you make any attempt to assure yourself that the tests performed by Intern 3 were properly administered and accurately scored?

*(Author's Note: Here we would simply call attention to the smooth way that DC is getting the testing correctly labeled as the work of an intern and not of*

*Doctor 4 as so frequently indicated by the witness. Further on he does the same thing regarding Intern 8. This not only corrects the factual situation but should take a little more off of EW's credibility.)*

A.   I have reviewed—Oh, yes, I did review the scoring. I do that.

Q.   So you vouch for his results?

A.   I don't remember whether there were any scoring errors at all. I can take a look, but I don't remember being impressed with a lot of them, as I was with the other one, and there may have been some. If you want—Do you want me to look?

Q.   Yes. I am interested to know whether you examined Mr. 3's work to determine whether it was properly administered.

A.   There was one scoring error on 3 [sic]. There were two errors on the comprehension subtest, two scoring errors, and one scoring error on the information subtest, both on the Wechsler Adult Intelligence Scale.

Q.   Were there any consequences to you of those scoring errors?

A.   Yes, there were. The information subtest score should be 7, instead of 6.

Q.   Is that all?

A.   That was the major consequence. It wasn't a big one but it was there.

Q.   Are there any other scoring errors made by Intern 3 that you are aware of?

A.   Not that I am aware of.

*(Author's Note: This moment or two of testimony could be almost lethal to EW's credibility. This would be even more likely if EW has been somewhat pompous or arrogant [we are not suggesting EW was] as big balloons tend to deflate rapidly when punctured. First of all, it would be necessary to establish just how many errors EW found in 3's scoring as the way it is stated, it is not clear. First of all, there is either a transcription error or EW has made a misstatement in saying "there was one scoring error on 3." We presume this was meant to be a scoring error on one of the subtests. Then as nearly as we can determine, EW finds two errors on comprehension and one error on the information subtest. However, the way the section reads, conceivably there could be a fourth scoring error, the one "on 3," whatever that was intended to mean. If the statement was as transcribed, of course this is another example of an erroneous statement made by EW, obviously a slip of some kind but nonetheless, if a patient did it, it would be taken as a sign of cognitive dysfunction. In this instance there is no self-correction either. However, referring back to the consultant's report, it should be noted that there is also the scoring error on the arithmetic subtest which apparently this outstanding expert did not detect. There is the glaring error in translating the raw score into a scale score of seven rather than twelve on the comprehension subtest which is acknowledged later in the testimony and the substantial error in calculating the I.Q. for P1 even based on the scores 3 had recorded, and the even larger error or discrepancy of I.Q. when the I.Q. is recalculated based on the corrected scale scores. Defense counsel does a good job of obtaining EW's statement that the three or four errors are all the errors he found although he had reviewed the scoring, and that there is nothing very significant in these errors. When forearmed with the knowledge that there are errors on a test such as the WAIS, counsel should always either subpoena or request that the witness bring with them a copy of the manual, so*

*that these errors can be demonstrated on cross-examination by having the witness read from the manual. The alternative is if one is going to be calling either a rebuttal or a consultant expert to have them read the portions of the manual that would be relevant. In any event, while a jury may tolerate one or even two wrong statements by an expert, as the errors pile up, the credibility of the expert fades away frequently to zero. Obviously one is reluctant to rely very much on an expert who makes numerous mistakes or who relies on material provided by someone who makes numerous mistakes. The testimony goes on to the testing by 8 and again, EW finds only one error whereas the consultant's report points out several scoring errors as well as several clear cut and some ambiguous errors of administration of the test.)*

Q. And now with regard to Intern 8, did you examine the tests which she administered to see whether they were properly administered and scored?

A. Let me go back and check one other thing on 3 because I have handled so much material lately I just don't remember.

Here is the sheet I was looking for. No. There were no problems with that.

And with Intern 8, I do not remember any problems but there may have been.

Yes, there was one problem in which she counted one point too high and it lowered the picture arrangement score, the age-graded picture arrangement score, from a 12 to an 11. And that was all.

Q. Dr. EW, in connection with your work in these cases were you given the psychological testing performed by Dr. J in December of 1981?

A. No.

Q. You have never heard of that?

A. It's the first I have heard of it.

Q. In particular, have you been given the opportunity by those persons representing P1 to examine and analyze the WAIS which was given to him on that date?

A. I have not.

Q. And, of course, you have seen none of the underlying data with regard to that examination?

A. No.

Q. I have used a shorthand expression, that is I have referred to a test as the WAIS, but you understand what that is?

A. I do.

*(Author's Note: Someone's credibility has to suffer when it is revealed that there was cogent information such as prior testing or prior examination which obviously was obtainable but which was not obtained or not even learned about by the witness. Either the interviews were inadequately conducted in failing to find out about this prior examination and in fact a prior visit to that hospital, or the interviewers attempted to find this out and were deceived by P1, or the other alternative which defense counsel may have somewhat hinted at, is that plaintiff's counsel knew of and/or had possession of the prior testing and did not provide it to the experts he was calling upon which is not likely to enhance his credibility in the eyes of the jury.)*

Q. That is the Wechsler Adult Intelligence Scale, which is a commonly administered test battery, is it not?

*(Author's Note: We would call attention to what defense counsel is doing here which we strongly recommend, that is that he not commit the sin of unexplained jargon that so often characterizes the expert witness. Here he is taking pains to make sure that the term WAIS is just a shorthand way of describing the Wechsler Adult Intelligence Scale.)*

A. The Wechsler. It's a hard "C."

Q. And is that a test that someone in your position is familiar with?

A. Yes.

Q. Now, let's talk generally about the neuropsychological tests that you have described at some length earlier. These tests, I gather, are collectively designed to allow a competent person in your field to draw some meaningful conclusions about how an individual is mentally functioning; is that correct?

A. No, they are not collectively designed. In other words, these are not tests that come from a single source where somebody says, "Well, now, I'm going to make a battery that will do everything," but rather this is a, I have selected out of the many, many tests available out there those tests that I felt would be most useful to me in understanding the nature of P1's problem, P2's problem, given the fact that they already had other tests that, had already taken other tests, such as the Wechsler Adult Intelligence Scale, which cover other areas of neuropsychological functioning.

Q. Dr. EW, what I attempted to ask you was whether the tests which you selected and gave, assuming that they were properly administered and interpreted by you, would tell you how P1 or P2 was functioning at the time the tests were given.

A. Yes.

Q. Now, the same thing would be true, wouldn't it, with regard to those specific tests given by Dr. 4's interns or Dr. 6's technician, assuming those were properly done?

A. Assuming those were properly done and the relationship was adequate and the examiner had helped the patient to perform at his best at that time.

*(Author's Note: This statement appears to be incorrect. The WAIS manual does not permit the examiner to help a patient to perform at his best. It does provide for limited assistance under some circumstances but is very clear that beyond that, no help is to be given. Therefore, if the examiner is going out of his way to help the patient to perform at his best, in violation of the instructions in the manual, one cannot legitimately apply the norms that have been obtained for the test and therefore the test is of virtually no use, particularly if one is using the best performance to estimate prior levels.)*

Q. Yes.

Now, measuring how P1 is performing in 1983 or 1984 or 1986 does not directly measure how P1 performed earlier in his life, does it?

A. It does not.

Q. And the same thing is true with regard to P2?

A. That's right.

Q. Therefore, if part of the goal is to decide whether P1's present condition—whatever that condition actually is—was caused by his exposure to paints and solvents, you have to determine what his condition was before the exposure to paints and solvents took place, don't you?

A. Yes, you have to make, in most cases, because we cannot go back and administer these tests retroactively, we have to do it on the basis of estimates based on historical information, what old tests are available, and the evidence in the current testing of prior functioning.

Q. And in the jargon of your business, you refer to that as the measurement of deficit, correct?

A. No, I'm not talking about the measurement of deficit now. I'm talking about estimating premorbid level, which you need to do in order to measure deficit.

Q. Then if you must or need to measure a person's—You have referred to premorbid ability. If I called it original ability, would we be talking about the same thing.

*(Author's Note: We would not recommend using terms such as "original ability," as this is probably not measurable at all, given any kind of present methodology. We would prefer use of "pre-morbid level of functioning" or avoid "pre-morbid" altogether and refer to "prior level of functioning.")*

A. Fine, fine. Original endowment is sometimes an expression I use.

Q. Fine. If you want to determine what a person's original ability is, I understand you can do it one of two ways. If you have a direct way to test it, such as a prior test score, that's very helpful; correct?

A. Yes.

Q. And if you do not have some direct way of measuring the original endowment, then you have to make an estimate?

A. Yes.

Q. Now, referring to that process as making an estimate, are we talking about just that, that is making our best guess as to what that original endowment was?

A. Yes. It's our best guess because we cannot, we do not have information available to know how good the person really was. The best we can do is say how good the indicators would lead one to believe, so that, for instance, P1 could have had superior premorbid, or original ability, and had been one of these kids who just floated through school and just horsed around on his tests so that his scores do not rise above high average. And there are very bright people who have done that and who leave no traces of their brightness behind them unless for some reason you come across it.

*(Author's Note: Here the witness is just speculating about why P1's performance was not better than it was and he has, so far as we know, no basis for those speculations in the case of P1. However, one might still make something out of it if one wants to pick up on the phrase "Just horsed around on his tests," because if he is a person who just horsed around on his tests before, there is no way to be sure that he is not just horsing around on his tests now.)*

So we don't know how bright he might have been and, therefore, our best guess is that he is at least high average. It's like somebody running a race. If you run a six-minute mile, you know, if you have run it once in your life, know that that person can run, has run a six-minute mile. You don't know whether with training and practice they may have been able to run a four-minute mile. But once you have evidence for the six-minute mile, you know that they have done that. And this is the same case here. We have evidence of high average functioning but we can only guess as to whether it would be any higher.

Q. Thank you for your observations, Dr. EW. My question to you was: if you don't have direct evidence of the original endowment, then it's true that you must make a best guess or an estimate; is that correct?

A. If you don't have direct—Yes, if you have no direct evidence at all. That is what I was talking about. We have no direct evidence of anything better than high average in P1's case.

Q. And whether any guess or estimate of original ability level is valid depends on the ability and willingness of the examiner to develop meaningful information about a person's prior life, doesn't it?

A. In part. It depends a lot, it varies from case to case. It depends a lot upon— For instance, if a person is a physician or a lawyer, you don't have to develop a lot to know that at least they were capable of a college education. So it varies.

Q. Well, with regard to a person that you have described as a working man, such also a P1, wouldn't the validity of your guess or estimate of his original ability depend on how much meaningful information about his prior life you obtained?

A. To some extent. There is a point at which you don't need a lot more.

Q. Dr. EW, do you have (one of EW's publication's) in front of you?

A. (Comments title)

Q. I refer you to page—

A. Uh-huh.

Q.—in which you are discussing the rationale of deficit measurement.

A. Uh-huh.

Q. (Here DC reads a passage in which EW has made among others, the following points:

Appropriateness of data from which premorbid ability is estimated is very important. In the best performance method sensitive attention to qualitative features of the test performance, good history which includes contact with family and other information sources including employers and schools is required.)

A. Yes.

Q. I accurately quoted from that?

A. Oh, yes.

Q. And you still believe that?

A. Yes.

Q. Now, in that regard, your neuropsychological report on P1 is dated May 27, 1984, is it not?

A. Uh-huh. Yes. That is the report.

Q.  Now, incidentally, it appears from the text of the report that the examination upon which you are reporting actually took place about 11 months earlier—

A.  Yes.

Q.—that is, in the first week of July, 1983.

A.  Yes.

Q.  Now, is that your custom and practice, to wait this length of time before writing a report after an examination such as this?

A.  No, it is not.

Q.  And do I gather correctly that at the time that you wrote this report you were relying solely on your memory and on your notes of the examination which occurred almost a year previously?

A.  Yes.

Q.  Fine. Now, I would ask you this, Dr. EW: on May 27, 1984, when you wrote this report concerning P1, did you have any information from which you could make a direct measurement of his original ability level?

A.  On that date the information I had was that he had been a shop steward, and I had Dr. 8's test data, which clearly indicated that he was performing at high average levels on those tests that are most likely to not change with brain damage, so that I was able at that point to estimate that he was at least of high average ability. Three of the verbal subtests, comprehension similarities and arithmetic, were all performed well within the high average range. And I had that information, and with that—plus the fact that he had been a shop steward—You don't have to have an infinity of information. I had sufficient I had this test information that demonstrated high average functioning in several areas.

*(Author's Note: First of all, it should be noted that which subtests "hold" [do not change] and which do not "hold" is a matter of controversy in psychology [see Volume II, Chapter 11]. We would note further that EW makes another error here inasmuch as P1 was not tested by 8 but by 3. Again, this error is not self-corrected. One might want to call it to the jury's attention by a question such as, "Doctor, didn't you make a mistake there when you said you had Doctor 8's test data?" Then the testimony goes on to state he was performing at high average levels on tests not likely to change with brain damage. This is not correct because he performed on that testing rather poorly on the information subtest, which is one of those generally acknowledged (and acknowledged in print by this witness) as one less likely to be affected by brain damage, and indeed, one that may be one of the best estimates of pre-morbid ability. Then there is the declaration that three of the subtests were well within the high average range which is not correct as of that testing date. Comprehension, we know, was a scale score of twelve, which if it is in what can be considered a high average range at all, is barely within it, not well within it. And arithmetic we know was a scale score of eleven which is not in the high average range at all, under any definition, so that again there are misstatements and misinterpretations of data by this highly credentialed expert. It is also of value to note and bring out in the testimony that the expert here specifies that these tests were all "performed" within the high average range. So that once again, we are talking about*

*performance as the gauge of ability, thus, again emphasizing the importance of his prior performance.)*

Q.  Perhaps we are having—

A.  So that is what you call direct information I had that direct, that data.

Q.  Dr., isn't it correct that in your (publication) you distinguish that sort of analysis from direct information, and that what you are really talking about in your prior and that what you answer is an indirect estimate of premorbid functioning?

A.  The indirect, the indirect will come from a variety of sources.

Q.  Yes. But perhaps we are having an auditory or comprehension difficulty here, but I thought I asked you whether at the time you wrote this report you had any direct information—

A.  Of premorbid functioning?

Q.  Exactly.
    Did you have any direct information?

A.  Yes. I had—I repeat. I had the evidence of premorbid functioning from Dr. 4's exam and from the fact that this man had been a shop steward, which means that he had risen somewhat above his peers and at a relatively young age.

Q.  Dr., again I ask you: doesn't direct information for a direct measurement of deficit require some sort of prior test results?

A.  No. You mean to have just the specific test results?

Q.  And isn't it true—

A.  I guess, okay, technically, I'll give that to you, technically it does.

Q.  I'm trying to understand what you wrote at Pages _____ and _____ of your—.

A.  Technically it does, it would require that.

*(Author's Note: Note that DC here has stubbornly persisted in his line of questioning despite the expert's numerous distracting, avoidant answers until he finally obtained a grudging confession that his point is correct. It is rarely good for a witness to have an answer such as this dragged out of him. It seems as though he has been trying to conceal the truth or been unwilling to grant that which is true. He would have been much better off to simply grant immediately that he did not at that time have direct evidence.)*

Q.  Now I go back. Did you have any such direct information?

A.  No, I did not have that kind of direct information.

Q.  So you were forced into the situation of making your best guess, or estimate, based upon the fact that he was a shop steward; and you looked at some results that 8 had developed in her test?

A.  That's right.

Q.  All right. Now, you mentioned in your direct examination relating to P1 that at some time you came into possession of some test given during school of general intelligence for P1.

A.  That was made available to me today for the first time.

Q.  That is what I was going to ask you because when I looked through your files on both P1 and P2 there is not in those files one piece of information concerning school performance, military performance or a job performance other than at company; isn't that correct?

A. That's right.

Q. Did you make any attempt to develop any information, such as school records, military records or job performance records, before writing your report for P1 dated May 1984?

A. No. On this I honestly do not know whether I had requested—I usually as a matter of course, when I take on a case like this, request the old school records and service records and I, frankly, do not remember whether I requested them or not.

Q. In my review of your files in this I did not see any such request.

A. It would not have been a written request. It would have been a telephone request.

*(Author's Note: The language "as a matter of course" is important here as indicating that EW does consider this kind of information important, otherwise why would he ask for it as a matter of course. It is also very clear that he drew his conclusions in this case without this information that he usually requires. Inasmuch as EW has been presented and presents himself as a "real pro" one could ask a question to point up the fact that if the request was made in writing, it would not be necessary now to try to rely on EW's obviously inadequate memory concerning this matter. Further, making the request in writing is more efficient from a standpoint that sometimes something jotted down from a telephone conversation gets overlooked or forgotten and the fact that with a written request made one can put a tickler on it to check again in two or three weeks to see if the information has been obtained. Also, it might be interesting to inquire, in view of the fact that EW has done another examination about a week ago, if he did not become aware at that time that this routine information was apparently not contained in the file, and why would this not alert him to again attempt to get it.)*

Q. And that is true with regard both to P1 and with regard to P2?

A. Yes.

Q. Now, apparently, then, when you wrote your opinion, report, dated May of 1984, the information upon which you relied in arriving at your opinion that P1 was a high average person before he began working with paints and solvents was the fact that he was a shop steward and had some test scores which you considered high on the examination performed by 8.

A. No. They were not test scores that I consider high, Mr. DC. Those are test scores that were well within the high average range as given by the standards and the norms for his age group for the Wechsler Adult Inteligence Scale. It was not my opinion at all. That was given by his performance. That is the range in which his performance fell, high average.

*(Author's Note: EW's credibility should be severely impaired here. Recall, he stated that he rescored the tests but as we know, he did not discover the error on the arithmetic subtest which reduced the raw score from fourteen to thirteen. Not a great deal was made of this in the consultation report because based on the regular norms, the change from fourteen to thirteen did not change the scale score. However, as EW is now utilizing age group norms rather than the*

*standard norms, the error becomes very significant because for P1's age group, a raw score of thirteen is a scale score of eleven rather than twelve and therefore is not by any definition in the high average group but is clearly simply average and is not as EW has been asserting all along, one of the basic props on which the conclusion of high average ability can be predicated. EW cannot dismiss this error as minor as it obviously makes the difference between being in his terms "high average" or just average. If the witness attempts to assert on this that it was after all only a difference of one second, the reader may recall that a correct answer within 10 seconds gets a time bonus, whereas from 11 to 60 seconds does not, and though the correct answer was given, the time noted is 11 seconds but nevertheless 3 had given the time bonus. If the witness attempts to assert that after all, it was only one second, this would open the whole field to argue that after all the difference between 12 and 11 is only one also. Also, again, note that EW continually refers to "performance." This is a point the defense will want to repeatedly make, that it is by his performance that you shall know him, because all of the evidence of his prior performance is that it was generally poor and definitely highly variable.)*

Q. With that correction, then, as to my terminology: was there anything else upon which you relied in arriving at your opinion which you gave in May of 1984 that P1 was high average?

A. I'll have to go back and take a look and see what else there was in the test data. That was awhile ago.

No. His performance on the verbal reasoning tests and on the arithmetic tests were the three specific indicators on which I relied, and the history I had supported the conclusion quite comfortably.

Q. And have you told us everything that, as of the date you wrote the letter, which in your opinion supported that conclusion?

A. Uh-huh. I'm not adding the hunting instructor because I don't know what level of expertise and capacity one needs to be a hunting instructor.

Q. Well, you have anticipated my next question because I want to know what level of expertise you believe is required of a shop steward in a facility such as this. Tell the jury what a shop steward does.

A. I believe the shop steward is the union representative.

Q. And what does his job entail?

A. And to the best of my knowledge—and I haven't made a study of this, it really is a lay knowledge—the shop steward is responsible for communicating between the members and the union. I believe the shop steward may be responsible for collecting dues, and I think he has to be an effective communicator. Probably there are times when he has to be an effective organizer, as well; and I also believe the shop steward helps the union members when they run into particular kinds of problems with management, or begins that.

Q. Is it your opinion that all shop stewards are of high average intelligence?

A. I have no opinion on that.

Q. Is it your opinion that while P1 was performing his functions as shop steward that he was able to do so satisfactorily?

A. Well, let me see what I know about that. That, I don't know.

Q. Do you know when he became a shop steward?

A. No, I do not.

*(Author's Note: In the above series of questions and answers, the ground is cut out from under another one of the few indicators EW relied on as to high average pre-morbid functioning and shows up EW as someone who is more or less talking through their hat on an issue about which they really do not know much. Interestingly, it starts out by EW stating, he would not base anything on the hunting instructor role because of lack of knowledge of the level of expertise and capacity needed for that. Then in the long paragraph about the shop steward, he admits he doesn't really know, all he has is lay knowledge and is not very sure of that as evidenced by use of tentative terms such as "may," "think," "probably," "believe," so that it is quite apparent that EW really does not have a very clear or firm picture of what is involved. Surely, if this was to be used as a basis for estimating pre-morbid abilities, one would have expected a highly competent and conscientious professional would have gone to the effort to find out what level of skills and abilities were required. Even if he had, he is forced in the next question to admit that he does not know that all shop stewards are of high average intelligence, therefore cannot say that holding such a position signifies high average intelligence. If there was any credibility on this issue, it is destroyed by the next two questions which show that EW does not even know whether P1 was performing satisfactorily as a shop steward or for how long he had been doing it. It is less important on this issue what the job actually entails and how well P1 was doing it than it is to highlight the fact that EW has gone off using this as a basis for a highly important conclusion, having failed to get anything remotely resembling the kind of information he would have needed in order to use it for that purpose. Here, EW seems to provide an illustration of confirmatory bias.)*

Q. Do you know how long he had been working there and theoretically been exposed to solvents and paint fumes when he became a shop steward?

A. That, I would have to look.

Do you want me to look in the records?

Q. Yes, if you have any record of that. If that was important to you, I would like to know it.

A. I don't know exactly, no, I do not know when he became a shop steward. I did not follow that.

Q. Don't you agree that a neuropsychologist is best able to do the job of estimating original ability level if the broadest base of data possible is obtained?

A. Where it's called for. It depends upon how much information you have.

The thrust of that statement has to deal with persons who are so demented that they cannot perform well on anything and you, therefore, need to go into the history to piece out what they might have been premorbidly.

When you have somebody who demonstrates on the kinds of tests that P1 demonstrated high average ability, then the requirement of going to the history is much less. If he had performed at low average levels on everything, then it would have been much more important for me to have gone into the history. But given that the data was there, that he had run the six-minute mile, so to speak, that he could perform at high average levels, then the need to look further becomes much less.

*(Author's Note: It should be made clear that psychological tests do not measure with the accuracy or reliability of a stop-watch.)*

Q. Thank you, Dr. EW.

I refer you to your (publication). Would you turn to page _____, please.

A. Uh-huh.

(Here DC quotes a passage to the effect that even a wide data base does not assure accurate judgments, but can appreciably reduce errors.)

A. Yes, I do.

Q. (Here DC reads a portion indicating that information about educational and work experience may be the best source of information about original intellectual potential.)

A. Yes, I do.

Q. And in this case, in fact, both of these cases, with P1 and with P2, at the time you wrote these reports you had absolutely no information concerning these patients' educational experience; isn't that correct?

A. That is right.

Q. And you go on to say on the next page, as well, that [here the material contains EW's observation that military records can provide important information].

A. Yes.

Q. And, likewise, for both of these individuals you didn't have that military information, did you?

A. I did not.

I had some—I didn't have the military records. I had some information.

Q. In that regard, Dr. EW, have you had an opportunity to review that, even as you sit here today, for either one of these two individuals?

A. Yes.

Q. Their military history?

A. I have glanced over it and we have talked about it.

Q. When did you do that?

A. This morning.

Q. I'm going to come back to the military history in a minute and ask you some specific questions about that.

A. All right.

Q. Now, as a matter of fact, at the time you wrote these reports for P1 and for P2 you relied in large measure on what you describe in your publication as the best-performance method of estimating a person's original ability level.

A. That's right.

Q. Now, that method, as I understand it, requires you to make the basic assumption that the performance level on any single test provides a reasonable estimate of a person's original ability on all other kinds of intellectual tasks?

A. That's right.

Q. Now, under that line of thinking, then, if someone scores high on a test of a specific intellectual function, that person should perform at the same general level on all other functions?

A. That's right, within a certain given error range. And it also depends on the function. This does not hold true for memory tests, for example. This does not hold true for attentional tests or for some other tests. But for most of the tests and the tests that P1 scored high on, it does hold very true.

Q. And if a person, using that same line of thinking, doesn't perform equally well across the board, so to speak, that is evidence to you of disease or cultural deprivation or emotional disturbance or something like that; isn't that correct?

A. Or it could be inattention, poor school work, something like that. There is usually something to account for it.

Q. But, Dr. EW, aren't normal people infinitely variable in their skills? For example, if someone on the jury is adept at fixing an engine, does that mean that that same person is skilled at writing a poem, for example?

A. We are not talking about writing poems, we are not talking about creativity now. We are talking about certain basic skills. If somebody is very clever about fixing electrical things, let's say, the chances are they are not stupid about practical reasoning and that they, chances are, given no particular problems in their life and an adequate opportunity at education, that they will have a reasonable vocabulary level, and chances are that they will be able to do basic math, the math that at least an average person can do, or person of high average ability.

Q. Are you saying, Dr. EW, that someone who is skilled at and good at humanities subjects in college, is going to do well across the board in science, physics, math, etc.?

A. No, I'm not saying that. I'm talking about ability, I'm not talking about skills. I'm talking about ability as we measure on these ability tests, such as the Wechsler Adult Intelligence Scale. I'm not talking about areas of specialized knowledge.

But if somebody does have the ability, for instance, to be able to write a learned paper about philosophers, this is generally somebody who spells well, who has got a good background in history, who can do math and who can put the puzzles together at a better than average level. And you will have to remember that the tests on which we are measuring them are tests that presumably *(Author's Note: "Presumably" indicates this statement has not been validated)*, a person can do well on without having had specialized training, in that area, and so this is how I am measuring people.

*(Author's Note: The argument EW is making is based on the following logic. He does better than average at cognitive task X. Therefore, he should do about as well on all other tests. Therefore, his ability on all cognitive things was previously above average. Therefore, if he now does not do about this well on some other tests, that shows he is impaired [has suffered a loss]. The counter-argument is that if he always showed considerable variability in performance, there is no reason to expect him to be different without any impairment [loss]. It is a widely accepted truism in psychology that the best predictor*

*of what someone will do is what they have done in the past. What can be brought out here is that the first argument, which is EW's position in this case, would incorrectly predict the past from the present. That is, for P1, school and military performances should have been high average according to this best estimate method. In contrast, the second or counter-argument correctly predicts the present from the past, that is, a high degree of variability on tests from the past, and also could predict the past from the present, that is, the present performance could predict a high degree of variability in performance in the past. In terms of what this lawsuit is all about, it seems clear that P1 is not any different than he was before the solvent exposure. That is, all of the objective records obtainable or obtained, show that for all of those times in his life he performed above average   on some things, average on some things, below average on some things and   way below average on some things. Also relevant to this argument is the statement of Professor Wechsler in the* Measurement and Appraisal of Adult Intelligence, *Fourth Edition, The Williams and Wilkins Company, Baltimore, 1958 at page 31, "It is certainly true that a good auditory memory does not go with a good visual memory. Persons who can repeat a poem after one hearing often have difficulty in reproducing a picture or a design and great chess players who are known to have extraordinary powers of visualization have not shown unusual memory span for digits." And Wechsler cites a reference for the chess player statement. These arguments could also be applied to the six-minute mile example. It seems almost certainly the case that there are people who can run the mile at speeds above average who would not be able to perform the shotput at even average levels as speed and strength are not necessarily correlated).*

Q. It is not uncommon, is it, Doctor, to have differences of up to 15 to 20 points between individual verbal and non-verbal intelligence scores?

A. I'm sorry, but I find that those statistical games make no neuropsychological sense and I don't use them.

Q. Does that mean you won't answer my question or you just won't use it?

A. What that means is if you want to ask me whether it is common for there to be as much as one standard deviation between subtests—

Q. I'll use a standard deviation, if that is what is comfortable.

A. Yes, I'm very comfortable. That is neuropsychologically meaningful.

Yes, because that is within the normal probability range of variation and what that means is that if somebody has a score, let's say gets a high average score on one subtest, it is perfectly reasonable for them to get a score in the middle of the average range on another subtest. When I'm talking about ability, I'm talking about ability within a statistically definable range. I'm not saying if they get a score of 12 on this they will get a score of 12 on everything else.

Q. Let's talk about that for a moment. Don't you agree that by chance alone there is a certain, a variation between test scores which can be expected for even the most normal of people?

A. By chance alone, one in 20 people would have a 5-point variation between two tests, and that is by chance. One in 100 would have a 6-point variation.

Q. So I guess your answer to my question is, yes, by chance alone a certain amount of variation is expected in normal people?

A. It is expected. It is statistically infrequent.

Q. In fact, for practical purposes in the work that you do, it takes a difference of 4 scale points on the WAIS, for example, to even approach significance, doesn't it?

A. No. Five. I don't touch a significant difference short of 5 points. I do not identify a significant difference until at least 5 points, a 5-point subtest differential.

*(Author's note: This case was tried before publication of Matarazzo et al., 1988, showing that differences as high as seven or eight points were common in the standardization population.)*

Q. And, in your opinion, a difference of 4 scale points, then, isn't significant at all?

A. No. I would have to leave that in the realm of chance, chance variation.

Q. And in order for there to be a significant difference there has to be at least five scale points of difference?

A. That's right.

Q. In order to take it out of just chance?

A. Right.

Q. I know you haven't had a chance—pardon the pun—to look at the WAIS record of the tests performed by Dr. J in 1981.

A. Who is Dr. J? I have never heard of him.

Q. He is a physician, I gather, that administered a WAIS while P1 was being examined at _____ Hospital (1981 test).

A. A physician?

Q. A doctor.

At any rate, I gather that Mr. CA has not supplied you with these records?

A. (Witness shakes head.) No.

Q. I have to unhook myself from the microphone, Doctor.

A. I caught that.

MR. CA: May I see that on your way up?

THE WITNESS: I would love to know something about Dr. J's credentials. You don't know whether Dr. J is an intern or trainee or where he studied or anything?

*(Author's Note: One might want to pick up on a statement like this. Is EW implying that if the testing was done by an intern or trainee, he would not have much confidence in it? This would certainly be inconsistent with the use he has made of work of 3 and 8.)*

BY MR. DC: (continuing)

Q. No. Do you?

A. I have never heard the name.

(Discussion held off the record.)

(A short recess is taken.)

THE WITNESS: Of course, I'm not in a position to rescore, since you don't have all of the material, do you?

MR. DC: This material has been subpoenaed and made available to both sides.

BY MR. DC: (continuing)

Q. Dr. EW, while we were off the record I handed you a photocopy of what I'm going to ask you to assume is part of the record of _____ Hospital on P1. Now, so that the jury will understand: that is a summary sheet of the raw score and scaled scores for a WAIS performed in December of 1981; is that correct?

A. That's right.

Q. Do you see any scaled scores there for him that are of statistical significance to you?

A. You mean by "statistical significance"—

Q. The difference. That is a difference of five?

A. Yeah. There is a significant drop on picture arrangement.

Q. From what?

A. From his comprehension and similarities.

Q. And is that 5?

A. It is 5 and 6.

Q. What is his scaled score for comprehension?

A. It is 13.

Q. And what is his scaled score for—

A. Similarities is 12 and picture arrangement is 7.

Q. I want to go to the report again, which is dated in May of 1984. It's mentioned in this report that he is a high school graduate. Did you do anything to check that?

A. No, I did not. I had asked him and he said that he was. That was—And I had no reason at that point to doubt that.

Q. Do you doubt it now?

A. Yes. I understand that he did not complete high school.

Q. He also reported to you, did he not, that he had sustained what he described as a mild concussion in a car accident in 1975 or 1976?

A. Yes, he did.

Q. Dr. EW, you are aware, are you not, that closed-head injuries of the concussive type can cause organic brain damage?

A. Yes, I am.

Q. And, as a matter of fact, in your most recent publication you go to some lengths to describe the frequency with which that happens, do you not?

A. I don't know if I talk about the frequency so much as what happens with head trauma.

Q. What I'm curious about is: did you do anything whatsoever to follow up and obtain a medical history which would tell you objectively the nature and extent of what he described to you as a mild concussion?

A. No, I did not.

Q. Did you learn, for example, whether or not he had been rendered unconscious and, if so, for how long?

A. I would have to go back to my notes.

Q. Feel free to do so. If you made note of that, please tell us.

(Discussion held off the record.)

THE WITNESS: My memory is refreshed.

He said "concussion" but then described it as a whiplash, so I didn't carry it any further.

BY MR. DC: (continuing)

Q. Did you ever up to the present obtain any medical substantiation as to the nature and extent of that concussion?

A. No.

Q. Your report also mentions that he was undergoing therapy at the Veterans' Administration Outpatient Center here.

A. That's right.

Q. Did you ask him when he began that therapy?

A. No, I did not.

Q. Did you ask him when he ended that therapy?

A. I wasn't, I didn't see him at the time that he ended.

You mean this last time? No, I did not ask him this last time when he ended that therapy.

Q. Did you ask him for the reasons for that therapy?

A. I'm trying to think whether we discussed it or not. I know—and I don't remember where this knowledge comes from, whether it comes from his wife or from him—that he had defined problems as being post-traumatic stress syndrome.

Q. That is what he or his wife told you?

A. Yes. But I cannot, I do not have a memory, a clear memory of somebody saying, and who it was who said this.

Q. At any time up to and including today has Mr. CA given you or have you obtained from any source the records from the Veterans' Center?

A. No, I have not.

*(Author's Note: What counsel is doing here is painting a picture of an examiner who has not been very thorough. He has attributed the alleged brain syndrome in this case to the toxic solvents without having adequately investigated the extent and degree of the concussion which, obviously to anyone, could play some role in any cognitive problems that P1 was having, and he has failed to investigate the diagnosis at the Veterans Administration. The lawyer should be aware that in almost any case of mental problems where it is known that there has been prior treatment or is ongoing treatment the examiner who is thorough would as a matter of course consult with the therapist. This would seem to illustrate the problem of selectivity of the clinician in regard to the data they will attend to and seems also to suggest a confirmatory bias, a sort of "I have already made up my mind. I do not want to be bothered by any possible contradictory facts.")*

Q. Now, I want you to assume for purposes of my question that he was seeking therapy there for a post-traumatic stress syndrome.

A. Yes.

Q. Will you do that?

A. Well, this is what I understood.

Q. Yes. Now, are you familiar with DSM III?

A. Not very.

Q. What is DSM III?

A.  DSM III is the listing compiled by a group of psychiatrists of what they consider to be mental disorders and the names that they give them and the numbers that they attach to them for classification purposes.

*(Author's Note: This statement is not untrue, but it is not a complete and accurate description and one might want to bring that fact to the attention of the jury. EW makes DSM-III sound like some manual put together by an ad hoc group of psychiatrists as their own private conception of mental disorders. It totally evades the fact that this is the official diagnostic manual put out by the American Psychiatric Association and used by the overwhelmingly vast majority of mental health professionals in the United States. While it is important for the jury to know that is the status of DSM-III, it is equally important for them to be able to see that EW is not giving an accurate picture here.)*

Q.  Have you examined DSM III to see how post-traumatic stress syndrome is classified or described?

A.  No, I have not.

Q.  Have you compared the symptoms and/or signs for post-traumatic stress syndrome to those symptoms and signs that you have described P1 as having when you examined him?

A.  I haven't in a deliberate manner because, having worked at the V.A., and in particular at a time that post-traumatic stress syndrome was surfacing and working with psychiatrists and psychologists who were working with post-traumatic stress syndrome, the likelihood that the kinds of problems and the extent of the problems that P1 was showing could be accounted for by the depressive and anxiety features of post-traumatic syndrome simply did not seem appropriate.

Q.  I take it, then, your answer is that you have not examined DSM III to compare the symptoms described there?

*(Author's Note: This is a good example of the lawyer bringing the witness back to his question and getting a clear answer to it.)*

A.  No, I did not examine DSM III.

*(Author's Note: On this issue one would want to make sure that the jury is made aware of the fact that three of the main symptoms described for P1— memory impairment, trouble concentrating, and irritability—are associated with post-traumatic stress disorder in DSM-III. Clearly then, the statement that PTSD could not account for the kinds of problems that P1 was presenting is not correct. It certainly could account for those kinds of problems.)*

Q.  Now, in your direct testimony in describing your qualifications you said that you went to a recent symposium in Sweden.

A.  That's right. I think it was _____, but I could look at my records in my C.V. It may have been _____.

Q.  Would your problem in that regard be an example of short-term memory loss or retrieval problems?

A.  It's a retrieval problem.

MR. CA: Objection.

THE WITNESS: It was as originally stated.

BY MR. DC: (continuing)

Q. Thank you. Did that symposium have to do with the neurotoxicity of organic solvents?

A. Yes, it did.

Q. Was it actually one which was under the auspices of the World Health Organization?

A. No. This was under the auspices of the Swedish industrial health organization. I don't remember the exact name. But it was organized by the Swedish group that was doing neurobehavioral research under the auspices, I guess, of their Ministry of Industry, or whoever it is that takes care of industrial health; and it was primarily for Scandinavians.

Q. Are you aware of the conferences and the debate at those conferences of the World Health Organization on the subject of organic solvents and the central nervous system?

A. I'm aware that there have been some questions raised. I'm not aware that they necessarily come from World Health Organization conferences.

Q. Specifically, in the case, or in the course of your research into this area, have you read the publications from the World Health Organization on this subject?

A. I don't believe so, and I don't know what the publications are. I would have to see them and then I could tell you.

Q. The articles which you cite in your treatment of industrial toxins in your (publication) seem to be all from either Denmark, Sweden or Finland.

A. Uh-huh.

Q. Is that correct?

A. That's right.

Q. In the course of your scientific work, since you wrote that book, have you kept up with the literature from those three countries to see how scientists in those countries are addressing these issues now?

A. I haven't kept up with those countries specifically. I have seen some of the more recent work from this country, and I'm trying to think whether I have some more recent papers—I'm not sure whether I have some more recent papers from the Scandinavian countries.

Q. So the answer is you have not kept up on the literature from the Scandinavian countries?

A. I'm not sure what I have seen that is dated _____ or later right now. I can't tell you off the top of my head.

Q. I notice that in your treatment of this subject in your publication you do not refer to any studies which criticize the methodology or conclusions of the Scandinavian research. Is that because you are unaware of such literature?

A. I do not recall seeing any that directly criticize the Scandinavian work at the time my publication went to press.

Q. Because you know now, as of 1986, that there is a substantial body of that criticism, don't you?

A. I don't know how substantial the body is. I do know of two papers that have been critical, one financed by, one of the big companies, the paper—and there are some problems in the paper

*(Author's Note: There may be a chance here to demonstrate the use of a double standard by the expert as he is asserting there are some problems, presumably methodological, in the cited article, and while we have not gone into and don't wish to get entangled with the criticisms of the Scandinavian literature, there are numerous flaws in those studies and in attempting to apply them to this case. One could focus on some of the major flaws and bring out the fact that nevertheless, EW was willing to rely on those findings. Interestingly, in light of the comment above, the three outstanding features of the painters syndrome according to the Scandinavian literature at that time were impairments of memory and concentration and irritability, symptoms that are, at least according to DSM-III, clearly associated with post-traumatic stress disorder.)*

—and the other that I have only glanced at that criticizes the Danish work. But the Danish contributions have been quite weak. The bulk of the contributions have been from Sweden and Finland.

Q. And I take it you are not aware at this time of any reanalysis or reassessment coming out of Sweden or Finland?

A. No. I would be very interested in seeing them and having them. If you could give me the references, I would appreciate having them.

Q. Did I understand you to say that you would generally expect verbal functioning of an individual who has brain damage to be minimally affected?

A. I said that there are certain verbal skills and functions that tend to be—I didn't use this word before but I'll use it now because it's a good one—that tend to be relatively robust when there is not focal damage involving the speech centers. And verbal functions tend to hold up well with many kinds of neurological disorders because they are used so much. By the time somebody is 35, 38 years old, they have been talking for 35, or 34 or 37 years and talking every day and using these same skills over and over and over again, so that these functions, again, if there is not, if there are not pronounced focal lesions right in the speech area, tend to remain and often serve as the best residuals, the best guideposts to what that person may have been prior to whatever happened that diminished their functioning.

Q. Did you find any evidence of any focal damage to speech centers for either one of these men?

A. No.

Q. My note says, to your direct examination, with regard to P1, indicates that one of the bases for your arriving at an opinion that he was of high average original intelligence was that he had a high average arithmetic score.

A. That's right.

Q. Are you referring to a scaled score on one of the WAIS-R's which you have reviewed?

A. Dr. 3 did not use age-graded scores. When I converted P1's raw score into an age-graded score so that I was comparing him to men of his age, that is men of 35, rather than to an age group in the range of 21 to 34, his was high average, his scaled score technically became 12.

*(Author's Note: As pointed out above, when the score on the arithmetic subtest is corrected for the scoring error that was made, the raw score is thirteen instead of fourteen, which for people in P1's age group still equates to a*

*scale score of eleven and not twelve. So EW is continuing to proceed on an er-*
*roneous basis. We realize that the attorney is not carrying around in his head a*
*table of scale scores for the WAIS. For this reason, we would stress the impor-*
*tance either of making sure that the witness brings the manual so one can look*
*at it, or of having a consultant available in the courtroom, outside the court-*
*room or by phone to check on the accuracy of any scores cited by a witness,*
*particularly if they are not in line with what one has expected.)*

Q. Did you have some sort of normative table that you referred to?

A. Yes, I used the normative table in the Wechsler manual.

Q. Then his arithmetic score became what?

A. 12.

Q. Instead of 11?

A. That's right, when comparing him to people his own age. I do not believe in comparing a person of one age to another age group, when possible.

Q. That is what I thought you had done. Now I want to discuss that.

A. Sure.

Q. So on the basis that he had a 12 on the scaled score on the WAIS-R arithmetic subtest—

*(Author's Note: It might have been better to phrase this question a little*
*more cautiously, perhaps in terms that the arithmetic score was "one of the*
*bases," which might have avoided the opportunity for the witness to deny the*
*question as it was asked and go off on a lecture.)*

A. Right.

Q.—you concluded that he is of high average intelligence?

A. No. On the basis of a scaled score of 12 on arithmetic, a scaled score of 12, on comprehension—now, both of those scores are 75th percentile—and a scaled of 13 on the similarities—and similarities is about the 82nd percentile, 84th percentile, something like that—it was on the basis of these three tests, not one indicator, but on—because one is much more likely to be due to chance—but on three, it was hard for me not to conclude that he had at least a high average original endowment.

Q. Perhaps you misspoke yourself but you said that he had 11 on the comprehensive subtest.

A. No, no. 12.

Q. You said he had a 12 on the comprehension subtest.

A. That's right.

Oh, yeah, I see what your problem is. That was 3's misscoring. You are looking there.

Q. He has a 7, doesn't he?

A. I know. That is a really gross piece of misscoring.

Q. You didn't tell us about that before.

A. No. I forgot about that.

I'll show that to you if you want to see. If you want to just compare him to even a younger group, you will see that a scaled score, that a raw score of 25 gives him a scaled score of 12, even for the younger group; and it's true for his age group, as well.

3 misscored.

Q. That is all well and good. Are there any other errors of this magnitude that you haven't told us about?

A. No, there weren't. I was only looking at my own scores and I forgot about 3 and I hadn't noted that. I can see now why you were so puzzled about my saying so definitely that he had these scores and why you didn't see where I was coming from.

Q. Because 7 definitely isn't 12?

*(Author's Note: Notice how counsel is keeping attention on this gross error and EW's omission of it so it will have time to sink in.)*

A. Because 7, that is not very good. But, no, he didn't have a 7 here, and he didn't have a 7 when tested on the WAIS at any other time, either. He had a raw score of 25, which translates for people both in the 21-to-34 age range and the 35-to-44 age range—It doesn't change in those two age ranges—it translates into a scaled score of 12, and there is no problem with that piece of data.

Q. What is the average? 10?

A. 10.
    Well, you have to think of it as a range, and it's the range, the middle 50 percent, which is 8, 9, 10 and 11, are within the average range.

Q. And 12 isn't within the average range?

A. No. 12 is high average, 75th percentile. 12 and 13 are high average.

Q. So you go two down from 10 and it is still average, and you go two up from 10 and it is high average?

A. Yes, because the average range covers the middle 50 percent of the population and, therefore, is the largest range of all.

Q. Isn't one of the things which people in your business worry about that unsophisticated people will take these scaled scores and make more out of them than they are actually?

A. That is why I report out in terms of ranges, rather than numbers, whenever possible.

Q. As a matter of fact, there really isn't any difference at all between a 9 and 11 is there?

A. Statistically, no. No. What a 9 means is that it's a range, it represents a range of scores. The range of scores represented be a score of 12 is higher than the range of scores represented by a score of 7.

Q. In fact, a score difference of two is more likely than not a chance variation, isn't it?

A. That's right.

*(Author's Note: If a score difference of two is likely to be a chance variation, then the difference between ten which is the mean and twelve which EW is asserting shows above average performance would actually be within chance variation and therefore no significance should be attached to it. That is, it is not further from the mean than could be expected by chance.)*

Q. If I understood your direct testimony, one of the things which you thought very important was that P1 had difficulty in reciting the alphabet backward.

A. Uh-huh.

Q.  And it's your opinion, is it, that any member of this jury could, assuming they are normal, just start repeating the alphabet backward without making a mistake?

A.  It's my opinion and my experience that most people, including most, many people with known brain damage, are able to recite the alphabet backward, but different kinds of brain damage, are able to recite the alphabet backward—I have them start from R, they don't do the whole thing—with reasonable speed and not more than one or two errors.

Q.  But he only made one or two errors, didn't he?

A.  He only made one or two errors but he had seven pauses of five seconds or longer. And typically people do not take five seconds or more between the letters of the alphabet. If you stop and count out five seconds, you will see that it's a considerable length of time when it comes to running thoughts through your head.

Q.  And another item of information or test result that you thought was significant was that when you gave him a paragraph and asked him to repeat it that it came out slightly twisted.

A.  Uh-huh Yes.

Q.  Is that correct?

A.  Yes.

Q.  Well, Dr. EW, are you familiar with a game, I don't know whether they still play it, but you start at one end of the room and you whisper something to someone and you pass it on and see how it comes out on the the other end?

A.  Yeah, I sure am.

Q.  You are not suggesting to the jury that that sort of twisting, if you will, is evidence of brain damage, are you?

A.  I'm suggesting that there is a difference between whispering quickly while you are all giggling and telling a story slowly and enunciating it carefully and then repeating it again. And my support from that is in the decades of data on paragraph recall tests. Typically people who, with a normal recall for this kind of information, will on first hearing remember about half or a little bit more of the items, so that there will be a lot of dropout in the specific items, but there won't be distortions. Distortions are very rare in normative populations, and actually don't occur a lot with many kinds of brain damage, either.

Q.  In describing P1's present condition are my notes correct that you said it was best summed up in his being able to give at this time an inconsistent and inefficient performance?

A.  Yes.

Q.  Now, with regard to that, isn't it correct that an inconsistent performance is one of the hallmarks of giving less than good effort on tests, or one of the hallmarks of malingering?

A.  No, no, I don't think so. That has certainly not been my impression or experience.

Q.  I have to go back to your publication again,

(Here DC reads material to the effect that inconsistency in performance levels or between such levels and claimed disabilities except where related to physiological conditions is the hallmark of malingering.)

A. I do, but we are not talking about inconsistency of performance levels. We are talking about inconsistency within a particular function. It is like having a flickering light; it is on-again, off-again, within that function. But there is not an inconsistency of performance levels in the sense of his doing well on something that people with his complaint generally do poorly on and vice versa. That is what I'm talking about.

Q. How about inconsistency between one test results and another? Do you consider that a hallmark of—

A. You mean when the tests have been repeated?

Q. Yes, sir.

A. It can be due to malingering, and I have seen that. It may also represent something else, such as being particularly nervous or anxious at a given time, or what I suspect—and I have already addressed the problem of inconsistent test scores here because I was very struck by it, too, Mr. DC. And I did note that the bulk of the inconsistencies piled up when 7 was the examiner.

Q. Who?

A. 6's technician.

And knowing and seeing how skittish P1 was with me, skittish in the sense, this man is so painfully self-conscious of his deficits that it's not difficult to believe that if he is with somebody with whom he feels threatened or who he feels may be putting him down, who may not be supporting him enough to keep his anxiety down, that you would have those, that kind of emotional reaction and he would do poorer.

*(Author's Note: There were as many inconsistencies in repeat test performance in the data of Doctor 5 as there were when Doctor 6's technician was the examiner. EW seems to prefer to ignore this. This could be utilized perhaps to indicate the presence of some bias. Also, it might be noted that on the repeated subtests, P1 did better on one of the subtests—information—for the technician than he had done in the 1983 testing for 3. So this might not be consistent with the notion that he is threatening or putting P1 down, although it should be noted that normally on the WAIS, the information subtest is the first one given. However, there were also several subtests on which he did not do any more poorly with the technician.)*

Q. So, in essence, you have searched and found to your satisfaction an explanation as to why you should not take the inconsistencies in the test results at face value?

A. I'm not taking, I'm not taking those low scores at face value. I'm also going back to one of 5's remarks, and that is on one of the testing sheets she made a comment to herself, "He seems embarrassed." And that certainly showed up with me. He apologized repeatedly for his poor performances, or even when he was doing fairly well and he felt that he was doing poorly. This is a man who is painfully self-conscious.

BY MR. DC: (continuing)

Q. Doctor, have you had an opportunity to examine P1's actual performance in school, as reflected by his grades?

A. Well,—

Q. Just yes or no first. Have you had that opportunity?

A. Yes.

Q. When did you have that opportunity?

A. This morning.

Q. Did you see his _____ Junior High School grades from age 12?

A. I saw the grades, but you couldn't see what they are in because the transcript was so lousy.

Q. Did you see the results of the California Test of Mental Maturity which was given him at age 12?

A. I don't know. I didn't see a California Mental Maturity Test. I think I saw, what I saw was an Iowa Test that was given somewhat later.

Q. Were you shown his grades from _____ High School for his freshman, sophomore and junior years?

A. Those—I didn't see the others. I saw the _____ High School grades, and those are the ones where I saw the grades but it was very difficult to make out what he got what in.

Q. Regardless of what he got what in, did you observe that he got 18 D's, 5 F's, 4 C's and 4 B's and two of those were in P.E. and Typing?

A. I didn't count them, but if it was my kid, he would have to stay home and hit the books.

Q. Did you have an opportunity to examine the Iowa Test of Educational Development given him at age 17?

A. Yes, I did.

Q. And, again, this was just this morning?

A. Yes.

Q. Incidentally, on either the California Test of Mental Maturity or on the Iowa Test of Educational Development are you familiar with the subtests to the extent that you can say what areas are being tested within each subtest?

A. No.

Q. Do you know the populations which are—

A. I just go by title. No, I do not. I have not reviewed that in many years.

Q. Do you know the normative scores for those?

A. The normative scores, yes, when it comes to percentiles, within any age group, I know that the norms are based on that age group. So if he took the test as a Junior in high school, then the normative group was either 17-year-olds or high school juniors, I don't know which, but it would be an appropriate normative group.

Q. Were you given an opportunity to see the U.S. Army Aptitude Test results for this gentleman?

A. No.

I'm trying to think. No, I don't think so. And I would very much like to.

Q. Were you given an opportunity to examine the GED Test scores which were given to him while he was in the military?

A. No, but I would like to see them.

Q. And along that same line, were you given an opportunity see the _____ National Guard Aptitude Test results?

A. No. Are you going to make them available?

Q. Your Counsel has them and has had them for a long while. And, yes, I will be glad to make them available to you.

A. Okay.

Q. Did you do any personality testing during your examination?

A. No, I did not.

Q. Specifically, did you administer the Minnesota Multiphasic Personality Inventory?

A. I don't use it when there is an issue of brain damage because I don't think it is an appropriate instrument for known or even suspected brain damage.

*(Author's Note: This answer should be subject to a motion to strike as it does not answer the question asked. However, one might not wish to make the motion in view of the fact that EW here is stating that 3/Doctor 4 utilized a test which he considers inappropriate for cases of known or even suspected brain damage, further implementing the idea the 3/Doctor 4 test results should not be employed. However, because there is the opportunity to take advantage of the responses on the MMPI, one might still want to go ahead and strike this and simply leave the answer that EW did not use the MMPI.)*

Q. The answer is you did not use it?

A. That's right.

Q. In your opinion, Dr. EW, should non-board-certified neuropsychologists render opinions in cases like this?

A. It's an interesting question to ask because the boarding procedure is relatively new and not everybody who would qualify has availed themselves of the opportunity. I think in each case you would have to go into the qualifications of each individual person.

Q. Now, I want to talk about something pretty basic for a moment to make sure I understand something. Am I correct in my assumption that all human beings don't begin life equally intelligent?

A. To the best of our knowledge, this is true.

Q. Why not?

A. I can name some very specific things. I mean, the most obvious would be birth damage. There seems to be a hereditary component. We know that the nutritional status of the mother, and even the grandmother, will affect intelligence. There is some data that suggest that children, children who are conceived in the late spring and who have their period of the fastest neuronal development during the summer may tend to have, be born with some less potential because the summer season is apt to be a more dry season. There are a number of different kinds. I have just named a few things here that seem to contribute.

Q. So it's not necessary, then, for a man or a woman to experience some organic brain damage in order for that person to perform below average intellectually; is that right?

A. That's absolutely right.

Q. Because of, among other things, the hereditary factor you have just spoken to?

A. Right.

Q. I guess all I'm getting at is that it is no secret or surprise in your field that intellectual deficits can be handed down from generation to generation in the same family?

A. If we are talking about garden-variety dullness, but we are not talking about garden-variety dullness...(the rest of this answer is omitted as it mentions someone not involved in this case).

Q. Let's test that by looking at P2 for a moment. Now, I know that you weren't given his military records or his school records until today. That's correct, isn' it?

A. That's correct.

Q. Now, I want you to—Do you have those in front of you by the way?

A. No.

Q. Where are the ones that you did see? Who has those?

A. I presume Mr. CA has them. I don't even know if they are here.

Q. Did you look at them here in this office?

A. No.

Q. Now, I think that the question which started all of this actually had to do with Mr. P2, and I asked you whether you had had an opportunity to see his military and school records before today and you said no.
Are you now aware of how P2 actually did in school?

A. Yes. He was a poor student.

Q. Now, he actually reported to you—

A. —that he was a poor student.

Q. Let's look at that because that was your testimony on direct examination. You testified on direct examination that he told you that he had mostly D's with a few C's.

A. No, mostly C's with a few B's.

Q. Okay.

A. I'm sorry.

Q. Yes. And that is a big difference, isn't it?

A. Oh, boy, it sure is. I am sorry.

Q. Would that be an example of a comprehension problem or a retrieval problem?

A. Neither. That was an example of a slip while trying to read rapidly.

Q. Now, as a matter of fact, now that you have seen his records, instead of getting mostly C's and a few B's, you see that he got almost all D's and F's, with a few C's; correct?

A. Uh-huh. That's what I recall.

Q. And, as a matter of fact, he graduated 409th in a class of 447 at _____ High School correct?

A. That, I don't know. You have to tell me.

Q. Did you see on here that on his California Test of Mental Maturity he is noted to have an I.Q. of 87?

A. I'm sorry, as I said before, those I.Q. scores I find very meaningless.

Q. Did you see it?

A. There was a percentile there that I would be glad to talk about.

*(Author's Note: Again EW is refusing to acknowledge an objective fact.)*

Q. You can talk about whatever you want to. Did you see it?

A. I saw it.

Q. Did I accurately state that, that it is recorded here that he had an I.Q. of 87—

A. Yes.

Q. —in 1958?

A. Yes.

Q. And it is also recorded here that in 1961 on the Iowa Composite he was in the 37th percentile?

A. Okay. That's right. So that we know he is well within the average range, which runs from the 25th to the 75th percentile.

Q. So, in your opinion you can be functioning at a level where 74 percent of the population is functioning better than you and be functioning at an average level?

A. We are not talking about 74 percent. We are talking about 63 percent. If you are the 37th percentile, 63 percent of the population is doing better than you. But the World Health Organization defines the average range as between the 25th and the 75th percentile, so that any score that falls within that range is within—that is what average means, statistically.

Q. Did his school records come as a surprise to you?

A. Not particularly.

Q. Did his military records come as a surprise to you?

A. I didn't go through them in any detail.

Q. Well, let's do that now.

I'm going to read to you a portion of his military records and see whether this is something that you focused on when you reviewed them this morning, and this is the Medical Officer's—Well, first I'll read the Company Commander's report. Quote: "He is unable to perform the simplest maneuvers."

Now I'll read you the Medical Officer's reports. Quotes: "This 18-year-old recruit was referred to the Recruit Evaluation Unit by a Medical Officer because of his inability to adjust to service demands. His GCT score is 50. He has been aboard for 48 days and has completed three days of scheduled training in one regular company. According to the man's own statement accepted by the Board, he completed the 12th grade of school with an average scholastic record. His social adjustments were inadequate and his work history sketchy. He has never participated in organized social activities. He has been extremely nervous for several years. He joined the Navy to further his education. Recruit's progress and training was indicative of lack of aptitude for the Navy. He was noted to be personally unclean and was found to be unreliable and depressed. His grasp of instructions was poor and he responded to authority with tears and timidity. He frequently visited Sick Bay with complaints of nervousness. Appropriate medical examinations failed to reveal any disqualifying defect. He spent approximately one month in the

Recruit Evaluation Unit barracks while necessary dental work was being completed. His overall aptitude for training was rated as poor. Psychiatric evaluation revealed an emotionally labile, inadequate recruit with minimal self-esteem, minimal stress tolerance and marked anxiety."

Did that come as a surprise to you?

A. There are so many, so much that can happen when a kid is 18 and goes away from home for the first time, I cannot get overly excited about it because, you see, I also know that this is the same man who put in 16 years with company. And he must have been doing something or else they would have let him go long before that.

Q. And not only—Well, it's very hard to get excited about something you don't know exists; isn't that correct? You didn't know this existed until this morning?

A. Yeah. But, even so, it's, this can happen with a kid who apparently was immature and not ready to leave home or do much of anything at 18.

*(Author's Note: This is pure speculation because EW does not know anything about P2 at that time. Also it shows the witness rushing in with a statement that is not responsive to the question which simply asks if he knew of this military record, which is a yes or no question. But here the witness is rushing in to explain away these data which would be detrimental to plaintiff's case, so that it may be an illustration of testimony biased to help the plaintiff or an illustration of the kind of hindsight bias which was discussed in Chapter 5 of Volume I of this text.)*

Q. Were you given this morning or at any other time the records of the State of _____ Civil Service Examination on P2?

A. No, I haven't.

Q. Were you aware that prior to going to work for Company he was employed by the State of _____?

A. No. You will have to tell me about it.

Q. It was apparently not brought to your attention that in 1966 he was refused rehirement with the following remarks, quotes: "Employee was unable to perform basic arithmetic necessary in work, i.e. addition, multiplication, division, etc." Were you aware of that?

A. No, but I'm not surprised.

*(Author's Note: One might consider here a question like "Doctor, does anything surprise you or are you always able to fit it into what you already believe?")*

Q. I was wondering about that because my notes indicate that both you and P2 expressed some dismay when you examined him earlier this month that he was suddenly unable to do long division.

A. I didn't say long division, I said short division. I said he was unable—He would set the problem up correctly and he was unable to divide a one-place number into a two-place number. I believe that was my direct quote.

Q. And you found that meaningful?

A. He was surprised and I was surprised because that is about 3rd grade stuff and his arithmetic performance is probably 4th, 5th grade, something like that.

Q. At that time you did not know that it was reported in the State of _____ records that before he ever went to work at Company he was unable to perform
basic arithmetic, such as addition, multiplication and division?

A. No, I did not know that. I do know that he can do basic arithmetic, basic
addition and subtraction and multiplication.

Q. With regard to this practice effect that you discussed earlier with Mr. CA, I
understand that that is the effect of taking one test after another?

A. And you learn how to take it and you learn some of the answers, you remember some of the answers faster.

Q. According to you, one of the major difficulties with both of these men is
that they have learning difficulties; correct?

A. Uh-huh.

Q. So if they have learning difficulties, by definition you wouldn't expect
much practice effect, would you?

A. And I didn't see much.

Q. And you wouldn't expect to see much practice effect in any subsequent tests
that they took; isn't that correct?

A. That's right, by and large.

Q. Dr. EW, in your publication—you have an entire section on the causes of—
the major classes of brain disorder "(title of section)"?

A. Right.

Q. In that, in describing and discussing the major classes of brain disorders,
you go from (not over 40 pages); and it's in that section that you devote
about one-half of one page to industrial toxins, correct, of all kinds?

A. That's right.

Q. And you acknowledge that (numerous other conditions) all cause brain
disorders?

A. Yes.

Q. At any time have you made a thorough review of either P2's or P1's prior
medical condition?

A. No, I haven't made a thorough review. I have read physicians'—I have read
the reports, reviewed the reports of physicians who have done a thorough
review.

Q. I wanted to ask you about that because the only one that is noted in P2's
report is a Dr. OM. At least I didn't see another doctor mentioned as having
given you a report.

A. That, I had seen the report, though, from the medical school. It is Dr. M's
report. And there is JW's report—Well, if I don't have it here, I have it
probably someplace else, but I did review another medical report, at least
one other. It's probably Dr. Z's report.

MR. DC: Dr. EW, I think that is all I have at this time.

(A short recess is taken.)

BY MR. DC: (Continuing)

Q. Dr. EW, I do have another question, and that is: have you yourself done any
analysis to determine how often the, quotes, pattern, end quotes, of scores
which you have seen for P1 or for P2 appears in normals?

A. I myself have not.

Q. Then my next question is: have you seen any?

A. Wait a minute.

I'm sorry, I take that back, I myself have. I have not looked specifically for that pattern but I have studied a group of 22 National Guardsmen and they were re-examined by many of the same tests that I have talked about here, first at six months, at a six-month-interval, and then a year later; and I do know how they performed and this pattern simply did not show up in that group.

Q. Those National Guardsmen are supposed to be normals?

A. Yes. They are representative of, they are folks who are volunteers from the community into the National Guard.

Q. Have you published this data?

A. Some of it has been published in here already. My reliability data is in here. The basic data had been presented in _____ in June of 19___, at the _____ Conference, that year. But I have not, I simply have not found the time yet to turn it into the major paper it should be put into.

MR. DC: Thank you.

### CROSS-EXAMINATION

BY MR. DC2:

Q. Just following up, Dr. EW, on the question that Mr. DC just asked you: did you use the same battery on these National Guardsmen that you used on P1 and P2?

A. Many of the tests were the same. If you put together the tests that were used by Dr. 4 and his interns and myself, there is a large overlap between those tests. It wasn't the exact, same battery.

Q. It wasn't the same battery?

A. It wasn't the exact same, but a lot of—

Q. And just going from your statement about the fact that this pattern of deficits that you found fits solvent exposure: have you done any studies yourself to tell what type of solvent exposure, when you say "solvent exposure"?

A. No, I have not.

Q. In other words, you have no idea what type of solvent itself you are talking about; is that correct?

A. That's right.

Q. You don't have any idea how much time exposure is involved to create this pattern of deficit?

A. You mean in terms of what I read in the literature or in terms of—

Q. No. I'm asking in terms of your opinion.

A. In terms of my opinion?

Q. Yes.

A. No.

Q. Or what concentration of solvent is required?

A. No, I do not know concentrations.

MR. DC2: That is all the questions I have.

## REDIRECT EXAMINATION

BY MR. CA:

Q. Dr. EW, I have a few questions on redirect.

There were some questions that you were asked about the quality of the examiner at various settings and also the steps that you took to rescore the results of the raw data that you were given. Is it true that as far as the testimony that you gave us in your explanation of the, both your explanation of the results that you had reviewed from other examiners, that this testimony was based on your independent conclusion as to the meaning of those tests?

*(Author's Note: Nevertheless, even the raw data is unreliable if the examination was not completely performed. We know there were a number of scoring errors by 3 and in addition to scoring errors, there were some errors of administration of the test by 8. Even EW's rescoring, we know, contained errors. The rescoring missed the error on P1's arithmetic subtest and it missed the error on the calculation of his I.Q. based on the correct age rather than the erroneous age. However, the main point is that the tests were administered by people who were trainees and who were not skilled examiners and therefore little credence should be based on them even though they were rescored to eliminate some of the scoring errors. That would not compensate for any problems with administering the tests, including possible examiner effects. One must consider there may have been errors on some of the other tests where errors are not detectable by inspection as they are on the WAIS-R.)*

A. Yes. I worked from the raw data.

Q. There were also some questions about the source of your information in terms of coming up with the estimate of what we call premorbid and original endowment, and you indicated that as far as the factual information, one fact was that P1 was a shop steward in the work at company. Were there other facts or information that you were given, either by P1 or by P2, that you used to determine the premorbid functioning level?

A. The—I suppose that the fact that Mrs. P1 reported him as having been a leader and he regarded himself as being a leader might be taken into account there, too.

But, you know, that again fits in with the fact that he was shop steward and he was the guy who was responsible, vis-a-vis his crew and the union.

Q. Now, there were also some questions regarding the records for P1 as to his school performance, and there were some comments made about the lateness of your ability to review those records. My questions involve the substance of those records.

In your opinion, do the records of P1's school performance substantiate or reinforce your assessment of his premorbid intellectual functioning?

A. No, they don't. The impression that I'm given is that, like many boys in their middle-to-late teens and perhaps even earlier, this guy just wasn't interested in school, he didn't like it, he obviously didn't perform well. And my opinion is that he obviously was an under-achiever, he was performing under his ability level, and that's why they give tests. For example, if grades were good predictors of ability, then they wouldn't have to bother giving the tests. But because the teachers know that grades are not good predictors of ability, and we all know, you know, how restless and disinterested in school and so on teenage boys can be, we give them tests to see whether they are working up to snuff or not.

*(Author's Note: First of all one might want to know where EW got the impression that P1 wasn't interested in school and didn't like it. It might be worthwhile at this point to ask a question to establish the fact that if EW had been thorough and gone to the trouble of getting the school records, he would have had information from which he could have sked P1 some questions to determine the reasons for the poor grades. It is a good place to raise some questions to the effect that if EW had done a thorough job and obtained the school records, he would have known about the poor grades when he saw P1 and could have inquired as to the reasons for the poor grades and at least have some better basis than this sheer speculation that he is engaging in. Actually, there is evidence in the MMPI that EW is simply dead wrong on this speculation. Item 173 on the MMPI asks if he liked school, and on both occasions, March of 1983 and September of 1984, P1 marked this true. We might also add in regard to the last statement, that tests are given to see whether people are working up to snuff or not, that this is true. This is the reason the I.Q. tests were developed, to determine if a student who was performing poorly had the ability to do better, rather than to punish a disabled student for not doing well, as had been the tradition around the turn of the century. But it should be noted that it is a full I.Q. that is used for this purpose, not the score on a single or a couple of subtests. In other words the idea was to try to tap into a variety of mental abilities, not just a single mental ability in order to determine what the overall ability level was.)*

Q. Then, in your opinion, which would be a more reliable indicator of original endowment, the grades that a person got or the result of a standardized test score in terms of percentile?

A. More likely the ability test. But ultimately—Let me say this. Ultimately you can have instances where a kid does poorly on tests. We all know people who freak out on tests and they do much better in *(Author's Note: We think this should be "than")* their score. So ultimately when you are looking for an indicator, for something to hang your hat on, you look for more than one thing. And, you know, so that is why you come back again to the cluster of test scores that were repeated when he was an adult, no longer a skittish kid, as a strong peg to hang my hat on.

*(Author's Note: First of all, EW now appears to be saying that the tests are not valid when working with a "skittish kid." It seems to contradict the reason he has just given for giving the test to people while they are in school. However, he is also indicating that there are people who don't do well on tests. In that case, it seems the jury should not want to rely on tests to determine how P1 functioned in the past, but rather to look at his actual past performances. But, overriding all of this is the fact that we have, in P1's adult life, objective measures showing exactly the same pattern as he had shown when he was in school. These are in the military records and that performance is described in the consultation report, and it shows him once again ranging through the entire range of levels of performance from above average to average to below average to very much below average. So that EW's excuse here simply will not hold water.)*

*However, it may once again demonstrate the lengths to which EW is going to try to throw out all data that is contrary to the conclusions he has reached. This seems to be another example of confirmatory bias.)*

Q. Now, there was also some questions about a report of a mild concussion some time in 1974 or '75. And in looking at your notes I believe you recharacterized that as a whiplash?

A. This is what he told me. I cannot remember it. I can only reconstruct from my notes, and apparently I had asked him as I generally do: have you had any other, anything happen to your head? And he said he had a concussion. And I asked for the details and he said, "I had a whiplash." And whatever else he said, obviously did not impress me as having that particular information be contributory to the problems he was having.

Q. I think you mentioned in response to a question that a closed-head injury, such as a concussion, could in the abstract be a source of brain damage; is that correct?

A. Yes.

Q. Now, if the concussion occurred there some time in the 1974-75 period, as it was reported to you, when would you expect to have the brain damage or the symptoms of the brain damage manifest themselves?

A. They would be most acute in the couple of weeks or months immediately following the damage, and the acute effects tend to resolve in 6 to 12 months. And then if there are residuals, then they would be present from then on.

MR. DC: I think the record should show that, although, Counsel, you keep using '74-'75, that is not what Dr. EW's, report shows.

THE WITNESS: '75-'76, I think. Thank you.

BY MR. CA: (continuing)

Q. Dr. EW, you expressed some familiarity through your work at the Veterans' Administration and also through the work of your colleagues there with the symptoms of post-traumatic stress syndrome, or stress disorder. Would in your opinion such an illness or a set of symptoms in P1 account for the constellation and type of mental deficits which you have identified in P1?

A. No. They simply would not account for the learning deficits he shows, nor for the more severe attentional deficits, nor for the visual spatial, visual perceptual problems that I discussed, or the visual memory problems, just wouldn't.

Q. Dr. EW, you mentioned that in your practice you do not utilize the MMPI in situations where there is or is suspected to be brain damage. Why is that?

A. Because that particular test, which was developed in the 1930's was, the normative—it was developed to be able to identify people with particular psychiatric disorders, and brain damage was never one of the issues that was involved in the norming of that test, or in the development of the test. That only came kind of stuck on years later.

But as a matter of fact, what happens—and I did do a study of this—is that people with brain damage tend to have, generally speaking, elevations on a number of the scales that contain complaints about numbness or difficulty in moving parts of their body and difficulties in concentrating and so on and so on. But so that if you use the MMPI, what you end up with is a profile which you then have a kind of psychiatric constraint about interpreting.

Moreover, I'm personally not comfortable with using the MMPI, even in a psychiatric situation, because there are enough false positives and false negatives. I think for institutional purposes, for research purposes, it's a very interesting instrument. For clinical purposes I think you run a risk of doing your patient a disservice, and I'm always afraid of that.

*(Author's Note: With regard to the MMPI, we think perhaps the question should be asked here to establish the fact that the MMPI is probably the second most widely used test after the WAIS by psychologists in the United States so as to establish EW as being definitely out in left field so far as practicing clinicians are concerned. Also, there is evidence that neuropsychological batteries have high false positive rate [see, e.g., Wedding, 1983; Leli and Filskov, 1981, in Chapter 15].)*

Q. Now, with regard to either of these—Let me ask you in the abstract. Would—We have talked about a number of factors that might contribute to problems with the type of deficits that you have reported to us here. Would low grades or even a low percentile in a standardized intelligence test be contributory to attentional or memory deficits that you have noted in both of these painters?

A. I think that you are asking me—I think I can answer this if I am allowed to paraphrase the question.

Q. Please do.

A. May I?

I think what you are saying is: what relevance does, would low scores—and by "low" I think you mean—what?—in the low average range, perhaps.

Q. Correct.

A. What relevance would they have to memory and attentional scores? Well, actually there is only one—Well, no. There are two subtests in the Wechsler set of subtests that are very, are particularly sensitive to attentional disorders. There are no memory tests, excepting the, you know, retrieval from old information on the Wechsler Adult Intelligence Scale. And those two tests correlate least well with the other subtests which have to do with what we may generally think of as intellectual functions.

The attention and memory, by and large—see how I can phrase it without getting too technical. Most of the tests on the Wechsler, tests of knowledge, tests of learned abilities, tests of learned skills, whether they be visual or verbal or whatever, tend to depend on cortical integrity, the integrity of the cortex of the brain. On the other hand, tests of memory and of attentional functions tend rather to be more reflective of the status of subcortical structures, a particular system, in fact—it is called the limbic system, and there are a number of structures in it—which is why attention and memory can be affected in a variety of ways.

And the attentional and memory deficits—Let me put it the other way. In persons of low average ability and better, by and large, if they are organically intact, there would be, there would not be the great differences in their memory abilities and attentional acts between them.

There is some effect of intelligence, and it seems to relate to actually— There is more of an effect of education. There is an education effect because the testing we do benefits from somebody who has sat in a school room for a long time and knows how to handle these kinds of questions and use their memory and so on.

But by and large there are not very great differences, so that most folks, 95 percent of people from the ages of 15, 16 to 70 will be able to get at least six digits forward and at least five digits backward, for example, and most of these folks will be able to subtract serial 3's without a great deal of difficulty and recite the alphabet and so on, and they will be able to learn 12 or 13 words at least of the 19-word list and retain that number, at the most minus two or three, 30 minutes later. So there is these differences because we are dealing with a different set of systems.

MR. DC: I move to strike his answer. It is not responsive to either Mr. CA's question or his own question as he rephrased it. It is in the nature of a speech.

MR. CA: I think it was quite responsive, at least I understood it.

Thank you, Dr. EW.

MR. DC: I have nothing further.

MR. DC2: Nothing further.

(Deposition concluded.)

Just to attempt to summarize what we feel has emerged in this direct and cross-examination and what we feel defense counsel would be able to use effectively in argument, it is the fact that different examiners got different results, illustrating possible examiner effects. EW has relied on data produced by examiners whose competence is at least questionable, and probably if he were going to use WAIS data, he should have administered the tests himself. He had failed to perform adequate investigation or to get adequate data that was available, such as the school and military records, which he said according to his own standards he usually gets. He has apparently displayed confirmatory bias and bias in favor of the plaintiff and an unwillingness to concede instances in which he was wrong, and further has made serious errors in calculating the scores and in selecting the scores he used upon which to some extent he based his conclusions. Given the above, one would not expect a jury to place much credence in this expert's testimony, despite the very impressive credentials he has presented. And indeed, as there was a total defense verdict, that apparently is just what happened. It should be mentioned, however, that in addition to the cross-examination, defense counsel was calling some experts who would testify to some of the matters we have touched upon. These were not experts who had examined the plaintiffs but experts who would testify about the issues raised in the various testings and reports and in the testimony.

# APPENDIX B

# A Homicide Case

*This homicide case includes analyses of reports by several clinicians and the testimony of a highly skilled expert with authors' comments on how his testimony could be dealt with.*

This is a valuable teaching case because it involves a highly skilled expert witness. It involves a charge of kidnapping, murder and attempted murder as well as lesser included offenses. As with all of the case material we report, every effort has been made to protect the identity of all parties involved. Therefore we have used no names except for the present author whose name appears in the context of the case and therefore could not be disguised. Otherwise the locations, times and other identifying material have been altered, except for that which plays an essential substantive role in the case. Also, for teaching purposes, the testimony and other evidence has been altered to some extent, so that it should not be construed by anyone that any portion of this actually represents anything said or done by anyone in the case.

Briefly stated, the facts of the case in a state in the Southeast are as follows:

Defendant (D) on the date of the shootings followed the female victim (FV), his former girlfriend, and her present boyfriend, the male victim (MV). He lost contact with them but after some driving around located them at a certain place. He approached the truck and forced them to drive to another location where he had them drive a small distance off the highway to where his car was parked. Once there he ordered MV at gunpoint to get out of the truck and stand by the truck while D went to his car ostensibly to get some pictures and letters to show him which would show FV had been involved with several other males sexually. According to FV, D then returned from his car and ordered MV to get down on his hands and knees. As MV began to comply with this order D, who was only a few feet from him, shot MV in the head and as MV did not fall immediately, shot him again at which point MV fell to the ground. It is noted that at some point prior to this, FV had stated to D that he wouldn't get away with this and D had told her to shut up or he would shoot her too. Following the shooting of MV, D came over to the truck and shot FV. As she continued to move he shot her again and then shot her a third time. FV, though still conscious, realized the best thing for her to do was to play dead, which she did. D then left the scene. MV died on the spot but FV survived and was able to relate these events.

D's version will become apparent in the testimony of Dr. 3.[1] Basically, his version consists of relating his belief that the two victims were out to get him, and that in that belief he had obtained the gun and went seeking them figuring that it was better for him to get them than for them to "get" him. However it is also indicated his purpose in going after them was to show the letters and pictures to MV, presumably so that he would lose interest in FV, with whom D was attempting to reestablish his relationship. The homicide took place in February. D then fled to another city several hundred miles away but upon calling friends in his home town learned that MV had in fact died, and at that point turned himself in to the police who notified the jurisdiction where the homicide occurred and D was returned to be charged with the crime.

He was first seen by Dr. 1, a local psychiatrist, at the request of the public defender "to determine if a basis existed for legal insanity or diminished capacity with regard to his alleged involvement" in the crime. Dr. 1's report follows below.

He was next seen by Dr. 2, a psychologist, who saw him on two occasions the following month after Dr. 1. (At the time of this writing Dr. 2's report and raw test data could not be located. The following material is based on Dr. Ziskin's notes.) Dr. 2 diagnoses a thought disorder and borderline psychotic, however in his report he indicates that D may be exaggerating, that he is obviously upset and anxious and has been strongly affected by being in jail. This is mainly the cause of his anxiety and confusion. He administered a WAIS as well as a TAT and MMPI. Because they have some significance later, his scale scores on the WAIS were as follows:

| | |
|---|---|
| Information | 5 |
| Comprehension | 7 |
| Arithmetic | 8 |
| Similarities | 7 |
| Digit Span | 10 |
| Vocabulary | 5 |
| Digit Symbol | 9 |
| Picture Completion | 7 |
| Block Design | 7 |
| Picture Arrangement | 9 |
| Object Assembly | 7 |

giving him a verbal IQ of 83, a performance IQ of 85 and a full scale IQ of 83 on that examination. A note on the WAIS reads, "Rapport OK; attention span, OK; misunderstands or mispronounces words; tends toward concrete thinking; doesn't look at global picture; tends to give up easily on more difficult problems; and lower than average frustration tolerance." On the sentence completion test that was administered, he indicates that he is suffering a good deal of confusion and anxiety, sleeplessness and other such symptoms due to being in jail and

---

[1] Because of D's questionable credibility, his descriptions of persons, events and actions should not be taken as necessarily factual.

that he "can't take being in jail." Thus he seems to be describing some pretty strong situation effects. His grammar and spelling are poor and his responses on the whole are somewhat longer than average but with one exception—the last item—could not be described as rambling. Note the instruction on this test is "complete these sentences to express *your real feelings*. Try to do every one. Try to make it a complete sentence."

On the TAT his stories are generally appropriate to the card and are not lengthy and rambling and in fact the examiner has to press him some to make the stories longer following which he does comply, but clearly his stories could not be considered exceptionally long or rambling. On the MMPI he showed a number of clinical scale elevations, however his MMPI is probably invalid because of a very high score on the F scale and on the F - K ratio (23), which was on a level which is very unlikely to be obtained by someone who is not malingering either by faking or exaggerating.

He was seen next by Dr. 3, an out-of-town psychiatrist, who was brought in for this case. He saw D twice, once in September, once in November. It should be noted that these examinations took place eight or nine months after the events, during which period of time defendant had been incarcerated. Dr. 3's reports follow below.

It is worth noting that FV testified that both D and MV were drug users. She was not sure of the extent, but the drugs included marijuana and cocaine. It should also be noted that D complained of harassment and poor treatment in the jail, but there may well have been a reality basis for this as a class action was filed by several inmates including D, and the judge apparently was aware that there were "problems in the jail."

After his first interview with D, Dr. 3 referred D to a psychologist who was a colleague and who shared an office with him for psychological testing and evaluation. This psychologist, Dr. 4, saw D twice in November in between the first and second interviews by Dr. 3. However, Dr. 3's second report is dated more than a week before Dr. 4's written report, which is very lengthy. Dr. 4's report follows below.

We will not deal at any length with the testimony of anyone other than Dr. 3, as he was quite clearly the "heavyweight" in the case and because his testimony provides an opportunity to illuminate a number of fundamental issues. This was an unusual case in that by virtue of agreement between counsel the present author, who would appear as a witness called by the prosecution, was allowed to sit in the courtroom during Dr. 3's testimony and Dr. 3 was likewise permitted to sit in the courtroom during the author's testimony. Dr. 3 is a highly experienced and very skilled witness. While we will deal with a number of items in his testimony, we feel the most important portions are those dealing with the basic issues such as those we have raised in Volumes I and II, the manner in which this witness dealt with some of these issues and the way in which his tactics could be countered.

Some preliminary information is important before getting into the transcript.

As Dr. 3 referred the case to Dr. 4 for testing and evaluation and in his testimony asserts that Dr. 4 is competent, some points about Dr. 4's report need to be noted. On the WAIS administered by Dr. 4, D obtained the following scale scores:

| | |
|---|---|
| Information | 7 |
| Comprehension | 7 |

      (This was incorrectly scored by Dr. 4. Correctly scored this
           would be an 8.)

| | |
|---|---|
| Arithmetic | 9 |
| Similarities | 8 |

      (Again, due to a scoring error this should be 9.)

| | |
|---|---|
| Digit Span | 10 |
| Vocabulary | 8 |
| Digit Symbol | 12 |
| Picture Completion | 8 |
| Block Design | 7 |
| Picture Arrangement | 6 |
| Object Assembly | 6 |

for a verbal IQ of 90, a performance IQ of 85 and a full scale IQ of 87 (corrected these would be 92, 85 and 88).

As noted above, Dr. 4 made several scoring errors on the WAIS and in some instance failed to follow the instructions in the manual on the administration of the test. Further, in reference to the MMPI, the report contains the statement, "The elevation on the F scale indicates extreme defensiveness on (D's) part." This statement is incorrect because the F scale does not measure defensiveness. The foregoing suggests considerable doubt concerning the competence of Dr. 4's performance in this case. However the report also states, "Emotional reaction demonstrated fear, anxiety and depression. Emotion instability was apparent. Affect was incongruous with thought content." This is a point to be kept in mind in relation to testimony to the effect that D lacked affect. Also Dr. 4's report made no mention of the fact that the automated interpretation of the MMPI that was used starts out with the statement that this MMPI should be interpreted with caution. In fact, no mention is made of the F - K score of 7, which while some clinicians would argue is borderline regarding malingering, at least deserves to be mentioned. Also the report consistently refers to brain damage indicating both tests and historical data evidence for this condition, but neuropsychological testing was not done. Also because Dr. 3 presents a great concern for saving public money it is noted that Dr. 4 was charging $125 per hour with services running over 30 hours for a fee in excess of $3,000 back in the early 1980s. (In fact, Dr. 4, with considerably fewer credentials than either Dr. 3 or Dr. Ziskin, was charging a considerably higher rate than either of them.)

As usual, Dr. 3's testimony begins with an exposition of his credentials, which will not be repeated here but can be summarized as very impressive, about as good as one is likely to run into. We would make the following comments however, as one of the qualifications is Board Certification. We would obviously suggest the line of questioning indicated above on that topic. With regard to other impressive credentials, we would suggest asking if those are based on a scientific evaluation of the accuracy of his psychiatric diagnoses.

## DR. 1, M.D.
## CONFIDENTIAL

April 24

Deputy Public Defender
Re: D

Dear DPD:

This report is in response to the order by Judge _____ and your letter of March 12. D was interviewed for a two hour period on April 15, and for a one and a half hour period on April 17. The following documents which you enclosed were reviewed:

1. Statement of FV
2. Statements of _____ and _____
3. Statement of R
4. Statement of _____
5. Statement of _____
6. Report of Lieutenant _____
7. Report of Detective _____
8. Interoffice memos from Officer _____ dated February 1, and February 4.
9. Academic transcripts from _____ Union High School District and _____ High School

## PRESENT PROBLEM:

The purpose of D's evaluation was to determine if a basis existed for legal insanity or diminished capacity with regard to his alleged involvement in the murder of MV and in the assault by shooting of FV.

The history of D's relationship with FV was described in such laborious detail that it consumed the time available for the first interview. He recalled meeting FV through her brother whose tragic death brought them together in January a year ago. D, in fact, lived thereafter with FV's mother, stepfather and grandparents in _____. Their intimate relationship apparently continued through the fall of that year but was clouded by the influence of FV's former boyfriend as well as by her relatives. He believed that a prior boyfriend had beaten her and "messed up her head." He believed that prior boyfriend took sexual advantage of her and participated with her in "affairs and orgies." FV moved to _____ in the past in order to obtain an abortion, according to D, which was possible because boyfriend's parents were "rich and ran the town." MV (the victim) was one of the prior boyfriends, who, during her relationship with D, frequently tried to obtain dates. D claimed that a prior boyfriend named _____ frequently contacted FV in order to persuade her to have sex with him. Complicating matters further was D's belief that MV was a "coke" dealer locally, "Which could be dangerous to me." FV relatives, [members of a particular ethnic group] except her father, were described as seductive and unreliable. He said that FV's sisters were prostitutes at the age of fourteen and that both sisters as well as an aunt solicited sex with him. D described FV's mother as "a tramp and a whore." D complained that FV's family was "always playing games" of deception and exploitation with him. The family was described as almost constantly battling, at times with "chains and club," in which D was involved. The combination of stresses emanating from FV's family and from her former boyfriends caused his break-up with FV in November and December together with his belief that FV, too, was exploiting him and being promiscuous. D said that he initiated the break-up but that she prolonged it by crying and pleading and even by the claim that she was pregnant with his baby. The final move evidently was FV's with her decision to return to MV.

In December there apparently was a poorly documented suicide attempt by D by an overdose. He said that he felt "screwed over" and "set up" by FV. He said that R and MV wanted to kill him. He claimed that he was aware of "heavy" criminal behavior in _____: "Drug dealings, orgies, killings, guns, crooked cops and judges." He believed that there were Mafia influences which could easily arrange a "hit." He claimed an ominous influence through local attorneys, citing that MV's mother was a legal secretary. He claimed that FV also had reason to want him dead because she was to receive a sum of [several thousand dollars of government ethnic group funds] which D's knowledge of her behavior could prevent. Further pressure during the last weeks was D's feverish attempt to get a good job "to show people that I can be out in society." During the final month D claimed that he had a number of telephone conversations with FV during which she was said to have pleaded with him for sex "because she was not satisfied by the other two."

By January 22 D had apparently spent a number of weeks almost constantly drinking beer and smoking marijuana. He felt at the end of his rope. He feared that in the noisy mill where he had gotten a job two weeks before the killing a "hit man could easily get to him." Because he felt "set up to be snuffed out" he felt that he must leave town. He obtained money. He obtained a pistol which he said was for his own protection. On the day of the killing he said that he passed the victims on their way to (someplace) and followed them for the purpose, he said, of confronting them with letters and pictures in his possession which he hoped would convince them that he needn't be killed. During that time he said that he "panicked when MV jumped at me." D said, "I guess I just flipped out. I don't remember too good. I guess I shot him again. I thought I saw her jump too, and I shot in the window. I guess I shot three times. I left scared and shaking."

D did, in fact, leave the area but voluntarily surrendered himself in _____. This decision to surrender included a number of factors. Through telephone contacts with friends locally he learned that MV had died, about which D felt "real bad." He also recalled feeling that "my head was all mixed up" and that he "needed help." He felt that "getting help" would improve his chances of eventually having a family of his own. D apparently began to realize that he was "paranoid" at the time of the shooting and "overreacted." This was also suggested by a spontaneous statement to the arresting officer to the effect: "it was either him (MV) or me." He also expected protection from legal custody from both the danger of his imagined persecutors and from the possibility of being shot as a fugitive. His apparent paranoia apparently continued after custody. The Interoffice Memos at the County Jail in early February strongly suggested persecutory delusions.

## FAMILY AND SOCIAL HISTORY:

D was born and grew up in _____. He was third youngest with five sisters and five brothers. He described an amicable relationship with siblings and parents. Apparently father is currently seriously ill, about which D revealed little emotion or apparent concern. D indicated that his family was incredulous about his difficulty but have been supportive of him since his arrest. Of interest and possible relevance is the current imprisonment of one brother for having shot a woman. D claimed that his brother's situation was somehow drug-related and he further stated that "the girl's dad knew the DA," as if that made the conviction a certainty. One sister had received psychiatric care according to D and one brother drinks excessively.

D's school records suggested a rather tenuous performance at best. He apparently was involved with the Probation Department during that time because of a series of juvenile misbehaviors involving a burglary. He said that he had had a brief stay in Juvenile Hall but otherwise had never been in jail or been arrested for a serious offense. Through the Probation Department he apparently left one high school and went to another high school, then, through the Job Corps, to school in _____. It was in _____ that his history of suspicion and beliefs of persecution apparently began. He believed that his "life was in danger" from drug dealers or minority groups. He returned to this area at the age of nineteen.

His occupational history involved a series of rather marginal jobs, mostly as a clean-up person, but he also mentioned being trained to drive loaders, dump trucks and cement trucks. His last job was for compacting compost, a duration of three weeks. He has also worked in the woods. D has never been married. His psychosexual history revealed an heterosexual orientation with intercourse beginning at age sixteen and continuing thereafter with a series of "four or five steady girlfriends." He denied homosexual experiences or fantasies.

"People like me," said D, claiming that he has a number of friends locally. He claimed to have attended church in the past but "forgot the name of it." Free time activities have included baseball in school, hiking, going to the beach, rock climbing, reading, and "sitting around drinking." His stated life goals were "a nice job, a nice stereo and marriage."

## MEDICAL HISTORY:

It may be relevant that D apparently was hospitalized at the age of nine when hit by a car, resulting in four days of coma and a two week hospitalization. There evidently was no skull fracture and no sequelae of this incident although he complained of episodes of weakness, a flushed feeling and physical collapse on at least three occasions in the last year, two of which were associated with drinking alcohol. None of these episodes was treated by a physician. The only other hospitalization was for tonsillectomy. "A few car wrecks" occurred thereafter without hospitalization.

Allergy to poison oak. Dental caries apparently exist.

Initial and middle sleep disturbances apparently occurred for the month prior to his arrest associated with beliefs and fantasies that "they would come" to his place and "break in or shoot through the window." He reported increased dreaming and dreams of violence. Appetite was reduced during the same period with ten pound weight loss to 130 pounds, 140 being about normal. He recalled pain in the abdomen and cramps. Energy was diminished. He felt like sleeping all the time. Mood was described as variable.

D had consumed cigarettes for nine years or more at a package or more per day. Two or three cups of coffee per day with occasional tea. He has utilized four or more Coca Colas daily.

Medications have included a hypnotic at the jail. He apparently had no pre-scribed medicine prior. In December he claimed an overdose with "two bottles" of Tylenol plus "red pills" resulting in vomiting but not being hospitalized. He said that he was "tired of violence" and the problems enumerated above.

D's use of alcohol began at the age of fifteen. "All my friends drank," he said. It began with two cases of beer among three or four people on weekends and progressed to every other day and then included whiskey and vodka. He claimed a capacity of being able to "split a fifth with a friend." That drinking pattern has continued to his present age though was interrupted for periods of three to four weeks at a time because of associated problems. He said that his burglaries were related to alcohol. Alcohol caused trouble with friends. It made him moody and short tempered causing him to strike siblings at times. He missed school in order to drink. He missed work because of hangovers. He was arrested for drunk and disorderly. Apparently at no time did he have a with-drawal syndrome or DT's according to him. At least he was not treated for it. He has never gone to AA or considered it. He was unsure whether he was an alco-holic: "I know I drink too much." Other drugs included diet pills in order to stay awake all night while drinking. He has used marijuana up to "ten joints a day" for a number of years for its relaxing value. He utilized "reds" once and LSD once resulting in a negative experience. He denied the intravenous use of drugs. He denied ever having sold drugs.

D denied prior psychiatric care.

## MENTAL STATUS EXAMINATION:

D was short and not well developed with moderately long, slightly curly hair and fair grooming. He had a boyish face, appearing younger than his stated age. He was moderately anxious, particularly in the first interview. His delivery contained such excessive detail, descriptions and repetitions that only the period of time between January a year ago and January this year could be covered in the first visit. His descriptions were rather fervent, emotional experiences. He believed that he indeed was being "set up for a hit." He believed that he was being maligned and manipulated since his arrest. He believed that there was a harassment at the jail and, in fact, D was involved in the recent class action to have conditions investigated at the jail. These beliefs appeared delusional. Hal-lucinations were not elicited at the time of the interview. An organic brain con-dition affecting memory, orientation or judgment was not obvious but also not tested in detail. Intelligence appeared in the average range or even higher, in spite of the school reports. His productions were logical and quite well articu-lated. He demonstrated a fair degree of insight. Mood was somewhat depressed.

His emotional responsiveness seemed otherwise rather bland. There was little demonstrated remorse about his behavior except to say that he "felt bad" when he learned that MV had died, although he apparently attempted to telephone FV's family from the jail in order to express sympathy. D viewed the shooting more as a self-defense than as a "kill or be killed situation." Except for the elaborate responses D was cooperative and pleasant during the interview. Some rapport was established. His self-esteem was quite low, partly related to his height of 5'7". His behavior expressed strong need for feeling adequate. As a result he tried hard to place himself in a more masculine or even "macho" image.

This seemed particularly reflected in his statements of sexual bravado indicated above and by his admission of consuming vast quantities of alcohol. These attributes suggested an inadequate, groping, boasting, surly misfit.

## DISCUSSION:

From the interview and documentation D appeared to suffer from a paranoid condition involving persecutory beliefs at the time of the killing and assault as well as an indeterminant time prior to and after the incidents. If his use of substances in the amounts claimed is to be believed, intoxications(s) could be viewed as a contributing factor. Some degree of exaggeration or fabrication in D's statements can not be ruled out, which leaves the questions of how believable is he?

D emerged from an environment which probably provided minimal nutritive interaction with parents. There was a virtual army of children in the family. D's school performance was marginal. Alcoholism began at an early age. The contribution of the apparent head injury at age nine is uncertain. Occupational performance has been meager and inconstant. His relationships with women have been a series of disasters. Delinquency began at an early age, perhaps the only social group with whom he could identify. Although he claimed a number of current friends this is doubtful. Intelligence may be in the average range. D has a powerful need to feel adequate and to be "somebody." Tragically, now he is.

My diagnostic impression would be inadequate personality disorder or borderline schizophrenia, with antisocial features. Either situation can result in paranoid delusions under sufficient stress. A related diagnosis is alcoholism and marijuana dependency. The presence of organic brain disease is unknown.

Was D legally insane? I believe that he was somewhat frightened and paranoid but he was also consciously "pissed." Telephone harassment of FV and MV during December and January would suggest a strong element of jealous rage. That he murdered MV as a direct result of his delusional beliefs appears unlikely. More likely is that his state of mind at the time was very shaky and that he overreacted as he claimed. Most likely perhaps is that D "executed" MV in cold blood and attempted to do the same to FV.

A diminished capacity may be more tenable than legal insanity if the impairments discussed above existed. His ability to reflect upon the gravity of the situation may have been substantially impaired.

I think I will conclude at this point with what is already a lengthy report. If you feel greater definition is needed regarding this man's personality strengths and weaknesses I would suggest psychological testing which might include an MMPI, Bender-Gestalt, and a TAT test. This would provide a personality description, projective testing and would give a look at organic factors. I would recommend for this Dr._____, Dr. _____ or Dr. 2.

I thank you for this most interesting referral. Please let me know if you have additional questions.

Sincerely,

Dr. 1

## REPORT OF DR. 3, M.D.

Doctor 3

September 30

Mr. DC

Re: People vs. D

Dear Mr. DC:

On September 27 I was privileged to perform a psychiatric examination of your client, D, at the County Jail. Prior to my examination I reviewed the transcript of the preliminary hearing, police reports, the psychological report of Dr. 2, Ph.D., and interviews or reports of interviews of several people.

Finally, I reviewed Mr. D's juvenile record which describes malicious mischief, burglary, runaway, and one or two additional minor misdemeanors. There was no medical or psychiatric records on Mr. D and it is represented to me that he has never had any formal psychiatric care.

### REVIEW OF RECORDS:

Of particular interest are the statements of R, FV and B. R states that the defendant came to him a week prior to the shooting and told him that "If you did not stay away from this girl this guy was going to kill him," that "He was scared someone would take a shot at him if he got out of the car," that "Something like this has happened to me before and this time I can't run...I'm scared...I have to get a gun before this guy gets me," although it was his preference that he simply get out of town.

B also learned from the defendant—several hours before the shooting—that he had need of a loan of $150 to go to _____...to get out of town before dark..."there's a guy that's going to kill me tonight." Neither observer felt the defendant to be abnormal, save for the anxiety implicit in his requests and at least in B's view, his demeanor.

The victim, FV, states that she dated the defendant briefly in early _____, and then the decedent in December of _____, although the defendant did ask her, after they had broken up and she had started to date the decedent, to marry him. She states that she broke up with the defendant in order to date the decedent, that the defendant did not wish this to happen and began to threaten her, saying that he would get even with her, called her a slut and a whore and assured her that she was going to pay for hurting him. She learned from the defendant's sister that he tried to commit suicide because of her, and continued to call her for dates. She believed that the defendant never called the decedent and made no threats to him until the day of the shooting when he said: "I'll teach you for saying that you are going to blow me away." MV said, "I never told you I was going to blow you away," to which FV added, "D, nobody said that to you. Why don't you just leave us alone?" FV said that the defendant replied, "You shut up or I'll kill you too. C'mon, MV, I want to show you some stuff I got so you will know what kind of girl she is." Apparently there were no letters or photographs, etc., and instead, the defendant simply had MV get on his hands and knees and then shot him, then came back to the truck where FV was sitting, and shot her as well.

The psychologicals performed on June 30 revealed a man with an I.Q. of 83 evincing a borderline thought disorder characterized by disjointed rambling, paranoid mentation, nervousness, anxiety, depression, hostility and suspiciousness. Dr. 2 quotes a study indicating that 68% of patients obtaining this profile are diagnosed as psychotic. Dr. 2 concludes that the defendant does have a thought disorder, "does not make good judgments, is not fully aware of the world around him, and likely sees events different from what most people would."

### PAST HISTORY: (OBTAINED FROM DEFENDANT)

D was born 23 years ago in _____, _____, the third youngest of 11, was raised there by his parents. He describes his father, a logger, as a strict man who was frequently disappointed that his son repeatedly strayed from the rules he laid down, and often expressed his displeasure with whippings. The defendant states that he had "hard feelings" toward his father at the time but they are much closer now and in fact the two worked together for several years in the woods. D states that his mother, a store clerk, is a loving woman who likes people and who was always liked by them.

Mr. D's childhood was often unhappy, and marred by financial hardship, the necessity of his having to work from the age of 9 on, and by disciplinary problems. Mr. D describes the latter in terms of other people's shortcomings— "It was this bunch that I used to hang around with that got me into trouble."

Mr. D knows of no mental illness in his family but believes that some of his brothers may be alcoholic. Some of his brothers have had difficulty with the law. An older brother who died several years ago at age ___ in an automobile accident, and another brother served time for forged checks and attempted murder, respectively.

Mr. D dropped out of school at the 11th grade because "I wasn't getting enough out of it." He then worked at a variety of skilled labor jobs but was primarily dependent upon lumber, and as a consequence was often out of work during the rainy season. He is rather bitter about his employment history and in some vague way felt that he was denied good jobs or they were taken from him.

Mr. D's physical health has always been good although he allegedly drank a bottle of vodka at about age 9 and then fell off a bicycle, was struck by a car hit his head and almost died. He has had no significant illnesses, accidents or injuries save that described, and denies significant drug use, but has been a heavy drinker of beer, about 15 cases per week (!). He admits to three "fainting spells" of some sort or another, but no frank blackouts, tremors, DT's, etc. He smokes several marijuana cigarettes daily and has experimented with other drugs but has never been addicted or a heavy user.

Mr. D had intercourse at the age of 16 for the first time and estimates he has had 9 to 10 partners since. He has had two serious relationships, one at age 18 with a woman named DO whom he dated and lived with for about a year until she "snuck out on me, broke our trust," and so he terminated the relationship; he reports that she lied to him, telling him falsely that she was pregnant in an attempt to bind him to her.

At age 20 he met one of the victims, FV, and dated her throughout _____. Again he maintains that he broke off the relationship and that toward the end, FV falsely told him she was carrying his child in order to bind him to her.

He describes FV as very smart, "outdoorsy," basically warm and loving, but a member of a mean and violent family and that when she was around them she would become like them, especially when drinking or using cocaine. He states that she liked to lead men on and get them involved with her, and then reject them. He maintains, however, that he ultimately rejected her, breaking up with her no fewer than three times—the first time when she was hitting at him while drunk, the second time because she was using him to provoke two other would-be suitors, R and MV, and a third time because R, MV and FV's family had started coming down hard on him and were all playing "head games." Indeed, near the end of their relationship in December of _____, purportedly "tired of fighting" with FV, her family, her girlfriends, her sisters' boyfriends, he made a suicide attempt around Christmas time. At the time, he was in turmoil, "trying to be so good to her family," while they were cruel to him, with various sisters, aunts, and even FV's mother trying to seduce him. FV even told him that she was pregnant by him.

Confused about his feelings, he saw a priest, and then around Christmas time made the suicide attempt. He states this was not because he was losing FV and insists the only reason he wanted to stay connected to her was that she was pregnant.

FV began dating MV, the other victim, in November, but Mr. D alleges that she really didn't love MV and in fact continued to use him and the fact that his penis was bigger to torment MV. She also played MV and R against each other and against him. Interestingly, this is the first time Mr. D was ever aware of having any homicidal feelings, although he insists, that others were out to get him.

**THE HOMICIDE:**

On January 22 Mr. D fatally shot MV and seriously wounded FV.

He alleges that one month before, FV invited him over to her house because she wanted to sleep with him. They had intercourse and he left about 1:30 in the morning. They had no more personal contacts thereafter although Mr. D states that he phoned FV frequently, even telling her that he would get even with her for all the head games she was playing—that he would stop her from getting money under the [ethnic group] act, would give MV and R pictures of him naked that she had taken (and which he was sure could be identified as her photography), and thus, people would know what she was really like. Somewhere along the line Mr. D became convinced that MV was out to get him or would hire someone to do so if he did not stay away from FV, that this attitude in him was provoked by FV who was taking advantage of the fact that MV had wanted her for over six years and he, Mr. D, continued to be a threat to his desires. He thought he represented a sexual threat to MV, particularly.

Mr. D denies any sexual problems except for occasional impotency "when drunk."

Mr. D states that his concerns grew to the point where about mid-January he asked his friend R to get him a gun so that he might "get MV before he got me," but when R failed, he stole a gun from another friend, one week prior to the homicide.

Mr. D states that he "couldn't handle what was going on." He would hide at home, go straight to work, and come straight home or go to a bar and drink himself into stuporousness. He took to sleeping on the couch rather than on his bed because "MV knew where I slept and could get to me easy there."

On January 21, the day before the homicide, Mr. D worked some extra hours, being joined by a day man who was living at the time at FV's house. He started pressing him with all sorts of questions so that by the time they finished working, at 10:00 P.M., Mr. D had all kinds of frightened and homicidal feelings.

He decided he would leave town, and the next day went to his boss, lied about having some outstanding traffic warrants, and got an advance on his salary. He then went home, got some clothes, got his gun, and a few beers, and tried to call FV about her intentions to have MV kill him. FV was not home so he said goodbye to his father, now terminally ill with cancer, and went to see his friend B to raise some more money, but B was flat broke.

Mr. D then decided to drive to to _____ see FV at her house, called en route several times, found her not there, decided she was probably at work, and drove to her place of employment. He saw MV waiting for her there, making some phone calls, "I'm sure he was getting me set up." Then FV came out, joined him, and he followed them both to FV's house. After a short while they left, and Mr. D, certain that they were now going to MV's house, followed them again but lost them. In fact they did not go to MV's house and it took considerable searching, accompanied by beer and marijuana, before Mr. D encountered them, explaining, "I guess I got lucky." He states he was frightened when he saw them but nevertheless, armed, went to their car, showed them his gun, and told MV, "I heard you want to kill me." He made MV get out of the truck to purportedly examine some pictures and letters which would reveal to him just what kind of a girl FV was and that she was "not worth killing someone for." While he was trying to take these pictures out of his knapsack, "MV made the move," and fearful for his life, Mr. D shot him. He thought then that maybe FV was going for the gun—"She can shoot better than any guy," and shot her as well. He then fled the scene, going to _____, where eventually he turned himself in, "to get help."

## MENTAL STATUS EXAMINATION:

Mr. D presents as a superficially pleasant, cooperative individual who comprehends all questions and replied with apparent candor, though in a markedly disorganized and paranoid way.

*Perception:* Mr. D is oriented to time, place and person, and is alert to his surroundings. There are no hallucinations or illusions.

*Mentation:* His narrative is rambling and pressured, with loosening of associations and paranoid ideation. He is always the aggrieved victim, always the good guy, always doing things for people, particularly FV's family, whereas everyone else was deceitful, violent, and promiscuous. Everybody is always "screwing him over." FV's aunt, age 30, and her mother, age 35, both tried to seduce him. A host of other people had plots of one kind or another against him. He is grandiose, incoherent, and delusional, with many of his ideas fragmented and blurring together. Performance of simple arithmetical computations and general fund of knowledge is adequate but interpretation of everyday proverbs is markedly concrete. Memory is good. There is no evidence of organicity.

Mr. D's narrative and thought processes can best be described by Mr. D himself:

"FV would rather see me dead than go out with a lot of other girls. I did go out with a lot of girls and she knew it and she'd say she'd kick their cunts in. She tried to run me over one day when I was talking to a girlfriend of my sister's. Then she cried and told me that she didn't want us to break up. It wasn't her fault that she was this way...She had a lot of problems. Her family beat on her. Her mother was a tramp and tried to come onto me and her father took out girls and gave them coke. Her girlfriends just wanted coke and sex. FV put MV up to all this like she tried to put me up to things and get R and MV to fight over her, show her pictures and so on, so I stayed away from town because I knew what she was doing and wanted R and MV and me to really get into it. I've gotten into two or three fights already because of her and her family where I had no choice. Her family begged me to stay with them. I made them laugh, I took care of them. We really liked each other but her aunt and her sisters were jealous and tried to get me into bed and her mother was always trying to pick up on me. My freedom means a lot to me. I just don't date any girl."

*Affect:* Despite the pressured speech and drama of its content, Mr. D presents in a superficially calm, flat, quasi-rational manner. Emotional tone is subdued and unremarkable save for its pseudo-normalcy and perhaps a bit of depression.

*Behavior:* Behavior is appropriate throughout.

## PSYCHIATRIC DIAGNOSIS:

Paranoid schizophrenia.

## CONCLUSIONS:

Mr. D presents a dramatic picture of a man projecting all of his own chaotic libidinal and homicidal feelings onto others. He is all virtuous and can maintain this self-portrait only by disposing of his own unacceptable feelings and impulses by laying them upon others. Thus, through these mental processes he surrounds himself with imaginary enemies, and by the self-cleansing process makes himself all the more innocent and their real or imagined transgressions against him all the more heinous.

In January he was suffused with uncontrollable feelings of jealousy and rage, but rather than admitting to or owning them, projected them onto MV and FV and then acting in "self-defense" against what were in fact his own intentions, mortally wounded one and seriously wounded the other.

There is a possibility that the mental processes so in evidence now have been aggravated by confinement, but it is quite likely that at the time of the homicide they were sufficiently in evidence to contaminate the mental processes by which he would premeditate, deliberate, form intention and malice, understand the wrongfulness of his acts and control his behavior.

Thank you for the opportunity to examine Mr. D.

Sincerely,

Dr. 3

## DOCTOR 3, M.D.

November 28
DC
Re: D

Dear DC:

On November 26 I was privileged to perform a psychiatric re-examination of your client at the County Jail. Prior to my evaluation I reviewed summaries of various taped interviews and a Sheriff Department interoffice memo. Interviewed were Mr. D's sister, who describes her brother's depression near the Christmas of _____ over the fact that he was going to be killed; another sister, states that when she saw her brother in jail he told her that the Mafia was after him; _____, another sister, spoke of her brother's suicide attempt, his depression over financial problems, gastrointestinal complaints, insomnia and weight loss, and concerns about a variety of threats he was receiving, although she had never known him to be violent; by contrast, C stated that the defendant picked fights when intoxicated; R, a friend of Mr. D, stated that the defendant was frightened and needed a gun to protect himself—that he was going to be killed; W reports that she was once kicked and beaten by FV (a victim) and her friends; Y, W's girlfriend, confirms W's statements; a Sheriff's deputy reports that the defendant told him that the Mafia or someone was out for his skin, and that further, he could not remember pulling the trigger when he committed his offenses, that he could trust no one, not even his attorney, that he hadn't slept in over a month and that he could provide information about drugs and firearms if he could get some sort of apparently necessary protection for his family; D's oldest sister reports that two weeks before the shooting, her brother told her that the Mafia was going to kill him and possibly injure other family members, and that FV and MV might well be involved—he was crying the entire time he told her this; a jail counselor found the defendant often incoherent and complaining of people trying to get him, that MV's mother was the driving force against him, collaborating with the District Attorney with whom she was sexually involved; former County Jail commander stated that D told him the Mafia and other people were out to get him and that for this reason he wanted to be placed in isolation—he said that D was obviously disturbed and that the District Attorney was pushing hard for political reasons.

Finally, Dr. 1 submitted a report dated April 24, describing his examinations of Mr. D in March and April of that year, finds him suffering either an "inadequate personality disorder or borderline schizophrenia with antisocial features," either one of which could "result in paranoid delusions under sufficient stress. A related diagnosis is alcoholism and marijuana dependency." He saw the defendant's defense as an amalgam of paranoid fright and jealous rage rather than the consequence of frank delusional beliefs, that he "overreacted," but in any event "executed MV in cold blood and attempted to do the same to FV." Dr. 1 felt that the defendant's "ability to reflect upon the gravity of the situation may have been substantially impaired," though he was not likely legally insane.

## RE-EXAMINATION:

The principal focus of the second examination was Mr. D's thinking prior to and at the time of the offense. Once again, there is a confusion between whether he terminated with FV or vice versa. He does acknowledge that there was a time when she was sexually intimate with both him and his rival. One day in November, for example, FV came home from _____ and they had sex. Ordinarily FV's vagina was "very tight," but not so on this occasion because she had had sex earlier with MV. On another day that week he caught her having sex with another man.

Mr. D states that he had carried a gun during the summer of _____ but sold it in the fall because "things quieted down." Toward the end of the year, however, he began to fear for his life again and so acquired a weapon. He states that the decedent had it in for him, and followed him home, threatened to kill him and that his family had great power; furthermore, MV realized that he, D, was the only one who could get between him and the woman he wanted, FV; FV also had reasons to fear him because he could get her [ethnic group] funds cut off with his knowledge that she was only [partly of ethnic group ancestry]. He saw MV and FV as threatening his life and this required dramatic action on his part. He tried to get help from a priest, tried to get out of town, tried to get help from his family but ultimately decided the night before the shooting that he'd simply better get them before they got him. He made a last-minute effort with some purported letters and photos to dissuade MV in the few moments prior to the shooting but became frightened and shot him and then FV. Even so, he feels he is somewhat at risk—that either MV's mother or FV will arrange to have him killed, especially if he goes to prison where that sort of thing happens all of the time.

## MENTAL STATUS EXAMINATION:

Mr. D appears much as he did in September, rambling and so tangential as to be almost non-responsive to many questions. He is still quite paranoid and still believes in a local Mafia though he is utterly unpersuasive in his documentation. He acknowledges suicidal thoughts and in fact were it not for his newly-found religion he would have killed himself many months ago. But he cannot stand the thought of living in prison the rest of his life and sees suicide as a possible option. He believes, however, that his new-found religion has enabled him to foreswear all violence although if once again faced with a situation of imminent danger and the need for "self-defense" he is not sure if he would not do it again.

## PSYCHIATRIC DIAGNOSIS:
Paranoid schizophrenia.

## CONCLUSIONS:
The second evaluation confirms the results of the first. It is clear that whatever simple jealous rage Mr. D may have felt as a rejected suitor was markedly contaminated by his paranoid thought processes and fragmented, chaotic thinking.

Thank you for the opportunity to re-examine Mr. D.

Sincerely,

Dr. 3

### DR. 4, PH.D.

December 7
DC
Re: D

## REPORT OF PSYCHOLOGICAL ASSESSMENT[2]
Name: D
Age: 22
Birth Date:
Dates of Examination: November 10, 17

## REFERRAL STATEMENT:
D, a 22-year-old Caucasian male was examined in County Jail in order to estimate past and present levels of psychological functioning. Mr. D is imprisoned awaiting trial for homicide and attempted homicide to two victims on January 22. On that date, Mr. D apparently borrowed a friend's car, drove to a secluded spot and fatally shot MV and seriously wounded FV. Prior examiners have suggested the possibility that Mr. D was mentally deranged at the time of the shootings. Medical examinations of Mr. D in County Jail diagnose him as both schizophrenic and paranoid.

---

[2] Dr. 4's report is quite long. It is not essential to read it to follow the case. Author's comments are to the effect that errors were made and many statements were highly questionable. The quality of Dr. 4's performance was put in doubt.

*(Author's Note: Here, Dr. 4 clearly states the conditions for preconception and confirmatory bias. It should particularly be noted that one of the prior examiners is a psychiatrist for whom Dr. 4 has great admiration, as noted in his testimony.)*

The present testing was undertaken to add further data to estimate Mr. D's frame of mind prior to, during and after the homicidal attack.

In conjunction with the preparation of the present report, the following materials were examined:

1) Psychiatric report dated April 24 by Dr. 1, M.D.
2) Psychological report dated June 30 by Dr. 2, Ph.D.
3) Psychiatric report dated September 30 by Dr. 3, M.D.
4) Deposition of FV, February 28.

## REVIEW OF MEDICAL RECORDS:

A psychiatric report dated April 24 by Dr. 1 states: "From the interview and documentation D appeared to suffer from a paranoid condition involving persecutory beliefs at the time of the killing and assault as well as an indeterminant time prior to and after the incident." The report further states: "My diagnostic impression would be inadequate personality disorder or borderline schizophrenia, with antisocial features. Either situation can result in paranoid delusions under sufficient stress. A related diagnosis is alcoholism and marijuana dependency. The presence of organic brain disease is unknown."

It was Dr. 1's opinion that Mr. D might have been frightened and paranoid at the time of the murder. Dr. 1 also feels that Mr. D was "consciously 'pissed.'" Dr. 1 also feels that Mr. D suffered a shaky state of mind and "overreacted as he claimed." Dr. 1 further feels that the murder was an execution.

*(Author's Note: Here, Dr. 4 distinguishes among Dr. 1's conclusions, treating the three alternatives he stated as though they were equal, whereas Dr. 1 made it very clear that his opinion was that it was more likely that the murder was an execution than a result of simply a shaky state of mind. This would seem to be an example of biased reporting or biased distortion of the data, which would support a notion that Dr. 4 was biased.)*

Dr. 1's report goes on to say that greater definition of Mr. D's personality strengths and weaknesses might be provided by psychological testing.

A psychological report dated June 30 by Dr. 2 states: "In summary, in my opinion, Mr. D does have a thought disorder, and is borderline psychotic." The report goes on to say: "The thought disorder and paranoid process coupled with a rather low intelligence level presents a picture of a person who certainly does not make good judgments and is not fully aware of the world around him, and he likely sees events different [sic] from what most people would do." In supporting his argument, Dr. 2 cites MMPI (Minnesota Multiphasic Personality Inventory, a basic psychometric tool) scale elevations suggesting a person with a serious thinking disorder and paranoid mentation "consistent with a paranoid schizophrenic reaction."

*(Author's Note: Dr. 4 cites Dr. 2's utilization of the MMPI he had administered. However, the author's notes show that on the MMPI administered by Dr. 2 that there was an F-K score of 23, which has to at least raise the issue of*

*malingering for anyone who is familiar with that measure. However, even without the malingering interpretation, that F-K would make the MMPI at least uninterpretable. Dr. 4 could be questioned as to whether he obtained Dr. 2's test data, not simply Dr. 2's interpretation. It is a good possibility that Dr. 4 does not know what the scores were on the validity scales of the MMPI administered by Dr. 2.)*

A psychiatric report dated September 30 by Dr. 3, M.D., states the psychiatric diagnosis: "Paranoid schizophrenia." In explicating this diagnosis Dr. 3 states: "Mr. D presents a dramatic picture of a man projecting all of his own chaotic libidinal and homicidal feelings onto others....There is a possibility that the mental processes so in evidence now may have been aggravated by confinement, but it is quite likely that at the time of the homicide they were sufficiently in evidence to contaminate the mental processes by which he would premeditate, deliberate, form intention and malice, understand the wrongfulness of his acts and control his behavior."

## RESULTS OF TESTING:

The following psychometric tests and procedures were administered to Mr. D in County Jail: The Wechsler Adult Intelligence Scale (WAIS); the Minnesota Multiphasic Personality Inventory (MMPI); the Clinical Analysis Questionnaire (CAQ); the Bender-Gestalt Visual Motor Test; the Forer Structured Sentence Completion Test; the Goodenough Draw-A-Person Test (DAP); the State-Trait Anxiety Inventory; the Depression Assay Scale; a Social History Questionnaire; and a Comprehensive Clinical Interview.

*(Author's Note: It should be noted that at the time of this testing, the Wechsler Adult Intelligence Scale had been replaced by the WAIS-R, the revised version, for a substantial period. Therefore, it can be brought out that Dr. 4, who is the highest-priced expert in this case, was using an obsolete form of the test. Also, with the exception of the MMPI, Wechsler, the Draw-A-Person test, and the Bender-Gestalt, the tests employed are not used by a majority of psychologists, and probably can be shown to have little validation research. So far as the Draw-A-Person test, the status of this test is described on the chapter on projective tests, and this literature will show the test to be, at the minimum, of very dubious value. Additionally, Dr. 4 made two errors of administration of the WAIS and several scoring errors. One of these errors occurred on the Comprehension subtest, which he asserts measures social judgment, and he asserts fell in the dull/normal range with a scale score of 7. However, with the score corrected to what it should be, the scale score is 8, which would be in the average range, and therefore would, according to Dr. 4's statement, indicate that D has social judgment that is within the normal range.)*

### Results of Intelligence Testing

On the Wechsler Adult Intelligence Scale (WAIS), Mr. D obtained a verbal I.Q. score of 90, a performance I.Q. score of 85, and a full scale I.Q. score of 87. The following scaled subtest scores were obtained:

**Verbal scaled scores**

| | |
|---|---|
| Information | 7 |
| Comprehension | 7 |
| Arithmetic | 9 |
| Similarities | 8 |
| Digit Span | 10 |
| Vocabulary | 8 |

**Performance scaled scores**

| | |
|---|---|
| Digit Symbol | 12 |
| Picture Completion | 8 |
| Block Design | 7 |
| Picture Arrangement | 6 |
| Object Assembly | 6 |

During this testing, Mr. D's scores were consistent with I.Q. scores obtained by Dr. 2, Ph.D., who administered this test to Mr. D in June. During this second testing, Mr. D obtained a slightly higher verbal I.Q. score, consistent with the fact that there are usually some practice effects in retesting with the WAIS. However, the overall scatter of test results obtained in the second testing confirms the first results. Mr. D essentially functions in the low-average to borderline range of intelligence. The comprehension subtest which measures social judgment fell in the dull-normal range on both testings. On both testings, the digit span subtest provided the greatest strength to Mr. D's profile. An adequate short-term memory is his greatest additional strength. He has benefited little from formal education. Thinking is excessively concrete. The Similarities subtest is generally viewed as a measure of ability to abstract (the opposite of concrete).

*(Author's Note: Dr. 4's scoring of 8 puts D in the average range on Similarities. The score corrected for Dr. 4's error is actually 9, even further up in the average range in ability to abstract. Also the Digit Span subtest with a score of 10 is not his strongest—Digit Symbol with a score of 12 is. Dr. 4 is simply wrong in this.)*

Mr. D was nervous and tense during intellectual testing. He felt that the testing was another means for people to "get at" him. Contents of testing suggest an extremely simplistic mentality. Mr. D subscribes to conventional moral values. However, his understanding of such concepts as punishment is childlike in nature. For example, he describes punishment as something you have to "pay so you don't get worst [sic]." Mentation such as this suggests that Mr. D does not see human beings as volitional.

*(Author's Note: This statement seems to simply be nonsense. We doubt that Dr. 4 under questioning would be able to produce any source data which would justify this conclusion based on the statement or the quote indicated. Even if his response is childlike in nature, most children by the age of five or six are aware that human beings are volitional and I doubt that any assertion that D's mental capacities are below that of a five or six year old child could be supported by the data. Such a statement would simply be ridiculous. Also, one has to wonder if drug and alcohol abuse represent conventional moral values.)*

In summary, Mr. D's mental processes are underdeveloped. Levels of intellectual ability are not adequate for normal school performance. The concrete nature of Mr. D's mentation limits his understanding of moral concepts. It also makes social judgments difficult for him to manage. Mr. D's intellectual style is essentially that of a reacting individual. He simply tries to manage situations at hand without much benefit of knowledge or social conditioning to help him interpret day-to-day events.

Mr. D's profile strongly suggests stunted intellectual growth. It is notable that Mr. D was struck by a car while riding a bicycle at age nine. He was unconscious for some time and hospitalized with severe head injuries afterward.

Mr. D's earlier developmental history also contributes to a picture of stunted mental growth. Apparently, Mr. D's mother had an untreated, severe kidney infection during her pregnancy with him. He was born immature and required several weeks of intensive care at birth. During interviewing, Mrs. D stated that she always considered her son "scarred." Poverty, ten siblings, and low intellectual attainment on the part of his parents have undoubtedly also contributed to Mr. D's limited intellectual development. The overall intellectual profile of this individual is that of dull normal intellectual development as a result of multiple disadvantaging factors.

### Results of Visual-Motor Testing

The Bender-Gestalt Visual Motor Test further suggests dull normal mental capacity. Mr. D's production contained elements suggestive of emotional disorder. Some figures were diminished in size. There was some evidence of perceptual disorder. Mr. D's performance was hasty and confused. Organic brain damage was neither ruled out nor confirmed by this testing.

*(Author's Note: Having given the Bender-Gestalt, which is a screening test for brain damage, the statement "organic brain damage was neither ruled out nor confirmed by this testing," virtually mandates that the psychologist go on and perform a battery of neuropsychological tests, or, if not competent to do so, have a neuropsychological testing done by somebody who is. One simply cannot justify giving the Bender-Gestalt, the only purpose for which, in this case, given the number of other tests that were given, would be as an indicator of brain damage or absence thereof, and then say the results are inconclusive, and then drop it. What was the point of giving the test in the first place? It is noted that at various points further along in the report, Dr. 4 continues to refer to possible or probable organic brain syndrome or brain damage.)*

This episode may have contributed to slow mental development. Mr. D has also engaged in excessive alcohol intake since age nine. Since adolescence he has also taken street drugs such as marijuana, cocaine, etc.

Again, the picture of Mr. D's mental processes derived from this test suggests inadequate or stunted brain development. Emotional factors appear to play a part in his minimal performance.

### Results of Objective Testing

On the Minnesota Multiphasic Personality Inventory (MMPI), Mr. D's profile is that of a confused, disorganized and acutely disturbed individual. The

Roche Psychiatric Service Institute interpretation of this profile states: "The test results on this patient are strongly suggestive of a major emotional disorder. The test pattern resembles those of psychiatric outpatients who later require inpatient care."

*(Author's Note: The report here quotes the automated interpretation of the MMPI, utilizing those portions which are supportive of his diagnosis. However, the report completely omits the cautionary statement provided by the Roche Psychiatric Service, which starts out by saying this profile has to be interpreted with caution. One would think that minimal professional responsibility would require that that statement be communicated to whoever would be reading the psychologist's report. It is misleading to make the statements from the report without including that cautionary statement. In addition, Dr. 4 seems oblivious to the fact that there is an F - K ratio of 7 on this test, and while that's a borderline, or grey area concerning malingering, at least it is high enough to raise the issue. However, as the testimony of Dr. 4 later shows, he is really not familiar with that measure.)*

The overall profile is supportive of the diagnosis "paranoid schizophrenia." In addition, there is strong evidence to indicate a major affective disorder. Patients with this profile can be expected to act out in bizarre and disordered ways.

An elevation on the F scale indicates extreme defensiveness on Mr. D's part. *(Author's Note: This is just plain wrong. K, not F, is the measure of defensiveness.)* On the clinical scales, Mr. D's highest obtained score was a 96 on the schizophrenia scale. Scores above 70 are considered above the high normal range. Mr. D also obtained an elevation of 86 on the psychopathic deviance scale, a score of 83 on the psychasthenia scale, a score of 82 on the paranoia scale, and a score of 81 on the mania scale.

With this profile, one can expect disordered thinking, hostile, antisocial acting out, a paranoid structure to thought processes, excessive sensitivity to slights of others, and an inability to control one's own behavior. Mr. D also has elevated symptoms and depression.

Mr. D's profile indicates a strong rejection of masculinity accompanied by a relatively passive effeminate non-compulsive personality. During testing he completed one item indicating that he is strongly attracted to members of his own sex. He has deep concern over sexual matters.

Paranoid trends were blatantly manifested. Suspicion and ideas of reference included the feeling that others have it out for him and are plotting against him. He feels he has been hypnotized and manipulated by others. He is not sure he is able to control his own mind.

During testing, Mr. D subscribed to statements indicating that he has bizarre hallucinatory experiences.

*(Author's Note: Dr. 4 is the only one of the four clinicians who finds evidence of hallucination. This should be borne in mind in light of Dr. 3's testimony that while there may be some quibbling about labels, the four clinicians essentially saw D the same way. Dr. 1 states that hallucinations were not elicited at the time of the interview, Dr. 3 also asserts there are no hallucinations or illusions. It would seem that either Dr. 3's interviewing was not adequate, in that it failed to produce evidence of hallucinations, or that D is inventing symp-*

*toms as he goes along, or that his condition has deteriorated during the period he has been in jail. In fact, on page 27 of his report, Dr. 4 indicates that if D is placed in a general prison population, or with jail staff untrained with individuals with his disorder, he would decompensate in most undesirable ways. Inasmuch as he had been in jail and it is not likely that Dr. 4 knows any more than we do what the make-up was of the population in that jail, that he, according to Dr. 4's prediction, could have severly decompensated by the time Dr. 4 performed the examination.)*

He feels he is prone to behaving in ways which he regrets afterwards. Presently he is experiencing a great deal of guilt, depression, and self-destructive ideas. Attempted suicides are a strong possibility.

Mr. D's MMPI strongly indicates that this patient is in need of psychiatric care. His testing indicates that he is presently suffering from paranoid schizophrenia with an affective disorder and inadequate behavior controls. He is presently a danger to himself. Paranoid ideation is strong and may cause him to strike out irrationally at others.

On the Clinical Analysis Questionnaire (CAQ), Mr. D's test results substantiated those results found on the MMPI. Again, he was found to have an inassertive tenderminded effeminant personality. However, he is prone to paranoid delusions which convince him that others are about to attack him. He has insufficient behavior controls and is likely to attack others on the basis that they might attack him.

Neurotic maladjustment was found to be high on the CAQ (7.8 on a scale of 10). Effectiveness of behavior controls was found to be below average (4.3 on a scale of 10).

Primary personalities found in testing were consistent with other testing results. Capacity for abstract thinking was below average. A mild conforming submissive personality was indicated. However, under stress Mr. D may become shrewd and aggressive.

Mr. D is essentially an introverted person who is a loner. His potential for leadership is below average.

On the Whaler Physical Symptoms Inventory, Mr. D indicated that he presently suffers from daily headaches, difficulty with sleeping, dental problems, and chest pains.

## MENTAL STATUS EXAMINATION:

Examination of the patient in County Jail found Mr. D to be an immature young man. Reactions on all dimensions are more similar to adolescence than to a man of his age. His general manner in interaction was cooperative but preoccupied. The patient's own mental trend of thought predominates his consciousness. He does not interact with full attention to the present. His general activity level demonstrated nervousness.

Mr. D's stream of mental activity was inaccessible due to his preoccupation. Nonetheless, his productivity was valuable. The harder he tried to cooperate, the more his ideas tended to take flight into nonreality. There was a self-absorption and a paranoid trend of thought which could not be penetrated by clinical techniques to bring his thought processes to the present. Progression of thought was illogical, irrelevant, incoherent, and demonstrated extreme blocking of affect and conscious thought.

Emotional reactions demonstrated fear, anxiety, and depression. Emotional instability was apparent. Affect was incongruous with thought content. Ambivalence of expression was noted throughout. Clinical symptoms of emotional deterioration were omnipresent.

Mr. D demonstrated continual symptomatology of disturbance in mental trend. The persecutory line of thinking dominated his preoccupation. Although Mr. D did not demonstrate overt hallucinations at the time of examination, his belief system includes many thoughts that were clearly not based on reality. Mr. D entertains delusions of influence. He believes there are others without and within the prison who are likely to cause him physical harm or to entrap or influence his mind.

Perceptive disorders in the form of overt hallucinations were not present at the time of hallucination [sic], however Mr. D described times when hallucinations were present. For example, Mr. D believes that FV's brother, who died in an auto accident, frequently speaks with him. In addition, Mr. D described trips to [ethnic group] enclaves where he regularly held discourse with spirits.

Sensorium, mental grasp, and capacity were limited. Mr. D has circumscribed amnesia, especially relative to the homicide event. His thinking relative to the homicide is clearly projective. Mr. D engages in confabulation, mixing real events with his clearly confused projected mentation. Thinking capacity is distorted. Mr. D suffers from a chronic thought disorder severely impairing his judgment and insight.

In summary, attitude in general, behavior, stream of mental activity, emotional reaction, content of thought, sensorium, mental grasp, and capacity are all severely disturbed.

## RESULTS OF CLINICAL INTERVIEWING:

The following information was obtained from Mr. D during clinical interviewing. The patient stated that his father is a retired _____ who presently has cancer—a brain tumor. A tree hit him in the head several years ago. Before the accident, Mr. D's father was described as a strict, honest, hard-working person. After the accident he would blow up.

Mr. D was born in _____ on _____, _____. He was the third-to-youngest of _____ siblings. Poverty was a problem with the family. Mr. D states: "I remember going to school—they were well off—I was embarrassed so I would leave to fish." Mr. D stated that he began working at age 9 for his own money. At that age he also began drinking. He stated: "I was on a bicycle and hit by a car. I drank one half-gallon of vodka." He does not remember being hit. He stated that he was unconscious for a few days and almost died. He stated that his face was torn up and he was incoherent when he woke up. Afterward, Mr. D stated that he had troubles in school. Essentially, his biggest problem was his inability to concentrate. He felt teachers did not care about him. He passed out several times and got dizzy spells regularly.

Mr. D described a childhood which was basically a street life. He stated that alcohol and drugs were prevalent in the peer group where he lived. By early adolescence he developed his alcohol intake to several cases of beer in a day along with ten or more joints of pot. He took diet pills, which kept him agitated and awake for two or three days at a time. (LSD "acid" trips were also common.) He believes he has taken six trips or so. Cocaine, psychedelic mushrooms, "reds" (barbiturates), and other substances have been used from time to time. He states there have been many times he didn't know what he was doing.

Mr. D's interviewing tended to ramble from topic to topic. He stated relative to drugs that he had tried to kill himself around Christmas time. He took 100 pills in that attempt. Instead of dying, he threw up blood, went into "the shakes," but did not go to a doctor. He then went into a long discussion of his ex-girlfriend's family, whom he claims is involved in drug dealing. He stated that his girlfriend got him "into a serious game—I tried to leave town. I didn't want violence. I went to a priest. I tried to tell him problems." Mr. D also went around with [minority group members] for moral support.

During his youth, Mr. D had poor examples in older siblings. An older brother was sent to prison for assault with a deadly weapon. Apparently another man was giving his girl drugs and wanted to be paid.

Another brother was incarcerated for bad checks. Mr. D himself had numerous arrests for juvenile crimes such as burglary.

During his youth, Mr. D had difficulties with his father. His father frequently beat him and called him a "runt." In addition, his father bullied Mr. D claiming that he was a homosexual because of his immature build and behavior. Mr. D stated that his father and he were not close until a few years ago. At that time, Mr. D became compassionate toward his father as he saw him suffer from cancer.

In describing his early sex life, Mr. D stated that he became active with girls at age 14. He said: "Girls afraid of pregnancy made me paranoid." He went on to describe an incident, saying: "This girl said she was pregnant so I wouldn't leave. She acted pregnant." Mr. D seems to have confused thinking and approach-avoidance feelings over pregnancy. This pregnancy problem played some part in his relationship with FV but it is unclear exactly what the story is. At any rate, Mr. D claims that at one time FV also said that she was pregnant, but then this turned out to be a lie.

At age 18 Mr. D went to trade school in _____ and tried to get a G.E.D. He said that doctors checked him over at that time and told him he was "weird." He saw psychologists during this period. He claims they told him "not to worry." Mr. D stated: "I grew up a lot different from other kids."

Mr. D retains fragments of events which are related in an unclear manner. He states that at age 18 a fight broke out and he was tipped off that he would be stabbed. He said that he wanted to go home and when he woke up he found himself in the middle of a sex orgy. There was a counselor on the premises that Mr. D claims to have watched have sex with four men. The context of this story is unclear.

Mr. D rambles on, describing his relationship with S, the brother of FV. He was killed in a car accident. Mr. D feels that he himself should have been killed in the same accident. He believes that the friendship he had with S gave justification to his romance with FV. He said, "S would have approved."

When Mr. D began dating FV he felt that he was there to protect her. Mr. D stated that FV's aunts and uncles beat her up. Mr. D felt that FV's mother was a "tramp" who used men. Mr. D stated that FV had earlier been involved with a man who had sex in front of her with other girls and "messed up" FV's mind. Mr. D attributed FV's manipulation of men to this event.

In describing his meeting with FV, he stated that they met in at a dance. Both were drinking and passed out. The couple had sex a week later. They kept their relationship quiet for six months. D said during this time many of FV's girlfriends, her mother and her sisters tried to seduce him into sexual activities. He stated: "A lot of girls wanted me but I was faithful to FV."

Mr. D dates the origin of his problems with FV to the time when her sisters tried to seduce him. Mr. D felt that FV's mother was turning her daughters into prostitutes. One of FV's friends, J, was described as taking cocaine and would go to bed for it.

Mr. D described FV as a person who used one man to tease and threaten others. Mr. D stated: "FV would lead R on and didn't tell them about me. FV would use R and MV. She'd tease them—go to bed."

At this point, Mr. D became confused again in his conversation, changing topics. He stated that the [ethnic group] were going to get [several thousand dollars in government funds] and he thought he should stop it. He stated: "They put me through hell. Tried to blame me for S's death." Mr. D experiences great amounts of internal conflict over S's death. In some way, he apparently feels responsible for that event, although he was nowhere near the premises at the time. His responsibility appears to relate to the depth of his friendship, feeling that if S died he should have died too.

Back again to his sexual relationship with FV, Mr. D stated that things went well until R and MV were involved in the competition. He stated that FV was offered $100, a house and cars, etc., if she would sleep with R, who was allegedly a drug dealer. Mr. D stated: "FV was shy. I got her over that. Her first boyfriend beat her up and had sex in front of her with other girls. I felt for FV. R and MV wanted to hurt her. But she started having sex with MV in November and with me."

Mr. D then related an incident which he felt was the turning point in his relationship with FV. He stated: "One day I had sex with her and I could tell she had sex the same day with another guy. She was lubricated. I asked her if she had been with MV. She admitted sex three times with MV. I broke up with her. Trust was broken. She lied to me—played with their heads—tormented them with my picture. I tried to tell her not to do that. FV turned them against me. FV tried to get MV to kill me. At her birthday, nobody knew who I was. MV followed me home.

"FV and I were breaking up. FV wanted to beat up girls that I talked to but she wanted to go to bed with other men. I told her she couldn't do this to me. I stood up to her when nobody else would.

"One day we stopped at a store. I talked to a girl. FV threatened to put her arms around guys to make me jealous. She and I had a fight in the car. I jumped out of the car. She tried to run me over with the car. I jumped in a ditch. I got back in the car. I told her I was tired of this shit. I told her to stay away from her family. We went to my house. I said 'We're finished.' She said no and cried. I said I'll think about it.' A few days later I said I'll try one more time. She told me that she was pregnant in November. I loved her a lot. I stayed with her. I wouldn't leave her. I found out later she was lying in December. We argued. She wouldn't see a doctor. I told her I didn't believe in abortion. I had delivered a baby for her cousin.

"FV and I in December were still having sex. Her family kept trying to break us up. I saw family feuds—beating each other up with baseball bats, shooting. They hit me in the head. Cops came. They knew I knew how to fight.

"I told them MV would kill me. FV told me that MV followed me. FV's mother threatened to have me beat up like she had done to FV's dad. FV's sisters were mad at me—called me names—tried to beat me up. FV beat off attackers.

"J (FV's friend) wanted FV to go out with MV to get cocaine. I took naked pictures of myself. FV broke out with hives when I left. FV showed naked pictures of me to tease R and MV to make J want to go to love with me. Homosexuals have approved me in jail. FV and J would tease me that I had a larger cock than most. I wonder if I had been to bed with FV's mother none of this would have happened.

"I was threatened by MV. I had naked pictures. I told them I'd get back at them. I put things behind garbage can [sic]. FV picked them up three weeks before.

"MV threatened to have me killed. I knew his family would do it. Italians. Mafia (Mexican). I knew they'd send somebody to get me. R and MV were making $5,000 bringing heroin and cocaine in tuna to get it over here from Peru. I tried to show him that FV was lying. I tried to leave town—no place to go. No money. I tried to kill myself. I took pills on Christmas day. She told me she was pregnant and I said I couldn't see my kid.

"FV called me over. I went to her bedroom and had sex. I told her I knew she wasn't pregnant. She seduced me. MV couldn't have sex with her anymore because MV wasn't a good lover. MV went out with older women. FV said I was better [sic] lover. I broke up with FV after she had sex with MV. I wanted to take FV away from drugs, etc. I was faithful to FV. FV was jealous. She tried to get me back. Threatened me. I gave letters to J's husband and told FV to lay off. I'll prove how FV and J were. Letters about sleeping around. I gave pictures. FV's mom turned against me. I knew I'd be killed. I had seen a lot of violence—knew the mob was after me. I tried to get FV. They humiliated me—tried to seduce me."

Mr. D's stream of consciousness then turned to a period two weeks before the murder. He stated: "I was going to work. I asked R to get me a gun. I was drinking, passing out. I told him I would be killed. There was a diary of days we had sex. The day of the murder I worked overtime. I wanted nothing to do with FV's family. I worked overtime. I knew they could kill me there. I was paranoid drinking. I had no sleep or food but sweets. My insides were tore [sic] up. Smoked a joint one hour before we left work. Riding a 10-speed—thought I'd be killed. Went up fast. People following me. Showered—10:45 got my .22 gun, slept on couch so they couldn't kill me. I didn't have to go to work, tired, didn't sleep for days. FV called me—I went back to bed—woke up, 9 or 10, called FV. MV was supposed to be fishing. FV lied to me. I knew I would be killed that day. We smoked joints. I borrowed a car.

"I asked for an advance on my salary to pay for a fine. (Not true.) Got gas. Tried to borrow more money to leave because I knew they would kill me. Tried to call FV. Got my backpack. Knew I had to kill or be killed. Knew the chances were against me. They would gun me down—professionals. I tried to stop them. Reason with them. They wouldn't listen. My head was going crazy—drinking— passing out. I didn't want my friends to get hurt. I tried to kill myself. FV didn't want to tell me she was a prostitute. I called FV, went to MV's. I knew FV's mother was having an affair with the D.A. My killer would have gotten off free—lesbians—I wanted to leave but had no money. I didn't want to kill but if I had to I would because I knew I would be killed. I followed FV and MV. They lost me. FV's stepdad had tried to kill me. I found them at. I was drinking and smoking dope. I tried to calm myself down. Tried to straighten things out. Didn't care about punishment. I came up on his side—showed my pistol. Said I knew you want to kill me. I was trying to show MV what FV was really like." At this point the patient rambled incoherently.

"I said 'I'll show you the pictures.' FV said, 'Are you going to kill me?' I didn't have the pictures. I told MV to stand in front of the truck—was going to get the pictures. I saw MV come at me. I told him to get down. I aimed and shot. I was jumpy. I shot him twice. I saw FV lean down. I shot her. I could have gone back to kill FV. She was moving but I didn't. I was sweating, shaking, crying. My mind was out of control. I couldn't remember anything. I turned myself in. I knew I needed help. I got a cab. I drank. I went to get a ticket for bus. I heard sirens. I went to _____—drank more—called home and said 'I killed some- body.' They told me to turn myself in. Smoked more joints. Sat by water. I was going to Mexico. I was at the bar for two hours. I got a ticket under a false name, drank more whiskey, and hash—it was a big nightmare. I was drunk in _____.

"I knew they would blow me away. I had thrown the gun away. I got on a bus to _____ to go to _____. I met a guy to take me to _____ and get me a job. Other guys tried to take me to _____. I turned myself in in _____—_____. I went to my old school. I went to a black bar and drank. A black guy said, 'You're on the dodge. The devil made you do that.' He wanted to take me to New York. He offered me girls, food, money and booze. He said, 'If you got gun, we can do business.' I rolled joints. I left. He wanted me to do holdups. I walked around for an hour and called my mom. I was going to Mexico. I thought about it. I turned myself in. My family talked me into turning myself in. I ordered breakfast. I called police who handcuffed me. They took me to the police station. I said, 'I got them before they got me.' I know I'm facing the death penalty. I had a dream when S got killed. I dreamed I'd be killed or go to prison."

During interviewing, the patient talked on and on, switching in a bizarre way from topic to topic. He related that he believes he has visions and can pre- dict the future. He stated: "I had dreams people try to kill me. I banged my head. I had leg irons. Cops tried to work me over. Put me in isolation. I won the lawsuit because I am the type to stand up for my rights. I was to win $28,000 but they blackmailed me. I always know things before they happen. I have dreams and can predict what will happen. I was here in other lives in western days and in the thirties. I was in the Army training post. They tried to hang me for something that didn't take place. I was saved at the last minute. I've had visions for eight years. I'm afraid people would say I was crazy. The [ethnic group] were the only ones who believed me. I was hunting bear with a .22. I spent a lot of time looking for bear."

"They [ethnic group] told me that FV's picture would be used to me. FV with S's picture was at the grave. Only S's picture was there. Things happened at the graveyard. I would pay my respects to S's grave. There were things around me that I couldn't see—evil spirits were watching me. E's cousins did it to me. S was like a brother to me. I was lucky I didn't die. [Ethnic group] were after me. They use their hair. I almost talked to a [spiritual leader]. Even in the Bible it says 'Even at the end, black magic and sorcery will rule.' We live by energy, vibrations and movement. When E's grandmother died, somebody did something to make S die. E came to take the spirit. S, C and H died in the car accident. I was supposed to be there but...(at this point the patient went completely incoherent)."

Mr. D rambled on: "I knew they died before I heard. I felt guilty that I wasn't with them. S talks to me through my dreams from the other world. FV's mom also had dreams. I know people who travel by astral bodies. Hypnotism can make you become an eagle.

"Right now I don't care if they give me life or death. It don't really matter. I figure I won't see outside. I'd rather be dead than live in here. I know I did wrong. My head was too messed up. Everybody (D.A.) is against me. My family and my lawyer have been threatened. If somebody tried to sexually assault me in prison I will have to stop them. FV's mom uses her body with the D.A. I wanted to hurt somebody six years ago when a 6'5" man beat me up in a poolroom."

## INTERVIEW WITH YOUNGEST BROTHER:

D's youngest brother recalls that people would tease D for being small. He recalls D's automobile accident when he was nine. He stated: "The family was mad at him for drinking and being in the hospital."

He related that their father hit both boys with a belt. He stated: "Father would be very critical of D. D never really trusted me—he was afraid I would tattle on him." He went on to relate that D went through a period when he would not come out of the house. During this time, D simply sat around and stared into space. At one time, D's brother recalls that D warned him that "People would try to get me if they knew if I was D's brother—to watch out."

He related that their father called D "dumb" and a "pothead" because he couldn't hold a job. D always had trouble in school and consequently did not go very often. He stated that FV couldn't be trusted because she lied.

In relating family life when D was young, he stated that all the brothers picked on D because he was smaller.

### INTERVIEW WITH OLDEST SISTER:

She related that she was in her twenties when D was born. D's birth was not planned. The parents were in their forties. She stated: "D was always little, sick, didn't catch on to things but then there were so many children. My dad picked on D." The father was described as too strict and the mother too lenient. D was described as uncoordinated and unable to find a job. She continued: "It was known that he was a slow learner."

In describing family life, she said that her father had a bad temper and said mean things to his own children. He would call his own daughters whores for no reason. He also called the sons homosexuals if they weren't married at 18 or 19. He has gotten worse with age. She stated that her mother told her their father threatened D physically with a belt. He whipped his children for no reason. The parents could not handle their last children.

She continued, stating that it was her opinion that D should have been in special education but wasn't. He needed glasses but broke them or wouldn't wear them. The parents were too poor to supervise these problems. Sometimes there was not enough to eat. One holiday the family starved. The father's work was not steady. Babies were too close together. The mother had no time for the babies. There were two before D, then D, then two after D with less than a year apart.

In relating the family history, she stated that the family came from Midwest in the hills. There was no education in their family. The mother was too embarrassed to talk about sex, birth control or pregnancy. The mother would not even tell her eldest daughter she was pregnant—she would say she was sick instead and turn out to be pregnant.

She stated: "My dad is so cruel that I try not to be around him. He calls my sons queer. He makes my children cry. He calls them fat."

She continued, stating the D was the slowest and smallest of the family. The whole family picked on him. The last year, D was never at home for a holiday. D called her husband daily to see if there was a job. Her husband couldn't help because D was too poorly coordinated to use a hammer. "My dad told D," said she, "not to be around FV and bad company.

She continued: "D tried to commit suicide. I got a phone call and called _____ and she said he was passed out. She couldn't wake him. What should she do. He had taken pills. They got him to throw up. He refused to go to the hospital."

"Since D started going around with S he was weird. D believed that he talked to S after S's death. He seemed to believe that he could communicate with the spirits. D would say 'I'm the only white man they let come to the [rituals].'"

She related that D and FV tried to borrow $5,000 to go into the cocaine business. She stated that FV's stepfather was in the cocaine business.

*(Author's Note: Here, according to Dr. 4's report, the older sister apparently believed that D and FV were going into the drug businesss. This is further implemented by Dr. 4's statements on page 24 of the report that it is impossible to determine whether threats actually were made, but the data strongly suggests*

*that there were. Obviously, if threats against him were made, D's belief that threats against him were made is not a delusion; it is a fact.)*

D called _____ and asked her for money, saying that FV was pregnant. _____ (a sister) lives with an [ethnic group man] who is a cousin to FV.

She related that D had been trying to get in _____ to get away from the people trying to kill him. D believed that the Mafia was trying to kill him. D gave _____ (another sister) a list of names in case he died. D had seemed really crazy for the last few years.

She related that D said "I've been set up." She further stated that D attempted to get a job every day from her brother-in-law. Again, lack of coordination was apparently the factor which kept D from obtaining employment.

D described to her strange delusionary experiences. For example, D talked about taking a rope and lassoing a fish. D also claimed that he delivered a baby for FV's relative right before the homicide episode. There was really a baby born, but it was born in a hospital. D believed that FV was pregnant. D said he wanted to marry FV to take care of them.

She went on to say that D had had a brother killed in an auto accident when he was about 10. She stated: "I have wondered if D did things to get attention from father. A neighbor told me that D was at her house and felt guilty and sorry for his mother who had been through so much."

## INTERVIEW WITH D'S MOTHER:

Mother related that she had a kidney infection during her pregnancy with D. She stated that the "kidney rotted out." She stated: "I went to Dr. _____—I have the infection the whole time I was pregnant. D was the smallest of the kids when he was born. He has always been smallest. D was in an incubator." Both mother and D were hospitalized for 15 days after the birth.

She related: "D has always been slow. He didn't talk much. He was a loner. He didn't like to play with other children. My husband is sick with cancer and on drugs. He says horrible things to us. He has had five operations and can't sleep. He's been worse in the last two years.

"The school told me that D was unable to learn—almost completely blind. I got him glasses when he was in grade school. The kids laughed at him and he broke the glasses and I couldn't keep him in glasses. The kids called him an old man. D was never close to me or to anyone else.

"When D was six or seven he climbed out of a window and ran away. My husband was in the hospital because a tree fell on his leg. He was in a wheelchair for two years."

She continued: "D was closest to sister of all the children." The school kept telling her that D could never make a decision. She related that when D was seven or eight he went to a ball game and got liquored up and a car hit him and his head was crushed and he was in the hospital for five days or so.

Describing family life, she stated that she worked for a store. She said that the family mostly ate bread and beans. There were a lot of hard times when there was not enough for the children to eat. There were cold winters and the family lived on unemployment.

She related that she and D never talked about sex. She knew that FV had said she was pregnant. As she recalled it: "FV may have said that. She had an abortion. D didn't want her to have an abortion."

She continued: "Before this episode D would stay in his room and stare into space. D had a friend S that was killed in a car accident. D would have been with him but he was taking garbage out at the time. D said, 'If I hadn't been hauling garbage, we could have gone together.'" D's mother believes that D had wanted to die from that time. She continued: "D stayed with FV and relatives. If he came home to shower they'd call him right back. FV would come and get him."

"D cried and said, 'I can't get over what they put in S's grave.'" The mother doesn't understand what D meant by this. She stated that D wouldn't sleep at night. He thought he heard spirits or the Mafia outside his window. He was depressed and tried to overdose himself with pills. She stated that he would not tell her why he did it.

## INTERVIEW WITH D'S FATHER:

The father related that D was always tiny and didn't grow very fast. He was smaller than the rest of the babies, but he "didn't give it much mind." He further stated, "Since then I read the Bible and it said I was too old to have children. We didn't want all these children. My wife had kidney problems."

In relating the auto accident, he stated: "D got run over by a car. He was riding a bicycle. I can't remember too much. I was sick and taking medicine. His doctors said he was brain damaged. He was unconscious for a long time."

Changing the subject, he stated that D recently told him that he had been contacted by the Mafia who wanted him to sell narcotics about one month before the episode in question. He said to his father: "Dad, I could make a lot of money but it's dangerous."

Father stated that there was a homosexual problem. He related that D and his brother went to a hotel where there were homosexuals. He stated that his older daughter told him that D was going to this hotel. He stated he had no idea why D had done this. During that time, D stayed in his room a lot. D tended to stay awake all night and sleep by day. He slept on the couch because he thought people were after him.

He went on to relate that D used to get beaten up a lot as a child and later. He stated that a big person beat up D about a year before this happened. He stated that the attacker knocked in D's teeth and his nose.

Father related: "D told me 'Dad, you won't believe this—there's Mafia over there with machine guns, etc.' The [ethnic group] told D that he was one of them. D believed the [ethnic group] would do anything for him. They raised marijuana and made a lot of money."

## INTERVIEW WITH ANOTHER SISTER:

She stated that D was always a crybaby as a child. Family and friends would tease him and he would cry over any little thing. He was frequently teased about being little and a loner at school. He was shy and not much interested in girls.

She related: "Our dad is strict. We don't care much for our dad. He punished us (especially D) no matter what we did. D got lots of spankings with switches and belts. We were poor. Dad would be gone a lot of the time. Dad would pull D's hair and hold him down and beat him and yell at him and leave welts from age six or seven—maybe younger. Dad would threaten D before the beatings. Dad doesn't seem all there. Dad was suspicious and would accuse D of taking drugs from fifth or sixth grade up.

"D and I were the closest. D told me he loved FV. S got killed. D said FV wanted to get married. D wanted to get out of \_\_\_\_\_ and get a job. He felt he was being watched because my brother had gotten in trouble. D became fanatic when S died. D told me that [ethnic group] accepted him after S's death. He believed in [ethnic group] spirits. He had seen [rituals]—took acid and pot—once he took enough acid and then there was a [ritual] and the [ethnic group] held a knife at his throat. D was so wasted that he just laughed. This meant that he had become S's [ethnic group] spirit.

"FV and D started arguing. FV's friends called and said bad things about D. D tried to kill himself. I came in and found him. The night before, FV had said she was going to break up with him. D would say things that were too off the wall I couldn't follow. He dreamed that S called him in his dreams. [Ethnic group] and Mafia were threatening him because of what he knew about drugs. Then he would talk about my brother, who had gotten into trouble. D didn't want to hurt mother and dad like \_\_\_\_\_ had. Around Christmas time he was nervous, shaking and smoked cigarettes a lot. D was afraid for his life and the whole family's. D was chaotic and incoherent—rambling.

"FV was never really pregnant but D believed she was. FV lied and said she was pregnant so he would marry her. FV was D's first serious relationship.

"D was accused of being a homosexual because he was small and never went around with girls. D came to me and asked me to get him out of town and hide him. He was so scared to go home or out—he was paranoid and crazy. He said he had to get away or they would kill him for what he knew and Mom and Dad. The Mafia and [ethnic group] were after him. I couldn't reason with him. He was petrified to be alone.

"D has never been violent. Even if people came after him he would back off." She stated that D was afraid of guns and afraid of jails. He was afraid he would get into trouble like his brother."

## FORMULATION:

Results of psychological testing, clinical interviewing, and review of voluminous records strongly support the diagnosis that D has suffered from paranoid schizophrenia for some years. Testing results and his clinical history strongly indicate that D suffered organic brain damage at a very young age. Multiple traumas appear to have contributed to his limited mental functioning. To begin with, he was seriously stunted as a newborn consequent to his mother's kidney infection during the entirety of her pregnancy with D. In infancy, he never was able to develop normally. He was slow to grow, slow to talk, and unsociable. As an infant he was neglected in terms of diet and environmental support. Even before the auto accident at age 9, his mother felt that this son was scarred or impaired.

At age 9, D suffered an auto injury which left him unconscious for a protracted period. According to interviewing with his father, doctors at the time felt that this injury brain-damaged the boy. It is strongly suggested that records of this injury be obtained to assess the probable outcome of that event. It is notable that friends and relatives have stated that D's inability to obtain employment stems from growth-motor disability which precludes him from working at laboring jobs. The observation that he is not coordinated enough to hold a hammer strongly suggests that there may be physical disability in addition to intellectual stunting as a result of this old accident. It is most likely that this trauma further contributed to slow intellectual and physiological development from age 9.

Clinical interviewing with all family members suggests that D was subjected to continual ridicule and stress during his adolescent years. He was unable to function in school, too uncoordinated to find employment, and socially withdrawn. He suffered from stunted physical size, which caused him embarrassment. His father further exacerbated his problems by suggesting that D was a homosexual. Apparently, he has had some encounters with members of the same sex, possibly lending further reasons for derogation at home. During testing, D admitted to being attracted to members of the same sex. It is very probable that he fell into an ambivalent sexual development early in his adolescence. Although D, during clinical interviewing, claims to have been primarily heterosexual in his development, it is clear that he is deeply threatened by homosexual fears.

It is known that paranoid mentation is frequently accompanied by homosexual fears and often homosexual behavior. Paranoia appears to be exacerbated by fears of homosexual involvement. There is usually an approach-avoidance aspect to the homosexual psychosexual adjustment of paranoids. The relationship between these two psychological adjustments is not clearly understood.

D's overall functioning has been further diminished by excessive alcohol and drug abuse throughout his life.

After the death of his friend S, D's drug abuse and association with people who abused drugs increased dramatically. He became friends with the [ethnic group], participating in their drug and psychic superstitions. At this point, it is probable that D was unable to distinguish between reality and the superstitious. Real experiences while under the influence of mind distorting drugs become permanently distorted. This increased drug usage undoubtedly contributed to D's loss of reality. It is clear that his feeling of relatedness to S had meanings for D which were not understood by others. Family members have testified that D appeared to want to die with S. D's psychological involvement with S is not entirely clear; however, it is evident that D's relationship to FV was colored in intensity by feelings which he had for S.

Clinical interviewing strongly indicates that D's relationship with FV was pathological. It is clear that FV wittingly or unwittingly contributed to his confusion. While the veracity of D's statements is open to determine, it is clear from other testimony that there was some trading of nude pictures back and forth which substantially aggravated D's feelings of persecution. FV testified in the documents reviewed that she and MV were at the beach that day reviewing four scrapbooks of her pictures. It is unclear what exchange of pictures actually took place, but it is certain that the picture theme somehow triggered D's paranoia. It is unclear what part FV might have played in exacerbating his paranoia through showing pictures to other men, etc. It appears that FV may have been exacerbating an insane person without entirely realizing it. However, from testimony which FV gave at the time when investigators were examining the pickup trucks and garage which were painted by D, it seems that she herself understood to some degree that D's mental stability was questionable. It is possible that actual counterthreats were made to D in order to control his earlier bizarre behavior. It is impossible from the testimonies given to determine this with any degree of certitude. However, data reviewed strongly suggests that there were cuing factors to D's paranoid trend, including some types of counterthreats.

D's paranoia appears further exacerbated by what he either experienced or imagined to be sexual proximity to MV. Either factually, or in his imagination, D had concluded that FV had been having sexual contact with both MV and D himself on the same day. This perception substantially precipitated D into his final dementia.

A further theme which appeared to trigger D's delusional system was the talk of pregnancy. Various people in his family substantiate the belief on his part that FV was either pregnant and obtained an abortion or claimed to be pregnant for some time. This time of psychosexual stimulation was undoubtedly more than D could manage. D apparently went from a condition of believing he was soon to be a father to a condition of believing that FV was planning to marry someone else and abandon him entirely. This sudden shift in focus undoubtedly further precipitated emotional problems for D.

A further aspect contributing to D's loss of reality appears to be some real drug trafficking involvement of the people in his social circle. Various people have been named in clinical interviewing as either regular drug dealers or as planning to enter the drug commerce. Apparently, D entertained many fears related to the sorts of people who might be involved in drug dealing. This may be the source of his fears that Mafia people or others might be coming to get him. His parents were aware that he and FV at one time contemplated entering a drug business. D apparently withdrew from this activity out of fear. It is unclear whether or not FV and her relatives planned to obtain [ethnic group] funds in order to enter this illegal business. However, enough testimony has been gathered on this subject to possibly suggest that there was some triggering of fears on D's part by an intent to enter the drug business.

Psychological testing results very clearly indicate that at the very least, D is a paranoid schizophrenic and has been for some time. The murder episode and subsequent jailing have probably exacerbated this condition to some extent. However, adequate testimony to D's confused mentation before the episode has been obtained from other family members. In addition, the type of theme building and behaviors commonly expected of an individual with this type of psychosis is strongly substantiated by all participants in this situation. Additionally, D has the type of clinical background which one typically finds retrospectively in paranoid schizophrenics.

The type of psychosexual theme which D has developed in is relationship with FV and his fantasies connected to it are typical of paranoid schizophrenics in a chronic condition. Further substantiation to the hypothesis that he was a paranoid schizophrenic prior to this incident is provided by such informants as D's mother, who claims that schoolteachers for years told her that her son was unable to make decisions, etc. Such behaviors are typical of early schizophrenic thinking. D's tendency to be withdrawn and a loner,...

...his tendency to stay indoors and stare into space, his proclivity for sleeping on the couch during the daytime to avoid nighttime fears and other early behaviors strongly suggest that D has been psychotic for some time.

The diagnosis of paranoid schizophrenia is consistent with other mental examiners who have seen D since this incident.

There is a further aspect of psychosis which appears in this latest testing. Both MMPI and CAQ results strongly indicate that D has a manic element to his personality. This particular characteristic is typical of individuals who have suffered brain damage. Essentially, it means that individuals so affected are likely to develop emotions which they cannot control. The elevation in manic affect also contributes to rambling, incoherent stories. When paranoid schizophrenia is complicated by affective psychosis, the behavioral outcome is considerably worse. It means that the individual so affected not only has a thought disorder, but is also likely to act upon his thoughts in an immediate and uncontrolled manner. This is what is meant by the diagnostic conclusion that behavioral controls are inadequate. According to psychological testing done at this time, D has inadequate behavior controls to manage his own affect. Early brain trauma may have substantially predisposed him to this condition. Later alcohol and drug abuse have further weakened his affective controls. At the time of this testing, D was found not only to have paranoid schizophrenia but also an affective disorder.

The summary of results obtained by psychological testing, review of records, and clinical interviewing strongly suggests that the relationship between FV and D essentially set off a time bomb of psychosis. It is strongly concluded that both the paranoid schizophrenia and the affective disorder existed prior to this relationship. Apparently, D began his final decompensatory disintegration around the time that his friend S died. He experienced some respite in his emotional relationship with FV. However, evidence strongly suggests that FV did engage in interactions and behaviors which D could not process emotionally or mentally. The switch in her affections concomitant with the entrance of drug traffickers into his immediate acquaintance apparently had the effect of triggering total mental and behavioral decompensation on his part.

At the present time, D is entirely unable to put together the pieces of his life. He is suffering from two virulent, overlapping psychotic disorders. Either one would be sufficient to require hospitalization and intensive treatment. Both the paranoid schizophrenia and the affective disorder make him totally unfit to interact with other prisoners or with jail staff untrained in the management of individuals with these disorders. If D is placed in a general prison population, he will undoubtedly decompensate in most undesirable ways in his interaction with others. If other inmates listen to his talk, they may be affected by his mentation. At worst, he may develop fears that other inmates are approaching or attacking him. He may see some of these people as extensions of the Mafia or the [ethnic group]. It would be unfair to him and to others to program this type of interaction.

On the other hand, D has inordinate fears of being left alone. Prior to this series of events, he slept by day and took drugs by night in order to ward off his fears of solitary existence. Imprisoning him by himself will also tend to exacerbate his decompensation. It is presently most strongly urged that this patient be treated by competent medical and professional individuals. Staff persons entrusted with D's care should be trained in the management of psychotic patients.

## DIAGNOSTIC IMPRESSIONS:

Paranoid schizophrenia complicated by measurable affective disorder. Etiology of the affective disorder is probably multiple brain traumas including birth injury, head injury at age nine, malnutrition, drug and alcohol abuse, and environmental deprivation of the worst magnitude. Affective disorder is the most usual psychological consequence of brain damage. It causes loss of behavior controls.

## RECOMMENDATIONS:

It is strongly recommended that D receive professional psychiatric treatment and housing. He is not capable of participating in his own defense at the present time. It is most likely that he will attempt to act out suicidal needs.

It is strongly suggested that medical records of the head injury D received at age nine be obtained. It is also recommended that D's gross motor coordination be checked. There are not only signs of stunted intellectual growth suggesting early brain damage, but clinical interviewing also reveals testimony that D has insufficient physical coordination to undertake simple tasks such as operating a hammer.

## ESTIMATION OF D'S MENTAL CAPACITY
## AT THE TIME OF THE HOMICIDE:

Psychological testing results, clinical data and records reviewed indicate that D was psychotic at the time of the attack. He clearly remembers some aspects of the attack but misinterprets most of the factual data. The construction of his paranoid system which motivated him to attack obviously contained some elements of delusion. D suffers from a complicating affective disorder which makes him lose control of his behavior under stress. It is probable that this affective disorder is most likely in an organic condition.

Thank you very much for the opportunity to examine this most interesting patient.

Dr. 4, Ph.D.

**DR. 4, PH.D.**

December 8
Mr. D.C.

Dear D.C.:

Enclosed is my report of psychological assessment of D, including interviews with his relatives. The report is somewhat lengthy, due to the rambling and fragmented nature of the clinical data.

In the course of my interviews, a strong drug theme developed which I believe you might wish to investigate. It seems that D told his father that he and FV were planning to obtain [ethnic group] fund money from the government in order to set up a cocaine business in order to support their supposed new family. It appears somewhat likely that FV was the instigator of this entrepreneurial plan. D was apparently frightened by the illegal nature of the undertaking, possibly because of the criminal problems of his brother. Ambivalence over this cocaine plan may have contributed to the romantic break-up between D and FV.

According to D, FV and MV intended to apply [to the government for several thousand dollars in funds] which would then be used to begin a cocaine trafficking business. The model for this dealership is apparently the ex-boyfriend of FV, R.

According to D, after the romantic breakup with FV he threatened the new couple (FV and MV) with disclosure of their intended plans to fraudulently obtain government funds to enter the cocaine business. It appears most likely that D did receive counterthreats as a result of his intention to thwart this illegal business.

It appears most likely that D's developing paranoia was put into full gear by fears that FV and her boyfriend might retaliate against him for obstructing their business. If this sequence of events, pieced together from my clinical interviewing data, should be true, then the fear of reprisal from MV was more justified in fact than we may have previously thought. The development of an extreme paranoia is then more understandable.

I have included this hypothesis in a separate letter because I feel that the testimony of individuals involved is subject to distortion. However, this theme was developed in a number of my interviews, and I feel that it bears investigation. If this sequence of events or some similar drug undertaking was really afoot, then D's paranoia was constructed not only around his sexual rejection, but also around some realistically expected threats as the result of his threat to blackmail the [ethnic group] funding of the cocaine business.

I feel that D may be somewhat defensive in revealing his own role in this situation. D probably still fears retaliation from informing on his friends. Furthermore, D undoubtedly feels some guilt if he himself contemplated entering this cocaine trade. My clinical interviewing notes strongly suggest that D did consider entering the cocaine business, but withdrew from the plan out of fear of illegal activity. This drug scenario, in addition to the psychosexual "games," strongly support a position that FV did in fact "mess up" D's mind—a mind already chronically psychotic.

Inasmuch as data taken from paranoid individuals must be checked out thoroughly, I feel a separate letter is appropriate to you on this issue. However, interviewing data with other family members strongly substantiates this hypothesis.

Thank you very much for the opportunity to examine the individuals in this case.

Sincerely,

Dr. 4, Ph.D.

*(Author's Note: The description of D as a loner is contradicted by his own description of himself, Dr. 4's use of the description, "people in his social circle," on page 25 of the report—loners don't usually have a social circle—and his score on the social introversion scale of the MMPI test which Dr. 4 has relied on a great deal is right about at the average point, which would certainly counter-indicate a description of him as a "loner."*

*Of course, the letter of December 8 to defense attorney clearly indicates Dr. 4's belief that there was adequate evidence for D's beliefs that he was endangered due to the drug trafficking, whatever it may have been. Obviously, Dr. 4's excluding this lengthy statement from the report creates serious concerns about his credibility and his integrity. The statement that the reason for the separate letter is because data taken from paranoid individuals must be checked out thoroughly seems to have no substance, in view of the fact that all the other statements made by the so-called paranoid individual are not subject to a request for further investigation by Dr. 4. It is difficult not to suspect that Dr. 4 did not want to include this in his report, because it would be somewhat damaging to the basis, or one of the bases, for the diagnosis that was made.*

*We have not dealt with a good deal of the material in this report consisting of Dr. 4's statements that seem clearly speculative, or those stated with such certitude that one should recognize that there is no body of knowledge which supports that degree of absoluteness.*

*With regard to Dr. 4's actual testimony, the transcript is quite lengthy, and we have made the decision that it simply is not worth the space it would take here and the time it would take to adequately comment on all of it.*

*In describing elevation of the MF scale on the MMPI, Dr. 4 states "D has marked the following items as true '[He is] very strongly attracted by members of [his] own sex. True.' That's sufficient to cause the scale to be elevated." This, of course, is simply wrong. No one item can cause the scale to be elevated.*

*Another statement is "Rigidity is measured by a high S scale, which is quite high here, meaning that he is not a psychologically flexible person. His father is one of the least flexible people I ever interviewed, and it would be natural that he emulated some of these traits of inflexibility." This is more psychobabble. While some sons do emulate their fathers, many sons do not emulate their fathers.*

*At another point, asked "What does the 'F' scale represent?" (referring to the MMPI), the response is "the basic measure of psychological flexibility." The author has considerable experience with the MMPI and its interpretation, and has never encountered such a statement in all the literature he has reviewed and in all of the reports he has ever read. If there is a statement somewhere in the literature which would support this description, it certainly flies in the face of what is generally given as a description of the F scale, which is a scale made up of items which are rarely answered in a scorable direction, even by people with known psychiatric disorders. When asked, "What is the 'K' scale?" the answer is, "The 'K' scale is a measure of the ratio between the two of them, and it is considered significant and it's another measure of validity..." and then goes on to say it is a measure of defensiveness. Then he refers to his low K score as being consistent with his high profile. However, the profile shows that the K score is a T score of 48, which is just about at the mean, or about as average as one gets. It is not low. A later answer indicates that the psychologist does not even know what the K stands for. "What then does the 'K' stand for, please?" Answer: "Well there's a statistical interpolation, that is you go from raw data to— eventually to T data, and K is somewhere in between," indicating that the psychologist does not seem to know that K is a correction applied to some of the raw scores in order to compensate for the degree of defensiveness that the individual has shown.*

*Asked to define diminished capacity, the answer is "That means suffering from a mental defect or mental disease. In my opinion, he has both." Clearly, this is not the definition of diminished capacity.*

*When asked what the term "validity" means in psychology, particularly what the term "coefficient of validity" means, the response is, "For instance, the MMPI has built into what we call 'validity scales,'" indicating that the psychologist is confused between the general meaning of validity in psychology and the narrow meaning applied to measures of test-taking attitude with the MMPI. Because Dr. 4 in his testimony comes on like "gangbusters" with terms such as "absolutely" and "certainly," revealing errors of this kind usually causes that balloon to rapidly deflate.)*

## TESTIMONY OF DR. 3

### DIRECT EXAMINATION:

*(Author's Note: This picks up after presentation of an impressive set of credentials.)*

Q. I'd like to ask you—you've indicated that you are a psychiatrist with some degree of experience. We've had another psychiatrist testify, but I'd like to have you tell us what is it that a psychiatrist does.

A. First of all, a psychiatrist is a doctor. He's an M.D. And I suppose he looks at emotional or mental problems much the same way a doctor who is limited to physical medicine would look at a physical problem.

He's interested in diagnosis and treatment.

Some of his patients simply have some problems in living, they don't really have a mental illness per se, but they may be stuck someplace in their life, they may have a marriage which is stuck and destructive, and so many of us are very good at getting people moving again and communicating better and putting aside some of the things that get in the way of a meaningful loving intimacy with their spouse, for example.

Or our patients may have a specific symptom. They are all right generally but they have a specific symptom. They may have an abiding fear of flying, for example. A phobic symptom. There are techniques by which we can help people to put that irrational fear aside so that they can get back on the airplane.

Or the symptoms may be many and coalesce into a pattern which we call a diagnosis. You connect the dots of the symptoms and a picture emerges, you know. A motorcycle cop upside down in a tree or whatever the case may be. The same process that an internist would connect dots to determine that you have had a heart attack; crushing chest pain, radiating down the left arm, smoke three packs a day, family history of coronary heart disease, dropping blood pressure, perspiration. These dots connect and they read out "heart attack." Well, there are psychological symptoms, too, when you connect them and the same pattern emerges over and over again, this person is schizophrenic, or you connect the dots and this person is manic depressive, or it may be just one dot, this person has a fear of flying.

*(Author's Note: The witness has done two things here. He has established an association, an identification, if you will, of psychiatric diagnosis with medical diagnosis in which most people tend to have a certain amount of confidence. Therefore, the lawyer would probably not want to just let this stand. He could ask some questions to bring out the fact that the level of agreement and accuracy in psychiatric diagnoses is not the same as it is for the diagnosis of a heart attack. The example is used effectively. One way of doing this is with a question such as, "Doctor, isn't there a substantial body of scientific and professional literature indicating that there is considerable disagreement concerning psychiatric diagnoses?" If he responds that there is also disagreement in medical diagnoses, a follow up question might be, "Doctor, doesn't the literature generally indicate that the degree of disagreement (and/or lack of accuracy) is somewhat greater in psychiatric diagnoses than in medical diagnoses generally?" Or, "Does the research clearly show that schizophrenia can be diagnosed with the same degree of reliability and validity as a diagnosis of heart attack?" [For more on this point, see the references to Dr. Seymour Pollack and others in Chapter 1 of Volume I.] The second point that the witness has established is that there are firm fixed criteria for psychiatric diagnoses which are applied the same way by all psychiatrists. He could be questioned concerning the plethora of material in Volumes I and II indicating this is not the case; or he could be questioned more specifically concerning schizophrenia, which is the diagnosis which will be at issue in this case, as to whether or not there is considerable disagreement in the field of psychiatry as to just what dots should be connected in order to establish this diagnosis and whether or not different psychiatrists not only connect the dots differently but in fact observe different dots. A quote in Chapter 12 of Volume II from the* American Journal of Psychiatry, *1973, Brodie and Sabshin, states, "The inability to identify a cluster of symptoms peculiar to schizophrenia affected all other areas of research in this widely studied affliction," and in the* International Journal of Psychiatry, *1973, Mosher and Feinsilver say, "A major obstacle in any attempts to reach agreement as to [what schizophrenia is] is the fact that confusingly diverse diagnostic procedures are used in different countries and indeed within a single nation." Other evidence on the diversity of diagnostic approaches to schizophrenia are available in that same chapter. If the witness should attempt to indicate that all disagreements have been resolved with the coming of the DSM-III (in effect at that time but the same would apply to DSM-III-R) then questions can be asked to*

*bring out the fact that the DSM's are ephemeral, transitory, to use the commit-
tee's expression, "way stations" on the way to diagnostic reliability and validity
and as such cannot be counted on. That is every few years the dots and the connections between the dots change. Additionally the point can be made that, particularly in the early years of a new edition of the manual (such as the time of
this trial), not only have the dots been changed but there has not been enough
time to evaluate the appropriateness of the dots. Alternatives to attempting to
establish this on cross-examination would be simply to ask the witness if he is
aware of scientific and professional literature as indicated above, and if he is
not he will appear somewhat ignorant if you then produce your own expert who
will establish such literature.*

*In addition, there are some facts available in the courtroom in this instance
which would either tend to support your contention that there is diversity in dot
connection or that if everybody is using the same dot connecting principles then
the condition has changed in ways that may be significant in the six months or
so between the examination by Dr. 1 and the examination by Dr. 3. That is, we
note in Dr. 1's report that he does not diagnose paranoid schizophrenia, with
his diagnostic impression hovering somewhere between inadequate personality
disorder or borderline schizophrenia with antisocial features. In DSM-III, borderline states are not classified under schizophrenia but are classified under
personality disorders (schizotypal personality disorder). Obviously inadequate
personality disorder was a personality disorder. Dr. 2's diagnoses, if they can
be called that, are thought disorder and borderline psychotic. The point being
made here is that neither of these individuals connected the dots at that time to
come up with a picture of paranoid schizophrenia such as Dr. 3 did when he
connected the dots. Therefore, either the dots get connected differently by different clinicians; or the diagnosis depends on who is making the diagnosis rather
than the true condition of the individual; or D's condition, whatever it may have
been, changed in a negative way between the time of the examination of Drs. 1
and 2 and the examinations by Drs. 3 and 4, a period of time in which D was
incarcerated facing a possible death penalty trial and at least according to some
of the evidence, being harassed and possibly mistreated by jail personnel or jail
conditions.)*

So he makes a diagnosis and then applies the appropriate treatment, which
may be psychotherapy, digging into the individual's past and uprooting
those things long forgotten that may be causing the problem, or putting the
individual on medication, which may correct a chemical imbalance. There
are many psychiatric conditions which may be caused or at the very least
mediated—mediated by chemical problems. So if you give them a different
chemical, theoretically it will straighten them out. Lithium is such a chemical. It helps people with manic depressive problems.

There are some who believe that schizophrenia is alleviated with drugs
and will make those symptoms go away.

Q.   You've alluded to the fact that you have a private practice, apparently, aside
from your various court appointments and that kind of thing.
What kind of problems do you deal with in your private practice?

A. Very much the spectrum of problems that I described today. It is a general psychiatric practice. I see all kinds of people, school teachers, housewives, plumbers, carpenters, a couple of psychiatrists, quite a few lawyers.

THE COURT: Judges?

A. Just one, your Honor.

Mr. DC: Stay away from the judge.

Q. Apparently these people that you just talked about are those persons who come to—they're not ordered to come see you by a court, they come by their own volition?

A. Yeah. Sure.

Q. How do they find you? How do people like that find you?

A. Well, they may have read about me, they may have a friend who had some mental problems, saw me and the problem went away, and thus was recommended.

Or another doctor may discover his patient seemingly with a physical problem really has a psychological one, and he refers me.

Q. I take it these people pay you fees, they pay you money, you charge them for that kind of thing.

A. Right.

Q. Can you give me an idea of the kind of fees that you do charge in those cases?

A. For psychotherapy I charge fifty dollars an hour.

Q. Okay. What about some of the other things?

A. Well, ranges, depending on what I am doing and how far I have to go. For legal work, which is a sub-subspecialty of psychiatry for which I have special training and experience I charge as much as eighty-five dollars, and in some rare cases as much as a hundred dollars an hour.

Q. Are those by and large the same kinds of fees that you charge in the court cases that we are talking about when you are appointed?

A. Yeah.

Q. Is that pretty much in line with what goes on in this state, to your knowledge?

A. I think probably I charge a little less. Usually when you're doing court cases, you know, it is coming out of the taxpayers pocket, and I'm sensitive to that. I feel in part it is a public service. A part. Also, the hours add up very quickly, and if it is an individual carrying that load, it is pretty heavy. I'm sensitive to that factor, too.

*(Author's Note: Here the witness seems to attempt to establish his character as a good guy who does his legal work partly as a public spirited citizen and charges less than others because he feels it is a public service and even if it is an individual, not a public taxpayer money case, he still keeps his fee down. However, regardless of all of that goodness, the fact remains that as a result of doing legal work the hours he spends in that work compensate him at a rate almost double or, in some cases, actually double the amount he would be receiving if he was helping those individuals who are suffering from psychological distress of one kind or another which is the usual psychiatric practice. As will become apparent below, his referral of this matter to Dr. 4 hardly saves the taxpayers any*

*money and the reasons for doing it appear rather weak. There will be more about his fees when the cross-examination takes place.)*

Q. The gentleman seated to my right, D, have you ever seen him before?

A. I have.

Q. When did you first see him?

A. Back in September. September 27th of last year.

Q. How many times did you see him?

A. Twice.

Q. When was the second occasion?

A. On November twenty-sixth of last year.

Q. At whose request did you see Mr. D?

A. Yours.

Q. He was not a patient of yours?

A. No.

Q. As you sit there now do you feel he should be a patient of yours?

A. Indeed. He should be a patient of somebody's.

Q. What was the purpose of the examination when you first saw him?

A. To find out if there was anything wrong with him, and you suspected that there was, and if there was, what that problem was and what relationship, if any, did that mental problem have on the fact that he killed one person and very nearly killed another.

*(Author's Note: The witness acknowledges that defense counsel suspected there was something wrong with D when the referral was made. If this is not a protected communication or if the protection has been waived by the witness's statement it may be worthwhile to find out if defense counsel communicated to the witness what the bases were for his suspecting there was something wrong. This might set the stage for questions on biases of various kinds including confirmatory bias or preconceptions. This issue does come up again on cross-examination where it is not particularly well handled by the cross-examiner.)*

Q. When I asked you to come in and take a look at Mr. D and conduct a psychiatric examination, I supplied you with certain records and documents involved in the case. I'd like you to tell the jury what documents you reviewed on this first occasion back in September.

A. All right. I reviewed the transcript of the preliminary hearing, the police reports, the psychological report of Doctor 2, and interviews or reports of interviews of the following people: (names of several friends, relatives, FV, officers) and the January twenty-eight statement made by the defendant himself to detective.

   I also reviewed an interview with (another friend), D's juvenile record, and then a batch more of things the second time around.

Q. Were there some of these things—I'm talking now back in September when you first saw D, were there some of these documents that you were provided that you felt were more important or more significant than others?

A. Yeah, yeah.

Q. Which ones?

A. Well, the first time around I thought statements of (two acquaintances and FV) were of particular interest from a psychological point of view.

Q. Why?

A. Why? Well, they gave me a view from the outside of D's head, and indeed, a view of Mr. D at times other than the moment of the offense, and even before the offense, and even enriched my picture of him, enriched my ability to make a diagnosis of him. It gave me some corroboration to his history.

His history giving is pretty spacy, pretty flaky, at least it was when I saw him, so it's nice to see someone who has all their wits about them to give me some comments from what they observed, from which I could draw psychiatric conclusions.

*(Author's Note: In a statement about his history, giving, "At least it was when I saw him," provides an opening for questions to indicate that the psychological state and psychological functioning of people fluctuates, the implication being that his history giving at some other time may not have been pretty spacey or pretty flaky.)*

Q. Referring to your first report—your Honor, I had an extra copy that has been referred to from time to time, marked for identification, and I made an extra copy for you and me, so the Court can follow along in case there's references to it.

You said you got a past history from Mr. D. I'd like you to tell us what that past history consisted of, that Mr. D related to you back in September.

PA: Excuse me, Doctor. Again, I would impose a hearsay objection, but I assume it would be subject to the same—

THE COURT: Yes, the history is taken for the purpose of making a diagnosis. I'll probably be giving an instruction that covers this. There is a general instruction dealing with statements made to a physician, and although I haven't gone over the instructions with the attorneys yet, I will be pretty sure that I'll be giving a formal instruction along that line, too.

THE WITNESS: I should emphasize that this is Mr. D's perception or perceptions of his life, and who he is and how he got that way, and I don't necessarily take these things at face value, but learned from him that he was born twenty-three years ago in, the youngest of eleven, got along well with his mother, whom he describes as a loving person, considerably less well with his father, who seems to be a strange bird, rather brutal, rather strict, whipped D, and particularly Mr. D, but the other kids as well.

He had an unhappy childhood, tremendous financial hardship. The family lived close to, and sometimes below, the level of poverty. Mr. D himself had to start working from the age of nine on. He believes two of his brothers are alcoholics, two had difficulty with the law, and lost an older brother several years ago in an automobile accident.

*(Author's Note: Now the witness had elaborated D's history in a manner to elicit a certain amount of sympathy for him. The lawyer may not want to focus any more attention on this but there is the alternative of attempting to defuse this to some extent with question to the effect that unhappy childhoods are not all that uncommon, financial hardship is not all that uncommon, that most people who grow up under circumstances of that kind do not ever kill anybody, and in fact that the majority of them do not develop disorders such as schizophrenia.)*

He dropped out of school in the eleventh grade because he didn't feel he was getting enough out of it, and then worked a variety of seasonal jobs, particularly in the lumber industry.

He's rather bitter about his employment history and in some vague way feels that he was denied good jobs, or they were taken from him, which is sort of a paranoid suspicion as to "How come I'm unemployed?" And of course, the reality is that many people in this area are unemployed because of the market.

*(Author's Note: The statement "in some vague way feels he was denied good jobs or they were taken from him, which is a sort of a paranoid suspicion" may be worth noting. First of all the witness is not very clear as to whether is it a paranoid suspicion. Secondly, however, he does use the term indicating that this is a paranoid suspicion and it might be worthwhile to ask if all suspicions which may not be true or correct are paranoid. He appears here to be demonstrating the well-known propensity of mental health professionals to over-pathologize. That seems particularly true where the belief, whatever it is, is quite vague. Normally to be paranoid requires somewhat more specificity than that.)*

Mr. D's physical health generally has been good. He allegedly drank a bottle of vodka at about age nine and then fell off his bicycle, struck his head, and was hit by a car.

He denies significant drug use, but has been a heavy drinker of beer, he tells me about fifteen cases a week, which is a rather extraordinary amount. He claims he has had three fainting spells of some sort or another, but no other signs of alcoholism and indeed, he is too young for most of the common symptoms, like DT's, to show up.

He smokes several marijuana cigarettes daily, and has experimented with other drugs.

*(Author's Note: Some of the other clinicians seemed to find this drug usage more significant than does Dr. 3. So there is some question whether they may be connecting dots differently. Also it is not clear how many marijuana cigarettes "several" means daily, and therefore somewhat difficult to determine whether it could be considered significant drug use. We would assume that there was some amount of marijuana smoking which some mental health professionals would consider significant. Inasmuch as Dr. 3 specifically mentions 15 cases of beer a week it would be worthwhile to inquire if he knows what the word "several" means with regard to marijuana as there seems to be a good chance he will not know. Given his style of testifying, there is a probability that he would answer by saying that he doesn't know but that if it had been a significant amount he would have noted it, which is a kind of "trust me" statement of which there are a good many in his testimony. In any event, there is at least the possibility of substance abuse here. Note that in Dr. 4's report the marijuana consumption is specified as ten marijuana cigarettes a day. If indeed D was smoking ten marijuana cigarettes daily and consuming approximately two cases of beer daily, according to his statement, along with three or four cups of coffee and other caffeine containing substances as well, according to Dr. 1's report, it is difficult to understand how these consumptions would not have some effect on his behavior or*

*mental state. For example in the DSM-III it is indicated that where there is sub-*
*stance abuse, social relations can be disturbed by display of erratic and impul-*
*sive behavior or by inappropriate expression of aggressive feelings. It would be*
*a matter of the attorney's judgment as to whether he wants to develop this issue*
*or not but it should also be noted that if there is evidence from friends, family*
*and so on regarding behavior that is symptomatic of psychopathology prior to*
*the crime, this could very well be accounted for on the basis of this fairly heavy*
*consumption of alcohol and drugs.)*

He had intercourse at the age of sixteen for the first time, and estimates he's
had nine or ten serious relationships—I'm sorry, nine or ten partners since
that time, two serious relationships, and the second serious one was FV and
the first with a woman named DO, who lived with him for about a year until, and I quote, "She snuck out on me, broke our trust." She lied to him and
allegedly told him falsely that she was pregnant, and so on. I don't know if
any of that's true, but again, this was the perception that he was somehow
cheated upon. At age twenty he met one of the victims, FV, and began dating her throughout a year. He maintains that he broke off the relationship
and that, toward the end, FV falsely told him she was carrying his child,
again, like DO had said, and I do have some skepticism about that, or at
least that's how he perceives it.

He describes FV as a very smart outdoorsy type, basically very warm
and loving, except when drinking or using coke. I guess nowadays you have
to distinguish between the beverage and the drug, and in this case I mean
the drug.

He believes that she initiated the relationship and that he terminated it.
He has some unpleasant things to say about her that she likes to play one
man against another, kind of tough lady playing head games, and apparently
she has a pretty interesting family, according to Mr. D, the sisters, mother,
also some relatives, who tried to seduce him. A lot of drugs, a lot of violence in the family, and that created a lot of problems for FV, too. Because
of problems he was having with his relationship with FV and problems that
be felt originated in her somewhat anti-social family, he became kind of depressed and started having suicidal thoughts and saw a priest, and then
around Christmas time of (year) he made a suicide attempt. He insists that
this was not because he was losing FV, but this corroborating evidence,
certainly at least in the time frame of his suicide attempt, is associated with
his loss of this woman.

He tells me that FV began dating MV in November, but that she didn't
really love MV and in fact just was using him and would torment MV over
the fact that he, Mr. D, had a larger penis than MV did. She played them
against each other.

Interestingly, this is the first time Mr. D was ever aware of having any
homicidal feelings, although he insists that others were out to get him.

*(Author's Note: Dr. 3's description here seems to establish that D's homi-*
*cidal urge was directly associated with the relationship of MV and FV, even*
*though apparently at that time he also had the belief that other people were out*
*to get him. There is no need to cross-examine on this as the statement seems to*

*stand by itself and can be woven in during argument along the theme that what
we have here, regardless of any psychopathology that he might have had, is a
fairly conventional motive, the love triangle-rejected suitor motive for the killings in this case, and that this appears to be the primary motive.)*

He takes what you would think is normal reaction against unpleasant
events, and projects them onto somebody else.

Q. Did you ask him questions about the day of the homicide, January twenty-
second, which is exactly one year ago today?

A. Yes, I did.

Q. What did he tell you about that?

A. He told me that on January twenty-second he fatally shot MV, and seriously
wounded FV. He alleges that a month before FV had invited him over to her
house. She wanted to sleep with him. They had intercourse. That right up to
and almost up to the time that MV was killed and FV was wounded he
maintains that FV was really interested in him. Although they had no personal contacts after that point, although they spoke a lot on the phone.

Somewhere along the line Mr. D became convinced that both FV and
MV, each in different ways, had it in for him and were out to get him. I
think he started to sleep under the bed or away from his bed, because that's
the usual place where people who are out to assassinate you, will find you.

And in MV's case, that was one largely of jealousy, because he had
wanted FV for six years and he saw Mr. D as a threat and continued to be a
threat to his desires.

There was something about that he had the goods on FV for using some
[ethnic group grant funds] inappropriately. There was some very vague confused stuff that I frankly did not understand about her being involved in the
drug world and the Mafia. In any event, there were things, vague feelings to
very acute feelings, that he was going to be put away, and that MV and FV
were the primary movers in this.

He states that his concerns grew to the point where about mid-January
he asked his friend to get him a gun so that he might get MV before MV got
me.

*(Author's Note: The declaration here seems to clearly establish that shortly
before the killing he was able to plan and premeditate [e.g., think ahead and
carry out a plan to avoid assassins by staying out of his bed. It may not be a
good plan but it is planning and deliberation], allegedly at a time during which
he was suffering from the disorder of paranoid schizophrenia, unless Dr. 3 is
willing to testify that at that time he was not suffering from paranoid schizophrenia. This, then, might be an instance of the "gap" referred to in Chapter 1
of Volume I, at least as demonstrating that someone with paranoid schizophrenia is not necessarily incapable of planning and premeditating.)*

Friend didn't come through, and he finally stole a gun from another friend
about a week before the homicide. He told me he couldn't handle what was
going on. He would hide at home, go straight to work, and come straight
home or go to a bar and get drunk to wipe out his fears. And this brings us
to January twenty-first, the day before the homicide. He worked some extra
hours, was beginning to get increasingly paranoid. There was a day man

that had been assigned to work with him and the discussion he had with his fellow worker was filling him with all sorts of fears and homicidal feelings. He decided to get the hell out of town and went to his boss and lied about traffic warrants and got an advance on his salary and went home and got his clothes, got his gun, had a few beers, tried to call FV about her intentions to have MV kill him, went to see (a friend), tried to get some money, I think, from him, who was broke, and then decided to leave the city to see FV at her house, called en route several times, found her not at home, decided she's probably at work, drove to where she worked, and, of course, by now it was close to five or late in the afternoon, and saw MV outside waiting for her, making some phone calls."I'm sure he was getting me set up," Mr. D tells me.

And FV comes out and joins him. He follows them both to FV's house. After a short while they leave, and Mr. D is certain that they were now going to MV's house.

He tries to follow them and loses them. He then searches around the area driving here, driving there, accompanied by beer and marijuana, and before Mr. D encountered them, explaining, "I guess I got lucky." He states he was frightened when he saw them, but nevertheless, went to their car, showed them his gun and told MV, "I heard you wanted to kill me." He made MV get out of the truck to purportedly examine some pictures and letters which would reveal to him just what kind of a girl FV was.

I realize this is inconsistent. He loves FV. He wants FV. FV is being misled by MV, but then MV is being misled by FV. There's nothing coherent in any of this. FV is not worth killing someone for. And while he was trying to get these purported documents out of his knapsack, MV quote makes a move as what Mr. D perceives as threatening, and he kills MV. He sees FV doing something, maybe going for her gun. FV apparently is a good shot, and he shoots her as well.

He then goes fleeing to _____ where he turns himself in to get help.

*(Author's Note: It seems possible that in fact there were some pictures and letters. Otherwise if it was D's intent to just get them before they got him he could have shot them while both were in the truck and not take any additional risks by giving MV the freedom of action he would have once he was out of the truck. If in fact this is true, this again would appear to be more of a lover's ploy designed to break up the existing relationship so that he could recapture his lost love than it appears to be the action of someone who is terrified of one or both of these two people who might try to kill him. Also the statement about turning himself in to get help is somewhat misleading. The fact is he did not go to _____ to turn himself in as simply as the sentence describes. Rather he called some friends and upon discovering that MV in fact was dead and one can almost certainly assume also discovering that FV was not dead and could and probably did identify him as the killer, he had sufficient "savvy," despite his alleged devastating disorder, to realize that he would be caught and to realize that he was truly in danger of being shot by the police if they recognized him on the street. There is also at least a suggestion in combining the statement that he needed help with some notion on his part that inasmuch as he was going to be clearly*

*identified as the killer, the only way out for him would be some kind of psychiatric defense. While it is obvious that he is not a highly intelligent person, nonetheless the lifestyle involved with drugs and so on would suggest that he is not without a certain amount of what are called "street smarts.")*

Mr. DC: What is a mental status examination?

A.   It's sort of a psychological X-ray of an individual as he sits before me, where I focus on perception, whether he sees and hears the same things the rest of us do. His mentation, his thought process, do his ideas hang together, what his sentence structure is like, what his memory is like, his general knowledge, can he handle abstractions, or is he very literal or concrete. Does he have any delusions or fixed beliefs which really don't make sense, and seem immune to reason, affect, or overall feeling down. Is he angry, is he depressed, is he out of it, bland, unemotional? And lastly, behavior. Does his behavior seem appropriate for the situation? Is it normal? Is he aggravated? Is he simply comatose? Does he have some pain problems or what have you?

*(Author's Note: One cannot allow the witness to get away with portraying the mental status examination as an X-ray, something that most people have had experience with and view as portraying an objective reality about a bone or an organ of the body. Questions could be asked here to establish the fact that indeed a mental status examination is nothing like an X-ray which is taken by a mechanical device. The personality and biases of the X-ray operator will have no affect on what the X-ray shows. It can be presented to others for them to look at in its raw form. However, the remainder of the statement can be useful to the attorney. Questions can be asked to establish that the mental status examination is a very important part of the psychiatric evaluation. Then the obvious can be brought out, that all of the things he is looking at are in an individual who has been in jail for several months with his life truly in danger due to the charges against him so that there is no way that the psychiatrist can determine from the mental status examination at that time and under those circumstances what D's perception, mentation, thought processes, hanging together of ideas, sentence structure, memory, general knowledge, ability to handle abstractions, fixed beliefs and so on were like prior to or at the time of the crime. If it is important to know these things, then nothing the psychiatrist says can apply to any time other than the time of the examination. To the extent that the psychiatrist relies on reports of people who observed D at or before the time of the crime, he can be asked if those people were capable of and in fact did go around making evaluations, for example, of what D's sentence structure was like or whether D could handle abstractions, as it is most unlikely that his friends and acquaintances were looking at him along those dimensions. Also here Dr. 3 discusses delusions or fixed beliefs and he should be asked if these are synonymous. There are two items here. One is with regard to ideas that don't make sense. There are some beliefs that some disordered people have which patently do not make sense. For example, the individual believes that he is the emperor of the world. No investigation is needed to recognize that is not possibly correct. However, a belief that one's life may be in danger because of some kind of drug related activities is not patently nonsensical. It may be untrue and without any kind of basis for*

*believing it. It may also be untrue although there are factual bases upon which a reasonable person could entertain such a belief. The point here is that one cannot per se label these kinds of beliefs as delusions without investigating to find out whether there is a substantial factual basis or, for example, without investigation one cannot know whether or not MV had behaved in a way or directly expressed something threatening toward D. The second item is the statement "seem immune to reason" which is in line with the definition of a delusion given in the glossary to the DSM-III, that is it must be a belief "firmly sustained in spite of what everyone else believes and in spite of what constitutes incontrovertible and obvious proof to the contrary." Therefore Dr. 3 could be asked what incontrovertible proof had been offered to D that his belief about MV was in error. If he does not have this information, which seems likely, he can then be asked if he attempted to obtain it in his interview and if so, how. It is important to make the distinction between a false belief, that is a belief that is incorrect, which almost everyone has from time to time, and a delusion which is a false belief held in the face of overwhelmingly convincing evidence to the contrary.)*

Q. Did you perform a mental status examination in September of Mr. D?

A. I did.

Q. What were the results?

A. I found him to be superficially pleasant, cooperative, individual, who I felt comprehended all my questions, and who replied with apparent candor, I thought he was telling the truth as he saw it, though in a markedly disorganized and paranoid way. I found him perceptually normal with no hallucinations. He was alert.

Q. What is mentation?

A. How his mind worked. He was patently abnormal. His narrative was rambling, and my impression was like all these things inside of him, he could easily talk to me for twenty-four hours and not run dry, and it would come out at a tremendous rate. His sentences didn't hang together. Sometimes indeed parts of his sentences didn't hang together to make a whole sentence. His sentences didn't hang together to make whole coherent paragraphs, and his paragraphs didn't hang together to make a whole coherent narrative.

I read the transcript of Mr. D's testimony and I'm sure you all got a feeling of what I'm talking about. In addition his associations are what we call "loose." He started talking about—let me see if I can come up with a real example. We would be talking about driving his car somewhere, and he would be low on gas, and gas, of course, is what is sometimes used by the Mafia to eliminate people. And there is no connection between those two ideas from gasoline, but when he thought in his sentence structure that he needed gas, then the next part of the sentence should be something about what he did about that. Was he worried the car would end up immobile on the highway or did he stop to get gas, or what did he do about the gasoline, but he leaps to some very tangential subject, where the only seeming connection is gasoline, which is no logical connection between the two subjects.

These subjects fly around all over the place, and he can't gather them together and follow a thought. Also a lot of paranoid ideations. In a more simplistic sense of paranoia, where people are out to get him and he does seem to be living in a hostile world surrounded by enemies, but more sophisticatedly he disowns all the unpleasant but imminent parts of himself, like jealousy, rage, anger, and he gets rid of them, cleanses himself by attaching them to others. It's not that he wants to punish MV or FV for injuring him, but rather they're trying to get him. That's how he gets rid of these feelings. "I don't want to harm anybody. They'll all after me."

This is an unconscious process, and it'a part of the paranoid process where these people cannot bear that they have any bare parts in their mind, kicks it out, and he connects the people that they're concerned about, people with whom they're intimate, and they see this all the time, people that are jealous of him, MV was jealous of his penis, and FV wanted to punish him. He had no unbridled sexual feelings. It was FV's family always trying to seduce him. He's lily white. Well, how do you get to be lily white? You have to get rid of that, and paranoids are good at that, and good at attaching other people. It's not my problem. It's FV's.

He's always the victim, good guy, always doing things for people, particularly FV's family, where everybody else is deceptive, violent, and promiscuous, particularly FV's family. Everybody is always screwing him over. FV's aunt, age thirty, her mother, age thirty-five, trying to seduce him, and a whole host of other people have plots against him. He has grandiose feelings when all these important people are out to get him, including the Mafia who is trying to get him. This is an illustration of your importance by the importance of the people who are your enemies.

I found much of what he said to be incoherent and flagrantly delusional.

He had a lot of ideas, which couldn't be true, they weren't distortions, they weren't simply pulling my leg, they were nutty ideas that he believed, but were blatantly false.

For example, he's convinced that the District Attorney was having a sex affair with the victim's mother, and that kind of stuff. There is a lot of his ideas that are blurred together.

You know, I'm giving you a fairly rapid narration of some complex material, and sometimes my ideas are blurred together a little bit, but by and large, I'm able to keep one thought separated from another, and move along fairly rapidly. Mr. D's are all blurred together in sort of an overcoat of porridge.

I found his performance of simple arithmetical computations and general fund of knowledge as adequate, but interpretation of everyday proverbs was markedly concrete. What do I mean by that? He takes a proverb like "People who live in glass houses shouldn't throw stones," and if you ask somebody what that means, and if they've gone through oh, at least tenth-grade education, they'll know that there is a moral to that story that, you know, if you're vulnerable in some ways, you keep your mouth shut, and not criticize others, something to that effect. But people who either have virtually no education or who have something wrong with their ability to go to the literal concrete, to the meaning or to the abstraction behind the concrete, will talk in terms of what that means. If your house is made out of glass, and people throw stones at it, the glass would break. There are several reasons why people would do this.

These are different kinds of disorders, people with organic brain disease, for example, who have some physical problems with brain structure, who talk like this, so will schizophrenics, but schizophrenics will often put a little twist to it, "If you live in the glass house the glass will shatter and some of the fragments will go in your heart." These are bizarre, in addition to being very literal and concrete. Well, Mr. D interprets things in this fasion [sic], both literal concrete and a little nutty.

*(Author's Note: With regard to D's difficulty in interpreting proverbs, it should be noted that there are some problems of this type, that is interpretation of proverbs, on the WAIS. These are in the comprehension subtest. One is item 7. The subject is asked "What does a particular saying mean?" As to Proverb 1, statistical data provided by Professor Wechsler in his book* The Measurement of Adult Intelligence, *based on the performance of more than a thousand subjects carefully counted and quantified, shows that one person out of four is unable to correctly respond to this question. That means that about 25% of the population, presumably not paranoid schizophrenics, are unable to abstract the meaning of this saying. It should be noted in this connection that D's intelligence level as measured by the two intelligence tests given by Drs. 1 and 4 is somewhere in the vicinity of the bottom 20-25% of the population. Therefore, D's inability to abstract a meaning is no more than one would expect given the level of intelligence asserted by two psychologists employed by the defense. It is not correct, as Dr. 3's statement implies, that anybody with a tenth grade education would be able to explain the meaning of not throwing stones at a glass house. It might be worthwhile on this issue to ask him where he gets his data or his conclusion as it may provide another opportunity to demonstrate the deficiencies of clinical observation as against more systematically gathered data. Just around this issue there are two more proverbs on the comprehension subtest. On the second only approximately one person out of three gets a creditable answer. On the third only one person out of five gets the answer correct. It should also be noted that these are answers which can be scored 2, 1, or 0, with 2 being given for a good abstract interpretation of the proverb, while 1 point of credit can be given for a concrete illustration which conveys an idea of the meaning but not in the abstract form. For example, on the hot iron example, while 75% get some credit, some portion of those are getting credit for answers that are on the concrete side. Dr. 3 states that D interprets things in the fashion illustrated, both literal concrete and a little nutty. We do not know what proverbs he administered nor what the answers were. It might be worthwhile to find these out, but in any event Dr. 3 is clearly utilizing this as one of the dots he is connecting to make up the picture of schizophrenia. One would assume that with elimination of that dot, given that it is easily explained without employing a complex concept like schizophrenia, that his picture would at least become a little "fuzzier." In addition, the Similarities subtest of the WAIS is generally described and viewed by many, if not most, clinical psychologists as a measure of the ability to abstract, abstracting being the opposite of concreteness. On this*

*subtest, according to Dr. 4, D obtained a score of 8 and with a corrected scoring his scale score would be 9, either of which are in the average range. Nine is well into the average range and eight would be about where you would expect him to be on the basis of his intelligence level. It also shows on the first four items according to Dr. 4's scoring and the first five items according to correct scoring that he got 2 point answers, which are the answers given for good abstractions, which would suggest again that he is not pathologically deficient in the ability to abstract nor is he pathologically concrete, nor is his concreteness, to the degree that such exists, a product of psychopathology any more than it is a product of his somewhat low intellectual capacity. As another side note, there is Dr. 3's reference below to his modest skills, which seems another attempt to sell himself as a humble good guy, but it should be noted that elsewhere in his testimony he clearly establishes that he has a very high opinion of his skills and considers himself considerably better than most of his peers.)*

Other than that, I didn't find any real evidence of organicity. If there is any brain damage, it's too subtle for me to pick up in my modest skills. I found that his narrative and thought processes were best presented by Mr. D himself, and I jotted down here rather extensive quotes.

Counsel, do you think in light of the fact that Mr. D has already testified, whether or not I should read that quote?

Mr. DC:

Q. I think—I think that it would—I think we are interested in what—you know, what he told you.

A. All right. Well, this is a direct quote and I am using this because I thought it illustrates how his ideas blur together and run together when you don't interrupt him with questions. If you try to structure him with questions, you can keep him on the point a little while because then your mental health helps his mental processes. But if you just let him go on his own, this is what you get. "FV would rather see me dead than go out with a lot of girls. I did go out with a lot of girls and she knew it and she said she'd kick their cunts in. She tried to run me over one day when I was talking to a girl friend of my sister's. Then she cried and told me that she didn't want us to break up. It wasn't her fault that she was this way. She had a lot of problems. Her mother beat on her. Her mother was a tramp, tried to come onto me, and her father took out girls and gave them coke. Her girl friends just wanted coke and sex. FV put MV up to all this like she tried to put me up to things and get (friend) and MV to fight over me. Show her pictures and so on. So I stayed away from town because I knew what she was doing, and wanted friend and MV and me to really get into it. I've gotten into two or three fights already because of her and her family where I had no choice. Her family begged me to stay with them. I made them laugh. I took care of them. We really like each other, but her aunt and her sisters were jealous and tried to get me into bed, and her mother was always trying to pick on me. My freedom means a lot to me. I just don't date any girl."

Q. That was one thought?

A. That was one thought.

Q. Expressed as one thought?

A. Expressed as one thought. See how they all kind of run together? There's a little connection, but not really a logical connection. Almost a concrete physical connection that these people connect literally in a sense and he goes on as if they're connected logically or abstractly.

Then we get to affect, which I defined as a generalized feeling. Despite that previous speech, the drama of its contents, I mean he is talking about some pretty hairy things here, he presents in a superficially calm, flat quasi-rational manner as if all that made sense and without the feeling. He's talking about suicide. He's talking about homicide. And he could be talking about what I am going to have for breakfast today. It is all the same.

Sometimes this sort of enthusiasm, but you can't—you don't get any despair, don't get any anger, you don't get any depression.

Just sort of a pseudo normalcy. I guess it is detachment. It is characteristic of the schizophrenic. I found his behavior appropriate throughout the examination.

*(Author's Note: With reference to the preceding "previous speech" Dr. 3 refers to lack of affect or inappropriate affect because the things referred to in the speech are "hairy." While they may appear "hairy" to Dr. 3 who probably lives in an upper middle class world, that does not mean that they were "hairy" to D or were anything extraordinary given the milieu in which he lived. Therefore, it is not clear what is meant by "he's talking about suicide, he's talking about homicide" because there's nothing in the speech about either of those. So far as affect is concerned or lack of it, Dr. 4's report portrays a considerable amount of affect. It is also noted in the next statement that one of the primary purposes, in fact the primary purpose, of conducting the examination was to formulate a psychiatric diagnosis, which was paranoid schizophrenia. We are just noting this at this point because later Dr. 3 attempts to denigrate the use of "labels" which of course a diagnosis is, and certainly the diagnosis of paranoid schizophrenia is a label. We simply suggest the reader keep this in mind when we get to the denigration of labels.)*

Q. I take it one of the purposes—the primary purpose of conducting this examination was to formulate a psychiatric diagnosis.

A. Right.

Q. What was that diagnosis that you formed?

A. I think Mr. D is paranoid schiz.

Q. Which means paranoid schizophrenia?

A. Right.

Q. And would you tell us what your conclusions—when you called all this together, what that led you to, that specific diagnosis.

A. Well, much of what I described here is characteristic of the paranoid schizophrenic. Just like the—as I say, you connect the dots, the way he thinks, the way he disposes of his unpleasant parts and projects them on to others, the slippage of his thinking, how things run together, the detachment of his thoughts from his feelings, separation of the two, the grandiocity, the perception that he is surrounded by evil, his inability to let go of FV, the blurring together of his identity and her identity so that when she started to move away from him, and I think she did, it was like losing a piece of himself. This is characteristic of schizophrenics, I mean all of us who lose someone we love dearly experiences almost figuratively speaking like losing a piece of ourselves, but the schizophrenic experiences it literally because his own—he has so much trouble telling where friends end and he begins, the boundaries are so blurry, and I think this is why he was so devastated by jealousy and loss of this woman. But I say that's typical of schizophrenics.

The confusion. Now, again, just like all of us could be a little jealous and all of us can be a little confused, it is the extent—the relentless immobile extent of the schizophrenic's thought confusion that is somewhat diagnostic.

The associations, how he leaps from one thought to another by superficial concrete section rather than logical ones is typical of schizophrenics. His problems with abstractions as represented, for example, in his interpretation of proverbs is somewhat reflective of a schizophrenic's thought process.

I may have mentioned this before, the projection, it's not that I'm a threat to MV and FV, but they're a threat to me is typical of a schizophrenic.

The depression, the suicidal act is not typical of schizophrenics, but schizophrenics probably have, you know, one of the highest suicide rates of all classifications. So, you know, that goes with the diagnosis even though it is certainly not pathognomonic.

His early life, apparently the father was really a very strange fellow and quite brutal, and we find that paranoid personality is typically from homes where there's a brutal father. Not every brutal father is going to create a paranoid child, but again there's a high statistical incidence, and I'm satisfied from what Mr. D has told me and more from what I read in interviews of others in the family that the father was a brutal man.

*(Author's Note: Earlier Dr. 3 gave a lengthy explanation of the dots he's connecting to make his diagnosis. Probably the best way to deal with this is in a lump indicating that there is considerable disagreement about the characteristics of schizophrenia, even to the present time. There are different diagnostic systems (systems for connecting dots) and while DSM-III represents the official dot system, it is acknowledged that DSM-III was a product of considerable discussion, disagreement, finally compromise, and political action and that there are many psychiatrists who do not agree with it. Further, the dots in this manual are different than the dots in the previous manual and may well be different in the forthcoming new manual, so that the dots are continually changing which means the picture is continually changing, and what is characteristic today was not characteristic yesterday and may not be characteristic tomorrow. He makes it clear that the difficulty with abstractions on interpretation of proverbs is one of the dots he's connecting and we have already explained why that dot does not necessarily belong in the picture. He talks about depression and the suicide rate but acknowledges that is not "pathogonomic," and it might be useful as long as he's raised the word to ask him what is pathognomic, as there is so far as we know no one thing which is what the term means, that is pathognomic of*

schizophrenia. That is, there are no symptoms of schizophrenia which are not also symptoms of some other disorder. One could ask here if he is aware the suicide rate of psychiatrists is also one of the highest of all rates of classifications.

Then he refers to the relationship between paranoid personality and a brutal father. He acknowledges the obvious, that not every brutal father will create a paranoid child, but says "there's a high statistical incidence." Dr. 3 could be questioned as to exactly what the statistical incidence is. No harm is done as he has already indicated that he knows. However, if it turns out that he doesn't know, some question as to his credibility is raised. If he knows what the statistical incidence is, he could be asked if it is possible to predict what percent of children from homes with brutal fathers will develop paranoid personality. That is in order to know there is a relationship between brutal father and paranoid personality, one would have to know the base rate for homes with brutal fathers which it is unlikely that anyone knows and then determine that the number of children who develop paranoid personality who had brutal fathers is out of proportion to the number who developed paranoid personalities who did not have brutal fathers. So another way to put the question to Dr. 3 is whether he knows the base rate or what percentage of homes in the United States have brutal fathers, based on statistical studies, not his guess from the patients he had dealt with. One thing he has definitely done is open the door here to questions about statistical incidence as it is apparently something he takes into consideration. Also, of course, one would want to know the source of the statistical incidence if he is in fact able to state what the statistical incidence is. Also DSM-III at 186 notes that among predisposing factors the diagnosis of schizophrenia is more common among lower socioeconomic groups for reasons that are unclear. Also note DSM-III states that certain patterns of family interaction have been hypothesized as predisposing the development of schizophrenia but that the interpretation of the evidence supporting those hypotheses is controversial. Regarding brutal fathers, DSM-III does not mention this as a predisposing factor in either Paranoid Personality Disorder (307-8) (in fact, DSM-III says there is no information on this) or in Paranoid Disorders (195-6) where some predisposing factors are stated but brutal fathers is not among them.

One additional item on this is an apparent omission by Dr. 3 of one of the significant dots given in diagnostic criteria for schizophrenic disorder in DSM-III, if it turns out that he was using DSM-III to derive his dots. That one is item B (189) "Deterioration from a previous level of functioning in such areas as work, social relations and self care." If he asserts that there was deterioration following the breakup with FV, this may be in conflict with his statements which follow shortly.)

I think that—I think that will do for now.

Q. All right. Did it concern you at all when you saw him that he had been in custody for the length of time that he had, and if so, what effect did that have on your conclusions?

A. Yes, it did concern me because the jail setting is a structured setting, it is a different environment than he had been living in. And environment can affect how an illness appears. If somebody, for example, suffers high blood pressure and lives a pretty tough life, the quiet structure of a prison setting is typically associated with their blood pressure coming down. They sit in their cell all day, there's really not much to do unless they're on some—you know, really violent floor.

Prison life is somewhat protective of cardio-vascular disease. On the other hand, if they're under particular stress, and some people do experience prison very stressfully, not just the first week, but week after week after week, it is a tremendous—they have difficulty with confinement, then their blood pressure can go up and be worse.

So I was concerned that possibly being in jail would distort to some extent what I was getting.

Q. Were you able to more or less weed this out, or what weight did you get that—give in your diagnosis?

A. I thought that Mr. D's schizophrenia was so rampant that any effect of environmental changes at this late stage of the game would be slight. I mean who he is and how his mind works was set in cement a long time ago. But I don't think the jail setting will either necessarily make it significantly worse or better unless he was placed on substantial anti-psychotic medicine, which sometimes happens, and I don't think he was.

*(Author's Note: In dealing with the situation effect of being in jail, he acknowledges the possibility of some situation effect but in response to the question whether he was able to more or less weed this out or what weight he gave this in his diagnosis he dismisses it on the basis that D's schizophrenia was so rampant that any effective environmental changes at this late stage of the game would be slight. Who he is and how his mind works was set in cement a long time ago and jail would not necessarily make it worse or better absent anti-psychotic medicine. Obviously one thing to do here is to get a commitment from him as to approximately when the paranoid schizophrenia became rampant, so rampant that no environmental change was going to substantially have any effect. The statement that his mind was set in cement a long time ago would suggest that the effects of the schizophrenia are very longstanding, the point being that if it was so rampant, more than eight or nine months prior to his examination, nonetheless with such a serious disorder D was able to function adequately without a need to be institutionalized which would suggest that despite his paranoid schizophrenia he could function in all necessary things to live outside of walls and avoid trouble except for the trouble that is encountered by paranoid schizophrenics when they are involved in a love triangle. Additionally on this point we have a statement from Dr. 2's report, unfortunately missing, to the effect that D is very anxious and confused as a result of being in jail. So at least someone is connecting dots differently than Dr. 3. It should be noted again that confusion is one of the dots he is connecting to establish the diagnosis. He is apparently saying he is not more confused as a result of being in jail whereas Dr. 2 is apparently saying that D is more confused as a result of being in jail. It should also be noted that Dr. 3 did not himself observe any of the dots that he is connecting prior to the time that D was in jail. What he seems to be saying is that he saw D in September and at that time he saw all of these dots which he connected which tell him that he is suffering from paranoid schizophrenia (note*

*again this is a label) and once he has diagnosed him as paranoid schizophrenia with some possible estimation of the degree, he can then say that he was suffering from all of this before he was ever in jail, which of course completely obliterates the fact that indeed he was suffering from extreme stress in jail as he might well have been, facing a death penalty, that much of the confusion and the other dots that Dr. 3 is using may well have not been present or, if present, not to the same degree prior to these incarcerations. A point that should be made whether it is attempted on cross-examination or through another expert is that there is no scientifically validated method for determining the extent of the situation effects. It simply doesn't exist. There is no way to do it. And there is certainly no verification of the ability of psychiatrists to do it. One form of question that may be useful for a witness of this type is something along these lines. "Dr., if someone didn't believe you when you said you can do this or when you said psychiatrists can do this, what proof could you offer?"*

*A series of questions could be asked to establish what symptoms he showed at the time of the examination and which of these same symptoms he had prior to the crime and prior to incarceration. Also it is necessary to keep in mind the fact that while both Doctors 1 and 2 found some symptoms similar to those found by Dr. 3, neither of them some months earlier had diagnosed paranoid schizophrenia. This raises the possibility that D's condition worsened as a result of being in jail and it may have worsened from the time of the incarceration to the time that Doctors 1 and 2 saw him. Obviously it will be necessary to establish what the meaning is of "how his mind works was set in cement a long time ago." All of the material that follows on the next three pages of the transcript has to do with Dr. 3's secondhand reading of interviews done by other people plus Dr. 1's report. One could question him as to the qualifications and skills of the people doing the interviewing, the possibilities of family involvement or desire of friends to help and so on. However, it should be noted in this segment of the statement that he was crying the entire time he told his older sister of his fear of injury or death. If so, two weeks before the shooting he was certainly capable of plenty of appropriate affect. Also he keeps intimating of knowledge of drugs and firearms and other illegal activities to an extent that it almost becomes imperative for some kind of investigation to determine what, if any, truth there was to those claims. There is so much of it that it appears to have a possibility of being true which would certainly change the whole picture. In this connection, attention is directed to the letter of Dr. 4 sent to D's attorney and dated one day after Dr. 4's report in which Dr. 4 clearly indicates some uncertainty at the minimum as to the likelihood that there was some truth to these claims of drug deals and so on. The report is pretty close to indicating Dr. 4 believes that there must have been some truth in all that. If that is so, many or all of the prior claims of fears of being killed and so on would make "normal," as opposed to psychopathological sense if, in fact, D was involved even tangentially in drug dealing or with people who were into drug dealing as it is well known that it is a dangerous business and a possibility of suffering death at the hands of one's associates or one's associates' associates is at least present, if not imminent. There is another item which lends some credence to this. In view of D's rather lean earnings, his consumption, if true, of fifteen cases of beer a week at considerable expense plus the expense of the ten marijuana cigarettes and the occasional cocaine and other drugs gives further credence to the possibility that indeed he was to some extent involved in drug dealing if for no other reason than to support his various habits.*

*Dr. 3's statement that Dr. 1 describes D as having paranoid delusions is not correct. Dr. 1 stated "The interoffice memos at the County Jail strongly is 'suggested' persecutory delusions," which is not the same as saying he "had" persecutory delusions and this comment may have been related to the class action suit over mistreatment in the County Jail. Dr. 1 says on page six that "D appeared to suffer from a paranoid condition," which could be anything from a paranoid personality up to paranoia involving persecutory "inner beliefs." Incidentally Dr. 3 does not report Dr. 1's declaration that "some degree of exaggeration or fabrication in D's statements cannot be ruled out, which leaves a question of how believable is he." Finally, on page 7 Dr. 1 diagnoses inadequate personality disorder or borderline schizophrenia with antisocial features. He distinctly does not diagnose paranoid schizophrenia, but he then goes on to say, "Either situation 'can' result in paranoid delusions under sufficient stress." The distinction is not necessarily a great one but it is indicative of Dr. 3 fudging a little bit in a direction that seems to make the case for D stronger than it actually is.)*

Q.  Okay. Let's talk about the second interview you had with him, again at my request. I think you said it was in November.

A.  Yes.

Q.  Where was he at that time, do you recall?

A.  Same place. In jail.

Q.  And can you give us an idea of what information, what further information was supplied to you between the first interview and the second interview?

A.  I reviewed summaries of various taped interviews and the Sheriff's Department interoffice memo. Interview with Mr. D's sister, who describes her brother's depression near the Christmas of over the fact that he was going to be killed. An interview with another sister, who states that when she saw her brother in jail, he told her the Mafia was after him.

Another sister, who spoke of her brother's suicide attempt, his depression over financial problems, gastrointestinal complaints, insomnia, weight loss and concerns about a variety of threats he was receiving. She'd never known him to be violent.

Another friend interviewed stated that Mr. D picked fights when intoxicated. An interview of another friend of Mr. D's, who stated he was frightened and needed a gun to protect himself, but he was afraid he was going to be killed.

A friend who reports that she was once kicked and beaten by FV and her friends. Another friend, confirms one of these statements about FV.

A Sheriff's Deputy reports that Mr. D told him that the Mafia or someone was out for his skin, and further that he could not remember pulling the trigger when he committed the offenses. He trusts no one, not even his own attorney. And he hadn't slept in a month. And that he could provide information about drugs and firearms if he could get some sort of protection for his family. Mr. D's oldest sister, who reports that two weeks before the shooting, her brother told her that the Mafia was going to kill him and possibly injure other family members, and that FV and MV might well be involved. *(Author's Note: This sounds more like a "belief" than a "delusion.")*

He was crying the entire time he told me this.

A jail counselor found Mr. D often incoherent and complaining of people trying to get him, collaborating with the D.A., with whom she was sexually involved.

Finally, I reviewed Doctor 1's report, who describes that Mr. D, who he saw about six months before I did, having paranoid delusions. He saw the defendant's defense as an amalgam of paranoid fright and jealous rage rather than the consequence of frank delusional beliefs, but he overreacted, but in any event, executed MV in cold blood and attempted to do the same to FV.

Doctor 1 felt that the defendant's ability to reflect upon the gravity of the situation may have been substantially impaired, though he was not likely to alleviate same.

Q. All right. After you reviewed that material, I take it you conducted another examination, a personal interview and examination of Mr. D?

A. I did.

Q. What did you find out in that examination?

A. The second time I focused on his thinking prior to—at the time of the offense. Once again, I found confusion between whether he terminated with FV or FV ended the relationship with him. He does state that there was a time when she was sexually intimate with both him and MV, his rival.

*(Author's Note: The confusion, if any, is 9 months after the crime and while in jail.)*

FV had a very tight vagina but on this one occasion she came back lubricated purportedly because she had just had sex with MV. He tells me he carried a gun in the summer of the year before the crime and sold it when things quieted down.

However, toward the end of the year before the crime, he acquired a weapon again. He told me that MV had it in for him, and followed him home and threatened to kill him and that his family had great power; that MV realized that he was the only one who could get between him and the woman he wanted.

He tells me that she also had reasons to fear him, because he could get her [ethnic group] funds cut off. He saw MV and FV both as threatening his life, and this caused a traumatic reaction on his part. First he tried to get help from a priest. He tried to get out of town and tried to get help from his family, but ultimately he decided the night before the shooting that he simply better get them before they got him.

He tells me he made a last-minute effort with some purported letters and photos to dissuade MV in the few moments prior to the shooting, but became frightened and shot MV and shot FV. Even so, he feels he is somewhat at risk—that either MV's mother or FV will arrange to have him killed, especially if he goes to prison, where he assures me that sort of thing happens all the time.

Q. Did you conduct another mental status examination in November?

A. Yes.

Q. What was the result of this?

A. Much as he was in September, rambling sometimes so tangential to the point of being nonresponsive to my questions. Still paranoid, still believes there's a local Mafia, although he gave me no data to support this conclusion. *(Author's Note: One might ask Dr. 3 if he or anyone gave D incontrovertible proof that there is no local Mafia. Is there any proof there is no local organized crime? The evidence of drug availability suggests there might well be some.)* He still has some strange beliefs about the District Attorney. Still having suicidal thoughts. Were it not for his newly-found religion, he apparently discovered Christianity while in jail, he would have killed himself.

Q. Any change in the diagnosis?

A. No.

Q. What then—how would you sum up your conclusions then, based on the total sum of information you had at your fingertips back in November after the second interview?

A. I think the loss of FV was a loss to Mr. D. It was a loss of a piece of himself. I think Mr. D is a fragile individual in many ways, including sexually. FV was very important to him and he started to unravel when she left him and connected with another guy. I don't know this for sure, this is somewhat—speculative, but it may well be that FV continued to have good feelings for Mr. D, so she didn't break clean. They may have continued. There may have been an overlapping period which caused more trouble. He was already having trouble separating himself from FV, and if FV possibly was occasionally giving him loving conditions, kept him on the string, it was probably more than he could handle.

He began to get filled with jealous rage; became increasingly paranoid. And instead of dealing with looking at his anger, his jealousy in a rational way and saying, "Look. I've got to put this woman aside and go on with my life" he started projecting it. He got rid of it that way, getting it out onto other people until finally the whole world was his enemy, but particularly MV and FV and all of his hostile feelings became tasks and he perceived them as wanting to get him.

If I may say one thing. Like the other day, my kids were playing with a Kleenex and one of the kids has a bit of the flu, and the Kleenex was kind of filled with the product of that particular illness, and one kid said, "Well, this is not my Kleenex. It's your's." And threw it at the other. The other said, "No, it's your's," and threw it back, and that's what the paranoid does, with considerably less conscious attention, where they say, "It's your illness. You're out to get me." And I think it's—this illness contaminated his thought process, in a word, why he did what he did.

Q. Incidentally, after your interview in November, were you provided with a copy of Doctor 4's report that he filed sometime in December?

A.  Yes.

Q.  And you reviewed it?

A.  I did.

Q.  All right. Doctor, in all the material that you reviewed in all the interviews, or both of the interviews that you conducted, did you ever find any trace of a significant history of violence to which you could attribute what happened?

A.  No. You know, I examine a lot of people in criminal matters, so possibly I'm somewhat inured to violence, but no, I don't consider Mr. D's history as being what I consider being a characterilogically violent person. He may have a big mouth sometimes, but he is of slight build, and any fight, he would inevitably get the short end of the stick.

And I cannot see anything in the records which I reviewed, at least or any of the interviews, and I read dozens, that would indicate that this man, absent a mental disorder, is a violent person.

Q.  Let's talk a little bit about the illness or the diagnosis that you've given us. You told us that he's a paranoid schizophrenic. Is that a good thing?

A.  I don't recommend it. It's perhaps one of the most serious mental illnesses that there is. There is a substantial variety of people that we have got to lock up in State hospitals who have schizophrenia.

And while most schizophrenics are peaceful and law-abiding people, sometimes their thinking can cause them to do what Mr. D did.

*(Author's Note: This statement seems to confirm generally the "gap" as demonstrating that schizophrenia does not prevent people from being peaceful and law abiding. Therefore, at least by implication, they possess the necessary capacity to obey the law and possess the capacities which would preclude them from exculpation. So far as "sometimes" their thinking can cause them to do what D did, a question could be whether they could also do what D did for the same reason as people who are not schizophrenic do what D did, such as, for example, in one of the common homicide situations, the love triangle. It should be possible to extract from him, unless he is going to be completely irrational, that if someone has schizophrenia and is in a love triangle and kills one or both of the other members of the triangle, this could be the result of the conventional motive in such situations rather than the result of schizophrenia. To say otherwise would be to say that never in any case could someone with schizophrenia who is normally able to be peaceful and law abiding, having the same passions as a nonschizophrenic individual has, could kill for the same reasons as a nonschizophrenic individual, which seems to be patently nonsense. Stated another way, there is no basis for saying that because he is schizophrenic a person with schizophrenia cannot kill because of a jealous rage.)*

So it's a messy business, schizophrenia.

Q.  Is this—is schizophrenia, this specific mental illness, is this something that you feel can be faked?

A.  No, no. There's a big difference between acting crazy and being schizophrenic. Oftentimes I see people who try to simulate mental illness, where they borrow a symptom from this disease, a symptom from that disease and one from that disease, and you connect the dots, and you get a squiggle. We see Mr. D fairly consistent, and all of the people that have seen him, doctors and even lay people, and I think, you know, we might quibble about labels, but I think he's pretty consistently nutty, and that nuttiness falls into a clinical familiar pattern as schizophrenia. They might see differences in how severe it was, and what contribution it made to his legal responsibility and so on, but I think most experts would find him schizophrenic. Even the computer found him schizophrenic.

*(Author's Note: Probably the best way to deal with an assertion by a clinician that schizophrenia cannot be faked is simply to ask him if he is aware of studies in which lay people did successfully fake schizophrenia and if he is, you can let it go at that unless he tries to explain it away. If he is not aware of it, you will have to introduce it through some other expert. He also indicates that there might be some quibbling about labels. This is his first denigration of labels but he insists that the doctors find D is pretty consistently nutty and that nuttiness falls into a pattern as schizophrenia. This is simply not correct. Dr. 1 was at best uncertain as to whether it was an inadequate personality or borderline schizophrenia. As noted above, borderline is generally thought of as a personality disorder rather than a psychotic state. He states that even the computer found him schizophrenic. We do not have available the computer printout if there was one from Dr. 2. However, the computer printout obtained by Dr. 4 does not state that D was schizophrenic.)*

Q.  We've been talking about schizophrenia now all this week, and to some extent prior to that time, and you are the third person with expert's credentials that has come forward and talked in general terms about the mental illness that Mr. D is suffering from, but nobody has really told us exactly what happens to a person's mind when he develops this illness. Can you help us out there?

A.  Well, to begin with, there were some studies which show that a schizophrenic has trouble screening out perceptual stimuli, that in a controlled study, when they're shown some dots and some colors and some numbers, they are asked to pick out a pattern and they have trouble, because they take it all in, and they can't kick out some of the underlying parts. It's as if you were looking at a page and some of the words were in big print and underlined and the rest weren't, and I asked you to read to me the ones that were underlined, but you're so overwhelmed by all the type on the page, you can't pick out the big words, the important words from the rest of the material, And there seems to be this kind of perceptual overload, at least in people when they are acutely psychotic.

And then they've done some studies, I recall one I think they may have done, it's in San Quentin, in any event, it was in a prison setting, and they put prisoners who were in there for white collar crimes in a chair, in a room all by themselves, one at a time, blindfolded, and then they would have somebody enter that room and the individual who was locked up for white collar crime would be aware of that person quietly kind of approaching him when they got within maybe twenty feet in front of him and ten feet behind him. And they did the same test with thirty to forty individuals who had committed violent crimes, so many of them bearing the diagnosis of paranoid schizophrenia, and the individuals became alert and uncomfortable when the person would walk into the room. There was only thirty feet in front of them, and twenty feet behind them. That is like their area of alarm was much bigger.

The County is really running out of money when it comes to chalk.

THE COURT: Yes.

Mr. DC: See if I can help you.

A. Writing with my fingernail.

Here's the person with the white collar crime sitting in the chair, blind-folded.

I'm okay now.

They become a little disconcerted when somebody approaches them. Let's say here is the front. Like that. Somehow people sneaking up behind you makes you a little bit more uncomfortable when they approach you from the front. People with more ominous diagnoses, they find, get jittery like this.

As soon as they approach them, the big—the circle of alarm is larger. So there's something going on even with their perceptual equipment. Then there's some studies which show that schizophrenics' thought processes are different, and really it gets kind of technical and I don't know if really I am equal to explaining, but you can demonstrate, like I tried to in very simple terms today, that they don't think the same way everybody does, and they have interesting ways of drawing conclusions.

They have boundary problems where people that they become connected with almost merge with them into their—it is hard for them to tell what's them and what's their environment. Sometimes they begin to project pieces of themselves onto the environment so it comes back to them as, for example, Mr. D's homicidal rage.

Q. I'd like to—

A. There's a separation of their thought and of their feeling. They may have fixed beliefs they manufacture seemingly out of the air that are patent nonsense that are at war with reality but which they determine their behavior. They may see this innocent person as a threat to themselves and go out and defend themselves against this person.

See, you're taking down what I am saying and then you're going to use that against me next week. I better be careful about you. That's the kind of thing.

There are some studies which suggest that there's some biochemical abnormalities of schizophrenics. There has been some twin studies, for example, which show that identical twins separated at birth, they have different parents, one twin is raised in London, the other twin is raised in another city, and the twin in the other city, let's say develops schizophrenia. Well, the chances of the twin in London being schizophrenic are much higher than you would expect from mere chance, so there's something inherited, some sort of biochemical susceptibility that contributes to this kind of problem. Doesn't always express itself, but there probably is some sort of biochemical basis for at least the origins of schizophrenia. I don't know if I have answered your question.

*(Author's Note: There are a couple of important things in the several preceding pages. Most important is that when Dr. 3 is asked to explain what happens to a person's mind in schizophrenia, he immediately starts to make reference to studies and in particular specifies at least one of them to have been a "controlled study." He makes four references to studies, presumably meaning research studies, although one would want to make sure that was what he meant. Obviously in the controlled study he is talking about scientific research so that when asked to describe the effects of schizophrenia, he apparently is relying upon scientific research, at least to a considerable extent. At no point here does he say, well in my experience it's this or that. All the reference here is to the studies. It may also be worth bringing up that in the San Quentin study of the individuals who have committed violent crimes, some of them were labelled "paranoid schizophrenic" and apparently some of them were not and we don't know which numbers there were of each, so that this was not a study of how paranoid schizophrenics think, but it was a study of how people who commit violent crimes think. Then he also becomes rather tentative with phrases like, "It is hard for them," "sometimes," "they may," "some studies which suggest." It may be noted that most of the studies cited in this lengthy answer do very little to answer the question, which Dr. 3 seems to recognize at the end.)*

Q.  Well, I'd like you to go one step forward, and then I think the Court might want to take a break, but let me go one more question.

I'd like you to relate that to what happened or what effect the schizophrenia had on Mr. D's mind in this case.

A.  I think it is the reason why he could not handle the amicus relationship with FV, the reason why he perceived them as threats, the reason why they became his enemies and the reason why he killed them.

Mr. DC: Your Honor, if we are going to have a break, this would be appropriate in terms of my presentation.

(Recess taken)

## DIRECT EXAMINATION (CONT.)

Mr. DC: Thank you, your Honor.

Doctor, we have been talking about Mr. D's schizophrenia that you've diagnosed. I'd like to ask you this: in your opinion did the schizophrenia, the disease, the mental illness that Mr. D has, do you feel that that had an effect on his ability to maturely and meaningfully reflect, premeditate, deliberate and reflect on the gravity of his acts on January twenty-two?

A.  Probably.

Q.  More particularly did it have an effect on the kinds of abstract thinking that we have to involve ourselves with here—let me go a little bit further with that before you answer. The kinds of thinking I mean are the mental thought processes to harbor malice, expressed or implied, premeditated or deliberated, to form the specific intent to kill; those kinds of things?

A.  Yes.

Q.  Can you give me an idea what effects it would have on those things?

A.   His paranoia would contaminate his thought processes, including those re-
     quired to form malice and harbor malice and form intent, premeditation and
     so on. That requires some pretty heavy thinking. This man's heavy thinking
     is contaminated by his nuttiness.

*(Author's Note: One could inquire here as to just what is the nature of the
"heavy thinking" that is required to form an intent to commit a crime and to
plan or premeditate. That is, what is the difference in the mental process required to intend and plan to steal a gun as contrasted to intend and plan to use
the gun? Unless Dr. 3 is going to testify that D stole the gun by accident or that
it was somehow just lying out in the open waiting for him to pick it up, there
seems to be little doubt that he did premeditate and intend to steal it. As this was
shortly before the time of the crime when presumably he was suffering from
paranoid schizophrenia, this would then suggest that despite his paranoid
schizophrenia, he could form an intent and make plans and execute them in accordance with that intent.)*

Q.   Have you—you indicated that you have reviewed the transcript of his testi-
     mony of a week ago, and you talked about, I think at some extent, we talked
     about delusional beliefs, and in the review of that testimony, can you give
     us some examples of those delusional beliefs?

A.   Yes. In fact, the example that I have here, not only shows his delusional
     beliefs, but also again are more examples of how foggy his thinking is. And
     he says here—this may be under cross, I'm not sure, but it's not important
     what question he's answering, because it's not responsive, but just to look
     at his thought processes, "Well, my head was so messed up I didn't want
     to kill nobody." I mean, that's an illogical thought, "My head was so
     messed up I didn't want to kill nobody." What does one phrase have to do
     with another?

*(Author's Note: First of all, while Dr. 3 reads this as a straightforward sin-
gle thought, actually in the transcript of the testimony there is a comma which
might suggest some kind of break. Also nearly all of the transcripts, as with most
transcripts, are replete with errors so that Dr. 3 could be asked if there is a possibility that this was really two sentences and simply was not transcribed that
way. However, more importantly, it seems as though what D is saying here is
exactly what Dr. 3 has been saying about him, that his head was so messed up
with paranoid schizophrenia that that is what caused him to do the killing, not
that he wanted to do it. Dr. 3 has just stated earlier that the way his head was
messed up prevented him from forming malice or harboring malice or forming
intent or premeditating, so it would appear that actually one phrase does have a
great deal to do with the other. This would be entirely congruent with Dr. 3's
insistence that D perceives himself as a virtuous person and that in this instance
he did not want to kill anybody as he has stated, but that he had to, presumably
again in line with Dr. 3's thinking, because of his paranoid schizophrenia.
Third, it would probably be worthwhile to make reference to a statement in the
transcript of Dr. 4's testimony where Dr. 4 has been questioned concerning the
absence of a listing in the 1980* Directory of the American Psychological Association, *whereupon the psychologist claims it was failure of a secretary and possibly because of a broken arm. Then questioned about membership in the state*

*psychological association, Dr. 4 claims membership in that, but to the question "Would you necessarily disagree with me, Doctor, if I say as of today it indicates that you have not been a member since (four years)?" Dr. 4 answers: "I really don't remember when or if it lapsed and I have been a member at one point of my career. These are voluntary organizations and they have seminars and I generally teach more than I attend." What does the second sentence have to do with the first? Then Dr. 4 states, "I spend my weekends doing forensic work." What does that have to do with membership in the state psychological association? We see no logical connection here at all, certainly less logical connection than for a defendant in a criminal case to say my head was so messed up I really didn't want to kill anybody. We also note that the response of Dr. 3 above is in answer to a request to give examples of delusional belief. Certainly there is no delusional belief here. If this was one of Dr. 3's dots, then it seems clearly to be a dot that should be removed so as not to further blur the picture.)*

"I tried to stop the whole thing when the whole thing was going on, and right now in this courtroom there's FV's cousin in here that was into a lot of other fighting that we were into, that put me under a lot of pressure, and if I would have got killed, these people would have got blamed for my death, because they already threatened me times and these were the same family, so if I would have ended up dead, these people would have been blamed, because a lot of people know I was already threatened by them, and MV would have gone scot free. And that's why I told my friend, I said, 'If I get killed tell my parents about MV,' and I told him to tell that to my parents, if I didn't make it, that's what I told him, because I knew MV's mom was a legal secretary and I knew she went out with lawyers and I knew the lawyer she worked for is very powerful and very rich, and I knew he would get off scot free."

Now, I don't know what the hell that is all about, but clearly it's a mangled mental process. Such mangled mental processes, I believe, were in evidence at the time he pulled those triggers, and we also see delusions here and grandiosity, "rich powerful lawyer, MV's mother going out with lawyers and works for a lawyer," somehow this is connected with him getting killed instead of someone else. It's a delusional smorgasbord of psychoses.

*(Author's Note: According to the glossary in DSM-III (page 357), "Delusions, grandiose. A delusion whose content involves an exaggerated sense of one's importance, power, knowledge, or identity. It may have a religious, somatic or other theme." There is nothing in the statement that we can see which involves an exaggerated sense of D's importance, power, knowledge or identity. It is possibly MV or possibly MV's mom or possibly the lawyer she worked for who is very powerful or very rich, and MV could get away scot free, not because D was important, but because MV or someone connected to MV had important connections. They have the power, not D. Also, D is not the object of the exercise of their power or importance as is sometimes the case with grandiose delusions such as, "The FBI is out to get me because I am an important person for some reason or other." Also Dr. 3 says he believes such mangled mental processes were in evidence at the time he pulled those triggers. How could he*

*possibly know that? We suspect that he, as well as most mental health profes-*
*sionals, will grant that psychotic states fluctuate so that one can be in a highly*
*psychotic state at one time and at other times be able to function in a non-*
*psychotic manner. Other than for the fact that he did perform the shootings,*
*there is little to indicate that at the moment of the shootings he was having man-*
*gled thought processes, and indeed that is what Dr. 1 indicated: that rather than*
*his thought processes being mangled, they were cold-blooded and deliberate.)*

Then, by the way, for reference that was page six twenty, and page five
seven oh, I think I've already alluded to this on direct, he feels he can't get a
fair trial here because the District Attorney is going with the victim's
mother. "Well, how do you know that?" you asked. "I found out and the
first lawyer I had did some checking. Some people says that him and MV's
mother did have dates."

And then on cross examination, this is Mr. PA, asks, "You found
out since this trial started that I have not ever dated the victim's mother,
Mr. D?" "Oh, I've heard you have." "Oh? still; is that right?" "No, not now.
I know you're married, and I know who you are married to." Question: "But
you still believe I did?" "Yes."

Now, that's a delusion. Where does it come from? It comes from his
perception that he is at risk, which is probably accurate. But it's not simply
enough that the prosecutor is going to do a workman part job, part of his
profession, to present the evidence as he sees it, but there's some sort of
conspiracy going on between this man and another woman connected with
the homicide, and that kind of delusional thinking which he sees as a connection, that do not exist. I think it plays a significant role in homicides, and
probably contaminated his thinking when he attempted such processes, as
intent and malice.

Q. In your interviews with Mr. D, and your review of the various materials that
you've been supplied were you able to determine whether or not Mr. D re-
gretted his actions?
A. I was able to make such a detemination.
Q. What was that determination?
A. He regrets it. He perceives of himself as a non-violent individual who
would not willingly take a life, and he regrets the loss he created to MV's
family, but even his regret is markedly contaminated and limited by his perception that these people were evil and out to get him, even now, after all
the evidence, that it was inevitable that he had no choice, and with the same
reasoning that led to their—led to the shooting, is to some extent in evidence now, even though he's loaded up on all kinds of medication.
Q. Is that to say that there was no bases for what happened?
A. I'm not sure how to answer that. Certainly there's no rational basis for his
killing these two young people, or shooting at least two young people and
killing one; no rational basis for it. Whether or not there is some germ of
truth in the reasons that he gives, I'm not competent to say, but the basis, of
course, is his schizophrenia, basically, although that—that schizophrenia
may embrace some sort of real grievance, but the grievance is small compared to the enormity of his decision to deal with it.

*(Author's Note: He could be asked here, given the fact of a "love triangle" situation, what would be a rational basis for killing the other two people in the triangle. We doubt that Dr. 3 would be able to come up with something other than that one of the other members of the triangle was imposing an immediate threat of death or injury, e.g. by holding a gun on the other individual, which would then seem to make this a meaningless statement since it is unlikely that other than that situation, there ever is a rational basis for killing someone in that situation. Typically in the love triangle, the motive is jealousy, or rage, or a combination. Similarly, Dr. 3 appears to acknowledge that there may be a germ of truth in the reasons that D gives and states he's not competent to render an opinion on that, which ought to lend itself to the prosecution viewpoint that in fact there may well have been some threats, some reality to D's perception of being in danger, such as a connection with drug dealing, or whatever, and he repeats this more or less in that the schizophrenia may embrace some sort of real grievance which is small compared to the enormity of his decision to deal with it. Again, he could be asked what grievance would be large enough for the enormity of such a decision?)*

Mr. DC:

Q.   Let me ask more or less the same question slightly differently.

But for the presence of the schizophrenia in Mr. D's mind, in your opinion would he have killed MV and shot and seriously wounded FV?

A.   I don't think so.

*(Author's Note: Dr. 3's answer here contains a certain amount of tentativeness. He has not come out saying there is no doubt about it, "I am sure it is so," but he puts it more tentatively that he "thinks" that is the case. Questions could be asked on this whether anyone with paranoid schizophrenia who is involved in a love triangle and has, let us say, been rejected, could shoot one of the other parties for the same reasons as someone who is not paranoid schizophrenic. If he acknowledges that is possible, he then could be asked if there is research showing what percentage perform such shootings as a result of their schizophrenia, and what percentage perform it as a result of jealous rage, like other rejected lovers? If he insists that all schizophrenics in such a situation would shoot because of their schizophrenia, then he would have to be taken through a laborious cross-examination to establish the fact that many things done by people who have schizophrenia are not the result of their schizophrenia. For example, if they go to the grocery store and buy groceries, they do that as other people do in order to have some food that they can eat. They would not refrain from going to the grocery store but for their schizophrenia. In other words, the schizophrenia does not cause them to go to the grocery store. They go to the grocery store for the same reasons that anybody else goes to the grocery store. If somebody throws a punch at them and they punch back to defend themselves, they are doing that not because they have schizophrenia, but because they are defending themselves as many people who are not schizophrenic might do. And so on to work one's way up to the point where there ought to be some concession that if somebody with schizophrenia kills another member of a love triangle it is not necessarily because of their schizophrenia, and they might have done*

*the same thing regardless of the presence of schizophrenia or the absence of schizophrenia.)*

Mr. DC: Your witness, Mr. PA.

Mr. PA: Thank you.

## CROSS-EXAMINATION:

*(Author's note: It should be noted that because of other responsibilities, Mr. PA was only able to confer with Dr. Ziskin after office hours, at which time he was quite tired and appeared to have difficulty absorbing information given to him. He was also quite tired when he undertook cross examination.)*

Mr. PA:

Q. Doctor 3, a few moments ago you were asked about your fees in these matters, and I have a couple questions, sir, I would like to ask you along those lines.

   Why, for instance, is it that you would charge more for cases in which you do legal work than say for a counseling or psychiatric treatment type of case?

A. Because it is a subspecialty I have special skills, I have had special training beyond that which the ordinary psychiatrist has. It is infinitely more draining and more time consuming. I don't charge for things like phone calls and—I have to—in order to equalize what I would earn if I simply worked as a psychotherapist, there has to be somewhat larger fees because of the things I don't charge for, whereas when you do psychotherapy you charge for every minute.

*(Author's Note: There are a number of things in the above statement by Dr. 3. Why is it "infinitely more draining" than seeing patients, particularly seriously disturbed patients of which Dr. 3 has stated or implied that he sees a great many? It would seem that if a witness is just telling the truth and not going beyond the knowledge in the field or his own competence, that there does not appear to be anything that should be more difficult than dealing with "nutty" or "crazy" patients, particularly where they are in an outpatient setting, and particularly if they are paranoid schizophrenics whose logic is faulty and who suffer from delusions, so there is at least a potential threat to the physical well-being and even the life of the therapist.*

*As to phone calls, it is unlikely that Dr. 3's practice is so much different from others where most therapists get phone calls from patients. So it would be worthwhile to find out if he does get phone calls from patients, and whether he charges them by the minute for those phone calls, which leads to the next obvious conclusion. In terms of attempting to equalize earnings, all he would have to do is charge his $50.00 an hour for forensic work and charge for the time spent on phone calls. Other than the minimal phone calls which take just a few minutes for which probably nobody even charges patients, it is certainly not difficult to keep a log of telephone conversations or other time spent as most lawyers well know from their own practices. Also, inasmuch as his forensic rate sometimes is double his therapy rate, one could inquire if he spends an hour on telephone calls in forensic work for every hour of examination and report writing. This seems highly unlikely. It might also be worthwhile to ask him if he takes* *phone calls when he is seeing patients, as it is unlikely that he would do that, and it would leave a bad impression if he did, so that he is not losing any ther-apy income because of the forensic work he does. The bottom line to all of this is that he likely makes a good deal more money from the forensic work he does on a time basis than he does from his therapy practice, so that he is not quite the good guy, the public-spirited citizen that he has earlier portrayed himself to be.)*

Q. Okay. So that would mean that you somewhat specialize in the field of fo-rensic psychiatry?

A. Yes.

Q. Again, I know the jury's heard it a couple of times, but we've gotten a cou-ple of different meanings, would you describe your view, please, of forensic psychiatry?

A. This is the study of the relationship between law and psychiatry on the happy assumption that there is a relationship.

Q. What percentage do you believe of your income is derived from your self—working with lawyers as a forensic psychiatrist, lawyers on either side, peo-ple like myself or Mr. DC or the courts?

A. It probably varies from time to time. Maybe a third, maybe a half.

Q. Does most of your court work consist of working in criminal cases?

A. No.

Q. If not, roughly what percent?

A. Forty percent.

Q. Now, can you tell us, sir, what your fee per hour will be in this case, or your overall fee, a rough estimate?

A. Right. I really can't. I have submitted some bills but I—I don't know what—I can't remember precisely what I submitted. Probably with air fare and so on, it might be as much as a thousand dollars.

Q. Okay. The total bill?

A. For the day, yes.

Q. For today?

A. Yeah.

Q. All right. You recall how much you billed for the testing and consultations and other work, your report that you prepared to date, prior to today?

A. No.

Q. Over a thousand?

A. Well, I saw him twice, so it is entirely possible.

Q. Okay. Now, Doctor, you are, I take it, familiar with Doctor 4?

A. Yes.

Q. All right. How long have you known him?

A. Quite a few years.

Q. How many?

A. I don't know. I don't know.

Q. Do you see him frequently?

A. Once a month.

Q. Okay. Are you anywhere—that is professionally, the physical locations of your offices, are they anywhere near each other?

A. One of my offices is, yes.

Q. Do you refer cases to, him, Doctor?

A. Occasionally. I referred him this one.

Q. You referred him this one?

A. (Nods head.)

Q. All right. Now, do you recall when or about when you referred this case to Doctor 4?

A. No. Would have to be the fall of (the year of the crime), but I couldn't narrow it down more than that.

Q. And was that by way of an oral communication or by a written communication?

A. Probably oral.

Q. Again not sure?

A. Right.

Q. Okay. And why did you refer this case to Doctor 4?

A. Seemed to me that psychological testing was an issue here. I can't recall what—what that was. It seemed to me that he had some psychological testing and a second opinion might be useful.
I am really at the very limits of my recollection.

Q. Okay. I guess what I would like to ask is, was it your decision, that is did you, sir, professionally feel that a further examination by Doctor 4 might be beneficial, or was that a decision that was—that you might have passed on to Mr. DC, he said, "Yes, who can I refer him to for more psychological testing"?

*(Author's Note: In view of Dr. 3's altruistic concern with saving public money, he is remarkably vague as to the reasons for the substantial expenditure that was incurred for the psychological evaluation by Dr. 4. There was already an opinion by Dr. 1 based on psychiatric interviewing, and an opinion based on psychological testing by Dr. 2. If he was as concerned with taxpayers' money as he stated, it would seem somewhat extravagant to incur this additional expense without a highly specific reason for doing so, and without a feeling that it was really necessary rather than "might be useful." It might very well be a good point at which to ask him if he would have been unable to render the diagnosis that he rendered without this additional input. If he says he was not able, then he would appear to have to depend on the work of Dr. 4, who, as indicated earlier, can be demonstrated to have performed with at least questionable competence in this case, and who clearly did make errors. If he says it was not necessary, then he seems inconsistent with his early statement about being sensitive to saving the taxpayers' money inasmuch as Dr. 4's fees came to a considerable amount, somewhere over $3,000, which in the early 1980's would have been viewed as a very high sum for a forensic evaluation.)*

A. Probably a mutual decision.

Q. What specifically, Doctor 3, were you asked by Mr. DC to do in this particular case when you were first contacted, and even though it is compound, were you contacted by him in writing or again over the phone?

A. I was contacted in both writing and over the phone. And was asked to evaluate his client to determine whether or not he had a mental illness, and if so its severity and its relationship to the offense, if any.

Q.  Had you met Mr. DC before that first or initial communication?

A.  I don't think so.

Q.  Were you asked—I notice you made some reference to it on your direct examination—asked by Mr. DC to determine whether or not the defendant in this matter was mentally competent pursuant to the provisions of to stand trial, that is understand the charges against him and assist in his defense?

A.  Was I asked to make such a determination?

Q.  Yes.

A.  No, I don't think so.

Q.  Did you make such a determination?

A.  No.

Q.  Do you have any opinion now as you sit here about whether or not Mr. D is at least able to understand the nature of the charges against him and assist in his defense?

A.  I have an opinion.

Q.  And that is?

A.  He is.

Q.  He is, okay.

Now, I take it just from noting at the recess that you do know Doctor Jay Ziskin.

A.  Yes.

Q.  You're familiar with his book, *Coping with Psychiatric and Psychological Testimony, Second Edition*?

A.  Yes.

Q.  In your opinion, Doctor, is that book widely used by members of your profession, that is the psychiatric profession, who deal in forensic work?

A.  No. I think it is directed at attorneys, and I think it is widely used by attorneys.

*(Author's Note: Here, Dr. 3 has rendered an opinion for which he could have little or no basis. Unless he has conducted a survey or knows of a survey that has been conducted by others, he really is in no position to render an opinion as to the extent to which Dr. Ziskin's book is used by psychiatrists who deal in forensic work. He could be asked how he knows that it is not widely used, and in the absence of some survey, it can be shown that he is willing to render an opinion on flimsy or no grounds. Further, inasmuch as Dr. Ziskin is scheduled to testify in this matter, it might be noted that he will be able to testify that in fact Dr. 3 is simply wrong in this opinion, as the book has been extensively purchased by psychiatrists and inasmuch as it is an expensive book, one cannot avoid the conclusion that they would not spend that kind of money unless they intended to use it.)*

Q.  Okay. Both for the defense and the prosecution or more on one side or the other?

A.  I think Doctor Ziskin would be a better source of that information. He sells the book. But since I think psychiatric testimony probably is more often used by the defense as a tool to explain how the homicide took place, then I would—I would imagine that a book designed to discredit psychiatric testimony would be more commonly in the hands of the prosecutor than the defense attorney.

Q. Have you cited or quoted Doctor Ziskin in any of your talks, lectures, Doctor 3?

A. I don't—I can't say that I haven't. I just can't recall specifically doing so. I would certainly have no qualms about doing so. I think it is a very useful book. I don't think I have ever specifically cited it. Maybe I have. Maybe I used it for reference. It is a very useful book.

Q. You're just not sure one way or the other if you have or you haven't?

A. Right.

Q. Or do you really believe it is more likely that you haven't?

A. I—I can't say.

Q. Okay. Is psychiatry, the study of psychiatry or even forensic psychiatry, for that matter, in your professional opinion, Doctor, an art or a science?

A. Both.

Q. Can you tell us how much is art and how much is science?

A. No.

Q. Assuming that's a round circle, would you be able to go to the board, Doctor, and indicate what piece of the pie or the circle was an art, in your opinion, and what part was science?

A. No.

Q. Do you have the opinion, Doctor, that it is a much—that the study of psychiatry is as much a science as it is an art?

Mr. DC: I'm going to object. That's been asked and answered. He said no.

Mr. PA: I don't believe that's been asked and answered.

Mr. DC: Well, it is all in the same point.

THE COURT: I think he could tell how much of each there was, which I think would be the same thing. If he feels he has any additional answer, he could answer it.

A. No.

*(Author's Note: Here the prosecutor has obtained the answers that he wanted, establishing that psychiatry is, to some unknown extent, an art, as well as to some extent a science, but that the extent to which it is art is not determinable, which will allow him to argue later that it may very well be much more art than science, and as such, less credible. We might note the way the skilled witness handles all this. He gives one word answers, giving up what he has to give up and drawing, or focusing as little attention as possible on this area which seems not beneficial to his testimony. The cross-examiner could have asked one more question here to the effect of whether the science part is used to evaluate the art part. However, with a witness as facile as this one, it may be that the cross-examiner did well to take his gains and go on to another topic.)*

Mr. PA:

Q. Doctor, at the time you wrote your first report, that is the one dated September, 30th, I believe, what other—that is medical doctors, psychiatrists or psychologists reports did you have at your disposal to review?

A. The psychological report of Doctor 2. Period.

Q. Did you—I take it you relied on that report.

A. I never know what people mean when they ask me if I relied. That's a word of art—or is it a word of science—that lawyers use.
   I read it. He's in an allied field, so I paid attention to it, but did I rely on it? Did it sway me in a different direction?
   I can't say it did, but it didn't necessarily sway me in another direction.
   I read it. I respected it.
Q. Maybe a clearer way of asking it is was it able to assist you?
A. I'd have to say yes to that.
Q. I don't want to ask then to what extent, but can you tell me then what portions of his report were significant in your mind?
A. I no longer have a working knowledge of that report, so I can't answer that.

*(Author's Note: The cross-examiner should stop the witness right at this point. He has stated that he can't answer the question. He should be cut off then, with a quick "Thank you," and asking another question. However, this is another instance where a productive result was obtained. He has already established that Dr. 2's report did assist him, which again raises further questions as to the need for referral to Dr. 4, but also in his answer which immediately follows, he indicates that other examiners may observe the patient in a somewhat different way. And while he portrays this as a positive, that is "a rich picture," we should also note that what it does mean is that there may be a lack of high reliability in what is observed by different examiners, which can then be tied in to the problems of situation and examiner effects if and when those are brought into evidence.)*

   I can tell you to explain my previous answer that it is always useful to have another view, another view always is—provides assistance, even if it is maybe a cursory evaluation. But just to have another man in there seeing the man, the defendant at a different time and looking at him in a different way, it is sort of like describing a house. If you're standing in front of the house, you get one picture of it, and if somebody is standing ten feet to your right, may pick up a little angle, maybe a little side of the right wall, you have a rich picture.
Q. All right. I realize it is some time ago.
   Right now, you can't remember what, if anything, was particularly significant to you that you pointed to in arriving at your diagnosis?
A. Right.
Q. What about Doctor 1's report, you didn't have that, did you, at the first time of the first report?
A. No.
   Didn't I see that afterwards?
   Well, in any event, to be responsive to your question, no, I did not. I didn't have it prior to my evaluation.
Q. Do you believe, Doctor, you would have come to the same conclusions about the defendant had you not had Doctor 2's report at the time you rendered your diagnosis at that time?
A. Yes.
Q. All right. Now, it appears as though for the second report at least you did have the benefit of looking at Doctor 1's report.

A. Right.

Q. All right. Is there anything particularly significant about that report that you relied on in assisting you with your re-examination and subsequent diagnosis?

A. Not particularly, no.

Q. Do you believe your second diagnosis would have been the same, regardless of his report?

A. Yes.

*(Author's Note: Here he is confirming that he did not need the psychological test data to make his diagnosis which, again, seems to make the referral to Dr. 4, for a procedure that at this point he appears to be saying is not necessary for him to make his diagnosis, questionable, particularly in view of the taxpayers' money that was involved.)*

Q. Do you recall, independently now, with my appreciation of the fact that it has been some time ago, Doctor 1's report, some of the conclusions that he arrived at?

A. Only to the extent that my own report refreshes my recollection, but I should be happy to—if you'd like I would look at your copy.

   In my own report, I made a note to myself that—well, little paragraph of page two.

Q. That is, Doctor—quoting now: "Doctor 1 felt that the defendant's ability to reflect upon the gravity of the situation may have been substantially impaired," close quote, even though he was not likely legally insane.

A. Right.

Mr. PA: All right. I guess I might have this marked for identification as People's Number Fifty-Two for identification, I believe.

THE COURT: Is that something that's already been marked, possibly?

Mr. PA: It is the report of Doctor 1, M.D., dated April 24th, regarding D.

Mr. DC: I thought it was marked, but I could be wrong.

Mr. PA: It is marked Defendant's 1 for identification.

THE COURT: All right.

Mr. PA: May I approach this witness, your Honor?

THE COURT: Yes.

Mr. PA: Doctor 3, can you just take a moment or two to look at that and tell me whether or not that refreshes your recollection as to whether or not you've seen that document before?

A. Yes, I have read this.

Q. Okay. Directing your attention to the last page, page seven, I believe of that report—

A. Um hum.

Q. Would you kindly take a moment to read to yourself paragraph number three?

A. Okay.

Q. The question concerning whether or not Mr. D was legally insane.

A. Okay.

Q. Might I ask you now are you able to render an opinion as to whether or not you agree with the last sentence of paragraph number three, that is most likely perhaps that Mr. D executed MV in cold blood and attempted to do the same to FV?

A. Um, I have difficulty with that question. And let me answer it, then I will tell you my difficulty with it.

No, I don't agree. My difficulty is that it goes beyond my competence as a psychiatrist.

I think that that kind of issue—that conclusionary statement really is for the trier of fact, who has not only the benefit of the psychiatric evaluation, which is what I had the benefit of, but it has heard a lot of witnesses who, you know, are going to have weeks of evidence, then on the basis of that will form what is essentially an opinion whether or not this is first degree murder.

*(Author's Note: PA should not allow the witness to alter the statement to an ultimate conclusion as to degree. The question concerned "cold blood" which is similar in meaning to "premeditated" and "deliberate" on which Dr. 3 has already rendered an opinion.)*

I don't think that a psychiatrist can do that or shouldn't do it.

I do believe that in this case the jury's task will be aided by the psychiatric testimony that they hear, but I do not believe psychiatric testimony to be controlling and does not lead inextricably to these conclusionary judgments.

Q. Now, it appears to me, I'm not trying to trick you or anything, but it appears to me as though you did not have the benefit of Doctor 4's report during the course of either examination on the defendant; is that fair to say?

A. I'm—let me see—

Q. Sure.

A. That's correct. That's correct.

Q. When did you first become aware of Doctor 4's report?

A. Well, we can safely say sometime after he wrote it, which was December seventh. See, there are some concretes in psychiatry, and I presume the second week in September [sic].

Q. All right. Now, did you prepare a subsequent—that is a third report after you read his report?

A. I don't think so.

Q. I don't have one if you did, I'm just asking you.

A. I don't have one, either, so if I did, I would really be alarmed.

Q. Okay. Was there anything then—I take it there was nothing about his report that would make you change the opinion you rendered in the first and second interview with Mr. D?

*(Author's Note: This is not a good question. If asked at all, it should be whether there was anything in the report that Dr. 3 disagrees with.)*

A. Correct.

Q. Okay. Now, you, I believe, testified on direct that you, at least during your mental examinations with the defendant, found no evidence of organicity, that is organic brain damage?

A. Right.

Q. Is that still your opinion today?

A. That I found no evidence of it?

Q. Yes.

A. Yes.

Q. All right. Is it your opinion that he is not suffering from organicity or from brain damage?

A. Well, no, it's not, because there was some suggestion of it on psychological testing, which is a more sensitive indicia of organicity, but it certainly wasn't gross organicity. But I'm going to have to defer to psychological testing which are better designed for determining that.

Q. Okay. Is it fair to say that there was nothing that was so close or so obvious that you noted, that compelled you to suggest to Dr. 4 or to someone else that a neurological exam be done?

A. That's right.

Q. All right.

A. Besides a man could have flagrant organicity and have—be neurologically negative. They usually are people who, for example, have—are so senile, that they have little blood getting to their cerebrum, so that they walk down the street without their pants and urinate in garbage cans. They really have got brain damage, and most of them are neurologically negative, or have substantial neurological signs.

Q. Thank you for your candor, Doctor.

    Do you believe that after reading Doctor 4's report that organicity contributed significantly to the ultimate conclusion that he is a paranoid schizophrenic?

A. No. They're separate diagnoses, one would not contribute to the other.

Q. What, incidentally is the best way, in your opinion, to detect organic brain damage, Doctor 3?

A. The best way is to send them to a good psychologist. Now, you know, that's another—that's another field, and while I certainly have read a few books on psychological testing, I'm not an expert, but one test that has been commonly used, and I understand picks up organicity fairly well, is the Bender-Gestalt test. Another one is the—I think Holstead Writer [sic] Test, which is a very sensitive test of organicity, due to drug use, but I'm not an expert, and I hope you don't press me too hard with your questions on those subjects.

Q. Okay. You mean about psychological testing?

A. No, testing.

Q. No, I'm not—would there be any value—would it be common for you if you detected brain damage to ask for—to ask that someone perform—such as a neuropsychologist, a CAT scan or something like that?

A. Again, the return would be very small. If we had unlimited funds, and we could do everything a hundred percent, sure, why not, but even if I found substantial organicity, the chances of a CAT scan being positive or positive in a useful diagnostic way, are very small. I'm very sensitive to the use of County money or anybody's money, unless I feel that you're going to get a decent return cost ratio, think it's too low with a CAT scan.

Q. But the Holstead Writer Battery of Neurological Testing is a better method, or a good method, at least?

A. I think your return cost ratio is higher with that.

Q. In any event, again, unless I haven't asked this, you didn't order that these things be done?

*(Author's Note: This whole line of questioning about brain damage or organicity is related to the fact that Dr. 4's report continually refers to the probability of brain damage. At some point, it should be brought out that in fact, Dr. 4 did not perform anything that could be considered a neuropsychological test battery, and certainly did not give the Halstead-Reitan.)*

A. No.

Q. Okay. I notice on page nine of your report, that is your report, your first report of September the thirtieth, that you described the defendant as "all virtuous." That's not a quote, it doesn't appear to be a quote. Might you explain what you meant by that, please?

A. That he has—he portrays himself as utterly without sin. He has a need to believe himself is without sin. Even without the normal black passions that all of us suffer from, from time to time.

Q. Would it be common or would it even be probable, perhaps, theoretically speaking, that one who committed an act such as Mr. D, even after the act, feel all virtuous?

A. Would it be common?

Q. Uh huh.

A. No, quite the contrary. Even people who are much more familiar and comfortable with violence than Mr. D, often have considerable remorse after committing a violent act.

Q. Is it common to feel all virtuous, even if you're paranoid schizophrenic, after such an act?

A. Yes.

Q. I notice on page one, that is the beginning of that report, your very first line you say, "On September twenty-seven, I was privileged to perform a psychiatric examination of your client, D, at the County Jail." Why was it a privilege?

A. There are lots of psychiatrists in this state, and Mr. DC respected my judgment and my work sufficient to ask me to come up here and assist him, and ultimately perhaps to speak to these people. I consider myself singled out.

*(Author's Note: There are a couple of items here that do not need to be dealt with, but could be. One is to ask how he knows what the defense counsel knew about his judgment and work. The second item, and it may be questionable whether to use it, is to ask if it is possible that he was retained simply because, according to his own statement, he is cheaper than most other forensic psychiatrists.)*

Q. Okay. What, Doctor, is interviewer bias?

A. It's—I guess the point of view of the examiner which might distort the perception of the examinee.

*(Author's Note: This answer is satisfactory as far as it goes, but it does not go far enough and the whole issue of examiner bias needs to be expanded and*

*clarified. The attorney could use a set of questions derived from materials in Chapters 5 and 6, Volume I having to do with not only the effect of the examiner on the examinee and in some detail, all of the aspects of the examiner such as his theoretical, political, social views and so on, but also various kinds of confirmatory bias, anchoring effects and so on. Here the attorney gets clobbered because he has asked poor questions and failed to follow a careful sequence. As indicated in a previous note, the way to set this up is by setting up all the ways in which bias can operate and affect data gathering and interpretation in the clinical interview. It is generally not a good idea to ask any witness if he thinks he was biased because first of all you give him a chance to say that he is not biased and secondly because it implies that the individual would know whether he is biased or not, which is really not the position you want to take. However, again, in this instance after the first question, after he got the answer that there was some bias it might have been very wise to stop there. The question below about his own bias is a poor question to put to an adverse expert witness as it opens the gates wide enough to drive a tank through and that is exactly what Dr. 3 did. However, even with this answer, it might have been possible for the cross-examiner to regain some ground by asking the kinds of questions he could have asked earlier. That is, he could have tried to get Doctor 3 to be more specific as to any reasons at all that defense attorney might have given him for thinking there was a psychiatric defense. Did the defense attorney say nothing about D's assertions that they were out to get him? About the Mafia? About all of the purported delusional material? It appears at the point Doctor 3 was contacted, the reports of Doctors 1 and 2 were already in and defense counsel would have had some suggestion at least of psychiatric disturbance. If any of this was transmitted to Doctor 3, then the potential for preconception and confirmatory bias is established and there is no need to ask him if he was biased.)*

Q. Now, you examined Mr. D on both occasions in the County Jail, sir?

A. Yes.

Q. And I take it that just you and he were alone?

A. Yes.

Q. Do you believe that simply because—you were, I take it, aware of the charges?

A. Right.

Q. And do you believe that perhaps because you were hired by the defense and the charges were so serious that there was some bias on your part?

A. Yes, there was.

Q. Tell us about that, please.

A. I sort of recall when I talked to Mr. DC initially, he quickly gave me some details of the case, and this is very sketchy, but this man had shot his former girlfriend and killed the new lover, that there seemed at first blush to be very clear, saying it's not a psychiatric explanation for the homicide, and I didn't, just from what I heard, did not think that psychiatric examination would be terribly fruitful. In other words, I came up here with the expectation that I might well find myself testifying for the prosecution. Again, just based on what little I knew. This was not the kind of case where often I come up with a difference of a bias, where the man leaves the State hospital with a shotgun and kills seven people, and I'm very satisfied that I will find substantial psychiatric data and I have that bias when I walk into the case, but I came up with a different bias this time.

Q. Okay. I have noted that throughout your report, correct me if I am wrong, and even throughout your testimony here today on direct examination, that you refer to the defendant always as Mr. D, yet you refer to the victims always as M and F. Any particular reason for that?

*(Author's Note: This is another example of a poor question. The facts are there, that this is the way he referred to the parties and if the lawyer wishes to make something out of it in terms of bias, he can do so. By asking the witness if there was any reason for it, he gives him of course the opportunity to explain it away, which he does.)*

A. Yes. It's how he referred to them, and most of what I presented was what he gave to me, he called them M and F. I call him Mr. D. I don't presume to call people by their first names.

Q. So when you say that M felt this, or M was frightening him to this extent, and F was going out on him, you're telling us that what, through Mr. D's eyes?

A. That's right. Not only Mr. D, but mostly the people that were interviewed called them M and F. So these are the terms I heard, M and F, rather than Mr. MV or Miss FV. *(Author's Note: Did these people—friends and relatives—refer to D as "Mr. D"?)*

Q. In your mind, I take it it would be rather unfair to imply the fact that you called the defendant Mr. D and the other people by their first names, not an indicia of interviewer bias, necessarily?

A. No, I don't think so.

Q. All right. I've noted in your report furthermore on page three, Doctor, that you indicated the defendant, in describing his work history, had a number of skilled jobs. Am I correct in that, that's the last paragraph on there?

A. Skilled labor jobs, yes, yes, that's correct.

Q. And do you recall what you include within the category of skilled labor jobs?

A. Logging would be; working in a mill.

Q. That's the impression you got, I note that's not in quotes, skilled labor jobs?

A. That's what I'm saying, that he wasn't digging ditches, but he has some skills.

Q. Uh huh.

A. Blue collar skills.

Mr. PA:

Q. Do you know what specific jobs in the mill that he held for—

A. I did back in September sufficient for me to feel that that was an accurate summation. I don't now.

Q. Did you note anything in particular about the defendant, make any observations after you learned what these jobs were, whatever they were now—then that you can't remember now that—to believe that he was an uncoordinated person?

A. An uncoordinated person?

Q. Person with poor hand motor eye—

A. Yeah. Not in any gross way. Seems to me there may have been some subtleties on testing, but he could certainly earn a living using his body.

Q. Okay. No problem with that that you could tell?

A. No.

Q. All right. You did become aware during your interview with Mr. D that he did drink a bottle of vodka at some point early on in his life, I believe everyone has said at the age of nine, and got into an accident where he was riding his bicycle and was subsequently struck by a car?

A. Right.

Q. All right. Did that to you indicate the possibilities that there might be organicity?

A. Yes.

Q. Not so much, though, as if you would—you would refer it for specific testing on that purpose.

A. Correct.

Q. What does concreteness mean, Doctor?

A. It means taking things at—literally rather than deeper abstract meaning.

Q. Okay. Does concreteness—can that be considered one of the symptoms of brain damage?

A. Yes.

Q. You noted that there was some concreteness with Mr. D?

A. Yes.

Q. Again, not enough to believe that there was organicity?

A. Not enough for me to diagnose organicity. Enough for me to feel psychological testing was in order.

Q. Okay. But you didn't personally demand it before you arrived at your diagnosis?

A. No.

Q. All right. And finally, just this morning I have noted in your report, I believe, that the defendant did tell you that on several occasions he actually fell down on the ground, passed out?

A. Right.

Q. All right. Is that consistent with brain damage?

A. No. I think that was part of a drinking pattern, not that—again, I wouldn't expect brain damage due to the extraordinary amount of alcohol he claimed to have consumed down the road. But again it is a matter of judgment, and I guess here's that interface of science and art. I know what the odds are of finding something here, and they're measurable. But I have to make a judgment and protect the county and its funds and recommend things I consider practicable. I just didn't think he would get much with a CAT scan or neurological exam.

Q. Okay. At least as you understood it, the passing out, the falling down was due to the degree of intoxication that he suffered rather than to something else that was causing blackouts or—

A. Right.

Q. Is that fair to say that?

A.  That's right.
Q.  Based on what you knew from him?
A.  Right.
(Recess)

## CROSS EXAMINATION (CONT):

Mr. DA: Doctor, when you referred this case to Doctor 4 for his evaluation and comments, what did you expect to get from him?
A.  Standard forensic psychological report.
Q.  What does that mean?
A.  A clinical interview, a battery of tests, a diagnosis.
Q.  Do you feel as though you got that?
A.  Yeah.
Q.  Now, you were talking this morning about cost ratio of I believe some of the psychological battery of tests, to measure brain damage and the CAT scan. Do you know what the cost of the CAT scan is?
A.  No.
Q.  Are you familiar with Doctor 4's work?
A.  Yes.
Q.  He has told us that he has known you for a period of some ten years. Would you agree with that statement?
A.  Sounds about right.
Q.  In your opinion, Doctor, is he a competent psychologist?
A.  Yes.
Q.  Do you feel as though he's any more or less competent than Doctor 2?
A.  No. I don't know Doctor 2.
Q.  But you had Doctor 2's report at the time you rendered your first diagnosis; did you not?
A.  That's true.
Q.  What did you expect then to get from Doctor 4 that you didn't get from Doctor 2?
*(Author's Note: It would have been sufficient to stop with the previous question and answer.)*
A.  Second opinion.
Q.  And in your opinion you did?
A.  Yes.
Q.  Are you aware of what Doctor 4's fee is per hour?
A.  No, not really.
Q.  He has told us that it is a hundred twenty-five dollars per hour.
A.  Uh huh.
Q.  He spent in excess of thirty hours for this particular case.
A.  Really.
Q.  Did you feel as though you got anything additional now, that you've had a chance to read his report, than Doctor 2 had provided you with?
*(Author's Note: These few questions are unnecessary, and particularly this last one is not a good question, again, giving Dr. 3 an opportunity to explain away what had otherwise been advantageous to the examiner.)*

A. Well, it's certainly more thorough and I believe he also spent a lot of time interviewing relatives to get that extra dimension. I think that's where a lot of the time went. Also the report itself is quite substantial, quite rich. And I think it gives us a very complete picture of Mr. D.

*(Author's Note: This is a vague answer but sounds as though there was value in Dr. 4's contribution. It may have been useful to pin the witness down to exactly what was of value to provide for weakening Dr. 3's credibility if he relied on it when it is shown that Dr. 4's competence is very questionable.)*

Q. In any event, the privilege that you felt, not necessarily suffered, but were given by being picked by Mr. DC from a number of psychiatrists, you passed on to Doctor 4 when you decided to refer it to him, for a psychological test; is that correct?

A. That's correct.

Q. And I take it then you held him as a rather somewhat of an authority in that particular field?

A. I think he is a competent psychiatrist.

Q. You mean psychologist?

A. Did I say psychiatrist?

Q. Yes, sir.

A. Thank you. He's a competent psychologist. He's well regarded in the community. I've always been impressed with the thoroughness of his work. He's not unwilling to travel, which is a hardship to leave one's patients and one's practice, and he's willing to do that, and he's comfortable working with attorneys. He does much more civil work than criminal work, but he's reasonably comfortable in presenting some sophisticated psychological material in somewhat of an adversary setting, so I thought he would do a competent job.

Q. He testified that he only testified, that is actually testified in criminal matters in three or four cases. To the best of your knowledge is that true?

A. Yes.

Q. Now, would it surprise you to know that, or to learn that he made errors on the scoring on the Wechsler test?

*(Author's Note: Surprise is not a good issue. A better question would be, "Are you aware that Dr. 4 made several errors of scoring and interpretation of the Wechsler?" Or even better, ask if a number of errors would affect his opinion of Dr. 4's skill.)*

A. Would it surprise me?

Q. Uh huh.

A. I don't know how to answer it. You mean some serious errors, or petty little errors? I don't know what you mean by an error.

Q. Let's say serious errors in the scoring of the Wechsler?

Mr. DC: I'm going to object. It assumes a fact not yet in evidence.

Mr. PA: I'm not asking it for the fact, I'm just asking if the doctor, after knowing him this way, would be surprised.

THE WITNESS: Yes, he's very conscientious.

THE COURT: Just a moment.

Mr. DC: We need a ruling.

THE COURT: I don't believe we have anything in evidence now. Are you proposing that there will be evidence to that effect?

Mr. PA: Yes. I can ask it in the form of a hypothetical.

THE COURT: Well, even for a hypothetical question it has to be within the range of evidence, but the Court can let something come in subject to a motion to strike, if it isn't presented later, that is the foundational part.

Mr. DC: The problem that I see with it, your Honor, is that we're dealing with serious or non-serious or minimal or whatever, and I think we ought to probably have some kind of offer of proof so that the Doctor, if he's able to, can make some comment on the size of the error, if in fact it does exist.

THE COURT: It could come in that way subject to a motion to strike, if the evidence about the error isn't brought together.

Mr. DC: That's fine.

Mr. PA: I guess we're going to have a problem deciding what you think is serious and what I think is serious so for now I'll just withdraw from that. Doctor, the People—what makes up the body of knowledge upon which the practice of psychiatry is based?

*(Author's Note: This is another open-ended question. What the cross-examiner is after is to establish that there is little scientifically validated knowledge in the field, and what there is is contained in the scientific and professional literature and it would be better to put the question in that form. However, some useful information comes out anyway, in that the witness indicates that he does use information gleaned from studies of other than his own patients. It may be necessary to get him to define "studies" in the hope that he is referring to scientific studies.)*

A. I don't think I could possibly respond to that question without—in any kind of meaningful way, without taking the weeks it would take to share with you all the books that I've read, and all the patients that I've studied and the information gleaned from studies of other patients. So I'll give you a very simplistic answer which is that it is based on centuries, perhaps of attempting to come up to some understanding of how the human mind works and where sometimes it goes awry.

Q. It includes, does it not, as a rather important factor, I would guess, education?

A. Whose education?

Q. The psychiatrist.

A. Yes, most psychiatrists are fairly well educated.

Q. His training, I take it?

A. Yes.

Q. Personal experience?

A. Yes.

Q. And you indicated, the things that he continues to read?

A. Right.

Q. What journals do you read, Doctor, regularly?

A. Read the *Archives of General Psychiatry,* regularly; *The Journal of the American Psychiatric Association,* regularly; the *American Journal of Forensic Psychiatry*; those fairly consistently.

Q. Okay. What about research studies, they're important, are they not, to the degree of expertise that psychiatrists rely upon?

*(Author's Note: This also is not a well-stated question. Again, what the lawyer is really after is to establish that scientific research is important to the knowledge base in psychiatry as a field, and it might have been useful to ask if the journals that the doctor has just referred to do not contain considerable numbers of research studies. However, again, there is an answer that could be useful, in that when he says research is on the forefront and predictive of what may be coming down the road in the following years, that is only a partial truth. They are also used to check up on what is currently being done or what has been done, or on clinical "beliefs," and there are a number of such articles published in the journals he says he reads. He should also be asked if he reads some of the other important journals.)*

A. Most research studies don't have too much bearing on the workday therapist. Those are forefront. They are predictive of what may be coming down the road in following years.

Mr. PA: Do you have anything more to add to that?

A. No.

Q. Would you consider then a minor—that is research studies a minor part of the things that you rely upon in continuing to gain experience in the field or knowledge in the field of psychiatry?

A. In the immediate moment, but I do think that research is important because those, of course, provide the resources for the future. Sort of like the research I did with, I did it back in 1965-66. It wasn't until 1979—I'm sorry, 1969-1970 that the fruits of my research had any impact on the work of psychiatrists in being able to utilize my discoveries.

Q. I think you indicated this morning with those circles that you relied on research to make a point, research about some people at San Quentin accused of white collar crimes.

A. Right.

Q. You use research, don't you, in developing further knowledge for yourself in your practice?

A. Well, as I say, I'm a work-a-day psychiatrist on the firing line. Most research doesn't really become meaningful to me or useful to most people in my field until many years later, and then when it becomes practical and becomes useful and it gives me a tool to put in my hands, it has any validity, by that time of course, there's a whole bunch of research studies which will come to fruition in 19___. So I can't really say it is very much a part of my life. I think it is important to psychiatry as a whole that we constantly examine what we are doing and try to expand into the frontiers of our knowledge. But I don't think much work-a-day psychiatrists really have much to do with research, which is a very specialized field. Have to wait until the dust settles. You have one study that says one thing and then six months later another study says other things. Take four or five years until the dust really settles, those studies begin to fall into something that is really useful to the humble everyday practitioner like myself.

*(Author's Note: Note that this question calls for a "yes" or "no" answer, but the cross-examiner does not obtain this and lets the witness take control of the situation. However, even though the answer seems to waffle all over the place, it does contain in it the concession that research takes time and that it is important to psychiatry to constantly examine what it is doing, which is what most of the materials in Volumes I and II are all about. They are about examining what psychiatry is doing. One might want to pick up on his statement of contradictory studies to point out that if the knowledge is needed and it's worthwhile for the expenditure of money and energy on doing the research, that until the issues are resolved, as he indicates, in four or five years, they have to operate in what is essentially a vacuum of knowledge. However, he also does concede that after some years the research is useful, and in fact he supports some of this in his next answer, which contains the statement that where the studies are in conflict, "you don't really know where you are.")*

Q.  Okay. Correct me—again correct me if I am wrong, I believe you indicated this morning in your testimony that there was some research that you agreed with that said there was in fact a genetic component as part of the diagnosis of paranoid schizophrenia?

A.  Well, it suggests that. Suggests that. We really don't know what causes schizophrenia. That's the trouble with studies. You have one study which shows one thing and then six months later another study shows the complete opposite, so you don't really know where you are, and after maybe five or ten years a certain truth begins to emerge from this barrage and often conflicting studies. But right now, I would say that most of us, most of the studies would seem to point at last some genetic predisposition in some kind of schizophrenia.

Q.  Now, you might not know this—I'm not trying to be unfair—do you know the name of those studies?

A.  Not to rattle off, no. I read so many articles and I'm lucky if I can retain the essence of what they say. No less than people who may have put their title to the article.

Q.  Would they be easily available to you, that is if you were going back this weekend, knowing you were coming back next week, would you be able to call me collect and let me know what they are if you find any?

A.  Possibly.

Q.  Would you make an effort to do that, sir?

A.  Sure.

Q.  Is there any scientific literature, Doctor, showing that psychiatrists can detect malingering—that's what we understand so far at least in the courtroom of the evidence to mean faking a disease, even a mental disease. Is there any research that shows that psychiatrists can detect malingering with any degree of accuracy?

*(Author's Note: This is a not a good way to ask the question. Use of words such as "any," or "never" are too extreme. His answer, and his reference to there being studies which he can't identify are probably best dealt with at this point by asking simply if there are also scientifically conducted studies which indicate that experts are not very accurate in detecting malingering, which*

*would then allow the examiner to confirm what the witness has said earlier, that in the face of conflicting studies, they don't really know where they are with regard to detecting malingering. However, in his answer which follows, he states there are sets of signs of malingering which have been well-established. It might be worthwhile to ask him to state what those signs are and whether and how they have been validated through scientific research methods. If they have not, one cannot be sure that in fact they are valid signs.)*

A. I would imagine so.

Q. Well, have you read any?

A. I read lots of things, including lots of studies on malingering. Presumably they are based on something.

Q. Can you think of even one study where that has ever been the case?

A. Again, I am limited to the fact that I read so much, so many books, so many journals, that I can't at this point bisect that out for you and pinpoint the specific source of my information. But I have read certain studies on malingering and certain reliable signs and symptoms of medical disorders as to people who simulate mental disorders, they are pretty clearly, I think, indicated on direct—we have a pretty well established pattern for schizophrenia. There are—somebody who attempts to simulate a psychosis, unless he is extremely sophisticated, one year of internship, three years of residency, read lots of books, he is likely to pretend to be nutty, but not likely to duplicate schizophrenia. It is certainly a well-prescribed set of symptoms. I have done some writing myself based on some studies of people who have attempted to malinger, and again there are a number of ways of indicating— you know, we find that there are maybe thirteen, fourteen things that come up again and again. Typical malingerer would reflect eight or nine of those. Even that doesn't necessarily mean that he is a malingerer, but it would be suggested that he is.

   I should mention that's not—that work is not done in a criminal setting, but in a personal injury setting. But there are studies of that sort, and they are reviewed pretty thoroughly in a number of books that I have read.

Q. There is research, is there not, Doctor, to indicate that naive people, that is people who are not psychologists or psychiatrists, have in fact, simulated organic brain damage?

A. Is that a question or an answer? I'm not sure.

Q. That's a question.

A. I don't know the study to which you are referring.

Q. Have you heard of Doctor Heaton?

A. No.

Q. Doctor Albert?

A. No.

Q. Are there any studies that you are aware of where naive individuals, that is people like myself, non-psychiatrists or psychologists, have successfully simulated paranoid schizophrenia?

A. Well, as I say, I'm—I have read a number of studies. I'm familiar with the book on your table. I have dutifully tried to track down and read at least some of the articles that Doctor Ziskin referred to. You can design a study to show just about anything you want.

*(Author's Note: Inasmuch as the witness has already, when asked about the mental workings of schizophrenia, described a number of "studies" such as the San Quentin study, which appears to be a study conducted according to scientific method, it would seem appropriate then to ask him if the researchers in that study designed that study to show just what it showed, that in fact if all research is designed to produce a predetermined result, there really is no point in doing it. Then one can ask further questions to bring out the fact that this is why, in order to have any effect, research is published, the method is described, and this allows other people in the field to see whether it was designed in a way that would necessarily produce that result. It might be worthwhile on this to go through each of the studies he cited and ask him if he knows whether they were designed to produce that result, because if he answers affirmatively, or that he doesn't know, then it would seem inappropriate for him to have used those studies to demonstrate what is known about the workings of the mind of a schizophrenic. As he is not familiar with the Heaton or Albert studies, you could ask if he knows that these studies were designed to produce the results they got.)*

Q. So there may or—you're not saying there aren't such studies?

A. No, I am not. I just don't consider myself competent to testify on them.

Q. Now, the people you treat in your private practice, Doctor, they don't necessarily have anything wrong with their brain; isn't that fair to say?

A. You mean brain damage?

Q. Brain damage.

A. Most of them do not.

Q. Most of them do not. They usually come to you with problems of more of a personal nature, as you indicated this morning, helping them get a new direction?

A. Right.

Q. Are psychiatrists, doctor, the only professional people who deal with problems of this type?

A. No.

Q. What other professionals do that?

A. Psychologists, social workers, marriage counselors, even pastors that are trained can sometimes do a credible job of helping people who are stuck, who have problems.

Q. You don't ordinarily, I take it, even though you are a medical doctor, perform a physical exam on the patient?

A. Not anymore, no.

Q. Did you at one time?

A. Yes.

Q. Would you tell us about that and why you did it, please?

A. Well, I used to be a real doctor, you know. So I did examinations.

Q. I meant as a part of your practice as a psychiatrist.

A. Yes. Once I got to psychiatry, my skills doing physical examinations, because they were exercised so seldom, got rusty. And I just don't feel that it is appropriate for me to use skills which are rusty.

Q.  Yeah. I assume now there's a lot of courses that you took in medical school that don't really have anything to do with your practice of psychiatry as it is today.

A.  That's right.

*(Author's Note: On this issue, it is probably best to stop here having established that much of medical training is not relevant to psychiatric practice. By going on, particularly with an open-ended question, the cross-examiner has given the witness again, an opportunity to make a long speech, which is to his advantage, and not to the cross-examiner's advantage. Some of the things are not correct, such as the three or four years of residency being comparable to a what a clinical psychologist gets academically. It also is not correct that clinical psychologists do not get education in physical aspects of psychiatric problems and biochemical origins as almost all Ph.D. programs require at least one and sometimes two extensive courses in physiological psychology as well as courses roughly described as psychiatric information for psychologists which deal with the physical aspects. However, this may be more than one wants to try to deal with inasmuch as physical aspects are not a particular issue in this case.)*

Q.  Okay. What are psychologists?

A.  Psychologist is somebody who, like a psychiatrist, has gone through college, but then instead of going to medical school, the psychologist will get a PhD. Usually a degree obtained over a three-year period in mental functioning—assuming that he is going into clinical psychology, as opposed to working with rats or with color and perception. So that individual may get three years in which he learns about the emotions and where they sometimes get us into difficulties. May learn how some of these psychological systems to which I referred earlier may coalesce into a recognized disorder, even may get some skills into helping people non-defensively look at what they're doing in their lives and possibly find alternative ways of dealing with the problems. The chap who is destined to be a psychiatrist during that same period of time will be going to medical school. While he may be learning the organic bases of some mental disorders, he is also learning other things that will probably serve him less well later on, like delivering babies and suturing up cuts. Then the psychiatrist or psychiatrist to be takes a year's rotating internship, where again he gets exposure to the various subspecialties of medicine. Then again, since the mind and the body are connected, he will begin to sharpen or prepare to sharpen up psychological skills. But the thrust of his psychological training doesn't come until the completion of his internship, although he may have two months rotation on a psychiatric service. Upon completion of his internship, he will then have a three or four year training in psychiatry, which is, I think, roughly comparable to what a clinical psychologist might have had. Plus, of course, an emphasis on the physical aspects of psychiatric problems, prescribing of drugs, biochemical origins, that most psychologists will not get during their PhD program.

Q.  All right. Most of the people, I think you will grant me, that do come to see you have psychological problems, correct?

A.  Yes.

Q. And you have an M.D. degree, not a PhD in psychology?

A. That's correct.

Q. Will you not think it more appropriate then to have people with psychological problems primarily treated by one with a PhD in psychology? *(Author's Note: This is not a wise or necessary question.)* [*]

A. More appropriate? I've had excellent training in treating people with problems. I get excellent results as a consequence of my psychiatric residency, so I don't think their coming to me would be more or less appropriate. In that respect, this is not to be in any way critical of a psychologist, but I am not going to be critical of myself, either. Again, without being critical of the psychologist I can look at an individual and can tell how much of his depression, for example, is a product of a problem in living maybe a lost experience, a problem which would be susceptible to psychological manipulation and how much of that problem is now mediated chemically and would respond much more quickly to antidepressants and which antidepressant. People whose depression expresses itself not only in despair but in insomnia, where they awake and it is the early hours of the morning and they can't get back to sleep, they respond best to one group of antidepressants, tricyclics, which people who are depressed and are so worried that they can't fall asleep respond to an entirely different group of antidepressants, oxidase inhibitors. I'm just giving you a little example of the kinds of things I have learned above and beyond my psychological skills that are extraordinarily serviceable to my patients, which generally are not available to the patients of a PhD psychologist.

Q. All right. Do you recall what formal courses in psychology that you took in achieving a doctor's—a medical doctor's degree in preparation for this profession?

A. You mean their titles?

Q. Yes. Or even how many.

A. Yeah, well, you know, you talk about courses, I think that is perhaps a difference of the psychologist's training and the psychiatrist's training. The psychologist does indeed take courses, he goes to school, he sits in class— whereas the psychiatrist, although he has had that medical school, he takes his courses as he goes as part of medical model, working with patients. He'll have seven or eight patients. He may follow that patient for a year. As he is working that patient, gets instruction around that patient. It is a different way of teaching. We do take courses. We take courses in psychotherapy. We take courses—some psychological testing just for the sake of completeness. We will take courses in psychopathology. We will take courses in schizophrenia. We will take courses in system's communication. We will take courses in family therapy, all of which I've had and in some instances taught, but the focus is always on, the patient and the courses are grouped around the patient as opposed to the traditional didactic discipline of a psychologist. I think that's the major difference.

Q. Okay. Well, is it at least fair to say that you, as a psychiatrist, would take fewer formal courses in psychology than a PhD in psychology?

A. That's right. We may get the same material.

Q. Right.

A. But in a less formal fashion.

Q. Do they spend a lot more hours studying things, reading things, whereas yourself it is a lot more practice, intern—

A. That's right.

*(Author's Note: The question which set off this whole line of examination is not a good question. It is very unlikely that you are going to get a psychiatrist to state on the witness stand that it would be more appropriate for treatment to be given by psychologists than psychiatrists. We really are not concerned with treatment as such, but with diagnostic evaluation, and on this score, the research literature shows psychologists to be at least as good as psychiatrists, and inasmuch as this is really pretty much the point the lawyer wants to establish, it would be better to go at it from that direction. It is also noted that again, the examiner does not insist on an answer to the question he has asked, which could be a simple "yes" or "no," but allows the witness to give another speech in which he is able to cite his success in therapy, which is attackable if you want to go to the trouble to do it.)*

Q. All right. What is your definition of a mental illness or mental disorder, or do you see a difference between the two?

A. Well, I suspect we are quickly going to get into splitting some semantic hairs, so let me start off as a lumper and say no. Disorder and illness are, for all purposes, the same. It would be a condition which expresses itself primarily in emotional or mental form as opposed to largely physical form, although there may be a physical component for which there may or may not be—though often is, a non-organic ideology [sic], which compromises the individual's ability to function in one or more major areas of human endeavor. Loving, working, being comfortable and so on.

Q. Is that any different from a thought disorder?

A. Yes.

Q. What is the difference?

A. A thought disorder would be a type of mental illness, but there are many people who are mentally ill who do not have a thought disorder.

Q. In rendering your diagnosis of the defendant in this case, as a paranoid schizophrenic, did you rely upon the use of the DSM-III or -II?

A. Only to the extent that I am knowledgeable. I mean, that part of the information has gradually seeped, with some resistance, into my brain, but I didn't look up DSM-III and check Mr. D out, but I've read DSM-III, and I think D would probably fit in there.

Q. Do you use the III or the II?

A. Well, I've read them both, and I as well, they keep changing the labels on me, and I find it rather dizzy. I find labels of really very little use, and Mr. D really is schizophrenic.

*(Author's Note: In the previous answer, that D would fit in the diagnosis of schizophrenia in DSM-III, this might be questioned as to criterion B, which is deterioration from a previous level of functioning as discussed earlier. However, what is important here is the witness's statement that he finds labels of very little use and immediately uses one, "schizophrenic," which is a label. In fact, he has*

*been using labels such as schizophrenia, thought disorder, paranoia, paranoid, and so on throughout his testimony. However, there may be little to gain by confronting him with this, except to give him another opportunity to explain. His statement is there, and his use of labels is there, and this can be pointed out on argument that he is inconsistent and, therefore, not a witness of high credibility on this basis, if no other. If a question is to be asked at all, it might be one asking whether all diagnoses are not in fact labels. Which, of course, is what they are. Whatever the reality or unreality of D's psychological state or condition, the word schizophrenia or schizophrenic is nothing more than a label for it, which Dr. 3 has used repeatedly. The next question is not well-stated. It would be better to ask if the scientific and professional literature does not show a considerable disagreement as to schizophrenia.)*

Q. There is, is there not—it is safe to say that there is quite a lot of disagreement among the members of your profession as to what schizophrenia really is; is that a fair statement?

A. I don't know if it's fair or not. It's so simplistic, it's hard to judge it by fairness. I think we all tend to agree that we don't know what it is, so that leaves a lot of room to speculate as to what it might be.

Q. Well, showing you then DSM-II, page Roman Numeral ix, second paragraph, when they mention schizophrenia, are you familiar with the DSM-II?

A. I read it five or six years ago.

Q. Could you please read that paragraph, paragraph two?

A. "Consider, for example, the mental disorder labeled in this manual as schizophrenia, which, in the first edition, was labeled schizophrenic reaction. The change of label has not changed the nature of the disorder, nor will it discourage continuing debate about its nature or causes. Even if it had tried, the committee could not establish agreement about what this disorder is; it could only agree on what to call it."

Q. Thank you. The Diagnostic and Statistical Manual I, II, and III, have been the official documents for defining psychiatric terms by members of your profession, do you agree with that?

A. Yes.

Q. Are you inclined to agree or disagree with that particular paragraph or any portion thereof?

A. No, I think that's a different way of saying what I said in my previous answer, so I would agree.

Q. You would agree. How much then of your study or your training, then, have you spent with this—what I perceive as a very difficult subject of schizophrenia?

*(Author's Note: This is not a necessary question, and again, gives the witness an opportunity to expound on his qualifications. However, in connection with the previous note, again, a poor question has produced valuable information in his statement, "I think you know a significant percentage of people bear that label." So that he himself is stating that the term is a label, which he says is of little use to him, although he has been talking with it all through his testimony.)*

A. Fair amount. I have treated a great number of schizophrenics over the years. I've read a great deal about the disorder. I couldn't give you any hours or weeks, but it's a major problem in this country. I think, you know, a significant percentage of people bear that label. A large number of people in State hospitals bear that label.

Q. These so-called mental illnesses, when they're put in these diagnostic and statistical manuals, are decided upon by vote rather than scientific procedure, are they not; that is, a vote by a body of elected representatives of your profession or association?

A. I don't know precisely what the committee finally—how they finally arrive at what language to use, but certainly it is some sort of consensus trying to find the most efficient label to a fairly complex descriptive picture.

*(Author's Note: Once again, the attorney has asked a "yes" or "no" type of question, and should have stopped the witness when he says he doesn't know what the committee did.)*

Q. Well, correct me if I am wrong, but going back to nineteen seventy-two or seventy-one, homosexuality was agreed upon as being a mental disease, was it not, by the people in DSM-III—or DSM-I, I guess?

A. It was considered to be an abnormality, yes.

Q. In seventy-two would you agree with me, if I said that?

*(Author's Note: This issue should be handled with simple direct questions and insistence on yes or no answers. Was homosexuality in the DSM as a mental disorder in 1972? Did the committee vote to change this in 1974? Did psychiatrists as a group then vote whether or not it was a mental disorder? Did they vote about 4000 to 3000 that it was not?)*

A. Well, it depends. You see, we get into a philosophical problem. When you say "the condition is abnormal," do you mean that the people are not functioning according to a certain happy standard, or are they simply a numerical minority. Most people prefer approaching a congenial member of the opposite sex, but ten to twelve percent of our population prefers someone of the same sex. Now, certainly these people are outnumbered, homosexuals are outnumbered. It deviates from the standard norm. Does that necessarily mean that they are less happy and functioning less well because they engage in a—with a sexual act that would not ultimately lead to children? And so psychiatrists are caught up in that philosophical dilemma perhaps a bit more than the lay population, and I really don't know myself. To get to your question where I stand on that, it's a dilemma. I know some homosexuals who are very unhappy because of their homosexuality, and feel—well, they feel as if they have a mental disorder. Now, is this indeed true or are they simply responding to the prejudices they have had to deal with over the years, or are they unhappy because they're homosexuals, or would they be just as unhappy, and have just as many difficulties in their lives if they were heterosexuals. This is the dilemma that this raises. What is real, however, is that however you label these people, and whether you label this as an abnormality, or whether you fall on the side of this philosophical argument, that there still are eight to twelve percent of the population who do indeed prefer sex with the same sexed people, and that is real. DSM-II, DSM-III, may be philosophical, but labels come and go, but homosexuals remain and stay as evidenced by the ten to twelve percent of them.

Q. And that ten to twelve percent, that's based on research; isn't it?

A. Statistical study, I don't know if you call it that, but statistical surveys.

Q. What I'm getting at, in nineteen seventy-two the people that wrote DSM-II, DSM-I, I'm sorry, officially diagnosed homosexuality as a quote mental disease close quote?

A. Right.

Q. And then isn't it also true in the very next year, in seventy-three, the coming of DSM-II, they diagnosed it was not a mental illness anymore?

A. That's right, for reasons that I just explained.

Q. All right. What did they decide in nineteen eighty in DSM-III; I don't know.

A. I think the die is cast now in that respect. We will not assume that just because somebody turns to a member of the opposite sex or the same sex and engages in a minority sex practice, we'll not automatically assume that that reflects an abnormality. It's been noted that there was homosexuality in animal populations, so that it may just be a normal variance on the sexual spectrum.

Q. Do you believe in the theory that there is homosexuality among some animal populations?

A. Yes.

Q. And you've read adequate research to convince you of that?

A. Not that I've read. I saw two male rabbits humping each other with my own eyes, and I presume from that that it takes place.

Q. Is that what you base that statement on, then?

A. It's helpful sometimes to see it with your own eyes, but no, I've read some studies to corroborate my observations on this one case.

Q. Now, is it necessary to be Board Certified to practice psychiatry?

A. No.

Q. By Board Certified, what do you mean?

A. It means you took an examination which has a written—all-day written test in psychiatry, and in neurology, and then a day or two of oral tests in psychiatry, and when I took it, neurology, and if you achieve a certain score on each of these various tests, then you're Board Certified. And you have to complete a training in an accredited institution before they let you in the door to take the test.

Q. So a regular doctor could practice psychiatry without being Board Certified?

A. He could call himself a psychiatrist, yes.

Q. Now, I think you mentioned earlier that you don't rely entirely upon your formal education in rendering a diagnosis, but much of the time on your experience?

A. Right.

Q. Is there anything else other than your experience and your education that you rely on?

A. Well, I bring to bear my intelligence, however modest that may be, to the extent that I am a bright, attentive and perceptive fellow, and it probably carries some weight in my skill as a psychiatrist.

Q. Let's talk about the clinical examinations you have performed with Mr. D. That was a very important part of your diagnosis; was it not?

*(Author's Note: Clinical examination is all right to open with but ultimately you want to establish the importance of the mental status examination and its elements which would be difficult to know as of the time of the crime.)*

A. Yes.

Q. Was it perhaps the most important part of your decision to render the diagnosis of paranoid schizophrenia like you did?

A. Yes.

Q. How much time did you spend with Mr. D during the first interview?

A. I don't remember.

Q. Well, three days, three months?

A. Oh, no, it was part of a day.

*(Author's Note: This degree of vagueness should not be permitted. His bill could be checked for this also.)*

Q. Pardon?

A. Part of a day.

Q. In the County Jail?

A. Right.

Q. All right. And during the second interview, how much time did you spend with him?

A. Part of a day.

Q. During these time periods was he on any anti-psychotic medicine?

A. I didn't think that he was.

Q. Do you know, to your knowledge, was he or not, at this point?

A. To my knowledge he was not, but I usually make a note of that sort of thing, and I did not, and that's an oversight on my part.

Q. Well, is it fair to say in any event that you didn't prescribe him any anti-psychotic medications?

A. No, and if there was some prescribed, he sure as hell needed more. *(Author's Note: Everything after "no" could be subject to a motion to strike. However, it may also provide an opportunity to demonstrate bias or advocacy with questions such as "Did I ask you if he needed it? Isn't the function of the expert witness to provide information that is requested, or is it to try to prove a point for his side with dramatic statements?")*

Q. Do you feel as though he needed more at the time you saw him?

A. Yes.

Q. Did you mention that to someone?

A. No.

Q. Why not?

A. Well, I wasn't called in as a treating physician.

Q. Well, did you—do you recall asking anyone if he was on medication?

A. No, I can't. As I say, I seemed to have made no note about it. My recollection is that he was not, but I feel a little embarrassed that I can't give you a better answer to that question. I should know—I should have known, but I didn't.

Q. To your knowledge is he on anti-psychotic medication at the present time?

A. Yes, he is.

Q. What, to your knowledge, is that?

A. It was a new name to me. I just learned it last week, and looked it up in the PDR, and it did have some anti-psychotic effects, but I don't remember the name, and it was introduced after his injury, so it wouldn't have any bearing on my examination.

Q. All right. You say it wouldn't have any bearing on your—

A. That's right. This drug that I did learn of I believe was given to him the first time in the hospital after his fall, and I saw him before.

Q. Okay. And since you just arrived last evening, I take it you have not had too much time to spend with him up until the present; is that correct?

A. That's correct.

Q. In your mind is his appearance or his state of mind any different than it was the last time you saw him?

A. I haven't had a chance to talk with him, so I don't know how much he's changed. The most recent data I have is the transcript of his testimony, and it was certainly much more of a structured interview, you know, direct and cross, being what they are, than the kind of interview I gave to him, but I thought there were times, at least where he presented himself in a very similar fashion to the picture that I had of him.

Q. Now, what time, when you interviewed him before, I note that your report didn't reflect it, did you interview him in the day? Was it early day, late day?

A. I don't know.

Q. Was it—it wasn't in the middle of the night, I take it?

A. No.

Q. Okay. Can the time and place of the exams make some difference as to how a patient responds?

A. I'm sure it does.

Q. Did you attribute the fact that he was in jail, had been in jail for some time, now, by the time you were finally able to get around to seeing him, nine months later, and the fact that he was charged with first-degree murder with special circumstances, enter into your mind as perhaps a—being account-able for some of his responses?

A. Yes, that would have to play a part.

Q. All right. In your state of mind, or to your mind, did it affect his state of mind?

A. You mean at the bottom was it a controlling factor or just a factor?

Q. A factor.

A. Yeah, sure.

Q. A very large factor?

*(Author's Note: This is not a good question, as it indicates the cross-examiner thinks the witness can determine the degree of influence of situation effects.)*

A. Not given the severity of his disorder, no.

Q. In any event, what role do you think it did play. Tell us—tell the jury what kind of influence it did have upon him, in your opinion, the fact that he was charged with this serious crime and been in jail that long. *(Author's Note: Open-ended questions such as this are unwise to put to expert witnesses as it gives them great latitude.)*

A. I think it would elevate his level of anxiety and depression. I think it would give him more data around which to build some of his fantasies about what was going on, give him the richness of his thought disorder, and he would take any situation, and then play with it, work with it and develop it, and then have fantasies about it and what it means. "The Mafia will get me in jail," and other psychotic thinking can develop in this time, and I think the fact that he's in a structured setting, at the same time works against the increased anxiety of being in prison, in that it shelters him to some extent. So they tend to cancel each other out. *(Author's Note: He could be asked if there is a body of research showing these factors would be exactly equal in order to cancel each other out.)*

Q. Well—

A. I should add one other thing, I don't think it's terribly important here, but, you know, I do a lot of examination of guys that have been arrested and guys who have been arrested a lot, and I see them in the jail, and I've learned to accommodate to this setting. It's almost like another office of mine, a jail cell, and so I have a baseline in my head that's different than my expectations in my private well-paneled richly-carpeted offices. And one of the things that I note is that some people that I examine will attempt to steer a psychiatric evaluation in the direction that they wish it to go, that there's much more self-serving or transparent self-serving action on the part of the criminal defendant who are being examined by psychiatrists than someone I might examine in my own office, and I am, over these years, pretty good at recognizing when someone is trying to direct the interview to a certain place to achieve a certain outcome. And I think a forensic psychiatrist has to weigh that factor and should be party to that factor, if he's to do a competent job.

*(Author's Note: He could be asked if there is research validating his opinion of how good he is. He could be asked if he is aware of research showing inverse relationship between confidence and accuracy of clinical judgment.)*

Q. Do you believe that because Doctor 1 saw the defendant in April whereas you had to wait until the end—the last day in September, or thereabouts, to examine the defendant, that he had a better opportunity, in your professional opinion, to make an evaluation of his state of mind at the time of the homicide than you did?

A. Yes, I think that the more proximate the examination is to the offense in issue, the better it is.

Q. Okay. Closer in time we can get to the incident, the more likely we're able to be accurate in terms of our prediction of what it actually was?

A. Right.

Q.  Doctor, isn't there a research—I'm not saying whether or not you agree with it, but considerable research to the extent that same—I mean different psychiatrists would interview the same individual differently?

A.  Well, there are all kinds of studies which address itself to diagnosis, and I don't know if they can be reduced to that sentence. What I have read is that there's a bevy of different diagnostic labels and different psychiatrists will often use different labels to describe essentially similar phenomena, and that the higher level of abstraction you demand of the interview, the more variation you'll get. By that I mean ten psychiatrists will come in and with remarkable concordance will find the subject agitated or depressed or complaining of insomnia. Then you get divergence where you try to pull those symptoms that are readily observable into a contentual diagnosis, like he was a manic depressive syndrome and he's schizophrenic and even then there are different labels for the same condition. You get more apparent divergence than is real.

Then finally, when you try to extrapolate beyond the clinical diagnosis into more sophisticated issues, is he suicidal, is he legally responsible, that's when you start to get a tremendous divergence, and I think the studies tend to bear that out. I've seen studies which show greater divergence. I've seen studies which show remarkable concordance, so once again the studies tend to cancel each other out.

*(Author's Note: Once again, the lawyer has asked a question which could be answered "yes" or "no" and has allowed the witness to make an extensive speech, without, in fact, answering the question, except that at the end, he indicates that there are contrary studies which tend to cancel each other out, which is all right, and probably could have been obtained without the lengthy speech. The upshot of this is that if there are studies going both ways, then no statement can be made, except that no one knows whether different psychiatrists would interview the same individual differently or not. Of course, it can be shown by an overwhelming weight of the research that in fact they do interview differently, or at least obtain different data, but it is not likely that that information can be produced from this witness.)*

Q.  All right. Can you give me any idea of the ones that have showed marginal discord?

A.  Well, again, I am not—I personally don't spend my hours compiling studies, and I think you'd have to be a scholar of source material and bibliography to do that. I'm too busy treating patients to be that kind of scholar.

Q.  So you can't remember any right now?

A.  No.

Q.  All right. Now, do you have any idea of the degree of accuracy with which you predict people's state of mind, looking at them after the facts for a criminal case?

*(Author's Note: This is a poor question, which gives the expert an entire field to roam in, and of course, almost any expert is likely to say that his rate of accuracy is pretty good. The question, if it is going to be asked at all, should be, "Doctor, has there ever been a scientific study of the accuracy of your conclusions performed by independent evaluators, people other than yourself?" And if*

*that answer is affirmative, then the next thing should be to attempt to find out where the results of such a study have been published, if they have, or where they can be obtained, or at the minimum, who the independent investigators were as something of a barrier to someone misrepresenting such an event. Similarly, with his statement below that he gets better-than-average results, he could not know this in the absence of a controlled study comparing his results with that of a certain number of other psychiatrists. He is talking about treatment success here, and again, as we know, this has been shown to not be a good indicator of correct diagnosis. You might want to pick up, if this kind of statement comes in, on his statement acknowledging that treatments are not disorder-specific, and try to get some kind of statistical evidence as to what treatments work anyway, and how many disorders a particular treatment may cover. The facts stated in his answer that others agree with him has nothing to do with accuracy, only with reliability.)*

A. Well, I—again, it depends on the level of abstract that you demand of me. If you mean—if you're asking me whether or not I am accurate at the pathognomic level—this person again is depressed, he's anxious, he's seething with homicidal thoughts, fairly simple chunks, then I would say I am accurate, and I base that on, among other criteria, first, when I go in with three other guys like we did here, and I come out and I find that we kind of see the guy the same way at that level, we all agree he's had a delusion, we all agree he is paranoid, we all agree he is depressed, we all agree his affect is kind of flat, we all see the same things, going to the next higher level, what does all that mean? Connecting the dots now and coming up with a nice terse diagnostic label. Ideas one, two and three. There I find there's a little more divergence, and so it is a little bit more difficult to measure my, quote, "accuracy." Then when it comes to translating the clinical diagnosis to is he sane, could he premeditate, then I think it's up for grabs and it belongs in these people's laps, and I don't think I am accurate at all. The other criteria by which I measure my accuracy—and it is hard because you know there are no answers in the back of the book of life—is that I will frequently follow my diagnosis with the treatment whose efficacy depends upon the accuracy of the diagnosis. If I misdiagnose somebody suffering from anxiety who is really suffering from schizophrenia, put them on librium instead of thorzene, he's going to get worse. After three or four patients battling your diagnostic brains in, you develop some skills in diagnosis and matching the treatment so that the treatment in a sense conforms to the diagnosis. Now, that's not a perfect method, because sometimes treatments work anyway, or the treatment may cover a variety of disorders. But I do get good results with my patients, better than average from what I hear. I get a lot of strokes, not only from them but from my colleagues, some of whom when stuck will send me their patients. So that must mean something. Maybe not a good deal but it must mean something.

Q. I take it, though, that you don't necessarily—or maybe you do—that is after you have testified in a case then do follow-up to determine whether or not at least lay people believed you in X number of cases? *(Author's Note: There is no point to this question that we can see. The lawyer is probably fortunate that the witness did no more than point this out.)*

A.  Well, I do, but that's surely—you must appreciate that there's a big leap between a jury's verdict and a clinical diagnosis. The jury may decide today to believe me, that Mr. D is a paranoid schizophrenic, but may decide that doesn't matter and that schizophrenic or not, he knew perfectly well what he was about, what he did, and he's not entitled to any consideration in terms of lowering his degree of culpability. So you can't draw one to one conclusions about that.

Q.  Are you familiar with the Rosenhan study from Stanford University some years ago?

A.  Yeah.

Q.  And didn't he find that several normal people presenting a single complaint were diagnosed by hospital staff as schizophrenic?

A.  Yes, sir.

Q.  Wasn't it concluded as the result of that study that a good number of those people after two weeks of observation were not in fact schizophrenic?

A.  Yes, sir.

*(Author's Note: With a witness who is as facile as this one, it is probably a good idea to stop at this point, where you have obtained a valuable concession from him and not try to push it further. However, the lawyer does push it and gets another speech. However, at the conclusion of the speech [page 1251 of the transcript], he justifies the diagnosis on the basis of the need to admit the patient, so he could be asked whether they could have been admitted without a diagnosis of schizophrenia, such as, for example, diagnosis deferred.)*

Q.  Isn't it also a fact that in that study, while the psychiatrists didn't recognize that these people were mentally ill, a number of the mental hospital patients themselves did recognize that these people did not belong in a mental hospital?

A.  Well, you have subtly shifted apples and oranges, apples and oranges into the same sentence. What the study shows was that if you come into the hospital complaining of a hallucination—and I think there were a few other little "minor" things of no great importance that I can't recall, something about hearing a thud, but the big thing was they complained of hallucinations—is my memory serving me correctly?

Q.  (Nods head.)

A.  Yeah. There the professional diagnosis in many instances especially in public facilities, will be schizophrenia. But it isn't enough, you see. It isn't enough to simply have hallucinations in isolation to be schizophrenic—a point that I have spent considerable time today explaining—that it is a symptom complex and indeed schizophrenics are—when they are actively psychotic, sufficiently different from other people, yes, lay people, including other patients would know that this person's nutty or this person is not. Schizophrenia is real, and these people weren't really schizophrenic. They presented themselves to a hospital, and I think we have the medical obligation when a patient comes in and says, "I'm ill," that is presumed, because he applies to a mental hospital and complains of hallucinations, you've got to take them in until we have some evidence that let them out.

Q. Is it fair to say that—I mean other than what you told us, that is about the pats on the back from your colleagues, the fact that you refer to the—you're referred—that you really don't know—that is scientifically what the degree of your accuracy is?

A. I don't know what you mean by scientifically. Certainly a standard for measuring accuracy that reaches the threshold of my comfort at least—and I am pretty hard on myself—in psychiatry would not suffice for physics, where you have to get a result to the fourth decimal point. The truth is that it's really—you know, it is hard to come up with a good standard for accuracy in psychiatry, and so it is really hard for me to tell you whether or not I meet that standard.

Q. Let's talk about your report for a moment, Doctor. Referring to your page eight of the September 30th report—

A. Page eight, you say?

Q. Yes

A. Okay.

Q. You use the words somewhere in here "despite pressured speech." Do you recall those words?

A. Um hum.

Q. What did you mean by that?

A. He talked very often like this, with all the ideas coming rushing out, and he has a lot to say, and he—and then I—I went here and then he went there—and so on and so forth.

Q. All right. Now, he told you—I believe you wrote in your report that on the night before the actual homicide, that would be January 21, he thought he should just go get them because it is just as well it should be them as him; right, or something to that effect?

A. Maybe we—since that's probably a very important point, we'd better get the exact quote. What page are you referring to?

Q. Okay.

A. Didn't he tell a friend that, something to that effect? Did he tell me that?

Q. All right. I'm sorry. It's your November 28th report, page three, in the middle of the first paragraph. That would be about the middle of the page. Nine lines up from the bottom of the first paragraph. Would you read that sentence beginning with "He tried to get help for us"—please?

A. I'm sorry, I still don't find it. Would you give me that reference again?

Q. Yes. Page three, November 28th report, and it would be, I believe, nine lines from the bottom of the first paragraph. Eleven lines.

A. Okay, I've got it.

Q. Okay. Would you read me that sentence, please?

A. "He tried to get help from a priest, tried to get out of town, tried to get help from his family, but ultimately decided the night before the shooting that he simply better get them before they got him."

Q. All right. Now, at the time then that you—you wrote that down, you got that information from him, did you have the idea that on the night before the killing he actually planned to go out and kill MV or get them, whatever that means?

A. Well, that's the crux of our problem today. What does that mean? Given the state of mind of the fellow who says it, what does it mean? I leave that to the trier of fact.

Q. Well, what did it mean to you?

A. It means that he perceived FV and MV irrationally as a threat to him, and that he had to do something about it. I don't think Mr. D himself knew exactly what he would have—what he was going to do about it at that time. But taking some vigorous action was one of the possibilities.

Q. Well, did it not occur to you that the words "get them before they got me" might be the same, and most likely probably is, to kill them before they kill me?

A. That's a possibility.

Q. Well, is there any other possibility that's closer than that in your mind?

A. Well, what I am saying is that I think this man is so confused that he probably changes what he means and what he intends from moment to moment. But certainly in social convention "get them" high up on the list would be to do away with them.

Q. All right. Now, he said that to you better than nine months after the offense?

A. (Nods head.)

Q. That on the night before he thought about getting them—whatever that meant—that is in your professional opinion, consistent with the ability to plan and then, since he did do this the next day, carry through with it?

A. Yes, it is.

Q. Now, does it necessarily follow that one who is today diagnosed as a paranoid schizophrenic could not develop such a plan and carry it out the next day?

A. Is that necessarily so?

Q. Yes.

A. No, it is not.

Q. So is it fair to say that even if Mr. D were a paranoid schizophrenic, assuming that he was on January 21st, that he did develop a plan to kill FV and MV and follow through with it?

A. He could well.

Q. All right. Mr. D has testified in this trial that—I'm trying to paraphrase it, but very accurately that he knew to shoot somebody was wrong, but he also knew he had the right to defend himself, and that's in the same sentence in answer to one of my questions. Do you recall reading that testimony last night?

A. I do, sir.

Q. Now, is a person who is diagnosed as a paranoid schizophrenic, necessarily unable to distinguish the difference between right and wrong?

A. No, he's not necessarily.

Q. Is a person who is a paranoid schizophrenic necessarily unable to premeditate?

A. No, he's not.

Q. Deliberate?

A. No.

Q. Have malice aforethought?

A. No.

Q. And briefly, if you will, and I'm sure you can do this in your own words, and again, I'm not trying to trick you or have you read exactly from a jury instruction, but would you give us your description of premeditated, deliberate and malice aforethought?

A. First of all I do have the jury instruction right in front of me, and they're perfectly serviceable. My working definition of malice is the purposeful, willful harming of another when knowing that society prohibits such an act. Premeditation would be anticipatory planning of such an act.

Q. All right. What is meaningful deliberation; what is your understanding?

A. Well, this is a legal phrase of art.

Q. Grant you that.

A. And I don't think I'm an expert on legal phrases.

Q. So you don't have a specific understanding of meaningful deliberation that you apply in comparing your cases for court, when you are assessing an individual's diagnosis?

A. I have my own opinion, but I feel I'm in a very special place here. I'm in a courtroom and I feel very sensitive about infringing on the prerogatives of others, and I don't think that my opinion as to how that is defined is worth any more than the jury's, and yet I've been called an expert and I don't want to over-presume my role.

Q. No. I'm not asking you to do that, but it would seem to me that if one didn't have an understanding, that is his own, even though it was wrong, of what the legal terms meant, and was asked to come to court and ask if that person had the ability to have that state of mind, that something is wrong?

A. Well, that's why I will not make a flat statement that such an individual does or does not have that state of mind. I will say that he has a mental disorder and that this mental disorder does this, this and this, it affects your thinking, it screws it up with some paranoid thinking, it makes you confused, it contaminates the mental processes by which one deliberates in a meaningful way. Now, whether he could, nonetheless, deliberate with sufficient meaning to reach a threshold of guilty, I think falls not to the clinician but to the trier of fact.

Q. Is it fair to say, then, your conclusion would be that given the fact that Mr. D was probably paranoid schizophrenic on the date of the alleged homicide, and in fact did have such an effect on his mental ability, that you're unwilling to say whether or not it had such an effect as to elevate it to the defense of diminished capacity?

A. That's correct.

Q. In fact—and you're not willing to say whether or not it was more probable or not that it did, based on your understanding of the law?

A. I would not be terribly comfortable in doing so, no.

Mr. PA: I appreciate your candor, Doctor. I think that's all I have for now, Doctor, thank you.

Mr. DC: I have just one or two questions, your Honor. I think we can finish before the break.

THE COURT: All right.

**REDIRECT EXAMINATION AFTER RECESS:**

THE COURT: Yes, everyone is present. Let's see. As I understand it, you have no further witnesses now, Mr. PA, but there are certain matters that the court is going to have to rule on that have been brought up by both parties, and those are still pending.

Mr. PA: Yes, thank you, judge. And with that statement the People would re-rest.

Mr. DC: Your Honor, for surrebuttal and for the purpose we discussed earlier regarding the book, I would like to call Dr. 3.

THE COURT: Let's see. You were already sworn, Doctor. You're still under oath.

(NOTE: The following took place after Dr. Ziskin's testimony.)

*(Author's Note: Due to the arrangement allowing Dr. 3 and Dr. Ziskin to sit in the courtroom to listen to each other's testimony, the transcript now picks up after Dr. Ziskin's testimony and this is therefore a continuation of Dr. 3's redirect. A copy of Dr. 3's transcript was obtained by Dr. Ziskin immediately after the trial. When the decision was made to include this case as an example, Dr. Ziskin attempted, by telephone call to the prosecuting attorney's office, to obtain a transcript of his testimony, however, he was informed that it was no longer available. Essentially, he had testified to the kind of material that is contained in Volume I of the Third Edition of this work, and roughly that which is contained in Volumes I and II of the present edition. In addition, he had pointed out the various errors that Dr. 4 had made, and also the MMPI indicators of malingering.)*

RESUME:

Mr. DC: All right. Dr. 3, Dr. Ziskin began his testimony yesterday, or at early stages of it, using an example, something about the notion that bleeding used as a medical technique had been discarded over the years. Does that example that he used relate to the evolution of medical techniques due to the use of scientific method?

A. Well, I think it certainly goes to the very heart of the basic disagreement that has emerged between Dr. Ziskin and myself; where I am, I think, the very personification of the clinician with a certain skepticism about the universal, use of the scientific method as it applies to medicine; and Dr. Ziskin, a very articulate disponent [sic] of the absolute necessity of using scientific method as something to be valid, and he used examples, I think paradoxically, of bleeding, which indeed was a leading therapeutic technique from the dark ages right through to the time when they managed to finish off George Washington, by precisely such a device. Now, I think Dr. Ziskin suggested that this has since been discarded, and somehow he was weaving this into an example of the inadequacies of the clinical versus the scientific method, that now medicine is at least approaching techniques where we don't use those techniques, such as bleeding, and discarded them for carefully controlled scientific reasons. But a point in fact, while bleeding was discovered and used through the clinical method, namely you observe patients, you give them treatment, see how they do, and something seems to work, and you retain that treatment, and if it doesn't seem to work, you discard it. And indeed, for better—I would—I would say largely it was this clinical method that created this clinical technique. So it was the clinical technique that caused it to be discarded, and not the scientific one. That is, in about 1850, when they finally did away with this, we did not then have the statistical devices whereby five hundred people were bled, and you have five hundred controls, or five hundred other patients were not given this technique, and we arrived at a validated study that bleeding is lousy. What happened was just as bleeding got started, a couple of physicians noticed that five out of six patients that they bled died, and maybe one or two noticed that one out of six that got better were the ones that had shortness of breath. Somehow, if you bleed a patient that has shortness of breath, they seem to benefit. The other five out of six either don't do well, or stay neutral, and he mentions this to his colleagues, and he says, "You know, I've noticed the same thing. I still bleed a few patients. I take a few drops of blood, because they expect it, just like people expect penicillin if you have a cold, but I don't believe it has any effect, but with shortness of breath, and for some reason that's when it seems to work." If these physicians are respected in the community, the word trickles down and after awhile it goes out of fashion, (a) because some sharp doctors noticed clinically, empirically, it doesn't seem to work except in different cases, and seems to draw the conclusion, although they cannot be scientifically validated, at least in 1850, and secondly, because in 1850 we got to know a little bit more about the human body, and it didn't make sense logically, to bleed most people. We understood that you have a certain blood volume and for some reason, people with certain disorders accumulate the serum from that blood volume in their lungs and get shortness of breath, and for that reason bleeding may achieve symptomatic relief but it doesn't make sense to bleed somebody with anemia or somebody with cancer or somebody with a broken leg or somebody with a headache. It's illogical, and it took us awhile to develop this anatomic logic to get that conclusion, and that's what the clinical method is all about. So the clinical technique wrongly led to inappropriate therapeutic measures. It's all the device which we discarded, and replaced it with things that are better.

*(Author's Note: This lengthy discourse contains a mixture of truths, half-truths and statements that at least convey an incorrect impression. It may not be necessary to deal with all of them. Number one, it can be shown that the practice of bleeding is used as a classical textbook illustration of the inadequacies of the clinical observational method. Second, Dr. 3 gives the explanation that they learn by trying things out, and if they seem to work, they continue them, and if they find out that they do not work, they discontinue them without conveying the full extent of this error. This was not a matter of something that was tried out for a year or two, but a method that was used for several hundred years. It encompassed an enormous amount of clinical observation, during all of which time,*

*whatever hundreds or thousands of physicians there were, were not observing, that five out of six patients who were being bled died. Nor did Dr. Benjamin Rush, perhaps the most famous physician of his time, who was treating George Washington, seem to grasp this problem either, as a result of which our first president died of Dr. Rush's ministrations. Now it may well be that some physicians early in the 19th century made observations that suggested that bleeding was not a good treatment for diseases other than some pulmonary diseases. No one is denying that clinical observation is useful for formulating hypotheses, which is what such observations would amount to. Unfortunately, for many who received this treatment fatally, as long as they were hypotheses, most physicians continued to utilize this form of treatment. It is, however, incorrect to state that no research was being done. Literature we have obtained [in Chapter 2, Volume I] indicates that a Dr. Louis, in France, was doing some kind of statistical study, or at least record-keeping which would allow for making the statement that over a significant number of patients, too large a number were either dying or not being helped by this treatment. Other research was going on as well, as noted in the chapter on scientific method. It is noteworthy that in spite of this proof that the method was not working, it was continued for a considerable number of years, and in fact, there are records indicating that the practice was continued even into the 20th century. These facts could be brought out. The witness could be confronted with this literature. In addition, however, probably the best way to handle this is by asking questions or pointing out in Dr. 3's own words that the reason they did not do away with this earlier was because they did not have statistical devices, that is they did not have scientific methods. So the question would be something like this: "Well, Dr. 3, wouldn't it have been wonderful for all of those people who were killed by the medical doctors who gave them this treatment based on clinical lore, if someone much earlier had been able to do a scientific study which would have demonstrated what the reality was?" We suspect it will not matter how the doctor chooses to answer that question, because it really answers itself. Further, although it was not available at the time this trial took place with the publication of the DSM-III-R, it is now possible to cite this official publication of the American Psychiatric Association to the effect that with regard to diagnostic categories and classification, they would give the greatest weight to the presence of empirical support from well-conducted research studies, clearly preferring such data to such items as clinical experience [DSM-III, Introduction, xii].)*

Mr. DC:

Q.  Do you feel that scientific method is useful?

A.  Of course I do.

Q.  In what way?

A.  I believe it is a device—not the device, but a device for making useful discoveries in fleshing out the dimensions of those discoveries already made, in sharpening them, in validating them, in pruning away those things that really don't fit. And I think the practice of medicine is greatly improved by the scientific method. Just as I think it rests very strongly on the clinical method, they are both useful tools, they both have a place. You know, dealing with human despair and ailments is a very difficult thing. And our tools, quite frankly, are rather puny, and I for one am not going to discard one of the two major tools available to me. I would use whatever I can lay my hands on.

*(Author's Note: In his answer here, Dr. 3 is rambling on in a manner which makes it sound as though clinical method and the scientific methods are roughly on an equal plane. Given the above statement in DSM-III-R, representing the position of an official publication of the American Psychiatric Association put together by presumed experts in the field of diagnosis, any expert who attempts to do this can be confronted with that statement. Also, in this answer, while no questions are needed, certainly most attorneys would want to make a mental note of his statement that the tools of psychiatry are "puny," which in our understanding, would be approximately a confirmation of all that the first two volumes of this work have attempted to say and would confirm the substance of Dr. Ziskin's testimony. The point could well be made in argument that there is little basis for giving credence to Dr. 3's conclusions about D in the face of his statement that they are based on "puny tools.")*

Q. If I understand Doctor Ziskin's position, he believes in psychotherapy treatment of patients, but he doesn't believe in making a diagnosis because somehow diagnosis—making a diagnosis is not a valid—is not valid. What's your position on that?

A. Well, I don't understand how you can treat a patient unless you know what you are treating. You know, that knowledge of what you are treating has to be a presumption, has to be tentative. When you first lay eyes on your patient, you make a tentative diagnosis *(Author's Note: This confirms "preconception.")* and you may wish to revise that as you go along. I'm not saying you are stuck with it. But you have to begin somewhere and you know the surgeons who take a spleen out of every hot belly that he operates on is going to have uneven postoperative results, you've got to decide which is the organ that is most likely affected and go after that one. Once you have the stomach open, you may change your diagnosis, but of course you have to have a diagnosis day by day, minute by minute.

*(Author's Note: First of all, the question misstates Dr. Ziskin's position. Ordinarily, in his testimony, Dr. Ziskin indicates that the research cited in the book and from which he testifies for the most part does not deal with psychotherapy, but deals with diagnosis. So it is not correct to say he believes in psychotherapy. He acknowledges in his testimony that some percentage of people go to mental health professionals with problems, and following seeing the mental health professionals they either feel better or function better, or both. It should be noted that the question is concerned with making a "diagnosis," and in this regard, if it has not already been brought out, it should be, that "a diagnosis," as that term is used, constitutes labelling. A diagnosis is a label. It is a shorthand way of describing a symptom or set of symptoms. Therefore, making a diagnosis would not be consistent with Dr. 3's declaration earlier that labels are of little use. He goes on in the answer to say you cannot treat a patient unless you know what you are treating. However, some forms of treatment do not typically make diagnoses, and their rate of success is not less than for those that do, according the literature. The rest of the statement here seems to provide*

*further reason to give little credence to his opinions, as he acknowledges that the diagnosis is simply a hypothesis, that it is tentative, that it may need to be changed as you go along in treatment, and that preconception is common, but of course, in this case and in most of the work that forensic mental health professionals do, they do not go on and treat, they simply do as Dr. 3 did here—see the individual once or twice—and they do not have the opportunity of anywhere from one to five times a week of daily observation and communication with the patient over a period of weeks, months, or years.)*

Q. There's been a lot of talk about the various studies, five hundred studies in Doctor Ziskin's book and what not, and there's been a lot of testimony about clinical work, clinical diagnosis and clinical analysis. Is there—can we say one way or another whether—which is the cart and which is the horse, so to speak? Does the clinician do his work based on the studies—or are the studies done based on something that is originally discovered by the clinician?

A. I'm sure there is a circular process, each feeds the other. But at least in the field that I know, medicine, specifically psychiatry, the scientific studies lag behind the clinical observations for about ten years.

*(Author's Note: The witness's answer here is an approximation of the truth. Certainly, scientific studies often follow, rather than precede clinical observations. No one quarrels with the proposition that much research is generated out of clinical observations. This does not mean that the clinical observations are valid or always turn out to be validated by the scientific studies. In fact, it is quite common for the studies to invalidate the clinical observations. However, this is the purpose of many of the scientific studies, particularly the study of the reliability and validity of diagnoses. While it is conceivable that one could wipe the slate clean and eliminate all diagnoses and then start to build up a classification system based on scientific research methods, that is not the way it had developed, or the way it is done. We have with us diagnostic systems that have evolved out of clinical observation over a period of a considerable number of years. It is obvious from the constant changing of the DSM that there are many flaws in that classification system. Thus it is the function of the scientific method to try to weed out, as Dr. 3 indicated in the previous answer, those diagnoses that do not hold up under scientific scrutiny. This would be a reason for the DSM committee to prefer scientific research to clinical observation, and why they are already aware that they are going to have to change the system that is currently in effect as more "research" comes in. If this point has not already been made somewhere in testimony, it is something the lawyer will likely want to get into evidence. It should also be pointed out that it is one thing to present hypotheses or make hypotheses for the purpose of beginning treatment, where one knows they will have the opportunity to modify those hypotheses as they go along, and quite another thing to present hypotheses as fact in a court on a serious matter where there is going to be a decision made that will, in almost all cases, be irrevocable, with no chance to try it out and see if it was wrong and change it.)*

You know, Doctor Ziskin honored us with a horror story of his own about the clinical method when he talked about his last child custody case, and I don't wish to refute that, but I think add another dimension to the picture. I'd like to share a horror story of my own about the so-called scientific method. About ten, twelve years ago I observed that all depressions were not the same and that specifically people whose depression was wedded to large amounts of anxiety had trouble falling asleep, whereas people whose depressions were wedded to a lot of physiological slowing down could fall asleep all right but would wake up too soon, and that certain antidepressants which had just come on the market in some instances seemed specific for the first kind of depression, and other drugs seemed to work better with the second kind of depression. Let me, rather than hit you with a big long chemical name, say the first group of antidepressants were medicine A and the second group were medicine B. So I began to pick and choose that all antidepressant medications were not the same and the kind of insomnia you had was a good clinical clue as to which antidepressant was likely to be most effective. Hardly a scientific technique. I didn't have five hundred patients and five hundred controls, I just had my practice. But I made this observation. I'm not saying, I was the only one that made it, but I was the only one aware of having made it at the time. I started getting excellent—much better results with these antidepressants than I had before. They went along for about two years, and the first scientific study of the kind Doctor Ziskin quotes came out, and do you know what most of them said? They said the antidepressants didn't work, period. That you got just as good a result with the placebo, giving them aspirin, as you got with these anti-depressants. Fortunately, I ignored these studies and continued to cure my patients. Over the next two or three years other studies started to come out and finally on balance—on balance, the antidepressants were found to be therapeutic. One of the problems with finding them therapeutic in the first place is that the earlier scientific studies did not make distinctions between when you used antidepressant A and which patient would respond better to antidepressant B. Then came out another series of studies which showed that all right, they work, but they are really all the same. Again, seeming to fly in the face of my own clinical observations. Finally, several years later the studies came out and said by golly, you know, these antidepressants are different and they do have different uses. We are now up to about three or four years. All this decade I have been treating patients in the face of these hair-raising scientific or so-called scientific studies with their statistical tables and what not.

*(Author's Note: This long discourse about his experience in using a particular treatment despite negative research evidence should be portrayed as what it is, simply one experience of one clinician. No one, including us, has ever asserted that all clinical observations are wrong. Almost everyone would agree that some clinical observations are correct. The purpose of using scientific methods is to try to determine which ones are correct and which ones are not. Probably the way to deal with this is with a question to the effect of something like, "Well, Doctor, when you risked malpractice to treat your patients, you must have been pretty sure that you were right. Isn't that correct?" We would assume that the witness would answer this affirmatively, and the next question*

*then could be, "Do you think or don't you think that the doctors who were bleeding their patients for several hundred years also felt pretty confident that they were correct?" Assuming this would be answered affirmatively—any other answer is difficult to imagine—the next question would be, "And in that case, Doctor, rather than saving lives, or sleep, as you assert you have done, they were in fact killing a good many of their patients. Isn't that correct?" Assuming the answer to that is affirmative, the next question could be, "Well, Doctor, it would have been better for those patients they killed if some scientific research had been done, and if the doctors had adhered to the findings." He goes on in this answer to considerably inflate his image, but it could be pointed out that the scientific method was not given up, and that ultimately, the validation for his treatment, if in fact it is valid, came from scientific studies. If his point is that scientific research can be wrong, of course no one would argue with that either. This is why most responsible researchers publish their results and the publications have a format that is almost always adhered to in which they describe the subjects they used, the methods they used, the kind of experimental controls that were employed, and what the results were, usually in a numerical form so that other researchers can do a variety of things. They can replicate or extend the study to see if indeed it comes out the way the first researchers claim, or they can, in another publication, point to the flaws in the study which do not permit one to draw the conclusions which were drawn. He also suggests further on in his answer that you have to look at scientific method with the same skepticism as the clinical method. If it is his position that neither one is any good, then once again, there is no reason for a jury to give credence to what he is saying. Then, there is simply no body of knowledge on which his conclusions can be based.)*

At about this time I found that there was some patients who not only could not fall asleep, but who awakened at three in the morning and couldn't get back to sleep. They had both kinds of insomnia. They had it coming and going. So I followed the logical clinical conclusion, I started to give them both kinds of antidepressants. The same patient would receive medicine A and medicine B. I gave him a slightly lower dose, but they got them both. And I got remarkable results with these notoriously difficult to treat patients who have such global symptomology.

At about the time I started using both medications, there were a series of studies which came out that showed that if you used both of these medications together, they would produce the ultimate side effect, death. One in one hundred thousand patients receiving both medications would have a cerebral hemorrhage and die. Of course, I—as soon as these studies came out, I told this to my patients and some of them declined to continue on both medications. Others said, look, it is the only thing that ever helped me. I will take the chance. So I hung in there, taking perhaps a small malpractice risk, until the inevitable studies came out which say, yes, that's true. One in one hundred thousand patients who use both these medications will die. But one in fifty thousand patients who do not use these will die. In other words, somehow using both medications protects you against premature death. I am not sure exactly why, whether people who don't get accurately treated commit suicide or what have you, but it turned out if you re-examine these figures in another way, there's really no harm in using both medications and that these patients have a better—a slightly better—I'm giving you very crude figures—please don't hold me to them—but the order of magnitudes are accurate. What I guess I am saying is that I am not putting down the scientific method as a whole or in general, I'm saying it has a place, but that you have to look at it with the same skepticism that Doctor Ziskin suggests you look at the clinical method. We each have our strengths and weaknesses. And there's some things you simply cannot do with the scientific method. It was designed to measure hard data, like they have in physics and chemistry. It begins to become less useful when you start to measure psychiatry and psychology. This doesn't mean, that psychiatry and psychology are lousy, it just means that it is hard to test it using the scientific method. You can devise a study scientifically, a controlled statistical study which will prove beyond a shadow of a doubt that the best surgeons in town, the ones with the longest training, the ones that get the highest fees, the ones that are viewed with the greatest awe by their colleagues, have the highest mortality rate. I'm talking, of course, about the neurosurgeons. They have a six year residency. They have incomes of three hundred thousand dollars a year. They are the king of the surgical spectrum. And yet, they lose most patients. Now, why is that? Studies show you don't go to a neurosurgeon if you want to live. The reason is they take they take the most difficult cases and a lot of brain tumors simply can't be cured, even by the most skillful surgeon. In fact, you can do another study which shows that barbers, who used to do surgery about the time we were bleeding patients, barbers did have a very low fatality rate. You can draw the conclusions from these statistical studies that if you have a brain tumor, your best bet is to go to a barber rather than a neurosurgeon. Obviously a little clinical common sense suggests that that is probably not a good idea.

*(Author's Note: This note deals with the statement above and some others which follow the note. His assertion about science being designed for hard data like physics and chemistry is correct to a degree. However, most of the studies referred to in this text are based on hard data. For example, when a study shows that experienced psychiatrists agree with each other in their diagnoses only about fifty percent of the time (actually a study will give an exact percentage, whether forty-eight percent or fifty-three percent), then that is hard data. You have either the spoken or written words of the two clinicians, or whatever number there are, in which one clinician says psychotic, and the other clinician says personality disorder. Now that is hard data. Studies on the predictions of psychiatrists also rely on hard data. If the psychiatrist says "this sailor will not make it through training, nor will he make it through his period of service," and the individual does make it through training and his period of service, that is hard data. When the psychiatrist says "this prisoner will not represent a danger to society if he is placed on probation," and he is placed on probation, and he goes out and commits a serious crime, that is hard data. If there are no predictions that can be made, and no kind of research that can be done to determine the validity of psychiatric conclusions about what is going on inside of somebody's head or somebody's psyche, then there is no way on earth of ever*

*knowing whether the psychiatrists are right or wrong, no way for them to learn from experience, and no way for anyone else ever to have any basis for giving credence to their conclusions. In other words, while the doctor may be correct in saying if you can't research something, that doesn't mean that it is lousy, it also means that you cannot ever say it is any good, either.*

*In the next statement about designing a study scientifically, a controlled statistical study to prove anything you want, he gives the example of his idea of a scientifically designed study about neurosurgeons. In so doing, he indicates that he apparently has little understanding of what is meant by a controlled study. It should be obvious to the first researcher on this topic, and if not the first, certainly one of the very early ones, that in order to compare the rate of fatalities of neurosurgeons, the best ones, who get the highest fees and are the kings of the surgical spectrum, obviously one of the things you would think of to control for would be the nature of the tumor or other brain problem that they are treating. Just as in our example way back in the chapter on scientific method, in order to test the two fertilizers or the two seeds, you would want to make sure that both brands were being applied to equivalent soil. That is, you would not want to do a study comparing the two fertilizers using one fertilizer on infertile soil, and using the other on rich soil. This obviously is the same issue as the kind of patient the neurosurgeon is dealing with. It would probably be useful to expose the doctor's apparent lack of genuine understanding of science and scientific method, which should tend to nullify almost any of the comments he has made about it. His reference to the postal service probably does not need to be dealt with, but one could point out that in all probability, the volume of mail that is being handled through zip codes and computers is much larger than that dealt with by the old neighborhood postman in the good old days. It also might be pointed out that in fact the zip codes and computers perform their operations before the mail ever gets to the postman on foot. It is a way of sorting mail so that the volume is manageable. It could also be pointed out that this example really does not have very much to do with scientific method, but with technology. One can further go on to point out that it is probably not likely that we would have been able to send astronauts up in spaceships and watch them walk around on the moon purely on a basis of clinical observation. [Just as a sidenote, we would call attention to the error in the transcript in describing a challenge to the "youthfulness" of psychology. Undoubtedly, the testimony employed the word "usefulness" rather than "youthfulness." This is in connection with Dr. 3's description of lack of logic in a statement made by D which has at least a reasonable probability of having been erroneously transcribed.] Then in his answer, he indicates that he is not competent to tease the studies apart, which again, ought to render him not expert enough to testify about research. So far as who is going to check the validity and reliability of the five hundred studies, this may be redundant, but it can be pointed out that they are checked all the time. They are made public—that's the meaning of the word "publication"—and they can be critiqued by anyone who wishes to do so, and they can be replicated by anyone who wishes to do so, in contrast to his clinical observations, which so far as we know, except in rare instances, are not made public. His methods cannot be exactly duplicated, because he himself is an instrument in his methods of treatment. That is, it is common knowledge that the doctor's relationship with a patient may have some effect on the outcome of treatment.*

*We would note that in using the example of diabetes (see below) in his testimony, Dr. Ziskin was unwise, an error which he has resolved not to repeat. That is, it is unwise to use medical analogies or metaphors unless you are thoroughly grounded in the material.)*

Years ago, postal—mail used to be delivered by a clinical technique. The postman would squint at the address and somehow get it to your house. Five years ago we shifted to the scientific method with zip codes and computers, and I don't have to tell what happened to the mail service since that time. So, scientific method is not a panacea. It has its place but so does the clinical method.

Q. You were in the courtroom yesterday, and like the rest of us, I think you heard Doctor Ziskin criticize psychology because it fails a number of, in his mind *(Author's Note: We would not want to leave the impression that these failures are in Dr. Ziskin's mind. They are in the scientific and professional literature.)*, scientific tests that relate to consistency and reliability and that kind of thing. Then he went on to cite the five hundred and some studies that he has published in his book to challenge the youthfulness [sic] of psychology.

What's your feeling on that?

A. Well, you know, I can't—I haven't—I have read some, but I have not read all the five hundred studies. I have got to take—as I say, you've got to take five hundred studies, however impressive, with a grain of Thorazine or something. I'm not competent to tease them apart. I just can tell you I have had experiences where these studies show one thing in one year and then they show another in the other. So, you know, who is going to check the validity and reliability of the five hundred studies? Doctor Ziskin makes the point that a lot of the bases for what we do in psychology and psychiatry are controversial, and he's right. He's dead right. But I think he himself uses the example by contrast of diabetes, and he says something to the effect that, you know, unlike psychological subjects of study such as schizophrenia, diabetes is something kind of solid, and there's not much controversy about that. We can all assume that it is there and it is a well-known and well-understood phenomena. But he is wrong.

There's an enormous controversy about diabetes. Sure, some diabetics have too much sugar, but there's a lot of controversy if that's really the problem. Some diabetics don't have enough sugar and are hypoglycemic. And we are not sure—there's controversy whether it really is a disease of sugar metabolism or basically a cardiovascular disease of which problems with insulin is probably just a small part. There's controversy as to whether the problem is a sugar problem or insulin problem or whether it is a lack of insulin or whether or not diabetics have plenty of insulin but they also have another chemical in their bodies which bumps off the insulin before it gets to the sugar. There's controversy about treatment, about whether or not diet is the most helpful and appropriate thing or whether we should be using oral diabetic medicine or taking insulin. I haven't even scratched the surface of the controversy about diabetes. But two things are for sure: one, that diabetes will cause alterations in mental function—it produces depression, produces premature senility, it produces hypoglycemic episodes where people become quite irritable—and the other thing about which there is no controversy is that we do have good treatment for it, if not yet a cure. The same holds for schizophrenia. There's a lot we don't know. There's a lot which is controversial. There is a lot of revisions that we will probably see in DSM-IV, DSM-V as to what schizophrenia really is and how to best handle it.

But like diabetes, though it may be controversial, the schizophrenics are real. Just like diabetes is real. It is there. And until the scientific method resolves all those controversies, if it ever will, we have got to go ahead and treat these people. We have got to diagnose them. We have got to do something with them. And that's where the clinical method comes in. I think psychologists and psychiatrists have performed a useful service to these people, even if we can't quite yet validate everything that we do. Regrettably in psychiatry there are no answers in the back of the book by which you can check to see if you were right, but you do the best you have with the tools at hand.

Q. If we were to completely discard the use of psychiatry and psychology in an effort to reach the decision that this jury has to reach, state of mind of Mr. D a year age [sic], what other tools are there?

A. Well, they had an opportunity to meet Mr. D himself. Now, I'm sure that was useful. You had an opportunity to eyeball him and listen to him, and begin to get your own sense that this man is mentally different than other people. How much weight they want to give it is another matter, but at least they had that opportunity. I think that's useful. I call that direct evidence. They have the opportunity to hear people in Mr. D's life, who had contact with him before and after the offense, and who gave, I think, a picture of him and his mental state, and I think that's the tool that the jury will utilize, but I don't know if that's necessarily enough. This may be the first schizophrenic the jury has ever seen. I've seen hundreds, even without knowing what schizophrenia is, at least I know one when I see one, and I have some ideas about what it means to be schizophrenic, which I think the trier of fact deserves to hear.

*(Author's Note: The "I know one when I see one," type of statement is simply another form of the "trust me" statement. We have cited in the section on schizophrenia under special diagnoses [Chapter 19, Volume II] numerous studies and abundant literature indicating that one psychiatrist's schizophrenic may be another psychiatrist's inadequate personality, or borderline personality, or paranoid personality, or whatever. And each one is likely to say about the diagnosis he has made, "I know one when I see one.")*

I don't think someone should just say thus and such, and that a jury should reach a certain verdict, but it's a very complex thing, the human mind, and I think my familiarity with psychiatry should be considered in a jury's decision. I think any little help they can get from someone with no axe to grind would be useful. And one of the best tools available to the jury is to hear people who have some more experience with this problem and who can cast a light on those processes, and that is all that I've done. I'm not trying to tell them what to do with that light, whether or not they should give it any weight at all, but they are required by law to take into account his mental state, and I know a thing or two about people's mental states because I work with them every day.

Mr. DC: I have no further questions, Doctor, thank you.

## RECROSS-EXAMINATION:

Mr. PA: You yourself, I believe you testified, that you have done research yourself, correct?

A. Little bit.

Q. Doctor, you mentioned three specific things you worked on that involved research, the detoxification of alcoholics, the differential diagnosis and treatment of depression, and you mentioned in your testimony, I'm quoting, "worked with hysterics"?

A. Yes, hysterics.

Q. And I take it—well, let me ask you this: Did you use a scientific method in any of those attempts to do research on any of those three subjects?

A. Well, yes and no. It was scientific in the sense I did set out to do a study, and I did explicitly state my hypothesis of where I was going, and I took pains to assess whether or not I got there, which is something clinicians often don't know, instead of going along and treating the patient and along the way they make a discovery, it was not scientific in that it probably did not reach or may not have been susceptible of reaching a statistical threshold. I could not use readily the kind of statistical validation techniques that you can with large series of patients.

*(Author's Note: His description of scientific method that he has employed, in response to that question, which he answers yes and no, is not scientific. The answer should be no. It says nothing about utilizing controls of extraneous variables, and apparently, it is not susceptible to statistical analysis, and apparently, it did not involve a sufficient number of subjects to allow for the drawing of any conclusions. So his answer probably should have been "no." Simply forming a hypothesis does not represent the use of scientific method. It represents only the starting point for the use of scientific method.)*

Q. You do, I take it, as you indicated before, rely on research in an effort to improve your knowledge about certain areas of psychiatry?

A. I certainly read it. My reliance upon it is tempered by the observations that I shared with you a few moments ago.

Q. I take it, just as the observations of people in Mr. D's life, that is, specifically his family, and the kinds of people that Dr. 4 talked to, it's equally necessary, I guess, for them to arrive at a decision as the opinions that were rendered by the police and the people who saw him on the day of the homicide?

A. Sure.

Q. Finally, Doctor, I guess since we have you both here, Dr. Ziskin ended his testimony yesterday by saying that he's thrown down the gauntlet around the country for the past three years to get just one person to challenge his thesis by supporting it with any research to show that experience does not mean a very great deal in the field of psychiatry or psychology; are you prepared to enlighten us with any such authority or such study, at this time?

A.  Unfortunately, that's not my line of work. I'm not a research scientist, so I have to say no, I'm not prepared to challenge Dr. Ziskin on his ground, but I would think that if there were a loved one in Dr. Ziskin's family who, because of the closeness of the family could not be treated by his wife, and needed someone to give him the best opportunity of making a sharp diagnosis and appropriate treatment in helping his loved one, Dr. Ziskin would probably want to come to somebody like me, in my humble clinical method.

Q.  Okay. I don't think he disputed the fact that treatment is a valuable sort of aspect. Would you say that his testimony indicated that he did not think treatment was valuable; that is, psychotherapy?

A.  That's true. He did not say he thought treatment not useful. I simply said that treatment is, after all, the essence of the clinical method, and if he honors treatment, then in an indirect way he is also tipping his hat to the clinical method.

*(Author's Note: His declaration that Dr. Ziskin would refer to someone like him is of course sheer speculation, and should be subject to an objection and a motion to strike. He has no way of knowing what Dr. Ziskin would do under those circumstances. His final statement that if Dr. Ziskin did not say that treatment is not useful, that he is tipping his hat to the clinical method, seems to also strain logic. It is difficult to see how if Dr. Ziskin did not say that treatment was not useful that translates into a statement that the clinical method is good. It certainly does not translate to a statement that clinical assessment or diagnosis is "good.")*

Q.  That's your opinion.

A.  That's all we're here to offer, counsel, opinions.

Q.  Have you been involved in treating Mr. D?

A.  No.

Mr. PA: Thank you, that's all.

Mr. DC: I have no further questions, thank you.

# APPENDIX C

# A Child Custody Case

*The material in Appendix C consists of a clinical report in a child custody case along with the analysis of this report by the author. The clinician was court appointed and, therefore, presumably unbiased. The analysis shows how biases were indicated, along with suggesting other bases for challenging the conclusions.*

## CASE I

Dear Judge D:

As requested, we have performed a psychiatric evaluation of the above-named domestic relations matter. We interviewed the minor children, D and S, their parents, F and M, and SM and SF. The parties were interviewed both alone and in various combinations for a total of 12 hours. In addition, psychological testing was administered to the adults. Projective drawing tests were administered to the children. Below are our findings, impressions and recommendations.

## PRESENT SITUATION:

Since early April of 1978, both D and S have been in the temporary custody of their father and stepmother. This situation evolved from a series of events in regard to custody which began about two years ago. At that time, all parties were living in the midwest and the children's mother, who had had custody of S and D since separating from her husband in 1973, decided to go to Portland for the summer. F claims that M had planned to move to Portland and because of this, two days before she was leaving he picked up the children to take them to the beach and went to court to get a temporary custody order. M denies that she had plans to move at that time and two days later reversed the court order and took the children to Portland for the summer. During this summer, however, she did decide to move to Portland and returned to the Midwest to make plans with F (who was now married to SM) regarding the children. At that time, M agreed to let D and S stay with their father while she established herself with a job and home in Portland. The plan was that S would stay with his father the entire school year and that D would be sent to her mother in December. Due to a series of miscommunications, both children remained with their father until June of

1977, when he and SM (who were moving to Washington) brought the children to M. They agreed to let S return to Washington in August, while D was to remain with her mother, who was now living with SF. All parties agreed that D and S should have frequent visitation with each other because of their closeness to each other. The misunderstandings between F and M escalated; this resulted in little contact between D and S. During this time, SM gave birth to a son, SB. F backed down on a promise to send S to Portland for his birthday in October. M thus drove to Washington with D but refused to allow D to sleep at her father's because she wanted both children to stay with her at her hotel. More fighting ensued. According to F, at that time D pleaded with him to let her stay with him and claimed she was lonely in Oregon because her mother worked. Disagreements between the adults continued, the most recent being M's refusal to send D to Washington for spring vacation, until this March when F went to court and got custody of D. M is now seeking to regain custody of both children.

**M:** M, age 30, an open, energetic, verbal woman, states that she wants custody of her two children because she has provided them with a good home in the past and has worked very hard for the last four years in order to be in a position to adequately care for them now. She feels that F should not have custody of the children because he has a violent temper, is not psychologically well-adjusted and is manipulative. She feels that both he and SM overprotect the children and that the nature of F's work (he is in sales and travels about eight days a month) keeps him away from home a lot which leaves the children in SM's care. She describes herself as a "battered wife" and reports incidents of her former husband hitting her in the presence of their children while they were married and reports that he went out with other women during their marriage. She has never received child support from F and feels that if he had helped her financially, it would have been easier for her to care for the children. She admits that the fact that she had to work full time in Portland made it difficult to spend enough time with S and D during the past year. Presently M has begun working for her boyfriend, SF, and she states that this allows her more flexible working hours and the opportunity to be home for the children after school.

M was the oldest of four children. She dated F in high school and was married to him at age 19. She worked part-time during the marriage in order to help her husband finish college. When they divorced, she decided to go to school and get training as a technician so that she would be able to better support her family. She attended school full time for two years, supporting herself and the children through welfare. M presents as a warm, extremely talkative, disorganized woman whose efforts to be flexible and reasonable with regard to the care of her children have resulted in confusion, anger and unpredictable rigidity and distrust. Her sincere desire to do what was in the best interest of her children had not always coincided with good or consistent judgment. Thus her decision to allow the children to live with their father and SM for a nine month period so as not to interrupt their schooling, while she worked hard to make money so she could provide a good home for the children when they did come out here—did not take into account the effects that so long a separation would have upon S and D. Similarly, her feelings that "a boy belongs with his father" and that it might be a good idea for S to be apart from his sister because he was overdependent on her, did not consider the effects of separating such a strongly allied pair of siblings. M focused so intensely on creating a good home for her children that she lost sight of their immediate needs and feelings. She tends to make spontaneous, impulsive decisions and, then, upon later reflection, realizes the mistakes she has made. When not under stress, she has the capacity for good judgment, but when angered or provoked, she suspends judgment and makes impulsive—often inappropriate—decisions. Despite her being deeply upset by the recent loss of custody, when interviewed with her two children M was calm and loving. She exhibited a great deal of warmth towards both D and S to which they were openly responsive.

**F:** F, age 29, a talkative, friendly, though guarded, man, stated that he wants custody of both of his children because he feels he is providing them with a stable family environment. He says he re-initiated custody proceedings for D after her visit last September to Washington, when she pleaded to come and live with him. He reports that D was alone quite a bit while she was living with her mother and would often call him long distance and tell him she was lonely. He accuses M of giving too many responsibilities to D in terms of taking care of S and feels she did not give D an opportunity to be a child. He admits that he is away from home quite a bit for his job but adds that that situation will improve in August when he will begin to travel by plane instead of by automobile. He also admits to acting violently while married to M, but claims that "that was someone else" and he no longer has a violent temper.

F was the second of three children. He was brought up in a Catholic home and attended a Catholic college. During his marriage to M, he received his B.A. and has been working with the same company since 1970. He married his present wife, SM, in 1975, and describes her as "the best thing that ever happened" to him. F presents as a somewhat self-righteous, suspicious man who is sincerely interested in the welfare of his children. He was cooperative and even-tempered throughout the interviewing procedures with the exception of the conjoint interview with M. At that time, M's refusal to listen to him provoked intense and verbalized anger on his part. He exhibited a close, warm relationship when with his children. While there is no evidence of a thought disorder, F's careful denial and guardedness when taking the MMPI is indicative of an evasive individual who needs to be seen in a good light, has little insight into his own conflicts and projects blame onto others.

**SF:** SF, age 28, an outspoken man, who was initially resistant to the evaluation procedure, states that he is willing to support M in any way possible in order for her to have the children. He said he was impressed with how totally committed M was to her children and to him. He admitted that he had little experience as a parent but that he was willing to learn. He felt his recent acquisition of his own business would help free up more time for them to spend with the children. SF presents as a straight-forward young man who appears to sincerely like D and S and is willing to develop a relationship with them.

**SM:** SM, age 25, a neatly dressed young woman, states that she wants custody of both D and S because she feels that M does not provide a good environment for her children. She states that she wants to give D a chance to be a child and that she and D frequently bake cookies and have long talks together and are like "sisters." SM presents as an extremely home oriented, perfectionistic individual who denies the existence of any type of problem. She reported that she tries to encourage the children to love their natural mother but that somehow S has begun to characterize M as the "bad mother" and her as the "good mother." She says that she discourages this and yet when S was interviewed he stated: "I would have been a mixed up kid if my parents had stayed together." When asked where he got that idea, he said, "SM told me that." This sabotaging of the children's relationship to their mother is in contrast to SM's expressed interest in the well-being of S and D. She has avidly taken on the role of mothering them. She has been careful to include them in the birth of her son, SB, and involves them in his care. She is very involved in the children's education and concerned about areas where they need improvement.

**D:** D, age 10, a verbal, friendly and bright young girl, began the interview by saying that she thought her mother would be better off without her. When asked what she meant by that, she said, "I don't know." She expressed a clear preference to be with her brother, S, and her new brother, SB. When asked what she would wish if she had three wishes, she replied: "That Dad wasn't married to SM, that Dad had stayed married to Mom, and that we all still lived in midwest," then quickly added: "But I know that won't happen because Mom and Dad fight so much they'll never get back together." It became clear in the course of the interviewing process that D felt left out of her father's new family and new home in Washington and had done everything she could to encourage her father to get custody of her. While she and her father exhibited a close and loving relationship with each other, it became evident that part of D's desire to be with her father was based upon feelings of rivalry towards SM, jealousy of S and a real desire to take care of SB. D's primary interest at this time seemed to be in taking care of her baby brother. In private, she told the examiner that she felt SM yelled at the baby too much. What was interesting, is that both F and SM stated they wanted custody of D so that she would have an opportunity to be a child. This is incongruous with the way D experiences her role in this family which is as a co-caretaker of SB, a "sister" to SM, and an older sister to S.

D presents as a strong-willed, mature and somewhat manipulative young girl who is greatly confused in terms of her primary identity figure. While she verbally expressed a preference to live with her father in Washington, she appeared to be almost play-acting the role of a happy child when with her Washington family. Her interaction with her mother alternated between a warm and spontaneous response to her and a withdrawal and covering up of feelings. While there is no evidence of any childhood psychiatric disorder, D's overtly calm decision to move to Washington, blankets the deep conflict she is experiencing in regard to her separation from her mother.

**S:** S, age eight, a quiet, sensitive boy expressed not only a clear preference to remain with his father and SM (whom he occasionally calls "Mom") but also a wish not to live with his natural mother. He is strongly allied to his Washington family and very attached to his older sister, D. S's expressed negative feelings towards his natural mother were, however, incongruous with his behavior when with her. During the interview, he stated a reluctance to ever visit his mother for the weekend, saying that he thought she would try to "spoil" them while they visited. Upon seeing his mother, whom he had not seen for a while, his face lit up and he stayed close to her for the remainder of the afternoon. S is clearly confused in regard to his feelings toward his mother. It is likely that M's decision to let F have custody of S and not of D was experienced by S as a rejection. He seems to have dealt with the pain of separating from his mother by very strongly identifying with his stepmother to the point of internalizing her attitudes toward M. While, in some ways, his alliance to his father and stepmother can be seen as an adaptive way of dealing with the initial nine month separation from his mother, it has created some deep conflicts in S in regard to his mother. He has incorporated the negative attitudes of F and SM towards M, but these attitudes are at odds with his actual experience in the presence of his mother. S's reluctance to visit his mother may be explained as his way of avoiding the conflictual loyalties he experiences in her presence.

## IMPRESSIONS AND RECOMMENDATIONS:

This is a situation in which a series of seemingly logical events and discussions in regard to the custody of S and D has resulted in anger and suspiciousness in the adults and deeply conflicted loyalties on the part of the children. The combination of F's subtle manipulativeness and M's vulnerability to being manipulated, coupled with her impulsive decision making has created complicated and confused feelings in the children. M's decision to temporarily allow the children to stay with their father and SM two years ago, coupled with the covert ways that F and SM undermine M has damaged the relationship between the children and their mother. The children's verbalized desire to live in Washington with their father and SM must therefore be viewed in the context of the events of the last two years.

What is apparent is that all involved adults are sincerely interested in providing a good home for S and D and that both F and M are capable of giving their children an adequate and stable environment. What is initially less apparent is the real attachment, warmth and closeness that both S and D experience when with their mother. It is crucial that these children have an opportunity to have as unhampered a relationship as possible with both of their parents. It is important that D, and even more so, S, have a chance to repair their damaged relationship with their mother. We feel that this opportunity will be interfered with if the children remain in the custody of their father and SM. F and SM's subtle yet powerful negative feelings towards M accompanied by their total denial of such feelings, make it confusing and difficult for the children to enjoy a close and loving relationship with their mother without experiencing guilt and conflictual loyalties. M, on the other hand, is open and willing to encourage the children to continue the close and loving relationship to their father and SM. We therefore recommend that the custody of both S and D be returned to M with the children spending six weeks of their summer vacation and at least one weekend a month with their father. Although we are aware that the children will initially be unhappy with this decision, we feel that their long range psychological well-being will be enhanced if they are returned to their mother at this time.

We feel it will be crucial for M to participate in post-divorce counseling and family therapy with S and D. M must learn more consistent parenting skills; we suggest that SF also participate in the counseling process. He can be helpful in terms of the children's re-adjustment to living with their mother. We are also concerned with M's lack of organization and impulsive reactions to F's behavior. She can greatly benefit from counseling which will give her support during this transitional time. She can obtain this counseling at our clinic.

If we can be of further service to the court concerning this matter, please do not hesitate to call on us.

Sincerely,

Dr. Ph.D., Psychologist

Dr. M.D., Psychiatrist

## CROSS EXAMINATION NOTES FOR ATTORNEY FOR FATHER (F)

At the outset, it should be noted that the first paragraph of this report seems to misrepresent the evaluation procedure that was followed. I am here specifically referring to the use of the word "we" several times. For example, "we have performed a psychiatric evaluation" and "we interviewed." It is my understanding that all of the interviewing was done by Dr. Ph.D. Thus, the manner of presenting the report seems misleading. This is compounded by the fact the signature of Dr. M.D. is on the document following the signature of Dr. Ph.D. Thus, one reading the first paragraph of this report and noting the dual signatures on the last page would be led to believe that in fact the evaluation and interviewing were done by Dr. M.D. with Dr. Ph.D. I understand that Dr. Ph.D. indicated she had discussed this matter with some of the other people at the Center, however, that is a far cry from the evaluation being done by them and it remains incorrect that the interviewing was done by a "we." Clearly, it was done by Dr. Ph.D. and Dr. Ph.D. only. There is a particular importance to this fact and I would refer you specifically to the chapter in my book titled, The Clinical Examination. In that chapter you will find numerous references indicating that the observations, that is, the purely behavioral, observational data of the clinical examination are quite unreliable, that they are inevitably incomplete and quite frequently slanted in the direction of personal, social, theoretical, or other kinds of biases and attitudes and the personality make-up of the examiner. Thus, when Dr. Ph.D. would discuss the case with other staff members, all the information they have is information she provides, particularly with regard to any interview material. Obviously, the test data is available to be seen by others. But the point is that their discussion with her is going to be based on the facts as she has perceived them and, as the research has shown, one cannot rely on the perceptions of an individual clinician.

I have the impression that Dr. Ph.D. is relatively young and I have some reason to believe that her Ph.D. is fairly recent. I do not find her name listed in the most recent Directory of American Psychological Association members nor do I find it in the most recent edition of the State Psychological Association Directory. As most reputable psychologists are members of these two organizations, I would expect to find her name listed unless her doctorate is so recent that she has not had time to become a member or not had her name submitted early enough to be included in these very recent directories. If she has had her doctorate for a considerable period of time and does not belong to these organizations, this would raise some other kinds of questions, but I am so strongly convinced that the answer is a recent Ph.D. that I will not go into them here. It is, of course, possible that she has a wealth of background and experience prior to obtaining the Ph.D. which might overcome the implications of its recency. However, guessing that she is probably on the young side, it would seem that her experience in this field would necessarily be somewhat limited if not quite limited. Assuming that the court appointment was to the Center, I think it would be appropriate to question the wisdom of whoever is responsible for assigning cases out to assign a matter of such serious and potentially lifelong consequences for a couple of young children to a relative novice. Along these lines I would also recommend asking Dr. Ph.D. if she holds the diploma of the American Board of Examiners in Professional Psychology, and the diploma of the American Board of Forensic Psychology, as these two diplomas purport to provide some evidence that the individual's competence as a clinical psychologist has been evaluated by peers and, in particular, competence in the field of forensic psychology. I note that her name is also not listed in the most recent edition of National Register of Health Service Providers In Psychology. Listing in this registry is a necessary prerequisite for insurance company reimbursement for providing mental health services.

It is very well established in the literature that various kinds of biases of the examiner color the data that is observed, recorded, recalled and the manner in which the data is interpreted. There is strong evidence of some kind of bias operating in Dr. Ph.D. in this matter. It is, of course, impossible to unzip someone's mind and determine what the contents are, therefore, bias can only be inferred from objective data. I believe Dr. Ph.D.'s bias will become apparent in the material to be discussed below. However, there are some speculations that may be worth pursuing. Note that she described SM as "extremely" home-oriented, while Dr. Ph.D. and M are working women, albeit at somewhat different levels. This raises the possibility that Dr. Ph.D. would identify more closely with M and may even have some problems of her own regarding the career versus wife and mother dichotomy that still operates to some extent in our society, despite the advances in the liberation of women. That is, it is not uncommon to find these conflicts in highly sophisticated, highly educated professional women, even today. Her use of the word "extremely home-oriented" seems to suggest something of this kind. Even with women's liberation, there are still a considerable number of women who wish to adopt the traditional role of wife and mother and are quite thoroughly invested in that, devoted to it, and this is in no way sick or abnormal. In fact, given the nature of wifehood and motherhood, particularly with three young children, it is difficult to see how one could be described as "extremely" home-oriented, as these tasks are likely to encompass virtually all of the time and energy of a woman who devotes herself to it in contrast to someone who has some kind of household help or is simply being somewhat neglectful in this area in terms of time needed to follow an occupation.

As further evidence of bias or else neglect or loose clinical work, it is noted that while the MMPI was administered to M, F and SM, it was not administered to SF (although see note below concerning SF). Also suggestive of bias is the fact that her report contained no mention of the fact that M had her tubes tied after "her last" marriage. I am somewhat puzzled by the statement "last marriage" as I am not aware that she'd been married more than once. It is also not entirely clear from that note as to when the tubes were tied, but it does at least contain a suggestion of a question as to M's genuine interest in motherhood. In any event, it seems to be a significant fact in this regard that at least merits some discussion in the report, however, it is not mentioned.

In connection with this whole evaluation, it should also be noted that psychology and psychiatry are really not very advanced in the knowledge of what is beneficial and what is harmful to children, other than some rather banal kinds of things that everyone knows about. It is well known that theories and practices in relation to child-rearing keep changing every few years like the swing of a pendulum so that there is no given time where one can say yes, at last we really understand all of the variables that go into normal development of a child. Dr. Ph.D.'s orientation appears to be that sibling relationships and reduction of divided loyalties are of paramount importance, more important than demonstrated parenting ability, stability in the child's life, stability in the parental figures, and that it is better to gamble on the efficacy of counseling procedures to make a good mother out of one whose deficiencies are extensive, according to the report, in contrast to proven parenting capabilities and I seriously doubt that these positions can be supported by a convincing weight of the literature. They are simply speculations based on what Dr. Ph.D. perceives as important. It would not be unreasonable to ask her how many predictions of this type she has made and in what proportion of those predictions utilizing appropriate methods, her accuracy has been proven, or even in how many of the cases has there been a scientific kind of follow-up.

It is essential to note the contrast in terms of potential surrogate parenthood between SF and SM. SF is described as initially resistant to the evaluation procedure and it will be quite necessary to determine what were the bases for his resistance, as Dr. Ph.D. does not find them important enough to even mention, although they must necessarily provide some kind of clues as to his parental attitudes. It is very strange that Dr. Ph.D. would get an MMPI from SM but none from SF, although he states that he is willing to support M in any way possible. However, he either refused to take the MMPI or was too busy, either of which conditions would raise questions as to the sincerity of his declaration. However, Dr. Ph.D. fails to make any comment about this and, as a matter of fact, in this regard the report contains another misrepresentation in that it is stated that psychological testing was administered to the adults. As all of the adults were named in the preceding sentence, I would take it that psychological testing was then administered to SF as well as the others. Either we have not been provided with those results or that is another incorrect statement. If Dr. Ph.D. says that it was simply a careless error, I would then assume that it is representative of the way she works and it is a kind of carelessness that diminishes the credibility of a professional. If the use of the word "we" and the failure to specify that SF was not psychologically tested turn out to be carelessness, one can then legitimately wonder whether Dr. Ph.D. is not overly sensitive to the efforts of others to do things right, a characteristic she apparently lacks and therefore using herself as a frame of reference could easily perceive the efforts of others to do things the right way as being "perfectionistic." However, due to the fact that she based her evaluation of some of the other parties in part on the MMPI, I cannot see where she can do other than say that she does not have adequate information to evaluate SF. That is, if you need an MMPI to evaluate F, you need an MMPI to evaluate SF. If you need an MMPI to evaluate SM, you need an MMPI to evaluate SF. If you do not have the information you need to evaluate the person, you cannot evaluate them and the only appropriate thing to do is to say so. However, we note that in the section on SF there is no mention of the fact that he could not or would not take the MMPI and thus this important item of information on him is lacking and for lack of that, it is unjustifiable for Dr. Ph.D. to make any comments with regard to what kind of environment the children would have living in his home. Also, while her notes indicate that SF was an only child, there is no mention of this in her report. Obviously, an only child would have little if any experience with how siblings interact in a family setting, which would seem to be a serious deficiency in terms of assuming a father role in a family where there are siblings. Contrast this to SM who was one of three children, and in addition, whose mother took in foster children such that SM would have had considerable first hand knowledge of sibling relationships and relationships of children within one home. It is clear from Dr. Ph.D.'s notes, that she asked all four adults about their family background. Therefore, one must conclude that this is an item of information of some importance, yet in her report she mentions only the family backgrounds of M and F and says nothing about the markedly contrasting backgrounds of SF and SM. If this kind of information is important regarding two of the adults, it is important regarding all of them and requires at least mention if not discussion in Dr. Ph.D.'s report. But the contrast here requires much more than mere mention. Note, for example, that SM grew up with a role model of a mother who was able to give love and care and attention to children who were not her own. In contrast, SF has not even had the experience of sharing attention and affection with others in his growing up period. This raises a serious question as to how he will react to having to share the somewhat limited time, attention and affection of M with another male in the house. I do not know the answer to that question but it is an obvious, significant question in this case and one which, in my experience, few clinicians would simply ignore. In addition, in going over Dr. Ph.D.'s notes where I assume she has taken down things told to her by SF, there is the statement everything D has done is for the kids. It seems clear that he meant M when he said D, therefore, clinicians in my experience would raise a question as to whether there is some confusion of identity between his girlfriend and her daughter. Sexual problems between "stepfathers" and stepdaughters are far from unknown in our society. This is another serious potential that has to be dealt with by a clinician making recommendations and even more particularly where this slip of the tongue suggests the possibility in and of itself. Yet, this problem is not even raised by Dr. Ph.D. (It may be worthwhile to ask Dr. Ph.D. if in her discussions with her other staff people they read her notes or her report or both and whether they also looked at the psychological testing and, in particular, whether Dr. M.D. had reviewed the data in its entirety, or only the report.) In addition, Dr. Ph.D. concedes that SF has had "very little" experience as a parent. I wonder what that means because it would seem to me that he has had no experience as a parent, unless she means what little he has had during the time that D was with him. I am also given to understand that he has spent virtually no time at all, perhaps a day or two, with S. Thus, it would be impossible to determine how that relationship is going to go. What kind of a gamble is that to take with a young person's life? She says that SF is willing to learn parenting. This, of course, is a worthwhile ambition and, of course, it is easy to say. No one can state at this time how successful he is going to be in that endeavor, in contrast to SM who, from all that has been provided, has very clearly been a more than adequate parent to these children. Again, what kind of gamble is this to take with young children?

The gamble of course is further compounded by everything that Dr. Ph.D. reports about M, whom she describes as "disorganized," "whose efforts to be flexible and reasonable with regard to the care of her children have resulted in confusion, anger and unpredictable rigidity and distrust and her lack of good or consistent judgment with regard to the children." Dr. Ph.D. also indicates that when not under stress M's judgment is all right, but "when angered or provoked she suspends judgment and makes impulsive, often inappropriate decisions." Contemplate that within two or three years D is going to be an adolescent girl in the home and judging by nearly universal experience, will anger and provoke her parents. Should she then be living with a parent who under those conditions suspends judgment, makes impulsive and inappropriate decisions? How could anybody make such a recommendation? Contrast this with SM, whose faults appear to be that she is very home-oriented, likes to do things right, and denies the existence of problems, the nature of which is not made clear so as to know whether there are any problems or not. And in contrast to F, whose faults are that he is somewhat guarded, needs to be seen in a good light, has little insight into his own conflicts and projects the blame onto others. (All of these latter conclusions, I believe, are obtained from the MMPI and are probably not correct for reasons which I will state below.) On top of all of this, there is the final statement of the recommendation that counseling for M and family therapy with S and D will be "crucial." This is tantamount to Dr. Ph.D. saying that at the present time and under present conditions the welfare of these children will not be best served by being with M. It will only be best served, if ever, if successful counseling and family therapy takes place. Unfortunately, the data on counseling and family therapy is such as to fail to offer great hope in this regard. No one can be certain of the outcome of such counseling and therapy nor can anyone even make a good prediction and the literature is quite clear on this. Therefore, the recommendation seems extremely risky. This is particularly true where apparently at the present time, being principally with the father, the children seem to be all right. No one has noted any kind of psychopathology or developmental difficulty in these two children. Why on earth should their welfare be risked by taking them out of an environment where they are getting along all right to put them in one where their welfare will be crucially determined by the success or failure of future counseling and family therapy? And, even worse, to do this over the objections of the children. While one can grant that children do not always know what's best for them, obviously their desires are of some importance and obviously there are serious potential detriments to being uprooted or deprived of living in the home where they want to live to be placed in one where they have both indicated they do not want to live. Certainly one would not expect them to have feelings that they have been well and fairly treated by the legal system.

It is not clear whether Dr. Ph.D. saw either or both of the children with SF. Absent such observation, obviously she has no way whatsoever of determining what the nature of that relationship is like.

It is also not clear that she saw either or both of the children with SM, so that she may be in no position to state what that relationship is like.

She saw D with both F and M. What she saw between D and F was a close and loving relationship, which she asserts, however, became evident that part of D's desire to be with F was based on feelings of rivalry toward SM, jealousy of S, and a real desire to take care of SB. Nevertheless, the behavior she describes is a close and loving relationship. She describes the interaction with M as alternating between warm and spontaneous response and a withdrawal and covering up of feelings. As between the two, this would seem to describe a better interaction with F than with M, discounting as clinical speculation the other comments of Dr. Ph.D. She concludes the paragraph by asserting that while D appears calm she is covering a deep conflict she is experiencing in regard to separation from her mother. This, of course, requires a crystal ball. All you can tell about a person is from the way they behave. I will comment on this further when I talk about projective tests.

While Dr. Ph.D. describes the interaction of S with his mother, she omits any description of such interaction between S and his father, which would seem to be a matter of some importance in this case. In the case of S, however, she notes his clear preference to remain with F and SM and not to live with M. She refers to negative feelings towards M although there is no supporting evidence given, except for his statement that she would try to spoil them while they visited which may simply reflect reality. I do not know. In any event, what is very important is that when he saw M, his face lit up and he stayed close to her. Dr. Ph.D. finds this behavior incongruous with his expression of desire to live with his father and not with his mother. I see no basis for concluding that that is incongruous. It would be natural, and actually what Dr. Ph.D. says she desires later in her recommendations, that S would wish to live with F and SM and not with M, although still being able to feel love and affection for M. I see nothing incongruous about that. She states that his reluctance to visit M can be explained as avoiding conflictual loyalties he experiences in her presence. I do not know what her basis is for her conclusion of conflictual loyalties. Apparently S is comfortable with his desire to live with his father and can still feel happy and "light up" and feel warmth toward his mother without experiencing conflict. It appears like one of those cases where the psychologist insists that conflict must be there even though it cannot be demonstrated and it is the kind of thing for which mental health professionals are notorious.

Apparently the basis on which Dr. Ph.D. is willing to take all the above-described risks, is that it is "crucial for the children to have an opportunity to have as unhampered a relationship as possible with both of their parents" and "it is important that the children have a chance to repair the damaged relationship with their mother." It is, first of all, highly questionable whether these goals outweigh the risks outlined above. It is also doubtful that the relationships with the mother have been impaired to the extent Dr. Ph.D. describes as indicated by the behavior she describes of both children with the mother. However, even if the foregoing questions are eliminated, further questions arise in changing the custody from father to mother at this time. For example, how will this affect their relationship with their father and SM. Will they feel that their father and SM have let them down by not arranging for them to be able to live with them as they desire? Will they feel that somehow by not obtaining custody that F has "covertly" rejected them? How will shifting the custody from one parent to another eliminate underlying negative attitudes toward each other on the part of both parents? We are dealing here with a divorce and child custody battle. It would be a rare couple who did not have negative feelings toward each other as a result of these kinds of battles. Dr. Ph.D. keeps referring to subtle and covert influences but there is no reason to believe that M is not as angry with F as F is with M, and that these angers may simply go on until the custody issue is settled finally. Normally what happens in that situation, assuming any kind of reasonable arrangement, is that the animosity of the parents drops away, they become less antagonistic toward each other, particularly if as described by Dr. Ph.D. they all sincerely love and are interested in the welfare of these children, they readily come to see that the important thing is for the children to be able to love both parents and they work toward that end. It is only the continuation of custody battles that prolongs the strong antagonism. Therefore, so far as problems in relationships with either parent, there is no reason to expect this will be any easier for the children if they are with M than if they are with F. It should be pointed out in this regard that it is true if the children have some negative attitudes that they may be experiencing some sense of rejection because she left them. That is simply a fact and such feelings would not be uncommon and would not necessarily be resolved by their being forced to live with her, which would then compound the rejection experienced from their mother by the fact that their mother has deprived them of the chance to live with their father, which they desire. This is hardly likely to improve their feelings toward their mother or their relationship with her. It would almost seem designed to do just the opposite. Dr. Ph.D. refers to F and SM's subtle yet powerful negative feelings toward M accompanied by their total denial of such feelings, that this makes it confusing and difficult for the children to enjoy a close and loving relationship with their mother without experiencing guilt and conflictual loyalties. Number one, apparently S had no such problems as she describes his behavior with M. With D, she did describe some apparent fluctuation of feelings and attitudes in the interaction with her mother. She attributes these to the subtle and powerful negative feelings of F and SM. However, it is to be noted that for the year prior to her seeing all of these people, D was in fact with her mother. This would seem to suggest that being with her mother is more likely to engender or aggravate such feelings than being with her father and visiting her mother. It should also be remembered that the proceedings were not generated by F and SM but were apparently initiated at the request of D. Additionally, Dr. Ph.D. describes M as open and willing to encourage the children to continue the close and loving relationship with F and SM. I am not aware of any reason in this case to believe that F and SM, being apprised of the need for the children to love and care for their mother, would not be able to conform their behavior to such a requirement. I doubt that they would need any kind of extended counseling or family therapy but it certainly might be useful for them to have one session with a counselor who could explain this need to them. So far as the operation of covert angers and hostilities, I again repeat there is no reason to believe that M does not have these the same as F. It would be highly unusual and, in fact, she expresses some anger in the notes taken by Dr. Ph.D. Certainly if she had been beaten, she would be angry. She certainly might be angry over the lack of financial support.

There is also in my mind some question about the physical living arrangements as between the two parents. I have the impression from the notes that M now has a new two bedroom apartment. Assuming that she and SF are living together, that's one bedroom, which would seem to mean that either the children, male and female, would have to share a bedroom, or one of them will have to sleep in the livingroom. This is hardly a desirable arrangement. There is no indication that I find in the notes as to what the living arrangements are with F. This would seem to be a highly significant omission.

Certainly one can recognize that there are psychological dimensions to life but there are also physical realities that make a difference to a child. Again, particularly here where we are looking down the road a couple of years to an adolescent girl who is certainly going to want and/or need her own bedroom. If Dr. Ph.D. obtained facts showing that the physical arrangements are far superior with F than with M, that should have been noted in the report. If, on the other hand, she failed to obtain this information, one has to question her proficiency in dealing with children as it is quite clear that physical arrangements for living do have an effect on the development of children. In fact, having dealt with several of these matters, I find it unusual. I believe this is one of the few cases that I have ever seen where there is no discussion whatsoever of some of the practical aspects of life, such as living arrangements, continuing in school, and so on.

Dr. Ph.D. indicates that both parents could provide stable environments. All the evidence points to the correctness of that statement so far as F is concerned. He has been married for three years, apparently is well established in his occupation, and so on. On the other hand, the statement seems highly questionable with regard to M. She is, first of all, in a relationship with SF that cannot be considered to have the stability that the marriage between F and SM has. I accept the concept of people living together and find nothing in that to object to, but it is naive to assume that there is the degree of commitment in an unformalized relationship that there is in marriage. Therefore, it is not reasonable to assume that the relationship between SF and M is a stable one. Further, Dr. Ph.D. makes the point of F's being away in connection with his work for extended periods of time, which I gather boils down to about eight days a month, and which will be less given the new arrangements for flying wherever he has to go. On the other hand, SF has apparently just bought a business and because it is new it may require excessive amounts of his time. It is well known that while it is nice to be the owner of a well established business run by help, that for most small businesses, mama and papa-type operations, most of the time the owner of the business works harder and longer hours than any employee would. Therefore, there is no solid basis for believing that SF's time will be any more available than F's. And we note that M works in the business too and if there are some times of stress they are both going to have to put in long hours. In contrast, even when F is away, SM is home and apparently the children feel comfortable and attached and secure with her.

I will comment briefly now about the testing. The first and most obvious thing is that it seems inadequate not to have given the MMPI to all of the adults involved. It is not clear how much Dr. Ph.D. is deriving from the test, how much from history, and how much from the interviews. However, it does seem clear that in the case of F she is drawing some conclusions from the MMPI. In particular, she states that his careful denial and guardedness when taking the MMPI is indicative of an evasive individual who needs to be seen in a good light, has little insight into his own conflicts, and projects blame onto others. You should be aware that while the MMPI is one of the more respected testing instruments, its reliability and validity are not such that one can place a high degree of confidence in conclusions from it. With regard to the conclusions about F, I have to guess that they are based on his L and K scores, although the profile I have does not show the L score but I am guessing it was somewhat elevated. For your information, on the left-hand margin of the profile, those numbers indicate T scores and you will see a heavy line drawn across from 50 with additional heavy lines at 70 and 30 and lighter lines at 60, 80, 90 and so on. What each of those lines indicates is one standard deviation from the mean. This is a statistical concept. For example, the range from a T score of 40 to a T score of 60 would represent the area of plus or minus one standard deviation from the mean, 50 being the mean. This area would encompass 68% of the population. The area from 30 to 40 and 60 to 70 includes an additional 27% of the population, or an additional 13-1/2% falls into each of those ranges. Generally speaking, it is scores above 70 that are considered to be in a pathological area on the MMPI. Thus, none of F's scores fall into the pathological area, and of course none of SM's do either. F's K score is apparently at approximately a T score of 70 or a raw score of 23.

This tends to be on the high side and this particular scale is thought to indicate defensiveness and both the K and the L do indicate efforts to try and look "normal" or "good." However, these are norms based on a fairly broad sample of the population. It is, for example, known that upper middle class or college-educated people tend to score higher on K than do people in general. I'm going to give you some ranges of scores. That is raw score of 10 to 15 is considered middle range, 16 to 20 high average, 20 to 25 moderately elevated, 26 to 30 markedly elevated. However, it is noted that college-level subjects typically score within the high average range, which would make this then the average range for college-level people. Taking 16 to 20 as the average range for college-level people, one can see that F's score of 23 is not really remarkable and the conclusions about him taken from that scale need to be qualified in terms of his level of education. This information comes from an MMPI Handbook, Volume 1, 1972, by Dahlstrom, Welsh and Dahlstrom. Scores on this scale, however, need to be qualified in child custody cases because of another factor. You will note this under situational effects in my book in the chapter on clinical examination. That is, it is almost universal in my experience that parents involved in a custody dispute tend to get elevated K scale scores for the obvious reason that they are, in fact, trying to look good. One would have to be some kind of a fool not to try to put their best foot forward in a child custody situation. Many of the MMPI items lend themselves to either a true or false response on the part of the individual taking the test. That is, many of them are borderline questions which one could honestly mark in either direction and it is only to be expected that an individual in a custody case will tend to mark them in the more favorable direction. For these two reasons, in addition to the fact that his score's not all that high anyway, no interpretations based on it are of any value in this case. Additionally to that, we must be aware that we do not know what SF's MMPI would look like because we do not have one so it would be inappropriate to draw conclusions about F and make recommendations based upon those conclusions from the MMPI in the absence of having this kind of material available with regard to SF. It is also to be noted that while Dr. Ph.D. comments specifically on the MMPI results as far as F is concerned, she does not comment on the results for M, although M has the only score on any of the three profiles that is clearly well up in the pathological range. While her high score on this Ma scale (#9) may be reflected in Dr. Ph.D.'s description of her as impulsive and showing poor judgment, there is no specific reference to deriving this from the MMPI. In any event, inasmuch as she used the test it would seem appropriate to make some comment about this, the only pathological score on all of the testing. It is also interesting that she makes no comment on the excellent mental health shown by SM on the MMPI where her scores were all in the normal range and which pretty clearly indicate, if the test is of any validity, that SM is a far more stable and reliable person than M. I might also note that on the profiles supplied to me, there appears to be material deleted in the Xeroxing and one can only wonder what that material says. It should be obtained before this matter goes to trial.

Dr. Ph.D. does not indicate what information, if any, she derived from the projective tests administered to the children. These consisted of what look to be the House-Tree-Person and some sort of draw-your-family tests. Not knowing what Dr. Ph.D.'s conclusions were, I will offer what I think would be the most likely conclusions that would come from clinical psychologists viewing this material. S's drawing of the family seems to indicate a rather closely-knit group with many smiling faces which would suggest that he's a pretty happy child after all these years of living with his father, and that he sees himself as closest to his sister and his father. D's drawing is perhaps more interesting to clinical psychologists as one of the things they try to get out of this draw-a-family technique is how the child sees himself in the family constellation and what family members they feel closest to. I think almost any clinician would look at D's drawing and see that SM is more or less the hub or center of the world and all the others revolve around her, and further that at the present time D sees herself a little bit outside of the family circle, which fits with her own description of the way she seems to feel not being able to live with the family. It is also notable, in terms of closeness, that she feels herself closest to SM and that as between her father and mother, probably a little closer to her father. This is just simply in terms of the measurable distance between the characters. She also portrays herself in a happy activity, going down a slide, and she also shows happy and smiling figures, which is usually taken as a sign of a happy child and one who sees parental figures as pleasant, happy people. It may, however, be noticed, at least it's my impression, that she draws SM as a much happier and pleasant-looking person than she does for her mother. I am not saying any of this is valid—only that these would be conventional interpretations.

To summarize, the risks involved in Dr. Ph.D.'s recommendation seem very substantial. The goals to be achieved by a change of custody, while not unimportant, would seem to be less important than the many risks involved, and, in any event, it is quite likely that the goals of the recommendation can be achieved through other means. Furthermore, it appears to be a fairly minimal kind of evaluation at best, lacking an adequate amount of testing and certainly lacking anything resembling a sufficient amount of information concerning SF. The report, in addition, seems biased, as indicated above, by focusing on the reasons why the children should be with the mother and why they shouldn't be with the father while ignoring many facts that are contrary to that position. In addition, the report is dealt with in a manner which seems to misrepresent the procedure that was utilized. All of the foregoing, of course, is in addition to the well-documented fact that there is no adequate base of knowledge nor adequate methodology with which psychologists can accurately draw the kinds of conclusions that have been stated here.[1]

---

[1] Initially, the judge refused to hear the challenge to the report and recommendations. After heavy argument he permitted it. After hearing the challenge, he rejected the recommendations in the report.

# APPENDIX D

# Direct & Cross Examination of Consultant Expert in a Personal Injury Case

*This presentation is adapted from actual cases and is provided to illustrate use of a consultant expert as a witness.*

We are omitting the expert's qualifications. It is assumed that a lawyer presenting such an expert would know that his testimony would be most effective if he has impressive credentials. These should include academic position, publications in the areas in which he will testify, and previous acceptance by courts as an expert. It is also helpful if he has held office in professional associations and has received honors from such associations.

Q: Doctor, what is the current status of assessment in psychology/psychiatry?

A: At present, there are doubts about the reliability and validity of psychological evaluations. There is not even an adequate classification system.

Q: What is the basis for your opinion?

A: I base my opinion on a substantial body of scientific and professional literature which is negative concerning such evaluation.

Q: Is there also literature which supports such evaluations?

A: Yes, but in the face of the quantity of negative literature, the best one could say is that there is considerable doubt within the profession or science.

Q: Are you saying that the scientists and professionals have not been able to resolve these doubts?

A: That is correct.

Q: What do you mean by the scientific and professional literature?

A: That refers to the journals, the articles and books that are published in these fields, and this is where the knowledge of the field is contained.

Q: What is the purpose of publishing these materials?

A: The purpose of publishing is so that whatever someone in the field thinks, thinks they have learned or discovered or have an idea about, when it gets published, it becomes public; it's exposed to the view and scrutiny of other people in the field and they can evaluate what those findings or ideas or conclusions are and usually some will perform tests of their own on those matters so as to determine whether the individual was correct, whether the finding was wrong, whether there are modifications needed.

But it provides a means for checking on two things: One, to bring an idea or belief or conclusion out into public view, and then to provide a forum for checking on it and communicating about it. So some of the literature consists of articles or books in which the person proposing the particular belief or point of view states that, and maybe or maybe not provides some evidence for it.

Then once it is published, other people in the field say, "It sounds pretty good, I think I'll do a study to see if I can confirm what he has described," because in most cases you are not going to accept conclusions based on one study or one publication. And they may confirm what he said or they may find out they get a different result or they may find his conclusions are way off.

This is a process that usually goes on for a good many years before the field begins to have a pretty firm sense of, "Well, we are on the right track" or "We have solved this problem." Or they may find out it looked like a good lead or a good notion but it turns out to be a dud; then they drop it or try another approach.

But the function of the scientific and professional literature, it's a way of having the knowledge of the field available to everybody in the field so they can look at it and know the status of some particular element of knowledge in the field. It gives you a place to go look it up and find out what is known, in contrast to something some clinician may believe in his head, but has never had such exposure. For example, many clinicians believe that their years of experience have made them more accurate in evaluations than less experienced clinicians, but there is a substantial body of published research that is contrary to that belief.

Q: Does the literature reflect concepts, such a validity and reliability as they pertain to the diagnosis of psychologists and psychiatrists?

A: Yes, some of the literature pertains to those concepts, but we will have to define those terms.

Q: We will get to that.

A: Okay.

Q: Is this an area you try to keep up on?

A: Yes.

Q: Now of those terms that were mentioned, I would like you to define those to the jury. Let's start with validity. Does that have any relationship to the field of psychiatry and psychology?

A: Both reliability and validity have relationship to the field of psychology and psychiatry. It's easier to go from reliability to validity.

Q: Let's start with reliability.

A: Reliability refers to the stability or repeatability or reproducibility of a particular observation, so that if a psychologist gives a boy an I.Q. test on Monday and he scores 85, and he gives him the test on Wednesday and he scores 120 and he gives it to him on Friday and he scores 97, that is unreliable. We don't know what his I.Q. is. The measure keeps changing.

Or in the same example, if psychologist Smith gives the test and the boy scores 120, but psychologist Brown gives him the test and he scores 90, again we don't know what his I.Q. is. It is not consistent over time and it is not consistent across examiners. That essentially is what reliability refers to.

Validity refers more to accuracy, to how the observation relates to something else, how accurate a conclusion or prediction or interpretation of some data is.

As an example, assume that both psychologists find the boy's I.Q. is 100. Then the question is, "What does that mean?"

Knowing his I.Q., can we predict that he will be a good pitcher in Little League baseball? We don't have much reason to feel that I.Q. has much relationship to pitching ability. But maybe it does. If someone thinks so, they can do research to determine if there is a relationship.

On the other hand, we have a body of research which has found that I.Q. is related to academic performance, so knowing his I.Q allows us to make some statements, for example that he has sufficient ability to earn a high school diploma.

That's what validity means. What does an observation or set of observations mean. If you know A, what if anything can you say about B, with reasonable security that you will be correct.

Those are really key concepts in the field of diagnosis or assessment. Can a diagnosis be made reliably and if so, what can you predict from knowing that is the diagnosis.

Q:  Doctor, could we define in layman's terms some definitions for psychiatric or psychological diagnosis?

A:  Well, diagnosis or diagnoses, plural, represents an attempt to classify, in this field to classify mental disorders so they can be organized into basic groups. And then within the group of disorders, broken down into specific disorders, primarily for the purpose of providing treatment, assuming that treatment would be specific to that disorder which may or may not be the case in this field, or to predict something else about the individual from the fact that this label applies to that individual.

Q:  Doctor, what does the literature, scientific and professional literature, reveal about the reliability and validity of diagnoses made by psychiatrists and psychologists?

A:  In general the literature has been negative regarding reliability. In recent years, the American Psychiatric Association has attempted to remedy this by publishing new diagnostic manuals which made the criteria for each diagnosis much more specific than they had been, hoping thereby to get people use the labels in the same way and knowing what elements are needed in order to constitute that diagnosis.

They published diagnostic manual number 3 in 1980, and concurrently in an appendix, they published data of their preliminary reliability studies. For some disorders, reliability met acceptable levels, for others it did not, and for some specific disorders, they did not report any reliability numbers. They have since revised that manual in 1987 and that one is called manual 3-Revised or manual 3-R, but they did not report reliability data for the revised manual. Reliabilities for DSM-III reported by other researchers were more negative than those reported in the manual.

Q: When you say negative, what does that mean?

A: They found in many cases that the reliabilities were low, did not meet acceptable levels. In a nutshell they found that the labels were not being applied consistently by mental health professionals.

Q: Are there specific studies reflected in the scientific and professional literature that give examples of lack of reliability?

A: Yes.

Q: Are you familiar with the Rosenhan studies?

A: Yes, but that's not a study of reliability as we have defined it here.

Q: That's a study of what?

A: That's a study of validity.

Q: Is that an example of a study that shows lack of validity of diagnoses by mental health professionals?

A: Yes, that's one of the studies in which it's known that the diagnosis was wrong in 100% of the cases.

Q: Can you describe that study?

A: [There follows a fairly lengthy description of the Rosenhan study which need not be repeated here; see Chapter 7, Volume I.]

Q: Are there other studies showing lack of validity or reliability?

A: Yes, there are several other studies.

Q: Are you familiar with the term "post-traumatic stress disorder"?

A: Yes, that is in the diagnostic manual.

Q: What did the reliability studies show for that?

A: In reporting the reliabilities in DSM-III they did not report any reliabilities for PTSD, as it is commonly called.

Q: Is PTSD an old, well-established disorder or something new and controversial?

A: There is a controversy in the mental health field both as to whether it exists as a separate entity, or if it does exist, what the criteria should be by which to diagnose it.

Q: Where can these criteria be found?

A: They are in the diagnostic manual number 3, published in 1980.

Q: Was this manual preceded by any others?

A: Yes, there were manuals 1 and 2 which were found to be inadequate, then number 3 in 1980, and the revision of 3, III-R, in 1987, and they are working now on manual number 4 which they expect to have out in 1992.

Q: Did PTSD appear in number one or two?

A: No, it appears for the first time in number 3.

Q: Are you familiar with how a named disorder, the actual name—for example, let's talk about PTSD. How does that get into the volume?

A: It is not by a scientific process but is a political process, a committee process whereby a chairperson is appointed by the American Psychiatric Association who then appoints a committee to produce a diagnostic manual. And he, in consultation with others, selects people to be on sub-committees to determine whether or not a certain diagnosis should be included and what the criteria should be. They discuss and argue and thrash it out among themselves and make compromises. Finally, they vote. That's why I call it a political process. In number 3 revised, they clearly state that they would have preferred to have established the diagnostic categories on the basis of sound scientific research but that for most categories they don't have that so they have to rely on other, inferior sources to do it.

Q: Does the DSM-III or III-R contain any other warnings?

A: The introduction has a caution against using these diagnoses in legal matters. They indicate they should be used for clinical and research purposes but that one should be cautious in using them in legal matters.

Q: Are there any articles which describe the process that is used to get a particular disorder into the book?

A: Yes, there is a recent article in the *American Journal of Psychiatry* by Mark Zimmerman and Robert Spitzer, who is the chairperson of the DSM.

Q: How did they describe the process?

A: What happened in this particular instance was, there were twelve people on this committee. In session, they finally narrowed things down to where they had four alternatives which are alternatives one, two, three, and four. They debated and then took a vote. Unfortunately it took some time and by the time they got around to voting, one of the members had to leave. So out of the twelve, only eleven remained.

The vote went like this: Alternative No. 1 got one vote, No. 2 had zero votes, alternative No. 3 got six votes, and alternative No. 4 got 4 votes. So by what was essentially a vote of six to five with one abstention, they voted in alternative No. 3. This is not science.

Then Zimmerman and Spitzer go on to describe how they worked out the criteria for the diagnosis, in this instance, melancholia. Ultimately these issue were resolved by a guess, their words, not mine, based on a belief, their words, based on two assumptions, their words. So that was the nature of the process in that particular diagnosis. To resolve differences by voting and to base a diagnosis on a guess, based on a belief, based on two assumptions could hardly be considered scientific.

Q: Have there been changes between DSM-III in 1980 and DSM-III-R in 1987 about the diagnosis of PTSD?

A: Yes.

Q: Do you have copies in your briefcase?

A: Yes. It will take a minute to get them.

Q: Did they do some adding?

A: Yes, they added four or five new criteria.

Q: Did they delete?

A: Yes, they deleted one of the criteria.

Q: Under the changes, is it possible that someone that could have been diagnosed using the manual in 1986 as having PTSD could not have been diagnosed in 1987?

A: That is possible and the reverse is possible: that someone diagnosed in 1987 couldn't have been diagnosed in 1986.

Q: So these things are in a period of change, is that correct?

A:  Yes, these are significant changes. There are about 10 changes in PTSD. Some are just wording changes. But by deleting a symptom, that means that someone who was diagnosed on that basis before 1987 and then somebody had seen him after 1987, they might not be able to diagnose PTSD because that symptom is no longer a symptom of PTSD.

The whole thing is laid out in sections. There are groups of symptoms, A, B, C, and D, and they moved some symptoms, for example from Group D to Group B, so that somebody who did not previously have any symptoms in group B now might have a symptom in group B, which might then meet the requirement to have a certain number of symptoms in each grouping. The person's symptoms have not changed, he can be diagnosed with PTSD now only because the manual has changed.

These are significant changes. There have been a number of recent publications pointing out that when they make all these changes what they do, in effect, is throw out all the prior research. They have to start over because you don't know if the population is the same.

Q:  Doctor, did the changes that appear in DSM-III and DSM-III-R, does that reflect that this is an experimental concept or well-established concept?

A:  It's clear that it is an experimental diagnosis. It's clear that it was experimental in 1980 and they found it was not adequate.

Now they have changed it, so descriptively it is a new diagnosis and we are looking again at several years of research before we will know whether it is an adequate definition. And by that time, DSM-IV is expected in 1992, so by the time enough research gets done on this, we don't know but what they will have changed it again and then the whole process has to start all over again.

But in the introduction they are quite open about this and they describe these as pretty much experimental. They are trying things out. They are groping their way along. There is no criticism of them for that. They have to do that. They are in the very early, baby stages as a science, where the first thing that has to be done is develop an adequate system of classification. So you can talk, study, make predictions about it and they are still trying to work it out.

Q:  Did you read the report and deposition of Dr. W [a psychologist]?

A:  Yes.

Q:  Did you find any errors in his procedures?

A:  He made two errors in the administration of the Wechsler Adult Intelligence Scale and five errors in scoring the test. He misinterpreted the meaning of one subscale score by calling the score of 8 below average. 8 is clearly within the average range. He also attached significance to a difference of 6 points between the highest and lowest scale scores on that test although such a difference is perfectly normal and occurred in a high percentage of the standardization sample, that is the people who form the basis for the norms for the test.

Q:  Did that cause you to question his conclusions?

A:  Yes.

Q:  Why?

A:   The WAIS is a test where you can find examiner errors. It is difficult or impossible to detect such errors on the other tests Dr. W gave, but I don't think, based on the extent of errors on the WAIS, that one can safely conclude he did not make errors on the other tests.

Q:   Was there anything else that caused you to question his conclusions?

A:   In diagnosing PTSD, he asserted that plaintiff has feelings of detachment or estrangement from others, restricted range of affect, and a sense of a foreshortened future. These are the only three symptoms he reports that meet the Category C requirement. However, I note in his report that plaintiff indicates she is going ahead with marriage plans which would seem to contradict at least two out of three of these symptoms. That is, one of the examples in the manual for sense of foreshortened future is that the person does not expect to get married. And one of the examples of restricted range of affect is that the person is unable to have loving feelings which seems inconsistent with getting married. Also, on restricted range of affect, he notes that she is angry with her former employer, she cries, and at one point he describes her laughing. All of these are forms of affect. So on two of the three essential criteria, he seems to be wrong and seems to ignore his own data.

Q:   Dr. W. indicates he bases his conclusion primarily on his 10 years of experience. Is there any literature on the relationship between experience and accuracy of evaluation?

A:   Yes, there is a substantial body of scientific and professional literature indicating that there is little or no relation between experience and accuracy. In this field, experience does not appear to be a good teacher. We have a clear example here that after 10 years he apparently has not learned to administer, score and interpret the WAIS properly.

Q:   Is there some explanation for the lack of improvement with experience?

A:   Yes, the literature indicates that lack of adequate feedback is the main problem. In other words, in order to learn from experience you have to have knowledge of results, you need to know when you are right and when you are wrong, in order to get rid of erroneous thinking or methods. In the field of psychological assessment, the individual practitioner rarely gets that kind of feedback because they are usually dealing with internal processes which are not amenable to objective determination.

Q:   I have nothing further.

*(Author's Note: This is a relatively brief direct examination. However, note that it has dealt with the importance of the scientific and professional literature, and has challenged the status of psychological evaluations, the diagnostic manual, PTSD, experience, and the competence of the plaintiff expert in this case. Obviously, this is easier than struggling to get these things from the plaintiff expert. However, it can be quite expensive and there will usually be some kind of attack on the consultant-expert [e.g., does not perform diagnoses, did not examine plaintiff]. Usually, if the expert stays close to the literature, his testimony should survive pretty well.)*

## CROSS EXAMINATION

Q: You are not currently engaged in the practice of psychology, right?

A: No, that is not right, I do practice psychology.

Q: Didn't you testify that you stopped practicing several years ago?

A: I stopped practicing clinical psychology, but I continue to practice providing consultation to lawyers.

Q: Alright, but you do not see patients, correct?

A: That is correct.

Q: How long has it been since you saw patients?

A: Around 20 years.

Q: For what period of time did you see patients?

A: About 5 years, I don't remember exactly when I stopped.

Q: And you're on the faculty of what institutions today?

A: I'm no longer on the faculty—well, I'm professor emeritus so I think I am considered to be on the faculty, but I don't do anything there. I have library privileges and parking privileges but I am not teaching anything now. I retired from the faculty.

Q: How long has it been since you had a teaching load?

A: Well, it would be before 1979 when I retired, so at least 10 years.

Q: How much did you get paid money-wise for your testimony in this case?

A: I haven't been paid anything.

Q: How much do you expect to be paid?

A: I don't get paid for my testimony. I get paid for my time and expertise. My fee for a court appearance is $2500.00.

Q: Pretty nice income; right?

A: It is a pretty standard fee for people at my level.

Q: What was the purpose of DSM-I?

A: The purpose was to try to reduce some of the chaos that existed with regard to psychiatric diagnoses, to have a set of diagnoses that people could follow with a higher degree of consistency. And—

Q: What was your—I'm sorry.

A: And another purpose is to help them do research on these various disorders.

Q: What was your contribution to DSM-I?

A: Nothing.

Q: What was the purpose of DSM-II?

A: Same purpose.

Q: What was you contribution to DSM-II?

A: Nothing.

Q: What was the purpose of DSM-III?

A: Same.

Q: And your contribution—the same?

A: Same.

Q: What was the purpose of DSM-III-R?

A: Same.

Q: And what was your contribution?

A: Same as for DSM-III.

Q: In other words, nothing at all?

A: Yeah, that's right.

Q: Were you asked to contribute?

A: No.

Q: Did you volunteer to contribute?

A: No.

Q: Weren't the DSMs, I through III-R, weren't they an attempt by the mental health professionals to attempt to classify various mental disorders?

A: Certainly, it was an attempt.

Q: And isn't the purpose of DSM-III-R to further refine the work that's been done by mental health professionals, the very people you're trying to discredit.

A: It's a further attempt to try to get it right.

Q: Okay. Did you ever write any of these committees on DSM-III or DSM-III-R and say, "Let me give you my input"?

A: No, but my views, my opinions about the degree of success they have had, would have been available to them in various publications of mine.

Q: Is the DSM accepted by the courts of this state?

A: I don't have any knowledge that it isn't.

Q: Well, you have knowledge that it is, don't you?

A: It's been used in a lot of cases I've consulted on, but I am not aware of any appellate decisions about it. So with that qualification, I would say it's accepted.

Q: Is DSM accepted by the Social Security Administration?

A: I believe so.

Q: Is it accepted by the Veteran Administration?

A: Yes.

Q: And by every mental hospital in the state?

A: Yes.

Q: Now, you say this—to get something in the DSM, even though you haven't been in the process or contributed, you say that's a political process, right?

A: Right.

Q: Isn't it a matter of negotiation and compromise among mental health professionals?

A: I understood that was one of the definitions of politics, the art of compromise.

Q: You mean, in other words, somebody says, "Well, I'll vote for your definitions of PTSD if you'll give me a job"? Do you mean that kind of politics?

A: No, I don't think that's what the word "politics"—politics doesn't mean that to me. It does mean compromise, it does mean voting. There was a certain amount of horse trading of inclusions and exclusions, but not for jobs.

Q: Now, are there people who have psychological consequences from being involved in traumatic events?

A: Yes, of course.

Q: Have you ever dealt with anybody who's been diagnosed as having post-traumatic stress disorder in any clinical setting?

A: Not directly, not to my knowledge.

Q:  Look at Exhibit Number 187 up there. Would you agree that—make sure I understand this. You think it might exist but you can't diagnose it, right?

A:  No, I think that there exists—there exist reactions to traumatic events. There may be one set of reactions that everybody who's in traumatic events gets; there may be several sets of reactions; there may be 5 different kinds of post traumatic consequences; there may be only one kind; there may be three kinds. To this date nobody has been able to establish what the components are. Many people don't have any consequences; many other people have some reactions but they get over them in a fairly short time.

Q:  Would you agree with me, Doctor, that post—to suffer from post-traumatic stress disorder, you have to have unwanted intrusions and reliving of events after the traumatic event?

A:  I would agree that that's one of the categories of criteria stated in the manual.

Q:  How many people did you say you had seen who had been diagnosed as suffering from PTSD?

A:  I don't know if I have ever seen any.

Q:  Would you agree that post-stress disorder requires a psychic numbing of feeling and hope?

A:  I would agree that is a category of criteria stated in the manual.

Q:  Would you agree that post-traumatic stress disorder requires a persistent hyperarousal?

A:  I would agree that that's one of the categories of criteria stated in the manual.

Q:  But you can't talk to us about practical experience in dealing and treating these people?

A:  If you mean people who have received diagnoses of PTSD, that's correct.

Q:  Well, let me ask you this from a practical standpoint then. How would you go about diagnosing post-traumatic stress disorder in somebody?

A:  Well, I would not diagnose PTSD or any other disorder until I saw a sufficient body of scientific research which demonstrated, with little equivocation, little likelihood of error, that these criteria X, Y, and Z identify PTSD and not any other disorder.

Q:  What if we don't call it X, Y, and Z? What if we call it 1, 2, 3, and 4?

A:  Same thing. It doesn't matter what the names of the criteria are so long as there is sufficient research evidence that they identify a cohesive disorder in a consistent manner.

Q:  In diagnosing PTSD, do you think it would be important to give any tests such as the MMPI test?

A:  If I was going to do it, the MMPI would be one of the better tests for that purpose.

Q:  Do you think people can be treated for PTSD?

A:  I think people can be treated for emotional distress, emotional problems, psychological problems of most kinds, probably including the kinds with symptoms that have been described under PTSD.

Q:  Well, how can you treat somebody unless you diagnose them, tell us that?

A: Well, it's one of the perplexing mysteries of the profession. The scientific and professional literature, a number of studies, have shown that there is a lack of relationship between diagnosis, form of treatment, and outcome. The literature indicates that other factors such as the "fit" between therapist and patient are more important in determining outcome. There is ongoing research attempting to get more refined in this area but so far, except for possibly some narrow relations between certain disorders and specific medications, they have not reached their goal.

Q: Let me ask you this, doctor: Post-traumatic stress disorder, the condition is not a new condition, is it?

A: That people suffer psychological consequences from traumatic events is not a new idea, correct. However, PTSD as defined in the manual is pretty new, less than 10 years old.

Q: Has it been called something else in the past?

A: There have been many names for consequences of traumatic events.

Q: Look at Exhibit 187 and I'll ask you whether or not you agree that post-traumatic stress disorder has been called different things throughout psychological history.

A: I would not agree with that because the descriptions of those things are different than the descriptions that go with the term "post-traumatic stress disorder."

Q: Would you think it would be fair if mental health professionals who were experts in the field of stress disorders keep trying to redefine things and refine things and trying to get better? Is that okay?

A: I applaud their efforts to do that. I think they should do that. But I don't think they should claim that they have arrived at a satisfactory resolution before they have. And the writers of the DSM don't make such claims.

Q: Can the symptoms be treated?

A: Oh, I believe most of the symptoms described under PTSD in the manual can be treated.

Q: Okay. Let me give you a hypothetical question. Let's assume for a minute that you have a teenage son who starts to act bizarre, erratically, and his behavior is otherwise unexplainable. Would you send that person to a mental health professional for diagnosis and treatment?

(Objection, overruled)

A: I think a mental health person is among the people I might consider sending him to for some kind of help with his problems. It might not be the only one.

Q: Who else would you—

A: Well, first of all I would send him to a real doctor, one who practices physical medicine, to determine if there was anything medically wrong, like a metabolic or neurological disorder. Then I might consider a clergyman, or a very good friend he could talk to in ways he might not be able to talk to me. Probably I would look to the literature to see where the best chances would be.

There is considerable literature indicating that paraprofessionals, people with relatively little training have about the same success as professionals. But I would not rule out mental health professionals if that seemed like the best choice.

Q: Well, wait a minute. I think I am confused now. Perhaps you can help me with this. You might send him to a mental health professional for diagnosis and treatment?

A: No, I would not send him for diagnosis. I would be interested in whoever I sent him to just helping him. I would prefer not to have a diagnosis when everything I know about it tells me that diagnosis is not likely to be related to outcome. And there is a likelihood that he will get stuck with a label that could create a lot of problems for him.

Q: How would—

A: There may be some rare exceptions where there are drug-specific medications.

Q: Well, how would the mental health professional know what to treat unless he diagnosed him?

A: Well, one of the ways is to just ask, "What is the problem," "What do we need to work on." That is not a diagnosis.

Q: Well, doesn't he say sometimes, "Let's take a look at your past history"?

A: Yeah, he might do that. Some don't.

Q: And wouldn't he also say, "Based on my experience, I'm going to give you a series of psychological tests, including perhaps the MMPI"?

A: Some would. Some wouldn't.

Q: But in any event, you would expect this mental health professional, who you sent somebody to who is having problems, to make a diagnosis before treatment started wouldn't you?

A: No, I would not.

Q: Just start treating him?

A: I would try to select a therapist who does not make diagnoses.

Q: If you—

A: One of the problems with diagnoses is that they carry a lot of excess baggage, and once the clinicians have made that diagnosis, it tends to stick even if it's wrong. Then they treat the person as though he—that the diagnosis is correct, and the person has all the characteristic of that diagnosis, which may not be the case at all.

Q: But what if the mental health professional says, "Well, I'm going to treat him but first I have to diagnose him," what would you say?

A: I would say, "Thank you, Doctor. Send me your bill for this meeting," and I would look for another therapist.

Q: So you'd search over and over—

A: Oh, it's not a big, hard search. There are lots of them.

Q: Did you ever in your few years of clinical work as a psychologist ever work with or treat a schizophrenic, the most common of all mental illnesses?

A: Well, I can't say for sure whether I have.

Q: Because you certainly never diagnosed somebody as schizophrenic, did you?

A: Oh, I did diagnostics as part of my training, you know; I had to do diagnoses as part of my training in a mental hospital and it's required there. You can't just say, "I'm going to treat this person for this problem or that problem." You have to say this person has schizophrenia or whatever because the hospital is required to keep statistics; so you know, I have done that, but not for a long time, not in my private practice.

Q: You talked earlier about the Rosenhan study, correct?

A: That's right.

Q: When was that study done?

A: My recollection is that it was published in 1970, in *Science,* the most prestigious scientific journal in the country.

Q: 19 years ago?

A: That's correct.

Q: What's the danger of a Rosenhan—of the Rosenhan study? Tell the jury what that is.

A: Well, one of the problems with the Rosenhan study is that while Dr. Rosenhan in another publication did state that he did replicate the study, he has never published the replication so we cannot evaluate what—he says the results were the same, but we don't know that. You don't know unless you look at the data yourself.

   So, that is a flaw in the Rosenhan study. But that study is just one of many, used as an illustration of massive psychiatric error. There are a number of studies showing psychiatrists overwhelmingly wrong in their conclusions.

Q: The fact that the Rosenhan study has never had a published replication of it, that certainly does not bother you about coming in and telling the jury about it, does it?

A: No, not when I see that there are so many other studies with more or less similar conclusions. The finding of extensive error has been repeated. That's one of the reasons for having research done, and having several studies; and that's one of the reasons it takes a long time, maybe 10 years or more, to allow other people to replicate the study, the lag in getting it published, and then the second cycle of studies gets published, and then somebody wants to do research on what they found, and it takes a long time. It's very slow, but when you see a number of different studies converging on the same conclusion, you decide it has legitimacy.

Q: Well, why don't you tell us, Doctor, why there's never been a published replication of the Rosenhan study.

A: I think you'd have to ask Dr. Rosenhan. I don't know.

Q: Have you ever asked him?

A: No, I haven't.

Q: Have you ever talked to him about the Rosenhan study?

A: Yes, I talked to him about the original study. As a matter of fact, let me correct my previous statement. Now you jogged my memory. I think I did talk to him because an article came out in the *Monitor,* which is a publication of the American Psychological Association, and in that, somebody had asked him, "Have you replicated this famous study?" And he said, "Yes, I have and we got similar results." And either I asked him or the interviewer—and

I don't know—I no longer remember—asked, "Why haven't you published it?" and he said, "I have gone on to other things."

Q: And you just now thought of that, right?

A: Well, as we were talking about it, my memory got refreshed. It's been a while ago.

Q: You have not examined plaintiff in this case, have you?

A: No.

Q: Have you formed an opinion as to whether or not she has PTSD?

A: No.

*(Author's Note: These questions should have been asked on direct examination to make the witness's role clear.)*

Q: I have nothing further.

Q: (by defense counsel) I have nothing further.